Handbook of Marketing
for
Continuing Education

Robert G. Simerly
and Associates

Handbook of Marketing for Continuing Education

Jossey-Bass Publishers

San Francisco • London • 1989

HANDBOOK OF MARKETING FOR CONTINUING EDUCATION
by Robert G. Simerly and Associates

Copyright © 1989 by: Jossey-Bass Inc., Publishers
350 Sansome Street
San Francisco, California 94104

&

Jossey-Bass Limited
28 Banner Street
London EC1Y 8QE

Library of Congress Cataloging-in-Publication Data

Handbook of marketing for continuing education.

(The Jossey-Bass higher education series)
Bibliography: p.
Includes index.
1. Continuing education—Administration—Handbooks,
manuals, etc.   2. Marketing—Handbooks, manuals, etc.
I. Simerly, Robert G.   II. Title: Marketing for continuing
education.
LC5225.A34H36   1989   374'.0068'8   88-46090
ISBN 1-55542-142-3 (alk. paper)

Manufactured in the United States of America

The paper in this book meets the guidelines for
permanence and durability of the Committee on
Production Guidelines for Book Longevity of the
Council on Library Resources.

JACKET DESIGN BY WILLI BAUM

FIRST EDITION

Code 8915

The Jossey-Bass
Higher Education Series

Consulting Editor
Adult and Continuing Education

Alan B. Knox
University of Wisconsin, Madison

Contents

Figures, Tables, and Exhibits

Preface

This *Handbook of Marketing for Continuing Education* is intended for continuing education professionals at four-year colleges and universities and at community colleges who have the responsibility for marketing any aspect of their programs. However, the principles, guidelines, and suggestions presented in this volume will also be useful to professionals at social service agencies, hospitals and other health-care providers, professional associations and societies, park districts, museums, and many other organizations engaged in serving the needs of lifelong learners.

The purpose of this handbook is to provide practical advice to enhance the marketing effectiveness of continuing education programs in large, small, and medium-sized organizations. The case studies, guidelines, suggestions, and advice offered here establish basic principles of effective professional practice. Each chapter stands on its own; and because this is a handbook, readers will probably want to scan the table of contents and read first the chapters that interest them most.

It is possible to adapt the helpful hints and ideas in each chapter to the individual needs of a wide variety of organizations. To make this easier, we have grouped the chapters into eight parts.

Part One provides an overview of the complex dynamics of marketing and establishes a framework for market analysis of continuing education organizations. The authors explain how to integrate marketing into strategic planning. This part contains practical advice on how to increase marketing effectiveness by making use of geographic, demographic, psychographic, and behavioristic data, and on exactly how to develop a marketing plan. A sample comprehensive marketing plan for a continuing education organization is included.

Part Two is devoted to an extensive discussion of positioning the continuing education organization and its programs in the market. This includes such important issues as aligning programs with the desired organizational image, choosing appropriate program locations, building a service component into the marketing plan, and determining an effective marketing mix.

Part Three deals exclusively with direct-mail marketing, because this is the primary form of advertising used by most continuing education organizations. We provide practical principles, suggestions, and guidelines for using direct mail to increase registrations. We also offer advice on designing and laying out successful brochures and catalogues, writing effective advertising copy, creating appropriate mailing lists, and setting up production schedules and checklists for direct-mail marketing.

In Part Four we discuss ways to develop effective public relations. The authors explain how to put together an overall public relations plan and budget and how to attract radio, television, newspaper, and magazine publicity. In addition, they make helpful suggestions for taking advantage of often overlooked publicity sources and tracking the results of public relations efforts.

In Part Five we analyze a wide variety of complex issues related to effective advertising. Chapters deal with such issues as developing an overall advertising plan and budget, designing and laying out newspaper and magazine ads, and writing effective brochure and catalogue copy. They include practical advice on how to work with an advertising agency and how to track advertising results.

Part Six focuses on developing personal sales as an important part of marketing. The authors tackle such issues as using all program staff as personal salespeople, developing successful telemarketing techniques, designing exhibits, and involving clients in the development and marketing of programs.

Part Seven ties together many of the central marketing concepts presented in the handbook. The chapter authors offer guidelines for organizing and staffing the marketing office, scheduling and monitoring marketing activities, budgeting for marketing activities and staff costs, and gaining organizational support for marketing.

In Part Eight we look toward the future and offer a comprehensive analysis of how to keep abreast of market changes. We present an environmental scanning model, seventy-five tips for avoiding the most common marketing mistakes, and a ten-step process to ensure marketing success. The resources at the back of the book identify valuable background information and lists of addresses and references to assist continuing education professionals in enhancing their marketing effectiveness.

In summary, this *Handbook of Marketing for Continuing Education* gathers together the expertise of professionals from a wide variety of continuing education organizations. These authors base their recommendations on years of successful research and experience in improving marketing of continuing education programs, products, and services. Their guidelines and suggestions will provide you with hundreds of ideas that can be implemented in your own organization.

Definition of Terms

Key terms related to marketing are used consistently throughout the handbook. To assist the reader, a brief explanation of these terms follows.

Marketing refers to the overall concept of studying, analyzing, and making decisions about how best to serve consumers through continuing education programs and services. We emphasize consumer needs and attitudes and the values of the sponsoring organization. Marketing is based on the principle of exchange: The continuing education organization exchanges its programs and services for its customers' money and time. Thus, both parties receive something they value. The customer receives educational programs and services; the continuing education organization receives money and public support through program registrations.

Advertising and publicity are both promotion techniques used to achieve marketing objectives. For the purposes of this handbook they have separate meanings, and to avoid confusion, it is important for readers to keep these distinctions in mind. The term *advertising* is used to refer to paid promotion. For example, an ad in a newspaper or a direct-mail brochure is advertising. The term *publicity* denotes any type of unpaid promotion. For example, a feature story in a newspaper or an interview on a local television program is publicity.

Acknowledgments

Many people were important in bringing this manuscript to press. First, of course, I am indebted to all the chapter authors, who took time out of their busy schedules to work on the project. The scope of this handbook required tapping the expertise of a wide variety of professionals. It has been a pleasure to work with these authors, who have been so willing to share the successful marketing ideas they have developed for their own organizations.

I also want to give special thanks to my secretaries, Peggy Flynn, Sandra Hannah, Dee Leonard, and Colleen Tingle, for their contributions to this work as we went through the many revisions. Their attention to detail, hard work, and many excellent suggestions have contributed significantly to making this project an enjoyable one.

I also wish to thank the entire staff at the Division of Continuing Studies at the University of Nebraska, Lincoln. I am constantly learning from them. It is through testing marketing ideas for continuing education in our own organization, whose programs serve 75,000 people a year, that we have been able to develop models, guidelines, and suggestions to enhance professional practice.

I am also indebted to the people who read initial drafts of the outline for the manuscript and offered suggestions: Dorothy Durkin, Gayle Hendrickson, and Judith Riggs. In addition, the following people reviewed the completed manuscript and offered many helpful suggestions: Charles Falk, Nancy Hancock, and Alan Knox. Others who helped by providing suggestions for certain chapters are William Bowmaster, Mary Bruning, and Robert Mortenson.

Last, I wish to thank my wife, Coby Bunch Simerly, for her encouragement. She is also my intellectual companion and best friend.

Lincoln, Nebraska   Robert G. Simerly
February 1989

The Authors

Robert G. Simerly is dean of continuing studies and professor of adult education at the University of Nebraska, Lincoln. He has served in a wide variety of faculty and administrative positions in both the United States and Europe, including as head of the Division of Conferences and Institutes, Office of Continuing Education and Public Service, University of Illinois, Urbana–Champaign; and director of the Extended Campus Program in the School of Education at Syracuse University. Simerly received both his B.S. degree (1961) in education and his doctoral degree (1973) with a major in educational leadership and minors in industrial management and higher education from the University of Tennessee, Knoxville. He is the author of numerous publications. Among these are *Successful Budgeting for Conferences and Seminars* (1983), *Strategic Long-Range Planning,* and *Strategic Planning and Leadership in Continuing Education* (1987, with others). As a behavioral scientist, Simerly is particularly concerned with helping organizational leaders improve their daily leadership effectiveness. He presents workshops throughout the United States on such topics as managing organizational conflict; improving personal and organizational communications, leadership effectiveness, and financial management; conducting effective problem-solving meetings; and carrying out strategic long-range planning and effective team building.

Katherine Livingston Allen is assistant dean for marketing and strategic planning at the University of Miami's School of Continuing Studies. Previously, she was assistant dean and director of professional continuing education at Metropolitan College, University of New Orleans, where she also served as coordinator of marketing for three years. Allen is a marketing and management consultant to universities and corporations, a frequent speaker at continuing education conferences and seminars, and an adjunct instructor of advertising for the School of Business at the University of Miami. She received her B.S. degree

(1979) in business from Florida State University and her M.B.A. degree (1983) from the University of New Orleans. She is the recipient of several honors, including excellence in marketing awards from the National University Continuing Education Association and, in 1982, recognition as an outstanding young woman of America.

Francis E. (Skip) Andrew is president of the Continuing Education Forum, a training and marketing consulting firm devoted exclusively to the meeting industry. He received his B.A. degree (1962) in liberal arts from Drake University and his J.D. degree (1968) from Northwestern University Law School. Andrew's continuing education career began with his work in the legal profession. He has worked in the seminar and conference industry for more than fourteen years. His consulting clients have included both medium-sized organizations and larger clients such as *Inc., High Technology,* and *Business Week* magazines; a consortium of twenty-four universities; and the Business Communications Review Federation. He teaches one of the leading seminars in the United States on how to market meetings, often serves as keynote speaker for national and regional meetings on marketing and quality, and writes seminar and conference brochures for clients. In addition to his consulting and copywriting, he brokers and selects mailing lists exclusively for meeting marketers.

Chuck Buck is president of Arnold.Buck.Inc., a Southern California–based marketing, advertising, and design company specializing in commercial real estate, high technology, and financial services. He has participated in the marketing launch of new products and services, has successfully repositioned companies, and has conducted successful advertising and public relations campaigns for a variety of clients. As one of the regional advertising agencies for McDonald's, Arnold.Buck.Inc. introduced new menu items and services such as the first drive-through operation and the McDonaldland park concept. Buck is credited with helping to originate the McDonald's community relations program for local restaurants. One of his principal interests is continuing education. As a member of the visiting faculty, he has taught advertising at San Diego State University and target marketing for the continuing education program at the University of California, San Diego. He is a director of the La Jolla Academy of Advertising Art, where he also teaches. He has been recognized for his broadcast production talent and counts among his numerous awards a 1977 Emmy for writing television commercials. Buck frequently writes on advertising issues, and he serves as the media analyst for KFMB-TV (CBS) in San Diego, commenting on consumer and political advertising trends. A past lieutenant governor of the American Advertising Federation in Southern California, he is also a lifetime member of the Advertising Club of San Diego. He received his B.S. degree (1965) in broadcasting from San Diego State University.

Carolyn R. Carson is head of conferences and institutes, Office of Continuing Education and Public Service, University of Illinois, Urbana-Champaign. She received her B.S. degree (1978) in American studies from the University of Southern Mississippi and her Ed.D. degree (1983) in adult continuing education from the University of Georgia. She has had extensive experience in planning conferences, as well as other types of continuing education programs, at the University of Southern Mississippi, the University of Georgia, Brunswick Junior College in Brunswick, Georgia, and the University of Illinois, Urbana–Champaign. Carson currently serves on the executive committee of the Division of Conferences and Institutes, National University Continuing Education Association. She has made numerous presentations on conference management, budgeting and finance of noncredit programming, developing internal support for conferences and institutes, adult development, and interpersonal interaction.

Susan Coats is conference center manager and chairperson of the university exhibit committee at Georgia State University in Atlanta, Georgia. She received both her B.A. degree (1976) in visual arts and her M.Ed. degree (1988) in educational leadership from Georgia State University. She has worked primarily in the area of facilities and space management and has successfully developed an active exhibit program for Georgia State University, which she manages through the Division of Continuing Education. One of her primary interests is in helping organizations improve their market potential by participating in the exhibit business. She has recently developed a set of internal guidelines, the "Facilities Guidebook," to assist conference coordinators in planning and conducting successful programs in downtown Atlanta.

Joann Condino is director of marketing and public relations at Wayne State University in Detroit, Michigan. She received both her B.A. degree (1972) in philosophy and her M.A. degree (1980) in adult learning from Wayne State University. In addition to pursuing her university career, she owns a business that provides marketing, design, and graphic production services for nonprofit agencies and small businesses in Michigan. Her company's clients include health-care agencies, small industrial firms, and nonprofit arts groups. Her current research focuses on the organizational view of marketing activity, the interdependence of marketing and other organizational subsystems, and the integration of organizational effectiveness strategies with marketing strategies.

Ralph D. Elliott is director of Clemson University's Office of Professional Development. He successfully markets more than five hundred programs a year, which attract more than 20,000 attendees annually. His marketing experience includes conferences, seminars, executive briefings, in-house sales, cassette tapes, international study tours, videotape marketing, teleconferencing, and residential executive programs. A dynamic seminar leader, Elliott has delivered presentations at various state, regional, and national conferences for organizations such as West Virginia College, the University Continuing and Community Education Association, the National University Continuing Education Association, the American Assembly of Collegiate Schools of Business, the Learning Resources Network, and the Marketing Federation. Elliott also presents an intensive two-day seminar that he developed entitled "Increasing Registrations and Revenue Through Effective Seminar/Conference Marketing." He is the author of over fifty publications, including a best-selling mailing list monograph and a book entitled *Effective Marketing and Selling of In-House Programs* (1986). He has consulted or presented in-house training for such marketers as Wright State University, Bryan College, Gaston College, the Instrument Society of America, INFOMART, Professional Education Systems, Inc., Sumter Area Technical College, Lead Associates Seminars, Wayne State University, Athletic Business Publications, Trident Technical College, the University of Nebraska, and the Council on Education and Management. Elliott received his B.S. (1967) and M.S. (1968) degrees in textiles and his Ph.D. degree (1972) in economics, all from North Carolina State University. He is professor of economics at Clemson University, where he teaches and conducts research on labor economics and collective bargaining.

Richard B. Fischer is an associate director of continuing education at the University of Delaware. He received his B.S. degree (1964) in personnel management and his M.B.A. degree (1966) in marketing and business management from Pennsylvania State University and his Ed.D degree (1980) in adult and continuing education from Temple University. He has held positions in both industry and academe and frequently acts as a workshop and staff development trainer. His major interests focus on establishing linkages between the education and business communities. He is the author of *Personal Contact Marketing* (1984) and a contributing author to the *Handbook on Adult Continuing Education* (1987). He also contributed articles entitled "Pricing Strategy" (1986) and "Competing for Contract Business" (1987) to the Jossey-Bass series New Directions for Continuing Education.

Kenneth S. Foster is director of marketing/communications for the Division of Continuing Education and is an adjunct professor of advertising at the University of Utah, Salt Lake City. He received a B.S. degree (1975) in mass communications and in music theory and is currently completing work toward his Ph.D. degree in marketing with a minor in psychology at the University of Utah. He has eighteen years of advertising and marketing/communications experience. He has worked for the last five years as a consultant to numerous corporations, advertising agencies, colleges and universities, associations, politicians, and business organizations. He has won over 350 awards for advertising creativity. Foster has written several articles and publications, including *Promotional Strategies for Recruiting Adults* (1983, with J. P. Pappas), *New Product Development in Continuing Education* (1986), and *How to Buy Word of Mouth Advertising* (1987). Since 1980, more than one thousand institutions have been represented at his lectures and seminars sponsored by the American College Testing Bureau and the Learning Resource Network.

Jerry W. Gilley is program chairperson of the human resources development program and assistant professor of adult education at the University of Nebraska, Lincoln. He received his B.S. degree (1974) in marketing from Mankato State University in Minnesota, his M.A. degree (1983) in human relations and supervision from Louisiana Technical University, and his Ed.D. degree (1985) in adult education and human resource development from Oklahoma State University. His professional background includes eight years in marketing and training, four years in school administration, and five years in higher education and consulting. He also taught marketing education at Oklahoma State University and at the University of Central Arkansas. He has authored over thirty professional journal articles and a monograph entitled "Professional Certificates: Implications for Adult Educators and Human Resource Development" (1986), as well as *Principles of Human Resource Development* (forthcoming, with S. Eggland).

Donald E. Hanna is associate vice-provost for extended university services at Washington State University and professor of adult and continuing education. He received his B.A. degree (1969) in history and anthropology from the University of Kansas, his M.Ed. degree (1974) in education from SUNY, Buffalo, and his Ph.D. degree (1978) in adult and continuing education from Michigan State University. He has previously held positions as director of continuing education and public service at Washington State University and as head of the division of extramural courses at the University of Illinois, Urbana–Champaign. He has served on the board of directors of the National University Continuing Education Association and the executive committee of the Council on Extension, Continuing Education, and Public Service of the National Association of State Universities and Land-Grant Colleges. He has also served on the board of directors of the Washington Higher Education Telecommunication System and the administrative council of the Southwest Washington Joint Center for Education. Hanna received a W. K. Kellogg Foundation National Leadership Program Fellowship in 1987. He has conducted research in the area of developing multicampus systems and has published extensively on the subject of faculty rewards in continuing education. His interests include organizational change in universities and the use of electronic media in higher education.

Doe Hentschel is dean of extended and continuing education and associate professor of educational leadership at the University of Connecticut. She received her B.A. degree (1963) in speech and dramatic arts from the University of Missouri, Columbia, her M.A. degree (1964) in speech from Northwestern University, and her Ph.D. degree (1979) in urban education/adult education from the University of Wisconsin, Milwaukee. Before joining the administration at the University of Connecticut, she served as dean of adult and continuing education at the State University of New York, Brockport, where her primary responsibility was to provide internal and external leadership for the tranformation of the traditional residential college into a metropolitan learning center for a diverse student population. She previously held administrative positions in continuing higher education at the University of Illinois and William Rainey Harper College in Illinois and a faculty post in administrative leadership/adult education at the University of Wisconsin, Milwaukee. Hentschel has served in numerous leadership positions in local, state, and national professional organizations and has published many articles in such publications as *Lifelong Learning: An Omnibus of Practice and Research, Adult & Continuing Education Today, The Learning Connection,* and *Planning & Changing.* She is a frequent speaker and presenter. Her current interests focus on the adult re-entry student in higher education.

Carol D. Holden is dean of the division of continuing education and professor of education at George Washington University, Washington, D.C. She received her B.M. (bachelor of music) degree, her M.S. degree (1970) in music education, and her Ph.D. degree (1975) in education from the University of Illinois at Urbana–Champaign. She has been a member of the faculty at the University of Illinois and Illinois State University and has held administrative positions at the University of Illinois and Eastern Illinois University. A recognized leader in the field of esthetic education, she has published articles on the role of arts education in general education and coauthored an award-winning book on historic preservation education (1980). In addition, she is the author of the monograph *The Conference Coordinator as a Continuing Education Professional* (1981).

B. Ray Holland is executive director of continuing education at Kennesaw College in Georgia. He is also assistant professor of political science. He received his B.A. degree (1966) in history and political science from the University of Montevallo in Alabama and his M.A. (1973) and Ed.D. (1985) degrees, both in higher education administration, from the University of Alabama. He has held several administrative positions in higher education including as assistant to the senior vice-president at the University of Alabama, Birmingham, where he was responsible for marketing the university, as assistant dean for marketing in special studies (continuing education) at the University of Alabama, Birmingham, and as director of admissions. He is the initiator of telephone marketing in continuing higher education at the University of Alabama, Birmingham, and is the author of "Telephone Marketing as an Effective Means to Enroll Noncredit Continuing Education Students." He serves as a consultant to institutions and businesses and conducts seminars and workshops in telephone marketing and customer service.

Deanna M. Maneker is vice-president of the Stenrich Group, a full-service agency in Richmond, Virginia, specializing in direct response. The Stenrich Group provides clients with response-oriented advertising, direct mail, and telephone marketing services. Her duties include supervising account services and handling several key accounts—American Express, Northeast Utilities, Mitel Corporation, and AT&T Information Services, to mention a few. She conducts seminars on a regular basis for private companies and at college and university programs, such as the Boston University Professional Development Programs and Georgia State University Continuing Education. Maneker earned her B.A. degree from Barnard College and is a former publisher of *Change* magazine and Change Magazine Press.

Judith A. Markoe is director of communications for the American Association of University Women (AAUW). She is responsible for advertising, marketing, public relations, conventions, and publications for the 150,000-member national organization. Prior to joining AAUW, she served as the director of marketing at the University of Maryland's University College. Markoe has a wealth of experience in marketing nonprofit organizations and has implemented innovative and successful marketing initiatives at the University of Maryland, the

University of Rhode Island, and the University of Houston. She received her B.S. degree (1968) in health and physical education from the State University of New York, Brockport, and her M.S. degree (1969) in counseling and student personnel in higher education from the State University of New York, Albany. She is a popular presenter of workshops throughout the country and consults for business and nonprofit organizations on various aspects of marketing, including brochure design, image development, market planning, advertising, and promotion. Markoe has won numerous awards for her work and is currently serving on the board of directors for the Advertising Club of Metropolitan Washington.

Dawn Marie Patterson is the dean of continuing education at California State University, Los Angeles. She supervises staff who develop urban lifelong learning programs for extension, instructional television, conferences and workshops, small business, the American Culture and Language Program (ACLP) in English as a second language, research and development, international affairs, the Center for the Study of Black on Black Crime, and administrative and financial services. She has also held administrative positions at Michigan State University and the University of Southern California. She received her B.S. degree (1962) in education from the State University of New York, Geneseo, and both her M.A. degree (1973) in counseling and student personnel services and Ph.D. degree (1977) in education administration from Michigan State University. She completed her postdoctoral studies (1983) in educational policy at the University of Southern California and the Institute for Educational Leadership in Washington, D.C. Over the past ten years she has provided leadership for developing university-level programs and their marketing publicity plans in collaboration with community agencies, associations, and other nonprofit organizations. She has edited newsletters for professional associations in Michigan and California and has authored articles in such journals as *The Educational Record: The Magazine of Higher Education* and the UNESCO *International Review of Education*. She is the hostess/producer of a cable television interview series, "Golden Eagle Opportunities," and is the executive producer of a videotape, "Come Study English at Cal. State, L.A." She has served on the boards and committees of several professional organizations and as an adviser to both for-profit and nonprofit organizations. She is president of CO-PRO Associations, a Los Angeles–based consulting organization.

Dennis P. Prisk is dean of continuing studies at the University of Alabama. He received his B.S. degree (1964) in education from Florida State University, his M.A. degrees in history (1965) and education (1971) from Appalachian State University, and his Ed.D. degree (1975) from Virginia Polytechnic Institute and State University. He has held administrative positions at Appalachian State University, the University of Southern California, and Indiana University. One of his interests is assisting other universities in reviewing their continuing education operations. He is the author of numerous publications, including "Organizational Models and Elements of an Effective Organization," in the *Handbook on Continuing Higher Education* (1987), and editor of *Policies and Practices in Continuing Higher Education* (1983).

Judith K. Riggs is director of development for the University of Illinois Foundation. She received both her B.S. degree (1962) in education and her M.S. degree (1965) in guidance and counseling from Indiana State University, Terre Haute, and her Ph.D. degree (1978) in adult and continuing education from the University of Illinois. She served at the University of Illinois, Urbana–Champaign, as director of statewide programming at the system level and as head of marketing for continuing education at the campus level. In addition, she is assistant professor of education. She has taught courses and conducted numerous workshops related to marketing in nonprofit environments.

Maris A. St. Cyr is director of public relations for the Johns Hopkins University School of Continuing Studies. Under her direction the school has garnered numerous publication, advertising, and publicity awards and honors. St. Cyr received her B.A. degree (1967) in English from Saint Francis College in Loretto, Pennsylvania. She has worked in education for eighteen years, and in continuing higher education since 1981. She teaches workshops in publication production and design and consults for business and nonprofit organizations about marketing and public relations. She currently serves as chairperson of the Division of Marketing and Promotion for the National University Continuing Education Association.

Edward G. Simpson, Jr., is director of the Georgia Center for Continuing Education and associate professor of adult education at the University of Georgia, Athens. He received his B.A. degree (1967) in history, his M.A. degree (1971) in history, and his Ed.D. degree (1977) in educational administration, all from Virginia Polytechnic Institute and State University (Virginia Tech), Blacksburg, Virginia. He has held a variety of programming and administrative positions in higher education, serving, for example, as administrator of the Western Region Consortium for Continuing Higher Education in Virginia and as director of the off-campus graduate program and assistant dean of the Extension Division at Virginia Tech. He has been actively involved in higher education program evaluation, both in this country and internationally, on behalf of the Commission on Colleges of the Southern Association of Colleges and Schools. His areas of particular professional interest include leadership, organizational renewal, and planning. He was elected to the 1985 class of Leadership Georgia. Also in 1985, he instituted the environmental scanning project, which he currently directs, at the Georgia Center for Continuing Education.

Dennis L. Tarr is dean of the School of Continuing Studies at the University of Miami in Coral Gables, Florida. He received his B.A. degree (1962) in international relations from the University of Redlands, his M.Div. degree (1965) in political ethics from Princeton Theological Seminary, and his M.A. degree (1966) in American politics from the Eagleton Institute of Politics at Rutgers University. He is the founder and former dean of the Center City Campus of Temple University in Philadelphia, where he taught international politics and served as assistant to the president, assistant vice-president for academic affairs, director of international programs, and dean of continuing education. Tarr serves on several international boards, is president of a consulting firm specializing in strategic planning and marketing for universities and corporations, and is a popular keynote speaker at national conferences. He has also been a Rockefeller Fellow at Syracuse University and has won over a dozen national marketing awards from the National University Continuing Education Association.

Mary Lindenstein Walshok is associate vice-chancellor for extended studies and public service and associate adjunct professor in the Department of Sociology at the University of California, San Diego. She is responsible for the university's continuing education programs, which serve more than 35,000 students annually, as well as for the summer session and television education. She received her B.A. degree (1964) from Pomona College and both her M.A. (1966) and Ph.D. (1969) degrees in sociology from Indiana University. After teaching in the California State University system, she went to the University of California, San Diego Extension, as director of women's programs in 1972. In addition to authoring numerous book chapters and articles, she is the author of *Blue Collar Women: Pioneers on the Male Frontier* (1981), based on four years of research funded by a National Institute of Mental Health grant. Walshok has been a Kellogg Foundation National Fellow and is currently writing a book on education's role in the economic development challenges facing a technological society.

Craig D. Weidemann is director of professional development and business programs at Johns Hopkins University. He received his B.S. degree (1973) in psychology from Illinois State University, his M.S. degree (1975) in human development counseling from Sangamon State University in Illinois, and his Ph.D. degree (1982) in educational psychology from the University of Georgia. He has been director of continuing education at Blue Ridge Community College in Weyers Cave, Virginia, and program director in the Division of Conferences and Institutes, Office of Continuing Education and Public Service, University of Illinois, Urbana–Champaign. He has conducted numerous workshops on customer service, listening skills, supervision, and communication and has published articles on memory and learning.

Handbook of Marketing for Continuing Education

The Components of
Effective Marketing

This *Handbook of Marketing for Continuing Education* utilizes the expertise of professionals in a wide variety of continuing education organizations. Their ideas are based on years of successful experience in researching and implementing improvements in marketing of continuing education programs, products, and services. Because they are practicing professionals, the authors are able, individually and collectively, to offer ideas that have been proven successful. Their guidelines and suggestions provide you, the reader, with hundreds of ideas that can be implemented in your own organization.

Part One is an overview of the dynamics of marketing. The first chapter, by Robert G. Simerly, establishes a framework for market analysis by describing three models used in continuing education organizations—traditional, exchange, and adaptive models. Case studies illustrate how each model works. In addition, nine important guidelines are identified to assist professionals in enhancing their total marketing efforts. Chapter One establishes an important theme found throughout the book: Marketing should be an integral part of an organization's total strategic planning. When this occurs, marketing and planning create a synergy that helps a continuing education organization respond to its environment, adapt its programs to changing consumer needs, and constantly engage in organizational self-renewal.

In Chapter Two, Robert G. Simerly analyzes the symbiotic relationships among an organization's mission, goals, objectives, and marketing. Guidelines are presented to assist professionals in implementing these ideas in their own organizations. In addition, advice is offered on how to avoid the mistakes most frequently made in articulating organizational goals and objectives. How design of effective marketing strategies can empower an organization is illustrated. Helping staff to create this empowerment should be an important professional development goal in dynamic continuing education organizations.

Dennis L. Tarr, in Chapter Three, illustrates how continuing educators can use geographic, demographic, psychographic, and behavioristic data to increase their marketing effectiveness. Because educational needs and preferences are so varied in today's marketplace, having good programs is not enough. Sophisticated marketing research that defines and analyzes market segments is necessary. This chapter contains a comprehensive analysis of how continuing educators can use market segmentation to their advantage.

In Chapter Four, Kenneth S. Foster shows how to develop a comprehensive marketing/advertising plan. Whether your continuing education organization is staffed by two hundred or two persons, the basic techniques for establishing a marketing/advertising plan remain the same. Also included in this chapter is a comprehensive outline of the components of a plan.

Foster devotes Chapter Five to presentation of a sample plan—the marketing/advertising plan currently in use in the Division of Continuing Education at the University of Utah. He actively demonstrates exactly how such a plan is constructed to meet the needs of a specific continuing education organization. Readers are offered many ideas that they can implement in drafting their own marketing/advertising plan.

Part One, then, establishes a framework for marketing analysis in continuing education organizations. Conceptual material leads into practical suggestions that can be implemented immediately in your own organization. Continuing education professionals in a wide variety of organizations will find dozens of ideas in Part One that will help them become more effective in thinking through a comprehensive marketing analysis for their organizations.

1

The Strategic Role
of Marketing
for Organizational Success

Robert G. Simerly

Marketing is an essential ingredient in any successful continuing education organization. Yet, marketing means different things to different people. To some,
marketing is mailing a brochure advertising a program. To others, marketing is
convincing people to come to a program. And still- others see marketing as a
complex series of interactions between the continuing education organization
and its many constituencies.

Rados (1981), for example, approaches a definition of marketing by first
noting two core concepts: "(1) the use of persuasive communications, notably
advertising and personal selling, to bring out superficial changes in opinions and
behavior; and (2) adaptations to existing patterns of behavior, by designing
products and services that are easy to use and by distributing them so they are easy
to find" (p. 17). He defines marketing as the use of these two core concepts "of the
many methods by which A tries to get B to do his will, where B has freedom to act
as he chooses" (p. 17). This has been the traditional view of marketing, especially
since marketing as a field of study gained prominence in the early 1960s.

Kotler (1984), however, sees marketing differently. For him the core
concepts are "needs, wants, and demands; products, value, and satisfaction;
exchange and transaction; markets; marketing and marketers" (p. 4). He defines
marketing as "a social process by which individuals and groups obtain what they
need and want through creating and exchanging products and value with others"
(p. 4). Thus, Kotler subscribes to an exchange model of marketing.

A review of the marketing literature reveals that most marketing experts
agree on the following items:

1.   It is difficult to establish a single definition of marketing widely accepted by professionals and the lay public.
2.   It is often easier to discuss and obtain agreement on core ideas and concepts related to marketing than it is to establish a widely accepted definition of marketing.
3.   Professionals who study and write about marketing tend to focus on major ideas and core concepts. This, in turn, leads to use of particular approaches or models to describe the complex activities of marketing.

Table 1.1 illustrates three basic ways to view marketing. These approaches are classified as (1) the traditional model, (2) the exchange model, and (3) the adaptive model. Probably no continuing education organization will ever use only one of these pure marketing models. Instead, most combine the three models.

Traditional Model

The traditional approach to marketing is directed inwardly toward the organization. That is, the needs, wants, and desires of the organization tend to override the needs, wants, and desires of the consumer. The guiding force behind this approach is that the organization creates goods, products, and services and then uses marketing to persuade consumers to accept them. Often, consumers are viewed as unreceptive. As a result, marketing is seen as the way to change their ideas, attitudes, and values so that they will buy. This approach to marketing is inner directed because the emphasis is on the organization and what it can do to get consumers to buy.

Like all approaches to marketing, the traditional approach has both advantages and disadvantages. The advantages are that there are fewer variables to consider when planning marketing activities. In addition, it is often easier to convince long-established internal political constituencies of the need for marketing the continuing education organization's goods, products, and services using this traditional approach. The disadvantages are that the traditional model tends to discourage change, can contribute to organizational neglect of its consumers, and, as a result, sometimes disappoints, angers, or frustrates consumers.

An example of the traditional approach to marketing is seen in the following case study.

Case Study 1. For years the continuing education program in a large urban university had made foreign travel and tour programs available to participants on a credit or noncredit basis. Three to five faculty went along on each tour and conducted both formal and informal classes related to the art, culture, and politics of each country visited. Program expenses for each tour consisted mostly of the cost of travel, accommodations, meals, and salary for faculty.

The study and tour program had once been very popular, but during the

Table 1.1. Analysis of Approaches to Marketing for Continuing Education.

Model	Orientation and Focus	Relationship to Environment	Guiding Force	Involvement	Advantages/Disadvantages
Traditional	Organizational orientation	Less responsive to environment	Marketing viewed as the vehicle for changing consumers' ideas, attitudes, and beliefs so that they accept the organization's programs, products, and services	Inner directed	*Advantages:* Fewer variables to consider, less complex, and often easier to sell to long-established political groups in the organization. *Disadvantages:* Discourages change in the continuing education organization, can contribute to organizational failure, and sometimes angers, disappoints, or frustrates consumers.
Exchange	Symbiotic relationship	Constant negotiation, trading, and information sharing, leading to decision making	Consumers are asked to exchange something they value (for example, time, money, old patterns of thinking) for something they perceive as a benefit (for example, programs, products, and services); focus on consumer and organization and exchanging things that each values.	Balanced	*Advantages:* The emphasis on needs assessment and negotiation encourages the continuing education organization to change. Often this change is gradual enough not to upset the dynamic equilibrium between the organization and its consumers. *Disadvantages:* Traditional internal groups in the continuing education organization can sometimes grow tired of the constant negotiation and exchange process.
Adaptive	Consumer orientation	Responsive	Organization changes its programs, products, and services to fit the changing needs, wants, and desires of consumers.	Outer directed	*Advantages:* Pleases consumers, encourages organizational renewal and adaptation, and actively promotes change. *Disadvantages:* Sometimes goes against organizational traditions and norms, can alienate traditional groups in continuing education, and can induce charges of not being interested in maintaining traditional standards.

last five years it had lost considerable money and had to receive large subsidies from the total continuing education budget. On arrival of a new dean of continuing education, an analysis of all programs was undertaken.

A detailed analysis of enrollments, expenses, the competition, and program content showed that the tours as they were presently being conducted probably could never recover their direct costs and become self-supporting. Therefore the decision was made to discontinue them, take a year to study the market, and possibly reinstitute them sometime in the future but probably with a very different and more highly targeted marketing effort. When the faculty associated with the tours were informed that the programs were to be dropped, they protested loudly. The substance of the protest was that the programs should be continued even though they lost money because exposure to new cultures and ideas was an invaluable learning experience for participants. They suggested that the reason why enrollments were so low was that Americans tended to be inner directed and uninterested in other cultures.

They overlooked the following facts. In the last ten years the city had experienced a marked increase in the number of groups who offered foreign travel and tour programs so that the university had much competition in this area. These other groups had become more sophisticated in segmenting the market and developing special tours to appeal to the individual segments. For example, the city's art museum offered trips to English country houses to study furniture and the decorative arts. The chamber of commerce, together with five of the major civic clubs, offered tours to China in which business people met with Chinese leaders to learn how to deliver a wide variety of products at low costs through importing. The local ballet company sponsored an annual tour that visited London, Paris, Copenhagen, Leningrad, and Moscow to attend ballet performances.

The university, however, had continued to offer the general foreign trip, a tour that they hoped would be appropriate for everyone—undergraduates, graduate students, people from the professions, singles, marrieds, retired people, and just people who were interested in foreign travel. This type of tour had been extremely successful a number of years ago; however, now it no longer attracted enough participants to break even. Providers of similar continuing education programs in the community who had segmented their market were successful. In fact, most of the nonuniversity tours were sold out an average of forty-five days before departure.

Analysis of Case Study 1. This case is a classic example of the traditional approach to marketing. The faculty planning and conducting each tour thought they knew what was best for the tour—a general overview of each country with visits to the usual tourist attractions in each major city. Therefore, they tended to attribute decreased enrollments to disinterest. Their proposed solution was to promote each tour more heavily by doubling the number of direct-mail brochures. The underlying assumption was that if everyone tried hard enough the program would be seen as desirable by more people.

They failed to realize that for the programs to be fully subscribed, the market would have to be segmented. The tours would have to be redesigned to hit highly targeted audiences that had similar interests. The program focus would have to be completely redesigned to appeal to the needs, wants, and desires of the target audience.

This short case represents the traditional approach to marketing. The emphasis in the traditional model is that the institution knows what is best for people. Educators create tours that conform to the vision of what is best, and believe that if enough colorful, elaborate brochures are mailed, people will register. Continuing decline in enrollments is attributed to ineffective advertising.

Exchange Model

The exchange approach to marketing is that advocated by Kotler during his many years of research in marketing. According to Kotler, marketing is "a social process by which individuals and groups obtain what they need and want through creating and exchanging products and value with others" (1984, p. 4). The key assumption underlying the exchange model is that the organization establish a symbiotic relationship with consumers. There is constant negotiation, trading, and information sharing leading to decision making. Consumers are asked to exchange something they value (for example, time or money) for something they perceive as a benefit (for example, programs, products, and services). The exchange approach to marketing focuses on consumers and the sponsoring organization exchanging things they each value.

This approach represents a balanced view of marketing. The advantage is that the emphasis on needs assessment and negotiation encourages the continuing education organization to constantly change. Yet, because of the constant negotiation, this change is usually gradual and thus does not upset the dynamic equilibrium that encourages constant interaction between the organization and its consumers.

The disadvantage of this approach is that traditional groups internal to the continuing education organization can sometimes grow weary of the constant negotiation and exchange process. When this happens they may drop out and withdraw their support because the time and effort involved in creating and constantly modifying programs may not be worth their effort. In other words, they may decide not to exchange something they value, such as their time and personal commitment, because they cannot see a sufficient payoff.

The following case study illustrates how the exchange model of marketing works in continuing education.

Case Study 2. A number of years ago the University of California–Berkeley Extension and the Art Museum Association, now merged with the American Federation of Arts, observed that museum leaders were having difficulty in their management roles. Through conversations with a wide variety of museum leaders, they learned that a major reason for this difficulty was that few museum professionals had any formal training in business or the behavioral sciences. Therefore, many of them lacked the sophisticated skills in accounting, conflict management, law, personnel management, negotiations, marketing, strategic planning, and computer technology required to bring good business practices to museums.

The University of California–Berkeley Extension and the Art Museum Association put together a planning committee and the result was the creation of a thirty-day residential professional development program called the Museum Management Institute. Careful evaluations were done after each institute, and the program content was modified to fit the changing needs of participants.

After several successful years, the J. Paul Getty Trust funded the Museum Management Institute as one of its operating entities. This enabled the Museum Management Institute to offer scholarships to thirty-five carefully selected participants each year. In fact, selection to attend the institute has come to be seen as a mark of professional achievement in the museum field.

Analysis of Case Study 2. The institute continues today and each year it is modified as a result of participant evaluation as well as input from an advisory committee of professionals from a wide variety of museums. The present program has many of the same themes found in the first program, for example, financial management. Today, however, there is more emphasis on understanding financial management concepts rather than just addressing accounting issues. There is less emphasis on computers because as a result of the explosion of personal computers in the workplace, it is possible to gain these skills locally in almost any community.

The development of this program represents the exchange model of marketing. Participants exchange something they value (their time and money) for something the sponsoring organization (the J. Paul Getty Trust in cooperation with the University of California–Berkeley Extension and the American Federation of Arts) has, namely, scholarships and access to professional expertise, resulting in a program that has come to be viewed as an excellent professional development experience for museum leaders. The program establishes a symbiotic relationship among the University of California–Berkeley, the J. Paul Getty Trust, the American Federation of Arts, and the museum profession. There are constant negotiation and trading of information that lead to program modification.

Adaptive Model

The adaptive model also uses a consumer approach. It emphasizes responsiveness to consumer interests and, as a result, is outer directed. The adaptive approach differs from the exchange approach, however, in that it places so much emphasis on responsiveness to consumer needs that it virtually ignores the needs, norms, and values of the sponsoring organization. A disadvantage of this model is that it can alienate traditional groups in the continuing education organization or parent institution. The advantage is that it does place an emphasis on pleasing consumers and thus promotes change. The adaptive approach basically assumes that anything the consumer wants or needs should be delivered whether or not such activities are consistent with the continuing education organization's mission.

The following case study demonstrates how the adaptive approach to marketing plays itself out in organizations.

Case Study 3. Almost every military base in the United States and abroad has an education office. In fact, the military is one of the biggest supporters of continuing education. They view the development of their human resources as a high priority. A large military base in a western state has 20,000 employees. To provide for their continuing education needs they invited fifteen different colleges and universities to set up and staff offices in their base education office. These fifteen institutions of higher education provided a wide variety of courses throughout the year.

A large university located in another state more than 450 miles from the military base offered more than twenty credit programs each semester at the base. As the university was located so far away, they relied exclusively on adjunct faculty. Although these adjunct faculty worked very hard and generally received good ratings from students, locally hired instructors did not have the opportunity to interact with the sponsoring university's academic departments.

As a result, the faculty in the academic departments at the university tended to discredit what they called a "bootstrap" operation. Over the years tension developed between many academic departments and the continuing education office at the university. Faculty in many departments began to refuse to cooperate with the continuing education office on different programs because they had come to feel that the office was not interested in maintaining academic excellence.

Soon a ground swell emerged and the faculty called for the resignation of the dean of continuing education and the closing of the program on the military base to concentrate on the university's main mission: "serving the people of our state with quality educational programs."

Analysis of Case Study 3. This represents a continuing education marketing effort based on the adaptive model. There was a need for education on the military base. The continuing education staff located at a university 450 miles from the base in another state saw a chance to fulfill the need and at the same time make some money to support their operation. There was even university-based faculty support from academic departments when the program was begun in the 1960s.

With the changing times, tighter financial resources, and a new concern with quality control of courses offered by all institutions, many of the faculty at the university no longer saw this type of outreach using exclusively adjunct faculty to be a mission of the institution. Thus, what began as the adaptive model of marketing—if the consumer wants it, it must be good and we must provide it—

led to severe conflict between the continuing education office and the parent institution. The dean resigned and the university's continuing education operation on the military base closed shortly thereafter.

Summary of Approaches to Marketing

Three models of marketing for continuing education have been identified and analyzed: the traditional model, the exchange model, and the adaptive model. These are the most widely used marketing models found in continuing education organizations today; however, they rarely appear in their pure forms. Instead, most continuing education organizations use a combination of these models.

No matter which model or combination of models is used, there are important issues related to developing effective marketing for continuing education organizations. Nine such issues are outlined here together with suggested guidelines for dealing with them.

Nine Guidelines for Developing Effective Marketing Plans

1. *Clear definitions of the differences among marketing, advertising, and publicity will assist in development of more effective marketing plans.* The terms *marketing, advertising,* and *publicity* are often used interchangeably (Lovelock and Weinberg, 1984; Bobrow and Bobrow, 1985; Kotler, 1985, 1987); however, there are important distinctions among these concepts. In this handbook, *marketing* is used to refer to the overall process of studying, analyzing, and making decisions about how best to serve consumers with continuing education programs and services. The emphasis is on the needs, attitudes, and values of the consumer as well as the sponsoring organization. Advertising and publicity, then, become promotional techniques that are used to achieve marketing objectives (Farlow, 1979; Aaker and Myers, 1982; Higgins, 1987).

Advertising is the term used to refer to paid promotion. For example, an ad in a newspaper or a direct-mail brochure for a continuing education program is advertising. The term *publicity* is used to denote forms of unpaid promotion, for example, a feature story in a newspaper, an interview on a local television program, or a talk to a local chamber of commerce group. Therefore, advertising and publicity are both important components of marketing; however, marketing is the umbrella term that refers to the interactions between an organization and the many publics it serves.

As direct-mail marketing is often one of the primary means of advertising in most continuing education organizations, it is easy to be trapped into thinking that attention to the production of effective brochures, catalogues, and flyers is effective marketing. In reality, careful attention to these areas of direct-mail advertising usually means that you have developed this one aspect of marketing. However, a comprehensive marketing plan for a continuing education organization will also address the following issues:

- What image do we want to convey to the many publics we serve?
- How can we analyze our actions to see if we convey our desired images?
- What plans are developed to involve these stakeholders in the success of the organization and its programs, products, and services?
- What kinds of data can we collect about our consumers so that we can better serve them?
- How do our programs, products, and services contribute to the betterment of individuals as well as society as a whole?
- What is the proper mix of publicity, advertising, and other marketing tools to achieve our marketing objectives, with particular attention to the realities of our financial constraints?
- If we constitute a subunit of a parent institution how do our unit's goals and objectives help the parent institution effectively achieve its goals and mission?
- What kind of research must we do to fulfill our overall marketing goals and objectives?
- How will this research be financed?

These are some of the important questions to answer in developing a comprehensive marketing plan. Chapter Four describes in detail how to create an effective marketing plan. Chapter Five contains a sample marketing plan that can easily be adapted to fit the needs of your organization. Effective advertising and publicity are difficult to achieve without such a marketing plan.

2. *Marketing, to be effective, must be directly related to achieving the overall mission, goals, and objectives of an institution.* Marketing cannot be effective unless it is directly related to achieving the institution's mission (Luther, 1982; Kinnear and Taylor, 1983; Hayes and Elmore, 1985). There should be active consideration of this symbiotic relationship in the development and implementation of the overall marketing plan. This, of course, implies that the institution has a clearly defined and understood mission and that specific goals and objectives have been developed to achieve this mission. If this is not the case, it is impossible to develop a marketing plan. What is possible if the mission, goals, and objectives are not clear is to develop advertising and promotion for specific programs, products, and services. In addition, it is possible to use the development of a marketing plan to assist the institution in clearly defining and agreeing on its mission, goals, and objectives.

It would be nice if all institutions acted like the idealized models of rational institutions that first develop a mission from which flow goals and objectives. These could then be used to create a comprehensive marketing plan that guides the development of advertising and publicity for individual activities. The reality, of course, is that many institutions have not followed this rational, logical process. Therefore, because an institution's mission, goals, and objectives often lack clarity, their marketing efforts often lack clarity. In such cases marketing usually turns out to be a series of loosely constructed activities that lack focus because they are not designed to achieve specific goals and objectives

(McDonald, 1985; O'Shaughnessy, 1984; McCarthy and Perreault, 1985; Rapp and Collins, 1987).

The relationship among these variables is depicted in Figure 1.1.

The bottom pyramid illustrates that advertising and promotion form the basis for developing comprehensive marketing activities. These marketing activities result from environmental scanning. Such marketing activities interface with the activities illustrated in the top pyramid, which includes issues related to how continuing education programs and services contribute to the institution's mission. In addition, it is important to determine how these programs, products, and services contribute to the betterment of individuals and society at large.

As Figure 1.1 illustrates, marketing is a complex activity that forms the central interface with overall institutional concerns. It pervades all actions and creates perceptions on the part of consumers. If these perceptions are positive, the public will be more receptive to purchasing continuing education programs and services. If these perceptions are negative, they will be less likely to do so (Robertson, Zielinski, and Ward 1984; Webster, 1984; Weiers, 1984; Sheth, 1985).

Therefore, marketing is much more than publicity, advertising, or personal selling. It is that complex series of activities whereby an institution

Figure 1.1. Relationship of Marketing to the Institution's Environment.

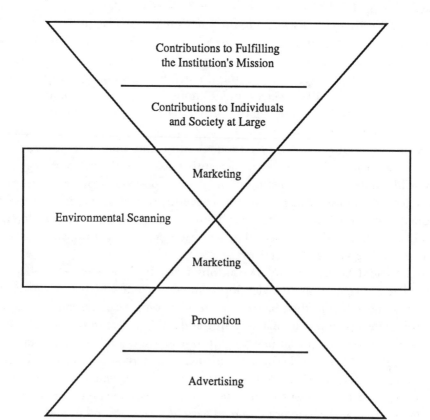

Contributions to Fulfilling
the Institution's Mission

Contributions to Individuals
and Society at Large

Marketing

Environmental Scanning

Marketing

Promotion

Advertising

exchanges information regarding attitudes, wants, desires, values, and needs with its environment (Kotler, 1984).

Chapter Two deals directly with articulation of institutional mission, goals, and objectives. Chapter Six shows how to align continuing education programs with the desired institutional image.

3. *Environmental scanning can help to make all marketing efforts more effective.* Environmental scanning enables continuing educators to gather information about issues critical to the success of the institution and its programs and services. Essentially, environmental scanning comprises those activities, both formal and informal, by which the institution takes in information.

Conducting focus groups to ascertain how people view your continuing education organization is a useful way to scan the environment. Participation in professional associations enables continuing education leaders to network and learn from others those issues that are most important in the field of professional practice. Reading widely in magazines, newspapers, and periodicals and analyzing how current issues can enhance the success of your continuing education organization is a useful environmental scanning technique.

It is important for any organization to establish a series of both formal and informal environmental scanning techniques that enable it to constantly monitor the environment (Mitroff, 1983). Thus, key issues related to achieving success can be identified and addressed. This is the primary way in which all institutions achieve change and adapt to their environment (Lippitt, 1982; Ehrenkranz and Kahn, 1983; Kirkpatrick, 1985). Chapter Thirty-One details effective environmental scanning.

4. *Developing a customer service orientation is an important part of marketing.* Continuing education organizations need to decide about the role of the consumer in relation to the organization. When the decision is made that the consumer is one of the most valuable organizational assets, then policies can be developed to achieve this. For example, listed here are some procedures established by one continuing education organization that decided to develop a comprehensive marketing plan based on the consumer as one of the most valuable organizational assets.

- Acknowledge all registrations for any program within twenty-four hours.
- Mail brochures or other continuing education information within twenty-four hours of the request.
- Answer all phone calls by the fourth ring.
- Create a computerized accounting system that reflects income and expenses for all programs and is accurate within the last twenty-four hours. Have printouts available on demand so that staff and clients can have accurate, quick access to financial data to ensure better decision making for all programs.
- Follow up any consumer complaint with a phone call and personal letter from the appropriate department head within forty-eight hours.
- Provide a toll-free phone number so that people can register for programs or

communicate with the continuing education organization for any reason without paying for a long-distance call.

- Institute a comprehensive staff training program to ensure that this new service orientation is effectively implemented.
- Ask for input from staff at all levels of the organization on ways to improve the service orientation. Take care to ensure that these suggestions are implemented.

Most continuing education organizations find that such a service orientation is difficult to initiate without (1) involving all staff, (2) clearly establishing this service orientation as an important goal, (3) having all the major leaders constantly communicate this to staff, and (4) developing ways to measure the success in achieving the many identified components of whatever service orientation is adopted. Development of an effective service orientation should be an integral part of marketing plan (Donnelly and George, 1981; Lovelock, 1984; Albrecht and Zemke, 1985; Heskett, 1986; Desatnick, 1987a, 1987b).

Chapter Eight discusses a wide variety of methods to effect this service orientation. Chapter Twenty-Four addresses this issue by analyzing how to use all staff members as personal salespersons.

5. *Psychographic and demographic data are important components of a marketing data base.* Demographic data are data on individuals and groups that are fairly well known and relatively easy to measure. Some examples of demographic data are number of people registered to vote in a community, average number of children residing in a household, age, educational level, and membership in clubs, societies, associations, or other groups.

Psychographic data are very different. These data are more abstract and not as easy to measure as demographic data. Nevertheless, market researchers are finding out that psychographic data are just as important as demographic data in developing comprehensive approaches to marketing. Psychographic data provide answers to the following questions. On what types of products, goods, and services do people with different life-styles spend their money? When do they spend this money? What values do they hold and how do these values influence their consumer behavior? What expectations do they have for themselves and their children and how do these expectations play themselves out in the marketplace? What are the key attitudes, values, and beliefs that will trigger them to be receptive to advertising? How do people in various occupations feel about different media used in advertising? Which medium do they feel offers them the most accurate and responsible message?

To develop successful marketing plans, continuing education organizations need to develop sophisticated methods to collect, analyze, and use both demographic and psychographic data as a basis for constantly modifying their marketing plans. Both types of data are equally important and necessary to a comprehensive approach to marketing (Mitchell, 1983).

Chapter Three analyzes this entire process of learning more about a specific market and shows how geographic, demographic, psychographic, and behavioristic data can be used to enhance marketing efforts of continuing education programs and services.

6. *Market segmentation is an important marketing concept for continuing education leaders.* There is no such thing as a general market for continuing education activities. Instead, there are many segments of a total market. Finding reliable and effective ways to segment the market for whatever continuing education programs and services are offered is essential to marketing success. For example, general programs on management supervisory skills are one way to segment the market for noncredit management workshops. Another way is to individualize the content and develop separate programs devoted to individually targeted audiences. For example, one continuing education organization has taken a general program on basic management supervision and adapted it to different markets using the following program titles for two-day workshops:

- "Principles of Supervision for the New Manager"
- "Management Supervision for Environmental Services Leaders"
- "Supervision for Administrative Assistants"
- "Supervisory Effectiveness for Managers in the Textile Industry"
- "Effective Supervisory Skills for Retail Store Managers"
- "Managing for Results: A Workshop for Hotel and Restaurant Managers"
- "Supervision for Leaders in Social Service Agencies"

Increasingly, continuing education organizations find that they must engage in this type of market segmentation to design and deliver effective programs. Consumers want to feel that the program content was designed to deal with their practical, on-the-job problems. This is difficult to do when participants come from a wide variety of backgrounds.

Perhaps no other aspect of marketing has gained so much national attention in the last decade as has the idea of segmenting the market and designing programs and services to deal with the individual market segments in ways perceived by consumers to be of value.

Throughout this handbook, market segmentation is emphasized. It is an important concept in development of an overall marketing plan for the continuing education organization as well as for individual programs.

7. *Tracking the results of marketing efforts is an essential step in the total marketing plan.* To evaluate the effectiveness of marketing, it is imperative to effectively track your marketing results. For example, if you advertise a workshop in a newspaper, it is important to track the number of inquiries and also to track how many of these inquiries result in actual registrations. In this way, the effectiveness of the advertising campaign can be determined.

If you mail a brochure advertising a program to 20,000 people using ten different mailing lists that you have carefully selected, it is important to code these lists and institute an effective tracking device so that you can determine which lists were most effective in producing registrations. Effective tracking systems enable you to analyze the results of your marketing activities, modify these activities as needed, and ultimately become more cost effective in all marketing activities (Hodgson, 1980; Harper, 1986; Holtz, 1986; Elliott, 1987).

Chapter Eighteen is devoted to tracking the results of public relations efforts, Chapter Twenty-Three analyzes how to track results of advertising, and Chapter Twenty-Five shows how to track the results of telemarketing.

8. *Development of a marketing plan is an ongoing process; it is never finished.* There is no such thing as a final marketing plan for a continuing education organization. Any successful marketing plan should constantly undergo modification. As new data are received from the environment, the plan must be changed. Various marketing activities will need to be redesigned. Publicity will need to be reoriented to meet constantly changing marketing goals. Advertising will need to be modified based on the results of tracking systems.

Marketing, like strategic planning, is one of those processes that is always in a state of change in any organization. All the chapters in this handbook emphasize this dynamic, flexible, changing quality characteristic of all marketing activities.

9. *A professional library of marketing resources can assist all staff members in becoming more effective in their marketing efforts.* People tend not to read, study, and analyze new marketing ideas if the resources for these new ideas are not conveniently located on site in the offices where they work. Therefore, an important step in developing a comprehensive marketing orientation is to establish an up-to-date library of marketing resources. The last chapter of this book suggests a wide variety of resources to include in such a library. In addition, an extensive bibliography is included at the end of this book.

Nevertheless, just having a marketing resource library on site is not enough. Key leaders in the organization must be encouraged to read, analyze, discuss, and adapt these marketing ideas for use on a daily basis. The literature on organizational change consistently points out the necessity for key leaders in any organization to actively encourage the introduction of new ideas into the organizational environment.

Summary

Attention to these nine important guidelines will lead to the development of more effective marketing plans in continuing education organizations. When marketing is viewed as broader than just advertising or publicity, it can be an important factor enabling the organization to achieve its mission more effectively. In this way continuing educators can develop dynamic, responsive organizations that meet internal organizational needs as well as external consumer needs.

As a result, marketing can be raised to a level of visibility so that all staff are aware of their role in the total marketing orientation. Each staff member becomes a personal ambassador for the institution. And, institutions staffed by such employees will be dynamic, flexible, and responsive to their environment.

2

Integrating Marketing into Strategic Planning

Robert G. Simerly

Continuing education organizations exist to serve society by providing a better-educated citizenry capable of solving the increasingly complex problems faced by humankind. We engage in marketing to establish a series of exchanges with our many constituencies which, in turn, leads to achievement of goals (Kotler, 1984, 1986). Thus, continuing education programs and other services are provided in exchange for support for these programs through registrations. As a result, marketing becomes an important process all continuing education organizations use to achieve their mission.

Before mission, goals, and objectives can be discussed, these must be defined. For the purposes of this analysis the terms *mission, goal,* and *objective* have very specialized meanings.

A *mission* is a short statement that provides the overall reason for existence for an organization. It should be inspirational, address how the organization serves society, and be of a visionary nature so that it can provide the direction for years to come. Basically, a mission statement should answer the question "Why does this organization exist and what should it be doing to help society?"

Goals are a series of statements that set direction for a wide variety of events in the organization. They are not easily measured; rather, they tend to be more abstract. They should, however, provide a rallying point for people and their ideas.

An *objective,* on the other hand, is very specific. It can be measured, someone can be assigned to achieve it, deadlines can be easily established, and methods of evaluation can be agreed on. An objective is thus a subset of a goal.

These three definitions must .be kept in mind in the development of effective strategic marketing plans for continuing education organizations (Simerly and Associates, 1987). Marketing plans then become an integral part of total organizational strategic planning because almost all actions of the organization are affected by marketing decisions.

Guidelines for Establishing a Mission, Goals, and Objectives

1. *An overarching statement of mission should be developed before goals are established.* Establishing a clear and achievable mission is the first step in setting goals, because everything the organization does should be measured against the mission to see if the fit is correct. The mission must be broad enough to take care of tomorrow's vision. For example, years ago the railroads established their primary mission as that of delivering goods via rail. If they had decided on a broader, more visionary mission, they would have realized that they were in the transportation business. Had this happened, the railroads would now be running the airlines. Similarly, the steel industry established its mission as being in the steel business. If they had established a mission of being in the materials and equipment supply business, they would be providing materials made of wood, metals, and synthetics.

Therefore, great care must be taken in deciding on a mission. A mission statement should be visionary and broad enough so that it can guide an organization for many years. If it is comprehensive and sufficiently visionary, it should not have to be revised very often. Goals and objectives may require frequent revision, but the mission should be able to remain virtually unchanged for long periods.

Listed here are some examples of mission statements that are effective for different types of continuing education organizations:

- *Continuing education division of a university.* The Office of Continuing Education is established to work with all academic departments to deliver the university's resources to the people of the state and beyond.
- *Training and development division of a major industrial corporation.* The Training and Development Division exists for the purpose of providing leadership in working with all departments in the organization to ensure that employees have access to quality professional development opportunities.
- *Training and professional development department in a large hospital.* The Training and Professional Development Department is established to work with all departments in the hospital to ensure that staff have access to the latest techniques, trends, ideas, and skills in their particular area of specialty. We believe that this constant attention to professional development will create the best possible working environment and that care for patients will be the best when this happens. Therefore, there will be no higher priority for this hospital than carefully nurturing this continuing professional development for all staff.

- *Human resource section of a large federal agency.* The Human Resource Development Office has been established to ensure that the quality of work life in the organization is excellent. We believe that this, in turn, will be the primary factor in helping the organization achieve its other goals and objectives. Therefore, we intend to create the kind of working environment that will enable staff to meet their professional goals and, hopefully, many of their personal goals. This emphasis on people will be a guiding principle for all our actions.
- *Large museum.* Henry Ford Museum functions as a national museum of history and technology that tells the story of how America changed from a rural agrarian society to the urban industrial nation it is today.

All of these mission statements share a common characteristic: they are not easily measured. At the same time they are visionary and set a tone and direction against which daily decisions can be made and for which goals and objectives can be developed.

2. *Goals should be large, generalized statements that cannot easily be measured in time and space.* A goal can be thought of as a large, generalized statement that contributes to the mission of the organization. It cannot easily be measured. It tends to be more abstract, inspirational, and visionary. It should provide a rallying point from which people move toward establishing specific objectives to achieve the goals.

Here are listed some goal statements for typical important areas in continuing education organizations:

- *Financial goal.* We will break even at the end of each fiscal year.
- *Human resource management goal.* There will be no goal more important in this organization than the continued professional development of all staff.
- *Program development goal.* This organization will specialize in developing a wide variety of continuing education programs that are innovative and do not duplicate those offered by our leading competition.
- *Physical facilities.* We will maintain our physical facilities in good repair within the constraints of our budget.
- *Marketing goal.* We will regularly conduct action-oriented marketing research within the organization to stay on the cutting edge of the most effective marketing techniques for our programs. This marketing will always be implemented in a manner appropriate for the overall tone, image, and quality of our institution.

The preceding goal statements provide a general but not a specific direction against which daily decisions can be measured. They are overarching and somewhat abstract, yet they communicate a set of powerful commitments on the part of the organization. For example, the goal for human resource management states that the continued professional development of all staff will be one of the highest priorities of the institution. This has an inspirational quality. Objectives can be created to implement this goal. And, most importantly, it clearly states an organizational philosophy designed to give specific and clear direction in the area of human resource management. Most organizations find that from five to eight goal statements are enough to clearly set direction. Then, as many objectives as necessary can be established to achieve each goal.

    3. *Objectives should be directly related to achieving goals.* Listed here are some sample objectives appropriate to the goal statements outlined earlier.

Financial goal

We will break even at the end of each year.

Objectives to achieve goal

Susan, our business manager, will provide each department with monthly financial reports showing all income and expenses for that month.

These reports will be in the hands of all department directors by the tenth working day of each month.

She will then arrange personal conferences with each department director to discuss each month's computer printout in relation to the total year's budget for that department. This will enable everyone to make adjustments in overall income and expenses as necessary. This meeting and any budgetary adjustments will be completed by the last working day of each month.

Human resource management goal

There will be no goal more important in this organization than the continued professional development of all staff.

Objectives to achieve goal

All department directors will submit their plans for the professional development of their staff by September 1 of each year.

These plans will be based on a survey of staff to determine their needs for professional development. Each director will complete this needs assessment by July 15 of each year.

All professional development programs will be evaluated by the participants. Results will be tabulated and available for all departmental staff.

In addition to specific professional development programs planned for the total staff, each director will work with each staff member to produce an individual professional development plan. This will be completed by October 15 of each year.

Program development goal

This organization will specialize in developing a wide variety of continuing education programs that are innovative and do not duplicate those offered by our leading competition.

Objectives to achieve goal

Each department director will submit a comprehensive list of programs to be offered by January 1 and July 1 of each year. This will also include budgets for all programs so that accurate budget projections can be made in relation to program development.

Each year Tom will do an analysis of what our five identified competitors are doing so that we can avoid doing similar programs. Tom will complete this by February 1. He will report the results for discussion at a staff meeting by March 1.

In addition to repeater programs, each department will plan and administer fifteen new programs each year. The department director will be in charge of ensuring that these are listed on the January 1 and July 1 updates of all programs.

Physical facilities goal

We will maintain our physical facilities in good repair within the constraints of our budget.

Objectives to achieve goal

Linda, our manager of physical facilities, will monitor on a monthly basis the condition of our physical facilities. She will arrange a meeting once a month to discuss physical facility needs with the director.

Linda will be in charge of seeing that routine repairs are made as the need arises. She will also manage her repair budget so that it breaks even at the end of each fiscal year.

A comprehensive list of needed capital improvements will be submitted to the director by June 1 each year so that these can be integrated into the budget planning cycle.

Linda will be in charge of supervising the custodial staff to ensure that the facilities are maintained in a spotlessly clean fashion. She will develop a comprehensive plan to achieve this by March 15.

Marketing goal

We will regularly conduct action-oriented marketing research within the organization to stay on the cutting edge of the most effective marketing techniques for our programs. This marketing will always be done in a manner appropriate to the overall tone, image, and quality of our institution.

Objectives to achieve goal

John, our director of marketing, will design a comprehensive tracking system so that we can monitor which lists produced how many registrants for each program. Preliminary plans for this will be discussed at a staff meeting by March 1. The permanent system will be implemented by August 1. Modifications will be made as necessary to ensure that this objective is met.

Each department director will arrange to meet with John at least four times a year to arrange special action-oriented marketing plans appropriate for that department. These meetings will take place by January 1, April 1, August 1, and October 1.

John will arrange a series of focus groups to determine what our clients think of our programs and services and to determine what they would like for future programs. He will report on the first series of focused group interviews by August 15.

By September 30, John will have

prepared a comprehensive marketing plan for the organization. This will be discussed at a staff meeting by October 30 and implemented by November 15.

A list of important principles of effective direct-mail techniques is being drawn up by the departments after a two-day retreat on direct-mail marketing. These important principles will be implemented for all direct-mail marketing taking place after December 15.

The preceding objectives share a set of characteristics. Someone can be assigned to implement each objective, a deadline can be set for achieving each objective, and an evaluation technique to measure the success in reaching each objective can usually be established before the project is begun. Although most organizations find that five to eight major goals are sufficient, for each goal the number of objectives is unlimited.

4. *A reliable feedback system should be established to periodically measure the organization's progress in achieving its goals and objectives.* It is one thing to establish goals and objectives on paper and it is another to actually achieve these goals and objectives (Hickson and others, 1986). To ensure success, it is important to establish feedback mechanisms to monitor the entire process (Steiner, 1979, 1982; Allen, 1982; Grove, 1983; Kilmann, 1984; Kilmann, Saxton, Serpa, and Associates, 1985). One of the easiest ways to accomplish this task is to generate a computerized list of all objectives along with the deadlines and the people assigned to implement the objectives. From this primary list, several secondary lists can be created, for example, an arrangement of objectives according to deadlines or according to the persons in charge of implementing the objectives. People can monitor their individual progress and an update can be done once a month at a staff meeting.

If such an ongoing monitoring process is not implemented, the establishment of goals and objectives will come to be viewed as an event that occurs only during planning meetings. This will not help the staff to achieve specific tasks by specific dates (Tannenbaum, Margulies, Massarik, and Associates, 1985). It is essential to establish a feedback system that is (1) easy to monitor, (2) reliable in providing a record of success, (3) reliable in providing an early warning where the achievement of an objective is in trouble, and (4) clearly understood by those with the responsibility for meeting deadlines.

5. *Goal attainment should be celebrated in ways that are meaningful to the organization's members.* In the busy work life of most organizations, it is easy to concentrate on problems and forget to celebrate successes. When objectives are achieved, they should be celebrated in ways that are meaningful to staff. For example, once a month at a staff meeting, the people who have met their deadlines for specific objectives should be praised. More elaborate systems can

also be designed, although lavish reward systems are often not nearly as effective as daily praise and thanks for a job well done. Finding appropriate ways to celebrate these successes will contribute to building a positive organizational culture in which all staff feel they have a part in defining the direction for the organization (Deal and Kennedy, 1982; Peters and Waterman, 1982; Bolman and Deal, 1984; Peters and Austin, 1985; Schein, 1985). Organizations that celebrate their success in achieving specific objectives empower their staff with a sense of accomplishment (Kotter, 1985; Lawler, 1986), which, in turn, encourages staff to reach out and try to achieve greater success. Research has demonstrated that being motivated by success seeking is much more rewarding than being motivated by the fear of failing (Mitroff, 1983; Phillips, 1985; Maehr and Braskamp, 1986).

6. *Marketing goals and objectives should always be designed to enhance the organization's overall goals, tone, and image.* It is important that marketing goals and objectives be compatible with the organization's overall goals, tone, and image (Crompton and Lamb, 1986; Greenley, 1986; Rapp and Collins, 1987). For example, a major university with a nationally recognized psychology department will probably not look favorably on a continuing education office that offers noncredit evening courses entitled "Astrology for Everyday Living." A training and development department of a Fortune 500 corporation will probably be most successful if it markets its offerings internally in a way that enhances the overall tone and culture of that particular organization. Thus, marketing objectives must always consider the history of the organization, its mission, its major goals, and the tone conveyed in the advertising message (Kotler, 1984; Lovelock, 1984; Lacznick and Murphy, 1985; Freedman, 1987). The fit between the marketing efforts and the institutional expectations must be compatible to achieve overall success.

7. *Internal marketing is just as important as external marketing.* Continuing education offices that are part of a larger parent institution have special marketing considerations. Not only do they need to market externally to their clients, but they must also market internally to the parent institution. Internal marketing has two purposes. First, it keeps the parent institution posted on the details of upcoming programs. In this way, all staff obtain a comprehensive view of the wide variety of programming provided by the continuing education unit. Second, it provides a chance to market to the parent institution information about the services and benefits provided by the continuing education organization. In this way it is possible to clearly establish how continuing education contributes to the overall mission of the parent organization.

This builds powerful internal support for programs, services, and benefits. It helps emphasize the importance of creating an effective fit between the parent institution and the continuing education office. In addition, it raises to a level of visibility the service orientation of the continuing education office and how this service orientation is important in helping the parent institution achieve its overall mission.

8. *Internal marketing and external marketing tend to be most successful when benefits to people are emphasized.* Articulating an organization's goals and

objectives is most successful when benefits to people through a service orientation are stressed (O'Shaughnessy, 1984; Heskett, 1986; Desatnick, 1987; Rapp and Collins, 1987). This applies to overall organizational goals and objectives as well as to individual programs. For example, an executive development program is judged to be of value because the quality of the content leads to specific benefits for people. (This is quite different from mere emphasis on the quality of the program.) For example, the copy in a direct-mail brochure for the program could read as follows:

As a result of attending this program, you will:

- Learn five new ways to manage conflict in your jobs and how this can help you become a better leader
- Find a renewed sense of personal accomplishment when you have to deal with difficult personnel issues at work
- Come to be seen as a powerful manager who knows how to cut through red tape to get things done
- Increase your effectiveness in working with superiors and subordinates
- Contribute directly to improved profitability in your organization because of your ability to develop a strategic planning process

This emphasis on benefits to people can carry over into a wide variety of interactions. For example, if you are part of a larger, parent institution you can develop marketing plans to let staff in the parent institution know how they can benefit from working with you. You can let external clients know how they can benefit from working with you to design in-house training and development programs. Emphasizing benefits to people throughout the process of articulating an organization's goals and objectives is an important marketing concept that can be adapted to meet the individual needs of all continuing education organizations.

9. *Development of effective marketing strategies can be an important step in organizational renewal.* An important reason for developing effective marketing goals and objectives is that it provides an opportunity for constant organizational renewal. Designing more effective methods to reach clients automatically spurs a rethinking of major procedures, programs, and policies (Bloch, Upah, and Zeithaml, 1985; Kotler and Fox, 1985; Heskett, 1986; Desatnick, 1987). Thus, the continuous definition of marketing goals and objectives is important to establishment of an automatic organizational renewal process. When all staff are able to participate in the setting of goals and objectives, it is possible to disburse the responsibility for effectiveness and efficiency throughout the organization (Ackoff, 1981; Lippitt, 1982, 1985; Beck and Hillmar, 1986; Tapor, 1986). Staff begin to feel an enhanced sense of personal power. Innovative ideas emerge with greater frequency (Boyatzis, 1982; Cohen and Cohen, 1984; Bennis and Nanus, 1985). Programs and people become more effective. The establishment, implementation, and monitoring of marketing goals and objectives can help guide this organizational renewal process.

Effective Articulation of Organizational Goals and Objectives

Once the decision has been made to engage in a comprehensive and systematic articulation of goals and objectives, it is important to analyze the factors that promote this process most effectively. Thus, the process of setting and achieving goals and objectives becomes a marketing process. Leaders should give attention to the following factors to ensure success:

1. Creating an environment where all staff can help establish appropriate goals and objectives consistent with the organization's mission. This is a psychological commitment to emphasizing excellence and service to clients.

2. Providing training in strategic planning. Establishment of a systematic way to define and achieve specific, measurable objectives is a new activity in many organizations. Therefore, training has to be provided to show people how to implement a planning process concerned with constantly emphasizing measurable outcomes.

3. Allowing people to fail when establishing and trying to attain goals and objectives. Reaching out to try new ideas and projects will result in some failures. Often it is much easier to celebrate success than to cope with failure. Therefore, it is important that any marketing or planning process allow for failure and provide support for staff to fail as well as to succeed.

4. Creating an organizational environment in which team work is rewarded. Often, it is easier to engage in individual entrepreneurship in organizations than it is to create cooperative team work situations. However, most important organizational problems require team work for effective solutions. Therefore, specific plans need to be developed to nurture and reward team work.

5. Realizing that higher levels of conflict are almost always evident in organizations that place high emphasis on establishing and achieving goals and objectives. Cooperative problem solving involves team work and team work often leads to conflict situations.

6. Assisting staff with managing organizational conflict for productive results. Change is always accompanied by conflict. If leaders manage conflict as a normal part of the problem-solving process, it can be channeled into productive results for the organization.

7. Establishing a system of early warning signs for goals and objectives that are not being met. Often, with advance warning, projects that are in trouble can be turned into successes.

8. Providing for open and honest evaluation and feedback on successes and failures. Opening up this feedback process so that it is honest and direct for both successes and failures leads to improved problem solving.

9. Asking people to constantly expand their visions and skills. Almost all people want to grow, develop, and constantly expand their horizons. Establishing this as an organizational expectation can encourage this process. People who are constantly encouraged to reach out for expanded responsibility and new projects usually become the most productive problem solvers in an organization.

Mistakes Most Often Made in Articulating Organizational Goals and Objectives

In analyzing what to do to increase effectiveness in establishing goals and objectives, it is equally important to analyze what not to do. Listed here are the mistakes most often made in this process. Leaders should plan to avoid these mistakes as they engage in the complex process of setting goals and objectives and developing both internal and external marketing strategies.

1. Failure to break goals down into measurable objectives.
2. Failure to delegate implementation of each objective to only one person to clearly establish accountability.
3. Failure to establish definite deadlines for each objective.
4. Failure to establish in advance how objectives will be measured.
5. Failure to provide a feedback system to establish how objectives can be achieved so that corrective action can be taken if necessary as projects proceed.
6. Failure to allocate the necessary human and financial resources to reach each objective.
7. Failure to realize that change is usually incremental and that small successes lead to larger successes.
8. Failure at the highest levels of management to support establishment of a clear mission, goals, and objectives.
9. Failure to create organizational readiness for setting goals and objectives. Change takes time and the organization must prepare for this.
10. Failure to utilize the expertise of staff in defining the problems of the organization and creating goals and objectives to solve these problems.

Empowerment

Helping staff to attain personal power is an important issue (Kanter, 1977, 1983; Pfeffer, 1981; Bradford and Cohen, 1984; Simerly and Associates, 1987). Power is sometimes viewed as a negative force. In reality, power is the ability to get a fair share of resources to do the job you were hired to do (Kanter, 1977, 1983). This is a positive definition of power. It is important that organizational leaders empower their staff by helping them create personal power in their organizational roles (Harris, 1985; Derr, 1986; Johnston and Associates, 1986; Block, 1987). People who see themselves as powerful apply their entrepreneurial skills to achieve internal organizational change. This internal application of entrepreneurial skills is known as *intrepreneuring.*

Empowerment is the opposite of *anomie,* which is powerlessness—the feeling that it is impossible to make an impact in the organization. Staff who experience anomie do not reach out to participate in problem solving. They do not define new directions for the organization. They do not create new projects and carry them forward toward a successful conclusion (Simerly and Associates, 1987).

Because the empowerment issue is so central to organizational leadership, it is important to consider what leaders can do to nurture this empowerment. These guidelines are helpful to continuing education leaders and constitute an important foundation for marketing the internal and external organizational goals and objectives.

1. Create consensus for goals and objectives. This will give staff members a psychological stake in achieving success for projects.
2. Clearly delegate responsibility for reaching a specific objective to only one person. Through the peer pressure of team work and cooperative problem solving, groups will develop a stake in helping individuals to succeed in achieving their objectives.
3. Provide the necessary human, financial, and physical resources to achieve objectives.
4. Integrate well-researched marketing concepts into all projects to help guarantee their success.
5. Pay equal attention to external and internal marketing.
6. Design deliberate reward systems at various stages throughout a project rather than reserving rewards for the end of a project.
7. Work in development of all staff; emphasize counseling, coaching, and straightforward feedback, whether positive or negative.
8. Establish two-way communication for all important organizational problem solving.
9. Deal with people's affective or feeling level during problem solving. This affective dimension of problem solving is as important as the cognitive issues.
10. Develop and use empowering language during individual and group meetings. Language forms the images for thoughts. Therefore, if empowerment is an important issue, this concept must be discussed openly and must be reflected in language and actions.

Summary

This chapter has examined the importance of articulating organizational mission, goals, and objectives. The marketing of this planning process both internally and externally is just as important as the planning process itself, which is in line with the major theme of this book—that marketing is much broader than the need to advertise continuing education programs more effectively. Integration of marketing concepts into all aspects of organizational problem solving can be a major force in achieving constant organizational renewal.

This constant renewal process keeps organizations vital and responsive to the changing needs of society (Kirkpatrick, 1985; London, 1985; Pfeiffer, Goodstein, and Nolan, 1985; Srivastva and Associates, 1986). It empowers staff and infuses a renewed sense of purpose and vigor into the daily routine (Bellman, 1986; Hall and Associates, 1986). As a result, there is a transformation wherein the organization begins to think and plan strategically (Sims, Gioia, and Associates, 1986; Simerly and Associates, 1987).

Marketing provides data for scanning the environment. It helps identify the stakeholders who are important for successful strategy implementation. It aids organizational renewal. It is the primary vehicle for reaching out to a wide variety of constituencies. It empowers organizations and their staffs. In all continuing education organizations, marketing should be an integral part of daily organizational life.

3

Learning More About Your Market: Sources and Uses of Data

Dennis L. Tarr

Educational needs and preferences are so varied in today's highly competitive marketplace that having good programs or services for adults is no longer sufficient. With so many options available to the discriminating adult customer, continuing educators who wish their programs to be successful and to flourish must provide more than excellent programs and services. They must also utilize sound strategic planning and be able to flex the marketing muscle that develops by use of the latest sophisticated marketing research.

Central to this effort is the process of learning more about your market, including the use of geographic, demographic, psychographic, and behavioristic data to develop a strong marketing strategy. In today's marketplace the competition for information and ideas is so intense, according to Rapp and Collins (1987), "if you don't know who, what, and where your true prospects are, or if you fail to go after them as individuals, you will lose ground to competitors who do" (p. 33). Thus, an alternate title for this could be "Why Segmentation Is the Key to Your Marketing Success."

What is market segmentation, how do you do it, and what difference does it make for the continuing educator? That is what this chapter is all about.

For many centuries some form of market segmentation has been practiced, consciously or unconsciously, by companies, political parties, religions, countries, and even universities. However, this idea did not receive academic legitimacy until 1956, when Wendell R. Smith published his now classic article in the *Journal of Marketing*, "Product Differentiation and Market Segmentation as Alternative Marketing Strategies." Since publication of that article, segmentation, or, as some writers describe it, "target marketing" (Rapp and Collins, 1987; Kotler, 1985; and others), has become a major marketing planning tool and the basis for effective strategy formulation in many companies and organizations throughout the United States and in Western Europe.

According to Weinstein (1987), market segmentation is "the process of partitioning markets into segments of potential customers with similar characteristics who are likely to exhibit similar purchase behavior" (p. 4). Segmentation is the most custom-made approach to satisfying a particular market. For example, a university may choose to distinguish among the various segments of alumni that make up its total market. It may choose to focus on one or two of these segments, such as recent graduates in engineering or law, and then develop programs to meet the specific needs of these subgroups.

Most textbooks in the field indicate there is no one correct way to segment a market. Many different variables can be used, singly and in combination. For example, it is possible to segment among all the medical doctors in the United States those who are pediatricians, those who are pediatricians and who also have a pilot license, and, further, those who are pediatricians, have a pilot license, live in the state of Wisconsin, and grow climbing strawberries as a hobby. The combinations and permutations are virtually limitless; however, the most useful ways to segment a market are based on geographic, demographic, psychographic, and behavioristic data. The choice and combinations among these segmentation variables will depend on the problem the organization is seeking to clarify.

In a very practical sense, all segmentation efforts need to be coordinated and managed to be effective. It is not possible to pursue every market opportunity that emerges, nor does it make economic sense. Strategic choices are required. We shall now look at each of the major segmentation dimensions as they apply to the practical work of the continuing education professional.

Geographic Data

Geographic analysis is the first step in segmenting your market. Based on the notion that consumers' needs and preferences vary by where they reside (in fact, where people live, work, and play has an enormous impact on their purchasing behavior), geographic segmentation divides the market by location. The market may be as large as several regions of the world, such as Western Europe and the Caribbean basin, or as small as a neighborhood in your own home town. For example, a major American university with an international reputation may choose to offer special executive seminars for electrical engineers who work for large corporations in French-speaking countries. The first step in segmenting such a market would be to examine the number of engineering firms in France, Quebec, West Africa, and other more remote parts of the world where French is the official language. This kind of marketing opportunity represents a wide range of geographic segmentation problems and settings. A community college, on the other hand, usually chartered to serve the educational needs of those who reside within a county or district, serves primarily a single geographic segment.

However, there may be many subcategories within that district including rural, urban, suburban, or municipal, to name a few.

In any geographic segmentation effort, there are at least two important subgroupings to consider: market scope and market measures.

Market Scope. Market scope comprises four broad categories: international, national, statewide, and local. At the global level you may have a worldwide market (as Coca-Cola does), an international regional market (such as Central America or the Middle East), or a selected international market (such as Japan or Korea). National scope could include the entire United States market, regional markets (Middle Atlantic or the Southwest), selected states (Idaho and/or Rhode Island), or selected metropolitan areas (Los Angeles or Chicago). Statewide scope would focus on one state only (such as the state of Texas), a region of that state (the Panhandle), selected counties, or selected cities (Fort Worth and Dallas). Local scope includes the county level, the municipality, the township, the zip code, or even a neighborhood focus within a zip code.

Market Measures. Market measures also comprise four broad categories: population density of a particular geographic area, climate-related factors, census classifications, and other standardized market area measures.

The population density of a particular area should be of considerable interest to the continuing education programmer, because the density of a region (either rural, suburban, or urban) immediately sheds important clues on where to locate a course of instruction, when to offer it, and sometimes even what to offer.

Climate-related factors include such regional categories as the tropics, the sunbelt, and the frostbelt. Courses in professional scuba diving cannot be offered in the frostbelt regions of the United States during wintertime, quite obviously, but persons from the northern tier of the United States are often prime prospects for such training year-round when it is conducted in the Grand Cayman Islands.

The major classifications developed by the Bureau of the Census, which are of particular utility to marketers in continuing education, include census blocks, census tracts, metropolitan statistical areas (MSAs), primary metropolitan statistical areas (PMSAs), and consolidated metropolitan statistical areas (CMSAs). The use of acronyms in the literature of market measures has proliferated; therefore, one of the first tasks is to become familiar with these acronyms. The Census Bureau, for example, defines a *metropolitan statistical area (MSA)* as either a city with at least 50,000 population, or an urbanized area with at least 50,000 and a total metropolitan population of at least 100,000. An MSA can include the county in which the main city is located, as well as adjacent counties with significant economic ties to the major county. The Census Bureau determines this primarily as a result of the data they collect among those commuting to work in an urban area. It is also possible for a MSA to cross state lines, as it does for Kansas City. The Census Bureau currently designates approximately 260 areas in the United States as MSAs. A *consolidated metropolitan statistical area (CMSA)* is a term the Bureau designates for an area that has a population greater than one million and meets other requirements as well (there are twenty CMSAs in the United States), including major components called *primary metropolitan statistical areas* (PMSAs), of which the Bureau has identified some seventy-one in the country.

As continuing educators become more and more sophisticated in their marketing skills, the usefulness of direct mail and other examples of individualized target marketing (as described in Part Three of this book) underscores the importance of gathering census tract and census block data when appropriate. Census tracts are defined by the Bureau as small geographic units with populations of approximately 4,000–12,000. Census blocks provide very specific data on individual streets in a community. By aggregating tract and block data, the continuing educator has precise and extremely valuable data to use in making marketing decisions.

The fourth category under geographic market measures, *standardized market area measures,* comprises Arbitron's areas of dominant influence (ADIs), designated market areas (DMAs), and A. C. Nielson's A, B, C, and D market measures. On the basis of measurable viewing patterns, the Arbitron Company has identified more than 200 ADIs in the United States, which define exclusive television markets. The A. C. Nielson Company uses a different system to segment viewing patterns. Defining markets by county size (A, B, C, and D, with A being the largest metropolitan areas and D the smallest), it also uses DMAs to measure television market coverage. On the surface, these market measures may seem relatively inappropriate or of minor importance to the continuing educator. However, if the goal is to learn as much as possible about your market, the television viewing patterns of persons in your primary geographic market area may provide significant insight for programmers, especially if telecourses are to be offered via public, private, or cable television networks. In addition, these market measures may also indicate useful information in terms of what the tertiary competition is providing to entice the adult learner in a market area.

The important thing to remember when reviewing the preceding classifications is that no category is absolutely exclusive. More than one variable should always be explored and thoughtfully analyzed.

Demographic Data

Demographic segmentation, the traditional approach, is the approach most frequently used by marketing specialists to describe consumers within a particular market. Simply stated, "Demography is the statistical study of human populations and their vital characteristics" (Weinstein, 1987, p. 69). Demographic segmentation, therefore, is a method of dividing a market into groups by typically using ten variables: age, sex, family size, family life cycle, income, occupation, education, religion, race, and nationality.

There are at least three reasons why knowledge of these demographic variables is so important to continuing education professionals. First, there is a very high correlation between these variables and consumer wants, preferences, and usage rates. Second, demographic data are easier to collect, define, and measure, and less expensive to obtain than are almost all other segmentation data. Third, even when describing a market in terms other than those reflecting demographic variables, to reach and ultimately serve a particular audience, one must know the key demographic characteristics of the desired market that influence the media they use and, therefore, the media must be used to reach them. In other words. you have to know the demographics of your market.

After a geographic market area has been selected, one can begin the demographic analysis. Using an analytical approach to the ten common demographic dimensions, one recognizes that these dimensions are interrelated and can be grouped into at least five categories: age and stage of life, men/women, market size, race/nationality/religion, and socioeconomic status.

Age and Stage of Life. Combining the characteristics of age distribution and family life cycle (marital status, presence of children, ages of children), this category is typically based on eight stages of life:

1. Bachelor stage: young, single people
2. New married couples: young, no children
3. Full nest I: young married couples with the youngest child under six
4. Full nest II: young married couples with the youngest child six or older
5. Full nest III: older married couples with dependent children
6. Empty nest: older married couples with no children at home
7. Solitary survivor: older single or widowed people
8. Other

The fundamental assumption underlying the factors of age distribution and family life cycle is that consumer needs and wants change with age and stage of life. For example, in most families the children are more likely to consume cereals or baby food, mothers and older daughters tend to use the most hair spray, and fathers consume the most beer. Teenagers purchase the largest share of record albums and tapes sold in the United States, middle-aged persons tend to buy the most life insurance, and senior citizens spend more on health-care services than other groups. It is important, therefore, to know the age and stage of life of your customers. This knowledge is valuable to programmers and to those offering individual services. It also establishes the appropriate time line for a product's life cycle. For example, the under-5 market will remain about the same in absolute size in the United States over the next ten to fifteen years—around eighteen million persons in total. The college-age group (18–24) will actually decline in absolute and relative terms over the next ten years. The number of traditional college-age students is approximately twenty-nine million or 12 percent of the population at present. In the next 12 years, the number will decline to approximately twenty-five million persons or 9 percent of the total. The age group 45–64, currently at seventy-four million, will grow to approximately ninety-six million by the year 2000, or from 31 to 36 percent of the total U.S. population.

If there are large numbers of teenagers in a college's local market, the college may want to consider offering special summer programs to acquaint high school students with college life as part of a strategic recruiting plan. If, on the other hand, there are large numbers of senior citizens in the market area, the college might consider offering an Elderhostel program or an Institute for Retired Professionals.

Men/Women. The men/women category focuses on sex and marital status. In 1960, men outnumbered women four to one in the work force. Today, the figures are closer to 54 percent male and 46 percent female. For hundreds of years, sex segmentation was the norm at all levels of education. There were separate schools and colleges for males and females, and the curricula were distinct. Men went into engineering and women became teachers or nurses. Although male-oriented and female-oriented products still exist in the marketplace, in education the segmentation by sex is somewhat different now. As women have entered the labor force in record numbers, and as traditional male–female roles have been redefined, the assumptions based on sex that once prevailed in the academy no longer have the same relevance. If anything, we are seeing a reversal of those assumptions during this period of transition. Even a cursory glance at current noncredit course offerings around the country reveals workshops entitled "Assertiveness Training for Men," "Auto Repair for the Working Woman," and "Homemaking Skills for the Macho Male."

An excellent example of market segmentation in continuing education for women is the work done by Nancy Greene at Indiana/Purdue University in Indianapolis (Kotler, 1985, p. 181). She divided all women in her geographic region into those who work at home and those who work outside the home. Those women at home were subdivided into homemakers and displaced homemakers (reentry women). Those who work outside the home were divided into businesswomen—clerical/technical and businesswomen—management/premanagement. Each of these four subsegments had different motivations for attending a university, different educational needs, and different special problems. By segmenting women in this manner in greater Indianapolis, the Division of Continuing Studies of the state university there was able to attract more women to the campus and to provide them with better service.

Marital status is also an important variable to many marketers. For example, if the divorce rate continues to fall in the United States, and young people get married sooner rather than later, a trend that is now emerging according to the Census Bureau's middle series household projections (*American Demographics*, May 1987, p. 70), the number of married couples should increase by 11 percent over the next fifteen years. On the other hand, even though the number of households headed by men with no wife present doubled from 5.3 million in 1970 to 10.5 million in 1980, and the rate has slowed down a bit during the eighties. It is now estimated that the number of men living on their own should reach 19.2 million by 2001. As a result of these changing life-styles, including increases in single-parent families, divorce rates, and cohabitation, research data on marital status are important to an understanding of the adult learner, and hence to more effective marketing.

Market Size Factors. This category includes population size, number of households or families, and household or family size. The essential ingredient in this category is the total population of the market being examined. If the community college can serve only the residents within the county in which it resides, the entire population of that county is an important comparative yardstick against which all other dimensions can then be evaluated. For example, by knowing the total population of the county, it is possible to declare that 31 percent of the persons living in the county are between the ages of 24 and 44 and that a possible goal for the next year is to serve 15 percent of those within that age group.

A similar measure is provided if you know the number of households or families in the county. In this case, however, the number of individuals may be less important than the number of buying units. For example, a nonprofit organization, like a YMCA, wanting to expand its membership would find the number of buying units in its market to be very helpful. If one member of a family were to utilize the service at the "Y," it is likely that the other family members might also join when they need recreational services.

Household or family size is a derivation of the other two variables. By dividing the number of households into the total population of the city or county, the average household or family size for an area is determined. In the greater Miami area, for example, the average family size is 2.3 people. That information is of great value in assessing market potential, especially for an organization that may want to consider providing a service with a very broad or family-oriented appeal.

Race/Nationality/Religion. The United States is a country of great diversity. We have different ethnic backgrounds, we have different countries of national origin, and we represent a wide spectrum of religious preferences. Such differences help shape our individual values, perceptions, beliefs, and needs and have a direct effect on our purchasing patterns.

Obvious examples of religious influence on buying patterns are the sale of kosher foods (mostly to Orthodox Jews) and the lack of market for coffee in Salt Lake City (Mormons do not drink it). Alsop and Abrams (1986, pp. 223–226) described a number of recent trends in religious advertising, including some designed for the "baby-boomers." Many baby-boomers drifted away from religion in the 1960s and 1970s, but are now settling down and starting families; one public-service ad targeted at this market depicts a parent teaching a child to ride a bicycle and then admonishes: "You haven't given them everything until you've given them something to believe in." An ad for the Episcopal Church features

Henry VIII with the message "In the church started by a man who had six wives, forgiveness goes without saying."

In the past decade or two, many research studies have been conducted on segmenting the black population in the United States. Although marketers recognize that no group of 26.5 million people can be considered a homogeneous market segment for all products, several studies comparing consumption patterns of blacks and whites suggest that (Kurtz and Boone, 1984, p. 190) blacks are very loyal to national brands; blacks save a higher percentage of their income than do whites; blacks spend less on food, housing, medical, and automobile transportation than do equivalent whites; blacks spend more for clothing and nonautomobile transportation; blacks and whites spend about the same on recreation, leisure, home furnishings, and equipment; and blacks buy more milk, soft drinks, and liquor than whites but less tea and coffee.

These principles are also illustrated in another growing population in the United States—persons of Spanish or Latin American origin. Although Hispanics represent the second-largest minority in the United States, they are not a segment of the population that is understood very well. Only in the past few years have studies of this rapidly growing ethnic group become available. Part of the statistical difficulty has to do with the fact that no one really knows how many persons cross illegally from or through Mexico into the United States. Another difficulty is that many Hispanics do not identify themselves as "Hispanic" on census forms; therefore, data on Hispanics in the United States are often underestimated. Given those qualifiers, it is generally agreed that approximately eighteen million persons in the United States are Hispanic, they are a large and expanding market, and their impact on business is growing. If it is assumed that the Census Bureau's highest projections on the Hispanic population are correct, soon after the year 2000 there will be twice as many Hispanics in the United States as there are today, or approximately 36 million. By 2030 the Hispanic population will quadruple to 72 million, and by the year 2080, there may be nine times as many Hispanics as today. These projections should not be ignored by those doing marketing research for continuing education programs, products, and services.

A recent study on Hispanic opportunities (Schwartz, 1987, p. 56) suggests that Hispanics in the United States are brand-conscious and brand-loyal. They prefer American-made products and the products of those companies that make a special effort to recognize Hispanic needs. Hispanics also constitute a young market, with a median age of only 23.6 years compared with 32 years for the U.S. population as a whole. They are loyal customers, and so once this market is captured by a company (or university or college) it will probably be held as long as the organization remains sensitive to Hispanic needs.

Although black and Hispanic populations are important demographic variables in many market areas, for some product categories, race, nationality, and religion have very little bearing on buying patterns. The smart marketer will gather, analyze, and use the information in those areas where such variables are important.

Socioeconomic Status. The fifth demographic group comprises the obvious relationships among income, occupation, and level of educational training. One of the fundamental tenets of the American dream is that the more education a person has, the higher is her or his chance of getting a better job and making more money. Although no two individuals or families spend money in exactly the same way, it is possible to predict with some degree of accuracy, if the person's income is known, what his or her wants are likely to be (Sheth, 1974). In some product categories, like automobiles, furnishings, appliances, and education, expenditures rise with income. In others, like food, they do not rise, or they rise very little. It is also important to know the income distribution according to geographic area. As educational products tend to sell better in markets with higher income levels, knowledge of the income levels by zip code in an area is essential to successful targeting of advertising.

In many ways, knowing the educational levels of the primary market area is the same as knowing the income levels. The higher a person's education, the more likely he or she is to have a higher income and to want to continue his or her education.

Occupation, like education, is also related to income in that certain occupations are traditionally better paying than others. However, the differential between white-collar and blue-collar incomes has been decreasing regularly over the past two decades. Yet, the spending patterns among different occupational groups earning approximately the same income can be quite different. For example, the white-collar clerical/salesperson spends substantially more for clothing, home furnishings, and continuing education than does the craftworker supervisor, although both spend about the same for recreation.

Other demographic variables need to be examined, including home ownership and social class. Homeowners tend to be better prospects than do renters for many products and services. The type of dwelling in which one lives (single-family home, multifamily home, townhouse, condominium, or apartment) also influences purchase behavior, as do household stability and mobility. Stability is based on the length of time households reside in a given area, for example, one to three years or more than five. Mobility measures the population turnover (influx and exodus) for an area within a specific time frame; for example, the mobility factor in a metropolitan area could be .28, which means that in the past year, 28 of every 100 residences have changed hands.

Dataman Information Services (July 1986), an Atlanta-based direct-mail firm that concentrates its marketing effort on the new homeowner, provides the following insights about new homeowners:

1. They tend to spend nearly ten times more in their first year in a new home than do established residents.
2. They tend to completely restructure their buying habits within the first thirty to ninety days in their new homes.
3. They are credit worthy, having just qualified for a mortgage loan.

4.   They have no point of reference yet. They are looking for businesses to patronize and are receptive to direct-mail and telephone solicitations.
5.   They are strong candidates for orientation to the community, for retraining, and for acquiring new skills.

Understanding these statistics can arm the continuing educator with valuable information on which to make important marketing decisions. It is generally more difficult for a new company (or university or college) to penetrate a stable community because the residents tend to be older and less flexible about new providers of goods and services. On the other hand, in a community with high turnover it may be easier to attract or recruit new customers as opposed to developing long-term customer relationships.

Another socioeconomic market segment that has received considerable national press is the young affluent professional. As companies and colleges have developed strategies to research the baby-boomer generation, a number of acronyms have emerged in the American language, including "Yuppies" (young urban professionals), "Yaps" (young aspiring professionals), "Yummies" (young upwardly mobile mommies), and "Dinks" (dual income, no kids). Although "Yuppies" constitute only approximately 5 percent of the total U.S. population, they have received an enormous amount of attention and have been the focus of marketers in nearly every product line, including the adult education market. Placing too much emphasis on such a narrow market, however, could be dangerous in the long run. By 1992, for example, most baby-boomers will be married, will have children, and will be homeowners. Just as the "Hippies" and "Yippies" became the "Yuppies," the "Yuppies" too will become something else. One writer (Russell, 1985) predicts the "Yuppie" will become the "Mechie" (middle-aged, exurban, computerized homeowner), representing a big market for home fitness and home entertainment, do-it-yourself projects, and technologically sophisticated household help.

Marketers have only recently begun to concentrate on the special characteristics of regional markets, often called "geodemographics" in the literature. The trend is underscored by Garreau (1981) in *The Nine Nations of North America* in which he argues that North America is divided into nine "nations" (regions) populated by persons who share distinct values, attitudes, and styles. This book should be required reading for anyone interested in the growing field of continuing education market research.

Although the general public believes that the national media and the fast-food chains have homogenized the United States into a single bland culture, the smart marketer is discovering the importance of regional differences. The new marketing trend recognizes local color and talent, caters to regional tastes and styles, taps local celebrities for testimonials, connects with local events, and sometimes showcases a regional version of a product. Using computers and laser scanners, companies are now able to analyze how buying habits change from store to store, making it possible to pinpoint problems and opportunities across the United States. By concentrating on the unique characteristics of a particular geographical area, large companies have gained market share, frequently at the expense of local competitors.

Knowing both the demographics and the geographics of the market area will provide some of the best clues to what people will buy. An example of geodemographics is a recent study by Selling Areas-Marketing, Inc., a subsidiary of Time Inc., which revealed the following number-one markets for selected products (Moore, 1985, p. 65):

Atlanta	Antacids and aspirin
Dallas/Fort Worth	Vitamins
Grand Rapids	Rat poison
Indianapolis	Shoe polish
Miami	Prune juice
New York	Laundry soaps
New Orleans	Ketchup
Oklahoma	Motor oil additives
Philadelphia	Iced tea
Pittsburgh	Coffee
Portland (Oregon)	Dry cat food
Salt Lake City	Candy bars and marshmallows
Savannah	MSG and meat tenderizers
Seattle	Toothbrushes

This list underscores the importance of understanding the demographics of a particular marketplace.

The ups and downs of the continuing education business are dependent to a great extent on demographic trends. By examining trends, one can observe today's consumers and look five to ten years into the future and predict many of the goods and services they will want tomorrow. Although no one can claim that demographics is the perfect or only marketing tool, it is one of the best predictors of consumption, of national moods, and of preoccupations. Demographics is a starting point in marketing, along with geography, and provides a valuable framework for strategic planning. Knowledge of both the ten variables of demographics and the geographic subcategories of scope and measures within a particular region is essential in learning more about a market.

Psychographic Data

As essential as it is, geodemographics is not enough. Two people, both aged 39 and both with an annual income of $55,000, may purchase different products depending on their life-styles. One may buy a BMW and the other, a Winnebago. Although both purchases are responses to the need for transportation, each purchase satisfies a different want. One fulfills a desire for status; the other, a desire for recreation.

If geodemographics is a means of segmenting and describing consumers through the use of data on location, age, income, occupation, sex, and education (among other variables), then psychographics is a means of describing consumers through the use of activities, interests, opinions, and life-styles. Such questions as "How do you spend your time?" (activities), "What do you like to do?" (interests), and "What do you think about various issues?" (opinions) lead researchers to examine consumers' responses in a search for a pattern or patterns that describe the common life-styles of significant groups of individuals. Therefore, psychographic segmentation, the third and very powerful approach to understanding your market, is based on "the entire constellation of a person's attitudes, beliefs, opinions, hopes, fears, prejudices, needs, desires, and aspirations that, taken together, govern how one behaves" and, in turn, "find holistic expression in a life-style" (Mitchell, 1983, p. vii).

Pioneered by Demby (1974) in an essay called "Psychographics and From Whence It Came," which appeared in the American Marketing Association's publication *Life-style and Psychographics,* the term has gradually developed to embrace the practical marketing information from both personality trait research and life-style research. Sometimes called "people research" (Atlas, 1984, p. 50), the concept was championed by Yankelovich in the early seventies when he began measuring the effects of social trends on consumers (1981, pp. XIV, 3), as did several advertising firms who carried out a number of elaborate surveys classifying consumers into categories and psychological types. Joseph T. Plummer, for example, was another early proponent of psychographics, especially in the life-style analyses he conducted for Schlitz beer in 1969 and 1970. He discovered that heavy beer drinkers were "real macho people who lived life to the fullest and didn't take any crap from anybody" (Atlas, 1984, p. 51), which led to the "gusto world" commercials still in production today in one form or another. But perhaps the person with the greatest influence in making psychographics a household word was the late Arnold Mitchell, who began working for the Stanford Research Institute in Palo Alto in 1948. He published a report in 1960 on "Consumer Values and Demands" (Cooper, Stern, and Mitchell, 1960) and then published, in 1983, the now classic book in the field, *The Nine American Life-styles.*

In this seminal work, Mitchell and his colleagues at the nonprofit research firm in Menlo Park, California, called SRI International (formerly the Stanford Research Institute), copyrighted the term *VALS,* which stands for "values and life-styles." The VALS typology that they developed divides Americans into nine life-styles or types, which are grouped in four major categories, on the basis of self-image, aspirations, and products used. The four categories are "need-driven," "outer-directed," "inner-directed," and "integrated."

As can be seen from Figure 3.1, the VALS typology is hierarchical, and shows the movement of an individual or a society from immaturity to full psychological maturity.

The need-drivens (11 percent of the adult population) are people who are especially limited in financial resources and whose lives are driven by need rather

Figure 3.1. The Life-Styles Double Hierarchy.

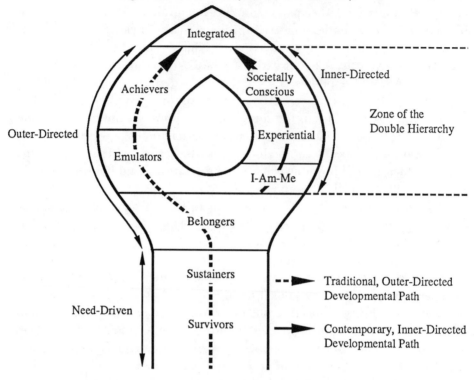

than by choice. Their values center around survival, safety, and security. They tend to be dependent, unplanning, and distrustful.

Outer-directeds (68 percent of the adult population) live in response to signals from others. Their attitudes and activities are based on what others will think. Outer-directeds tend to be among the happiest of Americans, being well attuned and creating much of the mainstream culture.

The inner-directeds (19 percent of the adult population), in contrast to the outer-directeds, live their lives in accord with their inner values rather than the values of others. Their primary concern is inner growth and development. Most seek intense involvement in their own activities. They tend not to come from need-driven or inner-directed families, but from outer-directed families whose values they have rejected.

The integrateds (approximately 2 percent of the adult population) are at the pinnacle of the VALS typology and are those rare persons who have gotten their act together. Their prime characteristics are maturity, balance, and a sense of what is "fitting" (Mitchell, 1983). They combine the power of the outer-directeds with the sensitivity of the inner-directeds and, in a psychological sense, have reached full maturity. They are capable of seeing many sides of an issue. They can lead when necessary and are willing to play a secondary role when it seems appropriate and fitting.

It is necessary to understand that these life-style segments are flexible and developmental. A person can grow from one level to the next, just as children grow from adolescence into adulthood. It is also possible to combine some outer-directed tendencies and inner-directed characteristics while one moves through the zone of the double hierarchy. Listed here are the nine life-styles, each with its distinctive array of values, drives, beliefs, needs, dreams, and special points of view:

1. *Survivors* make up approximately 4 percent of the adult population and are the most disadvantaged persons in American society. Survivors live in extreme poverty—many are in their old age—have low education, and have limited access to upward mobility. Caught up in the culture of poverty, they are people who tend to be despairing, depressed, and withdrawn. They also tend to be conservative Democrats.

2. *Sustainers* (7 percent of the adult population) are disadvantaged people struggling to get out of poverty. Better off and younger than the Survivors, the Sustainers have not yet given up hope. Though they seldom vote and may be angry at the system, they are determined to get ahead. They live for the moment, but hope for the future.

3. *Belongers* make up the largest group in the typology (38 percent of the adult population) and represent the solid middle-class segment of Americans who are conforming, conservative, "moral," nonexperimental and family oriented. The old-fashioned values of patriotism, home and family, and sentimentality are key elements in understanding the Belongers, whose essential drive is to belong rather than to stand out. They are people who know what is right and they stick to their values. They tend to be Democrats.

4. *Emulators* (10 percent of the adult population) are ambitious, upwardly mobile, and eagerly seeking to "make it big." Emulating the Achiever life-style, they are status-conscious, conspicuous consumers, competitive, ostentatious, unsubtle, macho, and distrustful and tend to be apolitical.

5. *Achievers* (23 percent of the adult population) are successful people, the established, who make things happen, who are competent, self-radiant, and efficient. They include many leaders in business, the professions, and government. They are hard-working, affluent people who have helped create the economic system in America. They work within the system, are defenders of the economic status quo, are well adjusted, enjoy the good life, are well satisfied with their place in the system, and tend to be Republicans.

6. *I-Am-Me's* represent only 3 percent of the adult population, and are in the short-lived stage of transition from the outer- to the inner-directed category. They typically are young and fiercely individualistic, to the point of being narcissistic and exhibitionist, are impulsive, dramatic, experimental, and inventive, are often into trendy products, and are rarely politically active.

7. *Experiential* (7 percent of the adult population) are often the more matured "I-Am-Me's," less intensely egocentric, and include other people and many social and human issues in their interests. Often physical fitness buffs, they seek intensity in all things and are adventuresome and liberal. Wanting direct experience and vigorous involvement, they tend to be very artistic and to get passionately involved with others.

8. *Societally Conscious* (11 percent of the adult population) are mission oriented, are leaders of single-issue groups, and have extended their inner-direction beyond the self and others to society as a whole and, sometimes, philosophically, to the cosmos. As sixties activists grown to adulthood, they are impassioned and knowledgeable about the world around them and are liberal and politically active, supporting such causes as conservation, environmentalism, and consumerism. Many are attracted to simple living and the natural.

9. *The Integrateds* (representing only 2 percent of the adult population) are at the top of the VALS typology illustrated in Figure 3.1. Possessing a deep sense of the fittingness of things, fully mature in a psychological sense, they are affluent, sensitive, tolerant, and self-assured.

Each segment of the VALS typology suggests a variety of potential educational needs and programs. For example, an urban community college would tend to attract primarily Sustainers and Belongers. If it wanted to reach out to Survivors, the college would probably need to provide special scholarships, loans, and a variety of special services, including child care and counseling, to motivate their attendance and to overcome the inherent distrust of education and of organized bureaucracies.

Why has psychographics suddenly become a popular and important method of segmenting the American public? Researchers now recognize that since the late sixties, so much of American society has become fragmented that people are considerably less predictable than they once were. For example, in the past, if you knew the demographics you also knew the life-style. That is not the case anymore. Several years ago it was much easier to make assumptions about the adult female consumer. Most of them were married, and most of them lived at home with their children. That is not true today. Even if they live at home, they have different attitudes toward their families, their careers, and their lives. Furthermore, their spending patterns are different. They tend to spend more on themselves. Such attitudes cannot be captured solely on the basis of the demographics.

The traditional demographic descriptions of age, income, sex, and nationality are not as penetrating or illuminating as psychographic research. In a typical demographic research project you could say that men earning $35,000 a year feel a particular way about the loss of groundwater. Psychographic research would suggest that one cannot draw much of a conclusion from only the demographics, because a man earning $35,000 a year might be a societally conscious school teacher who is active politically, or he might be a truck driver who is so exhausted at night that he collapses into bed and is never involved in political issues. It is important to know both the demographics and the psychographics of the group you wish to target in your marketing effort. The two approaches are complementary. If you were writing a press release targeted at Achievers, for example, you would want to know if they were young, middle-aged, or older. Achievers at 65 are different than they were at 25.

Psychographics can provide the continuing educator with a more complete arsenal of tools. Increasingly, psychographics is being used for four reasons: (1) to identify target markets with greater precision; (2) to provide more comprehensive insight into the behavior of consumers; (3) to assist organizations in developing a marketing plan; and (4) to lower the risk when introducing new products (Weinstein, 1987, p. 109).

Psychographic research in segmented studies is often very beneficial; however, there are also some limitations the continuing educator must be aware of. First, a well-designed psychographic study is often more expensive than other types of marketing research. Second, good psychographic research usually requires a large survey sample. There must be 100 to 150 people in most of the nine categories in the VALS typology to get a sense of what the people in each category are like. This means that several thousand people must be sampled, and some organizations do not have the personnel or the sophistication to administer such an instrument. Perhaps, this is why some organizations use psychographic data as thought starters rather than as a formal research tool (Zotti, 1985). Third, there is always the danger of oversimplification. People do not fall into neat and tidy categories; it is possible for an individual to be an Achiever in the VALS classification scheme in some areas and a Societally Conscious in others. Marketers need to be aware of this overlap because roles change in different situations as well as at different points in the life cycle. A person can be an Achiever in the office, Societally Conscious in the supermarket, a Belonger at the PTA meeting, and an Emulator at the computer store.

Given these pluses and minuses, the continuing educator should pursue the following guidelines in conducting or using psychographic research:

1. Use psychographics as one technique among many. Psychographics is the newest and flashiest technique and is a useful research tool, but marketers should not put all their eggs in the life-style basket. In particular, do not expect to substitute psychographics for demographics. The two should build on and complement each other.

2. Know how you will use psychographics. Make certain your expectations are realistic. Social value clusters are important tools in understanding specific segments of people; however, they are not the segments themselves. If you do not know how you will use the results of a study, you probably should not do the study.

3. Seek detail. As life-style is a complex area, the more relevant the data you collect the more valuable will be the results in helping you to market your products. Using focus groups to pretest the psychographic survey instrument can be of enormous help and an effective use of time.

4. Use the personal interview format. Given the amount of data to be collected, telephone surveys and direct mail are often not appropriate. The latter usually suffers from a low return rate and many incomplete questionnaires. Personal interviews, therefore, are often the best approach.

5. Get professional help. To develop individual profiles based on life-style, a large number of questions on interests, activities, and opinions must be included in the survey instrument. Additionally, a Likert five-point agree/disagree scale, or another similar scale, must be used to determine the degree of

agreement/disagreement for each statement. Unless you have had extensive experience in developing viable psychographic studies, professional assistance in this process is generally a good idea.

6. Do not ignore secondary data. Although most psychographic analysis is based on primary research, do not neglect secondary data in the data collection process. Information from past studies, as well as published or commercial resources, can contribute to your own efforts.

7. Never stop testing. Because values and life-styles are always changing, keep monitoring your psychographic segmentation system. As people move from one life-style to another, they shift in their attitudes, beliefs, and patterns of consumption.

One must remember that as helpful and exciting as psychographic research is, it is not a panacea. It is not the magic crystal ball that everyone has been looking for. Used well, however, it can enhance the continuing educator with critical insight to provide the added leverage in the marketplace.

Behavioristic Data

The fourth type of data important to development of a strong marketing strategy is behavioristic data. Response of consumers to a particular program of service, rather than their general life-style, personality, or demographics, is what many marketers believe is the most important variable in constructing useful market segments. Behavior has direct implications for the choice of college, university, or continuing education program by various consumer segments.

Consider your own individual purchase behavior. You buy some continuing education services or programs on a regular basis and others with less frequency or certainty. There are a vast majority of continuing education seminars and workshops that you have seldom bought and may never purchase. This reflection on your own buying pattern is the basis for product usage segmentation, or what is often called volume segmentation.

Volume Segmentation. In volume segmentation, persons are classified as light, medium, and heavy users of a product. An understanding of volume segmentation is important. Although heavy users may represent only a small percentage of your total market in total numbers, they may account for the major percentage of the total purchases of the product. It is what other chapters in this book refer to as the 80/20 rule: 80 percent of your products are purchased by 20 percent of your market. The time expended in learning everything you possibly can about that 20 percent will be time well spent. The goal of any marketing effort is to identify as many niches as possible of persons with like demographics, similar attitudinal characteristics and behavior patterns, and then provide them with the products and services they need and want.

User Status. In addition to volume segmentation, which focuses on usage rates, many markets can be segmented into nonusers, ex-users, potential users, first-time users, and regular users of your services and products. Much of this kind of segmentation of in-house mailing lists can be stored and analyzed on personal computers with hard disks.

Benefit Segmentation. Consumers of your products and services can be segmented according to the specific benefits they are seeking through participation in your program. Some adults, for example, are looking for a single dominant benefit such as a new skill. Others seek a particular combination of benefits or a benefit "bundle" (Haley, 1968).

Benefit segmentation extends beyond product features and focuses on asking the question from the consumer's point of view. "What is this product or service going to do for me?" Benefits serve to satisfy physical, emotional, financial, or psychological needs, and benefit segmentation examines the motives of the consumer buying a particular product. It is possible, for example, to compile the key benefits that motivate people to buy a product, and then to analyze the types of persons who cluster around a particularly identifiable benefit. Such a study identified ten benefit segments for categorizing prospective MBA students on the basis of their educational preferences (Miaoulis and Kalfus, 1983). Among these segments, "Quality Seekers" were those people who wanted the highest-quality education available in their communities. "Career Changers" were looking for a new job or employer and thought the MBA would give them mobility or opportunity. "Status Seekers" felt that graduate MBA studies would lead to increased income and prestige. "Avoiders" sought MBA programs that required them to invest the least effort. And "Nonmatriculators" wanted to take MBA courses without completing formal application procedures.

Benefit segmentation analysis is especially appropriate in the context of comparing psychographic and product usage information, as benefits are closely connected with these dimensions.

Loyalty Segmentation. Another behavioristic data approach is loyalty segmentation, which is a description of the strength of a consumer's preference for a particular product or service. The degree of loyalty can range from absolute zero to exclusive commitment. There are consumers who remain loyal to a brand, such as Pepsi; to an organization, such as the Democratic Party; to a college, such as Harvard; or to a person, such as a company president. Being loyal usually means maintaining a preference in spite of the pressure and incentives to switch to some other brand, organization, or person.

Schools and colleges often analyze the loyalty of alumni using four categories: (1) hard-core loyals on whom you can always depend for support; (2) soft-core loyals who may be devoted to two or three institutions; (3) shifting loyals whose loyalty is in transition from one institution to another; and (4) switch loyals who show little loyalty to any institution. An analysis of the hard-core loyals, to determine the basic satisfactions that have contributed to their feelings about the college, would be helpful in determining and creating the same kind of satisfactions for current students and other alumni in the region (Kotler, 1985, p. 184).

There are other ways to measure or organize behavioristic data, including stage of readiness and attitude segmentation. The former is based on the assumption that, at any given time, some potential consumers of a particular product or service are *unaware* of the product, some are *aware*, some are *informed*, some are *interested*, some are *desirous* of the product, and some *intend to buy*. Attitude segmentation is based on the assumption that markets can be segmented according to the attitudes of customers toward an organization and/or its services. For example, a number of university fraternities regularly interview the incoming freshman class to determine their attitudes about joining a fraternity. One study (Kotler, 1985, p. 185) revealed that 10 percent were *enthusiastic*, 20 percent *positive*, 30 percent *indifferent*, 25 percent *negative*, and 15 percent *hostile*. Each of these five segments had a distinct profile. The "enthusiasts" usually came from higher-income, better-educated families who lived in cities. With these data on attitudes, the fraternity was able to market itself more effectively to those members of the freshman class whose profiles more closely matched the "enthusiasts" and the "positives." The marketing effort was not wasted on those profiles matching the "negatives" or "hostiles."

The point of this discussion is to demonstrate the importance of knowing your customers and of using whatever behavioristic segmentation techniques are appropriate to gain enough information to maximize your marketing effort.

Summary

This chapter has explored four types of data that can be used to segment your market: geographic, demographic, psychographic, and behavioristic. The purpose has been to suggest how you can sharpen your strategic planning and strengthen your marketing muscle. These four types of data constitute only an introduction to marketing research and its importance to continuing educators. The ultimate goal, of course, is to have a sophisticated data base at your own disposal, in-house, that you can analyze and manipulate to build a subgroup of prospects for a specific marketing objective and to enable you and your programs to flourish.

4

How to Develop an Integrated Marketing and Advertising Plan

Kenneth S. Foster

Chapter Two discussed in detail the importance of establishing goals. The conceptualization of these goals may be tight or loose depending on the expectations of the people in the organization as well as the expectations of the publics being served, but all organizations must have some idea of what they are trying to accomplish. Thus, establishment of clear organizational goals and specific, measurable objectives designed to achieve these goals is an important step in developing an effective marketing/advertising plan. If the continuing education program is a department of a larger institution, its marketing goals should be subordinate to the overall institutional marketing goals, because to be most effective, marketing goals should be derived from institutional goals.

Goals state how the organization perceives its mission and whether or not the organization wants to grow. If the organization does not wish to grow in number of participants or number of programs, the goals should lead to enhancement of programs, products, and services and, thus, constant self-renewal. In other words, growth is not always expressed as increases in enrollments or programs. Growth can also be changes that enhance existing programs, products, and services.

Marketing specializes in analyzing the organization in relation to the marketplace. For example, consider an institution that establishes a mission out of line with its real identity in the marketplace. College A offers a variety of courses and programs in a blue-collar suburb. Management decides they would like to operate more profitably by attracting a higher-income audience. Marketing goals, then, are likely to concentrate on (1) increasing tuition to generate more income, and (2) enhancing the image of the elite aspect of the institution, thus appealing to a higher-income customer. The results are twofold, however: (1) no appeal to the new target audience because the institution is geographically located in a blue-collar area and historically has appealed to that segment of the population, and (2) loss of the existing market as new advertising has become snobbish and less appealing to the existing market.

The moral is that an organization should set realistic goals in line with what the institution really is before setting marketing goals and objectives. Some marketing goals that are typically found in a wide variety of continuing education organizations are to (1) achieve a specific level of profits; (2) obtain a defined market share; (3) be attractive and/or appealing to politicians, press, tax payers, and donors; (4) reveal a sensitivity to government and the community; (5) decide on the degree of financial risk that is possible to assume with continuing education programming; and (6) reflect the image or personality of the institution that has been established.

There are generally two forms of institutional marketing: long term and short term. Short-term plans generally are those that deal within an annual framework. Long-term plans generally extend beyond annual thinking, frequently as far as five years into the future. Factors that determine the length of the plan include (1) the development time of products, services, and programs; (2) the readiness of the marketplace (for example, do you want to market only to an existing need or go to the expense of creating that need?); (3) the availability of physical facilities; (4) the analysis of return on investment (for example, a program that takes longer to provide a return on investment will require a longer-term plan); and (5) the life cycle of a product, service, or program (for example, a shorter life cycle will require a shorter-term plan).

The long-range marketing plan is even more closely associated with the institutional plan than is the short-term plan, because it is generally produced by upper management and thus the plan's variables may be less applicable to the day-to-day tasks that lower-level employees perform. Some variables considered in the development of long-term plans are (1) assessment of the institution's strengths and weaknesses; (2) macro- and microeconomic forecasts; (3) forecasts influencing the education industry; (4) life-cycle patterns of the entire institution; (5) forecasts of individual performance of departments; and (6) forecasts of performance for products, services, and programs. For the most part, this chapter deals with the establishment of short-term plans.

No two educational institutions have the same interests, missions, or markets. Thus, educational institutions have vastly different goals. Consider how the goals of the following types of organizations may vary: universities, two-year colleges, community education, corporate education, private clubs, and professional associations. Then within each type of organization there are differences in size, enrollee profiles, geographic and demographic settings, economic circumstances, competitive circumstances, and a wide variety of other characteristics that make institutions unique. A marketing plan is the institution's or department's guideline for actively considering and dealing with the influence of these variables as it strives to achieve goals.

As noted earlier, marketing goals should be subordinate to institutional goals; however, they should be as specific as possible and should be expressed in measurable terms so that an effective evaluation of the marketing effort can be conducted later. Separate goals should be set for each program, service, or product for which a marketing effort is extended. Frequently, an organization will compile several different marketing plans, perhaps a plan for each product, service, or program. These individual plans are then combined into a master marketing plan which, in turn, might be incorporated into an overall institutional plan.

How do you begin to establish marketing goals? Simply ask: What do we want? How do we get it? What will we do with it when we do get it?

This process frequently results from the analysis of problems that are synonymous with opportunities in the marketing arena. Consider the following examples:

Problem: The institution is relatively new and lacks familiarity with the target audience.

Opportunities: The institution has the opportunity to start fresh and establish a unique position in the marketplace by marketing with a unified and well-defined image in mind.

Now we incorporate our three questions.

1. What do we want? We want to establish a unique image in the marketplace.
2. How do we get it? We decide what that image will be and what form of marketing will create the image.
3. What will we do when we get it? We will develop our continuing education products, services, and programs to reinforce the image.

Some typical marketing goals appropriate to a continuing education organization are (1) to increase market share—that percentage of the market that utilizes our services as opposed to the services of other providers; (2) to increase name recognition and/or top-of-mind awareness; (3) to increase dollar volume of products and services sold; (4) to improve profit (for example, an organization might decide to increase the efficiency of advertising to reduce the advertising budget 10 percent and thus improve profitability without losing market share); and (5) to improve customer service. It is apparent that these goals are based to some degree on a previous comprehensive market analysis and that the market analysis may influence the establishment of goals. Because of this chicken-and-egg relationship, flexibility must be incorporated into any plan. It is important to adjust goals as you gain market information that affects the goals.

Once the goals are set you can proceed with development of a marketing plan. A word of caution, however. Establishment of a marketing plan does not guarantee great success, and lack of a plan certainly does not guarantee failure. In fact, it is not uncommon for many organizations simply to engage in "sightseeing." Organizational sightseeing is similar to traveling in an airplane that takes off without having a specific destination. After flying around for awhile, and checking out the sights, it returns to the same location from which it departed.

Although success is not guaranteed, a well-written blueprint for marketing activities has proven to increase the chances for success in a wide variety of continuing education organizations. To avoid institutional sightseeing, however, it is important to analyze the benefits to be gained from developing a specific, but flexible, marketing plan. Most continuing education organizations find that these benefits include the ability to (1) better interpret variables in the marketplace as they impact the organization, (2) provide a unified marketing thrust for the organization so that all employees from the custodian to the president work toward the same goals, (3) ensure that a division's or department's marketing efforts are consistent with the parent institution's mission, (4) clearly define goals, (5) prioritize options, (6) establish and prioritize budgets, (7) identify strategies that will achieve goals, (8) establish schedules for production of marketing efforts, and (9) provide a means for evaluating marketing efforts to determine what works and what does not work.

How Do You Distinguish Between Marketing and Advertising Plans?

In business, an advertising plan is usually distinct and separate from a marketing plan. In the marketing of educational institutions, however, marketing and advertising within an organization are often so integrated with the administrative function that it is difficult to make distinctions. For example, marketing functions have been dispersed through most educational organizations to include decentralization of the establishment of profit margins, pricing policy for noncredit programs, and direct sales contacts. In addition, the marketing function is generally assigned to the same office responsible for advertising and publication. As a result, many educational institutions often consider the publication of a brochure to be marketing when in reality it is advertising. Marketing deals with the more global concept of establishing effective communication between the organization and its environment.

Because of the integrated nature of educational marketing, this chapter concentrates on how to develop an integrated marketing/advertising plan. However, an integrated marketing/advertising plan is not recommended if the institution has historically made a distinction between marketing and advertising or if the present marketing orientation reflects that distinction. If a nonintegrated marketing plan is to be undertaken, the following differences between marketing and advertising plans should be noted:

1. An advertising plan does not generally contain data on sales, profits, or return on investment.

2. The marketing plan generally gives no specific advertising or promotion programs such as "On July 4 we will have a booth at the city library Independence Fair."

3. The advertising plan generally does not reflect sales plan efforts such as "John Smith will make four new business contacts per day." Instead, advertising tends to address the media efforts to back up a sales plan.

4. An advertising plan is generally much more brief and to the point than a marketing plan. A marketing plan often contains a great deal of data and analysis leading to conclusions that result in specific aspects of an advertising plan.

Who Should Develop a Marketing/Advertising Plan? No matter what the size of the continuing education program or the type of organization, someone—one individual—must be responsible for pulling together a marketing/advertising plan. Because of the nature of the marketing/advertising plan, this individual will have to network with almost every department in the organization. The networking can be accomplished by formation of a marketing committee of key individuals from each department. This is especially advisable in the information-gathering stages. Committees are helpful in giving advice. Nevertheless, only one individual should be responsible for organizing and producing the final plan.

The basic philosophy of such a marketing plan should reflect the concerns of management; thus the support of upper management is necessary in the development of marketing and advertising goals. The implementation of a total marketing strategy will likely involve everyone from the president to the groundskeepers. Obviously, it is necessary to seek advice from many different people during the information-gathering phase.

A word of warning is in order at this point. With the involvement of such a variety of information sources, development of the integrated marketing/advertising plan can become an expensive effort—expensive in terms of the time of people who attend meetings and work on the plan. Also, it is possible to gather the wrong kinds of data, and the inapplicable information will decrease the utility of the data. The additional 5 percent of useful information that can increase the data's reliability may cost 100 percent more time, however. Generally, extra research costs extra money and an organization must make a conscious decision about whether they need or want to pioneer such marketing efforts.

How Much Time Is Required to Write a Plan? Normally, an integrated marketing/advertising plan is not compiled quickly. The plan is usually written from information gathered over a year and is updated annually. For this reason it is a good idea to set up a marketing/advertising plan file consisting of the major sections of the plan. As information filters in over the year, it is filed and then used when the plan is initially drafted or updated. The individual responsible for drafting the integrated marketing/advertising plan should set aside thirty to sixty hours of working time plus typing time to write the plan *after* the necessary information has been gathered.

Variables That Affect Development of an Integrated Marketing/Advertising Plan. The overall objective is not to write the plan; rather, it is to chart a direction for the organization. All of the elements of the marketing/advertising plan, beginning with overall national trends in education, lead to that point. Though every market is unique, ebbs and flows in national and international trends provide a direction that affects us all.

Next are listed some of these variables that affect the marketing of continuing education programs.

A. Macroenvironmental Factors
     The first set of trends concerns the global macroenvironment:
  1. Demographics
      a. Aging of the baby boom population
      b. Increasing number of women in higher education
      c. Low predisposition toward higher education of the babies of baby-boomers
      d. Dual-income families
      e. Emergence of ethnic groups and subcultures
      f. Geographic population shifts
      g. Emergence of alternative family situations
  2. Economics
      a. Forecasted information on U.S. and world economies
      b. Interrelationships among U.S. and world economies
      c. Forecasted economic pockets within larger economic areas, such as local and regional economies
      d. Forecasted slow growth rate and high interest rates of the U.S. economy
      e. Shifting and adjusting of employment types, such as the emergence of Japanese industrial production, the decrease in U.S. industrial production, the increase in U.S. service jobs, and emergence of new professions in information technology
  3. Technology
      a. Emergence of technologies providing for teacher–student interaction from remote classrooms
      b. Gradual acceptance of television as an educational rather than strictly an entertainment medium
      c. Possibility of satellite linkages that provide national and international classroom experiences
  4. Politics
      a. The move to decentralization and its effect on monitoring education

  b. Effect of decentralization on availability of grants and tracking of the shifts in grant money

  c. Expectations of lean, measurably cost-effective education organizations

 5. Other

B. Microenvironmental Factors

  In considering microenvironmental issues, an organization must analyze internal trends as well as those in competitive institutions.

 1. Markets

  a. Local demographic trends

  b. Local economic trends

  c. Penetration of technology

  d. Local politics

  e. Analysis and tracking of educational enrollment trends

 2. Consumers

  a. Shifts in preferences, perceptions of the institution, and brand loyalties

  b. Shifts in consumer behavior to include how far in advance consumers make decisions

  c. Shifts in consumer needs

  d. Competitive trends

  e. Secondary competitive influences

In considering these variables, and any others you discern to be influential, remember that you are examining them for a specific purpose. The important question is, "What do these mean to our organization?" Without a thorough analysis of these variables, the marketing/advertising plan simply becomes an interesting document to read and has very little practical value to the organization.

How Do You Structure a Marketing/Advertising Plan?

As each organization must meet its specific needs, there is no one correct integrated marketing/advertising plan. Therefore, the following outline of the components of an integrated marketing/advertising plan is proposed as a guide. Shorten it, lengthen it, add to or substract from it. Do whatever is necessary to make it suitable for your purposes. A complete sample plan is outlined in Chapter Five.

 I. Executive Summary

  The executive summary is a one- to two-page synopsis of the observations and recommendations of the marketing plan. It should include the major points of the plan without all of the detail. It is not unusual for the executive summary to be the only portion of the marketing plan read by some executives, so it should have sufficient information to explain the year's activities.

II. Situation Analysis

The situation analysis should include all pertinent background data. *Pertinent* is emphasized because there is a tendency among those who enjoy numbers to include information that has no bearing on the logistics of marketing. Graphics are useful in this section to prevent the report from becoming too wordy. Such graphics are easy to develop with personal computers and their many integrated statistical and graphics packages. In analysis of the statistics, many questions arise. If the information available is insufficient to provide answers, these questions will become topics in Section IV, Research Recommendations.

Some specifics must be dealt with in situation analysis:

A. Macroenvironmental Factors

The "big picture" trends, national and international, comprise (1) demographics, (2) economics, (3) politics, (4) technology, and (5) other variables that have an impact on marketing efforts. For example, the owners of a direct-mail company with which a continuing education organization works suddenly decide to retire without any plans to sell the company or replace their services. This will have an important impact on the execution of direct-mail marketing plans.

B. Microenvironmental Factors

These are localized versions of the same macroenvironmental variables.

1. Demographics

Local high schools may report a 15 percent decrease in the size of the graduating class, which means that you will have 15 percent fewer people to attract in the marketplace.

2. Economics

Local economies may be doing better or more poorly, which affects unemployment rates, which, in turn, affects expendable income available for educational or other activities.

3. Politics

The philosophies of newly elected officials frequently impact educational institutions, or the state of local economies may affect political decisions to fund education.

4. Technology

If an institution has acquired some of the newer educational technologies, such as microwave or satellite communications, products, services, and programs will need to be adjusted to address the new technologies. A conscious effort may have to be made regarding the money and time allocated to communicating the availability of these new technologies.

5. Other

C.   Product evaluation

       Every product or service offered by the organization should be analyzed with respect to its effect on sales. An outline is sufficient here because it is important to be brief. Only the relevant information that will affect present marketing efforts should be covered:

1.   The competition

       Analyze the strengths and weaknesses of your organization and those of the competition.

2.   Consumer needs and preferences

       Base these on surveys and information gathered with respect to the localized microenvironmental factors.

3.   Change in utilization of the product, service, or program

       Gather these data from instructors or others who have direct contact with the consumer and have observed new utilization patterns.

4.   New product, service, or program development

       How will marketing be done in these areas? How will this be received in the marketplace?

5.   Life cycle analysis

       This should be done for the organization as a whole as well as for the major departments. In addition, it is often appropriate to analyze life cycles of various products, services, and programs.

6.   Effective product image or institutional image

       Occasionally, a good product outshines the overall image of the institution or vice versa. Analysis can reveal ways in which the product and the image of the institution can enhance each other.

D.   Consumer profile

       A precise consumer profile will help determine the best possible medium for communicating messages. For example, a brochure targeted at "yuppies" may show a young person in preppy clothing standing next to a BMW (to use the stereotype), whereas a brochure targeted to the blue-collar community may picture an individual in Levis standing next to a pickup truck. The point here is not to stereotype or judge consumers but to communicate visually and verbally in their own terms. This section of the marketing plan provides an accurate portrait of the target market. It should be as specific as possible and include the following information:

1.   Demographics

2.   Geography—where most of the customers come from

3.   Psychographics—a personality and life-styles profile of consumers

4.   Behavior analysis

a.   Frequency of use of the product, program, or service. For example, an adult may register for one continuing education program a year or four programs.

b.   Purchase influencers. An entering freshman may be influenced by parents, or an adult student may be influenced by an employer.

c.   Institutional loyalty, which may be due to geography, parent, or alumni support.

d.   Present and developing attitudes. Information about attitudes toward the institution, program, service, or product based on confirmable evidence obtained through survey and evaluation forms.

e.   Observed changes in a–d. An analysis should ask why changes have taken place, what has caused them, whether the changes are good or bad, and whether anything should be done.

E.   Competitive analysis

It is important to identify the competition, understand what they will likely do, and develop your plan accordingly. Competitive analysis should include the following issues:

1.   Direct competition

Other educational institutions competing for some or all of the same consumers as your institution.

2.   Indirect competition

Other organizations competing for the time and money of your consumers. For an adult education program, indirect competition is anything that competes for that adult's time, such as movies, a good book, the theater, a concert performance, or a sports event. Analysis of the circumstance dictates the communications strategy.

3.   Marketing approach

How the competition incorporates marketing techniques and how this differs from your approach. You should also consider whether their approach is more effective than yours and in what circumstances would you want to imitate their marketing approach.

4.   Advertising analysis

As differentiated from the marketing approach, competitive advertising analysis examines specifically the media in which the competition is advertising, when advertising is done, and the nature of the copy appeal.

5.   Advertising strengths and weaknesses

Analyze your institution relative to the competition in terms of product, price, location, advertising/catalogs, and image.

F.   Pricing strategies

Pricing strategies, if not implemented under an integrated

marketing/advertising plan, would be considered only in a marketing plan. Marketing sets pricing strategies; advertising tells the consumer what the price is. Pricing is a complex and involved process. In education it is generally an integral activity of administration rather than the marketing office alone. This section deals with pricing strategies as they relate specifically to marketing, and there are some relevant items to consider.

The institution's economic objectives act as a last check ensuring that necessary profit margins are maintained.

Pricing should be appropriate for consumer needs and value perceptions. Price needs to be considered a good value by the consumer. If your continuing education program is a little more expensive, consumers need to be informed that they are getting more for their money.

Pricing should be appropriate to the phase of the life cycle of the product, service, or program. If a product is dying out, the price very likely should be lowered over time and less marketing effort should be concentrated in this area.

Pricing should be appropriate for environmental conditions. If your institution is located in a depressed economic area, price should reflect those conditions. Pricing in this circumstance may not necessarily result in a lower price, but instead in easy installment payments or credit card charges.

III. Marketing Goals

We have already considered marketing goals relative to institutional goals. Again, a marketing goal should be realistic and relevant, not grandiose and nebulous. It is often wise to think of goals in terms of the need of the consumer and the problems faced by the institution. For example, declining enrollment in an institution may dictate the goal of an increase in enrollment. Or if you have discovered by surveys the need for Saturday courses, the goal may be to provide courses on Saturdays and then to advertise them.

It should be noted that there may be long-range and short-range objectives within the annual marketing plan. A short-range objective might be one that must be accomplished over a year. For example, if you decide that the program Microcomputers for Business needs an annual increase of enrollment of 15 percent, you may decide to accomplish that task by conducting three campaigns during the year. The short-range goal then would be to send out a brochure within the four-month time frame. In addition, if long-range goals include drastic changes for the institution, such as moving away from credit evening courses to noncredit evening courses, short-range goals should address the gradual preparation of the consumer for the long-term goal. For the purposes of an integrated marketing plan, it is useful to suggest specific marketing strategies while discussing goals. Separating the section on goals from that on strategy in a marketing plan results in a lot of page flipping and is simply inconvenient. The marketing goals and strategies section should include the following:

A. Institutional objectives
    1. A pertinent history of the institution and past marketing efforts
    2. A mission statement
    3. Other organizational objectives
        These, for the most part, are reminders of what the marketing goals are attempting to achieve for the organization.
B. Marketing Objectives
    It is helpful to consider the basics of marketing when setting the marketing objectives.
    1. Marketing mix
        a. Product. What objectives do you have for the product?
        b. Price. What pricing goals will you need to set to accomplish the organization's goals?
        c. Place of distribution or location of product. What will be the distribution methods or individual locations required by the marketing effort?
        d. Promotion/advertising. What the industry commonly calls a copy or creative platform is a statement of the overall image or appeal that will be utilized to communicate all marketing, promotional, and advertising material to the public. How the advertising will position products, services, and programs relative to the competition should be considered. For example, a religious institution might position itself with the slogan "Devotion to Truth," utilizing words that not only suggest education but carry some spiritual meaning as well.
    2. A rationale for why the product is positioned in a certain manner
    3. Statement of consumer benefits as well as suggestions for the tone of the advertising messages
    4. Method of measuring response of consumers
C. Advertising strategies
    1. Schedule/calendar of events
        Made into a poster and hung on a wall, the schedule serves to remind you to prepare for next month's activities. It should include the applied analysis of which media will most effectively reach your previously defined consumer as well as when you want to reach them.
        a. Preevaluation of the media. The strengths and weaknesses of each medium used to reach the consumer.
        b. Media time schedule. What are the specific dates in which media events will take place?

        c.   Postevaluation. Some method of measuring the effectiveness of media selection.

    2.   Sales support

        This section covers coordination of media with direct contact through sales and promotion. For example, if you intend to have sales staff (programmers or department representatives) make contact with businesses for a stress management program for corporations, you may want to run an advertisement in magazines or newspapers that reaches personnel directors before your representatives begin their sales calls. The importance of such a strategy is exemplified in an advertisement that has run in many business publications. A stern gentleman sitting behind a desk faces a nervous sales representative and states, "I don't know you. I don't know your company. I don't know your product. Now what do you want to sell me?" Advertising can be extremely useful in softening up the target before your representative makes direct contact. It is also useful for informing the public about locations of promotional activities such as fairs, library displays, or shopping mall displays.

    3.   Media budget

  D.   Sales and promotional strategies

        More and more educational organizations are engaging sales representatives to help in their marketing efforts. Coordination of these sales activities with other marketing activities is essential in providing a unified image to target audiences.

        Sales and promotional events should coincide, as much as possible, with advertising schedules. Some form of evaluation is necessary to measure the effectiveness of sales and promotions. One popular method of evaluation is to list a specially installed phone number in an advertisement. Since the only place a person can get the number is from the advertisement, this provides a very effective tracking method.

IV.   Marketing Research Recommendations

V.   Total Marketing Budget

        Be warned: put nonmarketing budget items into the marketing budget. The marketing budget should include line items for the following expenses:

  A.   Staff salary expenses

  B.   Office/operational expenses

  C.   Research expenses

  D.   Media expenses

    1.   Printing

        a.   Art production

        b.   Print production

    2.   Direct mail

          3.   Broadcast
          4.   Print media
          5.   Other
    E.   Equipment expenses
    F.   Costs for membership in professional associations
    G.   Consulting costs (if outside consulting expertise is needed)

VI.   Evaluation

        The integrated marketing/advertising plan should clearly state how the overall marketing effort is to be evaluated. Generally, this entails a comparison of marketing accomplishments with goals, assuming that the goals have specific, quantifiable objectives. It should be noted that the evaluation is an important part of the following year's marketing plan that analyzes what changes ought to take place in implementing next year's marketing efforts.

VII.   Conclusion

        Inclusion of this section depends on who will be reading the plan. Frequently, the conclusions are covered in the executive summary. A concluding section is important, however, if the marketing staff is communicating to management that the plan meets the needs of a parent organization. It is an opportunity to sell the plan itself in more detail than the executive summary has done. Use this section to provide any further explanation of your conclusions, but do not make it too wordy.

Summary

This chapter has provided a basic outline of the component parts of a marketing/advertising plan. As you consider developing your own plan, you may want to include additional sections or delete some of those suggested in the outline. Chapter Five builds on this chapter and presents an actual marketing plan that includes most of the component parts of the outline in this chapter.

5

A Sample Marketing and Advertising Plan

Kenneth S. Foster

Chapter Four identified and discussed the components of an integrated marketing/advertising plan. This chapter presents a sample integrated marketing/advertising plan in use by the Division of Continuing Education at the University of Utah. The information contained in this abbreviated plan is accurate but edited to maintain brevity and confidentiality, while still highlighting critical areas. The sample plan deals only with the marketing of 1,200 credit and noncredit courses offered on the main campuses of the University of Utah; it does not include correspondence courses, television courses, special-contract courses, seminars, conferences, or in-house training courses offered by the division. It can easily be modified to meet the needs of a wide variety of continuing education organizations in higher education, business, industry, government, development and training departments, and professional associations.

The plan discussed in this chapter has the following components discussed in the preceding chapter:

   I.   Executive summary
  II.   Situation analysis
        A.   Macroenvironmental factors
             1.   Demographics
             2.   Economics
             3.   Politics
             4.   Technology
             5.   Other

    B.   Product Evaluation
        1.   Description
        2.   Competition comparison
        3.   Consumer perceptions regarding progressiveness
        4.   Student satisfaction
        5.   Market distribution
    C.   Consumer Profile
        1.   Demographics
        2.   Psychographics
        3.   Behavior analysis
    D.   Competitive Analysis
        1.   Direct competition
        2.   Indirect competition
        3.   Advertising strengths and weaknesses
        4.   Pricing

III.   Marketing Goals
    A.   Institutional Objectives
        1.   Mission statement
        2.   Background
        3.   Other
    B.   Marketing Objectives
        1.   Long-term objectives
        2.   Marketing strategy
        3.   Creative recommendations
    C.   Promotion/Advertising Recommendations
        1.   Schedule
        2.   Evaluation
        3.   Media budget
        4.   Problems
        5.   Opportunities

IV.   Marketing Research
 V.   Total Marketing Budget
VI.   Evaluation
VII.   Conclusion

Development of a comprehensive marketing/advertising plan is a very effective way to engage the organization in analysis of marketing and advertising. Through the collection, analysis, and presentation of data, the consensus for recommendations begins to enlarge, thus, building both internal and external support for continuing education programs, products, and services.

Integrated Marketing/Advertising Plan, Division of Continuing Education, University of Utah

 I.   Executive Summary
        The following recommendations and observations found in the various portions of this marketing plan are listed here in summary format

for convenience. The basis for the recommendations is explained throughout the report.

1. A more formal mechanism is needed to detect new subject areas that lend themselves to new course development.

2. All advertising and publications should be sensitive to the University's academic standards and image of quality.

3. The Division of Continuing Education should actively contribute to maintaining and enhancing the overall image of quality and excellence at the University of Utah.

4. Marketing efforts should help sensitize the administration and faculty to continue to utilize the Division of Continuing Education as the primary delivery system for serving the needs of nontraditional students.

5. Even though the Division of Continuing Education has an overall 85 percent satisfactory rating by students, additional research needs to be done to determine how student satisfaction can be improved even further.

6. More rapid payment for instructors is required to maintain faculty satisfaction with the administrative services of the Division.

7. Target audiences for continuing education programs have not changed significantly during the last few years. Female participation in higher education is up nationally and locally. For example, the majority of students in the Division of Continuing Education courses are female. However, audiences nationally and locally are aging, so research into the feasibility of targeting beyond the upper age limits of past target profiles is recommended.

8. Market share trends indicate that the Division of Continuing Education is still the dominant force in the local market and growing at a faster rate than any major competition except church-sponsored programs. Research indicates private business colleges have grown rapidly but in a different niche. Thus, they do not directly compete from a quality perspective.

9. Overall enrollment in Division of Continuing Education programs has increased at a steady rate after a temporary demographic plateau.

10. New competition in the marketplace has emerged, and the Salt Lake City market has been defined by the Census Bureau and several national studies as one of the key growth markets in the country.

11. Cross-selling is the distribution in class of promotional material for other classes. There is some indication that it has actually had a cannibalizing effect. This is especially true for no-growth subjects where course offerings have increased but total audience size has not increased.

12. In-class promotion efforts should be adopted. However, such efforts must be sensitive to the integrity of class time. For example, the hard sell does not do well when marketing liberal arts courses.

13. Studies have found that the Division of Continuing Education is rated more favorably among users than nonusers. Naturally, nonusers basically have no basis for making judgments. Hypothesizing a negative attitude toward the University as a whole by nonusers, we recommend further research into the nonusers' negative reactions. This should provide data useful in overcoming consumer objections to enrolling for courses.

14. Though our audiences have been well defined demographically and psychographically, the motives for taking continuing education programs continue to be highly diversified in the consumer decision process. For this reason, we recommend gearing our creative advertising messages to appeal to the broad market.

15. As we have recognized new secondary competitors, we recommend some new experiments in advertising media. These should include: use of theater advertising, expanded use of posters with targeted distribution points in such new locations as health spas, and expanded use of program ads in a wide variety of media.

16. Research has shown that our consumers like the *Class Edition* catalogue as is. We recommend only subtle, evolutionary changes for this publication in the near future.

17. The registration form stuffer will no longer be used in the *Class Edition* catalogue because of the phone registration system. Our experience has shown that most people prefer to register by phone. We should explore new facilitating methods for those who do not have access to the phone system.

18. Direct sales have proven to be successful for selling in-house programs to government and business. Therefore, production of sales aids for the new sales staff in the business programming area should be a high priority.

19. The Division of Continuing Education should develop a plan for assisting corporations looking to relocate and desiring affiliation with the University. This could actively contribute to the city's and state's economic development efforts.

20. Further research into reasons for various levels of satisfaction among students from competitive institutions is recommended.

II. Situation Analysis

     A. Macroenvironmental factors

         1. Demographics

Population shifts are continuing to affect the country, with five states losing population and the remaining states remaining stable or gaining population ("Demographic Forecasts: Marriage and Money," 1987). Past projections of the Utah Bureau of Economic and Business Research have indicated that Utah is among the fastest growing states, but growth has been due to birth rate rather than in-migration. For example, the current annual growth rate is estimated at only 8 percent, the slowest in twenty years. A net out-migration from the state was made up mostly of twenty- to thirty-four-year-olds, which is part of the traditional target audience for the Division of Continuing Education. Even though Utah's birth rate is declining, enrollment in public schools is projected to increase until 1993, when it will decrease. These factors do not necessarily mean that we will experience a decrease in the market for continuing education courses. During the next twenty years, the aging population will need to engage in additional study to maintain current skills as well as gain new skills. Thus, the aging audiences need to be studied further to determine if there is the potential for increasing the market share of people beyond the forty-five-year-old mark, which has been the traditional cutoff for our target market.

2. Economics

Personal income in the state has increased at 3 percent per year and is projected to increase 4.5 to 5 percent next year. It is hoped that this will provide more expendable income for education (Kelly, 1987).

The employment rate is decreasing and currently averages 6.3 percent. Most job increases came in the manufacturing and service industries, with construction decreasing and mining and government remaining flat (First Security Bank Annual Economic Report). The Division of Continuing Education should target the high-growth sectors, recognizing that most manufacturing organizations are serviced by trade education, not liberal arts.

Many high-tech companies look at Utah when considering relocation. These prospective employers should be actively courted by the University, and the Division of Continuing Education can play a key role in this recruitment process.

3. Politics

Close contacts with the University's lobbyists should be maintained in order to be sensitive to unforeseen issues. In election years there are many opportunities for special programming, especially for seminars and short courses related to the general political process as well as specific issues. Taxation, international economics, state/international trade, and corporate incentive programs have all been hot issues in the political areas this year.

4. Technology

The microwave system and the new education television station provide more programming options. We see little tie-in with national television efforts in continuing education in the near future, but there are many local opportunities based on past successes. For example, "Utah Geography" pulled well, as has "Photography." Both seem to have the common denominator of "hands-on" experience in conjunction with the TV experience, and the "Utah Geography" course has the added attraction of "Understanding Your Environment."

5. Other

The Canadian paper companies have increased prices, so an unexpected paper cost increase of approximately $3,800 dollars will need to be figured into the budget for printing the *Class Edition* catalogue. Availability of paper should not be a problem as our printer has ordered a year in advance for us.

Local television and radio stations have decreased their news staffs. We may see less cooperation as remaining staff receive extra assignments in addition to their normal beats.

Local newspapers have enacted a mid-fiscal-year price increase of 7 percent. We will have to adjust line-item media expenditures or decrease placement in newspapers to compensate for this increase.

B. Production evaluation

1. Description

The University of Utah Division of Continuing Education is responsible for the coordination and delivery of special services and activities to the nontraditional student. In this capacity, the Division serves as agent for the academic programs in the various colleges and departments of the University. The dean of the Division of Continuing Education reports to the vice-president for academic affairs. For all programs handled by the Division, whether credit or noncredit, both content and instructor must be approved by an appropriate college or department.

The unique function of the Division is to provide a wide variety of continuing education activities to the nontraditional student.

2. Competition comparison

The Division of Continuing Education leans heavily on the University of Utah for its image of quality. The fact that we are the University of Utah allows us to charge higher prices for our courses. In fact, the legislature dictates our prices for credit courses. No institution, with the exception of Brigham Young University, can offer courses at the same quality level that we do. Geographically, Brigham Young is not a serious competitor (even though they do have a Salt Lake City Extension Office) because they are located forty miles south of Salt Lake City.

We have no research to indicate the level of consumer satisfaction with our competing institutions, but that research is now underway. Our research does indicate a high level of consumer satisfaction with our programs. Our ability to offer a wide variety of courses and constantly develop new courses has been received positively by consumers as indicated in our survey. For example, in our surveys of the local market (users and nonusers) we found that 77 percent feel that the Division of Continuing Education provides good service, whereas 6 percent have negative feelings toward our service. Seventeen percent of the respondents fall somewhere between these two ratings.

We recommend further development of a sales staff for business courses and exploration of direct sales for other program areas. In the past, a special sales staff dealing with business courses has made sales calls to determine educational needs, create programs to meet these needs, and then market these programs in appropriate ways to the business community. Developing this customized service beyond business should be a high priority for the Division.

The new telephone answering machine has provided better phone service, but we recognize a further need for phone training for certain staff.

3. Consumer perceptions regarding progressiveness

Research indicates that 57 percent of the population rate the program in the Division of Continuing Education as high quality; only 6 percent give us a poor quality rating. Twenty-three percent had neutral attitudes toward quality and 14 percent had no opinion. Forty-six percent of the population rate us progressive, with 17 percent giving us a negative measurement in this area. Twenty-five percent gave a neutral indication and 12 percent had no opinion.

Because we depend on the University for our image, it is important to understand how the University is perceived. On a semantic scale of 1 to 7, 1 being "conservative" and 7 "liberal," the University has an average rating of 5. On a "national quality" scale, 1 being high quality and 7 low, the University has an average rating of 3.

Some variables affecting image of the Division specifically are important to note: on a scale of 1 to 7, 7 being "exciting," the Division's average rating is 5; with "geographical convenience" as a 7, the Division is rated 2.4; with "excellent faculty teaching" as 7, the Division's faculty is rated 5. (*Note:* In-class evaluations show a marked increase in instruction quality over the past three years.)

4. Student satisfaction

The Division of Continuing Education has an overall satisfaction rate of 85 percent. Though this is a very positive finding, further research is recommended to determine what we can improve to increase the ratings.

5.   Market distribution

The Division of Continuing Education currently has programs operating in the following locations: Salt Lake Art Center, Busch Forum in South Salt Lake, Redwood Road, Alta Ski Resort, Brighton Ski Resort, Campus Area, Canyon Rim, Whitmore Library, West Valley City Library, Park City Campus, Bountiful Campus, and Copperview Campus.

We show the highest level of consumer awareness of the presence of programs through the Division of Continuing Education in the east and southeast areas of Salt Lake City and the next highest level in Davis County: (1) 95.5 percent awareness in Holladay, (2) 93.2 percent awareness in Davis, (3) 91.7 percent in Avenues, (4) 90.5 percent in South Salt Lake, (5) 87.9 percent in Granger/Kearns, (6) 88.6 percent in Rose Park, (7) 85.9 percent in Salt Lake City, (8) 84.4 percent in Murray Midvale, (9) 81.3 percent in Southwest Salt Lake, and (10) 80.7 percent in Sandy/ Draper. A defensive marketing strategy suggests concentration of marketing and program development in those areas of highest awareness and highest past participation.

C.   Consumer Profile

1.   Demographics

A great deal of information is available nationally regarding the demographics of consumers of continuing education. The most recent information is from the Simmons Market Research Bureau (1986):

- 70 percent of the adult population claims to be continuing their education in some form
- 6.4 percent of the adults in the United States have taken an adult education course in the past 12 months
- 67.7 percent of continuing education consumers are female
    28.3 percent are employed
    28.3 percent are between the ages of 25 and 34
    51.1 percent have no children in the household
    34.4 percent read newspapers and magazines
    21.7 percent read *TV Guide*
    35 percent read *Parade*
    70.2 percent read a daily newspaper
    71.9 percent read the Sunday newspaper
- 32.2 percent of continuing education consumers are male
- 76 percent of all continuing education consumers are between the ages of 18 and 49
- 30.4 percent of all continuing education consumers are between the ages of 25 and 34

- 55 percent of all continuing education consumers have either graduated from or attended college
- 58 percent of these people have full-time jobs
- 30.1 percent are professional/managerial
- 69 percent are married
- 57 percent make $25,000 or more annually
- 45 percent come from a household of three or more people

Our surveys show that 92 percent of those taking continuing education courses at the University of Utah are between the ages of 18 and 49. This breaks down to 2 percent under 18 (special program), 32 percent 18–24 years old, 42 percent 25–34 years old, 18 percent 35–49 years old, and 6 percent 50 years or older.

The Division of Continuing Education (DCE) has two target audiences: "pure" DCE students and "total" DCE students. "Pure" students are those who take courses *only* through the Division of Continuing Education. "Total" students comprise the "pure" students and the matriculated students, those who are picking up extra hours through continuing education. We should continue to promote only to our "pure" adult students as they represent the way to fulfill our mission. Providing "pickup" courses to matriculated students is incidental to our mission. "Pure" students are older, more are employed full-time, they have higher incomes, they have a higher occurrence of divorce, they have higher education levels, and fewer belong to the predominant local religion. Media selection and creative strategy should reflect this profile.

2. Psychographics

In addition to the descriptive information we have found in our demographic research, we have conducted several independent studies of psychographic traits of those participating in programs through the Division of Continuing Education. This research reveals that half of our adult learners are under age 40. In addition to being young, those predisposed to learning are better educated and have higher incomes than those not predisposed to learning.

Interestingly, employed people are more likely to engage in formal course work than those who are unemployed. In addition, those who are employed full-time are more likely to engage in continuing education than those who are employed part-time. Less than one out of three retirees is engaged in formal course work.

Professional and technical workers are more predisposed to education than those employed in agriculture. Our research also indicates that there is a clear correlation between the amount of training required for an occupation and predisposition toward continuing education. In other words, the more you learn, the more you want to learn.

Other research indicates that adult students are more likely to live in urban areas (Simmons Market Research Bureau, 1986). Simmons shows adult participation in education is far below average where the population is less than 2,500 people.

Simmons also shows that adults in the Pacific Coast states are more likely to engage in continuing education than those in any other region of the nation, and adults in the South Atlantic states are less likely to participate than those in any other region. Making inferences to the Utah market with these data, we believe that the out-of-home, activity-oriented psychographics of the West causes a higher participation in adult education.

In general, it is suggested that adult learning theory as reported by Knowles (1972) and Knox (1972) and later by Cross (1981) and Long (1983) has psychographic applications to marketing. Adult learners have a desire to know, to reach a personal goal, to reach a social goal or a religious goal, to escape, to take part in any kind of activity, and to comply with formal course requirements. Some clinical observations have suggested that the latter is a matter of intellectual necessity, though we have not found survey data substantiating this. Commonly used variables show social relationships, external expectations, professional advancement, social welfare, escape, and cognitive interest as key motives to take courses (Taylor, 1985).

Our own studies have found that the age of a respondent is inversely related to job-related educational motivation, whereas personal employment is directly related to age. Our surveys have also found the following motives for taking continuing education courses: (1) degree or certification requirements, (2) learning for the sake of learning, (3) job advancement and the desire to improve income, (4) development of a recreational or a vocational skill, and (5) the opportunity to meet and interact with people. As a result of our knowledge of these diverse reasons that motivate people to register for continuing education courses, we must continue to offer a wide variety of courses and thus maintain our broad appeal. This has important implications for our continued program development as well as our advertising approaches to the market.

One study (Taylor, 1985) has shown that 83 percent of adult learners take courses or undertake learning to cope with changes such as those involving career, family, health, religion, or citizenship status. This too has important implications for our program development and its subsequent advertising, both of which should be directed to this perceived need.

Some mechanisms that seem to trigger these life transitions are being hired or fired, failing to receive a raise or promotion, getting married, or getting elected to office.

3. Behavior analysis

Our surveys of credit and noncredit participants indicate the following about people who register for both credit and noncredit courses through the Division of Continuing Education. Most people who take a credit class take another credit class within the next two years. This is not as frequent for noncredit courses. Thirty percent of all registrants are taking a credit class through the Division of Continuing Education for the first time. In the noncredit area, 35 percent of the registrants are taking a class for the first time. Fifty-seven percent of participants in credit classes pay their own tuition. As might be expected, employers tend to pay tuition for courses that directly affect an employee's work functions.

With respect to the frequency of use by participants taking credit classes, 67 percent of our registrants take two or more classes per year through the Division of Continuing Education, 48 percent take three or more classes a year, and 30 percent take four or more classes a year.

D. Competitive analysis

1. Direct competition

Nine public institutions of higher education, including two universities, constitute the Utah system of public higher education. In addition, there are five private universities (Table 5.1).

Institutions that represent direct competition for our Division of Continuing Education are Westminster College, various community education programs, Stevens–Henager College, the Latter Day Saints Business College, library programs, church programs, community arts colleges, professional conferences or meetings, technical colleges, the Brigham Young University Continuing Education College, the University of Phoenix, and two large community education programs in the Salt Lake District and the Granite District.

We have determined metro area market share through our surveys, which ask the general population in what programs they have participated:

Division of Continuing Education, University of Utah	24.1%
Westminister College	3.1%
Community schools overall	22.3%
Stevens–Henager College	5.5%
Latter Day Saints Business College	5.5%
Library programs	10.6%

Table 5.1. Utah System of Higher Education.

Institution	Location	Year Established	Type	Enrollment
		Public Institutions		
University of Utah	Salt Lake City	1850	University	24,603
Utah State University	Logan	1888	University	10,266
Weber State College	Ogden	1889	4-Year college	10,674
Southern Utah State	Cedar City	1897	4-Year college	1,966
Snow College	Ephraim	1888	2-Year college	1,127
Dixie College	St. George	1911	2-Year college	1,589
College of Eastern Utah	Price	1937	2-Year college	851
Community College	Provo	1941	2-Year college	4,130
Community College	Salt Lake City	1947	2-Year college	6,679
		Private Institutions		
Brigham Young University	Provo	1875	University	27,521
Westminster College	Salt Lake City	1875	4-Year college	1,365
Latter Day Saints Business College	Salt Lake City	1886	2-Year business college	1,044
Stevens–Henager College	Ogden/Provo	1891	2-Year business college	605
University of Phoenix	Salt Lake City	1985	4-Year business college	900

Church programs	32.1%
Community art programs	6.5%
Professional conferences or meetings	18.8%
Technical colleges	20.5%
Brigham Young University Continuing Education College	12.3%
University of Phoenix	2.1%
Salt Lake District community education	11.3%
Granite District community education	24.3%

The only significant rise in market share since our last study is in the community school area.

That these institutions really *are* competitive is clear when we note that 26.1% of Division of Continuing Education students have taken courses elsewhere:

Westminster	6.1%
Brigham Young University Extension	27.8%
Library classes	12.4%
Church-sponsored classes	40.2%
Community art classes	5.3%
Utah Technical College	12.4%
Brigham Young University	32.0%
Others	7.2%

That people are taking courses at places other than the Division of Continuing Education should not be surprising. It indicates the competitive nature of the education marketplace and reflects the independent nature of the adult student.

Table 5.2 is a sample of competitive course offerings and prices offered by the Division of Continuing Education, our major competition (Brigham Young University), and the Granite and Salt Lake school districts.

2.   Indirect competition

As demonstrated in the previous section, consumers of programs offered by the Division of Continuing Education are activity oriented. Basically any activity other than education can be considered indirect competition with our programs. These activities include television, sports, symphony, opera, ballet, movies, and health spas. That we consistently attract large numbers of people is gratifying considering the commitment required to attend class plus the reading and studying necessary during spare time to complete class assignments. It is obvious that those who do take classes are very committed to adult learning.

3.   Advertising strengths and weaknesses

The advertising strength for the Division of Continuing Education at the University of Utah is clearly that we dominate the marketplace in the mass media. Brigham Young University produces quality advertising but does not mass distribute as widely as we do. The other institutions utilize mass communications sporadically, with little continuity and with what appears to be very little targeting and no strong creative message or theme.

4.   Pricing

Pricing of programs for the Division of Continuing Education is flexible only in the noncredit area. Prices for credit courses are established by the Board of Regents. Our pricing should continue to recognize that we are, by legislative mandate, priced higher than the competition in most areas of credit programs. Operationally we are also priced higher than the competition in much of the noncredit area. Therefore, our product offerings and promotional efforts should carry messages that convey a sense of high quality and thus higher perceived value for the investment by consumers than that of the competition.

III.   Marketing Goals
  A.   Institutional objectives
    1.   Mission statement
The University administration is presently drafting an

Table 5.2. Continuing Education Fee Comparison—Salt Lake Area.

Subject	University of Utah		Brigham Young University		Granite School District		Salt Lake School District
	Credit Fee	Noncredit Fee	Credit Fee	Noncredit Fee	Credit Fee	Noncredit Fee	(noncredit fee)
Basic drawing	148	86	102			24	20
Watercolor	148	86	102			28	15
Private-Pilot ground school	148		102				15
General biology	169		153				
Accounting	127	70	153		27	20	
Management	148	70	153		27	20	
Real estate		90			27	85	125
How to start a business		70				7	50
Assertiveness training		75				20	25
Career change or planning	106	90				15	
Typing	88	53				30	22
Shorthand	157	89			27	20	25
Word processing		95				10	30
Business communications	127	81				20	35
Beginning photography	142	96	153			24	20
Ballet		110				9	18
Creative dance		77				11	12
Tap	85	35				13	18
Tai chi	106	75				12	18
Modern dance	106	75				13	20
Aerobic dance		40		35		25	18

Basic economics	169		153				18
Shakespeare	148	86			27		18
Kindergarten education	148	300	102			150	20
English as a second language						19	30
Creative writing	148	86				38	20
Weight modification	130	53				32	18
First aid and emergency	153	70	153			8	18
Stress management	106	75					10
U.S. history	169		153		27		20
Parenting	127	85	153			15	22
Beginning French conversation		75				22	15
Elementary algebra		85	102		107		
Group piano		85				20	40
Private piano	106	75				15	18
Beginning guitar	85	50					50
Ballroom dance	106	40				30	20
Exercise/fitness	106	35		35		22	18
Body building	106	30				13	20
Yoga (beginning)	106	40				22	20
Golf (beginning)				51		22	
Bowling (beginning)	114.5	43.50	51	35			
Tennis (beginning)		28	51	35		12	25
American government	169		153				
General psychology	169	73	153			21	20
Knitting (beginning)		21.50				21	20
Quilting	111	40					15
Basic acting	127	97					

extensive mission statement that, on completion, will require careful analysis to determine if the role of the Division of Continuing Education in the total University picture will change. The dean of the Division of Continuing Education has been involved in developing this document. Meanwhile, the Division continues to work toward goals that are within the definition of our overall mission statement, which suggests we are the agency through which people can gain access to the University's instructional resources.

2. Background

    The University of Utah has historically looked to the Division of Continuing Education to fill classroom space during off-hours; run the summer quarter program; program extension services; provide major University outreach along with our public TV and radio stations, athletics, hospital, and two museums; maintain its stature as a self-funding operation; and program for and service nontraditional students, that is, those who cannot attend full-time or during the mornings or early afternoons.

3. Other

    An important function of the Division of Continuing Education is to maintain academic standards and project an image that appeals to our target audience while maintaining an image complimentary to the main campus program. This suggests quality, concern, academic freedom, and a view of education as an important underlying variable affecting the economic well-being of the state.

B. Marketing Objectives

- To increase the share-of-market by .5 percent, from 24.1 to 24.6 percent. This translates into an increase of 10 percent in enrollment, which means a student head count increase of 900 students total in both credit and noncredit programs.

- To establish a positive and distinct image among our target audience and to help the University maintain its image of quality among the total population.

- To reaffirm the high quality of the programs offered by the Division of Continuing Education.

- To obtain a top-of-mind awareness of the Division of Continuing Education in light of the competitive advertising in the marketplace.

    1. Long-term objectives

        a. To maintain "brand" loyalty to the Division of Continuing Education so that consumers will continue to be loyal after having taken one or more courses.

        b. To continue to increase our market share.

    2. Marketing strategy

a. To continue to position the Division of Continuing Education against competitive institutions in the minds of our audience as being of higher quality and resulting in more satisfying and richer educational experiences.

b. To implement an internal and external marketing strategy that promotes our programs to the general public through the mass media.

c. To time our promotions to take advantage of peak periods during the fall and spring when people tend to register for continuing education programs. In addition, we want to position ourselves properly in the winter quarter to try to increase our share of market during this time. Historically, surveys have shown winter quarter to be the most preferred time to take a class, yet enrollment is lowest in the winter quarter. Careful positioning with winter holidays has helped us produce the highest growth of all the quarters during winter.

d. To be flexible to market conditions. That is, if we experience hard economic times in the state and nation, we should create new programs that reflect education as a source of solving problems caused by economic and other conditions.

3. Creative recommendations

      Advertising objectives should always correspond to marketing objectives. We recommend continuing to develop a creative strategy for each quarterly advertising theme. This will move us toward a slightly more academic approach. Therefore, we should communicate a more academic product mix in a more academically appropriate manner. This will allow us to react more quickly to the changing needs of the marketplace.

C. Promotion/Advertising Recommendations

1. Schedule

      Figure 5.1 is an annual media advertising schedule for the Division of Continuing Education. Such an overview illustrates the importance of the complex and integrative nature of planning and scheduling media promotion and advertising. All of these activities are carefully planned in relation to each other to accomplish specific objectives. Some specifics must be observed. Media schedules must always show the week or day the message hits the target audience. Each square must represent a simplified four-week month. Note the relationship and timing of the media. For example, outdoor billboard advertising, a

Figure 5.1. Advertising Media Schedule.

	JULY	AUG	SEPT	OCT	NOV	DEC	JAN	FEB	MAR	APR	MAY	JUNE
Direct-Mail Catalog			XXXX			XXXX			XXXXX		XXXXX	XXXXXXXXX
Newspaper Stuffer			X			X			X		X	
Newspaper Advertising		X	X			X X		X	X		X X	X
TV Paid Advertising	XXX								XX			X X
Public Service Announcement				XXX				XXX		XXX		
Radio Advertising			X X			XX		X X X	X X			
Magazine Advertising		X				X		X			X	
Outdoor Billboard Advertising		XXXX			XXXX			XXXX			XXXX	
In-Class Point of Purchase Advertising				X	X		X X			X X		

reminder medium, hits a week or two prior to direct mail. The media schedule must correlate with a production schedule and can be used as a reminder to start a project. Most projects should be initiated at least eight wccks before they hit. Some, like the catalog, need to be initiated even further in advance.

2. Evaluation

The Marketing Office continues to evaluate advertising effectiveness with methods standard to the industry but customized for education marketing. Using variations of the cost-per-order method, we utilize cost per student and cost per student credit hour (student credit hour refers to credit hours for which students have registered). The following chart shows how well we have met our goals (information on education industry standards for comparison is not available):

	Goal	Actual
Cost per order	$3.00	$3.38
Cost per student	5.50	5.56
Cost per student credit hour	1.25	1.39

Two factors need to be kept in mind as we examine advertising effectiveness. First, total cost-per figures do not reflect the impact of advertising of one program on another continuing education program. In other words, a customer may receive a brochure for the business program that reminds him or her to take a course in the engineering program. Second, cost-per figures represent only actual advertising costs rather than salaries and overhead.

Another means of determining advertising effectiveness is to analyze advertising expenditure as a percentage of the Division's total operating budget. The following chart suggests that marketing and advertising have been effective, as the Division continues to grow while advertising expenditures as a percentage of total have declined.

1980	15%
1981	14%
1982	13%
1983	11%
1984	9%
1985	7%
1986	7%
1987	7%
1988	7%

These data have important implications for promotion/advertising: (1) We have decreased the ratio of advertising expense to the total operating budget. (2) There is a relatively low cost per respondent for new students. (3) There is a low cost per student as compared with income per student.

In making advertising media expenditure recommendations, it is important to summarize the critical points in our research. *Our primary target market is women between the ages of 25 and 44; the secondary market is all adults between those same ages.*

Winter quarter is seen as the most preferred time to take courses; fall quarter is the second choice, spring the third, and summer the fourth. Though winter is the most preferred time to take courses, environmental conditions and competition with the holidays cause our enrollment to be lowest at that time. In fact, enrollment is different than preference. Fall produces the highest enrollment, spring the second, summer the third, and winter the fourth.

3. Media budget

The following figures represent the dollars allocated to general advertising for the current fiscal year. It is important to note that advertising budgets for individual programs are funded by each program. Therefore, these expenses are not listed in the following figures. Salaries and operating expenses also are not included.

Radio	$14,500
Television	34,000
Magazine	5,000
Outdoor advertising	26,000
Newspaper	10,000
Miscellaneous	2,000
Catalogue production	156,000
Newspaper supplement production	40,000
Additional direct-mail expenses	40,000
Total	$327,500

Media usage and expenditures over the past three years have remained fairly constant. The following chart illustrates the percent of change in advertising dollars allocated to different types of advertising during the last five years.

Transit	−100%
Institutional magazine	−100%
Outdoor advertising	+310%

Newspaper	+ 25%
Television	− 40%
Radio	+ 20%
Miscellaneous	+200%
Direct mail	+130%
Production of the direct-mail catalogue and preview	+152%

Direct mail is still the major form of advertising and thus is the major source of information for Division of Continuing Education students. However, outdoor advertising on billboards is now the most recognizable form of our advertising, with a public recall of approximately 60 percent.

Division of Continuing Education media patterns consist of using billboard advertising to supplement our direct-mail and newspaper-teaser advertising each quarter. Once or twice a year, depending on need, we use television advertising to develop new audiences. However, television has traditionally not been a good medium to reach those involved in adult education. Radio advertising is used two to four times a year depending on need. All media advertising is scheduled to run throughout the year.

Competitive institutions have traditionally depended on direct mail as their major form of advertising. In recent years, Westminster College incorporated billboard advertising, only to abandon it after three quarters. Brigham Young University has recently advertised on billboards in the downtown area of Salt Lake City on a limited basis and continues to use some newspaper advertising. Like most institutions, Brigham Young relies on direct mail as the primary source of advertising for its continuing education activities.

Local community education programs are using direct mail and supplementing this promotional mix with effective publicity programs such as feature articles in the newspapers.

The University of Phoenix relies heavily on newspaper advertising to develop its audiences and from all reports finds this approach effective. Phoenix has also used radio to supplement its advertising efforts. In tests, we have found that this university follows up immediately on consumer inquiries with brochures and explanatory literature. This same method is being used successfully by Westminster College.

4. Problems

Here are some of the major promotion/advertising problems we are encountering:

a. There are eleven educational institutions currently advertising in the Salt Lake City market. This means we face a possible loss of market share; certainly there is confusion among the public about our program.

b.   Continuing education enrollment has traditionally prospered in inverse proportion to the economy. The economy recently has been on the rise. Therefore there is some concern that our enrollments may have plateaued. Recent layoffs by Kennecott may have some impact on our enrollments. We predict that this will not be a major problem because their employees are predisposed to take continuing education courses with the technical colleges rather than with us.

c.   Enrollment has remained constant in the Division for the last several years. An analysis is currently under way but we hypothesize this as due to conditions in the economy rather than to the increased effectiveness of our competition.

5.   Opportunities

a.   The Division of Continuing Education has the opportunity to develop brand loyalty with the use of advertising as we have already set precedent in advertising continuing education programs in this marketplace. It will take other institutions several years to catch up in this area. An exception is the University of Phoenix, which has entered the marketplace in an entrepreneurial mode and has found a comfortable niche by taking overflow from the business schools of the universities in the area. The University of Phoenix appears to be little threat to us in the short run; however, we recommend watching them closely.

b.   The Division of Continuing Education has the opportunity to develop new audiences through the development of new programs. Overall enrollment for continuing education programs seems to have plateaued, but it appears that we can maintain our share of the market by offering a core set of popular programs and then constantly creating new programs to meet the rapidly changing needs of consumers.

IV.   Marketing Research

Research needs to be undertaken to explore the feasibility of attracting older audiences to the Division of Continuing Education. This research should determine if those who have participated in our program over the years will maintain their activity in adult education if we lose them to activities dictated by change of age and life-style, and if senior citizens will attend courses and other educational activities if the product is adjusted to fit their needs. The latter is of interest because of the recent growth in enrollment in Elderhostel programs and the increase in participation in the tuition-free seniors program.

An updated market study is recommended to aid in decision making where competitive institutions may affect the success of our programs. This should be a repeat of studies conducted over the years.

A feasibility study should be done on the potential of increasing programming in the downtown campus.

Further research into psychographic profiles is suggested to determine specifically the motivational factors that advertising might influence.

V. Total Marketing Budget

At this point in the marketing plan, rather than listing actual budget figures, we outline line items that should be listed in a budget. Thus, this section of the market plan can easily be adjusted to fit your individual needs.

A. Salaries
B. Travel
C. Supplies and expenses
    1. Honorarium or talent fees
    2. Office supplies
    3. Marketing research
    4. Telephone
    5. Print (noncatalogue)
    6. Print (catalogue)
    7. Radio
    8. Television
    9. Magazine
    10. Outdoor
    11. Newspaper
    12. Art production
    13. Memberships in associations
    14. Books and periodicals
    15. Repairs and maintenance
    16. Miscellaneous
D. Equipment
E. Income

VI. Evaluation

This year's marketing effort will be evaluated on the basis of ten factors:

1. Realization of an increase in student head count while maintaining present expenditures for marketing.
2. Development of at least twenty new courses generated from specific needs expressed by the market rather than from only the interests of academic departments.
3. Successful delivery of 95 percent of all programs; that is sufficient enrollments in 95 percent of the programs to enable them to be offered.
4. Projection of a measured positive image among the total population of users and nonusers of our program.

5. An increase in approval by present users.
6. Measurement of the effectiveness of new media as discussed in the media under Promotion/Advertising Recommendations.
7. Successful completion of research outlined under Marketing Research.
8. Successful use of data collected by the new computer system, which is in the process of installation.
9. Faster turnaround time for the quarterly catalogue as a result of installation of the new computer system.
10. Successful realization of goals as outlined under Marketing goals.

VII. Conclusion

The Marketing Office has achieved local and national recognition for its work in promoting the Division of Continuing Education, the University of Utah, and the state. This is due to the support of the administration, hard work on the part of the staff, good relations with the programming staff, and good financial support. The Marketing Office believes that if the items discussed in this plan are supported financially and otherwise, the Division as a whole will realize many positive benefits.

The Marketing Office believes that the most critical elements to focus attention on are the efforts to investigate the aging population to determine future direction for the Division and the University as a whole. An aggressive, creative, active marketing philosophy is alive and well in the Division of Continuing Education at the University of Utah.

Positioning Your Organization in the Market

Part Two is devoted to positioning of the continuing education organization in the market. Alignment of continuing education programs with the desired organizational image is discussed in Chapter Six, in which Donald E. Hanna identifies ten important issues to consider when planning programs that enhance the organization's image. The theme established is that to be successful, the continuing education organization should always align itself with the parent institution's values. Case studies illustrate practical ways to accomplish this goal in your own organization.

In Chapter Seven, Carolyn R. Carson provides a thorough analysis of the importance of choosing appropriate and advantageous program locations to the total marketing effort. She identifies the eight mistakes made most often in this area and suggests how to avoid these mistakes. Case studies and illustrations vividly show how professionals can make program location an integral part of their marketing plans.

Craig D. Weidemann, in Chapter Eight, explains how to build a service component into the marketing plan. Quality service and marketing must go hand-in-hand, and he provides specific examples of what continuing education professionals can do to enhance the service component of their marketing plans. Today, when a comprehensive marketing effort and image can be destroyed by dissatisfied consumers, this chapter provides timely advice on how to emphasize excellent service to consumers as a foundation for all marketing plans.

The four major components of the marketing mix are product, price, distribution, and communications. In Chapter Nine, Judith K. Riggs offers practical advice on development of a successful mix. She examines life cycle stages in product/program production and the importance of giving attention to this life cycle to the total marketing effort. Discriminate pricing is also considered with illustrations of how continuing educators can use this to their advantage.

Thus, Part Two offers a comprehensive analysis of how to position your continuing education organization in the market. All of the authors develop examples from the daily work life of organizations, list guidelines for success, and offer practical advice on how to avoid the mistakes most frequently made in positioning an organization in the market.

6

Planning Programs to Enhance Institutional Image

Donald E. Hanna

A continuing education organization is often part of a larger institution that has (1) a broader mission, (2) diverse goals, and (3) objectives other than those of the continuing education organization. Rarely is the parent institution concerned solely with continuing education. As a subunit of a parent institution, the continuing education organization must relate its programs to the mission, goals, and objectives of the parent institution.

Continuing education organizations operate within a variety of contexts. These contexts vary according to several key considerations, including the primary purposes of the parent institution, the types and formats of continuing education programs offered, the financial philosophy undergirding continuing education programs, the primary audience(s) served by continuing education programs, and special concerns, such as mandatory continuing education, job placement of successful clients or students, and the development of long-term relationships with and service to specific constituencies. Table 6.1 illustrates the wide variety of contexts within which continuing education organizations operate, depending on the purpose of their parent organization.

Table 6.1 demonstrates that continuing education organizations operate across institutional contexts that are dissimilar in many respects, including the programs offered, financial philosophy, and audiences served. Despite the variety of, and differences among, these contexts, continuing education organizations that maintain symbiotic relationships with their parent institutions share a common challenge. They must relate positively to the parent institution, including the definition and projection of its desired image. The importance of

Table 6.1. Organizational Contexts Within Which Continuing Education Organizations Operate.

Provider's Organizational Context	Primary Purposes of Organization	Program	Financial Philosophy	Audience	Special Concerns
Professional associations	Serve members	Continuing professional education	Membership services	Professional members	Mandatory continuing education Professional competencies State-of-the-art in profession
Governmental agencies	Provide service to publics	Staff development	Subsidized	Employees	Consistency
Nonprofit associations	Varied	Focused around organizational purpose	Low-cost, self-sustaining	Diverse	Volunteers
Higher education	Generate and disseminate knowledge	Focused around academic disciplines	Varies	Diverse/part-time	Appropriateness of content
Military	Meet need for effective national defense	Training to improve organizational effectiveness	Subsidized	Military personnel	Uniformity of training/education
Industry	Produce products/services that customers need	Training to improve organizational effectiveness	Profit motive	Those who can afford to pay Those targeted by company for training	Bottom-line measures
Schools	Educate for a productive life	Respond to community needs	Low-cost, self-sustaining, or subsidized	Dependent on client status and program	Community support Federal and state reimbursement

the parent institution's image to the success of programs offered by the continuing education organization is the focus of this discussion. Information presented in this chapter will be helpful to continuing educators who work within contexts such as those identified in Table 6.1.

Votruba (1987) suggests that the role of the continuing education organization is often to span the boundaries between the parent organization and its external environment. This function is illustrated in Figure 6.1.

The role of the continuing education organization in this model is to link appropriate resources available through the parent institution with educational needs of individuals and external organizations. This important concept articulates the contribution the continuing education organization can make in communicating important educational needs to the parent institution, carrying out the goals and objectives of the parent institution, and influencing the overall direction of the parent institution. To be effective in this communication interchange, it is essential that the continuing education organization consider the image of the parent institution as a major factor in arriving at programming decisions.

More specifically, the continuing education organization must (1) study the goals, objectives, and directions taken by the parent institution, including the image the parent institution portrays to its publics; (2) relate activities and plans to those of the parent institution; and, (3) be prepared to be evaluated on the basis of values, operating principles, and outcomes desired by the parent institution, one of which is promotion of the desired or preferred image.

Importance of Image to the Parent Institution

Every institution has an image by which it is identified. In some institutions this image has been purposefully created. In others it has evolved without careful planning or forethought.

Figure 6.1. The Role of the Continuing Education Organization.

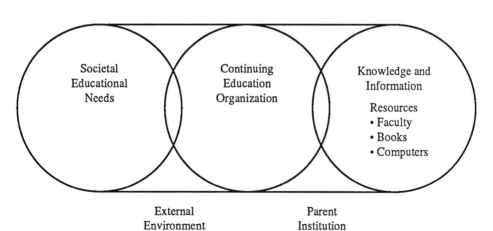

This image of an institution is not one dimensional or uniform but, rather, is a collection of many images held by many people. Kotler (1985) defines image as the "sum of beliefs, ideas and impressions that a person has of an object" (p. 38). Institutional image may be defined as a collection of individual images of an institution generated and shaped over time through experience. Institutions also develop global images that are composites of these individual images. For example, the image of the Peace Corps can be described in a very few words with a high degree of consistency by many different types of people.

Image is also dependent, as are beliefs and attitudes, on institutional values. One way to determine what an institution values most is to examine how its budget is allocated. Continuing education organizations can develop useful information regarding the values of the parent institution by analyzing this budget and noting, in particular, areas where resources are increasing rapidly. In the future, the parent institution will likely place major emphasis in these areas.

A positive image is essential to the long-term success of an institution. A positive image significantly affects the degree to which the public values and accepts its products, programs, and services. A positive image results in the institution assuming a preferred position with respect to the individuals, constituencies, and organizations it seeks to serve as a part of its mission and goals. A positive image helps the institution improve quality, secure additional resources, and expand its programs and services.

On the other hand, a negative image can be the death knell of an institution. Such an image can result in loss of public acceptance and support, a drop in resources and quality of programs and services, and the loss of key individuals within the institution.

As a result, most institutions pay close attention to their many images and carefully monitor their products, programs, and services to ensure consistency with their desired image.

Importance of Contributing to the Image of the Parent Institution

A major problem for continuing education organizations is that they have purposes and constituencies different than those of the parent institution. Therefore, the institution often has a tendency to consider continuing education programs as less important than other programs. As a result, continuing education organizations often are viewed as being "at the margin" of their parent institution. So negative is the internal perception of continuing education in some institutions that many continuing education organizations actually seek marginality and separateness from the parent institution so that they can have more flexibility in effectively and efficiently serving their own constituencies.

Although this strategy may be effective in the short run, it often results in reduced support from the parent institution. This most often occurs because the continuing education organization excludes broader institutional considerations from its program selection criteria. In some cases this approach has led to complete dismantling of continuing education organizations that had over time become disconnected from the parent institution.

When a continuing education organization is a part of a parent institution, it must first and foremost select its activities so that they contribute positively to the parent institution's images. The advantages of such an approach are many.

First, prospects for growth and vitality of the continuing education organization will be improved. The parent institution is more powerful than the continuing education organization, and continuing education programs rely on institutional support, either directly or indirectly. Budget support, centralized services, faculty, support personnel, and support from other offices are more likely to be provided to continuing education programs if they are perceived to be contributing to the overall positive image of the institution. Second, by systematically aligning programs with the image of the parent institution, the continuing education organization achieves broad-based relationships within the institution which provide sources of new information regarding program opportunities and needs. Third, the climate of the continuing education organization will be improved because the continuing education organization is contributing positively to the overall goals of the parent institution.

Assessing Organizational Image

Institutions maintain both an external image, which is a composite of images held by the institution's many publics, and an internal image, which is a composite of images held by its members. These images may or may not be similar, but the continuing education organization must relate its programs to both.

With both its external and internal images, the parent institution maintains a real image, which is the composite of existing images of the institution, and a desired image, which is the image the institution desires to project. The extent to which these are different, and they will always be different, is a key determinant in deciding on directions and programs to be offered. These concepts are graphically illustrated in Exhibit 6.1.

Continuing education organizations should carefully assess both the external and internal images of the parent institution and should select programs

Exhibit 6.1. Key Variables in Assessing Institutional Image: External and Internal Images.

Institution's Existing Public Image	Continuing Education Program Alignment "Safe Zone"	Institution's Preferred or Desired Public Image
Institution's Existing Self-Image		Institution's Preferred or Desired Self-Image

that do not detract from these images. Where a wide gap exists between the existing images of the parent institution and the desired images, the "safe zone" illustrated in Exhibit 6.1 is an important concept, suggesting that programs should be selected to contribute to the parent institution's desired images.

Kotler (1985) suggests several avenues available to institutions for assessing image. However this information about the parent institution's image is assembled, the continuing education organization should use it to influence key program selection decisions. Ideally, this information would include the public's (or key constituency's) perception of the parent institution's programs and services, their quality, their uniqueness, and the manner in which they are delivered.

The continuing education organization can make a significant contribution to the parent institution by carefully selecting programs that build the parent institution's desired image. For example, to control costs, a hospital wishes to improve its image within the community as a provider of high-quality outpatient services. To assist in creating this image, the continuing education director might propose a series of programs on health maintenance to be offered in the community. One component of this program might focus on alternatives to hospitalization and the efforts the hospital is making to implement this concept.

Aligning Programs with the Desired Image of the Parent Institution

Two general guidelines for aligning continuing education programs with the desired image of the parent institution have already been suggested: (1) studying the purposes, objectives, and activities of the parent institution and of other subunits and (2) making an accurate assessment of the desired external and internal images of the parent institution. Implicit within these general guidelines is the necessity for assessing what it is that the parent institution values. Also implicit is the need to relate these values to those of the continuing education organization.

Kotler (1985) suggests several broad criteria by which a continuing education organization might evaluate new program opportunities in relation to parent institutional values and image: "(1) centrality to institutional mission and purposes, (2) visibility likely to be achieved, (3) long-term program potential, and (4) present institution's capacity to mount the program" (p. 136).

Once these broad criteria have been established, the continuing education organization can develop more specific criteria for both the parent institution and the continuing education organization. For example, a list of values held by a parent institution might include programs that offer high visibility; are of high quality; are likely to generate additional dollars from gift grants; extend reputation and/or impact on society; cement important long-term external relationships; meet needs of important constituencies; and extend benefits across the institution.

A list of values held by the continuing education organization might include programs that attract large enrollments; will result in repeat enrollments;

generate revenue, institutional budget support, or recognition; are efficient to develop and manage; do not require excessive financial risk; result in other spin-off programs; and satisfy external constituencies.

These values can then be interrelated by placing all items on both lists on a grid, illustrated in Figure 6.2, on which each item is positioned according to its importance to the parent institution and the continuing education organization.

Programs that contribute to an objective rated as highly important to both the parent institution and its continuing education organization should be actively pursued. Programs that are important to the continuing education organization but less important to the parent institution should be carefully examined to determine what steps could be taken to increase their value to the parent institution. Additional support from the parent institution should be

Figure 6.2. Relating Continuing Education to the Values of the Parent Institution.

| | | Parent Institution | |
	Very Important	*Important*	*Less Important*
Very Important	Extension or building of institutional reputation High quality Fulfillment of needs of important consti- tuencies using insti- tutional resources or generated revenue Programs that achieve broad-based support across the institution		Generation of revenue to the continuing ed- ucation organization Large enrollments Repeat enrollments Efficiency in develop- ment and administration
Important		High visibility Extension of benefits across institution Cementing of long- term relationships	
Less Important	High-visibility pro- grams that deplete resources Important unfunded programs		Low or negative visibility Low enrollment Depletion of unit resources Low quality Benefit to neither con- tinuing education nor parent institution One-time efforts Poor faculty

Continuing Education Organization (row labels shown to the left of the grid: Very Important, Important, Less Important)

explored because programs important to the parent institution will often gain additional internal funding. Such discussions will increase awareness of the continuing education organization's contributions to the parent institution even if they do not result in immediate additional resources. And, finally, programs that are not important to the parent institution or to the continuing education organization probably should not have been started in the first place and should be discontinued.

After evaluating the values of the parent institution in relation to those of the continuing education organization, the continuing education organization should consider specific areas (some of which are discussed here) in developing strategies to align programs with the desired image of the parent institution.

Program Content. Is the content of the program consistent with the overall mission and goals of the institution? Does it contribute to stated objectives? Is it consistent with known strengths and/or the public image of the institution? Does it fit with emerging institutional priorities? Is the level of the content appropriate to the desired institutional image?

Faculty/Presenters. Who are the key instructors, resource people, and presenters? Are their qualifications consistent with the expectations of the parent institution? Are these qualifications reviewed by appropriate departments or individuals within the institution? More importantly, does the program offer the possibility of highlighting the expertise of the individual faculty member or presenter, and does this expertise reflect positively on the parent institution as a whole?

Program Marketing and Publicity. Does the marketing plan utilize positive images of the institution? Do brochures and other advertising pieces build the image of the parent institution in addition to highlighting the program? Are avenues created for credible individuals within the parent institution, starting with the president, executive director, dean, or content area leader, to gain ownership of the program by being asked to be part of the marketing strategy?

Are other subunits of the institution asked to lend support to the marketing effort? Such subunits might include those that (1) publish newsletters, (2) have frequent interaction with key constituencies, (3) offer access to various media, and (4) have direct influence on the presentation of the parent institution's image?

Location and Environmental Setting. Is the location and/or environmental setting conducive to proper conduct of the continuing education program? Is it one that the president of the institution and other leaders would defend if complaints were raised? If it is not, the location and/or environmental setting is probably contributing negatively to the image of the institution.

Cost. The appropriate cost for a particular program depends on many factors, one of which is the image of the parent institution. Given this image, is the cost of the program within parameters that the institution can defend? Is the cost set at a level that is consistent with the image the institution is projecting to its publics? Is the cost in line with the image being projected by other key decisions relating to the program?

Program Style. The manner in which a program is offered projects a certain image of the institution. Client expectations are based in part on the image of the institution offering the program. Are the style of presentation, degree of formality, use of various teaching techniques, and instructional technology consistent with the image of the institution? Expectations for a program offered in the use of computers in education by a large research-oriented university are likely to be much different than those for a similar program offered by a local school district.

Symbolism. Symbolism in any group setting is a highly effective way of communicating an image. Symbolism may include the use of common parent institutional identifiers such as logos and signs, use of prime institutional facilities, introductions and/or speeches by institutional leaders, and the quality of materials provided. Is the use of symbols a part of program marketing considerations? Are symbols planned in such a way as to take advantage of the parent institution's image, and does their use contribute positively to the desired image of the institution?

Program Evaluation and Follow-up. It is common practice in conducting continuing education programs to evaluate strengths and weaknesses of a program after its conclusion. This information is used as a method of program improvement and as a needs assessment tool. Rarely do evaluation instruments or questions focus on the image of the parent institution as a component of program evaluation. Such questions as "To what extent was the sponsorship of the American Association of Certified Accountants a factor in your decision to enroll?" can help provide important feedback to the parent institution about its image with the constituency of the program.

Quality of Service. The common saying "it's the little things in life that count" is certainly true when it comes to institutional image. A speaker who arrives late and/or unprepared, a clerk who uses poor telephone technique, or a program manager who is too busy to assist a participant can destroy months of excellent planning and can also negatively affect the parent institution's image. Because of the many details involved in a successful continuing education program, mistakes will occur. Those that are repeated or those that are not corrected politely can quickly reflect negatively both on the continuing education organization and on the image of the parent institution.

The continuing education organization must pay special attention to the service it provides, both for the immediate survival of its programs and for the long-term maintenance of the image of the parent institution.

Language, Style, and Tone of Marketing. Are continuing education programs marketed in a language, style, and tone that are consistent with those being used to market the parent institution? A hard-sell approach in an institution noted for reserved public presentation may alienate key individuals within the parent institution and lead to separation rather than alignment. A reserved marketing approach in a business setting may suggest that the program is of lower quality, does not contribute to increased competence or efficiency, or is too academic for practical application.

Which Comes First: Image or Program?

What is the relationship between image and program? How are images formed? What can be done to change an image? Institutions that have a history project an image to their publics. This image can be formed by first-hand experience, such as a visit to a campus, attendance at an activity, use of a product, through interactions with representatives of the institution, or through marketing efforts by the institution. Individuals also perceive the institution in different ways, based on their own values, frequency of contact, and the complexity of the institution. Once an image is formed, it tends to continue over time until individuals experience evidence that directly contradicts previously held perceptions.

Consider the activities of Lee Iacocca, Chief Executive Officer of Chrysler, on his arrival at Chrysler in 1979. Iacocca's first task at the failing automaker was to drastically alter the image of poor quality that had developed over the preceding decade. However, the company could not change this image without also improving the quality of their cars. Iacocca (1984) illustrates the dilemma very well: "When it came to a quality image, Chrysler had a really serious problem. With something so important, you can't just wave a wand and presto! Even if your product gets better right away, it takes time for the public to realize it. . . . Styling and values are what sells cars, but quality is what keeps them sold. When it comes to the public's perception of quality, advertising can't do the job for you. Neither can press conferences or other public appearances. The only solution is to build good products, price them competitively, and then go out and service them. If you can do those things, the public will start beating a path to your door" (p. 183).

Institutions with positive images try to maintain them. As suggested earlier, the continuing education organization can take advantage of these images through its program selection process. It is essential to the parent institution that the continuing education organization select programs that support the desired images and do not contradict them.

Conversely, a parent institution that is attempting to change its image offers a special opportunity for the continuing education organization to assist in this image modification. To the extent that the continuing education organization is able to position its programs in a positive way to improve the image of the parent institution, its value to the parent institution will increase.

Overcoming the Parent Institution's Negative Image

The image of the parent institution can be a hindrance in marketing continuing education program offerings. This can occur because of public dissatisfaction with the parent institution's programs, services, and activities, or as a result of the parent institution's inability to define and present itself to the public in a positive manner. It can also occur as the result of a single catastrophic event in the institution. Regardless of the cause, relating continuing education programs to the parent institution inevitably raises the issue of the credibility of the programs themselves and may ultimately cause their failure.

One response is to distance the marketing of these programs from the parent institution to the extent possible. Although this tactic may result in more enrollments, it does not address the more serious problem of negative image. Another approach is to develop relationships with other institutions through cosponsorship. Such arrangements usually cost very little. The broader sponsorship of the program expands both the commitment to ensure the quality of the program and the public's perception of its quality. A third approach is to identify and involve the very best faculty of the parent institution and work to ensure that these faculty are recognized, both tangibly and intangibly, for their contributions.

By using these approaches, the continuing education program is able to contribute to the improvement of the parent institution's image and at the same time improve the quality of program offerings.

Case Study 1

The campus of a state university is located in a midsize city. As it is the only higher education institution in the area, the community views it as a major educational resource. The campus has developed an extensive continuing education program serving thousands of students each year. To provide the community with a convenient access point, the university centralized continuing education in the early 1970s and provided the unit with several state-funded positions.

New staff, especially in the area of marketing, have been added as programs have expanded. The continuing education organization leadership prides itself on being able to identify a need early, respond to it in a timely manner, and find an appropriate instructor, who in many cases is not a member of the university faculty. The unit sees itself as dynamic, progressive, and acting in concert with the community and society. Members within the continuing education organization see the university as slow to change, unresponsive, and unable to meet the fast-changing needs of the public. As a result, interactions between the continuing education organization and the broader university gradually decrease.

With the arrival of a new president, the university is asked to undertake a self-study. It is discovered that while the university has developed several outstanding academic programs that are internationally recognized, the community is largely unaware of these developments and unappreciative of the quality of the faculty and the institution. Within the state, the university's image is largely unchanged from fifteen years earlier when it was viewed as a local alternative to more prestigious schools out of state. The president decides that the external image is out of balance with both the internal image and the desired image of the institution and is determined to address this. One of the president's first proposals is to create a central university relations unit and bring into this unit all individuals involved in marketing from across the campus, including those of continuing education, with the primary goal of ensuring that programs and services offered are publicized in a way that reflects the quality of the institution's faculty and academic programs.

As the leader of the continuing education marketing office, how do you respond to the president's initiative?

Clearly, one response is to demonstrate how effectively the continuing education program is marketed to the community, and to emphasize how focused the marketing research, brochures, and media must be to be successful in encouraging individuals to enroll. The end result of this approach is to stress the negative impact the president's proposal would have on enrollments generated by the continuing education unit. Unless these enrollments have a direct, and significant, financial effect beyond the continuing education organization, however, this argument is likely to be not only ineffective but counterproductive.

A second approach is to view the problem as the president does, that is, to examine how the image of the institution can be upgraded through more effective marketing efforts. Rather than arguing for the status quo, the continuing education director might suggest options that would (1) provide greater focus to the university's overall marketing efforts, (2) offer the considerable marketing base already established by continuing education within the community for purposes of highlighting university areas of quality, and (3) develop programs that bring visibility to key faculty and academic programs. The preferred approach is, of course, to have anticipated this development by being sensitive to key concerns of the parent institution through selection of programs and marketing efforts that highlight the parent institution in addition to the continuing education organization.

Case Study 2

The TECH Corporation has been in existence for forty years and produces a number of electronic devices used by other electronic manufacturers, research organizations, universities, and government agencies. The company has always depended on repeat business for much of its annual sales. As the computer revolution developed, the company's products became more sophisticated and a number of competitors appeared on the scene. As a result, consumer satisfaction with the company's product began dropping and repeat sales fell for the first time ever.

The TECH Corporation had for years maintained a small training force and continuing education staff, which was devoted primarily to internal training.

The company recently hired a new director after the previous director retired. The new director took two significant steps. First, she met with the leaders of those departments that had sent the greatest number of employees to the training unit and asked them to provide feedback about the training unit's responsiveness to their needs. Second, she met with each of the ten divisional vice-presidents to ask them to identify major challenges and problems faced by the corporation.

In the first step, she gathered valuable information about what directions the training department could pursue if it were to continue on its present course. In the second step, she gathered information that could be evaluated and discussed internally to decide if the training department could assist the corporation in solving its most pressing problems. What the director learned was that the company engineers felt that their products were better than ever and qualitatively outdistanced their competitors. Furthermore, the company's products were competitive from a cost standpoint. The major problem appeared to be that their increasing sophistication and complexity made them more difficult to learn to use. The company's manuals were no longer sufficient.

On the basis of this information, the director proposed that the training department be renamed the Customer Relations and Employee Education Department and that it be given specific responsibility for responding to customer complaints, information requests, and sales follow-up. The departmental staff began to ask customers in-depth questions about the company's products, pinpointing specific training problems, and in the process gathered valuable information for the company's engineers. With this information, the training department developed a series of seminars offered nationally that provided the company with a very effective solution to its problem. The director, by asking questions related to the parent company's concerns and problems, was able to chart a direction for the training department that placed it squarely at the core of the parent company's mission.

Both case studies illustrate avenues for integrating issues of importance to the parent institution with programming decisions of the continuing education organization. In Case Study 1, the absence of early consideration of the desired image of the parent institution placed the continuing education organization in a defensive posture with respect to the parent institution. In Case Study 2, early involvement of key individuals within the parent company in suggesting program directions for continuing education resulted in programs that met important needs and increased the centrality of continuing education. Such considerations are critical to maintaining a vital and dynamic continuing education program that operates within the broader context of a parent institution.

Summary

Continuing education organizations are usually subordinate to the parent institution, which has a broader mission, diverse goals, and objectives other than those of continuing education. The parent institution is concerned with maintaining its desired positive institutional image. The success of the continuing education organization depends to a large extent on the support of the parent institution for its programs and activities. To achieve this support, the continuing education organization must consider program offerings that contribute to the achievement of the parent institution's goals and to the enhancement of its image.

Once the desired image of the parent institution is determined, the continuing education organization must carefully plan programs by considering important factors relating to this image. Ten issues are important to consider when planning programs to enhance the parent institution's image: (1) the extent to which the program might contribute to results valued by both the continuing education organization and the parent institution; (2) the appropriateness of program content; (3) the selection of faculty, presenters, and resource persons; (4) the appearance and quality of marketing pieces and the extent to which they represent the parent institution positively; (5) program location and environmental setting; (6) cost of the program; (7) style of program presentation; (8) appropriate use of symbols; (9) quality of service provided; and (10) use of program evaluation and follow-up. Consideration of these factors will help the continuing education organization more effectively contribute to maintaining and/or building a positive image for the parent institution. The benefits of this effort will be returned to the continuing education organization in the form of increased centrality, greater influence, and more positive institutional support.

7

Choosing the Best Locations for Continuing Education Programs

Carolyn R. Carson

Whether you are planning a conference, a workshop, or a credit or noncredit course, choosing appropriate and advantageous program locations goes hand in hand with the program development process. Because good space is sometimes hard to secure, program planners usually want to reserve space as soon as possible. Location decisions, however, often cannot be made until the program design process is well underway. Where a program or course will be held is dependent on a clear understanding of program objectives, audience, promotional plans, and financial realities. The location will influence every step of the program development process, from setting goals and schedules to actual implementation and evaluation of the program.

Marketing is a crucial part of the program development process as planners seek to convey to potential learners why a specific offering is superior to other options available. Program location decisions are made on at least two levels. For some planners the first decision is global: the choice of region, state, city, or section of town best for a particular program. For example, in considering options for offering off-campus credit courses in engineering, planners may choose between several regions within the state of Georgia. After the decision is made to offer such a course in the Atlanta area, the choice is then between "inside the city" and "in the suburbs." Likewise, the coordinator must decide which suburb is most likely to be convenient and attractive to potential enrollees. This can be done reliably only by researching where engineers tend to live and work in the city.

At that point, program decisions are made on a local level. If different facilities are available, different variables come into play. With respect to the engineering credit course, planners must make a location decision based on such items as familiarity, accessibility, cost, size of group, and availability of instructional support equipment. For some planners, decisions are made solely at the local level, as their service regions are strictly defined.

This chapter focuses on location decisions made at both global and local levels, keeping in mind that education is not isolated from the program development process, but rather should be integrated with needs, objectives, resources, and learning activities. Although the value of the program itself should be the greatest selling point, planners often use location as an additional enticement. Location may make the difference in the perceived value of continuing education options.

Value-Added Marketing in Site Selection

Value-added marketing is concerned with adding something of additional value to the basic program, product, or service being marketed (Foster, 1972). In continuing education programming, planners add to the perceived value of the program by increasing user benefits. Components of the program that users value are called benefits, and benefits add significantly to the perceived value of the overall program. Location is often one of those components. The facility, community, or region where the program will take place can add to the perceived quality of the program, fairness of the price, expertise of the presenters, credibility of the sponsors, and attractiveness of the program in general.

Adding Value to the Perceived Quality of the Program. Continuing education program planners on college and university campuses take advantage of this potential regularly. A program held on campus, whether it is credit or noncredit, is often perceived as being of high quality because of its proximity to the academic environment. Programs that are offered in glamorous, highly desirable locales or in expensive hotels are perceived as matching the status of the location.

The effect of location on perceived quality works in much the same way as the effect of price on quality. Consumers tend to attach greater value to goods and services that cost more. In the same vein, learners tend to attach greater value to programs in locations that they consider attractive. The author has coordinated conferences in Washington, D.C., for recipients of federal funds for special education projects. Similar programs have been held in Des Moines, New Orleans, Denver, and Anaheim. Attendance increased dramatically for the Washington programs. The main reason is that attendees perceived more value in the program because the location afforded them greater access to administrators in the federal office located in the nation's capital.

Adding Value to the Fairness of the Price. Buyers, or in this sense, learners, evaluate price based on the combined benefits of the program. When the location is seen as highly valuable for whatever reasons, then a higher price is both expected and understood. Location is a very important variable in the perception of price. Just as consumers expect to pay more for a commodity in a speciality shop than in a department store, they have very definite ideas about price in continuing education programs relative to where those programs are to be conducted. The Institute for the Management of Lifelong Learning, held each year at Harvard, commands a relatively high price tag. Tuition is approximately $2,000. Because the program is held at Harvard, it assumes a high level of quality and credibility. Potential attendees accept the price readily.

Adding Value to the Perceived Expertise of the Speakers. When the presenters chosen for the program are not readily known to the potential audience, location can greatly add to perceived expertise. Again, the example of the academic world is germane, as consumers may assume that the instructor is somehow connected with the institution and thus more credible, even if that is not the case. Proximity to the learner is another way to add to the credibility of the presenter. Even when the speaker may be relatively unknown, the fact that such programming is available in a location that is nearby and convenient may compensate. Take, for example, the myriad of one-day workshops available to professional women. When such a program is available in a moderately sized city, there is an important convenience factor for women whose organizations may not be willing to send them to an expensive program in a large city. That the speaker may not be readily known becomes less important in evaluating the value of the program.

Adding Value to the Credibility of the Sponsors. Just as location can add to the credibility of presenters, it can also increase the perceived value of the sponsors. For many organizations, increasing credibility and visibility is a large part of the motivation to conduct a continuing education program in the first place. Professional associations, for example, conduct programs not only to benefit their membership, but also to increase membership by exposing professionals to their services. Associations that conduct programs in desirable locations are increasing the perceived value of the program itself and thus of their ability to serve their clientele. Sponsors who align themselves with high-status organizations located in specific places also tend to enhance their value to their significant publics.

Adding Value to the Perceived Attractiveness of the Program. In reality, programs are judged to be attractive for a variety of reasons. Topics, speakers, time of year, sponsors, location, and price all combine to influence the decision to participate. Where many options combining many of the same factors are available to the learner, location can greatly improve the likelihood that a specific program may be chosen. Consider, for example, programs in supervisory management skills. The number of these programs has increased dramatically in recent years as the growing service industry creates more supervisory roles and as business and industry realize that good leaders must be developed and cultivated. With so many programs to select from, location, in terms of either proximity, credibility, or attractiveness, may be the critical variable that produces the registration.

Selecting Appropriate Program Locations

As discussed earlier, location decisions are an integral part of the program development and marketing process. We will address the relationships between location decisions and three specific phases of the program development process: program design, audience, and budgeting.

Program Locations Must Be Consistent with the Program Design. Program planners must be careful to ensure that the location matches the goals, format, and tone of the program. If one of the program goals is to reward participants, then the location must be one that the participants perceive to be desirable. A program held in an economy hotel in a small, out-of-the-way community is not likely to be perceived as a dynamic, excellent program. On the other hand, if a program is designed for interaction, brainstorming, exploration of issues, and solution of difficult problems, a remote, retreatlike atmosphere can be effective in encouraging communication and minimizing distractions.

Locations must also match program formats and scheduling. One of the most common mistakes made in program planning for a conference is that of selecting a site where many exciting extracurricular attractions exist and then leaving no time in the schedule for participants to enjoy them. Conversely, program formats must be especially busy, varied, and stimulating in a location where there is little else to do besides attend meetings.

A third program design element to be considered when choosing a program location is that of program tone. A seminar for physicians on recent cancer research might be inappropriate for a hotel near an amusement park. However, that atmosphere might be very appropriate for a program where the subject matter is less serious or less formal.

Program Locations Must Be Consistent with the Audience. Audiences evaluate locations on the basis of their values, preferences, and taste. Academic groups like to attend programs on college and university campuses because they value the academic environment and are comfortable within it. Government employees, sensitive to costs and to spending the taxpayer's money, might feel that they should not attend a program held in a luxury hotel on Michigan Avenue in downtown Chicago.

A particular audience will also have had previous experiences that must be taken into account in the choice of location. One of the most important pieces of information about a group relates to where the group has met before for the same or similar programs. The author works with a group that has met at the same remote retreat for forty years. No one ever suggests an alternative location. In the experience of the participants, the idea of location cannot really be separated from the idea of the program itself.

Obviously, program locations must match the pocketbook of the audience. All the expert development and planning in the world will not make a program successful if a major portion of the audience cannot afford lodging in the conference facility and must therefore look for other accommodations. On the other hand, if participants are accustomed to paying $90 to $100 for a room, they will not expect very much from a location that costs $45.

Locations must often be acceptable to more than one audience. Meetings conducted for professional associations might be aimed at both members and vendors. Programs for government leaders might be aimed at civil service employees as well as legislators. Programs related to social services might involve professionals as well as parents. Many programs, in fact, are predicated on the need to bring together diverse groups. Those groups, however, may have very different attitudes about location, convenience, attractiveness, and cost.

Program Locations Must Be Consistent with the Budget. Although many facilities are likely to negotiate on room rates and meal costs, equipment rentals can often be very high in some locations. Devoting an inordinate share of overall financial resources to location, at the expense of other program concerns, can be detrimental to the program. A recent program for higher education faculty was held in a luxury hotel in a large city. Costs incurred in securing the facility were so great that there was little left over for paying speakers or for providing such amenities as continental breakfasts and informal social hours. In addition, the hotel was located in a part of the city where participants could not afford the meals available nearby.

Frequently, program planners using the same facilities compare rates secured in the negotiation process. The current industry norm among planners seems to be a focus on negotiating for the greatest possible concessions from the facility. Unfortunately, program concerns often suffer, as facility staff do not go the extra mile for a group that they feel wants more than it is willing to pay for. The "best price" is not always the "best deal." Driving too hard a bargain with respect to location can ruin a good program.

Integrating Location into the Market Strategy

Program Locations Must Be Consistent with the Overall Marketing Plan. As planners design and implement market strategies, they must decide what relative weight will be given to each of the "four P's": product, price, promotion, and place. As discussed earlier, location decisions fall under the category of place or delivery, and different kinds of programs rely in differing degrees on the aspect of place. Consider, for example, an executive training program. First and foremost, the program must be of high quality and offer benefits valued by the learner. Location offers a secondary attraction: if learners must have the skills offered by the program, and the location is convenient or particularly attractive, they are more likely to attend.

On the other hand, incentive programs, such as trips often offered as a reward for exceeding company sales quotas, might focus on location above program quality or content. Although such programs offer continuing education opportunities, participants are likely to be most concerned about the appeal of the location. If the company is willing to send the employee (often with family) to Acapulco, then the company must highly value the employee, and thus the employee also values the program more highly. In such situations, delivery is the primary feature of the marketing mix, with product playing a subordinate role.

Many continuing education programs, at least those related to enhancing professional competency, are paid for by employers. Again, locations must appeal to more than one audience, both to potential learners and to their superiors. Although the employee might find the location attractive, the employer may perceive the location to be frivolous, distracting, and more costly than other, less glamorous options. The position that place occupies in the marketing strategy must be determined with careful consideration of who is making the final decision about participation.

Converting Location into Promotional Copy. In explaining "how to market a facility," Suleiman (in a 1987 handout) suggests a series of questions designed to position the location in the integrated marketing strategy. These are shown in Exhibit 7.1.

Once location decisions have been made and these questions answered from the perspective of the audience, planners must convert information regarding the location into powerful advertising copy to attract learners. Three approaches are discussed here: the direct approach, the indirect approach, and the compensatory approach.

Direct Approach. The direct approach, of course, is the most straightforward approach. When the program location is highly attractive, the decision maker is also the attendee, and the price is appropriate for the audience, painting an irresistible picture of the location is relatively easy. In 1986, the Environmental Management Association met in Scottsdale, Arizona, in November. Costs were reasonable for the audience, the program was sound, and the location and season were appealing. Promotional copy for the conference stressed not only the program, but also the climate, the landscape, the charm of Scottsdale, and the variety of interesting things to do in the area. The approach was direct, upbeat, and effective—a program planner's dream.

Indirect Approach. What about those instances when a superior makes the decision about attendance? The location must be attractive to the potential participant but not overwhelming for the decision maker. Even when the attendee is also the decision maker, he or she must often consider the perceptions of others such as colleagues and subordinates. The indirect approach involves the use of subtle techniques to imply attractiveness of the location, while concentrating heavily on the value of the product. This approach is used frequently in planning programs. Locations often speak for themselves. When this is so, few will have to

Exhibit 7.1. Marketing the Facility.

1. What is the purpose of the meeting?
   A. Educational
   B. Networking/social
   C. Mandatory
   D. Combination of above
2. What is the kind of meeting?
   A. Seminar (small group)
   B. Conference (large group)
   C. One time
   D. Annual
   E. Permanent location
   F. Revolving location
3. Where is the audience coming from?
   A. Local
   B. Regional
   C. National
   D. International
   E. Combination of above
4. Where is the activity?
   A. Typical large city
   B. Typical small city
   C. Resort area
   D. Retreat
   E. On campus
   F. Special place (New Orleans, San Francisco, New York, Las Vegas)
5. In what kind of facility is the meeting being held?
   A. Hotel
   B. Conference center
   C. Retreat
   D. Chain
   E. Independent
   F. Club
   G. University
   H. Other
6. What is the quality of the facility?
   A. Clearly first class
   B. Standard
   C. Economy
7. How well known is the facility and location?
   A. Everyone absolutely knows it
   B. Some know it
   C. Never heard of it
8. How unusual is the facility for the program/audience/sponsor mix?
   A. Perfect match
   B. OK
   C. Audience will question
9. What is the approval process for participants?
   A. None required
   B. Nominal
   C. Rigorous

Source: Reprinted by permission of Anver S. Suleiman, The Marketing Federation, St. Petersburg Beach, Fla.

be convinced of the appeal of certain large cities, warm climates in winter, or locations with amusements nearby such as Reno or Las Vegas. Promotional copy should be detailed and specific with respect to intended outcomes, agenda of sessions with titles and speakers, and biographical information about the presenters that leaves little doubt about the credibility and excellence of the program.

Compensatory Approach. In reality, practitioners plan many programs without ever considering a Miami or a San Francisco as a destination. Many planners use "ordinary" locations for programs that are sound and successful. In the field of adult basic education, public school classrooms are often most appropriate to program goals and budgets. Other continuing education program planners work in moderately sized cities where three or four facilities are available. Choices of location are limited or nonexistent and often not obviously appealing. The challenge to the planner in these circumstances is to determine what is positive about the location, including the city, the area, and the actual building.

College and university programming often takes place in communities where the most marketable aspect of the location is the academic environment. Planners relying on the compensatory approach must give serious thought to what is attractive about the location. If nothing is attractive, then perhaps another location should be sought. Aspects of location to highlight in marketing include accessibility, convenience, surrounding institutions, privacy, and, as always, program quality.

Successful Use of Location in Programming: Three Case Studies

Case Study 1: Workshop on Physical Assessment for the Oral and Maxillofacial Surgeon. This five-day program was conducted for a national audience of oral and maxillofacial surgeons at a ski resort in Colorado. Housing was provided in condominiums, thus allowing participants to bring their families. The time of year chosen corresponded to the time when rates at such resorts are lower but the snow conditions are still good. Program hours were adjusted to allow for skiing during part of the day. Because physicians tend to be self-employed and certain types of educational expenses are tax deductible, the direct approach to marketing a learning/vacation experience was possible. The choice of location was completely compatible with the program goals and scheduling, as well as with the audience and its relative ability to pay for such an experience.

Case Study 2: Rose Hill College Leadership Retreat. Rose Hill College, a small private liberal arts college in the Midwest, conducted a weekend communications and leadership development program. A remote conference center, thirty miles from the nearest city, was chosen for the program. The location was consistent with program goals. Planners hoped to stimulate interaction and problem solving within a group of administrators. Participants worked together in problem-solving teams. They had little time for recreational activities because the program had been clearly billed as an intensive leadership retreat. The location was affordable on a tight budget. The beautiful landscape, remote environment, and intensive focus on issues important to participants compensated for tying up the weekend.

Case Study 3: Off-Campus Credit Programming. The University of Illinois at Urbana–Champaign conducts off-campus credit courses in the Chicago area along the "corridor" concept. Classes are located near the major traffic corridors going out into the suburbs. The idea is to attract individuals as they are commuting home in the late afternoon. Courses start toward the end of rush hour and accommodate major traffic patterns. Typical sites include public schools, community colleges, and libraries. Key issues are easy access from the interstates, early evening starting times, and accessible, secure, well-lighted parking areas.

Eight Common Mistakes in Choosing Locations

In the absence of careful and comprehensive planning, it is easy to make mistakes when choosing locations. The following eight mistakes are those most commonly made in choosing program locations.

1. *Failure to understand the goals of the program.* Lack of a clear understanding of program goals and objectives is perhaps the most common mistake made when choosing locations. Program committees and planners are sometimes prone to skim over program goals out of a desire to proceed with concrete plans. Although analysis of goals is conceptual and time consuming, it is essential for smooth functioning of the program development process. The goals of the program will greatly influence the choice of location. Because of the availability of space, location decisions must often be made early in the planning process. An analysis of goals must occur early as well. The two issues go hand in hand. Encourage planning groups to thoroughly analyze why the program is to be held and what is to be accomplished before proceeding with planning.

2. *Emphasis on location over programmatic goals.* In very few instances are program goals subordinate to location. If there is no need for the product (program) then there is no need for delivery (location). Even with incentive meetings, the purpose of the meeting is to reward people. Therefore, the attractiveness of the location is important to the participant. Nevertheless, even when location is of primary importance, planners must keep programmatic goals uppermost in their thinking.

3. *Underestimation of the power of location as part of the marketing plan.* An empty room with chairs and lights is rarely the only requirement with respect to location. Planners often underestimate the effect that location has on the perceived value of the program. People respond to programs with a combination of reactions. Not only do they evaluate the quality of the program, but they also assess how comfortable, convenient, threatening, and appropriate the location is for them. Remember that location can add value to the program, often at very little additional cost.

4. *Negotiation of too tight a contract with the facility.* In a recent issue of *Meeting Planners Alert* (1987), a hotelier made the following comment: "thousands of meeting planners . . . try to cut you to your knees, squeeze every penny out of a hotel company and then demand the finest suites, comps, the best food service, etc., 'insist' on a free (familiarization) trip over holiday weekends with their families and expect all food and two giant rooms picked up so they can 'site select'" (p. 1). Although this comment applies to a specific type of program, all planners would do well to negotiate fairly with all types of space providers. Negotiation implies that both sides give and take, not that one side reaps all of the benefits. Hotels and other space providers want to provide good service at a fair price, just as program planners do. It is difficult to generate enthusiasm and commitment for a program when the local facility staff feels as though they have been victimized. At the time of the program, planners will require some flexibility on the part of the facility. This is difficult to secure when no flexibility was demonstrated in the negotiating phase.

5. *Failure to negotiate for what is really needed.* On the other side of the coin, do not opt for less than what is really needed. If tables and chairs are essential for the program, do not settle for theatre-style seating. If participants have fixed per diem rates, do not expect them to subsidize sleeping room rates out of their own resources. If participants must travel to the program by car, do not schedule the program where parking is difficult. Space providers want to know exactly what is needed. They are usually prepared to be flexible, but they need to know what is really important.

6. *Failure to communicate goals of the program to facility staff.* Time spent in long, drawn-out negotiations for concessions from a facility can often be better spent communicating goals of the program and concerns of the group to the provider of the space. If the group is particularly sensitive to comfort and accessibility for handicapped persons, strive to overcome barriers rather than to shave a few dollars off of the room rental cost. If enhanced electrical capabilities will make or break the program, make that clear to facility staff and explore ways to ensure that those capabilities are in place at the time of the program.

7. *Failure to take into account multiple buyers.* Splashing palm trees all over the brochure cover for a program where participants must request authorization to attend from business managers in the North who sit in windowless offices day in and day out will surely kill a program. If program quality will not stand alone, the program should be reevaluated. It is essential to design advertising copy to appeal to all audiences.

8. *Failure to thoroughly investigate location before program.* Visiting the location before finalizing a commitment is perhaps the best way to investigate the location. Key reasons for site visits are getting to know the operational staff in addition to the front office, actually seeing the meeting space and sleeping accommodations if required, and observing other meetings in progress. Actual visits are not always necessary, however. In some instances, planners can evaluate space through assessments by other planners and through their own ability to judge the competence and integrity of the person on the other end of the

telephone. After years of experience, most planners know what they are looking for in a facility and in a staff, and are able to make safe judgments.

Summary

Selection of appropriate and advantageous program locations is an integrated part of the program development process. In designing a program and its marketing strategy, planners need to give careful attention to the location. Location decisions are made on at least two levels: the global level, which is essentially a geographic decision, and the local level, which is essentially a facility decision. The choice of program location can enhance the perceived benefits of the conference, seminar, or course offering. Locations can literally add value to the perceived quality and attractiveness of the program, to the expertise and credibility of presenters and sponsors, and to the fairness of the price.

Program design and, therefore, choice of location must take into account program goals, format, and tone. The audience is also essential, as audiences have specific values, preferences, previous experiences, and resources. In addition, program locations must be consistent with the goals of the program budget.

In the design of a marketing strategy for programs, location and delivery should be weighed against the other variables in the marketing mix: program design, price, and promotion. Marketing the location may follow one of three avenues: the direct, the indirect, or the compensatory approach.

Program delivery plays a vital role in continuing education programming. Quality programs are meaningless if not delivered appropriately. Successful programs, whether they be luncheon lectures, extension credit offerings, or extended intensive institutes, must be designed and promoted with careful attention to the importance and appropriateness of location.

8

Making Customers
and Quality Service
a Priority

Craig D. Weidemann

Good service is the key marketing edge in developing and keeping customers and must be considered when planning a marketing effort. However, many institutions ignore the relationship between marketing and quality service. Often, marketing and service efforts compete within an institution for the same dollars to the detriment of each. Quality service can make a significant contribution to the marketing effort of a continuing education program. Developing new customers is almost five times as costly as keeping present customers. In addition, through word of mouth, past satisfied participants are key marketers. Conversely, dissatisfied customers' comments can cause serious damage to an institution, resulting in an extremely difficult problem to identify and control. In the highly competitive continuing education market, an organization cannot afford to lose or alienate clients as a result of poor service.

Good customer service can be managed. Building a strong service orientation in an institution consists of developing a total commitment to service. This chapter analyzes how important it is that top managers embrace a service management philosophy, how to implement this philosophy, and how to assess and improve this delivery of service. According to Shostack (1984), services often fail because they lack a systematic method for design and control. Therefore, our discussion focuses on the customer and the three elements of service management: the service strategy, the service system, and the service people.

Today, almost 60 percent of America's work force is employed by a business providing an intangible service. This rapid growth in the service sector is anticipated to continue in the future. The first step in analyzing how continuing education programs can enhance their service orientation is to recognize that they are a part of this rapidly growing service sector, with customers to attract and to satisfy. Students are customers. Traditionally, users of continuing education services have been referred to as participants, students, and clients. Customers have usually been thought of as people who buy shoes, attend movies, and receive financial advice—not attendees at educational programs. Regardless of the terminology, continuing education users are "customers" and they respond to the quality of education services in the same way they respond to banking, eating, and lodging services. Good service results in repeat business and referrals. Bad service results in loss of business and negative comments.

Both Desatnick (1987) and Albrecht and Zemke (1985) report some significant findings about customers' reactions to service: Ninety-six percent of unhappy or dissatisfied customers do not complain about poor service; however, 90 percent or more who are unhappy will never come back. Each unhappy customer will tell an average of nine or ten people about their negative experience, and 13 percent will report their negative experience to more than twenty people.

On the other hand, 54 to 70 percent of customers who complain will return if their complaint is resolved; 95 percent if the complaint is resolved quickly. Each customer who receives a positive resolution to a problem will tell an average of five people about the experience.

Regardless of the strong evidence for providing good service, the quality of service in our country is considered poor (Albrecht and Zemke, 1985; Alderson, 1987; Kahn and Pearlstein, 1987). Shostack (1984) notes that in many surveys, poor service tops the list of consumer complaints. Good service anywhere, from the hospitality to the airline industry, seems to be the exception rather than the norm. Individuals can recount numerous incredulous tales of lost orders, blasé food-service people, and surly salespeople. Tom Peters, coauthor of *In Search of Excellence: Lessons from America's Best-Run Companies* (1982), points out in one of his videotapes that at each of his hundreds of presentations where he remarks about the sorry state of service in America, not once has one of the thousands of participants disagreed with him. Unfortunately, most participants lament that his statement is on target. Peters emphasizes that even when people provide adequate service, it puts their organization above the competition.

Despite the present standard of service, many industries are becoming aware that good service may be the only factor that distinguishes them from their competition. As a result, many service organizations are making intense efforts to improve their responsiveness to customers' needs.

The importance of good service is compounded by the increasing demands of customers. Not only are they cost conscious, but customers are tired of dealing with computers and machines. They demand courteous contact with real people. Naisbitt (1982) points out that as people's interactions with technology increase, the longing for human contact also increases. Koepp (1987) states that "Consumers want smiles more than ever because they have become strongly resentful of machines" (p. 52).

Continuing education organizations are not immune to the competitiveness of the growing service economy. Today, individuals and groups can receive education and training from numerous vendors, including churches, professional associations, hospitals, corporate training divisions, consultants, private businesses, colleges, and universities. Potential customers are inundated with brochures and catalogs announcing programs to address their particular learning needs. Quality service can differentiate your program from the plethora of organizations offering continuing education programs and influence an individual to attend your program as well as to return again. Plus, with a positive experience they may tell a friend.

Service Management

Think about the one store or restaurant to which you always return—the one place you drive out of your way to visit. This is the place you tell your friends about. Probably you are attracted to your favorite place by the quality of the product and the manner in which you are treated. The place makes you feel welcome, respected, and valued.

Institutions like your favorite place are being analyzed to find out what makes their service special (Peters and Waterman, 1982; Albrecht and Zemke, 1985; Peters and Austin, 1985). What is being learned is that good quality service does not just happen. Good service is not magical. It can be developed and managed. DeBruicker and Summe (1985) state that "successful companies choose and manage their customers with the same care they put into choosing and managing their product" (p. 98).

Superior service is not achieved solely through training front-line employees. Making sure your contact people are informed, courteous, and responsible is crucial to the provision of good service. However, there is so much more to managing the delivery of quality service. Good service is achieved through management of the total service process—the attitudes, values, and motivations of an organization and its employees. Albrecht and Zemke (1985) describe service management as the structured approach to the delivery of a product or service that promotes superior customer satisfaction and results for the institution. Their model depicting service management is a triangle, with the service strategy, the service system, and the service employees occupying the three points. The customer, or in continuing education the adult learner, is in the center of the triangle and the focus of the service management model. Close inspection of this model will show its value and application to a continuing education delivery unit.

Each customer is unique, acts precipitously, and possesses a faint loyalty. Customers are egocentric. They are not concerned about your institution's computer problems or if you are having a bad day. They care even less about rules and procedures that do not make sense to them. Customers are hard to recruit and hard to retain. Therefore, how does a continuing education organization satisfy its customers?

First, an organization must know its customers. Staying close to the customer is one of the eight principles consistently found in successful companies (Peters and Waterman, 1982). Many organizations, however, operate under the misconception that they know their customers' motivations, expectations, and values. Much has been written about why adults attend continuing education programs; however, it would be erroneous to respond to your customers by how they are defined in the literature.

Customers act on their personal perceptions and expectations. They have perceptions and expectations of what a continuing education program will cover, what it will be like sitting in the class, how an instructor will act, and also how they as learners will be treated. Problems arise when their experience in a class or program and their expectations are not matched. Customers' expectations are not met when continuing education providers focus on things not important to the customer, when they misinterpret their needs, or when customers' expectations are not known.

Understanding customers is a continual process and should be done on both a formal and an informal basis. Interests and needs can be formally assessed through mail and telephone surveys and through focus groups. Questions should focus not only on curriculum data but also on the respondents' expectations, needs, and attitudes. An ongoing analysis of the demographics and psychographics of the market, such as use of the VALS information discussed in Chapter Three (Mitchell, 1983; Sheth, 1983; Atlas, 1984), will provide valuable information to help structure your service to be client centered. Additional structured means to assess customers should be taken advantage of at every opportunity. Evaluation instruments addressing the quality of both course content and services should be incorporated whenever possible into the evaluation of continuing education programs. Even strategically located suggestion or comment boxes can provide valuable reactions to services and a better understanding of customers' expectations. Full evaluation instruments should be the norm with each course or program. Short questionnaires to gather data about customers can be included on registration forms, brochures, and folders. Not only do formal assessment instruments gather valuable customer data, they also convey to the customer that they are valued and their input is appreciated.

Informal assessment of customers can also provide a wealth of information. Invaluable opportunities to solicit customers' reactions and comments exist in interactions between continuing education staff members and customers at registration, during breaks for coffee or meals, and during telephone calls. Every interaction presents an opportunity to learn about the quality of service, how to improve service, and the general satisfaction or dissatisfaction of your customers.

Responding to information gathered from formal and informal customer assessment is crucial. It is in this response area where many continuing education organizations fail. Creating a structure to address customer assessment data is one way to ensure follow-up. For example, analysis of customers' responses and reactions to services can be a regular item at a weekly staff meeting. A continuing education organization must work hard to learn about its customers through both formal and informal methods and approach every customer problem as an opportunity to learn how to improve.

Service Strategy

Service strategy is at the apex of the service management model triangle. The service strategy is usually a one-sentence statement that describes the unique service provided by the continuing education organization. It is not a slogan or a mission statement. Service strategy is defined as the "distinctive formula for delivering service; such a strategy is keyed to a well-chosen benefit premise that is valuable to the customer and that establishes an effective competitive position" (Albrecht and Zemke, 1985, p. 64).

The service strategy serves as an organizing principle for mobilizing the efforts of all staff. It also describes the value to be offered to the customer. For example, a university conference and institute division's service strategy could be "total conference service." This service strategy states that the conference and institute office provides support from the first conference planning meeting through marketing of the conference, management of on-site arrangements, and provision for the final budget wrapup—"total conference service." This strategy is different from a conference and institute office that provides only on-site registration or marketing assistance.

A credit continuing education office that provides complete student services for adult students may have a service strategy such as "one-stop student services for nontraditional students." Their unique service proposition prevents students from having to travel all over campus to secure parking permits, purchase textbooks, and pay tuition. The service strategy for a training division that markets supervisory programs could be "excellence in development programs at moderate prices." A geriatric hospital's education division offering community education courses could set as their service strategy "accessible health prevention courses for the mature adult."

The service strategy must clearly define what is unique about the service you provide. Then this service orientation can be adopted by all staff. The service strategy lets both the customer and your employees know what type of service you provide and value.

The service strategy is developed from market research. It should tie in with the institution's mission statement and it should emphasize the values of the institution. To work effectively it is vital that this strategy be valued by the institutional leaders (Albrecht and Zemke, 1985).

Much has been written about the role of the manager as a figurehead or symbolic leader (Mintzberg, 1975; Peters and Waterman, 1982; Gardner, 1987). An organization takes its cues from the top manager. Successful implementation of a service strategy requires that the parent institution's leader model, value, and reinforce the service strategy through the commitment of time, resources, and personnel (Shostack, 1984; Desatnick, 1987). Then, leaders in the continuing education office must follow this lead. Nothing hinders front-line people from providing quality service more than lack of support from superiors.

A good example of commitment to excellent service from top management is illustrated by Magnesen (1987). He reports on a customer service training activity where employees describe their own jobs, emphasizing those factors that are most conducive to good customer service. A community college president describes his position in the college with the following statement: "I'm the college president and I have a very important job. My primary job responsibility is to serve students. I establish organizationwide conditions of commitment, recognition, and service and strive to get everyone moving in the same direction— serving students both in and out of the classroom in the best possible manner. I recognize that the college will be only as good as its people, and every person shares a responsibility for maintaining the college as a quality student-centered organization" (p. 53).

Establishing a service strategy shared by all employees is as important as defining the institution's mission statement. It is the key to building a service orientation in a continuing education organization.

Service System

The second component in implementing a service management approach is to analyze the system customers must negotiate to use the desired service. What process does a person go through to register for a course, workshop, or conference? Is your service system user friendly? Is your system designed to accommodate the needs of your institution, rather than to meet the needs of the customer?

With increased numbers of more sophisticated adult learners entering the continuing education arena and more organizations entering the education business, many continuing education providers have developed more consumer-conscious procedures. Nevertheless, it is important to continually evaluate and reevaluate the service system to ensure its user friendliness.

There are many ways to examine these service systems and procedures. One quick check is to go through the system yourself: register for a course in person and/or by telephone, attend a course, buy a textbook, and sit at the desks in a classroom. It is obvious that personally negotiating the system will give you a better perspective of what your customers must encounter.

Another method of investigation is to utilize the continuing education staff to evaluate the steps a potential customer takes to use your service. Identifying these steps with staff will yield a clearer understanding of what a customer experiences to use your program and services. It will give you an opportunity to evaluate and streamline the system and will be a good exercise to reinforce the importance of quality of service to your staff.

The following example of steps an individual must take to attend a continuing education credit course at a community college shows how this process can result in the identification of some real problems in the service system.

Step 1	Individual has need, desire, or requirement to attend course.
Step 2	Individual contacts college to request course catalogue.
Step 3	Individual must locate in the catalog the desired course and registration procedure.
Step 4	Individual must drive 15 miles to college to register after work.
Step 5	Individual must complete a college registration form, course selection form, and in-state verification form.
Step 6	Individual must wait in line to pick up registration card.
Step 7	Individual must wait to see an academic adviser for course selection approval.
Step 8	Individual must wait to pick up course selection card.
Step 9	Individual must wait to pay for course.
Step 10	Individual must wait in bookstore to purchase textbook.
Step 11	Individual must wait to pick up parking sticker.
Step 12	Individual must wait to have identification card made.

In these steps, it is assumed that individuals know what courses they want, that the courses are open, that the courses do not have any prerequisites, and that the textbooks are available. Customers must negotiate this cycle each time they elect to attend a course. Most continuing education organizations have refined their registration procedures to avoid some of the obvious negatives in the example. Nonetheless, when a staff reviews its customers' service cycle they can identify problems and obstacles in the service system that no customer should, or will, tolerate very long.

Jan Carlzon, president of Scandinavian Airlines, is famous for having led Scandinavian Airlines through a financial turnaround by emphasizing quality service. He introduced a method to evaluate the service system. President Carlzon, in referring to contacts between his organization and its customers, stated: "We have 50,000 moments of truth out there every day." To him each customer contact is a "moment of truth," where an individual develops an impression and makes a decision to use or not use his airline. Albrecht and Zemke (1985) conclude that "when moments of truth go unmanaged the quality of service regresses to mediocrity" (p. 34).

Application of the concept of "moments of truth" can help a continuing education unit refine its service system. The approach is very similar to evaluation of the service steps described earlier. This procedure also involves the continuing education staff. In a small group, staff members brainstorm about every possible customer "moment of truth" in which a potential or existing customer has contact with your continuing education institution. The following list of customer moments of truth was developed by the staff of a community education program.

- Individual reads newspaper listing of continuing education courses.
- Individual talks with community education staff member at church on Sunday about courses.
- Individual sees course flyer at YMCA.
- Individual telephones in registration for course.
- Individual discusses with instructor next session's course offerings.
- Individual sees a friend's community education course folder.
- Individual stops by community education office to pick up course schedule.

Through further discussion, the opportunities listed could be influenced to maximize each moment of truth or interaction with a customer. In addition, many new and existing opportunities are identified that can have a positive impact on customers' perceptions of your continuing education unit.

The service system, the process the customer must negotiate to take a course, must constantly be evaluated and improved. Customers will not become repeat customers if the steps to use your service are difficult.

Service People

The third element in the service management triangle consists of the people or staff of a continuing education organization. Creating a strong service-oriented staff requires a comprehensive management approach. Yet, many service institutions limit their customer service or front-line people to some type of "be nice" or "smile" training. This approach overlooks much of the motivation for working as well as customer wants. Desatnick (1987) points out that if you want your employees to treat customers well, you must first treat your employees well. Employees' attitudes toward customers often reflect their attitudes toward their place of employment. Thus, development of a quality, service-oriented staff requires specific service training and also involves a management approach that addresses the staff's needs.

From the customer's perspective, your front-line people *are your institution.* Shostack (1984) comments that "to the customer, people are inseparable parts of many services" (p. 136). Recognition of the importance of those individuals who represent your unit to the public, the secretaries and the other front-line people, is crucial. Daily operations should reflect the opposite of the organizational chart. Front-line service employees should be at the top of the chart, with all other personnel supporting the front-line people. Employees who do not have direct customer contact should be providing support to those who do.

Managers of service units must practice a participatory management style of leadership, utilizing coaching techniques, quality circles, or teams designed to share decision making. This is what helps to create a committed and service-oriented staff. Customers, in general, want front-line people to care and show concern. In addition, customers want to interact with people who are flexible and responsive and who have the authority to make immediate decisions. Front-line people want similar treatment from their managers.

An initial step in development of a strong service staff is writing job descriptions that emphasize the service commitment. Descriptions of positions from the top manager to the front-line people should include statements about their responsibilities for providing quality service to the customer. Specific job responsibilities and tasks need to be delineated in observable behavioral terms to promote better selection training, and evaluation of service personnel.

Desatnick (1987) notes that the next step in creating a quality service work force is in the selection, hiring, and orientation of new employees. New employees should be welcomed into an organization. Orientation for new employees should focus on three aspects: making the new employee feel comfortable, helping the new employee gain an understanding of the expected social behavior and norms of the organization, and teaching the new employee the required technical skills. Often, little effort is spent on new employee orientation even though it is the key opportunity to share an organization's service philosophy and to instill a strong service commitment. Those organizations that do orientate their new employees often focus more on the required technical skills than the expected social or human relations aspects. Again, if job responsibilities clearly list expected behaviors and tasks, initial technical and interpersonal training is much more effective.

Training of service personnel should include both job-specific and personal-enrichment programs. By providing resources enabling personnel to attend both types of training program, a manager demonstrates commitment to quality service and professional development of people.

Most job-specific training for service personnel is dictated by the unique demands of an organization. However, some training is generic for service personnel in any continuing education setting. All continuing education employees should receive training in communication skills, handling of difficult or angry customers, telephone techniques, stress management, and project and time management. Surveying employees for their perceptions of training needs begins the process of having employees committed to the training effort.

Consistent with a participatory management philosophy, personal-enrichment training or education programs should be encouraged and left to the selection of the employees. Support for participation in personal-enrichment programs conveys interest in the personal growth of employees. In addition, it develops a more well-rounded employee.

Training programs should reflect a participatory nature consistent with adult education methodologies. The following program on telephone techniques illustrates a service training program.

1. Have employees list the three biggest telephone problems, for example, telephone tag, not having information available for callers, or managing a heavy incoming-call load.
2. Lead participants through a lecture/discussion of what to say and what to avoid, how to answer the phone, how to clarify what a caller said, how to

handle delayed calls, what to do when the information is not at your desk, and how to screen calls and deal with irate and impatient callers.

3. Establish an officewide, step-by-step protocol for answering the phone.

4. Using some of the skills learned in the training program, address the most serious problems identified in item 1.

Keeping employees well trained is only one of the challenges facing the continuing education manager desiring to implement a strong service orientation. Managers must also motivate, reward, and evaluate employees' customer-service performance. The use of quality circles, or spirit teams, to address work-related problems can also motivate employees to improve the delivery of customer service. Desatnick (1987, p. 86) mentions some additional ways in which managers can reward as well as motivate outstanding service performance.

1. Honor the employee of the month.
2. Place complimentary letters in conspicuous places.
3. Use company publications to honor employees' service performance.
4. Arrange frequent parties or informal gatherings to say thank you.
5. Allow for flex time, compressed work weeks, or variable work days.
6. Hold a competition for customer-service representative of the year.
7. Establish monetary incentives for recognition of service.

Inherent in any performance reward is appraisal. If performance expectations are clearly shared with employees, periodic appraisals can evaluate and reinforce those expectations.

Finally, development of a service-oriented continuing education staff must also include the organization's instructors. Faculty members often have the most contact with the customers and are in the position to provide the best service. Unfortunately, many instructors in continuing education organizations are adjunct or part-time and are unfamiliar with the organization at which they are teaching. Nonetheless, faculty members must be familiar with the continuing education organization's service strategy and the value placed on quality service. Faculty handbooks should explain administrative procedures and educational programs and should emphasize the service orientation of the unit. Review of the handbook should be part of the hiring interview or the group orientation program. Inclusion of other continuing education personnel in the group orientation helps the faculty to learn the service strategy and to meet key personnel, and it reinforces the value of faculty members to the organization. Periodic class observations, banquets honoring outstanding teachers, monetary rewards for superior instruction, and student evaluations all help to motivate and reward faculty. Informed and caring faculty members can greatly enhance the quality of your service.

Summary

In the highly competitive arena of continuing education, service may be the factor that separates your institution from those of your competitors. In fact, provision of quality service is often the key marketing edge. Good service is not a natural outgrowth of being in business, however; rather, it is something to be directed and managed. The first component in service management is gaining a thorough understanding of the customers' needs, expectations, and values. The second component is establishing a service strategy. This strategy should be expressed in a short statement that delineates the organization's unique service proposition. User-friendly service systems must be developed. Finally, it is important to support the staff providing the service. Continual evaluation of how well your continuing education organization is addressing these components will ensure your success.

9

Determining an Effective Marketing Mix

Judith K. Riggs

This chapter focuses on the importance of the entire marketing mix as it relates to continuing education program planning. It deals with issues critical to the success of continuing education organizations, among which are (1) elements of the marketing mix such as product and program planning, pricing, branding, distribution, selling, advertising, promotion, packaging, servicing, and research; and (2) the market forces that influence the marketing mix such as consumer attitudes and habits, competition, and government controls.

Determination of a product and program policy is key to any organization's marketing effort. An organization's choice of continuing education programs influences all other elements in the marketing mix and has significant implications for other areas of the parent institution if there is one. For this reason, the major portion of this chapter discusses the product, which in continuing education is usually the programs, the product's positioning and planning, product mix decisions, and stages in the product's life cycle.

To better understand concepts presented in this chapter, it is important to distinguish between a marketing mix and a promotional mix. Often, the terms *marketing* and *promotion* are used interchangeably; however, the marketing mix is not the promotion mix. The marketing mix comprises product, pricing, distribution, and communication (the promotional mix, which includes personal selling, servicing, advertising, and other sales promotional tools) (Shapiro, 1981). Thus, the promotional mix is merely one part of the marketing mix. This distinction between these two terms will be made throughout this chapter.

Product

Decisions about continuing education products should focus on the programs, goods, and services offered for sale. To be effective, you must match the product resources of your institution with marketing needs and opportunities.

Every organization produces at least one of the following types of products: (1) physical products such as soap, clothing, and food; (2) intangible goods and services such as tours, insurance, consulting, and banking; (3) personal activity, for example, a statesperson who is trying to win the support of the public; (4) organizations, for example, the Republican Party or the American Medical Association; and (5) ideas, for example, a population control organization that is trying to sell the concept of birth control (Kotler and Levy, 1978). The product, then, is anything that can be offered to satisfy a need (Kotler, 1982). It could be a physical object, a service, a person, a place, an organization, or an idea. A product can be called an offer, a value package, or a benefit bundle. The product is the total package of benefits that customers obtain when they make a purchase (Corey, 1978). These benefits may be the product itself, the brand name, availability, the warranty, repair service, technical assistance, sales financing, or personal relationships.

A product must be defined in terms of the benefits to the buyer. The critical question that organizations must ask is, "What is the buyer buying?" Once that question is answered, the next step is to define what is being sold and to state the product in terms of its benefits to customers.

The 1988 Course Catalog of the Fund-Raising School, an entrepreneurial continuing education provider, lists such courses as Principles and Techniques of Fund-Raising, Getting Started Properly with Planned Giving, and Managing People, Ideas, and Things for Productive Fund-Raising. Although participants gain continuing education units for enrolling, the additional stated benefits should emphasize the opportunity to acquire knowledge that will make the fund-raiser more effective on the job; to meet other fund-raising colleagues across the country and exchange ideas; and to escape the routine of work and be rejuvenated. These benefits, among others, are the real reasons people buy the product (that is, register for the program).

There are several ways to focus on product decision making. Six factors considered here are: (1) core product; (2) breadth, depth, and consistency of the mix; (3) life-cycle stage; (4) consumer product adoption; (5) institutional product phasing; and (6) product portfolio evaluation.

Core Product

A key decision for administrators is to decide what product will stand at the center of their organization's total product line, in other words, their core product. This product should always be made available to the buyer in a tangible form. Kotler (1984) defines a product as having up to five characteristics:

1. *Styling.* A distinctive look or "feel." Sometimes, organizations discover that a style is no longer effective with a particular segment. For example, a long-established program attracts fewer and fewer enrollments and does not fit with the overall goals and mission of the institution. The style could be inappropriate because of program content, faculty participants, physical arrangements, or promotional materials.
2. *Features.* Individual components of the product that could be added or subtracted without changing the style or quality of the product (such as hand-out materials or planned meal/social functions at an educational program).
3. *Quality.* Perceived level of performance of a product, program, or a service.
4. *Packaging.* Container or wrapper around the product or service (support services, type of brochure, or physical features of hand-outs).
5. *Branding.* Anything that identifies the product as different from a competitor's offering, for example, name, sign, symbol, and design. Organizations should never overlook the power of their name or the image that the brand name carries.

Breadth, Depth, and Consistency of Mix

Administrators must also assess the breadth, depth, and consistency of the product mix. Breadth is the number of different product lines within the organization. In a higher education environment, the product lines may be undergraduate education, graduate education, athletics, performing arts, and student activities. In a health-care clinical setting, the different product lines include health care, ancillary care service, educational service, pharmacy service, and clinical research.

Depth relates the product mix to the average number of items in each product line. In a continuing education setting in higher education, where the product lines include conferences and institutes, credit courses, and independent study, depth would be defined in terms of total number of courses, number of courses for each professional group, number of offerings related to each college or department, or number of courses for each county in the home state may be studied.

Consistency of product is the degree of similarity between different product lines within an organization. In line with the previously cited example of a continuing education setting in higher education, consistency could be analyzed in relation to all offerings at the graduate level in each of the three major areas— conferences and institutes, credit courses, and independent study. Consistency could also be looked at in relation to education, or which professions are served by the three major program areas.

Often, suboptimal product mixes exist in institutions (President and Fellows of Harvard College, 1975). Suboptimal mixes include an overabundance of seasonal products, a large proportion of profits from a small percentage of product items, inefficient use of sales force contacts and skills, and steadily declining profits or sales in a particular product line or product mix. Again, using the conference and institute example, the offering of too many conferences in the summer without a proper balance the rest of the year may lead to a suboptimal mix. If profits for a conference office are too focused on programs for executives when the market is depleted or a stronger competitor enters, a suboptimal mix may result. The presence of a suboptimal product mix leaves three options: abandon, modify, or replace the particular product causing the problem.

Life-Cycle Stage. Evaluation of a particular product and communication of its benefits to consumers should take into account the stage of the product in its life cycle. There are five basic stages in a product life cycle: introduction, early growth, late growth, maturity, and decline (Kotler, 1982).

The *introductory phase* can range from several months to years of research and development. The resources necessary to develop the market and to ensure that the product will pass into the early growth stage can be very costly and may outstrip resource commitments to development of another product. Often, nonprofit organizations fail to invest enough time and effort in the research and development of a product or the potential market to ensure its success.

In the introduction stage, attempts should be made to educate consumers about the advantages of the product. Personal selling is important and advertising should educate consumers about features of the product that differentiate it from others. Prices may be set at a level that will not fully recover total production costs in the hope that the volume will build and that all costs, both direct and indirect, will be recovered at some later point.

For example, as director for continuing education at a YWCA, let us assume you decide to offer a series of programs aimed at women who are reentering the job market. Before introducing these programs, you should look at other similar offerings in your community: Who is offering similar programs? What is their content? When are they offered? How are they priced? Who is instructing? After analyzing the competition, you need to determine if there is still a need for your programs and how you will make your programs unique. Should you decide to enter the market, you need not only to promote your programs through direct mail and news releases, but you should try to take advantage of public speaking opportunities and television and radio talk shows.

The *early growth phase* is characterized by increasing sales. Typically, in this phase, the product differs very little from other products. Therefore, brand differentiation should be stressed in your communication messages. Prices tend to fall in this phase and competition should not be intense.

The YWCA programs mentioned before will probably begin with small enrollments, but should gradually increase in size if you have researched the marketplace correctly. Consumers need to be told repeatedly that your programs are different from those of competitors.

In the *late growth stage,* growth gradually decreases and there are fewer competitors, because those who were competing with your product either have bypassed you or have dropped out of the marketplace. Distribution at this point usually is very broad and price is often the most important competitive weapon.

By this time, the YWCA programs should have found a niche in the marketplace, word of mouth being one of the best means of promotion. To continue growth, if that is desired, the women's programs may have to be offered in other locations or at other times.

The *maturity stage* begins with a decline in sales growth; sales remain relatively constant and the product is sold to repeat users. Pricing should still be competitive and attempts to segment the market will rely not so much on packaging and promotional strategies, but on basic product distribution differentiation. Sales will eventually begin to turn downward as the product enters its decline stage.

The YWCA programs will stabilize in enrollments during this period and then eventually decrease in size. The marketplace will have been saturated with such offerings.

In the *decline stage,* annual sales decrease at a rate ranging from very gradual to steep. Decline may be caused by the growth of a substitute product or by a change in consumer needs that renders the product obsolete.

At this point, as director of continuing education at the YWCA, you will have to decide to stop offering the reentry programs, to modify them, or to find a new audience.

As an administrator in continuing education, it is important to take a look at your entire product line to determine at which point within the product cycle you have progressed. This could become a worthwhile task for your entire staff and a focus of discussions at staff meetings. How you treat each product and whether you begin to offer more or less of each product line is critical to your success and should force you to consider other marketing mix decisions—pricing, distribution, and communication.

Consumer Product Adoption. It is important as segmentation occurs that a communications plan be developed that takes into consideration at what point consumers enter the product life cycle. Capon (1978) divides the concept of product adoption into five major areas. *Innovators* are the first purchasers of a new product. They tend to be cosmopolitan, travel a great deal, and are socially mobile. They purchase new products in the introduction stage of the life cycle. *Early adapters* purchase a little later. These people tend to be more entrenched in the social structure of their communities and are among its leaders. The *early majority group* is slower to try new products, and enters the market only after their peers have adopted the product. *Late majority adapters* make their first purchases in the late growth and maturity phases of the product life cycle. *Laggers* are traditionalists. Products must be well into the maturity phase before they make their first purchase.

This classification suggests that continuing educators, regardless of their setting, should look beyond the commonly used demographics (such as age, sex, educational background, and geography) and delve into the psychographics of consumer behavior. Dennis Tarr discusses this issue in detail in Chapter Three. For each segment in which programming and service efforts will be concentrated, find out when and how each consumer group makes their purchase decisions. This information can be gathered in several ways: ask members of your advisory or program focus groups, read journals of the professional groups you serve, or ask conference participants key questions on program evaluation or follow-up forms. After collecting these data, use them to target your message and its timing for each appropriate segment.

Institutional Product Phasing. It is also important that administrators assess the type of organization in which they are employed and determine when their organization normally enters the product life cycle (Capon, 1978).

According to Capon, pioneer organizations launch many new products. If your organization is a pioneer, you should have a strong research and development component and be prepared to accept the failures and risks of research, as well as its successes.

Follow-the-leader organizations put their resources into development. They wait until a pioneer has launched a product and then monitor its progress. If they think it is going to be a success, they commit extensive resources into development.

Segmenter organizations enter during the late growth phase of the product life cycle. They modify the product to fit specific needs of a particular market segment. These organizations tend to invest substantial resources in product design, engineering, and segmenting.

Me-too organizations enter the market in maturity. They are very slim, carry a minimum overhead, have strong marketing tendencies, and have the resources to promote and price their product competitively in the marketplace.

As an administrator of a continuing education organization, you should consider product phasing from two perspectives. Determine both the philosophy of the parent institution and your own philosophy of continuing education as related to product phasing. The two philosophies should be compatible, if not identical. If your parent institution is not a trend setter or does not operate in an entrepreneurial mode, continuing education may be looked on as a maverick if it attempts to "buck the system."

Product Portfolio Evaluation. Another way in which an administrator can look at products is in terms of market share and growth of particular products. This is the portfolio approach. Most organizations have what Yip (1981), Kotler (1982), and others refer to as "cash cows," "dogs," question marks," and "stars." *Cash cows* are products that have a high market share and slow growth; therefore, they characteristically generate large amounts of cash for the organization. *Dogs* are products that have a low market share and slow growth; they neither generate nor require significant amounts of cash. *Question marks* are products that have high growth but low share; they require large amounts of cash to maintain market share and even larger amounts to gain share. *Stars* are products that have high growth and high share, but may be self-sufficient in cash flow.

The fundamental principle in designing successful marketing strategies is to use the money generated by cash cows to increase sales for stars and question marks in which the organization has a strong competitive footing. The goal of this strategy is to produce new cash cows. Dogs should be retained only if they contribute some positive cash flow and do not tie up capital that could be put to more profitable use (Yip, 1981).

Most of us could identify the products in our continuing education organization that generate a funding base on which we draw to support programs that are worthwhile but merely break even from a pricing objective. In post-secondary education environments, engineering, medical, computer science, and MBA programs are the current cash cows. They allow continuing education directors to offer programs that are in less demand or less profitable, but yet are important and needed, as in the fine and applied arts, the humanities, education, and social work. In addition, we all offer programs that do not generate enough money to break even but that others in our organizations believe should continue to be offered. The critical decision in management of products is to derive that balance among cash cows, stars, question marks, and dogs that satisfies the parent institution and its continuing education organization and also meets consumer demands, while maintaining a balanced budget or profit center.

Pricing

It is critical to determine objectives for pricing and to consider all pricing strategies and alternatives. Prices may be set for a number of different reasons (Corey, 1982). An organization may seek to gain or yield market share, or to discourage some competitors, or to forestall others from entering the market. In some instances, prices may be held high to avoid driving out less efficient competitors. Or prices may be kept low to meet a competitive attack or to offer a product or service to attract a new customer. A number of pricing strategies can be used, depending on the objectives. There are three major categories of pricing strategies: cost-oriented, demand-oriented, and competition-oriented (Kotler, 1982).

In cost-oriented pricing, prices are set largely on the basis of cost, either marginal or total costs, including overhead. Prices can also be set so that the organization determines the direct and variable costs of production and marketing, plus costs for administration, overhead, and desired profits (Marshall, 1980). This is called cost-plus pricing.

In demand-oriented pricing, the price is set on the basis of demand, rather than the cost. In some instances, an organization may want to get high margins for new products in order to promote them to discrete target market segments and to support high market development costs. This strategy is often referred to as "skimming" and should be used only when the consumer is relatively price insensitive. Costs can also be based on demand by penetration pricing. This strategy should be used when a large share of the market can be obtained quickly.

Competition-oriented pricing, which is the most popular type of pricing, occurs when an organization tries to keep its prices at the industry average. The organization does not want to offer programs at either end of the spectrum—too high or too low. Therefore, the price is kept at the average relative to the competition.

To illustrate these three pricing strategies, consider a hospital that offers a continuing education program on the latest techniques for open-heart surgery. Pricing for the seminar could be set using cost-oriented or demand-oriented pricing strategies. In this instance, the price for the seminar is set based on the costs of program development, promotion, physicians' honoraria, space, equipment rental, and staff time. This is cost-oriented pricing. If the fee is increased to include a profit for the continuing education office of the hospital to use for future program development, cost-plus pricing strategies are being employed.

Let us say that the program is conducted by one of the few heart surgeons who has perfected this particular surgical technique. There will be a great demand for this knowledge by other surgeons. Therefore, the continuing education director could set the price even higher than that set by the cost-plus strategy.

If, however, several competitors are offering similar seminars and one of the few resources (the acclaimed surgeon) is not available, then the price will probably be set using the competition-oriented strategy.

As part of your institutional marketing objectives, you must decide how you are going to use pricing. One way to use pricing is for discrimination in the marketplace. Price discrimination involves selling the same product at different prices to different groups. You can discriminate among market segments, geographically or through packaging, by using different brand names or making minor product modifications.

If you choose not to discriminate in pricing, prices could be set low. Normally, if you allow competition to set the ceiling on pricing, costs will set the floor, unless a decision is made to sell at a loss temporarily in the hope of gaining a foothold in the market.

There are several ways in which continuing education administrators become involved in discriminate pricing. Different companies may contract for a particular program of an organization and be charged different prices depending on the ability to pay, the number of employees who will receive training, or previously established relationships between the organization and the company. Pricing for the same program may vary with location and administrative overhead. Often, programs charge different fees for preregistration and late registration.

If price moves are initiated in the expectation that competitors will follow (price leadership), the organization should be fairly large, have strong distribution capabilities, and have technical leadership in the field. Organizations seldom reduce prices. If prices are reduced, it is usually in the hope of increasing market share.

In setting prices, seven major concerns should be addressed (Corey, 1982):

1. Set prices based on the product market objective.
2. Distinguish between perceived value and potential value for each target market.
3. Study the options available to the customer.
4. Establish whether the buyer can pass on the costs of the purchase.
5. Ensure that a modest price difference will overcome the purchaser's uncertainties about an untried product's quality, reliability, and service.
6. Raise prices only to reflect the supply/demand imbalance during shortages.
7. Prepare customers and competitors to accept price increases.

Distribution

Organizations must choose between selling directly to their customers through their own sales force or selling indirectly through independent agents. Many nonprofit organizations do not use direct sales for continuing education programs because it is too costly in terms of the number of potential consumers in the market; also, the markets are usually very disbursed, and many customers are not accustomed to the direct sales approach (Corey, 1978). Every organization needs to think carefully how it is going to make its products, programs, and services accessible to consumers.

There are a number of decisions related to distribution (Kotler, 1982). Two decisions are critical to administrators involved in continuing education. The first decision is determination of the level and quality of service that will be offered to the target markets. Will products be offered in one location or will there be multiple locations? The second decision concerns the design of facilities. Physical facilities should create the specific image that you want to project to your consumers. For example, executives and physicians accustomed to pleasant, plush surroundings may not be willing to enroll in a week-long seminar in a conference center that is remote from a major city and without such amenities as a gym, swimming pool, or bar. If meeting rooms are cold and not accommodating, participants may become disenchanted with the program, its content, and your organization.

Communication

A well-designed product, program, or service will not be successful unless (1) markets are aware of its existence, (2) target consumers understand what it is supposed to do for them, and (3) target consumers have at least some idea of where or how to obtain it (Quelch, 1975).

It is very important for those designing a communications program to understand the decision process involved in making a purchase. This process comprises five stages: (1) awareness of needs, (2) identification of alternatives, (3) search for information about the various alternatives, (4) selection, and (5) postpurchase reaffirmation (Corey, 1978).

Those involved in promotional efforts must also realize that several people may be involved in the purchase decision. It is important to understand each player's needs and motives and where they are in the decision-making process. For example, if a woman is trying to decide whether to go back to school to continue her disrupted education, her husband may be a critical player in her decision to return and in whether she resumes her studies full- or part-time. Other family members, relatives, and friends may also influence her decisions. To communicate effectively to this potential student, promotional copy must address the concerns and needs of these influential others, as well as the woman herself.

It is important to define the objectives of the communications program, the appropriate target markets, the message to be communicated, the breadth and depth of the message, and the most effective medium. There is always the danger that too many objectives will be assigned to a communications program. Promotion should center around communications programs in which the number of objectives is limited. One way to approach this problem is to develop different communications policies and messages based on the benefits that a segment of the market is expecting from a particular product.

Kotler (1982) classifies the various promotional tools into four major categories:

1. *Advertising.* Paid form of nonpersonal presentation and promotion of ideas, goods, or services.
2. *Sales promotion.* Short-term incentives to encourage purchase of a product or a service.
3. *Personal selling.* Oral presentation to one or more prospective purchasers for the product.
4. *Publicity.* Nonpersonal stimulation of demand for a product oftentimes obtained at no cost or nominal cost.

In using these tools to organize a promotional campaign, it is important to maximize communications goals within the constraints of your budget. Some of the more important criteria for evaluating individual media are (1) the cost of space/time; (2) the reach (the number of advertising exposures potentially achieved by whatever vehicle is chosen); (3) the audience composition; and (4) the impact desired with a particular medium (Farris, 1978).

To determine the information needed by a target segment, the questions asked should relate to the life-cycle stage of a particular product; the level of audience awareness; benefit expectations for each product; and perceptions of how a product or service compares with available alternatives (Quelch, 1975).

Remember that all elements of the marketing mix perform a communication function. Often, communication about a product is outside the control of the marketer and rarely is there a single best medium to which all communication dollars should be allocated. To select an effective mix of media, the role of each medium must be clearly defined. In addition, the message must be consistent across media.

Forces Bearing on the Marketing Mix

Three major forces bear on all components of the marketing mix (Shapiro, 1981). One force relates to consumer attitudes and habits, including motivation of users, buying habits and attitudes, and trends that affect living habits and attitudes. As an example, if an alumni association decides to offer continuing education programs for alumni in an area of the country remote from the campus, it must understand the graduates' attitudes toward participation in continuing education, their perceptions of the organization's ability to offer programs meaningful to them, the current status of their participation in continuing education programs, and factors in their personal and professional environments that would affect their participation.

The second force is competition. Is competition based on price? What are the choices afforded customers? What are the choices in terms of products, price, and distribution? What is the relationship of supply to demand? What is the position of the organization in the market in terms of size and strength relative to competitors? How many competitors exist and what is their degree of concentration? What is the indirect competition versus direct competition? What are the competitors' plans in terms of developing new products? What responses will competitors likely make to actions taken by the organization? To continue the example of continuing education for alumni, before launching a continuing education program, an organization should determine who is offering similar programs. To be successful, the organization will need to locate and price the program appropriately and communicate the benefits of its program versus that of the competitor(s), as well as appeal to the loyalty of alumni to their alma mater.

The third force is government control. As an administrator, you must consider whether controls exist over product, pricing, competition, and advertising and promotion, and if so, what is their effect on your organization as it operates in the marketplace. Some alumni may be involved in a continuing education program at another organization suggested by their employer or, perhaps, by a professional licensing body. You need to know if your organization is not recognized as a satisfactory provider of a particular continuing education program before you expend resources to develop programs in that area.

Uses, Abuses, and Misuses of Marketing

There are a number of marketing abuses to avoid (Lovelock and Rothschild, 1981). These abuses have implications for marketing for all nonprofit organizations and fall into the categories of product, pricing, distribution, and communication.

The product issues are basically two. The first is related to deviations from the consumers' fair and reasonable expectations of the basic product characteristics. An example of such an abuse is the award of certificates, degrees, or diplomas on the basis of fees rather than educational accomplishment. The second product abuse concerns provision of a product different from or inferior to that expected by the consumer on the basis of communications received. One example would be the delivery of instructional programs that are different in content or standards from those promised in the institution's literature. Another is the teaching of courses by faculty who are inferior teachers or who fail to live up to their responsibilities. Other examples are failure to provide adequate effective counseling and failure to provide support services such as libraries, labs, student accommodations, meals, health services, or other services that were promised.

On the distribution side, many times the way in which a product is actually delivered to consumers may offer legitimate grounds for discontent. If delivery is through videotapes or other electronic media, this must be indicated in the promotional literature so that participants know that they will not be in a classroom situation.

Lovelock and Rothschild (1981) address seven different potential pricing abuses that continuing education organizations should consider:

1. Failure to identify all program-related costs such as books, lab charges, and parking fees.
2. Failure to deliver educational services in return for the fees paid.
3. Unclear refund policies in the event of cancelation or withdrawal.
4. Failure to inform all students about the availability of loans, scholarships, and price discounts.
5. Failure to live up to stated refund policies.
6. Failure to offer the loans and scholarships advertised.
7. Failure to give adequate warning of changes in stated policies, such as a sudden hike in tuition or a cut in financial aid.

Communication abuses generally fall into two categories: abuses in the media, where false promises are made or facts are distorted or misrepresented, and abuses by employees, who may distort or misrepresent facts, make false promises, or apply unfair pressure to achieve desired behavior on the part of the consumer.

Summary

Although the four components of a marketing mix—product, pricing, distribution, and communication—must be analyzed by the continuing education administrator, product decisions are critical to the core of the institution. As an administrator, you must follow these guidelines to ensure successful programming and services:

- Ensure that the product line fits into the mission, goals, and objectives of the organization and capitalizes on the strengths and resources of the parent institution.
- Know the position of each product in its life cycle so that you can effectively communicate its benefits.
- Be aware of the responsiveness level of your organization in relation to product introduction and retention so that you can make the best product decisions.
- Assist your organization in setting its pricing philosophy and objectives.
- Decide the most effective ways to distribute your products and services based on consumer demands and competitive forces.
- Segment your target markets so that you can choose the promotional tools that will best communicate the benefits of your product line.

Effective
Direct-Mail Marketing

Most continuing education organizations use direct mail as their primary form of advertising. Therefore, Part Three examines how direct mail can be used effectively. In Chapter Ten, Ralph D. Elliott suggests a wide variety of ways to increase the effectiveness of direct-mail advertising. Effective use of direct-mail advertising techniques to increase program registrations is also discussed.

Chapter Eleven, by Judith A. Markoe, illustrates how to design and lay out successful brochures and catalogues. Her main thesis is that each direct-mail brochure or catalogue is an opportunity to influence how readers react to your organization. She analyzes the principles of design for both brochures and catalogues and offers many helpful suggestions for consideration. In addition, she addresses how one plans to create good design within the overall process of production of brochures and catalogues. Lastly, she provides guidelines for working with vendors in order to achieve the best possible product.

In Chapter Twelve, Robert G. Simerly presents a systems approach to writing effective copy for direct-mail brochures. He analyzes nine important components of brochure copy and illustrates how attention to these components can enhance direct-mail success. In addition, the seven mistakes often made in writing copy are outlined, with suggestions on how to avoid them. This comprehensive systems approach to copy writing ensures that a direct-mail brochure will be effective in meeting your advertising goals.

In Chapter Thirteen, Francis E. (Skip) Andrew maintains that mailing list selection is one of the most important aspects of direct-mail marketing. As he points out, because there are more than 100,000 separate mailing lists from which to choose, the decision on lists is critical to the success of programs. He analyzes seven mistakes most often made in list selection. A comprehensive checklist indicates what a house list should include and why. He also develops a set of practical guidelines for the use of outside lists.

Continuing with the direct-mail emphasis, in Chapter Fourteen, Robert G. Simerly develops and analyzes a production schedule and checklist for direct-mail advertising. As an example, a direct-mail advertising piece is moved through the many deadlines that must be met to ensure a successful advertising campaign. Twenty-five steps in this process are identified and discussed. Also included is a checklist for production of brochures that contains seventy-eight important items.

Thus, Part Three is a comprehensive summary of the important principles of direct-mail advertising. Case studies, suggestions, illustrations, guidelines, and checklists are provided so that you can begin to use the ideas discussed immediately.

10

Increasing the Success of Direct-Mail Marketing

Ralph D. Elliott

Direct-mail marketing is the form of promotion most often used in continuing education organizations. This chapter analyzes specific, practical methods to increase registrations through direct-mail marketing. The principles, suggestions, guidelines, and tips apply both to the large continuing education organization that mails millions of promotional items each year or to the small office with a very modest level of promotional activity.

Continuing educators choose direct-mail marketing to increase registrations for several reasons. First, direct-mail marketing is usually the most cost-effective technique because it yields a higher response relative to cost than any other advertising medium. Direct mail usually outperforms newspaper ads, magazine ads, radio/TV commercials, and such other media as outdoor signs, yellow pages, and package inserts.

Direct-mail marketing also permits selectivity. In contrast to other media, where the promotional message may be presented to a wide range of potential prospects, an educator can use direct-mail marketing to pinpoint audiences. The flexibility to target mailings makes it possible to select market segments that are likely to respond to a continuing education program offer. Then, by concentrating promotional dollars on the most responsive prospects, it is possible to increase enrollments and profits.

Finally, mail is effective because it allows you to tailor the promotional message. Again, in contrast to other media that give the same promotional message to all prospects, direct-mail marketing can be used to send a personalized message. Through mail marketing, it is possible to divide customers into clusters on the basis of common interests. Different appeals can then be designed for the different groups. For example, you might compose different cover letters to mail with a program brochure. In one letter to a potential attendee's boss, you stress the benefits that will accrue to his or her company as a result of sending a staff member to the program. In the letter to the training director, you might stress the instructional design and educational content of the program and then request that specified personnel be notified about the seminar. At the same time, you mail a third, different letter and brochure to potential attendees, in which you discuss the self-improvement that will result from attending the program. By keeping in mind each group's motives for supporting a continuing education course, you can present and discuss a program in the same way that the reader evaluates a course. Building in appeals on the basis of individual motives increases the likelihood that a prospect will either support or register for a program.

Mailing Lists: The Backbone of Direct-Mail Marketing

Your mailing list is the most important determinant of direct-mail marketing success. The mailing list comprises the prospects who will receive an offer. Ideally, the mailing list should comprise those individuals who are most likely to respond.

As a rule, individuals on an in-house house list are the most responsive. The house list contains all past customers. Having already attended one or more programs, past customers offer the greatest likelihood of repeat attendance. You should always include past customers when selecting lists.

Ideally, you should know a past customer's area of interest from your research on client groups. With knowledge of each customer's interests, it is possible to restrict the mailing of program offers to those prospects who are interested in a given topic. By concentrating direct-mail marketing resources on the highly interested prospects, you can achieve a high response.

You might further improve response rates or registrations by mailing only to customers who have made frequent or recent purchases. Past customers who attend courses frequently are more likely to attend or send attendees to upcoming programs than are past attendees who attend infrequently. At the same time, past customers who have attended a seminar/conference recently are more likely to attend again than are customers who attended long ago.

Another way you can build enrollment is through multiple mailings, that is, remailing to certain segments of the house list. In this case, you send a second or third mailing of the program brochure to the most responsive portions of the house list. For example, individuals who have attended a conference in previous years could be mailed a second brochure several weeks after they have received the first brochure. If time permits and response rates look attractive, you might complete a third mailing to these most responsive prospects.

To maintain responsiveness, you should take steps to remove the dead wood or unresponsive prospects from the house list. Each year, approximately 20 percent of the individuals on the house list will change their address or job, retire, or simply prefer to have their names removed from the file. With obsolete names, you may be wasting marketing dollars and potentially losing market share to competitors. For example, let us say that you have a house list of 20,000 names to which material is mailed fifty times per year. If the names are one year old, and if 20 percent of the file has become obsolete, you waste 4,000 promotional pieces per mailing or 200,000 pieces per year. If the cost of these promotional packages is $200 per 1,000 in the mail, you could be spending $40,000 per year on wasted mailings.

A number of actions can be taken to eliminate outdated names. Include an audit box similar to that shown in Exhibit 10.1 in the mailing panel on the brochure. As indicated by the box, mail recipients are given the opportunity to supply a new name, delete the name from the list, or provide an address correction.

You can also use an audit brochure to update the house list. With this approach, you routinely mail a brochure to individuals on the house list and request that they return the brochure if they would like to continue to receive mailings from the continuing education office.

As a last alternative, you might update the house list by dropping from the file the names of those people who have not responded within a particular period. For example, you might analyze your current attendance data and find that almost all individuals on the house list who have not taken a course or who have not requested information on programs within the last three years are not attending current programs. Given the lack of response with these older names, you probably would decide to delete them from the mailing list.

You may also rent outside lists to build enrollment. Of course you should ensure that you rent only highly responsive lists. First, develop a profile of the

Exhibit 10.1. Sample Audit Box.

ADDRESS ADJUSTMENTS OR ADDITIONS

To change an incorrect address, delete an address, or add a new name to the Clemson mailing list, please complete the following and mail to the address below:

☐ Please add this name to your mailing list
☐ Please delete this name from your list
☐ Please change my address to

Name _____

SS# _____

Company _____

Title _____

Address _____

City/State/Zip _____

Phone (Business) _____ (Home) _____

intended customer. In developing the profile, ask such questions as What job title will the prospect have? Which Standard Industrial Classification Codes (SIC) should be selected? What size organization will support the program? What are the demographic and psychographic characteristics of the targeted audience? What is the geographical distribution of potential customers? To answer these questions, analyze past attendance or customer records. Through analysis of historical data, it is possible to develop an accurate profile of past supporters.

Next, correlate the characteristics of past customers with the different programs and conferences in the product line. In Chapter Nine, Judith Riggs discusses the marketing mix and product lines in detail. By linking certain customer characteristics to specific courses, you can learn more precisely which type of person is most likely to attend an upcoming course. Once you have identified the highly responsive prospects, collect information on the available lists.

The most commonly used source of mailing list information is the *Standard Rate and Data Service Directory on Direct Mail*. This directory identifies lists, list owners, and list brokers. The business section contains information on approximately 25,000 different lists in 200 different categories. An index assists in locating the many mailing lists available for a particular course. In addition, mailing list directories published by brokers and compilers are available. The latter are available without charge. You need only have your name added to a publisher's mailing list to receive one.

Instead of using a directory, you may want to get in touch with a mailing list broker. Mailing list brokers are like stock brokers; they have available all of the pertinent information on lists just as stock brokers have the most recent information on stocks. The mailing list broker will recommend lists for your total product line or for a particular program.

Like any broker, the mailing list broker is an intermediary between the list owner and the potential user. The broker's role is to help you select the correct list and, at the same time, help the owners market their lists. The broker usually receives a 20 percent commission on the rental price of a list. The commission, built into the price, compensates the broker for conducting the transaction and is paid by the list owner.

Professional continuing educators who rent a large number of names each year should consider inviting several mailing list brokers to their office. During the visits, the broker should be asked to examine the various programs and then to recommend lists for particular programs and for the total product line. Having several brokers visit helps to ensure that you receive recommendations on the most up-to-date lists available to promote an individual course or series of courses. The personal visit also ensures that each broker better understands the market that you are serving.

To better evaluate a list, request that the broker supply a data card. A data card provides the information needed to assess the appropriateness of a list for an upcoming promotional campaign. Usually a data card is used to determine age of the list, the source of the names on the list, the selection criteria available, the minimum order, the addressing alternatives, sample piece requirements, and the average size of the transactions made by individuals on the list. Also, if you are planning to use the same list several times within a short period, you may want to check the data card or ask the broker for the cost of ordering extra copies. Extra copies can usually be purchased for about 50 to 60 percent of the original rental rate.

Expect to find duplication between the outside lists and the house list. The percentage duplication will vary with the similarity of the lists. A high percentage duplication is reassurance that both the rented lists and the house list are targeted to the correct market. If no duplicates exist, you may have rented the wrong list or may have been sent the wrong list by the mailing list broker.

To eliminate duplicates and thus avoid the cost of mailing to the same individual twice, you can do a merge/purge. In a merge/purge, all lists are put on magnetic computer tape, combined into a master file, and then unduplicated. To identify duplicates, you develop a special match code for each name and address in the consolidated file. Examples of various match codes for Mr. Jack Daniels are given in Exhibit 10.2.

As indicated, you can develop match codes with varying degrees of tightness. As the tightness increases, you are less likely to unduplicate a name that is not a duplicate.

The size of the files and the expected degree of duplication can be used to calculate the savings from the merge/purge. Suppose the outside list contains 30,000 names and that 20 percent of the rented names are already on the house list of 30,000 names. Elimination of the 6,000 duplicates on the outside list will save you printing, labeling, and postage costs. If these costs add to $140 per 1,000 brochures, you will save $840 by completing a merge/purge. Also, when

Exhibit 10.2. Match Codes of Increasing Tightness.

Mr. Jack Daniels
1277 Shore Drive
Paramus, New Jersey 07014

07014 DANIEL 1277	Zip code	5
	Last name	5
	House number	4
07014 DNLS 1277 SHR	Zip code	5
	Last name consonated	4
	House number	4
	Street name consonated	3
07014 DNLS J 1277 SHR	Zip code	5
	Last name consonated	4
	First initial	1
	House number	4
	Street name consonated	3

planning a merge/purge, you can negotiate a "net-name" rental agreement with list owners whereby you do not pay for duplicate names. Assuming a $60 per thousand rental rate, you can save an additional $360 ($60 × 6) from the "net-name" agreement, for total merge/purge savings of $1,200.

The cost savings of $1,200, plus the benefit of avoiding negative publicity by not sending duplicates, can be compared with the cost of the merge/purge to determine its feasibility. Merge/purge costs depend on compatibility of the consolidated files, the file size, and the degree of sophistication of the overall merge/purge. As a rule of thumb, estimate the merge/purge cost to be around $7.00 per thousand names checked. In the preceding example, 60,000 names were checked, so the merge/purge cost would be $420. Typically, you would obtain a cost estimate on merge/purge from a service bureau specializing in this. Names of merge/purge companies can be found in Standard Rate and Data Service's *Direct Mail List Rates and Data*, described in the Resources.

If the merge/purge does not appear cost effective, you may want to mail each list at a different time. Use of different mail or drop dates for each list spreads out the mailings, and it is hoped that those who receive duplicates believe that multiple mailings are being used to promote programs. Another alternative to a merge/purge is to place a message on the mailing panel telling prospects that outside lists have been used and asking them to pass duplicates along to colleagues.

As another alternative to a merge/purge, you can rent names from a public data base, which would contain multiple, unduplicated lists. For example, if your target is the business/industry market you might use the McGraw–Hill Business Leaders' data base, which contains the unduplicated names of subscribers to the company's eighteen different publications. More than one and one-half million names are available and can be selected on the basis of such variables as SIC, job function, home-versus-business address, geographic location, and gender.

You may want to add the house list to the lists in a public data base. In this way, you can retrieve your own names along with the rented names in an unduplicated, continuous zip string. Not only will the house list be readily available for personal use, but the public data base company will be able to rent the house file to other program providers, resulting in extra income for your organization. Each name on the list can bring as much as $3 per year. In other words, a house list of 20,000 names can yield $60,000 in additional income annually.

After you have identified all lists that might contain the names of responsive prospects, your next step is to determine how many lists to use.

Number of Lists

In evaluating house and/or outside lists, it is important to decide which list to use and thereby how many promotional brochures to mail to maximize profits. To determine list usage and mailing size, it is important to compare promotional costs and benefits. Weigh how much each mailing list adds to costs and to revenue. A mailing list that adds less to cost than to revenue should be used.

Suppose that your promotional costs (printing, labeling, list, and postage) per 1,000 brochures in the mail are $200. Assume also that the registration fee for the program is $500 per person, but that such variable costs as lunches, breaks, socials, duplication, and notebooks amount to $100 per person. Therefore, you net only $400 per person. In other words, each additional attendee contributes $400 toward all fixed or nonvariable costs (rental of meeting room, speakers' fees and expenses, registrar's expenses, and audiovisual costs). Let us also assume that you have seven different lists of 5,000 names each from which to choose. The seven lists could include different segments of the house list plus several outside lists. How many different lists should you use? Table 10.1 can be used to answer this question.

In this table, seven different lists are ranked in descending order by the number of expected enrollments or responses per 1,000 brochures. The response figures include allowances for cancelations, no-shows, walk-ins, and bad debts. As indicated, you expect the response rate to decline as more and more lists are added to the mailing. Response rates decline as mailing size increases because poorer quality names are used or because the geographical spread of the mailing increases.

As the response rate declines, the cost of attracting additional attendees increases. For example, at a cost rate of $200 per 1,000 mailings, your cost for one attendee is $200 when the response rate is one per 1,000 brochures. The cost per attendee increases to $400 if the response rate declines to one-half per 1,000. In other words, the promotional costs of $200 per 1,000 divided by the lower expected response rate causes the cost of attracting additional attendees to increase, as shown under Cost per Attendee in Table 10.1.

On the other hand, as shown in the last column, the added revenue from each additional attendee remains constant at $400. Now, how many different lists

Table 10.1. Optional Mailing Size.

List	Number of Names	Expected Responses per 1,000	Number of Attendees	Cost per Attendee[a]	Revenue per Attendee[b]
1	5,000	5	25	40	400
2	5,000	4	20	50	400
3	5,000	3	15	66	400
4	5,000	2	10	100	400
5	5,000	1	5	200	400
6	5,000	0.50	2.5	400	400
7	5,000	0.25	1.25	800	400

[a]Cost per attendee = $200 per response rate.
[b]Revenue per attendee = CP – VC = $500 – $100 = $400, where CP = course price, which is equal to $500 per person, and VC = variable costs such as lunches, breaks, socials, duplications, and notebooks, which sum to $100.

should you use? Lists 1 through 6 could be used. Why? Up to List 6, cost per attendee is less than revenue per attendee. Therefore, by including these six lists, you contribute more to revenue than to costs. With List 6, added revenue and costs are equal, but you might want to go ahead and use the list just to get the enrollment. Usage of List 7, however, would add more to costs than to revenue, thereby reducing profits, and should not be used.

The incremental revenue calculations in Table 10.1 do not include the value of having another customer name in your data base. If the name is rented, or if additional products such as tapes, books, and in-house training are sold, additional income is produced. With additional income, you would definitely use List 6 and, depending on the potential income, possibly List 7.

It is possible to further refine the decision-making process by considering the payoff from remailing certain lists. As a rule, remailing a list yields about 60 percent of the original response rate. Applying the 60 percent rule to Lists 1 through 7 yields response rates of 3.0, 2.4, 1.8, 1.2, 0.60, 0.30, and 0.15. If you wish to measure precisely the increased contribution of a second mailing, send one-half of the names a single mailing and the other half, multiple mailings. Given these respective payoffs, you should send second mailings to Lists 1 through 5, as these lists add more to revenue than to costs. These calculations are shown in Table 10.2.

As indicated by the analysis, income from mailings increases as mailing costs decrease, as response rates increase, and/or as the course price increases. Make your own calculations to determine the payoffs from different list choices and to decide on the optimal mailing size.

Mailing List Tracking

To estimate response rates accurately, consider testing different parts of the house list and outside lists. With testing, it is possible to obtain the response from sample names on each list. After obtaining the sample results, you can target mailings to the remaining names on the lists that had acceptable response rates.

You may want to consider sequential testing or pyramiding. Pyramiding is the process of sending out, over a specified period, successively larger samples to test a list's effectiveness. For example, mailings may be made to a random sample of 5,000 names from a list. If the rate of response is acceptable, such as 0.2%, mailings are then made to another sample of 10,000 names. If the response rate still holds, the next mailing may be to the remaining names on the list. Alternatively, you could identify those components of the list that are pulling the best and consider mailing to only the most profitable segments rather than to a larger cross section.

An important aspect of testing is tracking. To track the mailing list responses, instruct the broker to key-code the mailing labels with list identifiers, usually a series of numbers or letters or a combination of both. Thus, on return of the label with the response you can determine from which list the name was taken.

Table 10.2. Expected Payoff from Second Mailing.

List	Number of Names	Expected Responses per 1,000	Number of Attendees	Cost per Attendee[a]	Revenue per Attendee[b]
1	5,000	3.0	15	67	400
2	5,000	2.4	12	83	400
3	5,000	1.8	9	111	400
4	5,000	1.2	6	167	400
5	5,000	0.60	3	333	400
6	5,000	0.30	1.5	666	400
7	5,000	0.15	0.75	1333	400

[a]Cost per attendee = $200 per response rate.

[b]Revenue per attendee = CP – VC = $500 – $100 = $400, where CP = course price, which is equal to $500 per person, and VC = variable costs such as lunches, breaks, socials, duplications, and notebooks, which sum to $100.

Once the labels are key-coded, devise a system to retrieve them with the registration. This can be done in several ways. A simple method is to design the promotional piece so that registrants automatically return the label with the registration form. An alternative is to indicate to the recipient of the material that the "priority code" on the label should be written on the registration form to ensure speedy processing. This "priority code" also is helpful in telephone registrations. The telephone marketer can draw the caller's attention to the code so that the tracking process is not disrupted.

Other Important Variables That Affect Direct-Mail Marketing Success

In addition to the mailing list, several other factors can help ensure successful direct-mail marketing of continuing education programs. Mail program brochures far enough in advance so that recipients can include the program in their busy schedules. As a rule of thumb, most continuing education program brochures should be mailed twelve to fourteen weeks prior to the event. With the twelve- to fourteen-week drop, expect a three- to four-week "half-life" on the mailing; that is approximately 50 percent of the total enrollment is received three to four weeks after the *first* day of response.

To estimate optimal lead times more precisely, consider the variables that influence how far in advance a mailing should take place, such as program length, program price, level of the recipient in the organization, program location, prospect's occupation, repeat or new program, and first- versus third-class mail.

To find the best lead time for a particular seminar or conference, consider a split test, in which one-half of the brochures are mailed relatively early and the other half later. Once all the registrations are received, it is possible to determine the lead time that yielded the highest response and the greatest overall profit.

With further testing, it is possible to calculate an even more precise estimate of the lead time required for maximum response.

Next, provide plenty of options to recipients of your direct-mail advertising. In so doing, you make recipients feel that they are in control and, therefore, increase the likelihood that they will register.

One way of providing options is to list more than one date and/or location for a seminar. Potential participants are more likely to register when they have a choice of dates and/or locations. In addition, you might also allow participants to take certain portions of a program. For example, at Clemson University, a three-day "Fundamentals of Textiles" seminar is presented. Each day of the seminar is devoted to a different part of textile manufacturing. Day 1 is fiber and yarn formation. Day 2 is fabric formation, and Day 3 deals with dyeing and finishing. Participants can attend one, two, or three days.

You can also give participants a choice by offering several payment options, including "bill me"; "check enclosed"; "letter of intent enclosed"; "purchase order enclosed"; "charge the registration fee to my Visa, MasterCharge, or American Express card"; and "pay at the door." Finally, let prospects decide whether they would like to register by phone, mail, telex, or FAX.

Financial incentives constitute another technique useful in building program registrations and revenue. Examples are a price discount for two or more registrations from the same organization, a free registration for every three paying attendees, and two-tiered pricing whereby certain groups are permitted to register at a much lower fee. As in the case of lead times, it may be appropriate to split-test two different pricing approaches to determine which one, if any, yields the most profit.

A money-back guarantee is another inducement that might increase direct-mail marketing response. By guaranteeing a continuing education program, you may convince the prospect that the benefits of attendance are well in excess of the time and direct dollar cost of attending. Word the money-back guarantee so that it is convincing:

- You will be satisfied, or your fee will be refunded.
- You will save an amount equal to the registration fee in six months or your money back.
- You will be completely satisfied, or your registration fee will be refunded at the first coffee break.
- You will be completely satisfied, or the fee will be refunded at the end of the first day.
- You will be completely satisfied, or you will receive an immediate refund when the course is over.
- We are so convinced that you will be satisfied that we will give you a lifetime money-back guarantee.
- We are so convinced of our quality that if you find a comparable course of better quality, we will refund your registration fee plus pay for the other course.

The psychology behind these approaches is very sound. People are more likely to buy and think positively of your program if you offer them an out. The key to success here is to develop quality programming designed to hit the correct target group. When this happens, registrants are usually very satisfied with what they learn and will rarely exercise their money-back guarantee.

Several other inducement devices are offering a free book or some other promotional item to prospects as soon as they register, encouraging participants to send in questions they would like to have the program presenter answer, and limiting enrollment to a fixed number of attendees and listing that number on the promotional literature.

Again, you may want to split-test the impact of various incentives on response rates and profits so that the appropriate incentives are matched to the targeted audiences.

While considering incentives to build enrollment, take care not to build disincentives into appeals. Disincentives discourage participants from registering. Severe cancelation penalties are the most frequently used disincentives in continuing education programs. In some cases, program sponsors threaten to impound a prospect's registration fee if he or she cancels prior to the program. At the same time, these same sponsors hold prospects who have not paid but cancel or do not show liable for the entire registration fee. Sometimes other disincentives are used: requiring registrations by mail not phone; requiring payment with the registration; requiring payment before a program begins; establishing enrollment deadlines; charging a reduced fee for early payment and thereby creating a penalty for later payment; and not confirming, by mail, the registration as soon as it is received.

Before establishing a penalty, weigh the trade-off between elimination of a particular problem and reduction in overall registrations. In other words, penalties may solve one problem at the expense of overall reductions in enrollment. Again, you may want to test a change in policy on one-half of a mailing list to determine whether registrations increase or decrease relative to the original policy.

Appropriately written promotional copy and a properly prepared advertising package are two factors that help ensure direct-mail marketing success. Other chapters in the handbook discuss rules for writing effective sales copy and for designing effective promotional literature. The reader is encouraged to review and test the recommended changes. Some general rules should be kept in mind when writing copy: long copy outpulls short copy when selling. Short copy outpulls long copy when attempting to generate leads or inquiries. Benefit copy tends to outdraw feature-oriented copy. Serif type tends to outpull sans serif type. Ten-point type tends to outpull smaller type.

In Chapter Twelve, Robert Simerly discusses in detail how to write effective brochure and catalogue copy, demonstrating how to write copy in terms of benefits to prospective attendees rather than from the program planner's viewpoint.

In preparing a promotional package, most continuing educators insert a self-mailer. However, you may want to test different packages in an effort to improve the response rate. There are several possibilities:

- Including a cover letter along with a brochure in an envelope.
- Including a cover letter plus multiple brochures in an envelope.
- Choosing letter-size brochures in an 8½ × 11-inch format rather than smaller flyers.
- Using a third-class stamp rather than metered postage or a third-class indicia.
- Placing a message on the outside of the envelope containing the brochure.
- Using a window envelope rather than a plain, nonwindow envelope.

A Final Comment

Effective use of mailing lists is the most important determinant of direct-mail marketing success. Sending a poor package to a good list is better than sending an excellent package to a poor list. Of course, the ideal is to send an excellent package to an excellent list, and, at the same time, schedule optimal lead times on mailings, provide numerous enrollment options for prospects, incorporate appropriate financial inducements, and avoid disincentives that might discourage enrollments.

As all program planners know, a great amount of time can be spent on all the determinants of direct-mail marketing success. The time must be balanced with the relative return on each of the activities. This chapter has emphasized those techniques that yield a better return on the efforts expended on direct-mail marketing.

11

How to Design and Lay Out Successful Brochures and Catalogues

Judith A. Markoe

You should view each direct-mail brochure or catalogue as your opportunity to influence the readers' attitudes toward your organization. Effective design and layout can make the difference between brochures and catalogues that bring results and those that inform but do not move to action.

Your short-term goal is to get the reader to respond now. To be effective in the long run, this effort must be part of a larger plan involving marketing strategies and development of a desired image. That image requires a "look," a graphic representation by which your institution and its continuing education programs are quickly recognized. Examples of this instant recognition are the Coca-Cola logo with the red and white swirled line, McDonald's arch and yellow type, Apple Computer's multicolored apple, and the IBM striped logo.

Development of that look requires planning and time. If every communication looks different, your image will be confused. If your publications are unprofessional, unplanned, and scattered looking, your public will think the same about you. Decide on the attributes for which you want to be known. These will help you communicate to your graphic design artist what you want to achieve graphically.

Do you want to portray a traditional academic feeling? Do you want to be seen as friendly? Is your program large or small? Do you want to capitalize on that or change attitudes about it? For example, if you have a very large program and the criticism is that people feel like numbers, you need to address this in your copy and look. You may want to look warmer and more intimate. For example, a headline used in the University of Maryland University College catalogue read,

"Last Year 30,000 Students Put Their Futures in Our Hands." This statement acknowledges the importance of each and every student and also implies that all 30,000 students are satisfied enough to entrust the university with their futures. The headline was set in italic upper- and lowercase type, which is much warmer than all-capital, nonitalic type. In addition, potential students could identify with the catalogue photograph of students in an actual classroom setting.

Principles of Design

Make your brochures and catalogues stand out. Professionals receive piles of mail each day. Most do not have time to sort through it, much less read it. You have three to ten seconds to catch the attention of readers before they set the brochure or catalogue aside. The title and the design are the two tools most likely to accomplish that goal. The elements of design with which you work are graphic design, color, type, and space. Giving careful attention to these design elements is important whether you are producing a single brochure or a large, elaborate catalogue.

Design. Design can be a complicated undertaking. Professionals spend a lifetime studying this topic. It is critical that continuing education professionals learn the effective components of design so that they can create effective communications. Yet it is just as important to realize that graphic design is a highly skilled art. *Do not try to do your own design.* Invest in the services of a professional graphic designer. You will be rewarded with professional-looking advertising. With brochures and catalogues that do not intrigue and capture the reader, the best program will be unsuccessful. Determine what the reader reads and use this information well. Generally, much more time is spent on the copy than on design. As a writer you need to rewrite, refine, and reorganize text. As a designer, you need to experiment with type and design and move elements around on the page, changing the balance. This takes time. Allow the designer two weeks to come up with some rough sketches, of which you will choose one or more, and which the designer will then refine. Then, depending on the designer's workload, count on one to two weeks for each of these steps: receiving a more detailed layout of the entire brochure, and receiving mechanicals (the boards to which camera-ready art work is attached).

The optical center of a page is slightly above the horizontal midline. Your design should take the reader's eye to that point or through it to another point.

The balance of your piece will be disturbed if too many competing elements are set on one page. Balance is affected by the form, the number, and the size of elements. For example, if all type is the same size, then nothing seems more important. It is critical to rank-order the type on the cover and throughout the brochure or catalogue. Effective balance on a cover leads the eye to the most important point. The various formats used to achieve this balance are commonly called the *T*, *Y*, and *S* formats.

In the *T* format, the title, or most prominent part of the design toward the top of the page, is set above the optical center. The supporting copy or graphics follow a course down the middle of the page.

The *Y* format is similar to the *T* format except that it may have two important and complementary elements in the upper section of the page. Supporting copy and art would flow from this point down the center of the page.

The *S* format has prominent portions at the top and bottom of the page, although the bottom is usually less prominent than the top. In this format, the copy and other art would be more likely to fill a wider portion of the middle of the page.

As you experiment with various elements, you will find that most successful designs usually follow one of these formats. Mixing formats results in an unplanned and scattered appearance.

Few of us have the resources to follow these formats within the brochure or catalogue, but elements of these formats should carry through. Thus, it is to your advantage to use graphic elements on the cover so that they can be continued within to carry the reader from one point to another and to emphasize the most important points in the copy. Photographs, abstract designs, or design elements that relate to the topic of the program can be used.

It is not advisable to use photographs of buildings (unless you are advertising a seminar about architecture) or to use your name and logo as the primary design element and focus. Unless you use a variation of your logo to connect all of your brochures, it is unlikely to attract the attention you want to one individual program. If established and used effectively, your name and logo reflect your reputation. They will not, however, capture your readers unless the topic or design intrigues them.

Color. Color can be a powerful tool. It can attract or offend and as a result it needs to be considered carefully as an integral part of your design strategy. Color can be used as background to draw attention to the page. It can be used in conjunction with the design to make the reader's eye move to the point on the page you want emphasized, or it can be used to move the reader through the copy.

Color conveys feelings. For example, navy blue and white imply tradition or sophistication. Red implies high energy or warmth. Sea green and peach are considered trendy or contemporary. In general, dark and neutral colors are more formal; lighter colors tend to be more informal.

Color can be used to highlight. Frequently used highlighting methods are underlining and setting headings in blocks of color, shadows, boxes, and screens. If you want a word or phrase in a paragraph to stand out, underline it in a second color or set the actual words in the second color. Use a graphic element in a second color next to a heading to bring attention to it. Consider reversing out the heading in a block of color so that the heading is the color of the paper.

Box an area you wish to stand out and either set the box in a second color or use a percentage of the color (such as 10 percent) to "screen" the box. The entire box will then be a very light shade of the second color and will stand out on the page. Shadows can be used effectively; not only can they highlight, but they can also give the part shadowed a three-dimensional appearance.

Color can also be used as a background. Extending the color to all edges of the paper is called *bleeding*. Although this process is usually more expensive, it makes the brochure appear more professional and more expensive. It may be worth it to you. You can also use a colored background with a border around the edges. The border operates as another design element that may add to or confuse your message depending on how it is designed.

If the background color is light enough, printing the copy over the color can work well. However, reading an entire brochure or catalogue this way may be tedious for the eyes.

Color can be used to connect all of your brochures and communications. For example, you may use the color red in every brochure. If every printed communication always has some element of red, preferably used in the same way in a logo or a design, it acts as a subtle connector.

However color is used, make it part of your total design strategy. A word of caution is in order though. Do not mix too many of these methods, because the result may look scattered, confused, and unplanned. Instead, use color to make brochures and catalogues stand out.

These guidelines on the use of color should prove helpful:

1. Colored stock can be used to add color. It may be less expensive than using a second color of ink, especially if your printer has a low-cost paper in stock, and it gives the impression of an additional color.
2. The use of screens in two-color jobs can make it appear that three or more colors have been used. Screens can be very effective in highlighting important copy.
3. Yellow should be used only as a background or highlighting color. Yellow type is difficult, if not impossible, to read.
4. Black and dark blue are the easiest colors to read. Dark brown and green may be used, but they tend to tire the eyes.
5. Photographs should be printed in black ink. Sometimes, when combined with black, another color at 10 or 20 percent can give the photograph a more three-dimensional effect. This is called a dual-tone process. It can be tricky, however, and you should be certain that both your graphic designer and printer have experience working with dual tones. Avoid printing photographs in color unless a special effect is required. For example, printing in brown results in a vintage look. A forest scene printed in green might enhance the effect. Otherwise, color tends to make people look sick or at least strange. Use photographs to help the reader identify with the people in the photos and then with your program. Readers will not identify with strange, sick-looking people.
6. Type reversed out of a dark or bright color is more prominent than dark type printed over a light color.
7. When using large areas of color, select tightly woven paper. Paper that is too

porous will soak up the ink, resulting in the use of more ink and hence increased costs. On paper that is porous, such as newsprint, it is more difficult to achieve an even spread of the color on the page. The color will probably appear blotchy. Higher-grade newsprint that is more tightly woven and whiter in appearance is available.

Space. The most common mistake is to fill every inch of a brochure or catalogue with copy and artwork. The reader needs space to "breathe" visually and will stop reading if the piece seems too overwhelming. If the direct-mail piece is too crowded, the reader may not be able to find important information, which could result in failure to register for a program or unnecessary calls seeking information. Space can be used to highlight. Surround important items with space, or couple space with design to highlight nearby copy.

One design guideline that can be used is the grid concept, where either a two-, three-, or four-column format (most commonly two or three columns) is used on each page of your catalogue or brochure. Hence, an imaginary grid exists. Let us use a three-column grid as an example. To add some "air" visually, on each title page of a new category, you might leave the first column empty, fill the second and third columns with copy, and set the category title in large type across the top of the empty column. You might also use a photo or quote below the title or on selected pages throughout to add emphasis. Consistency is important in the use of grids.

Space needs to be planned and integrated with copy and design to avoid a scattered and loosely focused appearance, even if the words in the copy are effective.

Type. Thousands of typefaces exist. Type can be used to set a mood, establish a quality, and vary the balance and design of the page. Ask your typesetter to show you the typefaces available.

The different styles (or classes) of type are Roman, gothic, italic, script, and novelty. Roman type consists of vertically shaped letters with serifs, which are lines extending from the ends of the body of a letter. Gothic is type without serifs (sans serif). Italic type consists of slanted letters. Script looks like handwriting. Novelty types have a distinct and special feel suitable to nontraditional approaches to text and graphics.

Typefaces that have the same general appearance and characteristics are said to belong to the same family. Members of the same family vary to the extent that they are light, bold, italic, condensed, or extended. Cheltenham, for example, has more than twenty variations.

A type font is an assortment or set of type all of one size and style. Each font includes lowercase letters, capital letters, figures, punctuation marks, and often fractions, asterisks, and other special characters like percentage marks.

Type is measured in points. A point is one seventy-second of an inch measured vertically. Type is usually 6 to 72 points, but 3- to 144-point type can also be found. Text type is commonly 8, 10, or 12 point.

The equipment used by typesetters today can modify existing typefaces in many ways. For example, typefaces might be condensed, obliqued, expanded, or reversed to attain the desired effect. *Kerning* is the tightening of space between individual letters; it can often make the feel of a word or headline change. Kerning also allows adjustment of the spacing between letters on a line, resulting in looser or tighter lines of type.

Type is a critical element of design. Its proper use can introduce variety into an otherwise dull or overwhelming page. Bold type makes words within a paragraph stand out. The size of type in headlines indicates importance. The use of all capital letters also indicates greater importance, and the use of a variety of types or weights can indicate differences. These methods should be used sparingly. If any method is used too much, the elements will compete with each other.

In general, all body copy should be the same style. Although they may vary in style, size, or weight from the body copy, headings should be set in type of the same family.

Computers and Type. Computers have revolutionized typesetting and editing. They have cut editing time and costs by two-thirds. If you are not currently inputting your copy into a personal computer and arranging to have your type set without rekeying at the typesetters, you are wasting time and money.

When you give the typesetter copy on paper, the typesetting operator inputs every letter by hand, and you pay for this work by the hour. In addition, typesetters are human beings and are likely to make mistakes. You have to read every word to ensure that mistakes have not been made. You then make corrections, send them back to be reset, and proofread again. Meanwhile, the cost in dollars and time continues to increase. If you give the typesetter a disk or transmit the copy by wire, the copy simply needs to be formatted and the style and size of type designated. This takes one-third of the time. If the copy is proofread and run through a computerized spelling checker before it is sent, a random check for correct placement, type size, type style, and format will suffice afterward. Multiply your savings on one piece by the number of pieces you have typeset over a year, and you will probably find that you have paid for a personal computer.

Consider these guidelines related to type:

1. Serif type is more legible than sans serif in body copy.
2. Numerals are more legible when set in sans serif.
3. Italic type should be used sparingly in body copy because it slows reading.
4. Boldface type slows reading and large blocks of it produce eye fatigue.
5. Reverses retard reading by almost 15 percent.
6. Because italic, bold, and reverse type slow reading, they can be used more effectively to highlight certain copy or to make the reader stop where you desire.
7. Full capitals reduce legibility and reading speed. They also require 30 percent more space.

8. Legibility is lower when columns are wider than 22 picas (6 picas = 1 inch).
9. Legibility is lower when line width is less than 14 picas.
10. If you take the time to plan your use of type, your brochure or catalogue will be clear and flow smoothly.

Up to this point we have analyzed principles of design for all direct-mail advertising pieces—brochures and catalogues. However, brochures and catalogues have some separate requirements. Therefore, in the next two sections, specific suggestions are offered on the design of brochures first and catalogues second.

Design of the Brochure

The following approach to design of the brochure considers graphic elements and copy. The design portions have been emphasized and combined with some copy as it relates to the goal of each brochure section. (See Chapter Twelve for a detailed discussion of the components of brochure and catalogue copy.)

Cover. Your goal on the cover is to grab the attention of readers and make them open the brochure. You have approximately three to ten seconds to do that. It is, therefore, critical to bring the eye to the most important point. Do not put too much on the cover. Take time to determine the copy and use copy that appeals to readers' goals, aspirations, and desires. A design element can be used to draw attention to the title or cover. In addition, photos or drawings can be used to convey information that would otherwise require many words.

Copy. Most brochures contain a lot of copy. Use your design and type to facilitate reading. Arrange copy in short, well-organized blocks. Use white space and/or graphic elements to move readers through the piece. Different items are important to different people. Use headlines that help readers find the sections in which they are interested. Make each item graphically easy to find.

Overview. Give a synopsis of the program in one paragraph. Because people may have only sixty seconds to read this brochure, entice them with an item important enough to return to later. If the program is at a specific level, such as beginning or advanced, state it here.

Benefits. In bulleted, fragmented sentences, list the tangible benefits that readers will receive by participating in the program. Emphasize the skills they can acquire that will affect their life.

Who Should Attend. Indicate, in a bulleted list, the job titles of people who should attend this seminar. Do not be too greedy. If every job is listed, readers will think the seminar is not worth their time.

Program Description. Once you have sparked interest, you must elaborate with details so that readers can decide if the substance is worth their investment of time and money. Because the program description can be fairly extensive, be sure to use an outline form so that the reader can easily pick out key elements. If the brochure is designed before the final schedule and session titles are completed, use a topical outline, illustrating the basic plan and complexity of the program. If the actual schedule of events could be important to the reader, or if the program is unique in design, it would be to your advantage to print the schedule with days, dates, times, and session titles. In this way, the reader can pinpoint when major speakers or sessions are scheduled.

Special Features. Every program has some facet that can be highlighted, and these should be set apart graphically. Such features include a major speaker, a special format, location, instructional methodology, or particular tour or event.

Accreditation. Receipt of a reward for effort is an important incentive to those who must carefully allocate their limited time. Many professions require continuing education for continued certification. Continuing education credits of some sort can be offered for most learning experiences. If you offer these, be sure to say so and highlight this section in a subtle manner, perhaps in a screened box.

Testimonials. Quotes from individuals who have attended your programs can establish a credibility that your own words cannot. These quotes can be used within the copy blocks or as a graphic tool in margins. Include the job titles of people along with their quotes. These titles should be similar to those listed under Who Should Attend.

Location. If location is a selling point, it should be prominently displayed. If not, it should be a part of general information. Locations with special features, such as recreational facilities, historic tours, or cultural events, may influence potential participants, and this information should be stated and, if appropriate, pictured.

Organization Identity Statement. In a short paragraph, sell your organization and program. Discuss other opportunities such as in-house and upcoming programs. Depending on their extent, highlight one or more of these other programs.

General Information. Registration information, fees, refunds, and further information, such as tax deductions or equal opportunity statements, should be given under General Information. Grouping these items can help the reader find them more easily and can help you graphically. If space in the brochure is limited, print this section in a smaller type size or in a tighter format with less space between paragraphs. Readers still must be able to find the information easily, so number the steps in the process or set boxes to checkmark.

State all items included in the fee. Do not scrimp on what you offer in your program. You want to offer the highest-quality educational experience for participants.

Make it easy for people to register. Reduce your process to specific steps and number them. This is your opportunity to prevent unnecessary telephone calls; answer all of your readers' questions here. Include refund policies and such things as printed matter, meals, or special events that are included in the fee. State clearly how to register by mail, phone, or in person. Mistakes can be avoided if you design the registration form carefully. Use the registration form to gather other information such as the name of a friend who might be interested in learning about the program, other programs in which the reader might be interested, or important demographics that will help you market future programs more effectively. Design the brochure so that the registration form is on the back of the mailing label, enabling you to retrieve the mailing label. Ensure that the form can be tracked by the codes on the mailing panel or on the registration form. For those readers who are not interested in registering now, add a box that they can check if they want to receive future mailings.

The name and phone number of the person to contact for further information should be prominently displayed. If you want to encourage individuals to call for more information on how you can work with them to design in-house programs, include an appropriate check box on the registration form allowing them to request this information. Follow-up quickly on any of these responses.

Announce all relevant upcoming programs in each brochure. In addition, include announcements of upcoming programs in the confirmation letter that goes out to all registrants.

Design of the Catalogue

Cover. Like the brochure cover, the catalogue cover must gain people's attention and make them want to open and read the catalogue. One of the most common mistakes in designing covers is to put the name of the organization in the largest, most visible type. Readers need to find out what this publication *is*. Make this easy for them. The largest type should be reserved for the title—"Catalogue of Classes, Spring Semester," or "Learning Unlimited." Of course, the organization's name must appear on the cover, but less prominently. The entire cover will be identified with your organization. A design element can be used to draw attention to the title or cover, or photos can be used to convey information that would otherwise require many words.

Organization. It is critical to organize the headings and sections of the catalogue. Headings must be consistent. The most important headings should be equal in importance, in size, and in type. The same holds for the second most important, the third most important, and so forth. In large catalogues, as many as fifteen to twenty different headings may be necessary for clarity. Compose the major headings, making them as broad and logical as possible. Put yourself in the place of the reader. For example, if you have a number of aerobic, dance, hockey, and karate classes, use them as secondary headings under the larger heading "Physical Fitness." If you have classes for senior citizens, adults, and children, you might organize your headings on a different basis: "Seniors," "Adults," and "Children," could be the primary headings; "Physical Fitness," the secondary; and "Aerobics," the tertiary. Each class then would be a fourth size or variation. The sooner your readers find the specific classes in which they are interested, the higher will be the enrollments.

If potential students in your community are most likely to choose location first and then subject, organize your catalogue by location. The format of the listings should be consistent under all locations. If your community is small and subject is the primary drawing card, organize by subject. Note different locations under the course description with time, location, date, and fee as separate lines. These items should stand out in some way from the course description. For example, the words "day, date, time, fee, location" could be set in boldface or italic type with the information in regular type. The title of the course should always be set in prominent type.

First Two Pages. Your inside cover and first right-hand page are the most prominent pages in a catalogue. They should contain the Table of Contents (or Index), some information on what the reader can find inside, and critical dates. New or special courses might also be appropriate here. Many organizations list their leaders or county or city boards of directors on one of these pages; however, the reader has no need for such information at this point. Place it toward the back with the general information. If the purpose of such a listing is to let readers know who is sponsoring the program, consider inserting a short paragraph explaining who the sponsors are and what they mean to the community. Highlight this paragraph, perhaps through the use of a box or a screen. This may have more visual impact than a list of officers.

General Information. Most general information should be at the back of the catalogue. Readers do not need registration information before they have even the classes from which they must choose.

Remaining information on registration information, accreditation, and upcoming programs should be organized according to the design guidelines suggested previously for brochures. The overriding principle for both brochures and catalogues is to put yourself in the reader's place. Design the piece so that your reader can follow the story and register for the programs.

Planning

The best program does no good if no one finds out about it in time. Good brochures and catalogues take a great deal of time to prepare. Consider these four guidelines when preparing brochures and catalogues:

1. Establish schedules that allow adequate time for all steps in the production process, including rewrites and mistakes. Stick to these deadlines.
2. Provide instructors with a form on which they can summarize the course information in an established format. This eliminates the problems that too often arise when the writer edits the instructor's copy.
3. Whenever possible, market programs in a series and arrange them together in the brochure or catalogue. This allows you to spread the cost of the piece over a number of programs. It also results in a higher-quality publication and permits you to send out more than one mailing. Most important, it shows the reader that you offer many programs, which implies an impressive organization with a comprehensive series of programs.
4. It is cost-effective to employ a professional graphic designer to design your brochures and catalogues. The money you invest will be returned manyfold in the enhancement of your image, the consistency of your direct-mail pieces, and the time you save by following predetermined formats whenever possible.

Effective scheduling, then, is a critical component of the entire design process. Effective direct-mail advertising pieces do not happen by accident. Rather, they are the result of the highly skilled work of a wide variety of professionals, such as program planners, copywriters, graphic designers, typesetters, and printers. It is essential that you incorporate into the planning process the time needed by these professionals to do the best job possible.

Working with Vendors

The time you spend on copy writing, design, and layout is wasted if the quality of the printing is poor or if the brochure is late. The printing business is complex. It is important to become as familiar with it as you can. One way to do this is to ask vendors for tours of their plants during production processes in which you are interested. Vendors appreciate educated consumers because their work is made easier.

Consider the following suggestions when working with vendors:

1. Schedule at least two weeks for typesetting.

2. If possible, enter copy into a personal computer. The typesetter will then be able to convert the copy into type in one-third the time and for one-third to one-half the cost. After your graphic designer has selected the type, he or she can usually expect to receive galleys of typeset copy for long brochures within twenty-four hours. This represents an enormous savings in time and hence money.

3. Proofread your copy carefully. You pay by the hour for corrections. Even if you use a computer, thereby eliminating the need to rekey type, each time the type is rerun from the machine, the expenses climb.

4. If you are working with a designer, clarify the budget, purpose, schedule, and any other relevant information about the brochure. For example,

do you prefer a formal or informal feeling? Is this one in a series of brochures? Are there intangible messages you want to communicate in the brochure?

5. Schedule at least two weeks for each of the following design steps: (a) rough sketches from which you will choose the design; (b) a more detailed layout of the entire brochure; and (c) "mechanicals," or the boards on which camera-ready artwork and the actual copy are laid down.

6. Copy should be proofread at the typesetting stages so that no changes are necessary on the mechanicals. Although changes are very expensive, the mechanicals should be proofread very carefully. Check that all the headings are in place and that the more important ones look more important (that is, they are larger or stand out because of design). Check that the brochure flows smoothly.

7. Involve your printer at the beginning of your job. Discuss your budget, types of paper, color, and size. If possible, your designer should accompany you. Printers are professionals who take great pride in their work. They can offer very useful advice both to you and to your designer.

8. Develop a relationship with each of your printers. They can help you to avoid problems and can educate you about the many technical complexities in the printing process.

9. Divide your work among two or three printers, thus ensuring that no one printer assumes that you depend entirely on his or her firm. In this way, printers will be encouraged to do the best job possible every time because they want your continued business.

10. Discuss the kind of press, size of paper for the run, and how many brochures or catalogue pages will fit onto each sheet. Sometimes, by reducing the size a bit, you can get one more brochure or catalogue page on the sheet and thus save in page costs and in time on the press. Discuss the possibility of running more than one job or all of the covers of your catalogues at once. Called "gang" printing, this too can save you money because it is volume printing.

11. Schedule another two weeks for printing. This includes having the printer photograph the boards and produce a "blueline" or photoimpression of the brochure on treated paper. The blueline is a sample of what the actual product will look like when it is printed. Proofread the blueline for last-minute corrections. Remember that at this point, corrections are very expensive and complicated; new type must be ordered and set, negatives reshot, and new plates of the corrected pages made. In the final phases of production, press inspection is made, if you choose, and the job is run. Leave enough time to rerun the job in case there is a real problem. Always assume the worst possible scenario when planning your schedules.

12. Get estimates on all jobs before you begin. When you contract with the printer, indicate that all variations from the original estimates must be cleared with you. Any change you make, no matter how small you think it is, can cause serious delays and increases in costs.

13. If coated paper and reply coupons are to be used for a brochure, select a type of paper that is not too slick to hold the ink when the registrant fills out the coupon.

14. Consider type and weight (thickness) of paper when selecting coated stock. Take care not to place photographs on folds because they could crack.

15. Leave enough time in your schedule to get a blueline. Never omit this phase. It is your last chance to exercise quality control.

16. If using four-color, obtain a color key. The color key is similar to a blueline except that it is in color. Again, this is your last chance to exercise quality control. Do not omit this item in the overall production process.

17. The printer is not responsible for your mistakes. In addition, the printer is not responsible for a printing mistake if you approve it or sign off on the mechanicals or bluelines. Most printers will ask you to initial each page of a blueline to indicate your acceptance.

18. Check each stage of the production process carefully.

Summary

The design and layout of brochures and catalogues is a complex and time-consuming process. The key to success is planning. Determine the image you desire and plan to portray that image graphically. Combine design, color, type, and space to make your communications consistent and clear. If you take the time to plan, you will find that the process is more complex; however, it is also more effective, exciting, and rewarding. When you give adequate attention and time to planning, you will be rewarded with a higher-quality product that will attract your readers' attention. And getting the readers' attention is the first step in securing a registration.

12

Writing Effective Brochure Copy

Robert G. Simerly

The demand for continuing education programs has grown rapidly during the last decade. In coping with this demand, continuing education leaders have used the expertise of professionals in many fields to help them improve their program delivery. Important to the enhancement of this delivery is expertise in direct-mail marketing. Today, almost all continuing education programs use direct-mail brochures as the primary means of publicizing their programs.

It is not unusual for large continuing education offices, such as those in universities, public school systems, professional associations, community colleges, hospitals, business, and industry, to mail hundreds of thousands of publicity pieces each year. In smaller offices, direct-mail brochures are produced in more modest quantities, but they still represent the primary method for communicating information about programs.

No matter what the size of the continuing education organization, the principles of writing effective copy for brochures are the same. These principles apply whether you are planning one program or 1,500 programs each year. In this chapter copy writing is analyzed from a total systems point of view. Through analysis of the parts of a brochure, you can easily adapt the basic principles to the individual needs of your own organization.

Effective copy should have three main goals: (1) to enhance the overall image of the organization and program it represents, (2) to provide comprehensive and accurate program descriptions, and (3) to secure the number of registrants required to meet financial goals.

Components of a Brochure

The parts of a brochure vary slightly from organization to organization. Most commonly, brochures are divided into the front cover, introduction/ background, who should attend, special features, program content, presenters' biographies, general information, registration, and back cover.

Front Cover. A cover should have only one purpose—to attract the attention of potential participants so that they open the brochure and read about the program. The following guidelines are helpful in meeting this goal.

1. Create a title that accurately describes the program.
2. Whenever appropriate, use action verbs to give the program a dynamic character.
3. Display the program title in large type.
4. Prominently display the name of your organization.
5. Include the names of cosponsoring organizations or departments. This can add credibility and build support for the program.
6. Consider carefully what copy should be included on the cover that would cause the reader to look inside. Begin the story line on the cover if appropriate.

To achieve these goals for the cover it is almost always advisable to use an 8½ × 11-inch or larger format for the production. Brochures of this size allow enough room to accomplish the goals; smaller advertising pieces rarely provide enough room. In addition, we are all conditioned to handling 8½ × 11-inch letters, reports, and announcements. Anything smaller may be lost on the desk of a busy person. Or even worse, smaller brochures may look less important and tend to be ignored by readers.

Introduction/Background. Headlines across the tops of the inside pages, called header copy, should be designed to reemphasize the title as well as the dates of the program. However, it is usually the introduction/background statement inside the brochure that begins to describe the program. The introduction/background statement should be designed to (1) further establish the image of a quality program, (2) provide the necessary background to tell why the program is being presented, (3) generate enough interest to encourage the reader to read all of the copy, and (4) enhance the credibility of the program.

The following copy, written for a one-week residential program entitled "Executive Supervision: A New Professional Leadership Institute," is a typical introduction/background statement. It is important to include a comprehensive background statement for shorter programs too.

The Executive Supervision Institute in Environmental Services Management is a four-year program of executive development for leaders in the environmental services industry. This program has been planned by a national team of leading practitioners in the field. During the planning, leaders across the nation were asked to describe their major supervisory problems. Then we designed this special program to help leaders like you deal effectively with these practical on-the-job problems encountered in the environmental services industry.

The nine-year history of this program has shown that leaders in environmental services enjoy entering a program of continuing education to enhance their management skills. Each year, the evaluations by participants in the institute are very high. This confirms the fact that individuals as well as their sponsoring organizations value this intensive management development experience.

This example effectively communicates six positive ideas in a short background statement:

1. The tone of the message is that the institute has been carefully planned to meet the needs of the field.
2. The institute builds on a nine-year history of effective programming.
3. The institute offers the promise that by their attendance managers will be able to improve their daily leadership skills.
4. The employing organizations will benefit from the increased expertise leaders will gain as a result of attending the program.
5. The message emphasizes that the program has been planned to make learning enjoyable.
6. The institute deals with everyday problems that practitioners experience in their supervisory duties.

The most effective introductory/background statements are those written from the viewpoint of the potential attendee. In other words, the statement should answer the question, "What is there about this program that makes me want to attend?"

Who Should Attend. Program planners usually have a very clear idea of potential program participants. As a result, they assume that the readers will discern whether the program is appropriate for them. This assumption, however, is often incorrect. All brochures should tell readers exactly for whom the program has been designed. The copy should spell out very clearly who should attend so that readers do not doubt the appropriateness of the program. To accomplish this goal, it is important to analyze the readers' unspoken concerns.

Readers of brochures often have many questions about the program and its appropriateness. Table 12.1 lists some of the questions and their implications. These questions need to be viewed at two different levels of meaning. Level 1

**Table 12.1. Two Levels of Meaning Behind the Questions
People Have When Reading Brochure Copy.**

Level 1 *What Readers* *Ask Themselves*	*Level 2* *What Readers* *Really Mean*	*Implications for* *Securing Registrants* *as a Result of* *Brochure Copy*
Is the program suitable for me?	Will I be able to understand the material that is presented and thus be able to succeed?	I may have to convince my boss to send me. The program copy must help me to secure commitment from my organization.
What kinds of people will be attending?	Will I be thrown into a learning situation in which many of the participants are far ahead of me?	I probably will not attend if the majority of people are at a much higher skill level. I want to be able to meet with and talk to people like me.
I already have a lot of experience. Is the program too elementary?	I'm a busy person and I do not have time to waste.	I can't tell from the copy exactly what I will learn. Will attending be worth the time I invest?
Can I get this information somewhere else?	Will I be wasting my time if I attend?	Demonstrate through powerful copy that people will be able to explore ideas, learn new skills, and update their knowledge.
How much does it cost?	I don't mind paying if I get something of value for my money.	Determine the values of your potential audience and describe them in the program copy.

comprises the initial questions readers often ask themselves. Level 2 consists of the more complex and subtle questions. Often, receiving a satisfactory answer to a Level 2 question determines whether the reader will actually attend the program. Therefore, it is important that brochure copy address both levels of meaning simultaneously.

As most readers will not pick up the phone and call the office sponsoring the program to discuss their concerns, the writer must anticipate, in the Who Should Attend section, the readers' questions and the levels of meaning. For example, note how this concern is handled effectively in brochure copy for a three-day management workshop entitled "How to Become an Effective Supervisor":

This program has been planned specifically for the following kinds of participants:

- People who are thinking of becoming entry-level supervisors.
- People who have recently become supervisors.

- Current supervisors who want to learn the basics of how to be more effective in their positions.

The entire workshop has been planned to be an introductory course to the latest practical methods on effective leadership and basic supervision. The program will emphasize practical ways to become more effective in all of your leadership roles.

The following brochure copy was written for a twelve-week course, which meets three hours one evening each week, entitled "Personal Financial Planning: How to Manage Better During Inflationary Times."

Anyone who wants to find out about how to end up with more money at the end of each month will benefit from this course. The course emphasizes the kind of information you need in order to make better informed choices about how to manage your personal finances. The course is designed for people with all levels of income. No accounting background is required. The emphasis is on a wide variety of very specific things that the average person can do to improve his or her personal financial management.

Program Content. People lead very busy lives. The public is constantly bombarded by radio, television, magazines, newspapers, and billboards and by the many brochures that they find in their mailboxes. Each day people make many decisions about what they will read, listen to, and respond to. It is this "respond to" item that is of major concern to continuing educators writing brochure copy.

Usually, busy people quickly make the decision to read an entire brochure. Vivid, concrete, detailed descriptions of program content can be a major factor in persuading readers that the program has something for them.

Most people do not want to attend programs unless they are absolutely sure that they can learn specific things that they do not know and can benefit in some other very specific manner, for example, meeting colleagues and making new friends.

Therefore, how the content of the program is described in the body of the copy becomes very important. In fact, next to the front cover, it is probably the single most critical area in the brochure. The following examples illustrate two different ways in which program content is often described: an ineffective approach and an excellent approach.

The copy for a one-day workshop entitled "How to Plan and Run Effective Meetings" follows a fairly standard format often seen in brochures.

How to Plan and Run Effective Meetings

| 8:30–9:00 | Registration and Coffee |
| 9:00–10:15 | Introduction to Planning Better Meetings |

10:15–10:30	Coffee Break
10:30–12:00	Clinic Session on Running Meetings Followed by Discussion
12:00–1:00	Lunch
1:00–3:00	Practical Techniques for Running Effective Meetings
3:00–3:15	Coffee Break
3:15–4:15	Question-and-Answer Session, Program Wrapup

Note that this copy is basically a timetable of the workshop. It is not effective in persuading people to attend. The preceding copy fails to indicate how people can become better at running meetings by attending the program.

The second example effectively describes the content of the same one-day program.

How to Plan and Run Effective Meetings

The following topics will be covered during this one-day practical workshop:

1. *Creating the Effective Meeting Environment*
   a. How the seating in a room can be arranged to contribute to a successful meeting.
   b. Planning for the effective use of your psychic energy during a meeting.
   c. How knowing the phases all groups go through when working together can help you become a better meeting leader.
   d. How time management can contribute to a productive meeting environment.
2. *Building an Effective Agenda for Your Meetings*
   a. Getting input for establishing successful agendas.
   b. Hints on how to work through an agenda for maximum effectiveness.
   c. Proven techniques for structuring agendas to achieve successful meetings.
3. *The Importance of Meeting Leadership*
   a. How your leadership style can determine the success of a meeting.
   b. How to choose an appropriate mix of leadership styles during a meeting.
   c. How to use participative decision making effectively.
   d. How to develop an action plan to expand your repertoire of leadership styles at meetings.
4. *Managing Conflict for Productive Results*
   a. Analysis of the role of conflict in meetings.
   b. How to use conflict to produce a better decision at a meeting.
   c. Managing conflict for win–win outcomes.
5. *Steps to Productive Meetings*
   a. How to tap the hidden potential of your group.
   b. Easy-to-implement suggestions on how to get everyone to contribute to the success of a meeting.

    c.   Designing ways to help all participants become more effective at meetings.

    d.   Using proven techniques to get people to work effectively for you during meetings.

6.   *How to Train Your Staff or Committee to Contribute to Successful Meetings*

    a.   Effective evaluation techniques to help you improve your meetings.

    b.   How to turn the meeting blocker into the meeting helper.

    c.   How to develop an action plan to take home to your organization to improve the running of meetings.

In the preceding copy, the schedule is omitted; it can be placed in the general information section. Most potential participants want to know what topics the program addresses, not at what times the topics are addressed. Potential program participants want to be given clear and compelling reasons to attend, and a detailed, accurate, comprehensive description of program content achieves this goal. The copy in the second example more effectively communicates the specifics to potential participants. It is the kind of copy that encourages readers to register for the program. And the outline format is an effective method of presentation.

Special Features. All continuing education programs have unique or special features. We interact with people, we learn specific skills and concepts, we create plans to take home, we discuss ideas, we receive printed handouts, we get new ideas, and we meet professional colleagues who share good ideas. These special features, when properly identified and made an integral part of the brochure copy, can provide important incentives for registration.

    For example, a brochure for a three-day workshop for dance criticism in the media listed the following special features:

- You will attend three different performances of the Murray Louis Dance Company.
- You will have the opportunity to receive feedback and an analysis of your dance criticism by Jack Anderson of the *New York Times* and Suzanne Shelton of *Dance Magazine.*
- You will view and analyze dance films as a way to improve your critical skills.
- You will participate in movement classes especially planned to sharpen your dance perception. These will be simple classes intended for writers, not dancers.
- You will be provided a forum for discussion of problems in the field and in different areas of writing about dance for newspapers, magazines, radio, or television.
- All participants will write a review for group discussion of one performance of the Murray Louis Dance Company.
- You will work with Jack Anderson and Suzanne Shelton in an informal workshop setting designed to enhance your professional skills.

These special features constitute powerful copy that emphasizes the uniqueness of the program. Concrete reasons for attending are provided. There is an emphasis on interaction with distinguished faculty and on learning new ways to think and write about dance. Thus, including this description of special program features directly contributes to telling the overall story of the program. People interested in writing dance criticism will be very attracted to the quality of the learning as described in this Special Features section.

Presenters' Biographies. One reason people attend continuing education programs is to learn from presenters who are experts in the field. Therefore, integrating comprehensive biographical copy into a brochure can provide readers with reasons to attend. This copy should legitimize the expertise of presenters so that readers will say, "Yes, that's a person who has good credentials, experience, and expertise. I could learn a lot from this person. I ought to attend the program."

Ask yourself the following question when writing biographical copy: Is the biological information about the presenters extensive enough to swing an undecided person to register for the program? Good biographical copy should encourage readers to attend a program. The following guidelines are helpful in writing copy:

1. List the person's job title and organizational affiliation.
2. Describe the person's educational background, including degree programs, relevant internships, and other appropriate experience.
3. Include honors and awards that are relevant to the person's expertise as a program presenter.
4. Describe relevant experience and jobs in ways that are meaningful to the reader.
5. Consider including relevant organizations with whom the presenter has consulted.
6. List any relevant publications to legitimize the presenter's experience as a leader in the field.

The following biographical copy is for the main presenter in an executive development program.

> Dr. Fred Luthans teaches and does research in management and organizational behavior at the University of Nebraska–Lincoln. He received his Ph.D. at the University of Iowa and taught at the U.S. Military Academy—West Point while serving in the Army. He currently holds the George Holmes Chair of Business Administration at Nebraska. He is the author of over a dozen books and close to 100 articles. One of his books, *Organizational Behavior Modification,* was named by the American Society of Personnel Administration as the major contribution to human resource management a

few years ago. It is in this area of the behavioral approach to human resource management and the measurement of leadership research that Professor Luthans does his basic research and is best known. His O.B. Mod. model is widely used as a behavioral management technique and his leadership research is currently funded by the Office of Naval Research. Dr. Luthans is on the editorial boards of the *Academy of Management Review, Behavioral Management Journal,* and *Akron Business and Economic Review.* He is also consulting coeditor for the McGraw–Hill Management series which contains many of the leading books in the field. He is very active in the Academy of Management where he served as President and is a Fellow of the Academy. He is also an active consultant for a number of retail, industrial, and public organizations and management firms.

General Information. Often referred to as "boilerplate copy," general information is all the important information participants need to register. General information is usually most effective as a special section at the end of the program description but before the registration form. It should include the name and number of the person to call with questions; the address to which the registration form should be mailed; all costs associated with registration; the date, time, and place for registration check-in and for the first session; details about the cancelation policy and refunds; and other appropriate information. Consider these important guidelines when writing general information copy:

1. Clearly state that people can register by phone as well as by mail. Many continuing education organizations find that at least 50 percent of their registrations are by phone. It is thus important to offer this option, which makes it as easy as possible for people to register.
2. Clearly state the cancelation policy to avoid later misunderstandings.
3. Clearly state all costs for the program.

Registration Form. The registration blank is to direct-mail marketing what the closing line of a sales meeting is to a salesperson. By this time, if your reader is not interested there is little you can do to encourage her or him to register. If the reader is interested, however, you can do much at this point to increase the chance that he or she will register. The major goal is to make it easy for the interested person to register.

From the standpoint of the sponsoring organization, the easiest thing to do is to ask the reader to fill out the registration card, enclose a check, and mail it to your office. However, this procedure does not take into account the registrant's needs. Therefore, it is important to include those options that facilitate registration for potential participants. Here is a list of the most common strategies used in the registration process:

1.   Some readers want simply to fill out the registration card, enclose a check, and show up at the program.
2.   Other readers cannot tolerate forms. They are accustomed to handling their business transactions immediately. They want to phone in their registration immediately to ensure an immediate confirmation. This may be the critical factor that converts the interested reader to an actual registrant.
3.   Some readers interested in attending do not have the money immediately available, but are able to charge the fee to a credit card.
4.   Other readers, particularly those working for large organizations that will pay registration fees and expenses, know that it will take at least four to six weeks to initiate the paperwork, get it approved, and obtain a check from their business office. Keeping track of all of this paperwork can dampen the enthusiasm of even the most interested potential participant. You can offer such participants the option to be billed later or to use a purchase order. The latter is particularly helpful for attendees whose fees are paid by a government agency. Both options encourage readers to sign up for a program while their interest and enthusiasm are at a peak.
5.   The option to send a partial deposit should also be offered. Full payment can be collected before the program begins or when the participant registers. This is a particularly good option to consider when the majority of the potential participants are paying their own way and the program fee is high.

Program planners who offer their participants as many options as possible for paying registration fees often find that attendance rises dramatically.

Back Cover. The back cover has several important purposes. It usually provides a place for a mailing label and a logo, and often it contains the general information and the registration form. In addition, it should be thought of as valuable advertising space designed to catch the reader's attention and to reinforce the message inside. Consider these items when designing the back cover:

1.   Does the back cover containing the mailing label look important enough to be delivered to the addressee quickly?
2.   Many people pick up the brochure with the back cover facing them. Therefore it is important to include the title, date, and location of the program. The back cover, like the front cover, should encourage people to open and read the brochure.
3.   As the back cover is just as important for advertising, has the same care been given to its design as has been given to the front cover?

Avoiding the Most Commonly Made Mistakes

By taking the time to analyze copy writing from an overall perspective, it is possible to increase the effectiveness of advertising. It is also important to avoid mistakes.

Mistake 1: Failing to Schedule Enough Time to Write Good Copy. Often, in the rush to wrap up the program planning, insufficient time is allocated for writing effective copy. Enough time should be allowed for criticism by several people, such as members of your own staff. Excellent copy is often preceded by several revisions.

Plan all advertising production deadlines so that there is adequate time to write and rewrite copy. As a rule of thumb, the average continuing educator takes about four to eight hours to write good first-draft copy for a four-page 8½ × 11-inch brochure. Approximately another one to three hours are required for each rewrite. Three rewrites are about average for most programs. Add to this the turnaround time for criticism.

Professional copywriters employ the one-week rule to what they consider their last draft. They set it aside for one week without looking at it. Then they review it one last time. This one-week break often brings fresh insights.

Mistake 2: Writing Copy from Your Own Point of View. Copy for continuing education programs is often written from the point of view of the program planner rather than from the point of view of potential program participants. Always try to step into the shoes of potential program participants when writing copy. Consider asking people in the target group these questions:

- What ten things would you like to learn from this program?
- What would cause you to attend?
- What would cause you to stay away?
- If you have attended similar programs, what did you like about them? What did you not like about them?
- About how many pieces of direct-mail advertising do you receive each month?
- What causes you to read or not read brochures?
- What do you think are the five hottest, most controversial topics related to this potential program?
- What would you tell a friend about such a program?

The answers to these questions will provide many ideas for improving copy. Further, copy incorporating these answers will motivate potential participants to register.

Mistake 3: Failing to Consult Program Presenters. Sometimes the copywriter does not consult the program presenters to confirm the accuracy of the copy. It is important from the standpoint of professional ethics that program presenters be able to deliver on all the promises made with respect to program content.

Always work closely with program presenters to ensure that copy related to their portions of the program accurately reflects their plans. As they are experts in their fields, they will usually be able to provide good advice on the tone and language appropriate to the target group. Program presenters are usually excellent sources.

Mistake 4: Underwriting Brochure Copy. It is almost impossible to write too much copy for a program. When copy is overwritten—that is, there is too much and it will not fit into available space—it can be edited or the brochure size can be increased. However, underwritten copy comes across as just that—underwritten copy. It gives the negative impression that the copywriter could not think of anything to say.

Always be sure that the blank space in a brochure is the result of a conscious decision by you and your graphic designer. This decision should be based on the fact that blank space rather than copy is more effective in describing this particular program. Never use blank space by default, that is, because there was not enough copy to fill up the space and not enough time to write more copy.

Mistake 5: Devoting Too Much Front-Cover Space to Pictures, Drawings, or Other Designs and Not Enough Space to a Bold Display of the Program Title. Drawings, pictures, or other designs should be directly related to the program. They should never be used merely to fill space. The program title on the front cover should be large and in boldface. It should not be understated. The title must reach out and actively invite the reader to open the brochure and read. The date and location of the program and the name of your organization must also get the attention of potential participants.

Mistake 6: Failing to Highlight Major Sections of the Brochure. Each major section needs to be highlighted appropriately. Front and back covers are automatically highlighted because of their unique position. Large, boldface headings can attract the readers' attention to other sections.

Develop a checklist of important items to include in each major section. Be sure that no section on the checklist is omitted without a clearly thought out reason. Most copywriters for continuing education programs include on their checklists at least those sections previously identified as components of the brochure.

Mistake 7: Failing to Display Prominently the Name and Phone Number of the Person to Contact Regarding Questions. This item is very important. It makes it very easy for the reader who has questions to phone for answers. It is also important to train your staff to convert phone inquiries into actual registrations.

Even if readers do not have questions for the person listed, they react positively to the prominent display of such copy. They are comforted in knowing that someone with the answers is available should a question arise. Perhaps most important, it communicates that your organization consists of real people. Readers are given the name of the actual person who will be handling the registrations.

Summary

Approaching brochure copy writing from a comprehensive systems approach ensures that each part of the brochure achieves specific goals. These parts interact with each other in important ways. By ensuring that each important part is included and that strong, effective copy is written for each part, direct-mail marketing of continuing education programs can be enhanced.

Enhancement of the programs and the copy that describes them provides important benefits to the sponsoring organization as well as to program participants. The sponsoring organization improves its image and maximizes the chances of increasing registrations. The program participant is able to decide whether or not a particular program is appropriate. Thus, chances are increased for producing excellent programs that attract the required number of registrants to be successful.

13

How to Find and Select Mailing Lists That Get Results

Francis E. (Skip) Andrew

Escalating paper, printing, and postage costs force continuing education marketers to make their mailings more efficient. A proper understanding of the use of mailing lists results in more precisely targeted marketing, thereby reducing waste and thus costs. Computers make this function easier and, at the same time, more complex, more competitive, and more productive. Surprisingly, you will find that you do not have to rent the most expensive mailing lists to be effective in direct-mail marketing. In addition, many important lists are available without charge.

Continuing education programs throughout the United States fail every day because they select the wrong mailing lists. Mailing list selection is one of the most crucial decisions in the direct-mail promotion of your programs.

Chapter Ten offers excellent advice on how to select mailing lists. This chapter extends the ideas presented in Chapter Ten and concentrates on such additional important issues as types of lists, the mistakes most often made in list selection and their avoidance, preparation of a house list that can be sold, and guidelines on the use of outside lists.

Types of Lists

Your choice of list depends on your audience, advertising objectives, and budget. Consider the options.

Consumer Versus Business Lists. Consumer lists include names, home addresses, and other information on consumers. Business lists include names, business (and sometimes home) addresses, and other information about decision makers.

To decide which list you need for your promotion, ask yourself "Who will pay for this continuing education program?" If you expect a business to pay registration and other expenses for attendance at a continuing education program, choose the business list. Conversely, if you expect the consumer to pay, choose the consumer list. It seldom works to mail business mail to a home, although it sometimes works to mail to consumers at their business addresses.

Outside Versus House Lists. Business and consumer lists are further subdivided according to the source of the name. Names generated by the activities of your organization are found on the house list, whereas other names are on outside lists.

Compiled Versus Response Lists. The crucial distinction is how the name got on the list. Either the names were compiled from membership rolls, directories, government records, or other similar listings (compiled list) or the names are those of persons who responded to previous direct-mail marketing appeals (response list). The next section analyzes why response lists provide direct-mail marketers of continuing education programs with the best opportunities for securing program registrations.

House Lists

Your best customer is your present customer. In continuing education, direct-mail marketing efforts bring such a tiny response rate (for example, 0.01–10 percent per 1,000 pieces of advertising mailed) that it is very expensive to acquire customers. Only a few step out from the masses and say, "Hey! I'm on your side. I like you. I want to come to your program!" We want to please these respondents, keep them, and resell to them. If we have good-quality programs, our present customers will return to us repeatedly, and at a fraction of the cost of acquiring a new customer.

The best new customers are those acquired with information on your present customers. This is called cloning. Every institution has its mission and style, and the institution's image in the marketplace attracts customers unique to that institution. Therefore, if you want more customers, look at your present customers and determine their profile. Then, rent those lists containing people as much like your present customers as possible. This very important principle of direct-mail marketing cannot be emphasized too strongly.

Common Mistakes. Although current customers provide us ongoing revenue, many of us in continuing education make mistakes when dealing with our clients. Seven common mistakes are made in handling customer lists and should be avoided:

1.   Failing to update the list. Americans are very mobile; up to 25 percent of the population moves each year.

2. Failure to make verifiably correct entries, for example, addressing a promotion piece to a male as "Ms. Jan Smith."

3. Failure to separate actual customers from people who have merely inquired about your program. Each of these groups requires a different approach, and this cannot be achieved unless these two groups of names are separated.

4. Failure to maintain a backup house list in a remote location (thereby risking the demise of your business during a fire or theft).

5. Failure to treat your customers with special care by mailing specially targeted and useful information to them (so they do not feel like they are buried in your junk mail).

6. Failure to have the proper information in your house list (you need more than name and address to profile and clone effectively).

7. Failure to computerize your list (no manual system can beat a computerized competitor).

Leveraging the Value of the House List. A well-maintained house list enables you to target mailings more precisely to those customers and potential customers with the most propensity to buy the specific program or product offered in the promotion. For example, if you promote a seminar entitled "Time Slashers for Executives," your house list will identify those customers and companies that have provided the best responses to previous time management courses. You can save marketing money and increase response rates by limiting your mailing only to those customers. For knowledge of such propensities, you need much more than names and addresses. To profile customers and thus precisely target mailings, include the following information for each customer in your data base:

1. *Name, address, and function.* Allow for nine-digit zips, because the postage savings for bulk mailings sorted by nine-digit zips are considerable. Make your software require entry of company names in ALL CAPS to avoid such common errors as "I Bm Corporation." For job descriptions, include both job title and function; for example, "director of promotions" is a marketing function and "vice-president" alone does not identify the functional area. You need both title and function for effective marketing. The Direct Marketing Association in New York City publishes excellent references for industry conventions on the format for names and addresses. (See Resources for the address.)

2. *Contact history.* All of the following help you to identify customers according to their loyalty and interest in you: change of address, purchases, refunds, complaints, referrals, and multiple orders or registrations for programs. The last item is particularly valuable.

3. *Purchase history.* The acronym FRATS summarizes the data you need. You want *frequency* of purchase because it identifies your most active customers; *recency* of purchase because it indicates those most ready to buy; *amount* because it shows relative value; *type* of purchase because it enables you to

target by program or product; and *style* because it helps you to predict by associating life-style with type of purchase.

4. *Interest codes.* Indicate the topical interests of attendees. Solicit this information by mailing customers questionnaires or by asking them about their interests on program registration and evaluation forms. Types of programs actually attended will give you accurate information about propensity to buy the same or related program topics. An interest indicated by opinion or desire, rather than by actual program registration or product purpose, has significantly less value even though it may still be useful.

5. *Relevant segmentation of data.* Describe your customers in ways relevant to predicting their propensity to buy. Be careful here to gather even possibly relevant information, because you will sometimes discover surprising or unexplainable associations between personal characteristics and propensity to buy. Table 13.1 lists discriminants you should consider including in the personal information you maintain within your customer data base. This information can greatly enhance your success in direct-mail marketing.

6. *Source and date of origin.* Specify where this name came from (for example, a particular mailing list, a program walk-in, referral by a previous customer, an advertisement, a public relations piece).

7. *Postage saving.* The U.S. Postal Service gives significant discounts for carrier route and other sorting. The requisite information and sorting capabilities must be part of your data base if you are to take advantage of these cost savings.

8. *Unique identification number.* Each record for each name in your data base should be given a permanent identification number. This procedure can speed your use of the data base and avoid such common problems as guessing which one of seventeen John A. Smiths called to have his address changed.

Building such a comprehensive and useful data base takes time, money, and extreme care; it is a project that obviously requires planning, expertise, and staged implementation. Whatever the size of your organization, you can benefit tremendously from such a data base if you make repetitive mailings and offer multiple programs each year.

Parlaying Your House List into a Gold Mine

You may wonder, "What on earth would I do with all that information?" We do not gather information for its own sake. We use it to make our marketing better, easier, and less expensive. We want only actionable data. To decide which items in the preceding checklist can be acted on, their use must be understood.

Profiling. Profiling is describing in as much detail as possible your present customers or, in the case of a new product or program, your target audience. The old adage "birds of a feather flock together" applies more than ever to the marketing of continuing education programs, products, and services. Seldom do

**Table 13.1. Market Segment Discriminants to Consider for
Your Customer Data Base.**

Geographic
    Zip code
    Telephone and area code
    Region
    County size
    City or census area size
    Density
    Climate

Demographic—Organizations
    Age
    Life-cycle stage (startup, growing, mature, declining)
    Size (dollars and/or employees)
    Industry (Standard Industrial Classification codes)
    Class or size of advertisement
    Telephone and area code
    Fortune/BusinessWeek/Inc. Rankings
    Office type (headquarters, branch, foreign)
    Fortune markets
    Addressee's title and function

Demographic—Individuals
    Age
    Sex
    Income
    Housing
    Auto ownership
    Occupation
    Education
    Religion
    Race
    Nationality

Psychographic
    Family life-cycle state
    Social class
    Life-style (for example, studies of values and life-styles)
    Personality

Behavioristic
    Purchase occasion
    Benefits sought
    Type of problem
    User status
    Usage rate
    Loyalty status
    Buying structure
    Decision process stage
    Primary referral agent
    Primary approver
    Attitude toward us
    Sensitivity to promotions

Adapted from Kotler (1984, pp. 95–96).

people with widely disparate economic, social, and life-style characteristics attend the same program. If you were to list all the characteristics of attendees at one of your heavily attended programs, you would probably find that those characteristics cluster rather distinctly. This provides you with attendees' profiles for that program.

The more information you gather, record, and correlate, the more accurate a profile you can construct. Two keys used for profiling are Sectional Center Facilities and Standard Industrial Classification codes. Sectional Center Facilities, often referred to as SCFs, are large postal areas designated by the first three digits of a zip code. Standard Industrial Classification codes, often called SICs, designate each type of business in the United States.

For example, if I know that single adults, 22–28 years of age, working in clerical positions in retail establishments of twenty or more employees in SIC No. 53 and zip codes 959__ and 949__ register for my evening program series "How to Become an Executive Level Manager," then I will not waste money mailing to senior citizens and professionals, other types and sizes of companies, and other Sectional Center Facilities. I will use only those outside mailing lists that match my profile, again maximizing my response while cutting promotional costs.

Obtaining the Data. You can elicit a surprisingly large amount of segmentation information from customers at registration and evaluation: you can also obtain this information through list enhancement services. Large list compilers incorporate great amounts of data into their data bases. They know more about our customers than most of us do. Organizations like Donnelly Marketing, Dun's Marketing Services, CCX, CACI, and MetroMail are all listed in Standard Rate and Data Service's *Direct Mail List Rates and Data.* To order this publication please refer to the Resources. These organizations can run your computer tape against their tape and add to your names much of the segmentation data listed in Table 13.1. As a result, your list is enhanced. This enhancement will pay for itself many times over if you have large and accurate lists and if you utilize the techniques of data base marketing.

Making the Best Use of the Data. Data base marketing consists of building and using a data base for the purpose of nurturing a long and mutually satisfying relationship with your customer by targeting only those mailings your customer really wants to see. Thus, your customer comes to know you as a provider of service rather than a purveyor of junk mail. You can do simple data base marketing just by using profiling; however, if you administer a large continuing education program, you can derive greater benefits by using the model-building and multivariate statistical analysis tools fast becoming the hallmark of data base marketers who waste very little mail and, therefore, enjoy enormous profits (Stone, 1984; Baier, 1983; Andrew, 1987).

Pyramid of Response. Think of the world as a pyramid with your best customers at the top; they are followed in order by occasional customers, those who inquire about your programs, those who express some interest, and those with no interest. Targeting mailings to all of these levels is a waste of money. The customers at the top levels, however, deserve special attention, multiple mailings, and customized packages because they will provide the best responses. Data base marketing helps you determine who is in which level so you can mail more efficiently. Mailing efficiency means greater response at lower costs.

Outside Lists

Utilizing the concepts discussed so far, you can maximize your mailing list selection and usage by following seven key guidelines.

1. *Know your program and its target market.* Nothing matters more in selecting lists.

2. *Follow the law of similars.* Lists similar to those that have worked for you in the past will probably bring similar results for future programs. The best response is elicited from those persons who have attended similar meetings held in similar circumstances, at similar prices and locations.

3. *Test two to four list brokers.* Brokers link you to the list owner, helping you to select the best lists and then to order them. Paid by the list owners, brokers should be used as advisers, not deciders. Determine who gives you the best service and the best results. Analyze your response rates and track them by list so you can determine which lists, and which brokers, did the best for you.

4. *Do not let brokers make the final choices unless they are consultants who also know your business and market as well as you.* Treat mailing list brokers like real estate brokers; let them show you around according to your criteria, but reserve the task of final selections for yourself. Brokers differ in the level of quality, competence, and service. Brokers may have biases not consistent with your business goals.

5. *Use brokers instead of list managers.* Either way you pay the same. Brokers, however, are independent businesspersons who work for you to obtain the best list available for a particular direct-mail advertising campaign. They compare lists from many different companies and recommend the ones most appropriate for your particular needs. List managers, on the other hand, work for a particular company and manage its lists. Therefore, they have a vested interest in recommending only that company's lists.

6. *Always profile and clone.* Because your best customers tell you who responds best to you, profile them and select lists containing people who match, or closely match the profile.

7. *Test, track, and analyze.* Unless you test, you cannot know whether your list selections work better than other list selections. To test, you need one control list (one that did best for you last time) and a number of test lists. Code all labels so that the returned registrations tell you the lists on which the respondents' names appeared. Burnett (1983) and Stone (1984) provide excellent advice on testing. In addition, Chapters Ten and Twenty-Three address the importance of tracking and offer practical tips.

Obtaining Outside Mailing Lists

Consider lists before you design your program, product, or service. Too many marketers forego substantial profits by considering lists after they have developed a product, program, or service. Consider lists first, because lists delineate the markets available to you. A seminar on "How to Manage Your Career Change" cannot succeed unless you can find lists of persons in the midst of career change.

Start with Standard Rate and Data Service. Do your own research before calling a broker. Brokers, list managers, and lists are described extensively in Standard Rate and Data Service's *Direct Mail List Rates and Data,* a quarterly catalogue (and the primary mailing list directory). This service is also available on-line through your computer and a modem-connected telephone. See Resources for information on ordering this publication. SRDS, as it is commonly called, gives you extensive indexes by subject, list name, and list owner. But *SRDS* lists only some of the lists available. Consider every publication, association, and business a potential source of mailing lists. Consult *The Encyclopedia of Associations and National Trade & Professional Associations of the United States, Standard Periodical Directory, Oxbridge Directory of Newsletters, Thomas Register of American Manufacturers* and *Thomas Register Catalog File,* and *Dun's Business Identification Service.* In addition, the *Directory of Directories, Guide to American Directories,* and *Business Information Sources* (Daniells, 1985) will help you find almost any list or organizational membership.

Order list data cards. You can request these from the list owner or manager specified in *SRDS.* Brokers can also supply you with cards. Data cards tell you the list owner's name and address, the conditions under which names from the list will be rented/sold, charges for using the list and various selections and related services, how the names were obtained, and sometimes the number of names in various market segments (for example, number of chief executive officers in each sectional center facility). *SRDS* provides much of the same data in summary form, enabling you to make initial choice there.

Use free lists. You can often get lists just for the asking or by arranging cooperative sponsorship of a program. Many publications and associations provide lists in exchange for having their name publicized as a cosponsor. Consider establishing an advisory board of representatives who can provide you with free lists from their organizations. Ask your advisory board members to secure such lists. Some organizations, including your competitors, will exchange lists with you. Enthusiastic attendees and customers can sometimes lead to free lists as well. A word of caution is in order. Check to see when these lists were last updated. Some organizations have very old lists and do not know when or how their lists are updated.

Examine sample mailing packages. Order, directly from list owners, sample mailing packages used to generate the names on the lists you are interested in renting. These packages show you the offer, slant, style, and target audience, enabling you to judge their suitability for your mailing. In addition, you may gain ideas on how to reach these same audiences.

Study the list data card to find selections close to your profile. Data cards provided by list owners and brokers specify the numbers of names listed in the various categories or selections. A selection is a part of the list; for example, if your customer profile is male professionals in selected zips, then you will rent those segments of the lists.

Research. You want to know how useful a particular list is to your campaign. Your key inquiry "How and when did each name get on this list?" leads to other important questions. Was the name-generating offer a loss leader, a special discount, or a free offer? When was the address last updated and how? To reduce expenses, ask about rental charges, multiple mailing discounts, selection charges, reimbursements for "nixies" (undeliverables), and insurance against competing offers mailed at or near the time you mail to the list.

Contact list brokers. Now that you have done your preliminary research, contact the brokers. Do not tell brokers which lists you think will best suit your campaign. Instead, describe your target market, send them a sample of your proposed package, and ask them to make recommendations. Not biasing the broker with your own preliminary research gives you the opportunity to get fresh, experienced insight from an outsider. Give brokers adequate time to do the professional job they want to do.

Construct a spectrum test of lists. Your testing program is one factor in your decision on the number of pieces to mail. In a spectrum test, lists are divided into three categories: those with closest affinity to your audience (the highest scores on the screening matrix), those with some affinity (midrange scores), and those with only speculative affinity (lower-range scores). Mail most heavily to the first group, less to the second, and even less to the third. Track your results to determine which categories produced the most responses and, therefore, deserve further mailings.

Decide whether to buy or rent lists. Most list owners will let you rent their lists one time only, and they seed their lists with decoy names to discover any breach of this agreement. List rentals are quoted on a per thousand basis. If you plan to do multiple mailings to the same lists, get discounts by renting the names for multiple use at the outset. Some large list compilers such as National Business Lists and Dun and Bradstreet sell you their names. This is an advantage only if you plan multiple mailings within a fairly short period, as the lists quickly become outdated.

Consider a merge/purge. In a merge/purge, tapes of house and outside lists are run against each other to eliminate duplicates, update addresses, and identify nixies. *SRDS* lists service bureaus that can provide this service, which is valuable if your mailing is large enough.

Finalize copy, design, and mailing strategy according to the types of lists used. Because you reach your market for continuing education programs through lists, base your decisions on the brochure, final package, and mailing strategy on your final list selections. Determine how to elicit responses from those well-qualified potential customers who are interested in your program or product but do not yet want to buy. Every response you get, buyer or not, becomes a name you can keep. The more names you capture from a mailing list, the fewer you need to rent in the future.

Order the lists. If you order lists on magnetic tape, you must specify net names, tape layout and/or sample format, and instructions for return of the tape to the owner. If you order labels, specify key code imprints (the codes you use for tracking results). You need a careful system that can keep all of this straight. Mailing houses can help you with these tasks for larger mailings.

Clear your mailing piece and date. Some list owners require that you submit a sample of the package you propose to mail to their list and that you request a mail date. Your contract and industry practice require that you mail that package on that date. Generally, however, this does not prove to be a problem in the marketing of continuing education programs.

Summary

Two simple principles underlie effective list selection and management: Your best customer is your present customer, and your best new customers are derived by cloning your present customers. Implementation of these principles requires a thorough enhancing, profiling, and analysis of your house list. You can then use that profile in shopping for the best outside lists. By following the guidelines presented in this chapter, you can choose and use lists to your maximum advantage—mailing as few pieces as possible to get the most responses.

14

Setting Up
a Production Schedule
and Checklist for
Direct-Mail Marketing

Robert G. Simerly

Scheduling production deadlines for direct-mail marketing is essential to the development of effective marketing plans. Brochures and catalogues must be mailed far enough in advance of events to give registrants the necessary time to arrange their schedules to attend. To accomplish this, it is necessary to schedule a deadline for each step of the production process. Exhibit 14.1 is a typical production schedule for direct-mail marketing. Such a production schedule can be adapted to different organizational settings by addition or deletion of tasks. This type of deadline planning sheet should be part of every continuing education program marketing plan.

Analysis of Tasks in Exhibit 14.1

Planning the production of a direct mail-marketing piece involves construction of a comprehensive time line encompassing all major tasks in the production process. Because such a production process comprises many separate tasks, it is necessary to base all deadlines on the day on which potential registrants should receive the advertising piece. The following step-by-step analysis corresponds directly to the schedule in Exhibit 14.1

1. *First draft of program copy completed.* Most program copy requires several revisions. It is important that the first draft be completed so that others have time to react to it. This first draft should contain all the components of a brochure discussed in Chapter Twelve.

Exhibit 14.1. Production Schedule for Direct-Mail Marketing of the Program "Leadership Strategies for Peak Performance," Program Date October 15.

	Deadline	Activity
1. ___	April 1	First draft of program copy completed.
2. ___	April 5	Copy reviewed by co-worker for critique, suggestions, and revisions.
3. ___	April 12	Program copy revised.
4. ___	April 12	Mailing labels ordered.
5. ___	April 14	Arrangements for labeling and mailing completed.
6. ___	April 19	Final copy approved by those who have input. All final revisions made. (*Note: no changes in copy allowed after this date except to correct typographical errors.*)
7. ___	April 20	Final copy to graphic designer.
8. ___	May 4	Graphic designer completes rough sketches, negotiates final design with program director, and sends copy to typesetter.
9. ___	May 8	Typeset copy returned to program director for proofreading.
10. ___	May 12	Galleys returned to typesetter for corrections.
11. ___	May 15	Corrected galleys returned to program director for final check.
12. ___	May 17	Final corrected galleys returned to typesetter.
13. ___	May 19	Typesetter returns all corrections to graphic designer.
14. ___	May 24	Graphic designer completes pasteup.
15. ___	May 26	Program director checks pasteup.
16. ___	May 28	Graphic designer makes corrections on pasteup.
17. ___	May 29	Pasteup sent to printer.
18. ___	June 7	Blueline to program director and graphic designer for final check.
19. ___	June 9	Blueline returned to printer.
20. ___	June 14	Brochures printed.
21. ___	June 15	Brochures delivered.
22. ___	June 28	Two weeks of wiggle room for unforeseen delays.
23. ___	June 30	Brochures labeled and sorted in mail room.
24. ___	July 1	Brochures dropped in mail for delivery.
25. ___	August 1	Brochures in mailboxes of prospective registrants. (For most programs the brochure should be received a minimum of ten to twelve weeks before the program.)

2. *Copy reviewed by co-worker for critique, suggestions, and revisions.* This outside perspective is important. The writer is so close to the content that he or she may overlook items others will catch. An ideal arrangement is for writers in the same office to review each other's copy.

3. *Program copy revised.* Schedule the necessary time to revise copy based on the suggestions of others. Copywriters find the "one-week rule" useful (see Chapter 12).

4. *Mailing labels ordered.* Because mailing labels must often be ordered from different sources, it is important at this point in the production schedule to define the mailing list, establish the number of names on the lists, and order mailing labels. This will also make it possible to complete the budget because this decision determines the number of items to be printed.

5. *Arrangements for labeling and mailing completed.* Particularly if you work with an outside mailing house, it is important to schedule labeling and mailing work far in advance so that you can obtain price quotes and reserve time

on their schedule. It is advisable to check with several places to get competitive bids.

6. *Final copy approved by those who have input.* Often, planning committees, other members in the department, or clients need to sign off on final copy. Warn these individuals that beyond a certain date, no changes can be made except to correct typographical errors. Any substantive changes after this point would delay the production process and add considerably to costs. Failure to establish this principle is one of the mistakes most often made in the production process. Copy should not be changed after it goes to the graphic designer.

7. *Final copy to graphic designer.* After the final copy is approved, it is sent to the graphic designer who chooses appropriate typefaces and arranges the copy and art work to communicate the message effectively. It is important at this step to have an in-depth discussion with the designer regarding the tone and image desired for the direct-mail piece. Emphasize that the direct-mail piece should enhance the image of the sponsoring organization and be so compelling that the addressee will pick it up, open it, and read the message.

8. *Graphic designer completes rough sketches, negotiates final design with program director, and sends copy to typesetter.* Depending on the length of the piece and the graphic designer's workload, several days to several weeks are needed to complete this step. Work out this deadline with the graphic designer in advance to avoid interference with other production deadlines.

9. *Typeset copy returned to program director for proofreading.* Typeset copy is usually returned in long sheets called "galleys." Several people should read the galleys for typographical errors. Some professional proofreaders read the copy once straight through to ensure that content has not been omitted; on the second reading, they begin at the end and read backward. In this way, they look only at words and do not read for sense. This makes it easier to catch spelling errors.

10. *Galleys returned to typesetter for corrections.* Theoretically, all typographical errors will have been caught by having several different people read the galleys.

11. *Corrected galleys returned to program director for final check.* The program director should do one final check for errors.

12. *Final corrected galleys returned to typesetter.* At this point, any additional corrections, if any, are made. If extensive corrections have not been made, it is safe to proceed to the pasteup stage at this point. If there are extensive corrections, however, another proofreading is advisable.

13. *Typesetter returns all corrections to graphic designer.* As just stated, in the absence of extensive corrections, the graphic designer usually proceeds to the pasteup.

14. *Graphic designer completes pasteup.* The pasteup is the first chance to see what the final piece will look like. Changes to the pasteup, except to correct typographical errors not previously caught, are very costly and time consuming.

15. *Program director checks pasteup.* Program directors keep much information on the subtleties of image, program tone, and audience in their

heads. This check is their opportunity to work with the graphic designer to make the final changes necessary to achieve the best possible marketing piece. Any changes made after this point have serious consequences for both the final price and the completion date of the product. Therefore, this check should be used to correct last-minute mistakes that may have occurred, not to initiate revisions.

16. *Graphic designer makes corrections on pasteup.* Invariably, corrections will need to be made after the initial pasteup. Sometimes the copy is too long to fit the available space. Although spelling errors should have been caught earlier in proofreading, some may have slipped by. The layout may also require alteration to present the best possible visual image.

17. *Pasteup sent to printer.* These production boards, or pasteups as they are usually called, are sent to the printer, who photographs them. Then begins the complex, technical work involved in converting the pasteup into the final printed product. Graphic designers are trained to prepare pasteups for transport to the printer. If the pasteup is not prepared properly, small sections can easily fall off the boards.

18. *Blueline to program director and graphic designer for final check.* Before proceeding to the final printing, it is wise to request a blueline from the printer. The blueline is a preliminary draft of the printed product, usually printed in light blue on cream-colored paper. (The terminology varies from printer to printer; some printers call this a "silverline," others a "brownline," and yet others "proof.") The program director and the graphic designer can check the quality of printing including the reproduction quality of all art work and photographs. Flaws in printing negatives will show up on the blueline and can be corrected before the actual printing job is run.

Bluelines represent the last opportunity to correct errors. In the light of time and cost considerations, however, only major errors should be corrected on the bluelines, for example, an incorrect program date.

19. *Blueline returned to printer.* The printer will ask the graphic designer and/or the program director to initial each page of the blueline, indicating acceptance of the quality and accuracy of the job. Initialing the blueline gives permission for the printing to proceed. Any errors on the final product are your responsibility not the printer's.

20. *Brochures printed.* Good printers can always tell you the day on which the job will be completed. This deadline is influenced by such variables as their workload, the complexity of the job, the necessity for machine or hand work (collating, stapling, or binding), the amount and quality of art work and photographs, and the condition in which the final production boards are submitted. Keep in mind that once printers have reserved time for your job in their production schedule, if you miss a deadline you lose your place in the production schedule and have to go to the end of the line. For example, if the final production boards are scheduled to be at the printer on Monday and they are not delivered until Friday, your printing job will most likely be delayed two weeks rather than the four days you were late. Why? Printers must keep their employees working; they cannot wait to receive your job.

When the printing is finished, a representative sample of the finished product should be checked for printing quality control. Never, in any circumstances, ship the brochures directly to a mail room for labeling and mailing until this quality control check has been made.

21. *Brochures delivered.* Depending on the size of the job, it may be more convenient to have the brochures delivered directly by the printer to the mailing center.

22. *Two weeks of wiggle room for unforeseen delays.* In almost all direct-mail campaigns, deadlines are missed because of unforeseen events. Therefore, include two weeks of wiggle room in the production schedule. Scheduling this wiggle room (at the end of the production process, rather than at the beginning), allows for maximum flexibility in adjusting deadlines as the various tasks proceed.

23. *Brochures labeled and sorted in mail room.* If the labeling and sorting are done in your office, you can control the time and plan deadlines accordingly. If you use a commercial mailing house, it is important that you work out these deadlines with them for separate mailings. Incidentally, many continuing education organizations find that it is almost always more cost effective, in mailings of more than 1,000 pieces, to use a commercial mailing house. Labeling machines can attach up to 30,000 labels an hour. In addition, postal regulations require that all bulk mailing pieces be bundled separately according to zip codes. Mailing houses are set up to handle these tasks in a quick and professional manner.

24. *Brochures dropped in mail for delivery.* The best advice is to work with your local postmaster to determine how fast the post office handling your work turns around large mailings. Professional direct-mail marketers often use the following guidelines for bulk mailings. Bulk mail addressed to people in your state takes an average of four to fourteen days to reach the addressee depending on the workloads at the post offices through which the mail must pass. Bulk mail addressed to people in your region takes an average of eight to twenty-one days for delivery. Bulk mail sent across country takes from fourteen to thirty days depending on workloads.

Therefore, for a national mailing, assume that it will take bulk mail thirty days to reach its destination, and schedule all production deadlines accordingly.

25. *Brochures in mailboxes of prospective registrants.* For most continuing education programs, a prospective registrant should receive the direct-mail piece ten to twelve weeks before the event. Develop a data base in your organization related to this issue. Some direct-mail pieces will require longer lead time for maximum marketing effectiveness; some will need less. If brochures arrive late, there must be a clear and defensible marketing reason. Failure to meet production deadlines is not a marketing reason. It is better to change the dates of a program than to fail to provide the necessary lead time for maximum marketing effectiveness.

Exhibit 14.2. Checklist for Brochures.

General Principles

_____ Is the brochure 8½ × 11 inches or larger?
_____ Does the entire graphic design have a boldness about it to attract the reader?
_____ Is white or light-colored paper used to increase readability?
_____ Do photographs or art work overlie printed copy, thereby decreasing readability?

Front Cover

_____ Is the front cover bold?
_____ Is the title large and eye catching?
_____ Is the sponsorship accurate and used effectively?
_____ Do the dates appear on the cover?
_____ Does the story begin on the cover or are teasers used effectively?
_____ Is there more than one reason to open the brochure and read the story? What are these reasons?

Introduction/Background

_____ Does the inside of the brochure begin with a background statement that provides useful information about why the program is being offered? Does this statement help set the tone for the entire program?
_____ Does the introduction/background provide a natural lead-in to the comprehensive description of the program content?

Who Should Attend?

_____ Is the list of who should attend the program realistic?
_____ If a Who Should Attend section is not used is there a compelling and logical reason to omit it?

Special Features

_____ Are special features clearly spelled out so that the reader does not have to infer what they are?
_____ Does this section appeal to a wide variety of motivational needs?
_____ If a Special Features section is not used, is there a compelling and logical reason to omit it?

Program Content

_____ Is there a comprehensive outline of program content?
_____ Is this outline displayed in a bold visual way?
_____ If appropriate have you included the statement "At This Program You Will Learn . . ."?
_____ Does the description of content emphasize the latest trends, findings, research, and issues?

Presenters' Biographies

_____ If the program has a small number of presenters, is there extensive biographical copy?
_____ Is the biographical copy concrete enough to legitimize the expertise of the presenters?

Exhibit 14.2. Checklist for Brochures, Cont'd.

Testimonials

_____ Have testimonials been considered for use in repeater programs?
_____ Are enough testimonials used to create a powerful message of support for the program?
_____ Do testimonials contain name, title, and institutional affiliation of the person making the statement?

General Information

_____ Have you included two easy ways to register—by phone and by mail?
_____ Are the time and location given so that people do not wonder where and when to show up?
_____ Is the information on fees correct and clear?
_____ Are the options of registering by credit card, being billed, or submitting a purchase order offered?
_____ Are the name and telephone number of the person to contact for additional information given? (This item should be boldly displayed.)
_____ Are registration times listed?
_____ Are beginning and ending times for the program stated?
_____ Is information about meals and other social events included?
_____ Is appropriate information about hotel reservations included?
_____ Are special tie-ins with airline and/or car rental agencies outlined?
_____ Is the refund policy clearly stated?
_____ Is there a clearly designed registration form?

Back Cover

_____ Is the back cover treated as valuable advertising space?
_____ Have the title, dates, and sponsorship for the program been listed boldly on the back cover?
_____ Is the back cover bold enough to invite the reader to pick up the brochure and read it?
_____ Has "boiler-plate" copy been included if appropriate?
_____ Has a routing box (where the recipient can list those people in his or her organization to whom the piece should be circulated) been included?

Mailing Label

_____ For brochures to be mailed to organizations, is there a routing box on the label?
_____ Is the correct return address listed? (Boldly displaying this address helps play up the name of the sponsoring institution.)
_____ Is the appropriate postal indicia printed on the brochure?
_____ Is an affirmative action statement, if appropriate, included (preferably at the bottom of the mailing label)?

Inside Design

_____ If inside header and footer headlines, which should almost always be used, are omitted, is there a clear and logical reason to do so?
_____ Does the copy tell a story and lead the reader in a logical way through the story?

Exhibit 14.2. Checklist for Brochures, Cont'd.

Tone

Is there a bright, upbeat tone to
_____ the brochure copy?
_____ the overall graphic design?
_____ the color of the printing?
_____ the color of the paper?
_____ the illustrations?

Use of Illustrations

_____ Do illustrations directly relate to the content of the program?
In illustrations of people, is there an appropriate balance of
_____ males and females?
_____ cultures and/or races?

Use of Color

_____ Is color used to enhance readability? (For example, yellow against white bleeds out and is very difficult to read.)

Type Style and Size

_____ Is the type easy to read?
_____ Is all type in a point size large enough so that people with bifocals can read it easily? (This is particularly important for general registration information which often is printed in type smaller than that used in the rest of the brochure.)

Paper Selection

_____ Is the quality of the paper appropriate to the overall quality represented by the program?
_____ Is the paper white or a light color so that printing shows up clearly and boldly? (*Note:* darker colored stock is almost always inappropriate for direct-mail marketing because it makes the type harder to read.)

Special Issues

_____ If you are awarding continuing education units have you included this information as an important part of the copy?
_____ If you are awarding certificates, have you included this information as part of the copy?

Mailing Format

_____ Have you mailed the brochure in its 8½ × 11-inch or larger format instead of folding it? [Brochures that arrive unfolded stand a better chance of attracting attention and being read.]

Computer Check

_____ Has a computer spelling check been run on all copy?
_____ Has *all* copy been printed double spaced before going to the graphic designer?

Exhibit 14.2. Checklist for Brochures, Cont'd.

_____ Have you arranged for electronic typesetting from your word processing package so that copy does not have to be rekeyed at the typesetters?

Final Check

_____ Are the dates correct? (Check one last time.)
_____ Does the entire brochure design and copy represent your best effort at creating an effective piece for direct-mail marketing? If not, make the necessary revisions.
_____ Have you gone through everything on this checklist and actually checked off each item?

A special note about computerized typesetting: The advent of sophisticated word-processing software for personal computers has made it possible to go directly from copy prepared by word processing to typesetting. Thus, the copy can be run through a computerized spelling check, transmitted to the typesetter, and returned in a form identical to that produced by your word processor. The middle step, keyboarding at the typesetter, is eliminated. Use a word-processing package compatible with your typesetter's equipment. It eliminates keystroke errors in typesetting, except for the occasional end-of-line hyphenation error, it saves time and provides at least twenty-four-hour turnaround on typesetting, and it cuts typesetting bills approximately in half. It is very easy to implement if you have not already done so.

Checklist for Effective Direct-Mail Pieces

Creating effective direct-mail pieces is a complex process. In addition to the production checklist, another checklist should also be used to highlight the components of brochure or catalogue copy. This checklist acts as a reminder. Exhibit 14.2 is a checklist designed for a direct-mail brochure. It refers to all the components of brochures analyzed in Chapter Twelve. It can easily be adapted to production of a catalogue. Items can be added or deleted according to the needs of the particular continuing education organization.

Summary

This chapter has attempted to provide (1) a comprehensive checklist for production planning related to direct-mail brochures and catalogues and (2) a comprehensive checklist related to important parts of brochure copy as discussed in Chapter Twelve. Each checklist can be adapted to meet the individual needs of a particular continuing education organization. Utilization of such checklists encourages staff to think strategically about the production planning process as well as the components of a brochure or catalogue for which copy must be written. This systematic planning and analysis lead to production of the best possible direct-mail pieces. Professional marketers always develop and use such checklists for all their direct-mail projects.

PART FOUR

Effective
Public Relations

Part Four is devoted to analysis of effective public relations as an integral part of a comprehensive marketing plan. In Chapter Fifteen, Dawn Marie Patterson discusses a wide variety of very practical approaches to public relations that have been used successfully in continuing education organizations throughout the United States. She shows how to meticulously plan public relations efforts and how this fits into a total marketing plan. A central theme of the chapter is that a public relations plan should parallel the organization's business plan. The steps are similar and, when these two issues are considered together, they create an important synergy that improves organizational effectiveness and success.

In Chapter Sixteen, Jerry W. Gilley describes how to attract free radio, television, newspaper, and magazine publicity. Included is a comprehensive list of possible events for continuing education publicity releases. He provides guidelines and a four-step strategy for attracting free publicity. Guidelines for creating news releases are provided along with suggestions on how to write an effective release. He also includes hints on how to attract an editor's attention to increase the chances your story will get published or aired without cost.

Mary Lindenstein Walshok is an expert in taking advantage of often overlooked publicity sources. In Chapter Seventeen, she provides a detailed analysis of how to do this. Central to success in this area is establishment of two-way communications between the organization and its many publics. She analyzes such important concepts as how to be a personal representative of program values, the importance of becoming an information and relationship broker, and the need to participate in the larger life of one's community. According to Walshok, "the most often overlooked public relations opportunities are ones which arise as a function of ongoing relationships among peers and professionals.''

Once public relations programs have been designed, it is important to track their success. In Chapter Eighteen, Joann Condino shows exactly how to go about this by illustrating why it is important to establish publicity as an interactive communication process. Her systematic, practical approach to tracking response to publicity provides many useful suggestions for continuing education professionals. She provides a detailed model for conducting telephone surveys as well as suggestions for tabulating the data so they can be easily utilized to improve the total marketing effort.

Part Four provides the continuing education professional with a detailed analysis of how to plan and execute effective public relations plans. At all times there is an emphasis on practical ideas along with a description of the benefits to be derived from implementing these ideas.

15

Developing an Overall Public Relations Plan and Budget

Dawn Marie Patterson

Public relations is an essential function in the total marketing plan. It may be thought of as advertising, image building, and the creation of goodwill. At times it is noncost visibility, but at other times it is a series of very expensive activities. Public relations planning is the responsibility of owners and managers of small businesses; of publicity chairpersons of professional associations; of officers of civic, cultural, fraternal, religious, or service clubs; and of leaders employed by nonprofit entities, such as museums, churches, hospitals, universities, and public schools. In a highly competitive, fluid, and changing economy, a comprehensive public relations plan is essential to accomplishment of the bottom-line purposes of most organizations.

There are many sound reasons for developing a comprehensive, cohesive communications plan for continuing education organizations. Among these are the changing world, increased competition, and the quest for clients, customers, members, or volunteers.

Although there are thousands of public relations professionals, there are thousands more who are managers, executives, administrators, and officers with public relations responsibilities. Many of these leaders have little or no experience in the appropriate methods for carrying out the tasks. This chapter provides an overview of public relations strategies written by and for those administrators, officers, or leaders who are not public relations experts. Yet these people must be the primary promoter, press agent, lobbyist, image shaper, opinion influencer, and public relations campaigner in addition to their many other responsibilities. This chapter is intended for those who have a very small or no support staff, but who want to achieve visibility for advancing their programs, products, and services in a highly productive manner.

Public relations represents an emerging professional field with an increasing number of descriptive publications about its philosophy, policies, practices, standards, activities, and placement in organizations. There are hundreds of terms and definitions of public relations in this growing body of literature. The public relations function is also called public affairs, public information, community relations, corporate communications, and customer relations.

No matter which term is used, public relations is an inevitable and constant activity in organizations. In a highly competitive, rapidly changing environment the public has opinions about organizations. As a result, each organization has a reputation or distinction within the community whether the organization is aware of it or not. If an institution has a strong, positive position in the community, public relations planning will be relatively easy. If this is not the case, the task of planning for effective public relations will be challenging. In any case, leaders in continuing education must take charge of their image. A strategy or plan will assist in influencing the collections of ideas or perceptions held by various observers. A plan also will help to meticulously groom positive impressions and direct public awareness to an organization's resources. The sooner leaders take command through an orchestrated strategy, the more positive objective and subjective impressions of the quality and desirability of an organization will evolve or emerge.

When a department, division, or facet of a parent institution designs a public relations plan, it is important for the continuing education unit to be a part of the institution's total public relations efforts. The public relations portrayal of a division is only as strong as the foundation provided by the entire organization. The parent institution will impact the philosophy, the policies, the procedures, as well as the magnitude of the budget under which public relations is conducted.

Often, implementation of a plan requires legal review or official authorization. Developing a successful public relations plan requires a thorough knowledge of the parent institution's policies, principles, standards, and practices for public relations. Many groups have "muzzle clauses" in their bylaws that prohibit university deans, hosptial administrators, or association chapter officers from conducting campaigns without approval. Find out if this is the case in your institution before designing a public relations plan. Know who must approve initiatives, plans, and statements before they are developed or released.

A democratic society requires factual publicity free of deception and, therefore, free from the threat of libel. A public relations philosophy and policies should coincide and be consistent with those of the parent institution or association. The quality of an organization as well as its commitment, determination, resources, support, and resourcefulness will determine its ultimate public relations plan.

Definition of Terms

Prior to development of a plan it is important to distinguish clearly the differences among advertising, marketing, and public relations. A good public relations plan includes all three of the following activities.

Marketing. Marketing is the broad concept that embraces paid advertising, good public relations, and an overall philosophy of competition in the marketplace to achieve goals. It includes the process of research or needs assessment where the data are used to devise the direction for planning. It is sales oriented to encourage consumers to purchase a product, program, or service.

Advertising. Advertising is a paid commercial activity where money is spent on services or products or bartered for specified public visibility in the mass media. A purchased message is usually printed or broadcast at the requested time in the appropriate medium that will reach a carefully targeted clientele. Direct mail is one form of advertising.

Public Relations. A subset of marketing, public relations is a complex series of tools, techniques, activities, and strategies that educate the public about an organization. It is a systematic approach toward garnering positive visibility of an organization's programs, products, or services in broadcast media, newspapers, billboards, bulletin boards, posters, bookmarks, and other media.

A public relations plan is successful when it employs a variety of approaches. Whenever people read, listen, or watch they receive data about an organization. Magazines, newsletters, professional journals, leaflets, and mail offer some dimension of information. Good public relations is also achieved through public speeches. It is achieved through personal contact—conversations and discussions at breakfasts, brunches, lunches, cocktails, buffets, and dinners. It is achieved through letters, telephone calls, recorded messages, videotapes, and slide shows. Effective public relations consists of getting the right message to the right public via the right medium at the right time so that they will purchase, join, participate, or contribute money, time, or energy to your programs and projects.

Public relations may be a relatively inexpensive activity to gain visibility for an organization through a number of noncost promotional techniques. It may also be a complex, costly, broad-based initiative with special events and a staff to support them. Either way, efficient and effective public relations requires a carefully planned strategy with activities appropriate to an organization's desired image.

The Public Relations Planning Process

Assumptions About Public Relations Planning. There are several helpful guidelines to follow in the development of a comprehensive public relations plan. Successful public relations is achieved through imagination, interest, initiative, commitment, and skill. A carefully orchestrated plan includes a variety of strategies and techniques that ethically and appropriately portray an organization's programs, products, services, or resources to the internal organization and to external groups.

No person knows an association, product, program, or service better than those who are part of its creation. The best public relations strategies emerge from the organization and its products, programs, and services. These must be of quality or they must be upgraded to be worthy of public visibility before any public relations plan can succeed.

The major elements of a public relations plan should constitute a subset of the institution's general business or strategic plan. A business plan includes in its formula (1) a mission statement, (2) policies, (3) long-term and short-term goals, (4) objectives, procedures, or activities to achieve goals that are listed in priority order with flexibility for implementation, (5) a time line or milestone chart, (6) a budget, and (7) evaluation criteria.

Analyze and Define the Continuing Education Organization's Role in the Parent Institution and in the Community. Answer the following questions to determine this role. What is your purpose, your business, the reason for being in your enterprise? Determine your position or strategy and what makes you different from your competitors. In what ways are your programs, products, or services unique? Use market research to point the way to the appropriate position and strategy for public relations.

Determine Your Goals. Goals will lead to strategies for accomplishing your public relations plan. Who are your special or unique audiences, clientele, or public segment for each facet of your activities? Why do people use or why do they not use your programs, products, and services? What is appealing about them? What makes you different from your competitors?

What is your institution's image in the community? What does each member of your staff think? What does the public think about your quality and standards? What do people believe and say about your institution? What is your reputation? What beliefs, attitudes, and impressions do different people express about your institution?

What image do you want to have in your community? What must be done internally to achieve that image? Identify how you want to be perceived. Then ensure that all of your activities and strategies help to shape public perception. How can publicity strategies contribute to your efforts to enhance a positive image?

Analyze the Heterogeneous Publics You Serve. Determine the profile of your ideal clients, whether they be customers, consumers, opinion shapers, patients, board members, stockholders, students, suppliers, or patrons. Most cities are becoming highly populated pluralistic communities. This is a nation of many nationalities and diverse cultural groups rooted in a variety of ethnic traditions, values, and motivations. Determine for all continuing education programs and services the ideal purchaser's characteristics or background. What are some of the precise characteristics of each group of people who would be interested? Are they men or women? How old are they? Where do they live? What are their incomes? What are their levels of education? What are their interests, ideals, attitudes, and values? What motivates them? What are their needs, their aspirations, their hopes, their fears?

What do they read? What do they watch? What do they listen to? Where do they go? What radio and television stations appeal to them? What newspapers, magazines, and newsletters do they read? What billboards do they drive past? Will they read a direct-mail piece such as a letter, brochure, or pamphlet? In what groups do they hold their memberships? What publications do they receive? Would they attend a special event? Identifying constituent groups through a variety of research strategies is a critical activity for your public relations plan. Chapter Three provides a detailed analysis of how to use demographic, psychographic, geographic, and behavioristic data to learn more about your market.

Identify Benefits to the Consumer. Determine answers to the question "What's in it for me?" In other words, how will your consumers live better, feel better, and achieve more? What will they gain for investing their money, time, themselves in you and your resources? What media organizations interact with the people and the groups you need to cultivate? Develop a list with correct names and titles of contacts who will assist your public relations effort and update it regularly.

Take sufficient time to focus on and answer the preceding questions and to do the research and data analysis that will serve as the basis for the public relations plan. It will determine the goals that lead you to your strategy. Then every activity, tool, and technique can be designed to contribute to the accomplishment of that plan.

Review the Long-Term and Short-Term Goals in Your Business Plan. Every well-managed organization should have some form of business plan or strategic plan. The public relations tactics should evolve from this overall plan. Be certain that the scope of aspirations is realistic. Are they within the organization's resources, capabilities, and the time available? Always have a fallback strategy. An organization's goals and objectives will logically lead to identifying public relations goals. What are your parent institution's strategic goals in view of the social, economic, political, and environmental trends in the local, regional, national, and international arena that influence your direction? Listed here are some possible goals your business plan might include:

1.   To increase sales by 5 percent over three years
2.   To increase profits by 1 percent over two years
3.   To increase internal support by having an increased allocation of $50,000

4. To increase community support through increased contributions of $100 from ten current members and to acquire fifteen new contributors
5. To increase membership by 5 percent over two years
6. To increase volunteer activities with three new or reorganized committees

With these specific, measurable goals in mind, it is possible to decide on specific public relations strategies for the continuing education organization. Several public relations strategies could be used to support these goals:

1. To increase media coverage with five published announcement articles per month through press releases to 100 newspapers
2. To be involved in one radio or television interview twice a year
3. To be quoted by radio talk show hosts or make a news program item once a month in the broadcast media
4. To conduct two major special events per year
5. To deliver one speech per month to civic or cultural organizations
6. To hold office or serve on the board of a high-visibility community group
7. To submit two feature articles for publication
8. To conduct news conferences for four activities
9. To offer a program in collaboration with five different groups who will jointly publicize the event

Having decided what you want to accomplish in public relations, who you want to reach, and how to get to them, the next step is to decide what *news* story the organization has to tell. Determine what constitutes human interest stories. Develop a file of ideas of an angle, a draw, a sales pitch, the particular focus that will attract editors, producers, broadcasters, writers, photographers, and publishers. Remember that the goal is a carefully planned strategy to attain free news media coverage for the continuing education organization.

Public Relations Planning, Tools, and Strategies

A number of generic activities or strategies should be considered in developing a public relations plan:

- Special events to attract the appropriate public to facilities, programs, products, and services
- Printed news releases about the achievements and activities of your staff
- Public speeches to civic, cultural, and social groups
- Feature articles in the print and broadcast media
- Press kits that describe the organization and are distributed at press conferences where the media are invited to hear a carefully organized, brief presentation, allowing reporters and broadcasters an opportunity to ask questions of the highest official related to the topic of the news conference
- Public service announcements on radio or television

- Membership and active participation in community, cultural, civic, religious, social, and fraternal groups
- Collaborative activities with appropriate organizations featuring jointly sponsored speakers, conferences, or programs.

The following list of types of public relations activities can help continuing education leaders as they consider the appropriate mix of activities to achieve their public relations plan.

1. Electronic media, commercial, or public broadcasts
    a. Computers
          On-line access
    b. Movies
    c. Networks
    d. Radio shows
    e. Slide shows
    f. Television shows
          i.   Cable
          ii. Commercial
          iii. Satellite
          iv. Microwave band
    g. Videotapes
    h. Video text monitors
2. News conferences
3. Press kits
4. Public gatherings
    a. Advisory committees
    b. Ceremonies
    c. Exhibitions
    d. Lectures and seminars
    e. Trade shows
5. Public service announcements
6. Publications
    a. Annual reports
    b. Books, brochures, and bulletins
    c. Calendars of events
    d. Catalogues
    e. Financial reports
    f. Handbooks
    g. Inserts in mailers
    h. Magazines
    i. Newsletters
7. Publicity releases
    a. Announcements
    b. Feature articles

      c.   Interviews
      d.   White papers
  8.   Speakers' bureau
  9.   Special events
 10.   Volunteer, support, and/or advisory groups

Special Events. Special events are centerpieces for publicity. They are an attempt to organize a unique occasion to gain recognition and attention for an organization. Whatever event is chosen, it is essential that it carry the appropriate message for the targeted audience. Every detail must be carefully planned and carried out. A news release may act as a medium for generating visibility in newspapers, in magazines, or in radio and television broadcasts.

      The following list shows the wide variety of types of special events that can be used to engage in effective public relations.

Anniversary celebrations

Announcement of a new personnel appointment or a new product, program, or service

Athletic competitions

Auctions

Awards

Balls

Bazaars

Benefits

Building openings, remodelings, or closings

Celebrity-hosted programs

Conferences

Contests

Contributions to fund-raising of other organizations such as public television stations

Dedications of rooms, art works, buildings, or major collections

Dinners

Displays

Donations

Exhibits

Fairs

Fund-raising campaigns and updates on achievements

Giveaways such as a product, program, or service

Holiday or seasonal tie-ins to programs or events

Lectures

Meals—breakfasts, brunches, lunches, cocktails, buffets for important constituent groups

Membership receptions

Open houses

Pageants

Parades

Personnel hirings, promotions, or retirements

Presentations

Previews or sampler events

Receptions

Rummage sales

Scholarships

Seminars

Speakers, authors, politicians

Sports events such as walk-a-thons and marathons

Symposiums

Testimonial dinners

Trade shows

Tours of homes, historical sites, and facilities

Volunteer recognition functions

Workshops

Special events require planning as well as follow-through on details, budget, timing, facilities, and location. The nature and scope of the event, the amount of planning time, the quality of planning, and the budget will determine the ultimate success or failure of any public relations project.

Press Releases. Having identified the event, its purpose, and whom you want to participate, prepare a press release. Work to develop sensitivity for newsworthy events. Try to imagine what the readers of newspapers and their editors find newsworthy. In addition to invitations, advertising, and brochures for the activity, plan to attempt to have a free announcement in the newspaper.

There is a distinct format for a press release. Farlow (1979) provides excellent examples of effective press releases. In addition, Jerry Gilley in Chapter Sixteen discusses how to write an effective news release. Learn the journalistic style and follow it meticulously. Typewrite a double-spaced, one-page crisp, coherent statement on 8½ × 11-inch unlined white paper. Use your official stationery or create a distinctive logo for your news releases. Be concise in your presentation. In the press release provide answers to these questions: Who? What? When? Where? Why? How? Be accurate in your factual statements. Always be truthful. Be meticulous with the spelling, syntax, and grammar. Avoid jargon, cliches, and scientific and technical language. The first paragraph should tell the essential facts. Succeeding paragraphs should amplify the details and stimulate interest, but could be eliminated without loss of essential information should an editor want only one paragraph. Include your address and the name and telephone number of the individual who can provide additional information or verification of the news release data.

Organize the press release according to the intent. Is it (1) a feature article? (2) a public service announcement? (3) a public affairs interview for television, radio, the newspaper, or a trade journal? In the preparation, define as precisely as possible the audience it is important to reach. Consult representatives of that audience for recommendations of strategies for communicating with them. What do they read, watch, or listen to for their information?

Get to know local editors and producers. Make yourself known to those key people in the media with whom it is essential to work. A formal announcement of your appointment, a letter of introduction, your business card with a suggestion of your areas of responsibility, and a follow-up phone call will be helpful in developing a productive rapport. Meticulously follow the format required by the newspaper, radio, or television station. Prepare all statements in the form acceptable to that particular medium.

Subscribe to the paper you appeal to for publicity and watch the programs on which you hope to be interviewed. Become familiar with the variety of special columns in each publication. Become familiar with the radio or television programs on the stations on which you hope you or your announcements will appear. At a minimum, work to get a line or paragraph in the special columns or pages created for announcements such as "Club News," "Community News," "The Calendar of Upcoming Events," "Religious News," "The Digest," "Weekly

Events," "the Society Column," which give information about meetings or people.

Develop a careful time line of planning to meet the publication or production deadline. All promised material must arrive on time. Clearly indicate the date when the information should be published. For example, indicate whether the press release is for immediate release or whether it can be published only after a certain date. Be available for a follow-up interview to the press release. In an interview, tell only what you want to see in print or hear on the air. Keep a file of all releases and track results. Use a clipping service or be organized to keep a record of results.

Constantly cultivate your contacts. Most newspapers receive more releases than they can possibly publish. Many groups compete for the limited space. If the editors are familiar with you and your organization, you may be more successful in having your releases run. Call or send a note of compliment to the person responsible for publishing or broadcasting your news. Thank them for their interest in your organization.

Feature Articles. Feature articles are anecdotal articles, accolades, or human interest stories that go beyond the news-oriented brief announcement press release. They may be more imaginative embellishments of announcements or they may be several-column multipage articles. In either case, they should provide the basic who, what, where, when, why, and how. Feature articles are not usually subject to the same time constraints as news articles.

Examples of items that can be turned into effective feature articles are an employee who has attained special prominence, a unique event or series of events or programs, and the assistance provided by your continuing education programs in community or economic development. The strategy is to call editors, columnists, or reporters or to send a brief letter describing the concept of the article and the audience to whom it would appeal. Include an offer to develop a longer article with a couple of photographs.

Press Conferences. When you have a particularly newsworthy item, you may want to call a press conference. This consists of inviting print and electronic media reporters to your facility. Usual reasons for a press conference are a major event and introduction of an important new program, project, product, or service. Press conferences are held because a news release will provide insufficient data, although a news release and/or an invitation may stimulate the curiosity of professional reporters and photographers to attend and have their questions answered. The location and the individuals who will participate should be carefully selected. Distribute press kits to reporters as they arrive.

Press Kits. A press kit is a packet or folder of carefully selected inserts that provide information, key ideas, personnel profiles, program or product descriptions, quotations, and photographs which may assist in the development of a reporter's story on the subject of the news conference. It also should contain a summary of all of the pertinent data that will be discussed at the press conference. Distribute the packets to those who attend. Mail or send by courier a press kit to those reporters who were unable to attend. They may still help publicize your event if the packet is well designed.

Speakers' Bureau. Work with members of staff, advisory, and volunteer committees to organize a speakers' bureau. Together generate a list of those in the group who could be interviewed, act as a speaker, or appear on a television or radio interview. List each person's expertise and various topic titles. Remember to include hobbies and avocational interests as well as professional expertise. Develop clever titles and eye-catching descriptions that highlight the attractiveness of speakers to community groups. Create a card or computer file by subject area. Maintain an updated brief resume on each speaker. Index only those staff members and volunteers who will give a credible presentation.

A public speaking opportunity allows staff to discuss an organization's philosophy, purposes, and programs. Identify your spokesperson by title. Develop a short adaptable slide show, viewgraphs, or a videotape that demonstrates the organization's ability to enhance the listeners' world. A speech provides a chance to demonstrate commitment to the community and give examples of how an organization fulfills each special audience's needs. If introduced as a representative of an organization, be certain to follow all the standard guidelines for knowing the audience and for delivering effective speeches.

A speaking engagement may also be an opportunity to learn how effective publicity is in reaching an audience. Usually, a member of the group will have an opinion about the quality of your products or programs. Take the opportunity to gain feedback, do some informal needs assessment, and develop contacts for other speaking engagements.

Having created a speakers' bureau, and knowing what you want to accomplish through speeches, identify the numerous organizations that create annual programs and are always seeking speakers. Be sure the content or subject matter is of interest or value to the audience. Some of these organizations are chambers of commerce and civic, social, service, cultural, fraternal, and professional organizations. Notify them of your staff's availability.

Broadcast Media Interviews. Another effective way to inform the general public about your unique resources is to arrange broadcast interviews. A quick review of commercial, cable, and educational television and radio schedules uncovers a broad range of local talk shows, public affairs programs, interviews, panel discussions, news programs, and other information-based programs. Nearly every listener or viewer wants to live better, achieve more, or learn something new. Interviews on these shows will help you demonstrate the way your continuing education programs can enhance people's existence. Television producers welcome film clips to expand your interview comments.

Public Service Announcements. Radio and television stations often run free public service announcements related to upcoming community events. Although there is no regulation requiring them to run these public service announcements, many of them do so as a means of providing service to the community. Public service announcements are very brief, factual statements thirty or sixty seconds long. They can be used to highlight your institution or special event. The statements are prepared like news releases. You can augment the television public service announcement with a slide or film clip. If you have access to broadcast-quality cameras, a brief videotape will enhance the effort. Public service announcements are rarely broadcast in prime time; however, they may reach the late-night or early-morning listener or viewer. In major urban areas, competition for public service announcements is strong. When one is broadcast, the return on investment makes the effort well worthwhile.

Membership and Leadership in Community Organizations. Every member of the staff should be involved in a variety of community activities and organizations. Create opportunities to represent your institution. Take leadership roles. Volunteer to serve on project committees, especially high-visibility ones. Have professional business cards printed and distribute them. Seek collaboration opportunities with appropriate groups to multiply publicity efforts. Participating in leadership of community organizations can be one of your most effective strategies for developing effective public relations.

Public Relations Plans for Difficult Situations

Every carefully designed public relations plan should have a policy for managing the press in critical circumstances. Inevitably in the life cycle of organizations, there occur emergencies, crises, or catastrophes that may elicit negative comments in the press. Occasionally, a story, misinformation, or rumors may be spread to the public. Such situations require very careful management. Therefore, public relations policies and procedures should include guidelines for managing such situations.

A previously agreed on set of policies and procedures will help staff to respond to inquiries by the press. Each staff member should know to whom a reporter should be directed for information concerning the organization. Prior to such an occasion, try to develop a list of potential issues that could pose problems. Then devise a meticulous response guide to those sensitive, potentially negative news topics.

The first principle is to remain calm and determine the appropriate positive steps that must be taken. There are some essentials in difficult situations: Determine who should be notified immediately when a disaster, emergency, or crisis occurs so that appropriate action may be initiated. Decide who will manage the situation and who will meet with the news media. Develop a log of facts and determine when it will be appropriate to comment. If necessary, be prepared to set up a news center for the media near the problem area, but not at the immediate scene so that reporters do not interfere with the emergency personnel efforts.

The Public Relations Budget

Once an ideal plan has been created and priorities have been established, a budget must be prepared for implementing the plan. It is important to emphasize that the plan should precede the budget. However, the realities of limited financial resources may force the plan to be divided into several phases for development. A list of preferred activities and their estimated costs will assist with the decisions. Publicity is rarely a free activity. It can be relatively inexpensive or it can be a major cost factor in a continuing education organization's fiscal plan. Whatever direction is chosen, a well-planned vigorous public relations campaign requires a budget. Publicity requires time, energy, and money. It is essential that good public relations be a daily concern and a daily activity with a return on investment related to bottom-line accountability. The type of plan devised will determine the budget. An organization's internal budgeting system will have a strong influence on format, time line, and magnitude of the budget. Budgeting is one of the most competitive elements in any organization. As public relations must compete with every other function within an organization, it is imperative to identify every individual in the system who may approve or veto the public relations line item. Cultivate their interests and be perpared to defend each cost in the budget proposal. The following list illustrates the items typically found in a comprehensive public relations budget. Use it as a guideline to develop a budget that meets the individual needs of your continuing education organization. You may need to omit or add line items to fit your individual requirements.

Personnel expenses
Consultant/agency to assist in devis-
    ing strategy based on hourly bill-
    ing costs per hour (This can be one
    of your most expensive costs.)
Clerical support
Entertainment/special event func-
    tions and discretionary meetings
Art work
Reproduction/photocopying
Office supplies
Publicity packets
Mailing list acquisitions
Typesetting

Printing costs
Mailing/postage
Communications/telephone
Travel
Equipment
Messenger service
Subscriptions
Clipping service/broadcast reports
Photographs
Miscellaneous/discretionary items
Contingency or inflation allowances
    of at least 10 percent
Indirect overhead charges

Always include an inflation factor in the budget. And always expect to revise the budget a number of times throughout the fiscal year. Monitor expenditures to ensure that all activities are within the planning projections to make certain the public relations plan is implemented across the entire year.

Budget preparation is a fundamental form of planning. It also functions to control plans. In all goal settings, cash flow determines public relations priorities and the ultimate quality of the implementation of the public relations plan.

Tap the Expertise of Your Staff. All members of the organization, whether in a line or a staff position, need to be aware of their responsibility for public relations. In their daily interactions within the organization and the community, all staff can be a force for goodwill. They determine what people experience in contacting your office. All people who interact with your continuing education office form an opinion of the organization based on the people with whom they interact. Therefore, participatory planning is essential for a successful public relations plan.

Sharpen everyone's nose for news and ask them to be alert for the story that will generate space in newspapers, in magazines, or on radio or television talk shows. Everyone, from the custodian to the chief executive officer, must be concerned with public relations. Every staff member has contact with a facet of the internal or external constituency. All staff members, by their actions, influence the public's perception and therefore all staff play an important role in creating the organization's reputation and image. Giving conscious, active attention to involvement of all staff in planning for effective public relations is an important part of the organization's total service orientation. Time and money must be set aside for the professional development of staff in these areas.

Subscribe to a Clipping Service. The clipping service acts as your third ear to monitor the success of your public relations efforts. Successful articles reflect the quality of writing, the time of release for distribution, and publication frequency. They may also serve as an early warning device for emerging problems, such as negative articles, editorials, or letters to the editor. Staff can also be helpful in monitoring print and broadcast success.

When your clipping service or the staff returns copies of favorable articles, make copies and circulate them to department directors and volunteers as examples for them to consider in developing additional publicity releases for their areas of responsibility. Send a copy of the published article with a letter of compliment to the individual who is the subject of the positive public relations. The sense of pride achieved through this simple courtesy may motivate others to contribute in similar positive ways to public relations efforts. Major clipping agencies are listed in the Resources at the end of this handbook.

Summary

Building internal political support for a public relations plan is essential. Participatory planning for strategies and angles will ensure the staff's commitment to the implementation of the plan. They will also recognize when adjustments need to be made or when opportunity suddenly appears. Keep them informed and working with you.

A plan must be implemented. Begin working with small items and build on each success. Innovation does not occur until the ideas are implemented and tested and the activities are visible to the appropriate publics.

Public relations is a vast, complex range of activities employed to influence the attitudes and actions of the public. Effective public relations is costly in energy and time. It can be inexpensive or expensive financially. Public relations involves risks. There is no certainty that any of these tools, techniques, or strategies will be effective in all geographic areas. Managers, administrators, and other organizational leaders responsible for making their continuing education organizations positively visible must constantly work alone and with their staff to use their imagination, intelligence, and energies to create and implement the best possible public relations plans. These strategies must be based on sound principles, practices, and procedures standard to those who are public relations professionals.

16

How to Attract Radio, Television, Newspaper, and Magazine Publicity

Jerry W. Gilley

Continuing education organizations, like individuals, develop a personality or image over time. The way a particular continuing education organization is perceived by the public is important because it helps determine consumer acceptance of the organization's programs or services. When consumers approve of an organization, they are more likely to purchase its programs or services; however, when consumers are indifferent to or dislike an organization, the opposite is true.

The image people have of an organization influences all aspects of its operation. Good relationships with the organization's publics—such as its employees, students, taxpayers, elected representatives, educators, and government agencies—are helpful in winning greater acceptance in the marketplace.

Good relationships with the public require much attention to detail as well as recognition of the importance of the needs of the various publics. The most common type of goodwill exchange is known as publicity. It often takes the form of a news story transmitted through a mass medium—newspaper, radio, television, magazine—at no charge. This creates a nonpersonal stimulation of demand for a program or service.

For our purpose, publicity is primarily a communications tool used to advance the marketing objectives of a continuing education organization. For the purpose of this discussion, note the following important differences between publicity and marketing (Kotler, 1986): (1) Publicity is primarily a communications tool, whereas marketing also includes need assessment, program development, pricing, and distribution. (2) Publicity seeks to influence attitudes, whereas marketing tries to elicit specific behaviors, such as purchasing, joining, or voting. (3) Publicity does not define the goals of the organization, whereas marketing is intimately involved in defining the business's mission, customers, and services.

Comparison of Publicity and Advertising

Although publicity and advertising are both transmitted via mass media, they are different in many respects. Advertising messages tend to be informative, persuasive, or both, whereas publicity messages are mainly informative. Advertisements for continuing education programs are usually designed to obtain registrants or responses. Communications through publicity, in comparison, are low-key and subdued. When advertising is used, the sponsor pays for the media time or space. In the case of publicity, an organization does not pay for the use of time or space. Communications through publicity usually are included as part of a general public service announcement, editorial, feature, or news story. Advertisements are usually separated from the broadcast programs or editorial portions of print media so that the audience or readers can easily recognize, accept, or ignore them.

Thus, communications through publicity may have greater credibility among consumers, as the presentation is often in the form of a news story and thus may appear more objective. Finally, paid advertising provides an organization with the opportunity to repeat the same messages as many times as desired. Publicity does not provide an opportunity for such repetition (Ferrell and Pride, 1982).

Types of Publicity

The news release is the tool most commonly used to generate publicity. It is usually a single page of typewritten copy containing fewer than 300 words. Additional information shown on a news release is the organization's name, address, phone number, and contact person. A widely used form of publicity is the feature article. A feature article is a longer manuscript, up to 3,000 words, that usually is prepared for a specific publication. A captioned photograph is the third kind of publicity. The fourth type is a press conference used to announce major news events. Media personnel are invited to a press conference and usually are provided with a package (press kit) containing written materials and photographs. Letters to the editor and editorials are also prepared and sent to newspapers and magazine publishers. Finally, the fifth kind of publicity comprises tapes and films that are distributed to broadcast stations in the hope that they will be aired.

Selection of the specific types of publicity to be used depends on a variety of factors, including the type of information to be presented, the characteristics of the target audience, the importance of the information, the receptivity of media personnel, the importance of the news item to the public, the amount of information to be presented, and the relationship of the organization with the media.

Publicity is especially useful for organizations that have a good story to tell but have too limited a budget to support large-scale advertising. Publicity tends to be the least utilized of the major marketing communications tools, although it has great potential for building awareness and preference with the public (Kotler, 1985). Kotler identifies four steps in the effective use of publicity: (1) to establish the objectives for publicity in support of the broader marketing objectives; (2) to select the publicity message and vehicles that would be most cost effective; (3) to implement the publicity plan by seeking the cooperation of media people and arranging planned events; (4) to evaluate the publicity results in terms of the number of exposures achieved, changes in awareness/comprehension/attitude in the target audience, and, ultimately, increases in usage by the various publics as well as an improved organizational image.

Publicity is often viewed as being underutilized in relationship to marketing. In many cases, publicity creates the kind of memorable impact on the public that other activities such as advertising cannot accomplish. As the organization does not pay for the space or the time, publicity can be viewed as a very cost-effective approach to image enhancement. The staff time needed to produce interesting and important news stories is, however, paid for by the organization, so publicity is not completely free. In comparison to advertising, however, it is an excellent value. Furthermore, publicity often possesses more credibility as news than as advertising.

Step 1: Establish the Objectives of Publicity. The effective utilization of publicity begins with identification of the objectives to be accomplished. Objectives are the things that the organization believes it can affect or change as a result of publicity. Schwartz (1983) has identified four primary objectives of publicity:

1. *To obtain a favorable image.* A large part of the publicity program in many organizations is designed to gain maximum coverage in newspapers, magazines, and other media. Press releases about new, improved, or modified services, programs, organization-expansion plans, personnel promotions, and social contributions to the community are sent to editors in an effort to obtain favorable mention. Remember that a good news story is often more effective than regular advertising because people are more inclined to believe statements that are not paid for.

2. *To humanize the organization.* To many consumers, large organizations seem aloof and too busy to care about them. To counteract this feeling of indifference, many large organizations sponsor an assortment of activities designed to convey the impression that they are just a large family of ordinary people.

3. *To counteract rumors or negative publicity.* On occasion, publicity campaigns are used to counteract rumors by clarifying the organization's position on an issue or to win support for its stand in a public controversy.

Positive publicity work may also be needed to offset negative publicity about some of the organization's operations. This is done by playing up the organization's positive contributions to the community.

4. *To be accepted as a good citizen.* Many organizations consider it in their best interest to develop community respect for the organization as a good citizen. To accomplish this objective, they encourage staff to participate in a variety of community activities. For example, they may encourage staff to run training programs for handicapped people or for the hard-core unemployed, to donate surplus products to charity, and to take the lead in various civic improvement projects.

Each of these objectives can best be accomplished if the publicity offered by the organization is newsworthy, credible, and personable. First, a news story is considered newsworthy if it is directed at the needs and interests of a specific audience within the community. In addition, it needs to be written in such a way that readers can easily identify with it. It is also considered newsworthy if it involves individuals to whom the community can relate. Second, stories that are interesting, thought provoking, and controversial are often viewed as more newsworthy than stories lacking these characteristics. Finally, publicity is presented in an editorial context. Therefore, news stories written about continuing education programs, services, and/or the people that offer them are viewed as highly credible. In other words, the readers believe the message being communicated and trust that the information is true in the same way they trust other news stories. One thing that is guaranteed to stimulate others' interest is appealing to their self-interest. Continuing education programs and services that promote personal happiness, health, professional development, family and/or other personal factors are going to command interest. Each of these characteristics must be accounted for in order for publicity to achieve its objectives.

Step 2: Choose the Publicity Messages and Vehicles. After selecting the most appropriate objectives, the organization must determine whether there are any interesting stories to tell about its programs and services. For example, suppose a university's continuing education division with low visibility adopts the objective of achieving more public recognition. The publicist will review the division's various components to see whether any natural stories exist. Do any staff have unusual backgrounds or are any of them working on unusual projects? Are unique courses being taught? Are any unusual students enrolled? Are any interesting events taking place at the continuing education center? Is there a story about the architecture, history, or aspirations of the division? Usually, a search along these lines will uncover many stories that can be fed to the press to create much more public recognition of the continuing education organization.

If the number of acceptable stories is insufficient, it is important to create newsworthy events. For example, the university could organize a major academic symposium/seminar featuring well-known speakers and arrange press conferences to promote the event. Listed here are some of the many events that can be used to create news for a continuing education organization.

> *Marketing developments*
> > New programs
> > New uses for old programs
> > Research developments
> > Large contracts or grants received
> > Successful bids
> > Special events
> *News of general interest*
> > Meetings of advisory boards
> > Anniversaries of the organization
> > Anniversaries of an invention
> > Holiday tie-ins to the organization's activities
> > Annual banquets and picnics
> > Pageants in which the firm participates
> > Special weeks, such as Continuing Education Week
> > Foundation meetings
> > Conferences and special meetings
> > Open houses to the community
> > Awards of merit to employees
> > Laying of a cornerstone
> > Opening of an exhibition
> *Personalities—names are news*
> > Visits by famous people
> > Accomplishments of individuals
> > Employees' promotions
> > Interviews with organization officials
> > Organization employees serving as judges for contests
> > Interviews with employees
> > Staff accomplishments
> *Slogans, symbols, endorsements*
> > Organization's slogan—its history and development
> > Creation of a slogan
> > Organization's trademark
> > Organization's name plate
> *Reports on current developments*
> > Reports of experiments
> > Reports on new discoveries
> > Speeches by program presenters
> > Analyses of economic conditions
> > Organization appointments

Step 3: Implement the Publicity Plan. To obtain the maximum benefit from publicity, an institution should create and maintain a systematic and continuous publicity program. An individual or a department within the organization should be assigned the responsibility of managing the program. This could be an administrator who is responsible for maintaining a linkage between the media and the division of continuing education, or, in a larger continuing education organization, it could be a director of marketing. This person should try to establish and maintain good working relationships with media personnel. Personal contact with editors, reporters, and other news personnel is often necessary to determine exactly how a publicity program can best be designed to attract the attention of the media.

Remember that media editors want interesting, well-written stories and easy access to sources of further information. Therefore, continuing education administrators assigned the responsibility of implementing the publicity plan should look at media editors as a market to satisfy so that, in turn, these editors will be inclined to use the stories they receive. Another important point is that media editors reject a considerable amount of publicity material because it lacks newsworthiness or is poorly written. Thus, the continuing education administrator responsible for publicity must establish policies or procedures to ensure that publicity releases are acceptable. The following guidelines (Govoni, Eng, and Galper, 1986) are sometimes helpful in achieving these goals.

1. Publicity releases should emphasize news aspects of programs or the organization and should be written with the specific medium's audience in mind.
2. Individuals writing publicity releases should respect the integrity and independence of the editorial decision process. No attempt should be made to sell a publicity story on the strength of the organization's advertising commitment to the media. Editors have strong negative reactions to suggestions that editorial space is owned by large advertisers.
3. Publicity people should be aware of and meet deadlines. Media schedules must be strictly adhered to.
4. Publicity people should keep up-to-date on the editor's policies and needs. This will require personal contact that should not be ignored.
5. Editors, like publicity directors, expect to receive fair and equitable treatment. When major stories are breaking, equal access is an appropriate doctrine to follow for building goodwill.
6. The development of positive media relations must be viewed as a long-term process. It is important to be persistent yet patient in dealings with the media. Concentrate on building a reputation for integrity and fair play with editorial staffs. Confidence, trust, and mutual respect constitute the cornerstone of effective media relations, and they are not achieved quickly.

An alternative to these guidelines is to send an editor a personal letter about new developments in your organization. This novel format can spark enthusiasm, whereas the traditional news release may appear routine and not be noticed.

Another approach is inviting a reporter to participate in one of your programs. When a reporter has the opportunity to test or use a program or service, interesting and positive coverage often results. It is unrealistic to expect positive coverage on the part of the media without making your program available for their review without cost.

It is also very important that continuing education professionals be able to write an effective news release—one that meets the standard of various media editors. Exhibit 16.1 provides much of the information needed for a well-written news release.

A well-written news release has five components: who, what, when, where, why, and how. In other words, the news release should provide the reader with all the essential information about the program or service offered by the continuing education organization. In addition, the name, title, address, and telephone number of the individual to call or write regarding the story should be provided. It is important to enclose the release date and dateline (that is, the city, state, and date of origin) with each news release. This information is vital to the editor and can make the difference in the ultimate decision to publish the information. Exhibit 16.1 is a model news release illustrating the six components: who, what, why, when, and how.

Step 4: Evaluate the Effectiveness of Publicity. A continuing education organization needs some way to measure the effectiveness of its publicity efforts. Publicity is often evaluated on the basis of how many inches of coverage are published or how many minutes are broadcast. To accomplish this, an organization can hire a clipping service, a firm that cuts out articles for print media and sends them to subscribers. This makes it possible to monitor print media to determine which releases are published. Measuring the effectiveness of broadcast news releases is more difficult. One way of handling this is to enclose a card with publicity releases and request that the station record its name and the dates when the news item is broadcast. As station personnel do not always return these cards, follow-up calls may be necessary.

Limitations to the Use of Publicity

Although publicity provides a significant financial advantage, it is not without limitations. For example, news stories are usually altered to comply with a publisher's space requirements or a broadcaster's time requirements. As a result, the most important part of a story may be deleted during the editing process. Publicity releases are used at times and in positions that are most convenient for the media. Thus, they may not effectively reach the audience for which they were intended. Finally, messages and stories presented must be perceived by the media as newsworthy. All too often, institutions present messages that fail to meet this qualification and, as a result, spend considerable time and effort trying to convince media personnel of the news value of their releases. This tends to reduce the credibility of the institution in the eyes of the media, and thus reduces the interest in using future releases. And finally, the most important thing to

Exhibit 16.1. News Release.

19 March
For Immediate Release
Contact: International Board of Standards
for Training, Performance, and
Instruction
6947 Highway 73
Evergreen, CO 80439
Tel.: (303) 670-1194

At Last! Definitive Performance Standards
for Instructor Competency

WHO WHEN WHY

IOWA CITY, Iowa — What do competent instructors do that incompetent ones don't do? After more than three years of development and validation, the International Board of Standards for Training, Performance, and Instruction has the answer. It is in the form of their latest publication *Instructor Competencies: The Standards*, a volume in which the Board has such confidence that it is advertised with the slogan "The Standards. Need we say more?"

The IBSTPI is a nonprofit, elected body of instructional professionals who have delved into the persistent problem of a lack of uniform standards for performance in the field of training and development.

WHAT

This new set of instructor competencies follows their first effort in the development of standards, *Instructional Design Competencies: The Standards*, a publication now in wide circulation. As with the earlier volume, *Instructor Competencies: The Standards* is not designed with any specific instructional context in mind, espousing instead a generic approach to the examination of effective instruction as observed across its many applications.

WHAT

All competencies concentrate on six key training functions: (1) evaluating the quality of training delivered, (2) identifying the professional development needs of current instructors on your staff, (3) developing job descriptions for instructor positions, (4) evaluating prospective candidates for instructor positions, (5) developing and/or selecting courses or curricula to train instructors, and (6) developing systematic approaches to delivering training to be used by instructors in the organizational setting.

WHAT

Fourteen core competency areas form the framework of the IBSTPI approach. They include such issues as preparing the instructional site, establishing and maintaining instructor credibility, and demonstrating effective questioning skills and techniques. Each of these broad core competency areas is then broken into observable, measurable performance events that together constitute a total picture of a trainee's grasp of the competency area.

WHAT HOW

A typical page in the durable loose-leaf manual clearly defines and explains the performance required for demonstrating a competency, the conditions under which performance would normally be observed, the specific behavior or set of behaviors required for competent performance, and a checklist of criteria for assessing a learner's attainment of the competency.

WHAT HOW

Other specialized checklists, for instance, for managers with institutional responsibility for instructional quality are also included in the manual. "In" terms and other forms of jargon have been carefully eliminated from the text to enable users from any instructional venue to deal successfully with the manual. A glossary of legitimate training terminology is, however, included for easy reference.

HOW

The team who participated in the development of *Instructor Competencies: The Standards* are seasoned members of the training community dedicated to sparing the training professional from the fate of the novice golfer whose head is so full of techniques and advice that he misses the ball all together. Although truly a comprehensive set of instructional performance competencies, this instructional program is first and foremost an approach that *itself* performs competently.

WHERE HOW

Instructor Competencies: The Standards is available from the International Board of Standards for Training, Performance, and Instruction.

remember regarding publicity is to be honest with respect to the value of the message and act accordingly.

Roles and Activities in Publicity

Today's continuing education professionals responsible for publicity play a variety of roles. Each of these roles is vital to the effectiveness of organizational publicity:

Press relations. The aim of press relations is to place newsworthy information into the news media to attract attention to a person, program, or service offered by the continuing education organization.

Lobbying. Lobbying is the effort to deal with legislators and government officials to defeat unwanted legislation and regulation and/or to promote wanted legislation and regulation.

Counseling. Counseling refers to providing general advice to the public and media about what is happening in the community and what can be done to address or effect change.

Continuing education professionals also perform two other essential activities related to publicity:

Program publicity. Program publicity involves various efforts to publicize specific programs and services through the news media to improve participation and the image of the organization.

Organization communications. This activity covers internal and external communications that direct attention to the organization.

Getting Published: An Overlooked and Underestimated Form of Publicity

Every month thousands of articles are published in trade and professional journals. Two fundamental types of articles are common—those written for practitioners and those written for research academies. Each type is a special form of publicity. Many continuing education professionals have discovered publishing of trade and journal articles as a form of publicity. The average article for practitioners is approximately three pages long. Most include the name of the author and the organization he or she represents. Some even include additional information regarding authors and their organizations. Now consider the cost of three full-page advertisements in the typical journal. At as little as $750 per advertisement, a journal article represents $2,250 worth of coverage. If a journal were to charge $1,500 per full-page advertisement, this would represent a $4,500 investment. Thus, getting published represents a major cost saving for the organization. In addition, published articles can enhance the image of the author as well as that of the organization and position each effectively in the marketplace.

Getting published, however, is more difficult than writing an article and submitting it. Most journals maintain an acceptance rate below 30% (Cabell, 1984). Therefore, it is important to develop a strategic approach to getting published. These ten steps will help:

1. *Establish a long-term strategy.* Such a strategy includes the type of article to be written, its purpose, and its importance to the literature.
2. *Target the manuscript.* Select a journal and determine its focus and the types of articles it most often accepts. Also determine the types of articles that have failed to appear recently. An article should be developed and written with this information in mind.
3. *Discuss the article with colleagues.* Do this prior to developing the article. Incorporate their suggestions and recommendations. If your article is similar to others, it may fail to maintain the newsworthiness necessary to get published.
4. *Call the editor and discuss your idea.* Also do this prior to developing and writing the article. It will help you to focus the article as well as determine the editor's level of interest. In addition, the editor will better remember the article when it arrives for consideration, which may be the edge you need to get published.
5. *Be willing to adjust.* Be willing to change an article to comply with editorial considerations and/or journal style. As long as the principal content remains, it is not essential that the article appear in its exact form.
6. *Research the journal style, intent, and purpose.* Such knowledge will enable you to write an article that is compatible with editorial policies.
7. *Obtain feedback from editors.* If an article is rejected, obtain a copy of the reviewer's comments. Getting published is a learning process, not a personal assault. The most important consideration is to learn the process.
8. *Contact the editor.* During the interview process it may be appropriate and necessary to contact the editor and discuss the idea further.
9. *Prepare a well-written and professional-looking cover letter.* Also send the manuscript in an attractive envelope and/or binder.
10. *Develop a professional and attractive manuscript.* Remember the product is your signature. Find out in advance the required manuscript style for submission to the journal.

Summary

Publicity can be communication in news story form. Such communication can be very effective in describing a continuing education organization and its programs and services. The most effective way of utilizing publicity is to develop a four-step strategy to (1) identify objectives, (2) select the message and the medium by which it is to be transmitted, (3) implement the publicity plan, and (4) evaluate the publicity results.

In today's competitive society, continuing education professionals must rely on every available resource to maintain their share of the market.

Publicity is one resource that does not require large capital expenditures. However, it does require skill in utilizing such publicity vehicles as written materials, audiovisual materials, organizational identity, speeches, and telephone information services. It also requires that continuing education professionals engage in a wide variety of activities such as press relations, lobbying, and counseling.

17

Developing Ongoing Relationships in the Community

Mary Lindenstein Walshok

An effective publicity and public relations program involves more than the strategic placement of news stories, announcements, and calendar items with appropriate media. It also involves creation of an image, an "aura" about the institution and its programs, a reputation among targeted constituencies for special qualities or services that result in greater visibility of and attention to the institution, even when it is not trying to sell or promote specific programs or services. In addition, an effective publicity and public relations program develops a context in which ongoing, two-way communications can take place, thereby enriching the program development process and providing feedback on how effectively the institution is achieving its goals and objectives. Publicity and public relations in support of excellent academic programs can build prestige and credibility so that word-of-mouth referrals and the general attitude or social climate of a community strongly favor participation in your institution's continuing education programs over those of a competitor. Such a market position means that the continuing educator has to worry less about "selling" and more about serving his or her various publics.

The achievement of this kind of market position, particularly for institutions providing professional or developmental continuing education rather than part-time degrees, is greatly enhanced by the ability of staff to participate collegially in a variety of contexts in which the institution's constituencies move. Such constituencies include users of services, such as clients or students, and important stakeholders in the services, such as leaders in business, professional associations, government, or even the parent institution. In addition, regulators such as campus faculty, certifying agencies, and legislators need to be considered. With all these groups, it is important to have ongoing relationships—relationships built around mutual substantive interests such as engineering, public school teaching, or the fine arts. These relationships should be built on a sense of ongoing colleagueship and professionalism rather than on contacts made only when a favor is needed or something specific needs promoting. These relationships should open up the continuing educator to sharing resources and doing favors as much as seeking resources and asking for favors.

One of the most underutilized public relations resources is the continuing educator himself or herself. Continuing education leaders can become visible, involved, and collaborative. They can manage personal time and energy as well as institutional resources in a manner that allows for a modicum of external involvement. Even a low-key person can function as an expert and a valued community resource. This, in turn, can have significant public relations value for the organization. We cannot all be Lee Iacocca but we can, in our own ways, be spokespersons among a variety of community constituencies for the ideas and services our organizations represent.

This chapter suggests three general strategies for achieving these results: (1) being a personal representative of program values, (2) being an information and relationship broker, and (3) participating in the larger life of one's community. Each can provide access to and exposure in social networks and publicity vehicles not typically utilized by continuing educators.

Personal Representative of Program Values

Leaders of continuing education organizations are in a unique position to help establish and clarify the market position and special value of their particular organizations by strategically positioning themselves within a cluster of special interests and skills both internal and external to their own institution. What that exact cluster is, is less important than development by the continuing education enterprise of a reputation for a certain kind of emphasis. It should become best known for something, some type of quality programming. Continuing education leaders can then identify with important program content issues as well as the qualities the program represents. For some institutions this means the provision of flexible, learner-responsive programs supported by student services highly sensitive to adults. In such a situation a leader might self-consciously become a spokesperson for the special needs of adults; a resource to the press and community organizations on setting up responsive services for adult students; an expert on the social and economic constraints affecting the learning choices of adults.

In one institution, continuing professional and developmental education may be the emphasis. In such a situation a leader may be a more active participant in the economic development interests of the community. Such a leader may be knowledgeable and articulate about labor market trends and employment shifts, about the economic and political factors influencing the job market, and as such may be quotable on these issues. The leader may need to be someone who can relate the existence of a highly trained and up-to-date labor force to the economic needs of the region and position continuing education programs as an essential component in the region's economic development strategy.

In still another situation, the continuing education program may have a significant liberal arts and humanities focus. In such a context, the dean's or director's public relations responsibilities would be as spokesperson for the value of the humanities throughout the life cycle, even in the execution of professional roles, because of the clarifying contributions he or she can make to understanding historical trends and cycles or ethical issues. Such leaders might make themselves available as a board member to local cultural and arts organizations, as a resource for speakers, or as a source of ideas for pockets of funding in support of programming in the arts and humanities.

It is difficult for any one person to penetrate every sector of the social and intellectual landscape surrounding continuing education. It is difficult for a single continuing education organization to be all things to all people unless it enjoys the size and diversity of a UCLA Extension or a New York University School of Continuing Education. In such large operations, half a dozen professional department directors may be functioning in separate communities of ideas and interests and positioning their programs as significant resources, with unique characteristics. However, the vast majority of continuing education enterprises are smaller in scale and often lack the breadth and depth of professional staff to move with ease in multiple communities. In these circumstances, leadership has to decide on an emphasis as a way both of drawing attention to the organization and of establishing a perception of strength and depth within the community of learners one is committed to serving.

Over time these emphases can change. One may spend a few years solidifying market position as a partner in economic development and then move on to strengthening programming and visibility in the liberal arts. However, the simultaneous execution of positioning in a variety of markets is difficult without a large staff because the time and energy required to develop a sense of colleagueship and to establish personal as well as institutional credibility are substantial.

What is being advocated here is a view of the professional continuing educator as a representative of more than the general needs and rights of adult learners. What is being advocated is locating the continuing education enterprise at the center of broader social and economic issues. This is a strategy for building legitimacy and support for our vocation as a whole, as well as a strategy for increasing the probabilities of success for specific programs. But, to any continuing educator concerned with the problem of building organizational credibility and building support for programs simultaneously, the community relations and public relations role leaders play may become an important responsibility.

Like the president of a college or university, the leader of a continuing education program has to play a combination of internal and external roles.

Why? The job of the continuing education leader, like that of the president, involves a continuous process of external resources acquisition and political support that occurs simultaneously with internal academic program planning and support of students and faculty. That is why in the next section I describe the role of the continuing educator as a broker. Increasingly, continuing educators must develop resources as well as academic service. What has been emphasized in this brief section is the significant spokesperson role leaders can play. Such a role not only positions the organization, it humanizes it. Potential students and supporters associate a real person, a person with ideas, values, and feelings, with the program. This both enhances the attractiveness of the program and highlights the benefits of being associated with it.

Information and Relationship Broker

Personal relationships are at the core of all contemporary business, political, technical, educational, and corporate enterprises. In fact, as the world becomes more complex and the futures of organizations are increasingly interdependent and affected by external forces, it can be argued that personal relationships have become more important rather than less important. Intimate knowledge of the needs, interests, resources, and special problems of potential clients, collaborators, financial underwriters, and political supporters greatly facilitates goal achievement. Goal achievement is not just a problem of internal planning and monitoring. It is dependent on fluctuations in the external environment. It may depend on the decisions of people who may not even be members of one's organization or direct beneficiaries of one's services or products. This is the reality of the highly institutionally interdependent character of modern life.

Thus, multilateral communications become the watchword of effective public relations. Continuing education leaders have a unique opportunity to position their organizations in a network of relationships. We must be able to think about ourselves professionally not simply as vessels for program planning and administration but also as brokers between the providers of knowledge and the users of knowledge. Building on the metaphor of broker, we must see ourselves as people who have feet in both worlds, who can work both sides of the street, who are equally at home in the world of ideas and the world of practice. Rather than seeing the continuing educator as the advocate for the adult student on the one hand, or as the champion for the parent institution on the other, the broker metaphor urges a definition of the continuing educator as a builder of relationships based on the knowledge, personal connections, and trust they have been able to foster in all partners in the educational transaction.

Active participation by such leaders in groups and organizations that are the potential beneficiaries or supporters of educational programs and services is an essential part of being a broker. Through such participation, ongoing communications are enhanced, access to significant gatekeepers—be they intellectual leaders, institutional decision makers, or resource managers—is fostered, and knowledge about how best to communicate and promote information on specific educational programs is acquired. In an environment where a professor can as easily provide a one-day topical workshop for an off-campus proprietary organization for a high fee as teach in a campus-based extension program or where an employer can as easily refer workers to one of a dozen providers of continuing engineering education on business communications, it is often the personal relationships that determine which decision that professor or that employer makes.

We as educators are fooling ourselves if we see everything as determined by price. We must not buy into the stereotype that professors go where they will get the most money or employers go where they will get the lowest fee. All of these issues are negotiable. The best continuing education reflects the strengths and resources of all participating parties in the educational relationship, and it is our job to bring all sides of the transaction into alignment. By facilitating these sorts of relationships and helping to design collaborative programs, we are actually building our business and our credibility. An example from the University of California, San Diego, may be appropriate here.

A few years ago, in reaction to an unsuccessful attempt by the city to attract a multimillion dollar computer company consortium to San Diego, the director of the city's Economic Development Corporation approached the chancellor of the University of California, San Diego, a campus prominent for its basic scientific research and links to high-technology enterprises. He was interested in the possibility of setting up an academic program in entrepreneurship to attract new businesses to San Diego and to foster indigenous new business development. The obstacles to developing such a program at the University of California, San Diego, were formidable, especially the degree program advocated by the Economic Development Corporation. UCSD possesses no school of management or business school, for example, and therefore had no on-campus faculty doing research or teaching on even remotely related topics. Other academic initiatives also precluded establishment of such a degree-related program on campus.

Nevertheless, the inclusion of the dean of the Extension Division in the early discussions allowed the initial idea to evolve into a rather different program achieving the same goals. Today, both the university and the community take great pride in this program. CONNECT, the UCSD Program in Technology and Entrepreneurship, is analogous to a small business development center, except it focuses on the development and nurturance of small, high-technology enterprises, places a significant emphasis on technology transfer and technical briefings for nontechnical business people (something UCSD *is* capable of doing), and receives no government funding. It provides courses, seminars, lecture series, a quarterly newsletter, and one-on-one advice to high-technology startups as well as to scientists and engineers with ideas they feel have commercial potential. It is partially funded by an annual $2,000 membership base of approximately 75 service companies, such as accounting, venture capital, and law firms, for whom new business development opportunities are tied to the growth of high technology in the San Diego region.

Many of CONNECT's one-day seminars receive underwriting from more prosperous high-technology companies and commercial real estate developers who are the more direct beneficiaries of this sort of supportive business education program. The program hosts an annual luncheon for its benefactors and beneficiaries and receives continuous news coverage as a result of its links to both cutting-edge research and new business successes. It is about to begin a year-long postbaccalaureate fellowship program for young adults interested in intensive exposure to small-business principles and practices prior to entering business or law school or securing a first job. This is to be financed through a proposed endowment to be established by a local entrepreneur.

The relationships and activities centered around CONNECT have resulted in major financial contributions to on-campus teaching and research programs in the sciences, and university faculty actively participate in the governance of the program even though it is entirely noncredit. The relationships built through the CONNECT program have also aided the Extension Division as a whole in generating corporate contributions to teacher education programs in science and mathematics and in securing on-site training contracts with important employers. The opening of Extension's downtown center was also partially underwritten by financial contributions from business service firms in accounting and finance, many of whose first involvement with the Extension Division had come through the CONNECT program.

This brief example illustrates the educational and organizational payoffs of functioning as a broker of ideas and relationships that can benefit the intellectual and research interests of an institution of higher education on the one side and the economic development or more practical concerns of the consumer on the other. Phil Nowlen of the University of Virginia's Continuing Education Program frequently talks about the importance of participating in the various conversations central to the university to learn the values that animate the institution and the pragmatic limits and opportunities that frame the life of the institution. These conversations occur within numerous subgroups in the larger community. Continuing educators who are contributors, not only to the conversations but to the clarifications of issues, the formulation of solutions to problems, and the negotiation of alliances and compromises among many interested parties, are building a solid social and financial foundation for their enterprise. As with the success of UCSD's CONNECT program, employers and community groups with education- or training-related needs or problems tend to come to UCSD before they approach other institutions. This is due in part to the fact they have had a good experience, trust the people who run the programs, and have an ongoing one-on-one relationship with them.

In more routine ways it is important for continuing educators to have ongoing involvement in such relevant associations as the Chamber of Commerce or Rotary. Professionals in charge of engineering programs should be involved with local professional engineering societies such as the American Electronics Association. Education programmers should be involved with professional teachers groups such as the Association of Teachers of Social Studies. Arts programmers should connect with local arts commissions. Such involvement creates opportunities for conversation, collegial relations, collaborative program development, and joint promotion. The personal relationships that develop from these interactions not only enhance public relations and promotion strategies but represent an important source of early information on new opportunities and emerging constituencies for learning. This involvement can also provide clues about how to price and fund programs. All of this information greatly increases the potential for program success which feeds on itself because people, and especially institutions, like to be associated with success.

There is another critical factor related to this issue which will be addressed in a separate section because it is such an underappreciated dimension of the work we must do to build visibility and support for our programs. It is reciprocity, which is tied to ongoing participation in the life of one's community. For the continuing educator this means both the larger life of the parent institution as well as the life of the town, city, or state.

Participation in the Larger Life of a Community

In the marketplace economy in which continuing educators find themselves, they must become involved in a wide range of community service activities, both because reciprocity is important in the service sector and because it is an essential business development strategy. Through such involvements, organizations as well as individuals become known, favors are exchanged, business collaborations evolve, and clients are referred. One must know how to raise and give money to others, not just how to get money for one's own programs. One must be able to share institutional resources in support of the community, not just solicit community support for education. One must share in the social and leisure activities of the community, not just expect the community to support arts and leisure activities on campus.

There are a number of specific examples of how continuing educators can be good citizens; one is participation in the life of the campus. Here, as everywhere, the role of the continuing educator as broker is central. Continuing education typically serves diverse constituencies. Again, I would like to cite an example from the University of California, San Diego.

For more than ten years the extension program has sponsored a membership-based educational program for retired persons known as the Institute for Continued Learning, which is modeled on the pioneering Institute for Retired Professionals at the New School for Social Research. Over the years, the UCSD program has grown to more than 350 members who spend a few hours each day participating in study groups, lecture programs, special field trips, study tours, and a variety of social activities. The group has also become a valued asset and public relations tool for the University's Extension Division because of its relationships with other campus entities. Members, primarily college graduates with fascinating career experiences in their backgrounds, audit campus classes. They are so appreciative of the faculty and conscientious about reading and written assignments that they have become a kind of cadre of goodwill ambassadors for adult learners and, as a consequence, for the Extension Division. Many have lived abroad and volunteer as English language tutors for the on-campus International Center, which serves 1,000 foreign students in undergraduate and graduate programs at UCSD. In addition, many volunteer to house foreign students who come to the University for shorter intensive language programs. Finally, as people with rich and varied career experiences, they are formal resources to the on-campus career planning and advising center and frequently help students with career information and contacts.

This reciprocity has built a lot of campus support for this group as well as benefited faculty and students. The CONNECT program, described earlier, is involved with the undergraduate student management society and the student entrepreneur club. Business leaders help get industry speakers for these organizations, hire them as student helpers in their programs, and arrange for student internships in industry.

In broader terms, continuing education organizations are in a position to advertise campus events of potential interest to adult students in their catalogue, thereby helping on-campus groups reach audiences. They can note relevant on-campus events and programs in more targeted newsletters, which are often published by extension units in disciplinary areas such as teacher education, engineering, or public policy. They can make a point of sharing guest speakers for continuing education programs with relevant campus units.

Participation in the community life off-campus is more diffuse but no less productive. Professionals in continuing education, particularly those involved in professional and developmental continuing education rather than part-time degree programs in traditional disciplines, need to be engaged in the communities and interest groups whose educational needs they wish to serve. This enables them to function as brokers in the manner described in the previous section. It also enables them to function as peers and colleagues with those individuals with whom they wish to work and for whom they can provide services and from whom they may solicit resources.

The tenor of the times is such that one does not want to be in the position of supplicant or dependent. The tenor of the times is such that guaranteed government funding and philanthropic support for adult and continuing education are seen as a less significant priority than early childhood education, improvement of the undergraduate curriculum, and augmentation of the engineering work force. Therefore, astute continuing educators must build their support base strategically. It is important both to the direct benefits and support in the community for program development and to the indirect benefits of external credibility in the face of frequently scarce campus resources.

Support comes only when the activities of continuing educators, the programs for which they are responsible, the institutional resources they are willing to share, and the social and psychic rewards they make possible are experienced by the community. Here are some examples to illustrate this point. Once again I call on the experience of my own institution, the University of California, San Diego. For many years, the Extension Division has run an educational program that represents an alternative to incarceration for first offenders apprehended for drinking while driving. The program represented hundreds of thousands of dollars in annual revenues to the Division, and though it had virtually no connection to on-campus activities, other Extension Division academic programs, or the larger life of the San Diego community in terms of health, public safety, or policy issues, it was sustained on the grounds that it was a "cash cow," making other less profitable Extension Division programs possible. A new vice-chancellor for academic affairs seriously questioned the appropriateness of such a program at the university, both because the "students" were in some sense involuntary participants and because the direct services provided had no relationship to campus or medical school research and no confirming evidence of effectiveness. There are some discussion of trying to extricate ourselves from the program and the various financial dependencies that had developed over the years.

Within the Extension Division, the decision was made not to extricate ourselves from the court school program but to deepen it intellectually and to expand our role within the community of practitioners. To this end a professional, for many years involved in the issue and the local community, was brought onto the staff to define a new direction and establish new linkages both with the on-campus research community and with the off-campus policy-making and practitioner community. What has evolved in recent years is a program of quarterly conferences aimed at bringing researchers and practitioners together on topical issues of significance in the field of alcoholism prevention and treatment. We now publish a quarterly journal, *Prevention File*, which communicates research findings and information on a variety of prevention and treatment issues to a readership of thousands.

There has been an infusion of federal funds in support of the dissemination of research findings from campus groups and regional medical centers outside the university. These are used for alcohol education in the schools and for a variety of community forums on alcohol issues. The director of the program is building a national reputation as a broker and serves on regional and national commissions, lectures at conferences, and leverages his on-campus resources and budget for numerous co-ventures. He is not just "selling" educational programs to an audience. He is involved in a continuous relationship—exchanging ideas, resource people, his professional time and energy, and the institutional and financial resources available to him with regional, state, and national organizations concerned with the issues his program is designed to serve. This broad-ranging participation has not only enhanced the intellectual and social credibility of the program, it has resulted in revenue increases.

Another brief example, this time from the liberal arts, may be useful. In a growing community such as San Diego, membership development and general social visibility constitute a continuous challenge for museums and performing arts groups. Education in the form of lectures, tours, and behind-the-scenes visits are often one strategy among many utilized by these groups to develop audiences, subscribers, and members. The problem for such groups is they usually lack the marketing staff, the publications development capacities, and the large mailing lists to reach the numbers of potential participants they would like to have. In contrast, colleges and universities often have these capacities but lack the array of more appealing experiences and services that capture the imagination of adults. Joint programming often results in greater success for both, because the community arts groups have access to appealing individuals and venues and because the campus has access to the adults who would be interested in such activities.

For these joint efforts to be established, however, there must exist opportunities for interaction between the professionals, the voluntary leadership involved in the cultural and arts organizations, and the continuing educator. If the continuing education professional is a member of a community arts commission or a symphony or museum board of directors, opportunities for collaboration are more likely to develop. Familiarity and trust make people more willing to try new things, to develop mutually beneficial alliances, to share scarce resources. They are also more willing to share joint credit for a job well done or joint responsibility for a failed effort. This is equally true in applied arts fields. Credentials in a relevant disciplinary field, participation in the relevant professional communities, and contributions through voluntary service, proposal writing, fund-raising, or resource sharing are often the secret to why some continuing education programs are so esteemed and successful while others struggle to meet minimum enrollments.

Many campus extension units bring well-known distinguished visiting lecturers to special programs such as symposia or topical lecture series on health, film, journalism, or the arts. Such guests often are very appealing to the broad community and the orchestration of community-hosted receptions or small lunches or dinners can be a meaningful way to facilitate town/gown interaction. Recently, on my own campus, we gave the local press club an opportunity to host a visiting Soviet journalist at a reception and facilitated a number of brunches and dinner parties in honor of visiting Extension Division lecturers such as the photographer Duane Michels, South African parliament member Helen Suzman, and novelist Lady Antonia Fraser. By this means, community leadership becomes involved in a very personal and satisfying way with the continuing education organization. Thus, leadership often can be a source of political clout, program referrals, and financial support for adult-oriented initiatives.

Participation of the sort described in this section is not just good citizenship. It is good business. In the service sector, of which we as continuing educators are a part, networking and reciprocity are critical components of business development. They are part of the culture of professionalism. Accountants, bankers, and attorneys have been quicker to pick up on this reciprocity than we have in continuing education. The advantages that accrue are both direct and indirect. In the process of community participation, one may serve with the president of a high-technology company, the superintendent of a school district, or a leader from the Hispanic community with whom relationships are built as equals around such a common area of concern as drug abuse or the viability of the symphony orchestra. These relationships can be called on at other times and for other purposes because of the credibility and trust established in the more neutral territory. The chief executive officer might be a resource in selling a contract for the provision of on-site educational services for engineers at a sister company. The school superintendent might exercise his or her influence in helping the university secure state funding for a special teacher education program. The Hispanic leader might be an ally in developing a marketing strategy for a new curriculum in communication skills for bilingual professionals.

What is critical is that the first contact with these people was not to ask for a favor or for cold support. Rather, the first contact was involvement in mutually engaging community affairs. In such circumstances the interaction grows out of an established relationship. It is within this context that advice and favors can more than likely be easily and gladly reciprocated down the road, because the relationship is not limited to the favor.

Summary

The most often overlooked public relations opportunities are those that arise as a function of ongoing relationships among peers and professionals. One does not need to have a large public relations staff or a personal public relations adviser and speech writer to be effective. Clearly, such professionals make significant contributions to press relations, the development of news stories, and special events that bring attention to the organization or individuals associated with it. Inches of news coverage is not an adequate measure of public relations effectiveness, however. Public relations should help raise people's awareness of the existence of a program, their ability to identify the distinguishing characteristics of the program, and their willingness to participate in some ways in that program.

The strategies discussed in this chapter can go a long way toward achieving that goal and can happen even without a formal public relations plan and professional staff. This is because they represent a means of locating a key person in a variety of social and institutional contexts that may yield dividends for the continuing education effort. These strategies are premised on the belief that personal relationships matter. Institutional credibility is based on positive, direct experience with the institution or a person who is a part of that institution. Continuing education leaders can become that positive symbol of the parent institution through the values they articulate, the ideas they contribute, the problems they help solve, and the contributions made and resources shared for non-self-serving purposes.

It is also important to emphasize that although personal charisma, speaking ability, and sociability can be helpful in this role, they are not the crucial qualities. Intellectual depth, clarity of vision, generosity of spirit, integrity, and a sense of humor are more significant attributes than force of personality in the execution of this part of the leadership role. With such attributes, continuing education leaders can become a valuable public relations resource, not only for their division but for the institution as a whole. They can achieve this position by (1) being a personal representative of program values, (2) being an information and relationship broker, and (3) participating in the larger life of their community.

18

Tracking the Results of Public Relations Efforts

Joann Condino

Traditionally, publicity has been an important promotional tool used by many types of organizations. Unfortunately, tracking the effectiveness of publicity use has not been an important priority for many managers. In most cases, success has been indicated simply by the continued existence of the organization. For example, success indicators have been the number of tickets sold for performances by a symphony, registrations recorded for training courses, or the number of patients enrolled in a particular health plan at a clinic. Although this tracking system is uncomplicated, it also lacks sophistication. The analysis usually indicates a causal relationship without the support of any hard data. Today, this type of rather unsophisticated analysis is referred to as "the bottom-line" approach, because participation is seen to equal degree of success. The analysis of publicity practices outlined in this chapter is not presented as unfeeling criticism of these practices. Rather, it is presented with full awareness that continuing education leaders are in a constant fight for survival. As a result, it is necessary to develop comprehensive strategic plans for effective publicity. In addition, such plans should contain systematic, reliable ways to track the effectiveness of publicity efforts.

This chapter discusses the problem and process of the tracking of publicity effectiveness in this new, expanded-use environment. The backdrop for this discussion is public relations in a market-oriented environment for continuing education organizations. The chapter will address the purpose of and need for a tracking system, the analysis of the data it provides, and finally the tracking tools.

A marketing plan, such as the one discussed in chapters Four and Five, is a partial articulation of the organization's strategic plan. The publicity plan translates and communicates these marketing objectives to the publics. Publicity planning includes (1) the definition of the publicity messages, (2) the choice of media, (3) the actual plan and execution or placement of the messages, (4) and the evaluation of the process—the tracking system.

Humorously, good publicity managers are often described as being able to walk on water. For a manager with this gift, every event is successful. As a result, the organization is usually in the news so much that the local papers appear to be its own newsletters. To explain this phenomenon, a colleague once asserted that "To walk on water, you have to know where the rocks are." My response was, "Of course you know where the rocks are. *You* put them there." Putting the rocks there is an important part of publicity efforts.

If you throw publicity randomly to many sources, without thinking of a plan, you may end up like the person who jumps in the ocean and quickly sinks to the bottom. A few key questions should be considered before taking the plunge. Where is my destination? How do I get there? What tools do I need? Will I be able to return? A plan is formulated and the "rocks" are laid. Thus, walking on water is no longer a magician's trick. Instead, it is a marketer's potential success story.

The plan must not only get you where you are going; it must allow for the return trek. In the world of marketing this means a tracking system. Planning is "making tracks" and the evaluation is thoughtfully retracing those steps.

Publicity must be an interactive communication process. Knowledge that a message has been sent is not sufficient. It is important to know (1) that the message has been received, (2) how it was received, and (3) what action, if any, it has caused. Initiating a publicity effort without a tracking mechanism is like sending a letter to a stranger requesting information but not including your return address and being angry when a response is not received.

For example, every year as a service to the community, an admissions office at a university in a large, metropolitan area publishes a full-page insertion in the daily newspapers entitled "An Open Letter to High School Students and Their Parents." The letter states the required preparatory courses for college. Is it a helpful letter? Does it help students better plan their high school curriculum? Who knows? How can you know if this letter is truly viewed as a beneficial service?

It would be possible for the admissions office to answer these questions by making a small change in design and content and, thus, providing a feedback mechanism. This could be in the form of a simple response coupon with the heading "We Want to Hear from You." When this format change was tried, much to the surprise of the skeptics, over 200 were returned per insertion. Many of the coupons included comments, such as "Thanks for giving me direction" and "Thanks for asking for my opinion." Teachers even responded with "Thanks for the reinforcement regarding course selection." The coupon also became a vehicle for requesting information about specific programs. These new respondents were then added to the admissions office's mailing list. In addition, an evaluation of applicants' transcripts over a four- or five-year period will provide hard data on changes in curriculum planning of high school students as a result of this effort.

Communication is a two-way process—sending and receiving informa-tion. Every publicity effort should be planned in such a way that it not only sends useful information to the public but also provides a method for receiving information in return. This feedback can help the institution evaluate promo-tional activities and, in addition, plan future promotional campaigns.

A Practical Approach to Tracking Response to Publicity

A Systematic Process. When the professional decides that communicating with the public and collecting response data are important priorities, a tracking system must be developed. The process involved in developing such a system can be described as follows:

1. Define your audience. Carve a slice from the big public pie and begin to define segments of your audience that can be studied and analyzed.
2. Establish tracking techniques for each publicity effort.
3. Develop a meaningful system for collecting responses. Log inquiries in a rational way that fits your particular needs, conditions, and environment.
4. Tabulate the results so that the data collected have meaning to the organiza-tion. Display the data graphically to facilitate their interpretation by your organization.

Each of these ideas is now discussed in detail.

1. *Define your audience: Use questions as tools.* Think about your many publics and what you want to ask them. Consider how you might engage in a typical daily conversation with them. The important questions are to be determined by you and should be formulated by your experience, your environ-ment, and the organization's objectives. Consider these suggestions:

*   What do you want the publics to tell you about themselves and your message? What is the anticipated response?
*   What message do they want to transmit? Are you prepared to receive the unexpected? How will you design your response vehicle to allow for all possible responses? Do you want all responses?
*   How will the data be collected? By whom?
*   What types of responses will be tabulated? How will they be tabulated?
*   How will the response data be communicated internally? To whom will the data be communicated?

2. *Devise tracking techniques.* Some sort of tracking technique has to be attached to your outgoing communication in order to receive an incoming response. Two techniques are especially useful: the mailed coupon and the tele-phone information line.

Coupons can serve as a response vehicle. They provide information on programs and services by functioning as minisurveys. Returned coupons also help build a mailing list.

For example, the Detroit Zoo has "$1 off admission" coupons printed at no cost in several regional travel magazines. These coupons, when used by zoo visitors, serve as a tracking device for tabulation purposes. As a different design, color, code, or message is used on coupons from different insertions, the effectiveness of the different magazine publicity vehicles can be determined. In addition, some coupons contain a special offer, such as a free map and/or future promotional brochures, to provide incentive and to ensure a higher response rate.

Another technique is to have the reader call an information number. Users of your service receive a free concert schedule, catalogue of course offerings, calendar, or additional information concerning office hours or other pertinent details. The call is greeted with a recorded message ending with the question, "Where did you get this phone number?" A telephone answering machine with record-a-call and counter capabilities is necessary. This mechanism tabulates only the number of calls the publicity effort generates. Although this system is effective as well as inexpensive, it has minimal appeal to the true market researcher because it leaves so many questions unasked. Caution must also be exercised in using the telephone answering machine. The public may be unhappy with such an impersonal greeting. Initially, however, organizations wanting to track publicity efforts are often unwilling to commit both the money and the human resources necessary to operate a fully staffed information telephone line.

An alternative plan that is a compromise between the answering machine and a real person is to staff the information line for a limited number of advertised hours, for example, mornings only. Data collection must begin somewhere. Although limited, the data generated by this system can provide enough ammunition to push the organization toward giving additional support to your department for a fully staffed telephone information line and more sophisticated research.

Establish a telephone information line to serve as a data collection center by using a designated phone number in all promotional materials. Operators receiving calls at this data collection center can administer a short survey; record information requests; mail the requested information; and register the caller for seminars or workshops, sell concert tickets, or accept museum memberships.

3. *Collect responses.* The data control center need not be an elaborate operation with state-of-the-art equipment. A data center can be as simple as a designated phone line answered by a trained receptionist, student, or volunteer. The individual answering the telephone information line must understand the specific goals of the service and be trained to effectively administer a telephone survey. If respondents are handled professionally and courteously, this system can provide an invaluable service by gathering information, tracking publicity efforts, and building a positive rapport with your publics. Experience will sharpen and develop the information-gathering system. There is no excuse for

not attempting data collection. Starting small and thinking big are more tolerable than thinking small and not acting.

4. *Analyze your data.* At the minimum, tabulate your responses for a specific period. To accomplish this, the publicity activities must be separated in time from all paid efforts. There must be an attempt to make them independent variables for the purpose of evaluation. Tabulation itself is not enough of an evaluation. More information can be gained by the use of a survey; an analysis of survey results provides a profile of the audience you have attracted. A well-designed survey indicates the effectiveness of publicity vehicles, but cautious evaluation of the survey results is necessary. It is important to realize that the survey provides only indicators and that responses do not ensure expected behavior.

Effective use of graphs and charts to explain the data helps everyone to visualize the effect of publicity. Any response rate traced over time becomes a valuable factor in the strategic planning process of an organization. Obviously, if one publicity effort produces more phone calls or coupons than another, it should be considered as part of your advertising mix. In a sense, effective publicity planning, tracking, and evaluation can serve as a test market tool providing feedback before an organization enters into a multidollar advertising campaign.

A Case Study

This case study illustrates the important elements in a publicity tracking process. The event to be promoted is a training seminar to be given on January 22. Discussion will center on (1) the promotion time line, (2) the tracking and collection of inquiries, and (3) analysis of the data through the tabulation and graphic display of the inquiries.

Promotion Time Line. The time frame is a sixteen-week period including the months of October, November, December, and January. The promotional activities occur in the following order:

Activity 1   A paid advertising effort in the form of a direct-mail bro-chure is delivered to households during Week 3.

Activity 2   The first publicity effort is news releases, which appear in the print media during Week 10.

Activity 3   The second publicity effort is feature stories, which appear in the print media during Week 11.

Activity 4   The third publicity effort is public service announcements, which are aired during Week 12 on local radio stations.

The time separation between paid and unpaid effort has been exaggerated slightly to state the case for adequate time separation between promotional efforts. Separation of this sort makes it possible to suggest some causal relationship between publicity effort and response. Although there is very little control as to when a publicity effort will appear in the media, the continuing education professional is in control of the dissemination of the message whether it is paid or unpaid. Because there is little control over when the message will be printed by the media, special attention should be paid to determining when publicity communications will be sent to the appropriate channels. Make sure sufficient time is allowed to meet the demands of publication and insertion deadlines. In this case study, the time line presents an ideal situation. In practice, the suggestion is simply to attempt to separate in time the paid from the unpaid efforts so that the tracking of the responses provides some indication of effect.

Collection Method. The tracking technique in this example is the telephone information line. A single telephone should be designated in all promotional efforts to call for information on this seminar. The telephone information line provides an excellent opportunity to administer a short survey. The survey formalizes the collection of information, and its use as a research vehicle provides for consistent data collection over time. The collection of response data is not an empty exercise to be completed in isolation for each event, course, or campaign. Careful collection over time provides a historical picture of responses to your organization's communications. It enables you to more effectively plan future program development.

The design of the survey is important. Random information is of little value. By determining objectives before you initiate the survey and by carefully wording the questions, you can ensure that the information gathered will be useful to the present plan as well as future promotions.

The telephone survey consists of five important sections:

1. The date on which the call is made is critical to separation of publicity efforts. If calls are clustered, no significant variation will appear.
2. The demographic information provides mailing list data and can provide data for further tracking.
3. The type of request determines how the respondent has reacted to your messages. For example, the caller may wish to register or may simply want more information.
4. The survey questions have the primary function of determining which publicity or advertising activity created the response.
5. The instructions to operators regarding the interview process ensure standardization of the resulting data.

Exhibit 18.1 is an example of an effective telephone survey instrument.

The survey attempts to measure recognition and recall of your publicity message, method, and medium. Keep in mind that telephone surveys must be short. The sample survey assumes that the caller's first response will be the best, that is, a response elicited without any prompting by the operator. Such an answer has more value than one given after a response cue. The questions you write will determine the type of response. Therefore, formulate them carefully. Consult the many excellent books on survey design formats and question construction techniques before designing your own survey (Cook and Campbell, 1979; Converse and Presser, 1986).

As shown in Exhibit 18.1, the caller is asked to give the name of the publication or radio/television channel where the publicity was encountered. If the caller does not remember where he or she saw or heard the publicity, the operator is instructed to read the list of possible sources to prompt a response. To ensure the accuracy of the data, the list must include all possible sources. In addition, by including the category "Other," you are prepared to receive a message that may not have been anticipated. Though these answers are more difficult to tabulate, they may be significant identifying options that should have been considered in the original survey.

Take advantage of the opportunity to solicit information regarding your public image. This section of the survey can be used to measure the attitudinal or affective impact of your promotional campaign. A variety of closed-ended questions are available for recording survey responses (Kotler, 1985).

1. The amount of agreement/disagreement (Likert scale). For example, "Larger hospitals generally provide more state-of-the-art care than smaller hospitals." Agreement/disagreement is measured on a 1 to 5 scale.
2. The degree of importance of an attribute (importance scale). For example, "For me, attending a performance by a well-known performer is. . . ." Degree of importance is then measured on a 1 to 5 scale.
3. The rating of an attribute (a rating scale). For example, "Wayne State University's professional development courses are. . . ." Degree of excellence is rated on a 5-point scale.

Tabulation of the Data. Tabulation of responses is more than simply counting. A common error made in the analysis of such responses is to aggregate data over too long a period. This can distort or hide important trends in the data. Compare Tables 18.1 and 18.2.

Table 18.1 summarizes all the calls received in each of the months of a hypothetical promotional campaign. Let us say that publicity activities occurred during the third week in April and during the fourth week in May. Table 18.1 indicates that neither activity influenced the number of calls received. In contrast, Table 18.2, which tabulates the calls received weekly for the same three-month period, shows the same total number of calls but tells a different story. Clearly, the publicity efforts have had a major impact on the number of responses received. Table 18.2 also indicates that their effect dissipated rapidly. By choosing the proper period of aggregation, the ambiguous data in Table 18.1 became strategic information to be considered in the planning process.

Rather than tabulate the data, you can display the number of calls received per time period graphically. Figures 18.1 and 18.2 are bar charts of the same information presented in Tables 18.1 and 18.2. Again, Figure 18.1 shows no

Exhibit 18.1. Design for Telephone Survey.

DATE _____   SURVEY _____

Information Line Survey

Demographic section

Name _____

Address _____

City _____ State ____ Zip _____

Phone _____ (D) _____ (E)

Action requested

Registration _____

Mail Information ⌐

Type(s) requested

Do you want to be on our mailing list?   Yes _____   No _____

Would you assist us in our marketing research by answering nine short questions?   Yes _____   No _____

Question 1   *How Did You Get This Number?*

┌─ *Instructions to phone operator* ──────────────────
If response is immediate, go to the next question.

If necessary, probe for response by reading list provided.

Note: a. Newspaper ____ (continue with Q 2)
List   b. Magazine ____ (continue with Q 4)
all   c. Radio ____ (continue with Q 6)
possible   d. TV ____ (continue with Q 8)
sources   e. Friend ____ _____
         f. Other ____ _____

Question 2   *Which Newspaper(s)?*

┌─ *Instructions* ──
If response is immediate, go to Q 3. If not, probe for response by reading list.

Note: For example: **Question 3**   *In what form was it?*
List   a. Detroit News ____   a. Feature story
all   b. Detroit Free Press ____   b. Community calendar ____
sources   c. Observer Eccentric ____   c. News item ____
         d. Unspecified ____   d. Other _____

Question 4   *Which Magazine(s)?*

┌─ *Instructions* ──
If response is immediate, go to Q 5. If not, probe for response by reading list.

Note: a. Detroit Monthly ____   **Question 5**   *In what form was it?*
List all   b. Metro Detroit ____   a. Feature story
sources   c. Other _____   b. Community calendar ____
                             c. Unspecified ____

Question 6   *Which Radio Station(s)?*

┌─ *Instructions* ──
If response is immediate, go to Q 7. If not, probe for response by reading list.

Note: a. WHYT ____   **Question 7**   *In what form was it?*
List   b. WJLB ____   a. Public service announcement ____
all   c. WWJ ____   b. Talk show ____
sources   d. WJBK ____   c. Unspecified ____
         e. Unspecified ____

Question 8   *Which TV Station(s)?*

┌─ *Instructions* ──
If response is immediate, go to Q 9. If not, probe for response by reading list.

Note: a. Ch 7 ____   **Question 9**   *In what form was it?*
List all   b. Ch 9 ____   a. Commercial ____
sources   c. PBS ____   b. Interview ____
                           c. News show ____

**Table 18.1. Number of Calls
Received per Month.**

April	30
May	30
June	30
Total	90

**Table 18.2. Number of Calls
Received per Week.**

April	1	5
	2	0
	3	0
	4	25
May	1	25
	2	5
	3	0
	4	0
June	1	30
	2	0
	3	0
	4	0
Total		90

Figure 18.1. Number of Calls by Month.

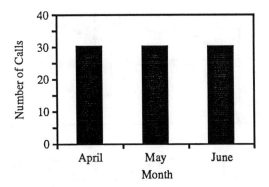

Aggregation of responses by month hides the
impact of marketing activities in April and May.

Figure 18.2. Number of Calls by Week.

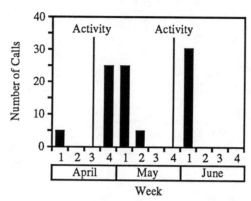

Aggregation of responses by week shows the
impact of marketing activities in April and May.

Figure 18.3. Number of Calls and Registrations per Week.

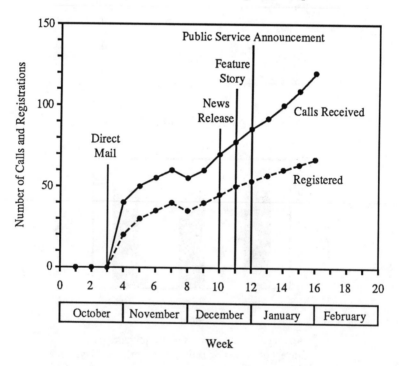

This plot shows two types of responses to four different marketing
activities.

Figure 18.4. Responses to Types of Publicity.

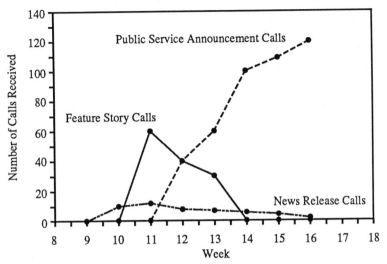

Responses are tracked by week and by type of marketing effort.

effects from the two publicity activities that occurred. Figure 18.2, however, where the horizontal axis reflects weeks rather than months, clearly indicates the effectiveness of publicity activities.

To return to our case, Figure 18.3 is a line graph of results obtained from the telephone information survey. The line graph indicates a functional relationship between two variables. The variable on the horizontal axis is weeks, and the frequency variables displayed on the vertical axis are the calls and registrations. The lines parallel to the vertical axis indicate an intervention or publicity activity (McBurney, 1983). This graph would be uninterpretable if the data were displayed by months rather than by weeks.

Breaking out or disaggregating the data graphically, as shown in Figure 18.4, further translates the data collected into miniprofiles. This line graph depicts the effect of the particular activity on the frequency of calls during the specific time frame of Weeks 9 to 16. Figure 18.4 indicates that the number of calls produced by public service announcements grew consistently during Weeks 9 to 16. Initially, the feature story appeared to be a strong vehicle; however, its effect quickly dissipated. The news releases produced the same low level of calls throughout the time frame.

Summary

Publicity performs a vital function within the continuing education organization. Publicity messages and vehicles must be planned and then evaluated through an effective tracking and collection system. A tracking system allows the continuing education professional to perform as a player, observe like a spectator, and evaluate as a coach–analyst in the promotion process. With this global perspective, and armed with the ability to constantly interpret the messages from the environment, the tracking of publicity will become an important part of your total marketing efforts.

PART FIVE

Effective Advertising

Part Five deals with effective advertising. Katherine Livingston Allen begins with Chapter Nineteen, which is devoted to development of an overall advertising plan and budget. She identifies ten key steps that should be followed to ensure maximum results from advertising and provides a detailed analysis of each step with practical illustrations. She also describes five ways to determine appropriate spending levels for advertising and shows how spending money on advertising is always cost effective as long as the expenditure is less than the revenue it generates.

In Chapter Twenty, Deanna Maneker presents a step-by-step process for design and layout of newspaper and magazine ads for continuing education programs. Included is a detailed analysis of when to use newspaper versus magazine ads and how to weigh the benefits of each. She also provides practical ideas on choosing your design emphasis in an ad, using color in the design, making the decision to use a photograph or illustration, and choosing type size and style. Her chapter emphasizes the necessity of using layout and design in ads to promote the natural synergy with other marketing tools.

In Chapter Twenty-One, Robert G. Simerly identifies eight principles of successful advertising copy writing. These eight principles are illustrated with examples and suggestions from a wide variety of continuing education organizations. In addition, a checklist of items to include in direct-mail brochures is provided as a handy reference. A central theme in the chapter is that people register for continuing education programs to fulfill their unmet needs. Therefore, to be most effective, advertising copy must be written so that it concretely demonstrates how people can fulfill these needs by accepting the direct-mail offer and registering for your continuing education program.

Often, continuing education organizations find it helpful to work with a professional advertising agency to meet some, if not all, of their advertising needs. In Chapter Twenty-Two, Chuck Buck, an agency professional, gives practical advice on how to do this effectively. He addresses such important issues as (1) how to determine what kinds of services you will require from an agency, (2) how to evaluate the relative costs of these services, and (3) how to determine with an agency how success for projects will be measured. He also presents a complete analysis of the pitfalls to avoid when working with an agency. As an agency professional with extensive experience with continuing education organizations, his advice proves to be helpful and practical in considering the advantages and disadvantages of seeking the help of an advertising agency.

Chapter Twenty-Three, by Maris St. Cyr, is devoted to the tracking of advertising results. She provides hints on how to code ads for tracking and how to maintain charts to tally responses. She considers the special techniques of tracking telephone responses to advertising and how this can prove to be an excellent source of information about consumers. In addition, she illustrates how to track the results of broadcast media, and how to organize and display the analysis of conversion information so that it can be most helpful in improving advertising campaigns. A checklist for tracking is included at the end of the chapter.

Thus, Part Five builds on the previous sections of the handbook by analyzing a wide variety of issues important to success in advertising. The chapter authors, all with many years of professional experience in advertising continuing education programs, collectively present a comprehensive overview of the most important principles, guidelines, and tips for you to consider.

19

Developing an Overall Advertising Plan and Budget

Katherine Livingston Allen

This chapter concentrates on the placement of advertisements in print and electronic media. An advertisement can be distinguished from other forms of promotion in that it is considered nonpersonal mass communication, paid for and placed in various media by an identified sponsor who seeks to inform or persuade a particular audience about a product, service, or idea (Dunn and Barban, 1986; Nylen, 1986). In the field of continuing education, advertising is typically utilized in two important ways: (1) as institutional advertising that promotes the organization as a whole and (2) as product advertising that focuses on individual programs or courses of study. A series of ads may appear as part of a unified campaign, or individual ads may be run on a limited basis in selected media.

The primary goal of these types of advertisements is simply to communicate. It is rare that an advertisement alone can influence a prospect enough to make an actual purchase (Ray, 1982). Because of this weakness, advertisements are often considered less cost effective than other forms of advertising such as direct mail (Suleiman, 1982). Moreover, ads are usually viewed as useful in generating inquiries, but not necessarily helpful in securing direct registrations. The production and placement of advertisements, especially in large urban newspapers or national magazines, can also be expensive.

Many people think that the planning of an advertisement or an advertising campaign begins with the creation of a brilliant headline. It doesn't. In fact, an advertisement represents only the tip of the iceberg (Dunn and Barban, 1986), that tiny portion of the entire advertising planning process that is visible to the consumer. What the consumer does not see, of course, are the many steps an advertiser must go through to facilitate the creation of that dazzling headline.

This chapter, then, illustrates how continuing educators can, through careful planning, maximize the results of their advertisements.

The Planning Process

Whether you intend to do your own advertising or to employ the services of an outside agency, ten key steps should be followed to ensure maximum results from advertising:

1. Develop an understanding of the overall mission and goals of the organization.
2. Analyze the product, the consumer, the marketplace, and the competition.
3. Define advertising objectives.
4. Pinpoint the target market(s).
5. Determine the budget.
6. Formulate the message strategy.
7. Select the optimal media mix.
8. Coordinate advertising with other elements within the promotional mix.
9. Execute the campaign.
10. Measure results and evaluate effectiveness.

Each of these ten steps is now described in detail.

1. *Develop an understanding of the overall mission and goals of the organization.* Long before one begins thinking about the development of a specific advertising campaign, a thorough knowledge of the history, mission, goals, and objectives of the organization is critical. To achieve this level of understanding, continuing education leaders must become familiar with the philosophy and strategic plans that shape the direction of their operations. For example, if an organization wishes to become the preeminent provider of expensive, executive-level seminars, its advertising must be carried out in such a way as to reflect and reinforce this goal.

Effective advertising does not happen by accident. Careful planners arm themselves with every available bit of information and immerse themselves in data, including a review of previous advertising efforts. By knowing what produced results in the past, as well as what failed, managers benefit from the lessons of history.

In moving from the past to the present, it is also imperative to spend the time to conduct a "SWOT" analysis. By uncovering the strengths, weaknesses, opportunities, and threats facing their organizations, planners are more likely to design advertising campaigns that exploit competitive advantages and make strategic sense.

2. *Analyze the product, the consumer, the marketplace, and the competition.* Advertising planners must also concern themselves with acquiring an

intimate knowledge of these four factors. As Ogilvy (1983) advises, "You don't stand a tinker's chance of producing successful advertising unless you start by doing your homework. I have always found this extremely tedious, but there is no substitute for it. First, study the product you are going to advertise" (p. 11).

The product for continuing educators may be a single course offering, a special service, or an entire series of programs consisting of hundreds of courses or seminars. Regardless of how the product is defined, it is important to identify the unique attributes of the product, what stage has been reached in the product life cycle, how the consumer perceives the product, the cost of the product and the pricing strategy, and the availability of similar products from competitors. Chapter Nine discusses in detail these important aspects of the marketing mix.

Development of a consumer profile is also essential. It is necessary to have reliable answers to the following questions: Who uses the product and why? How often do they use it? How does the use of the product satisfy the needs of the client? These and other types of audience segmentation questions should be addressed before devising an advertising strategy.

Likewise, an assessment of the marketplace in which the product competes, as well as the identification of the competitors themselves, must be undertaken. The continuing education professional must stay abreast of environmental factors—economic, regulatory, social, political, and cultural issues—that could impact total market sales. Furthermore, it is critical to monitor the competitive situation, the activities and advertising of others, to ensure that one's market share does not begin to erode. This kind of market analysis provides important information in setting advertising objectives and positioning the product (Nylen, 1986).

3. *Define advertising objectives.* Advertising objectives flow logically from the knowledge gained in the first two phases of the advertising planning process. Unlike longer-term marketing goals, which focus on increasing sales, advertising goals emphasize the dissemination of particular communication messages to key target audiences, with the hope that these messages will ultimately lead to greater sales volume.

One of the most well-known approaches to setting objectives is the DAGMAR method: Defining Advertising Goals for Measured Advertising Results. Developed by Russell Colley back in 1961, this model uses a hierarchy of buyer readiness—awareness, comprehension, conviction, and action—as the basis for 52 possible advertising objectives. However, these can be collapsed into three major categories—informing, persuading, and reminding (Kotler, 1982)—that parallel the stages within the product life cycle.

For example, suppose the continuing education division of a suburban hospital has just begun offering a new program on nutrition for teenagers. The advertising objective might be to create awareness of the program within three months among at least 30 percent of the mothers of adolescents living within a ten-mile radius of the hospital.

Note that this objective is very specific and includes a quantifiable measurement on which results can be evaluated. The statement also identifies the target market segment and a time frame for realizing the objective. Most importantly, the objective provides a clear focus on which other key decisions, such as media and message strategies, can be based.

One of the most difficult tasks, however, is to set realisitc objectives. Organizations, both public and private, often make the mistake of selecting goals that are impossible to achieve through advertising alone. The question, then, to test the validity of a specific objective is "Can this objective be accomplished through advertising?" (McDonald, 1985, pp. 105-106). If not, the goal is not a proper one and must be reconsidered.

Although defining objectives is a time-consuming and complex task, the process offers great benefits to the advertising decision maker. First, goal setting suggests specific guidelines as to what is to be accomplished. Second, it enhances the communication process within the organization because everyone clearly understands the big picture and what advertising is supposed to achieve. Finally, it provides a formal means of measuring and evaluating the effectiveness of the advertising itself.

4. *Pinpoint the target market(s).* It is neither desirable nor affordable to attempt to reach all potential buyers in the marketplace with a shotgun approach. Instead, advertising planners should use the rifle approach and seek out specific groups whose needs can best be met by their particular products.

Returning to our previous example, recall that the hospital sought mothers of teenagers for its nutrition program. How could this prospective group be segmented? Through careful research involving focus groups or surveys, it could be determined that four targets exist: (1) traditional mothers concerned about their families' health, (2) mothers working outside the home with limited time to devote to meal planning, (3) mothers of children who are either under- or overweight, and (4) mothers of athletes.

One goal of market segmentation is to recognize subgroups within the potential consumer pool that are both accessible and of sufficient size to warrant special attention. Once identified through the use of demographic and psycho-graphic characteristics, subgroups can be prioritized based on the relative potential each has to offer. This information, in turn, assists the advertising planner in determining exactly which audiences to reach and with what frequency.

Understanding the similarities and differences between target groups is also critical. It may be that some segments are similar enough to respond to the same advertising message (Ray, 1982). In that way, the advertising budget can be maximized to reach as many prospects as possible, as often as possible. Decisions regarding the appropriate advertising message and media mix (to be discussed more fully in Steps 6 and 7, respectively) are more easily made when the planner understands clearly to whom, and how often, the advertising is to be directed, as well as what will motivate prospects to respond.

5. *Determine the budget.* The advertising budget, perhaps more than any other, is the product of much guesswork (Patti and Murphy, 1978). Nonetheless, there are a number of ways in which the continuing educator can determine an

appropriate advertising budget. Before enumerating these, however, it is important to mention that no single method is correct. A combination of several approaches seems to work best and provides a series of checks and balances before arriving at a final budget figure.

One of the most common budgeting methods used in continuing education is the all-you-can-afford or arbitrary approach. After allocating funds for all other expenses, the residual is earmarked for advertising. Although this method is simple to use, it does not consider the optimal level that should be spent to maximize registrations. Moreover, the advertising budget, through default, does not focus on achieving specified goals.

A second popular methodology is to link advertising to some performance criterion such as enrollments, number of courses offered, or revenue. For example, the advertising budget might be set at 15 percent of revenue, or $20 per student, or $250 for each course or seminar offered. Although past experience will help define what these rule-of-thumb factors should be, it is far more logical to use forecasts of anticipated performance goals, rather than last year's figures, as the base on which to apply these formulas. Thus, the planner recognizes that sales are dependent on the dollar amount expended for advertising.

Competitive parity is a defensive strategy for determining the advertising budget. Here, the competitors' promotional activities are monitored to ascertain what they are spending, which then serves as an expenditure guideline. This copycat method, although recognizing the importance of competition, assumes that the objectives of others are similar to yours and that others are using advertising efficiently. This, of course, may not be accurate.

Yet another means of budgeting is the objective task, or zero-base-budgeting method, which seeks to build the budget from the ground up. Tasks are defined and prioritized, costs are determined for each, and the budget is put together project-by-project until all have been accounted for or until available funds are exhausted. The strength of this approach is that it forces planners to set objectives and to justify their actions rather than resort to a business-as-usual mentality.

A final method, payout planning, views advertising as a long-term investment, allocating dollars over time to secure a strong market position in the future. Often utilized for new products, the strategy suggests combining the advertising budget for the first several years and then expending a greater amount, say 60 percent, in the first year, with lesser amounts, perhaps 20 percent, in each of the second and third years. Although this approach is extremely logical, many continuing education organizations, especially those in the public sector, would have a difficult time employing it because of the fiscal calendars under which they operate.

In summary, the five ways just described can be used to determine appropriate spending levels for advertising. Regardless of the method utilized, however, it is always cost-effective to continue spending money on advertising as long as the expenditure is less than the revenue it generates. This is true both for institutional advertising and campaigns and for specific advertising focusing on individual programs or courses.

Many continuing educators find that by combining their generic, all-purpose advertising funds with those earmarked for special projects and specific courses or programs, their total advertising budget is suddenly much larger than it appears at first glance. By lumping together all available monetary resources and then reallocating them based on institutional priorities, rather than on source of funds, planners can often stretch their budgets to accomplish more.

Professionals in the field of continuing education often wonder how much of their total budget should be devoted to advertising. Unlike other industries, no single percentage of advertising-to-sales ratio exists, primarily because continuing education organizations vary so widely in terms of their economic situations. However, two different organizations, the Learning Resources Network and The Marketing Federation, have indicated that successful providers look for a four-to-one return on the cost of their promotional activities. This means that up to 25 percent of anticipated revenue may be invested in the overall marketing program, with advertising representing just a part of that total expenditure. With any rule-of-thumb, however, planners must consider their own situations and goals to determine the applicability of the measurement.

6. *Formulate the message strategy.* Once the advertising objectives, budget, and target market segments have been defined, the focus turns to the creative program to determine what message is to be communicated. At this stage, the emphasis is *not* on how the message will be delivered but rather on the content of the message itself.

Four major issues should be addressed before an attempt is made to devise a creative strategy. The first issue is identification of the product's unique selling proposition, the one distinctive characteristic or attribute that sets the product apart from all others. Related to this is the second issue—determining the key benefit that consumers will reap as a result of attending. The third consideration is image. What kind of personality or reputation should be projected about the institution or program? The fourth factor is positioning, which suggests that to succeed in our media-oriented society, an organization must carve out a competitive niche for itself in the prospect's mind. This position must consider not only the organization's own strengths and weaknesses, but also the strengths and weaknesses of its competitors (Ries and Trout, 1981).

By clearly understanding the competitive advantages of the program or institution, as well as the motives, needs, and problems of the consumer, the advertising planner will be well prepared to begin generating creative strategies. Brainstorming sessions with past attendees, faculty, instructors, and staff are useful in compiling a list of possible appeals to buyers. Research indicates that ideas that can be expressed succinctly in one sentence have the best chance of being successful (Ray, 1982).

Strong message ideas seem to share a number of common characteristics. Based on these factors, the following questions are useful in evaluating alternate creative strategies for continuing education programs:

- Does the message make a meaningful promise to the prospect?
- Is the message single-minded, simple, and specific?
- Is the message distinctive and interesting enough to stand out in a crowd?
- Does the message have staying power and durability?
- Is the message believable?
- Does the message successfully position the product vis-à-vis the competition?
- Is the message directed to the right target audience?
- Is the message tasteful and appropriate, enhancing rather than undermining the desired institutional image?
- Is the message conveyed in the same language used by the prospect?
- Is the message persuasive enough to stimulate the desired action?
- Does the message support the established advertising objectives?
- Does the message fit strategically into the overall marketing goals of the organization?

Obviously, the more "yes" a particular message idea generates, the stronger it is. Weak-scoring messages should be discarded no matter how clever or creative they might seem.

7. *Select the optimal media mix.* To efficiently utilize advertising time and space, it is important to match the target market to the media vehicle. The stronger the correlation between the two, the more likely it is that dollars will be spent on reaching the prospects for whom the product has the greatest appeal (Barban, Cristol, and Kopec, 1976).

The starting point, then, in determining an appropriate media strategy is to understand the profile of your target market segments, which by this stage in the advertising planning process should be readily evident. The second step is to become knowledgeable about various media options, which include daily, business, community, and national newspapers; consumer, business, and special interest magazines and trade journals that are published locally, regionally, nationally, and internationally; AM and FM radio, offering a variety of formats from news/talk to religious, rock to classical; local television and cable stations; supplements and inserts in advertising circulars, weekly shoppers, and cardpacks; but transit and outdoor billboard advertising; point-of-purchase displays; and specialty promotional items. Add to this traditional list a variety of new and unusual media, ranging from trayliners at fast food outlets to hot air balloons to ads on pizza delivery boxes and take-out videocassette containers. Suddenly the choices seem endless, and perhaps a bit overwhelming. Of course, not all of these forms are appropriate for advertising continuing education programs. However, it is important to identify and consider the feasibility and appropriateness of a wide variety of media options.

Alternate media choices can be narrowed down, first through a qualitative approach, and second through analysis of reach, duplication, frequency, cost, continuity, and impact. By considering the nature of the product and its price, the advertising objectives, the target audience, the budget, the image of the institution, the creative message strategy, and other components within the promotional mix, the advertising planner can immediately eliminate many of the media choices that seem inappropriate. Through research and the use of a variety of sources, such as Simmons Market Research Bureau and Standard Rate and Data Service, which provide information about media patterns, specific choices can then be made and the media plan can be finalized. Consider these factors:

- Reach—How many prospects will be exposed to the advertising at least once?
- Duplication—What overlap in audience exists between two or more media vehicles?
- Frequency—How often, on the average, will prospects receive the message?
- Relative cost—How expensive is it to reach prospects, as expressed by CPM (cost per thousand)?
- Continuity—How long a period will the advertising span (density versus longevity)?
- Impact—What is the total impression created by the media strategy and how well does it meet stated objectives?

Media selection is based on creativity, compromise, and allocation of limited resources. For example, there exist trade-offs between reach and frequency. Given a limited budget, as reach goes up, frequency goes down. As repetition enhances retention, it is usually desirable and cost effective to hit a smaller, selective audience with the advertising message more often than to hit a larger population only once. Likewise, concentrating advertising is almost always more successful than spreading out the schedule. Ten ads in ten days will have far greater impact than one each month for ten months. Advertising planners must be alert to these and other trade-offs that exist in media planning and remember that there is no single approach that works best.

8. *Coordinate advertising with other elements within the promotional mix.* Advertisements should not be planned in a vacuum. Rather, they must be considered in the light of other promotional activities such as direct mail, publicity, and personal selling. Because of this interdependency, advertising objectives must reflect decisions made about other marketing efforts (Nylen, 1986).

To illustrate this point, assume that a university-based continuing education division plans to offer a course entitled "How to Succeed in the Import–Export Business." The marketing plan might begin with the mailing of 25,000 brochures, followed by the insertion of three ads in the business section of the local paper. Personal visits to ten of the largest import–export firms in the county, as well as a presentation to the leading industry association, might then be scheduled, along with the release of calendar announcements and public service announcements. Through the careful coordination of all of these activities, a synergy is created, enhancing the effectiveness of each element while increasing overall results.

9. *Execute the campaign.* Now that the advertising strategy has been carefully planned, it is finally time for implementation. The actual advertise-

ments and commercials need to be produced, a budget itemizing estimated costs must be prepared, and the exact media placement schedule has to be finalized.

Chapters Eleven, Twelve, Twenty, and Twenty-one explain in great detail how to write effective advertising copy and how to design print ads. Chapter Twenty-two is devoted to working with advertising agencies, as some large continuing education organizations utilize outside services to develop and implement their advertising strategies. Regardless of who has the final responsibility for execution, however, note that coordination is the key. With so many details to manage and control, it is easy to miss deadlines and deviate from the stated advertising plan.

10. *Measure results and evaluate effectiveness.* Although Chapter Twenty-three is devoted exclusively to the tracking of advertising results, the process deserves special mention here. This type of evaluation is the final step of the advertising planning process, but one that is often overlooked.

According to the legendary John Caples in his classic book *Tested Advertising Methods* (1974), the secret to success is "testing, testing, testing." Even small advertisers, he claims, can devise research methods that are inexpensive and easy to use, yet highly effective. Conducting focus groups, coding coupons, and reading copy aloud are just a few of the techniques he suggests.

The evaluation process cannot be left to chance. Testing should not become an afterthought. Instead, it should be planned well in advance. Setting advertising objectives early in the planning cycle (step 3) helps to ensure that performance criteria are clearly defined and that results can be measured against an established benchmark.

Writing the Plan

After proceeding through the ten planning steps, you undoubtedly have a mental outline. At this point, however, it is critical to formalize plans by committing them to paper.

Depending on the nature of the organization and the number of educational programs it offers, it may be necessary to create a separate advertising plan for each program. Normally, plans are prepared on an annual basis. But during the year, they should not be relegated to the back of a file cabinet. Instead, they should be used as a management tool and reviewed periodically to ensure that tasks are being accomplished on schedule.

In addition to keeping the advertising activities on target, the written plan offers other important benefits:

1. It forces a thorough review, at least once a year, of the opportunities and problems facing the institution.
2. It stimulates the creation of realistic advertising objectives.
3. It provides a clear focus for the organization, charting a course of action that

is based on sound reasoning and logic instead of intuition and questionable assumptions.

4. It ensures that a favorable and consistent institutional image will be projected.

5. It enhances the coordination of a wide variety of advertising and promotional activities.

6. It encourages creativity, communication, involvement, responsibility, and delegation among staff members.

7. It sets control standards and provides a means of measuring advertising results.

8. It creates a permanent document, useful as a starting point for future planning efforts.

9. It ultimately saves both time and money, and prevents painful mistakes.

Summary

Admittedly, the advertising planning process is a long one. It begins with an understanding of the goals of the organization, as well as the product, the consumer, the marketplace, and the competition. Next, advertising objectives are set, target market segments are identified, and the budget is established. The development of message and media strategies follows, along with a consideration of how advertising will support other promotional efforts. Once these steps have been completed, the tactical execution of the advertising campaign can finally take place. Lastly, results must be measured against stated objectives to determine the overall effectiveness of the advertising activities.

It is important to prepare advertising plans at least once a year and to commit them in writing. By so doing, the continuing education organization will reap substantial benefits while exploiting the medium of advertising to its fullest.

20

How to Design and Lay Out Newspaper and Magazine Ads

Deanna M. Maneker

Advertising is a creative endeavor. To be as successful as possible in this endeavor, professionals must follow certain guidelines to create an ad that meets the objectives set for it. Such advertisements help continuing educators sell their programs, products, and services. These guidelines are based on research, experience in the marketplace, and historical data.

To create an ad that meets the objectives set, the wide variety of factors that contribute to an ad's success must be analyzed. Before one even thinks about the creative side of advertising, he or she should step back and consider three factors: objectives, strategy, and tactics.

The first step is to establish a clear objective for the ad. What do you want to happen as a result of the advertising? Usually, advertising has three objectives: to create awareness of a continuing education program, product, or service; to ask for a registration or purchase; to create awareness of your organization as the program sponsor. Typically, a newspaper or magazine ad for a continuing education program asks the reader either to call or write for more information or to register for a program. The decision on the objective, then, is an important first step in designing and laying out newspaper and magazine ads.

Next, a strategy must be developed to meet the objective. The strategy is the means by which an objective is met. Often, there is a choice of strategies. Either you are uncertain as to which strategy will work, or you have several alternatives to accomplish the objective. For example, you might decide to select a spokesperson or location that will create the desired image. If you are looking for a response, you might include a return coupon as an integral part of the ad.

Tactics concern the implementation of the strategy. Tactics consist of a step-by-step plan to design an ad that fits the strategy and meets the objective. For example, you plan to run quarter-page newspaper ads twice a week to meet the objective of developing public awareness of your organization and its continuing education programs. If your objective is to create a response, you might design the ad so that around the coupon is a heavy dotted line on which is inserted a graphic of a scissor cutting the line, making it clear to the reader what response you want. Such visual graphics can be powerful motivators that encourage the reader to take the action you desire.

Newspaper Ads Versus Magazine Ads

The decision on whether to place an ad in newspapers or magazines should be based on the market you wish to reach. However, there is a design implication in using the newspaper ad: Newspaper ads are usually larger, are printed on poor-quality stock, do not reproduce color well, and are expected to be thrown out after the first reading.

Newspapers call for bold graphics, more use of type than photographic material, and simple, clean design. The type size is usually larger than what is used for a magazine ad because the newspaper reader is assumed to be skimming the material, not reading in depth. Magazines, on the other hand, usually have an 8½ × 11-inch format, use a finer-quality paper stock that will reproduce color printing if required, and have a life expectancy until the next publication date.

Consider the following important guidelines when deciding to use newspaper or magazine ads:

1. *Plan a copy strategy or product strategy for the ad.* Decide on the key elements of the ad in advance of creative planning. For example, if you wish to visually feature a product or service, then allocate more space to this than to copy. On the other hand, if you wish to focus on the copy, then it and the headline must take the prominent position.

2. *Plan in advance what you want the reader to do after reading your ad.* This ties in with your objectives. If awareness is your key objective, then you might be looking for recognition from the reader that he or she has heard or read about the program or service before. If your focus is on image, then you want the reader to feel good about your organization after reading the ad. And, if you are looking for a response, you must define what that response is and what readers will experience when they give the desired response.

3. *Clearly define whether your ad is being used to support another marketing program.* As advertising is usually combined with other marketing steps such as direct mail, telephone marketing, or live sales calls, your advertising strategy, design, and layout must support and mesh with all other marketing steps. One of the biggest mistakes often made is creation of a newspaper or magazine ad to support direct-mail marketing in which neither the copy, the design, nor the offer is appropriate for direct mail. Because advertising is not

conducted in a void, and is usually the first step in the marketing ladder, care should be taken to look at the total marketing plan before creating a layout.

4. *Recognize that design and layout of ads is not a pure science.* Advertising is often unmeasurable as far as the ultimate results are concerned. If your objective is to elicit a registration, note that newspaper and magazine advertising for continuing education programs is often not powerful enough to pull the best possible response. Direct-mail advertising is usually more effective in securing registrations. Nevertheless, newspaper and magazine advertising often proves excellent in garnering requests for your direct-mail brochure or catalogue. Thus, it is important to be attentive to the principles—what works and what does not work.

What Newspaper Ads Can and Cannot Accomplish. Certain issues affect design decisions regarding newspaper ads. For example, newspaper advertising is perceived as immediate and time-sensitive information. People do not expect to reread or retain a newspaper. On the basis of readership studies, we know that newspaper ads are often only scanned. People look at what catches their eye. Therefore, an eye-catcher must be incorporated into the ad.

In the light of this information, we should use newspapers for announcements and introductions of new programs, products, and services or to generate requests for more information. Newspapers also lend themselves to simple messages and ideas. Newspapers demand large, bold type and graphics. Any photographs or illustrations should be simple and clear. Intricate design or photography is difficult to reproduce because of the mechanics of high-speed printing on newsprint. As color cannot be used with a high degree of reproduction reliability on newsprint, most newspapers use black and white photography. Therefore, if your advertisement must be in color, newspaper ads will probably not be effective. However, if your objective is to create a response, newspapers lend themselves very well to generating telephone responses.

Copy for newspaper ads should be brief. Readers who scan do not indulge in large copy blocks. The large type size that complements the large graphics called for in newspapers will further slow the reader and thus reduce readership.

What Magazine Ads Can and Cannot Accomplish. Magazines offer a completely different formula for advertising. First, people retain magazines, reread them, and refer to past issues. Second, the editorial content of many magazines is such that it attracts the committed reader who reads everything—articles and advertising copy. Third, color is an option because of the paper stock and the quality of the printing techniques. In addition, because of the flexibility of a magazine's graphics and design, you are not restricted to specific types of ads, as is the case with newspapers. Copy-heavy ads, product or program ads, technical information ads—all can be done well in magazines.

An important guideline concerning the decision between newspaper and magazine ads is this: Do not try to accomplish in newspaper or magazine ads what is best done by direct mail, telephone marketing, or a live sales call. For example, newspaper or magazine ads rarely are effective in closing the sale of a program or service. What you can do with newspaper or magazine ads, however, is to generate leads. Magazine and newspaper ads usually are not large enough to convince a dubious prospect to actually register for a continuing education program.

Implementing the Strategy

After a strategy for newspaper or magazine advertising has been established, it is important to develop a specific plan for implementing the strategy. Note these suggestions:

1. *Choosing the design emphasis.* In creating effective and striking advertising, your first step is to decide what will carry the overall emphasis. For example, will the emphasis be conveyed through headlines, body copy, logo, photographs, or a call to action? Any one or several of these elements might be emphasized. The decision on what to emphasize should tie in with the objective and strategy. If you have a key benefit or a very special offer, you might want to put it in the headline for attention, thereby increasing the chances that it will be read quickly and promptly. On the other hand, if your message is complex and requires a thorough explanation, the body copy should take precedence over other design elements. If your objective is to build a strong organizational image or to reinforce the existing image, it may be important to emphasize the logo and place it in a position of prominence. Or, if the continuing education program, product, or service speaks for itself, you might use a photograph in a position of prominence. If the objective of the ad is to elicit a response, you might place a coupon or a telephone number in a key position.

2. *Using color in the design.* The criteria for the use of color may be set by economic reasons or production reasons. Can you afford four-color art or a second color in your advertising budget? Does the newspaper or magazine offer you the option of full color or additional color? If you have the option of using color, use it wisely according to these guidelines:

- Set a key word or phrase in the second color.
- Use color to call attention to the key design element.
- Set your logo in color as it is often seen and recognized by its color hues.
- Use full color in your photograph if it enhances the shot or if your program, product, or service is usually shown in color.

3. *Deciding on use of a photograph or illustration.* Most people absorb information more quickly through pictures than through words. As a result, a photograph or an illustration can often convey an idea effectively; however, a poor graphic is worse than no graphic. Invest in a photo or illustration that has good composition and is of high-quality resolution. The preference for a photograph over an illustration is based on the fact that most people easily relate to photographs. A good-quality illustration prepared by an artist might be

slightly less expensive, but usually the difference is not large enough to affect the decision. People relate to what they see. People relate to photographs because they can see themselves in that particular situation. As a result, photographs are almost always more powerful as an advertising tool.

Basic Ground Rules for Copy

Headlines have proven to have good readership. For a long time, professional copywriters have used the rule of thumb that a headline should not contain more than thirteen words. In some instances in newspaper or magazine advertising, however, it is appropriate to use longer headlines. What is crucial to the success of headlines is their content. State the major benefit, state your offer, or describe your terms in the headline.

Graphically, the headline should be set in 24-point or larger type. The preferred style for a headline is a sentence, with the first letter of the first word a capital and all other letters lowercase. In the second best style, the initial letters of the key nouns and verbs are capitals, but the other words remain lowercase. The least desirable style is to set the entire headline in capital letters. People have a tendency to slow down when reading all capital letters. And once they slow their reading speed, they usually stop reading.

The headline should be set close to the body copy to which it refers or to the appropriate photograph or illustration. When a headline is set too high, the white space between body copy and headline tends to separate thoughts which, in turn, causes the reader's mind to wander.

For ease of reading, it does not matter whether headlines are set centered line under line or set flush left. We do know that headlines set flush right produce an unusual design; however, this different design may also upset the reader. In the flush right format each new line starts at a new place and the reader quickly becomes annoyed. Such headlines should almost always be avoided.

As copywriters have modified their thinking about headline length and now write longer headlines, so too have professional advertising agencies rethought their policy concerning the number of lines in a headline. For years it was tradition not to stack a headline over three lines deep. Now we find that readers do not object to a stack four, five, and even six lines deep.

In setting up the headline, watch for "widows": The last line of the headline should be at least half as long as the preceding line. If it should not, then rearrange the copy. Note the following examples.

Correct

> In 1985, we introduced the world's most
> successful financial management
> computer software.

In 1985, we introduced the
world's most successful
financial management
computer software.

Incorrect

In 1985, we introduced the world's most
successful financial management computer
software.

Body copy is another important issue. Short body copy is usually fifty words or less. As it has little graphic bulk, it tends not to engage the reader. Thus, it is important that short copy be set in a highly readable type.

There are two factors in setting body copy—typeface and type size. Typeface is the design of the type. Many typefaces have been designed over the last hundred years, and each has a specific name. Some of the typefaces most often used in newspaper and magazine advertising are Times Roman, Palladium, Melior, Century, Souvenir, Helvetica, Optima, and Lydian. Preference for typeface is very subjective. Except for very stylized typefaces, it often makes little difference what typeface is chosen. The basic typefaces, such as those just mentioned, are the most readable. Remember, your goal in choosing a typeface for advertising a continuing education program, product, or service is to increase the readability of the ad.

Pay particular attention to decisions on expanded or condensed typeface. When a typeface is expanded, the letters are drawn out so that they are wider. This type is much harder to read and, when used for body copy, will quickly tire the reader. Condensed typeface is narrow and also is difficult to read in extensive body copy. One group of readers has adjusted to the condensed typeface— engineers and scientists; however, most readers will quickly tire of reading copy set in condensed face.

There are two major typeface categories: serif and sans serif. Serif typeface has little curlicues on the letters, as in the letters *r, y,* and *g.* These curlicues help focus the eye on body copy. Sans serif typeface has a clean-cut look with no curlicues. Readers tend to skip lines when extensive body copy is set sans serif. The remedy for this problem in newspaper and magazine advertising is to insert extra white space, called "leading," between the lines of type; the white space helps the reader to track easily.

Serif italic typeface is difficult to read and, therefore, should be used sparingly in ads and then only for subordinate material. Many people make the mistake of using italics for emphasis. Unfortunately, it often has just the reverse effect. Rather than emphasizing the content, italic makes the content more difficult to read.

Type size refers to the largeness or smallness of the type and is expressed in points. One point equals one seventy-second of an inch. The letter is measured from the tip of its ascender to the bottom of its descender. The midrange of the letter is called the "x height" and is the height of the letter *x* of that design and size.

Having gone into this depth of explanation, let us discuss the value of this information. Body copy is best set in a serif typeface, with an "x height" 60 percent of the total point size and a type size of at least 10 points. Twenty-five percent of the population is wearing glasses by age 18. Beyond age 40, deterioration proceeds more rapidly and larger type tends to be easier to read.

The following guidelines are useful when setting newspaper or magazine ad copy longer than fifty words:

- Make your paragraphs seven to nine lines long.
- Use lead-in phrases or key sentences to allow the reader to scan the material. Highlight the lead-in phrases by setting them bolder than the remaining copy.
- If the copy is arranged in columns, set the right-hand margins unjustified, cutting the use of hyphens to a minimum; that is, set the type "ragged right." Hyphens at the ends of lines decrease readability.
- Set blocks of copy from the text in large type to serve as "illustrations."

In general, when setting advertising copy, remember that the reader tends to read in the following order: (1) large captions or headlines; (2) graphs, charts, and tables; (3) captions for photographs; and (4) subheads within the body.

Copywriting style is also an important consideration for newspaper and magazine ads. Certain styles have more impact than others. The choice often depends on the mind-set of the reader. For example, if your reader is knowledgeable about your program, product, or service and is not hostile to your premise, then a friendly and telegraphic approach works nicely. On the other hand, if your reader is not aware of your program or might be hostile to your premise, then a more subtle approach is appropriate.

If your reader is not aware of your program or service and might well be hostile or disinterested, you should consider including testimonials, statistics, or case histories in the ad. Telling a story that makes the point about your program or service puts the reader in the position of relating to the story. This too is often very effective.

Basic Ground Rules for Design

There are two key ingredients to good design of newspaper and magazine ads: balance and proportion. Balance is based on the "weights" of the elements in an advertising piece. To grasp the concept of "weights," take note of the following facts: (1) A photograph "weighs" more than copy. (2) Color "weighs" more than black and white. (3) Unusual shapes "weigh" more than usual shapes. (4) White space has "weight" in and of itself.

Keep in mind that there are two forms of balance—symmetrical and asymmetrical. In a symmetrically balanced ad, the left and right and sides are mirror images of each other. Although easy to produce, this form is less interesting and does not capture the reader's attention for long. Asymmetrical balance is achieved when uneven pieces are balanced by a variable, for example, the use of a small color photograph to balance a large block of blank type.

In a well-balanced ad, the eye does not naturally seek the top of the page or the geometric center. The reader's eye is drawn to a point slightly left of and above the geometric center of the page. This, then, is the point at which you want to establish the key element and create the eye path.

Proportion refers to the relationship among the parts of the ad. The most pleasing proportions are 5:3 or 3:2, for example, the 8½ × 11-inch page or the 5 × 7-inch photo. Ads that stray from these proportions will certainly attract attention but not the benevolent, receptive attention that enhances readability and involvement. Displeasing proportions include a square or even an extreme rectangle of 6 × 2 inches.

In addition to being balanced and in proportion, advertising should be fresh and creative. Cliches should be avoided. Listed here are suggestions on how to avoid cliches in newspaper and magazine advertising:

- Do not set body copy on an angle because it will be hard to read. Slanted heads and subheads create a feeling of movement and are acceptable; however, slanted body copy is annoying and reduces the chances that the reader will persist long enough to read your message.
- Do not reverse out headlines unless they are set in very heavy type and therefore are easy to read.
- Do not set type up the side of the page (vertically) because it is unreadable and irritating.
- Do not cut a photograph into the shape of some object such as a snowflake or a tree. This ruins the composition of the ad.
- Do not cut a window in a photograph and insert another photograph in that window. The composition of the larger photo will be destroyed and the design will be busy and distracting.
- Do not run your headlines across photos and onto the blank page. This interrupts reading, making it difficult for the reader to internalize the message.
- Do not reverse out a headline over a photograph as this will distract from the photo and also make the copy hard to read.

Some graphic techniques can be used to emphasize the key points of an ad:

- Lay out the ad so that a part of the photo or illustration points toward a key element.
- Use a series of smaller photos instead of one large photo to lead the reader through the ad to the end.
- All color photographs for an ad should have the same background color and

the same dominant color, and should be on the same scale. Such photos look related and direct the reader's eye.

- Use a second color to emphasize a key word or call attention to a specific element.
- Set the "big" words in advertising (such as new, announcing, free, first time, only) in a bolder typeface or several points larger, or both.
- Highlight a key idea or element of the ad in a burst or circle.
- Arrows, dashes, little scissors for coupons, and even miniature hands pointing to a key idea or image are helpful in directing the reader's attention.
- In photographs, persons using your product or service should never appear in an inappropriate pose or outfit, for example, a woman in short shorts sitting on top of the desk next to your computer! The reader will reject your whole premise.

Use of Layout and Design to Promote the Natural Synergy with Other Marketing Tools

To elicit a response from your ad, highlight the response mechanism. If you want people to call, consider using a graphic of a telephone or a photograph of a person answering the phone. Set the telephone number in bold type or in a second color and place it in a prominent position. If you want to promote a written response, then insert a coupon requesting more information in a prominent position. Such response coupons are most effective in the lower outside corner of the page, where they can easily be clipped. Work with the advertising department of the newspaper or magazine to ensure that the return coupon is placed correctly.

If you are using direct mail and newspaper/magazine advertising simultaneously, consider similar headlines and graphics so that the two forms complement each other. Ads should run first, about seven to ten days before receipt of the mail, to increase the response to the direct-mail advertising. Direct mail almost never increases response to an ad when it precedes the ad.

Radio and television advertising can also work well with print advertising if they share common headlines, graphics, key phrases, and tone or point of view. If the ad is running on television, then you should use color for newspaper and/ or magazine advertising as well to achieve maximum synergy for the total advertising campaign.

Summary

To place the principles of newspaper and magazine advertising in perspective, convert these recommendations on layout and design into a checklist appropriate to your continuing education organization. The staff can then use this checklist as a guide.

Determine the objective of your ad first; then formulate your strategy and choose your tactics. Select the key elements. Include ideas you wish to emphasize. Next, list the items that must be included in the ad. Construct a checklist appropriate to your organization that can be used by your staff to create the best possible newspaper and magazine ads.

21

Writing Effective Advertising Copy: Eight Principles for Success

Robert G. Simerly

Writing good advertising copy is a fine art. The most successful copy for continuing education programs incorporates a set of eight basic guiding principles that have proven to be effective. Each principle is designed to involve readers so that they respond the way you want them to respond. Usually, this response is a registration for a program or a telephone call or returned coupon requesting more information. Each of the eight principles discussed in this chapter has been tested in a wide variety of continuing education organizations, such as training and development departments, the health care professions, colleges and universities, for-profit seminar and meeting providers, government agencies, museums, and industry.

These eight principles are easy to incorporate into the advertising copy writing of any continuing education organization. In the following discussion, each principle is analyzed and concrete examples of successful copy writing are provided. If you review the principles before each copywriting job, it will be easier to incorporate them into an assignment. Then, a review once again at the end of the project serves as a check that no basic principle has been omitted without a clear and logical reason to do so.

1. *Clearly define your target market before writing.* The best copy writing in the world will not be effective if it is not written for the target market. Therefore, before writing advertising copy, clearly define your target market. This can be done in several ways. Markets for continuing education programs tend to be targeted according to (1) job title, (2) life-style category, (3) age,

(4) income level, or (5) some category relevant to the market for a particular program, such as all previous program participants who have taken a business-related workshop within the last two years.

Writing copy for programs aimed at people with a particular job title is one approach, for example, a three-day workshop entitled "How to Avoid Legal Problems in Your Personnel Department" targeted to personnel directors. If such a course deals broadly with the latest legal issues in the personnel process, it would be appropriate for all personnel directors regardless of the type of organization in which they work. It would be relatively easy to obtain a mailing list of personnel directors. In a major metropolitan area, you might decide that your target market is all personnel directors within an hour's driving radius from the program location. Now you can begin writing the copy. Knowing exactly who you want to reach determines the approach you take in writing with respect to the use of appropriate language, images, and examples.

The same is true if you are targeting an audience on the basis of life-style or income level. You might, for example, aim a one-day seminar entitled "Investing for Results in Inflationary Times" at established professionals between the ages of 35 and 50 who earn more than $90,000 per year per household and live within a forty-five minute driving radius of the program. A list broker would have no trouble in securing such a list. This information about the audience tells the copywriter that he or she is writing for the established professional who has a significant amount of disposable income and is interested in seeking better long-term investments. Such knowledge determines the content of the program, the approach to instruction, and thus the approach to copy writing.

Probably the most frequent copywriting mistake is failure to clearly define the target audience before writing. The result often is a confused message that is designed to appeal to everyone but is effective for no one.

2. *Know the needs of your target audience and write with the purpose of helping them to fulfill their needs.* Marketing research consistently confirms that one of the major reasons people make purchases, whether material possessions or educational experiences, is to fulfill unmet needs. For example, there are many different types of laundry detergents; however, advertising for one of the best sellers ensures purchasers that by using that particular product they can avoid the embarrassing "ring around the collar." The need fulfilled here is to look good and avoid social embarrassment. Realistically, any of today's modern laundry products would probably eliminate the ring around the collar. Yet, Wisk detergent successfully linked their product with this phrase and effectively helped purchasers fulfill their unmet need to be socially acceptable.

Interviews with continuing education participants consistently demonstrate that people attend these programs also to satisfy unmet needs. People want to better themselves and thus be more effective in their personal relationships and in their jobs. They want to acquire new skills that they hope will lead to promotions or better jobs. They may attend personal enrichment courses to meet interesting people.

The lesson is clear. Advertising copy must demonstrate clearly and accurately how people can meet their needs by participating in continuing education programs. Copy can actively demonstrate to readers that their needs will be met, as shown in this example from a two-day executive development program entitled "Managing the Difficult Employee." The copy is the program content, which appears in the middle of a four-page brochure.

Brochure Copy for Program Content	*Unmet Need Fulfilled by Attendance at the Program*
At This Program You Will Learn . . .	
• Three effective ways to encourage people to take responsibility for solving their own problems in the organization.	To avoid feeling guilty for not solving other people's problems.
• How to turn a difficult person blocker into a supportive problem solver during meetings.	To gain control over negative situations and channel energy into productive results.
• Fifteen different strategies for managing conflict on the job.	To develop new skills to overcome feeling of ineffectiveness in work situations.
• How to help your staff become more effective in team problem solving.	To help staff become more effective and thus be better liked.

Naturally, copy for a direct-mail brochure should have a much longer description of content. As a rule of thumb, 30 to 40 percent of the copy in a brochure should describe in detail the content of the program. Throughout the project, the copywriter should ask "How does my copy help readers meet their needs?" If there are no clear answers to this question, readers will not understand how their participation in the program can help meet their needs. The copywriter must spell it out.

3. *Emphasize benefits.* As just discussed, people participate in continuing education programs because they perceive that their unmet needs will be fulfilled. They regard the fulfillment of those needs as a benefit of value to them. How are benefits conveyed in advertising? Note this example from a one-week summer workshop entitled "Transformational Leadership: A Workshop for High School Leaders." The target group comprised high school students entering their junior and senior years. The copy is taken from the Special Benefits section of the direct-mail brochure used for this program. Beside each special benefit is the rationale for the copy. The rationale was for the copywriter's benefit and was not part of the final copy.

Stated Benefit in Copy	*Implied Benefit*
You will receive a 200-page note-book of practical leadership tips that you can put into practice as soon as you return home.	You will be smarter and more highly skilled as a result of attending. The workbook will be evidence of the many new ideas you have explored.
You will have the chance to meet other people like yourself and learn their practical tips on how to be a more effective leader.	As a result of informal social interaction, you will make new friends and learn new skills at the same time. Learning will be fun.
You will take five self-assessment instruments designed to help you assess your strengths as a leader.	You will develop deeper personal insights about yourself. This self-knowledge will help make you a better person whom others respect.
You will have the opportunity to engage in a two-day leadership-simulated exercise in which you play the role of a high-level industrial leader running a large business.	You can test on a first-hand basis the wide variety of problems leaders tackle every day on the job. You can learn much about the real world of business through this role playing.

The preceding copy enhances program content by describing special benefits to participants. This is very different from simply stating the content of the workshop. Program content is always more effective in engaging the reader when it is described in terms of benefits to participants. Descriptions of content are impersonal. Benefits are personal and they provide readers with a wide variety of psychological reasons for signing up. To be really effective, most direct-mail brochures should contain ten to thirty "special benefits."

4. *Catch the reader's attention within the first three to four seconds.* Research on reader behavior consistently demonstrates that you have approximately three to four seconds to catch your reader's attention with your advertising message. Therefore, the entire advertising piece must be designed to catch the reader's attention and quickly engage him or her. There are many ways to achieve this goal. For example, bold headlines provide an arresting visual engagement. Powerful, action-oriented titles for programs also catch the reader's attention. Color is an attention getter as is the overall graphic design.

A major job of the copywriter is to write copy that immediately attracts the reader's attention. Given here are some examples of how this has been accomplished in different continuing education settings.

Do Not Call This Number .... 857-3857!

Unless you want to receive the free catalogue of credit classes for the fall semester.

This newspaper ad had only one purpose—to generate inquiries for the catalogue. Additional copy in the ad provided information about the college sponsoring the evening credit classes. The copywriter took a unique approach in asking people not to call the number. Such a direct, negative order in a newspaper catches the eye, causing readers to pause. They read several more lines of copy and find that the ad is for a catalogue of credit courses. Then they decide whether to request the catalogue. The important copywriting principle is to get the reader's attention within three to four seconds.

A training and development department of a Fortune 500 company advertised its internal five-day beginning management development program in a brochure with a large banner at the top:

Would you like to help earn an additional $185,000 for the company?

The copy that followed explained the program in detail. Also mentioned was a recent research study that demonstrated that attendance at this workshop had enabled new managers to streamline their operations and save their companies, on the average, $185,000 within the first year of completing the program. The headline caught the attention of everyone in the company who received the brochure. Almost everyone read the entire brochure because of the equally strong and effective copy in the eight-page brochure.

5. *Engage the reader*. Professional marketers in the business sector have been especially effective in refining this technique. For example, each year the Publisher's Clearing House has its annual sweepstakes. You first learn of this through television ads. Next you receive an announcement that the official information will be mailed the next week. When you receive the official announcement you are asked to return the enclosed postcard to participate in the sweepstakes. Sometimes a pencil is included for your convenience. Other times, you are asked to use the "No" label (to enter the contest but not order magazines) or the "Yes" label (to enter the sweepstakes and order magazines). As a result, most Americans know about Publisher's Clearing House.

Recently, an ad in a Silicon Valley newspaper was designed to draw people into a dealer's showroom to look at new cars. The ad asked the reader to return the coupon with a check for three dollars. For this amount, you would receive a computer disk with all the specifications for all models and options handled by the dealer. Respondents could thus use their personal computers to design the car they wanted. Also included was a computer game in which the dealer's name and car brand appeared frequently. The copywriters knew exactly who they wanted to attract—computer professionals in the Silicon Valley. Through their design, they deliberately engaged these people.

Incidentally, this ad was so effective that within three months of receipt of their computer disks, 22 percent of the respondents had actually visited the car dealership. It was the most successful advertising campaign in the history of the company and also one of the most cost effective if the expense of the campaign is measured against the high-potential buyers it attracted (Rapp and Collins, 1987).

The principle of reader engagement can be adapted to almost any continuing education program. Simply ask the question, "How can the reader be engaged in a manner that is both cost effective and appropriate to the image of the organization?" The following examples illustrate how continuing education organizations have effectively engaged readers in their advertising.

- Ask people to call or return a coupon for more information.
- Ask people to call or return a coupon to receive a current update on the latest research in their profession—research that is related to the content of the continuing education program—even if they do not plan to attend. Such respondents always represent your best candidates for future registrants.
- Ask people to take a quiz printed in the brochure and provide the answers. Relate the quiz to the content of the program and make it difficult enough that most people will not pass. Explain that by attending the program they will get detailed answers to these and many other questions, answers that can make them more effective on the job.
- Lay out the advertising message so that the reader is led logically through a complete story to the decision to register.
- Make the advertising piece, especially if it is a catalogue, so attractive and of a high enough perceived value that people will not discard it. Many of the most successful catalogues strive to be coffee table conversation pieces.
- Demonstrate through powerful copy that people can fulfill their important unmet needs by attending the program. This technique is very effective in engaging the reader.
- Ask past participants to tell your story through their pictures and quotes. Such testimonials actively engage readers in the lives of these past participants. Readers then visualize themselves in the same situations, developing skills that people just like them have found to be valuable.

These are only a few examples. The important principle is to engage your reader in a manner that is appropriate in tone, style, and technique to the organization and the program you represent.

6. *Use action words and powerful messages that have a sense of urgency and encourage action on the part of the reader.* Effective advertising copy deliberately stages the response desired from the reader. If you want an action-oriented response, such as a registration for a program or a telephone call or mail-in coupon requesting additional information, use action words liberally throughout the copy. Tell readers clearly what you want them to do. Tell them what they will learn by attending your program. Action words can be effectively incorporated into (1) the program title, (2) headlines above and below the main

advertising copy, (3) the program copy, and (4) the Special Benefits or Special Features copy. Strong action words create powerful messages and a sense of importance, urgency, and dynamism that gets the reader's attention, focuses that attention on the entire copy, and leads the reader to take the action you desire.

These six sets of titles illustrate how action words can be used to strengthen program titles in direct-mail brochures. Each set comprises a weak title and a strong title for the same program. The difference is achieved through strong, action-oriented words designed to create powerful images.

Weak Title	*Strong Title*
Leadership Skills Workshop for Supervisors	Dynamic Leadership for Results-Oriented Managers
Prospects on the Future of Agriculture Economics	Challenging the Future: What Agriculture Leaders Can Do to Turn Around the Farm Crisis
Improving Your Business Writing	Powerful Business Writing Skills
Financial Planning for Retirement	How to Invest Now for a Secure and Carefree Retirement
Planning Successful Conference Budgets	Fifty-seven Ways to Save Money When Planning Your Next Conference
Coping with Difficult People	How to Manage the Difficult Employee for Productive Results

The strong titles use action words, suggest that skills will be improved through attendance at the program, have a sense of urgency and power, and/or recommend practical approaches to problems.

Another way to use action words effectively is through headlines above or below the main advertising copy. For example, in a newspaper ad announcing the new university catalogue for evening credit courses offered, the banner across the top of the ad might read

Call Now for Your Free Catalogue!

and the banner at the bottom,

Come to the University as Our Guest . . .
And Leave as Our Friend.

The next example is taken from a direct-mail brochure for a one-day program entitled "Powerful Business Writing Skills." The banner at the top might read

After Attending This Workshop
You Will Be Able to Write . . .
　　more effectively . . .
　　more easily . . .
　　more powerfully . . .
　　more clearly.

Become More Successful at Your Business Writing in Just One Day!

And the banner at the bottom of each page of the eight-page brochure,

For fast, easy registration call toll free
1-800-354-7793

The banner for a one-day program on time management, "The Time Trap," read

Techniques to Save You Two Hours a Day!

The following copy appeared in bold type on the cover of a brochure for a one-day program devoted to training continuing education office staff on effective ways to deal with clients.

Train Your Whole Staff to Be Marketers!

Your Staff Will Discover:

- How to treat continuing education participants as customers.
- Ways to convert inquiry phone calls into registrations.
- Four easy methods for collecting testimonials to use on your next brochure.
- Eleven important principles office staff should know about direct-mail marketing.
- How to handle complaints so that you convert the complainer into a friend.

　　The preceding approaches are effective in catalogues, individual program brochures, and newspaper and magazine advertisements. They are very effective when the readers are told exactly what you want them to do or what they will learn as a result of participating in the program. Make such bold headlines an integral part of all advertising unless there is a clear and logical reason to omit them.

　　You can also use action-oriented words and images in descriptions of the special benefits participants will receive by attending a program. An eight-page brochure for a three-day executive development program entitled "Dynamic

Leadership for First Time Managers" contained the following copy under Special Benefits:

> As a result of attending this workshop you will be better able to

- Deal with problem employees
- Bridge the gap when moving from beginning supervisor to experienced manager
- Redirect your feelings of anger for productive results
- Promote effective problem solving even in highly charged emotional situations
- Reduce the amount of time you spend in following up on delegated tasks
- Improve your ability to see problems from the viewpoint of others
- Promote the kind of organizational culture that emphasizes confronting problems
- Use a wide variety of leadership styles depending on the demands of the situation
- Handle difficult personnel problems with confidence
- Sell your ideas to others so that they will want to implement them
- Apply principles of conflict management to solving difficult situations at work
- Employ a wide variety of methods for developing and running effective problem-solving meetings
- Practice principles of effective time management in order to increase your efficiency in the organization
- Implement action plans that address both short- and long-range leadership issues
- Raise morale by giving away power
- Upgrade the quality of problem solving by all staff
- Decrease in-fighting in the organization and refocus this energy on productive problem solving
- Diminish the amount of time you have to spend in checking to see if things have been accomplished on time
- Advance the organization's mission by finding ways to achieve specific goals and objectives
- Foster a climate of team problem solving
- Cultivate better working relations with all people who report to you
- Create a dynamic organizational culture that emphasizes shared responsibility for problem solving
- Reward all staff for a job well done in ways they will appreciate

- Work for long periods of time without interruption by applying three easy-to-use principles of time management
- Activate the best leadership qualities in all staff
- Deliver on measurable goals and objectives
- Define problems and alternative solutions so the important work of the organization gets done
- Manage the inevitable conflict that occurs in all working situations as people work together to solve important problems
- Learn from your mistakes and the mistakes of others
- Concentrate on setting priorities and defining ways to achieve these priorities
- Change the problem employee into a productive employee

Note that each benefit begins with an action verb. After reading this list, a reader will begin to feel the power behind the statements. In essence, this list provides thirty-one different reasons for a person to attend. The list describes not only benefits, but also program content, and ultimately leads to a request for a registration.

7. *Arrange copy so that it leads the reader through the message to take the action you want.* This concept is explained in greater detail in Chapter Twelve. Basically, advertising messages should lead the reader through a logical series of steps to take the desired action—usually to register in the program or to telephone or send a written request for additional information. In a previous example used in this chapter, the short copy for a newspaper ad read

Do Not Call This Number . . . . 857-3857!

Unless you want to receive the free catalogue of credit classes for the fall semester.

(Additional copy in this ad provided information about the college sponsoring the evening credit classes.) This ad first tells the reader what not to do and then actively invites him or her to phone for the catalogue. Such short ads are very effective. The copywriter gets readers to (1) notice the ad, (2) read the entire message, and (3) phone for a catalogue. This type of ad is cost effective compared with mass mailings of catalogues, because it narrows the audience to those interested in receiving the catalogue. The ad is clear: Phone for the catalogue if you are interested in taking a course. Do not phone if you are not considering taking a course.

Longer advertisements such as direct-mail brochures incorporate the same principles. They attract the reader's attention and then lead the reader step-by-step through a logical sequence of messages, concluding with a request to register for the program. Brochure copy is discussed in detail in Chapter Twelve.

8. *Test! Test! Test!* Copy writing is not an exact science based on fool-proof rules. It is an art that is learned and that can be enhanced by adherence to

the eight principles discussed in this chapter. This last principle emphasizes the need to test all advertising copy to determine whether it produces the desired results. There are three basic ways to test new copy: (1) Test the copy on colleagues. (2) Test the copy on members of the target group. (3) Test the results through tracking.

Test all copy with your colleagues. Ask them to read the advertising copy and suggest improvements. Can they tell you what you want the reader to do? Do they view the copy as action oriented? Do parts of the copy seem weak or inappropriate? How do they feel about the quality and power of the copy? Make a pact with your colleagues—promise to read and comment on their copy if they read and comment on yours.

Next, ask at least one member of the target group to read the copy. Does he or she think the language is appropriate for that particular group. Ask the following questions: What would you like to learn if you attended such a program? What special benefits would encourage you to attend? What biographical information about a presenter would cause you to view this person as someone you would like to hear? What improvements would you make in the advertising copy?

Finally, design a tracking system to determine the effectiveness of the copy after the event. Does a brochure containing a list of benefits result in more registrations than one without a list? Does inclusion of testimonials attract more registrants? Which arrangement of copy is better—a brochure prepared as a four-page typewritten business report or a brochure designed by a graphic designer?

The real test is whether or not the advertising copy produces the desired results. If you (1) know exactly what results you want, (2) determine whether or not these results are realistic, and (3) know precisely your target market, it is possible to write copy, test it, and determine whether it is successful.

Therefore, development of methods to test the effectiveness of advertising copy should be a high priority in every continuing education organization. It enables leaders to constantly experiment with variables in the copy to see what works most effectively with specific groups. Patterns of success and failure in copy writing begin to emerge. As a result, you are able to develop comprehensive guidelines for your staff—guidelines based on the individual needs of your organization.

Summary

Eight principles of effective copy writing have proved successful in a wide variety of continuing education organizations. The following checklist is based on these eight principles. It, or your own individualized checklist, should be reviewed before and after each copywriting project. Even the best copywriters can fail to incorporate one of the eight principles if they do not use a checklist. Originally developed for direct-mail brochures, this checklist can easily be adapted to newspaper or magazine ads or to catalogues. In addition, it can be modified to fit the individual requirements of any continuing education organization.

1. Clearly define your target market before writing.
    —— Do you know what mailing lists you will be using?
    —— What are the job titles of the recipients of the advertising?
    —— What are their life-styles?
    —— What is the average educational level?
    —— What is the average household income?
    —— To what professional and social organizations do they belong?

2. Know the needs of your target audience and write with the purpose of helping them to fulfill these needs.
    —— Have you talked to or surveyed members of the target group to determine their needs?
    —— Does the program content assist them in fulfilling these needs? How?
    —— List at least fifteen needs of the target group. Keep this list in front of you while writing.

3. Emphasize benefits.
    —— Include in the copy at least ten to thirty benefits people will receive by attending.
    —— Place these benefits in a Special Benefits section.
    —— How have you accurately determined that these benefits are perceived as valuable by the target group?

4. Catch the reader's attention within the first three to four seconds.
    —— Is the copy on both front and back covers bold and action oriented?
    —— What about the title emphasizes action, urgency, importance, and excellence?
    —— Does the program title reach out and grab you?

5. Engage the reader.
    —— What about the copy immediately engages the reader?
    —— Does the copy tell a complete story?
    —— Is the copy presented in a logical sequence?
    —— Does the copy actively encourage registration?
    —— Is it easy to register?

6. Use action words and powerful messages that have a sense of urgency and encourage action on the part of the reader.
    —— Can you clearly identify at least fifty action and/or power words in the copy?
    —— Are there powerful and action-oriented headlines on each page of advertising?
    —— Does the title emphasize results?

7. Arrange copy so that it leads the reader through the message to take the action you want.
    ____ Have you tested the logic of this arrangement on at least one colleague and asked for feedback?
    ____ Have you tested the logic of this arrangement on at least one member of the target audience?

8. Test! Test! Test!
    ____ How do you plan to test the effectiveness of your copy?
    ____ Have you devised a system to track the effectiveness of mailing lists?
    ____ Have you set the copy aside for several days so that you can revise it with a fresh perspective?
    ____ Does the copy represent your best efforts?

22

How to Work
with an Advertising Agency

Chuck Buck

Often, continuing educators believe that only organizations with large staffs and large annual budgets can afford to use an ad agency. Although usually it is the large continuing education organizations that make extensive use of ad agencies, small organizations also use such agencies. Therefore, if you work in a small or medium-sized organization do not automatically exclude the services of an ad agency. You will find that use of these agencies can be very cost effective.

Advertising agencies can assist an organization in the creative interpretation of a continuing education marketing plan as well as in the implementation of an advertising program. This chapter describes how to (1) decide what kinds of services you will require from an agency, (2) evaluate the relative costs of these services, and (3) assess, with the agency, how the success of projects will be measured.

Advertising agencies can bring to life the continuing education organization's marketing position in an advertisement. They can create the appropriate image through a brochure. They can persuasively communicate the organization's programs, products, and services to a highly targeted audience. In addition, they provide professional advice on how to reach this audience in a cost-effective manner through an appropriate mix of media. As an advertising agency's work will reflect the marketing plan and other elements of the advertising program, it is important to consider the kind of agency services needed and the extent to which resources can be allocated for those services.

Most agencies provide such services as primary and secondary research, creative development of newspaper and magazine advertisements and radio and television commercials, outdoor and transit advertising, and a variety of collateral design projects, including brochures, flyers, statement stuffers, and annual reports. In addition, advertising agencies, acting on behalf of their clients, analyze media options relative to audience delivery and cost-per-thousand of reaching a targeted audience. They purchase media for which they are compensated through commissions paid by the media. In the case of newspapers, which do not pay commissions, agencies add a surcharge representing a percentage of the total cost—normally 15 percent. These services are only a few of the services traditionally provided by advertising agencies.

In recent years, some advertising agencies, to respond to the changing needs of their clients and the marketplace, have supplemented traditional services with services typically offered by highly specialized communications companies. Therefore, certain agencies will probably be able to provide corporate identification programs, graphic design, direct-response marketing programs, executive recruitment advertising, sales promotion support, and audiovisual production services.

Considering an Advertising Agency

In deciding how an advertising agency might play a role in the marketing program, review the internal and external factors before selecting the advertising agency. Address the (1) costs of internal sources, (2) costs of external services, (3) availability of internal resources, (4) total program costs, and (5) alignment of the organization's needs with outside services.

It might be in your best economic interests to deliver some promotional services internally, using available resources. Or the particular advertising program might require specialized services not readily available internally, for example, a television or radio commercial, which should probably be executed by an experienced agency broadcast producer familiar with residual talent payments, music rights, and labor laws.

Costs of Internal Sources. Compare the costs of services available from an advertising agency with the costs for similar services available in your organization. Include labor, materials, and overhead; agencies include these costs in their estimates. The true cost of a product such as a brochure or newspaper ad reflects more than the time used to produce the work. For example, if you have a graphic designer or production artist and a copywriter on your staff, use the actual time spent and their base hourly rates to calculate the cost of producing the brochure. Since the base hourly rate may not include health insurance costs, taxes, and overhead, set up a procedure for computing that information. You will then be able to determine the real cost of labor for a project. Such data are invaluable in comparisons of internal costs with cost estimates provided by agencies and outside vendors. You might find that it is less expensive to produce advertising internally; however, you can draw such a conclusion only after an objective analysis.

Costs of External Sources. Agencies typically arrive at hourly rates that are competitive within the marketplace. Into those rates is usually added a multiplier factor of 2½ to 4. This factor represents the profit returned to the agency. The multiplier will vary with the agency and depends on the total annual billing relative to their total annual expenses. The lower the multiplier, the more likely the agency is to bill significantly higher to offset overhead costs. Conversely, an agency with a high multiplier needs to charge more per job to reach its profit goals. Generally, advertising agencies have competitive rates based on their talent and competence. Because these agencies are in business to make a profit, they rarely reduce their rates to gain clients.

In addition, agencies are likely to charge a commission, normally 15 percent of the out-of-pocket expenses for such items as photography, engravings, typography, color separations, and printing. This commission covers the time the agency expended on these purchases and thus represents a kind of handling charge or overhead you pay for not having to handle these transactions yourself.

The client and the agency should agree in advance on the tasks that the agency is to undertake, as well as the costs for those tasks. If the costs are not covered by commissions the agency expects to earn on advertising space and broadcast time, then usually a fee is negotiated to make up the difference. This fee can be paid monthly or on a project-by-project basis.

Agencies use many different methods to charge for their services. Since the 1970s, agencies and advertisers have been wrestling with inequities inherent to the commission-only basis of payment. Advertisers have long believed that agencies should not be paid only through commissions earned by placing advertisements, particularly because media costs have outpaced inflation. Agencies, experiencing shifts in client budgets away from media to promotional mix programs such as direct-response and sales promotion, have been looking for methods of compensation that return an equitable profit for their time and money. This would allow them to reinvest profits into their businesses to improve services.

If you decide to use an agency, review compensation plans, hourly rates, fees, and commissions, and compare them with competitive market rates and with the cost of handling the project internally.

Availability of Internal Sources. The marketing plan for a continuing education organization should clearly describe the kinds of promotional programs (newspaper, magazine or broadcast advertising, direct mail, telemarketing sales promotion) required to promote the organization and its programs, products, and services. For instance, if advertising and direct mail are the recommended promotional mix in the advertising plan, the tools that need to be produced should be described. Will there be magazine ads as well as newspaper ads? Will the direct-mail program require the production of a brochure, business reply card, and an incentive?

One of the first steps in assessing the availability of internal resources is to list the communications tools needed to implement the advertising program. Matching that list with the organization's available internal resources should indicate whether the resources necessary to create the communications tools are available. In addition, this assessment should indicate the extent of the need for outside sources. Determine the time required to produce the recommended tools to see if your staff can complete production of work in the allotted time.

Total Program Costs. Just as the marketing plan outlines each of the advertising programs, it must consider the costs for these items. Program costs, together with all other costs relative to overall revenues, determine the financial viability of the marketing plan. Therefore, the list of communications tools, along with the anticipated production and printing costs, indicates how much work should be done internally versus externally.

To calculate your advertising costs, predict the amount of time necessary to complete each project internally. For example, if the product is a brochure, determine the number of hours the graphic artist will spend on conceptualization, overall layout, type selection, and stock specifications. Add the number of hours required by a staff member to write, edit, and rewrite copy. Estimate material and labor costs for photography, engravings, color separations, and typography.

These calculations will provide a valid estimate of the cost of producing the communications tools internally, and can be used to judge the cost of producing a similar product externally. The cost of each tool must be similarly estimated. Printers, color separators, and typesetters can estimate the external cost associated with each tool.

Another important consideration is the staff experience level. Can they objectively interpret and persuasively communicate the features and benefits of your organization and its products and services? The level of staff experience in the many different phases of production will determine how much more time might be required on their part to complete tasks or whether their time could be better spent on other aspects of the advertising program.

Alignment of Needs with Outside Services. In many cases, advertising agencies are expected to creatively interpret the marketing goals of the organization and develop the appropriate communications tools (brochures and other direct-mail pieces, for example). In some instances, clients rely on agencies to develop elaborate corporate identification programs, including letterheads, business cards, on-site signs, and annual reports. With the knowledge that these services are available, you must align your needs with the resources of the agency you are considering.

In contemplating use of an agency, answer these two questions: (1) To what extent can the agency interpret and create an appropriate marketing image for your organization and its programs, products, and services? (2) With what level of skill can the agency create and deliver that marketing image—consistently and cost effectively—across a broad spectrum of communications tools to well-defined targeted audiences? If you determine that these services can be better provided externally, then develop criteria for selecting an agency.

Selecting an Advertising Agency

Advertising agencies come in a variety of sizes and shapes, with varying levels of competence across a wide range of services. Interview the agencies you are considering. You can expedite the interview process if you communicate to the agency your organization's advertising needs, budget, and availability of internal resources. You can thus use the interview to discuss the cost and time constraints under which the agency is expected to perform.

Interview a variety of agencies to gain an understanding of their respective talents, strengths, approaches, and, just as importantly, the people who will be assigned to your account. Specifically you should consider (1) overall agency size, (2) scope of services, (3) comparable experience level, and (4) compatibility. Advertising agency personnel are frequently interviewed by prospective clients and they are not at all uncomfortable with the process.

Overall Agency Size. The relative size of the advertising agency and your anticipated billing are important considerations. Billing is the total money to be spent by your organization for services and media. You want to know how the agency spends your money compared with the monies of other clients. Usually, an individual client's budget is small relative to the agency's overall budget. Therefore, the time that agency personnel can spend on an individual account and still maintain overall profitability is limited. On the other hand, an agency that is not large enough to provide all the services expected by your continuing education organization can be an inappropriate choice.

Scope of Services. Use the list of recommended advertising programs and anticipated communications tools as a framework against which you compare the agencies under consideration, with respect to the services they provide. Not all agencies offer the same kinds of services. Some, for example, are more qualified in research and design than in media buying and broadcast production.

Comparable Experience. You should compare different agencies with respect to both type of experience and level of experience. Generally, most advertisers seek agencies with experience in similar industries. This is especially true of health care organizations, financial institutions, and high-tech firms. The more experience an agency has in your particular industry—continuing education— the less tutorial time must be expended on members of the agency. In some cases, a lack of experience within the specific industry can be offset by experience in other areas important to your organization.

Cost of Services. Most agencies price their services competitively within the market. Agencies in major markets such as New York, Chicago, or Los Angeles charge somewhat higher than agencies in regional markets. More important than the relative costs for services of various agencies, however, is how those costs fit into your overall advertising budget. The cost for completing the project internally is a good benchmark against which to compare the costs for services offered by outside sources. Moreover, if you should discover that the various agencies offer comparable services but at prices different from your internal estimates, you might want to reexamine your budget. It is easy to underestimate production and media costs.

Compatibility. Most agencies agree that the best work is accomplished when agency and client exist in an environment of mutual trust and respect. As you are relying on the agency to provide honest, objective counsel, establish a relationship that encourages independent thinking. Encourage debate. This is possible only if your organization and the prospective agency are compatible. You can probably sense compatibility during the interview. All other factors being equal, your decision may depend on compatibility.

Working with the Agency on Your Advertising Program

After carefully selecting the agency, organize a system to manage the relationship. Consider these guidelines:

1. Define the client/agency relationship.
2. Assign key people to the account.
3. Agree to the creative development process.
4. Develop the criteria for measuring success.
5. Establish effective communications between you and the agency.

Management of the client/agency relationship from the beginning will do much to ensure clear communications in day-to-day activities.

Defining the Client/Agency Relationship. Review in detail the scope of the agency's anticipated involvement in your advertising program. Will the agency review your research materials and data bases? Will the agency be responsible for the development of advertising materials, brochures, videos, and other forms of communication? Will the agency be in charge of placing such materials? Will you seek their counsel on public relations issues, organizational identity programs, or sales promotion? To keep future communications clear, review the full range of anticipated involvement.

In addition, review and discuss individual projects that you have assigned to the agency. Each project should be fully described and include a profile of the target audience, a time frame for the project, and its cost relative to other projects in the advertising program. Write this description so that it can be shared both with the agency and within the organization.

Assigning Key People to the Account. In most cases, your advertising account will be managed by an account executive selected by the agency. Agencies select the person best qualified to supervise the internal as well as external activities associated with creating and implementing your advertising program. The account executive relies on others within the agency to provide expertise in such areas as creative development, media buying and placement, copy writing, and broadcast production. Just as the agency assembles its team, assign key individuals from your organization to work with the agency. Select a primary contact who will represent the concerns of your entire group.

Agreeing on the Creative Development Process. The best creative solutions can miss the mark if they do not evolve from a thorough analysis of the marketing problem. For each project, provide the agency with a written fact sheet that addresses the following issues:

1. Establishing a profile of the consumer or end-user
2. Defining consumer or end-user benefits
3. Agreeing on the problem that advertising must solve
4. Identifying the primary competition faced by your organization
5. Developing approaches that differentiate your organization and its programs, products, and services from others
6. Setting overall objectives for the advertising
7. Agreeing on the inclusion of disclaimers

Most agencies will see this discussion and the agreements that result from it as a productive path to creative solutions. Inform the agency, in writing, of who will be responsible for supplying information, providing technical resources, selecting subjects for photography, and approving concepts, copy, final art work, and proofs. Also note the timetable for the completion of those tasks.

Anticipate changes during the course of the creative development process because these may affect the budget. All changes should be documented and the reestimates resubmitted and approved before proceeding to the next step in production.

Developing Criteria for Measuring Effectiveness. Before authorizing the agency to begin the creative work, both you and the agency should review and agree on the criteria to be used in evaluating the effectiveness of the advertising program after its implementation.

1. For each program, determine the response expected from the target market.
2. Establish time lines for projects relative to the overall marketing plan and in consideration of seasonality in the target market.
3. Understand the relative value of creativity for all projects.
4. Determine the cost of each advertising project relative to the expected revenues.

It is also important that you agree on how effectiveness will be measured. It is usually measured as the number of inquiries received in response to advertising, the percentage increase in sales or advertising awareness, or the number of products, programs, or services sold within a given period. Success also hinges on timely implementation, particularly if the program, product, or service is seasonal.

Different parts of the advertising program require different levels of creativity. Should the quickly produced flyer have the same creative input as the comprehensive catalogue? Should the magazine advertisement be in black and white or in four color? Ensure that both you and the agency agree on such issues.

Collectively Measuring Results. Review and analysis of program effectiveness should be an ongoing activity in both your organization and the advertising agency. Not only do you want to measure response to each project, but you want to determine how much the entire advertising program has contributed to the success of the marketing plan. Typically, reviews are conducted toward the end of a year or a project. If yours is a year-long program of promotional projects and activities, review its overall effectiveness during the last three months of the year. You then can use the evaluation in preparing next year's program.

Compare the effectiveness of the program with the goals of your organization's marketing plan. For example, if one of the marketing objectives was to increase penetration of a program, product, or service within a certain market segment and advertising was the recommended promotional tool, it should be determined whether advertising actually created sufficient awareness. If a marketing objective was to increase overall sales for the organization, was the money allocated to the advertising program disproportionate to the revenues generated? Simply put, did it cost too much to achieve the marketing objective?

Alignment of the advertising costs with the marketing objectives is important because of the many internal and external changes taking place in the market. Continuing education marketing is conducted in a dynamic environment, and change is to be expected. Control over certain factors can help keep marketing objectives realistic and, consequently, in line with budgets.

Pitfalls to Avoid When Working with an Agency

Advertising agencies are completely dependent on you for the internal information they need to perform the tasks assigned to them. They can gather external information and evaluate it independently as it relates to the organization and the market it serves. Thus, lack of communication is the single largest pitfall in dealing with agencies. There are other pitfalls:

1. *Failure to allot sufficient time to projects.* Inadequate planning is usually the cause. The importance of early planning and of contingency planning cannot be stressed too much. To avoid this pitfall, establish a deadline for each task and review progress regularly.

2. *Failure to prepare an adequate budget.* This pitfall has several causes. The original budget may have been incorrect, budgetary control may have been lacking during the implementation stage, or external factors, such as competi-

tion, may have made the planned budget obsolete. The solution is to insist on rigorous budgeting accountability from both the agency and your own organization. If it becomes apparent that there is not enough money to complete all tasks, reduce the number of planned projects, scale them down, or rethink the advertising strategy itself. Make sure that the estimates under review are accurate and current. Budget review must be considered an important daily procedure both within your organization and at the agency. Be prepared to take steps to keep costs in line or to alter the present course of action if costs escalate beyond the budget.

3. *Failure to clearly define marketing objectives and strategies.* Marketing objectives must be quantifiable, attainable, specific, and complete. Strategies are the action plans through which objectives are achieved. When marketing objectives are ill-defined, ambiguous, or too ambitious, the corresponding strategies are inappropriate and adversely affect the advertising programs. As the marketing plan is executed in a constantly changing environment, continuous reevaluation of objectives is wise. Determine whether the objectives are still valid. If they are not, modify them and make the corresponding changes throughout the plan, down to the smallest details.

4. *Failure to set realistic expectations.* Too often, anticipation of the success of an advertising program leads to unrealistic expectations. Even seasoned professionals are sometimes disappointed when they equate advertising effectiveness with sales performance or when they assume that a good promotional campaign will overcome external forces that doom a program, product, or service to failure. To overcome this pitfall, set realistic goals for the advertising program. At best, advertising creates awareness and helps to project the personality or image of an organization. You must set a realistic and mutually agreed-on expectation level with the agency. In addition, keep expectations in line with market realities.

These very common problems can lead to stress between client and agency. It is important to consider all these issues because they affect the success or failure of advertising. The point is clear. Discuss these issues openly and frankly with the agency.

Summary

Before securing an advertising agency to implement all or part of your advertising program, list the anticipated tasks, prepare a budget, analyze your internal resources, and determine whether the program can be handled internally.

Once you have determined that it is to your advantage to work with an advertising agency, use the guidelines discussed in this chapter. If you facilitate clear communications, the advertising program will be executed as planned and within budget. When it operates in an environment of mutual respect and agreement on goals, an agency can breathe fresh life into a continuing education organization's marketing program.

23

Tracking the Results of Advertising

Maris A. St. Cyr

You have identified your advertising theme, approved final copy, kissed the mechanicals good-bye, and signed off on the media plan. Now it is time to sit back and hope for the best. But what *is* the best and how will you know if you have it or not?

Advertising results are seldom what we expect, often less than we want, and sometimes all that we hoped for. But how can we arrive at any of these conclusions without a reliable means for measuring outcomes and assessing results?

In this chapter, we will explore several ways in which you can monitor the results of ad placements. We will examine why tracking is important to your campaign, how tracking procedures can be incorporated, how tracking results can be traced and reported, and why collected data should be viewed from more than one perspective. The chapter focuses on tracking as a viable and intelligent measure of ad effectiveness and provides guidelines on development of a tracking system that suits your special organizational needs.

Tracking—The Whys and Wherefores

Tracking the results of advertising makes good sense. And it can be done by most advertisers if they take the time to devise a tracking system that suits their needs. Tracking provides important feedback, allows for analysis, provides accountability, and creates a basis for informed and responsible decision making. Need more convincing?

1. Tracking will allow you to assess and analyze your advertising efforts. By measuring response, you can determine if advertising has been an effective part of your promotion mix and whether your ads are having the desired impact on the target audience.

2. Through tracking, you begin to evaluate your advertising expenditures in the light of the income generated. Over time, you are able to weigh the cost effectiveness of your placements and determine those types of advertising that are appropriate for your program or service.

3. When you track results, you are, in effect, doing the research for your next marketing effort. By evaluating response *this* time around—which medium drew the best response, which generated the greatest income, which most effectively sold what products—you can better target your next campaign. Knowing what works and what does not work will help you to fine-tune future advertising strategies.

4. As you accumulate tracking results, you increase your chances of predicting downward trends, before they have an adverse effect, and upward trends, before your competitors spot them. In addition, your tracking histories may reveal seasonal surges or geographic hot spots that can work to your advantage in the next campaign.

5. Tracking can assist you in testing the variables you believe have an impact on the success of your ads—from design elements and page position to coupon location and day of placement. A good tracking system can provide you with the means to test some of your theories.

With forethought, planning, and staff cooperation, an advertising tracking system can tell you more about your efforts than you have ever known before. As a result, you will be in a better position to design effective advertising strategies for your continuing education program.

Getting Started—The Basics of Measuring Response

Tracking Procedures as Part of Your Advertising Plan. Once you have decided to track, immediately incorporate tracking procedures into your advertising plan. Be sure that you have a trackable campaign, that is, a program intended to generate an immediate response from a target audience (an image campaign, for example, is not expected to generate an immediate response). You will need to address certain issues early in your planning:

1. *Ad design.* What response method are you going to use? If you are tracking for the first time, you may select a response method that is relatively easy to track. Many find business reply cards accompanying ads or reply coupons included in ads effective response vehicles; others prefer telephone response exclusively. Some use both methods. Choose the response method early because the response mechanism must be part of your ad design.

2. *Ad copy.* Clearly state the response method in your ad: return the coupon,

call today, write for more information. This raises several important questions: Who will receive the responses? What return address will be used on the reply card/coupon? Whose telephone number will appear in the ad?

3. *Ad response.* As you develop an advertising tracking system, it becomes crucial to anticipate response. What is the anticipated volume of response? Will it be possible to handle response within your own operation and with current staff? Must several staff people be assigned to handle incoming mail? Will you need several telephone lines to accommodate a large volume of calls? Does your media plan include electronic media placements that are broadcast outside of working hours? Are ads placed at times when there is no one to answer an ad line?

4. *Ad tracking time frame.* What are you defining as the tracking period? Although most responses are received within the first five to seven days of ad placement, response time varies according to the medium. How long should you plan to collect responses? Take a look at your media plan and determine a reasonable tracking period.

5. *Tracking methods.* What are your capabilities? If you have a relatively small operation, is manual tracking the most reasonable approach for getting started? Or do you have computer support that will allow you to track electronically? And, if so, can your software be programmed to record responses and match them with later sales/registration logs?

By taking a close look at each of these items, you can begin to outline the mechanics of a tracking system.

The Tracking Code—The Key to Measuring Display Ad Response.

Perhaps the single most important element in measuring display ad response is a tracking code. Codes are devised according to your needs, and each ad placed is assigned its own specific code. Codes can be as simple as A, B, and C or they can be keyed to represent the ad publication and appearance date. For example, BBJ2/14 can be used to represent a placement in the *Big Bargain Journal* on February 14. Develop a coding system that addresses your computing needs. Whatever the coding system, remember that a tracking code should be assigned to *every* display ad, either on the coupon or on the reply card.

The tracking code can be printed anywhere on the coupon or card. Of course, it is a good idea to place the code where it will not interfere with the information you are requesting from the respondent. Review your media plan *before* you place your ads and assign a code to each placement. The artist can then place the code on the mechanicals. You can also apply it yourself with press type (in small point size) purchased at any graphic supply store.

If you decide against a return coupon and include only a response address, consider incorporating a tracking device into the return address. In this way, a look at the return envelope will tell you the ad to which your client is replying. Distinguish between ads by varying the name of the addressee (Registrar, Coordinator, Sales Director) or the return address (102 Beed Hall—A, 102 Beed

Hall—B). Just be sure that the code does not interfere with postal regulations or delivery of your mail.

Coupons, reply cards, and return envelopes are easy to separate and can usually be tallied on a daily basis. A daily log and a sheet of weekly totals will give you a quick indication of how your ads are doing. Over time, your tally sheets become historical data that you can use for comparisons. Exhibit 23.1 is an example of an easy-to-maintain response tally sheet.

If you are not logging respondent information elsewhere and if the response mechanism is not an order to purchase, retain your coupons and reply cards. You will need them later in the tracking process to determine whether or not respondents actually purchased your product or attended your program. Of course, all of the respondents who have demonstrated an interest are potential customers, and their names and addresses should be retained on your mailing list.

Telephone Tracking—When the Question Is Key. Today, most display ads provide a telephone number for immediate and convenient response. Telephone responses must also be tracked; therefore, early in the planning stages of your ad campaign, determine whether your organization can handle telephone responses. Consider the anticipated response to your ad. Can your office deal with additional telephone traffic? Will your staff be at work during the hours respondents are most likely to call? Do you have an appropriate answering system that can be used during nonworking hours (answering service or recorded message)? If you believe that you are unable to field telephone responses in-house, you should consider using a reputable answering service.

Should you decide to handle telephone response calls in-house, there are several items to consider before you begin: telephone equipment, development of a telephone call slip, and staff training.

Exhibit 23.1. Daily (Weekly) Ad Response Tally Sheet.

Date   Monday, August 10 (Week of August 16)

Ad Placement	Telephone Response		Coupon Response		Total Responses
BBJ7/31	_____	+	_____	=	_____
SSM8/1	_____		_____		_____
CF8/3	_____		_____		_____
BBJ8/4	_____		_____		_____
	+ _____	+	_____	+	_____
Total	_____		_____		_____

Adapt this grid to serve as a daily or weekly tally sheet.

1. You may find it helpful to investigate the installation of a special advertising telephone line to be used exclusively in ads. This line would never be used for outgoing calls. Thus, when the ad line rings, you know that the incoming call is an ad respondent—you need only learn which ad prompted the call. The volume of calls may force incoming calls to other extensions. Consider instituting a second exclusive line if volume is very heavy.

2. Once you have decided to handle telephone response, design a telephone call slip that covers the information you need from each ad respondent. If you are loading information directly into a computer, create a screen that prompts for the needed information. Clearly show what information is needed, putting the most important information first and providing space in which the data can be entered. Exhibit 23.2 is a sample call slip for recording responses. It can easily be adapted to fit your individual needs. The call slip should conclude with your key tracking question: *Can you tell me how you learned about our product/service/program?* It is an easy question to ask once rapport is established with the caller. It is also the most important question for the purposes of tracking. Provide space for the answer. Remember, the caller has dialed your special ad line, so you can be certain that she or he is responding to an ad.

3. Staff need to understand the concept of tracking and must be committed to collecting the information that makes tracking possible. The time spent in preparing your staff will pay off when your ad calls start coming in. Take the time to explain what you are doing and how the information gathered will be used. Review the call slip with everyone who will answer ad lines. Give staff an opportunity to devise their own ways of asking how the caller learned about your service, but stress the importance of obtaining an answer to this question. Encourage staff to coach the respondent, when necessary, with such questions as Did you see the ad today? Do you recall in which publication? Might it have been in the *Big Bargain Journal?* Most callers are happy to tell you where they saw your ad after a little prompting. If your media placements are relatively few, you might even insert a checklist of ads at the bottom of your call slip. Staff can simply check the appropriate ad or location.

Again, a daily tally of call slips gives a quick overview of ad response activity. With your coupon and telephone tallies in hand, you can calculate your week's total response and begin to visualize the progress of your campaign.

The Display Ad Report—A Key to Understanding Ad Results. From the data you have collected thus far, a simple report will give you important feedback on the performance of your ad placements. With tally sheets in hand you are ready for analysis.

First, determine the number of responses generated by each ad placement. The results may be surprising. A publication you thought perfectly suited to your audience might have drawn far fewer responses than one you had considered a

Exhibit 23.2.

Sample Call Slip   **Telephone Call Slip**
                                        Code _____

Date _____

           Mr.
           Ms.
Name   Dr. _____

Address _____

           _____

           _____
                              City   State   Zip

Item Requested   **Interest Area**

__ Graduate catalogue   __ Noncredit brochure   __ A&S   __ Ed

__ Undergraduate   __ Other _____   __ Bus   __ ABS
   catalogue

How Caller Learned About Program

__ General knowledge   __ SCS catalogue

__ Word of mouth   __ Noncredit brochure

__ Student or former student   __ Letter

__ Employee   __ Other _____

__ Ad _____   _____
            Publication name/TV or radio station   Date

__ Article _____   _____
                    Publication name   Date

---

marginal advertising vehicle. A placement you had selected primarily for sales of program X may have generated more inquiries about program Y. A publication with a limited circulation may have drawn better for your service than the broad-circulation piece you thought was a sure bet.

Next, compare your telephone and coupon figures. Did more respondents call or write? Did the writers request information about one program while the callers asked about another? Were more registrations generated by phone or by mail? How does this information influence your next campaign?

And last, what did each inquiry cost you? Divide the cost of your ad (a two-column by four-inch ad in the *Big Bargain Journal* cost $1,500) by the number of February 14 ad respondents (number of individuals who called or wrote in response to the BBJ2/14 ad). The answer will give you a rough idea of the cost per respondent:

$$\frac{\text{(cost of ad placement) \$1,500}}{\text{(number of respondents) 150}} = \$10 \text{ (cost per respondent/inquiry)}$$

Are you shocked? Are you pleased? What are the relative cost differences between placements? Have you learned something you did not know and is it information that you will consider when you prepare your next campaign?

Although you may now have more information than you have ever had about the performance of your display ads, there is more to be learned. Do not discard the poor performers yet.

The Mechanics of Tracking Radio/Television Response

Plan the tracking of broadcast media well in advance with your creative director and media buyer. As with display advertising, some decisions must be made early in the advertising planning process—decisions that will affect your ability to track advertising response. One of these is the method of response. Because of the immediacy of television and radio, most advertising experts encourage telephone response, though response by mail is not out of the question.

So, what must you consider as you devise the tracking system? Again, you must determine whether you are adequately staffed to field the response calls. What is the projected response? Will your staff be available during the hours the ads run? Must the ad include a tag line requesting that calls be made only between certain hours?

Next, do you plan to use your standard ad line telephone number or to install a special line? If you are airing ads on a variety of stations, how do you determine which station the caller was listening to? Are separate numbers available in-house that would allow each station to have its own response number?

Encouraged to call right away, and given a simple mnemonic (Call COL-LEGE right now!), the listener/viewer who dials your number expects someone to answer the phone and to provide the necessary information. The staff person must elicit tracking information from the caller. After collecting the information outlined on your call slip, staff should again close with key questions, prompting for answers: Can you tell me how you learned about our product/service/program? Do you remember on which station you heard the ad? Can you recall the station or program you were watching when you saw the ad?

Once again, the telephone call slip (or specially designed computer screen) is essential to tracking response. In addition to this basic information, you may wish to note the time the call came in, when the caller heard the ad (morning/evening), what stations the caller regularly watches/listens to, and whether the caller has ever purchased a similar product. The call needs to be handled quickly, however, and a lengthy set of questions is not recommended.

If you are located in a large market and determine that you are simply unable to handle the volume of calls expected in-house, or if your ads will run during nonworking hours, you may consider working with a reputable answering service. Again, early planning is essential. Meet with a representative of the service and make your needs clear. The service may be willing to use your telephone tracking slips to collect the information you need. Call slips can be prepared in advance and specifically geared to the phone answerer who does not know your product. You may also consider buying several different extension numbers. In this case, each station buy can have a separate response number, allowing you to determine with greater accuracy exactly how many calls were generated by each station.

Work closely with the answering service's representative to ensure that all of your concerns are addressed. Call the various numbers yourself early in the campaign to check that respondents are being handled as you directed. And let your representative know right away if you discover any problems.

In collecting simple data from your broadcast media ad respondents, you learn several things about the effect of your campaign: number of respondents to radio/television, number of responses generated by each station, and cost per respondent. If you have used various time slots, or tested different delivery formats, you may also derive information on the tastes of those you have targeted through broadcast advertising.

Your telephone tracking slips are valuable records of information. Not only should these be retained for the next tracking step, but the respondents should be added to your mailing list.

Conversion Data—The Rest of the Story

If you have never tracked advertising responses before, then what we have discussed thus far will provide you with some basic data on your ad placements. There is, however, another level of tracking and analysis that will further enhance your understanding of what your organization's advertising dollars are achieving.

Although it is important to know what response each ad placement garners, it is even more important to know which ads actually sell your product. Taking the next step—review of conversion data—will help you to analyze your placements by determining which ad respondents actually became buyers, how much income each ad generates, and how much it costs to sell to each customer.

The value of this information can be readily seen, especially when you remember that current tracking information is research for your next campaign. Up to this point, you may have been delighted with the ad placement that generated an exceptional response. On further analysis, however, you may learn that the ad converted (or translated into sales) quite poorly and that another placement, drawing a more moderate response, converted very well. Or, you may learn that although two ads converted equally well, the respondents to ad A spent a great deal more on your products than did the respondents to ad B. Thus, one placement generated more income than the other. Whatever you learned from your initial tracking data now takes on added meaning as you look at qualitative outcomes.

From Respondent to Customer—What the Numbers Tell You. To determine how many of your ad respondents became paying customers, check the respondents' names and addresses (from coupons and telephone call slips) against your sales or registration records. To assess the conversion rate of a specific ad, determine how many respondents to that ad purchased the program/service. Then divide the number of paying customers by the total number of responses generated by the ad:

$$\frac{\text{paying customers who responded to BBJ2/14}}{\text{total number of respondents to BBJ2/14}} = \text{conversion rate}$$

You may find it worthwhile to analyze this same information in the light of telephone and coupon responses. In this case, divide the number of telephone respondents who became paying customers by the total number of telephone respondents. Did your telephone respondents convert better than your coupon respondents or vice versa? Will this information change your strategies for the future?

The Paying Customer—What the Dollars Tell You. As you check your ad respondents against sales or registration lists, take a close look at what each customer spent. You may be surprised to learn that the *Big Bargain Journal* ad generated significantly higher income than another ad that produced the same number of paying customers. Watch for these income indicators and through your tracking histories determine whether they are trends or flukes. An ad placement that consistently generates good response and excellent income may get the nod when budget considerations force you to make some hard choices.

You may also be interested in learning how much it cost you to capture each paying customer. If your ad placement cost $2,500 and 50 respondents actually bought your service, then your cost per buyer was $50.

Outlining conversion information in a brief yet concise report will let you see at a glance how each placement performed in the long run. The report may include the total number of responses to the ad, the number of respondents who became paying customers, the conversion rate, the income generated by the ad, and the average amount spent by each customer. Conversion information, in the final analysis, is what you have been seeking all along.

The following chart illustrates how to organize and display this analysis of conversion information.

Ad	Responses	Sales	Conversion	Income	$ per Customer
BBJ2/14	175	40	22.8%	$8,000	$200
WAK3/13	473	65	13.7%	$9,750	$150
MJK9/4	195	28	14.3%	$6,300	$225

At first glance, you might focus on the excellent response generated by the WAK3/13 ad. Sales and income for this ad also look good until you examine the conversion rate, which shows that only 13.7% of the ad respondents actually purchased the product. On the other hand, although the BBJ2/14 ad generated a more moderate response, 22.8% of the respondents actually purchased the product, generating $8,000 in income.

MJK9/14 generated a moderate response and had a 14.3% conversion rate. The converted customers, however, spent an average of $225 per buyer, significantly more than the converted customers of the previous two ads.

As you evaluate these data, it is interesting to calculate the cost of these ad placements. If the least expensive placement was BBJ2/14, you may have a winner on your hands. In any case, you now have data that should assist you in future ad placement decisions.

For a detailed analysis on how to analyze response rates using an electronic spreadsheet, see Chapter Twenty-nine.

Recovering Conversion Data. The method for recovering conversion data depends on your organization's structure and resources. It is up to you to assess the most efficient resources, staff hours, computing capabilities, and information feedback systems available. In a small continuing education operation, staff time may be needed to manually match the names on sales or registration lists with the telephone call slips to determine how many respondents registered for a program or purchased a product. This method is workable but slow and, in addition to significant staff time, requires readily available sales/registration lists and careful hand calculations. Many operations begin harvesting conversion data with a manual operation and then shift to a more effective and cost-efficient mechanized system. Often, by working through the steps of a manual system, you are better able to articulate your tracking needs when mechanization becomes possible.

A computerized tracking system is ideal for organizations equipped with competent computer support. It is worth the investment of time and money to work with your computing center/information systems unit to devise a program or adapt a software package that meets your tracking needs. If input at the time of the ad respondent's inquiry is accurate, respondents can later be matched with sales, registration, or contract lists to determine which respondents registered, the source of their original inquiry (identified by the code), and the income generated by that advertising vehicle.

Yet another option is to enlist an outside firm. Computing services will work with you to devise a system, provide the necessary data input, and generate reports that address your areas of concerns—all for a fee. A large operation or an operation in a large market may find it more economical to pursue this line of action. It is important that you know what you want to learn from a tracking system, how you want reports generated, and the time frames in which you will need to receive them. The success of the system may depend on your ability to articulate these needs, your willingness to work closely with those who will develop the system, and your patience in working through various trial runs.

Whatever method you choose, it is always helpful to talk with others who have covered the ground you are about to traverse. Network with colleagues, talk with software vendors, and explore tracking systems that are currently serving organizations similar to yours. And do not forget to consult your staff, especially those who speak directly to your ad respondents. Their insights—about questions callers ask, response hours and patterns, difficulties in obtaining certain pieces of information—can help you identify important items that may influence the system you devise.

Summary

Tracking the results of advertising is a valuable and effective means of keeping on top of your advertising efforts. One caution, though, must be offered. The data you collect must be viewed in perspective within a broad set of evaluative criteria. There are many variables to the success or failure of an ad campaign, and your collected data must be judged within a balanced framework. Remember, the customer who responds to this week's ad may do so because he or she saw a number of previous placements, and the ads placed this week may prep potential clients who will not respond until your next campaign. The intangibles of advertising are difficult to calibrate and the long-term effects are often too complex to measure.

Keep this brief checklist for tracking handy.

1. Make tracking part of your advertising plan.
2. Use a tracking code on every print ad.
3. Reserve one telephone line for all advertising response.
4. Design a telephone call slip that can be used by staff to record necessary data.
5. Train all staff to ask the key question.
6. Keep a daily/weekly/total count of all ad responses.
7. Calculate how many ad respondents are converted to customers.
8. Do a final report on ad response, conversions, and income.
9. Analyze tracking data before launching the next campaign.
10. Keep a log of ad results and review it periodically.

Tracking the results of advertising provides feedback on the measurable parts of a complex activity. By balancing this information with your own knowledge of the market, the media, your product, and your organization's advertising needs, you will be in a better position to make informed decisions and to develop effective strategies for the future.

PART SIX

Effective
Personal Sales

Part Six analyzes how to be effective in using personal sales in the continuing education organization. The thesis of Chapter Twenty-Four, by Carol D. Holden, is that by involving all staff as personal salespersons, you can increase registrations and sales volume without increasing payroll and advertising costs. She gives many examples of how successful continuing education organizations are accomplishing this and creating a dedicated, loyal work force with a personal ownership in the success of the continuing education enterprise.

In Chapter Twenty-Five, B. Ray Holland looks at ways to increase registrations through successful telemarketing, a form of advertising often overlooked by many continuing education organizations. Holland provides step-by-step assistance for thinking through this type of comprehensive advertising campaign. Integral parts of the chapter are actual telephone scripts used for telemarketing campaigns and suggestions on how to maximize the effectiveness of such scripts. Telemarketing in continuing education works and Holland demonstrates how to use it successfully to increase program registrations.

Susan Coats uses Chapter Twenty-Six to explain how exhibition at conferences, conventions, and trade shows can be an integral part of the total marketing plan. She presents guidelines on budgeting, preshow and exhibit promotion, staffing, effective product demonstration, and avoidance of the most frequently made mistakes. In addition, she explains how commercial exhibit preparation and setup people can provide professional assistance. Her lists of professional people and organizations specializing in exhibit preparation are invaluable to those involved in creating effective exhibits.

Involving clients in the development and marketing of programs can actively contribute to an organization's overall marketing success. In Chapter Twenty-Seven, Richard B. Fischer describes many creative ways to accomplish this goal. He analyzes how this often overlooked assistance with marketing can be important in creating highly innovative marketing programs. He examines the use of written surveys, interviews, planning groups and advisory boards, open houses and public hearings, events, focus groups, and client visitations to achieve this special form of marketing. Included as appendixes to this chapter are a topic preference scale survey, an advisory committee questionnaire, a client interest survey, questions for structured telephone interviews, a peer invitation, and a confirmation letter suitable for use with advisory board members. All of these samples can easily be adapted to fit the individual needs of your continuing education organization.

The central idea in Part Six is that development of effective personal sales techniques is essential to establishment of an effective continuing education organization. Personal sales can be one of the most effective ways to reach consumers with information about programs. It is a very important aspect of a comprehensive marketing campaign.

24

How Every Staff Person Can Be a Salesperson

Carol D. Holden

All continuing education organizations have a potential untapped sales force—their own staff. Sometimes, as managers, we tend to compartmentalize our people and think narrowly about the jobs they perform. What we must realize is that our staff needs to understand the marketing process and become involved in it. Aside from program planning and development, marketing is probably the single most important factor in the success of continuing education enterprises. Leaders need to be sure that everyone on the staff understands and participates in the total marketing process.

By involving your staff in the creative marketing process you may increase attendance, registrations, and/or sales volume without increasing payroll and direct-mail costs. With printing and mailing costs rising, it is even more important to utilize all available help in the marketing of programs. In addition, staff involvement in the marketing process has the potential to increase morale and promote stronger team efforts in program development. In this chapter, methods that take advantage of this marketing potential are explored.

The Continuing Education Organization

How is your continuing education operation organized? Is there a separate marketing office or sales staff? If not, have you thought of adding professionals with direct responsibility for selling and promoting programs? Do you see your organization as having a sales and promotion mission or do you envision it as merely providing support to the teaching or service side of the parent institution?

Perhaps you are unhappy with the concept of selling in education (Freedman, 1987). If you are, then you are a member of an ever shrinking minority. Nearly all colleges and universities rely on their continuing education organizations to sell programs, as well as provide program development and logistical services, at least for programs older than the traditional daytime programs. Hospitals and health management organizations also depend on their marketing staff to promote their continuing education programs and their services. Fund-raising for many large organizations, including symphony orchestras and charitable organizations, is dependent on a strong marketing orientation. In all of these organizations, it is important to ensure that quality in programming equals quality in marketing (Freedman, 1987).

Many parent institutions expect that the continuing education division will return a sizable surplus for administrative overhead. This is true for colleges and universities as well as other not-for-profit organizations, such as hospitals and clinics, museums, and charitable organizations. A well-developed marketing and/or public relations function is becoming standard in organizations. Marketing strength is essential to success in continuing education organizations.

In any case, even if you are not expected to return a surplus to the parent institution, you nearly always need to make sure that individual programs break even. This is very difficult to do without setting a realistic break-even point (Simerly, 1984). Therefore, it is necessary to coordinate the budgeting process with the marketing plan to ensure both financial and program success.

Credit Programs

When marketing credit or noncredit continuing education programs for your organization, remember that you are marketing the very essence of the organization. The primary business of educational institutions is providing credit courses and degree programs. If you work with an organization other than a college or university, either for-profit or not-for-profit, the primary product is the quality of service. Many times, excellence is the only variable that distinguishes products among competing schools or organizations. Most colleges and universities have similar degree programs. What is distinctive is the quality of the faculty or the variation in a degree program that serves a specific market segment. Therefore, to remain viable, continuing education must serve two masters: (1) the faculty or the professional staff of the sponsoring organization, and (2) the public and its need for high-quality continuing professional education.

An overlooked, natural marketing staff for credit programs sponsored by institutions of higher education comprises the faculty and the deans of the schools and colleges. They know the programs and courses intimately and they have an abiding interest in the success of these programs. They are interested in finding qualified degree candidates for the programs and will help in the marketing effort if it is properly orchestrated.

The briefing (an invitational information session for the purpose of recruiting new students into the program) is an excellent marketing tool and, if handled properly, will help to seal a successful partnership with the academic faculty. The briefing is a means of informing potential students about the merits and particulars of your degree program at a time and place convenient for the working adult. It is cost effective, as it reaches the target audience with minimum financial outlay. Briefings depend on the sincerity and the collective salesmanship of your staff and selected faculty for their success. Those who attend briefings are very strong candidates for your program and the hope is that many will convert to registered students.

Briefings should be held prior to the start of each semester and should be scheduled after a major direct-mail campaign. The format of the briefings is simple: A welcome and overview of the specific educational program, given by the academic dean, are followed by a more detailed discussion of the program by a faculty member who is actively involved with, and enthusiastic about, the program.

It must be emphasized here that as a marketing tool, briefings are only as effective as the speakers. Particulars on the registration and application process and other procedural details should be handled by the continuing education staff. Graduates of the program are often the most enthusiastic promoters of the program so do not fail to include them at these sessions. Allow time for questions and answers. Emphasize that networking with professionals is a very positive outcome of participation in continuing education classes. In some instances, the opportunity to make professional contacts outweighs other considerations. For the nontraditional student, class location is a very important element of the program. Combining quality with convenience for the working adult is the essence of most successful continuing education programs.

Hold the briefings either at or close to where the courses will be taught, and schedule them at a time convenient for the working student. Do not invite recent graduates of the program merely to attend. Ask them to give short talks on how the program helped them and what they liked about it. Let potential students know how the graduates of the program are doing. You do not want to promise employment, but you do want to leave the impression that recent graduates have fared well in the job market because of the program.

Design a survey to gather vital information about attendees, such as the possibility of tuition reimbursement by employers and other logistical issues important in serving the adult or part-time student. Attendees are also excellent prospects for the in-house mailing list.

Remember that these briefings may well be the audience's first real exposure to the college or university and its continuing education degree program. The briefing will determine their impression of the institution and its continuing education program. The commitment of your staff to all aspects of the briefing activity is critical. Participants will be able to suggest new target groups to you if you allow them to participate in marketing meetings. You should always have members of the staff attend the briefings to welcome students and speak about the program. A sensitive staff member is very often able to convince adults of the value of continuing education.

Noncredit Programs

A crucial stage in the planning of conferences, institutes, or seminars is the exploration of target audiences. Spend time with your program planning staff in identifying the target audience at a preliminary meeting. Your staff may know other professionals who might be able to share insights on marketing a particular program. Invite a member of the marketing team to join the program planners in the initial planning stage. This will increase involvement in the total continuing education enterprise. Experienced marketers may have some special insights on how to reach the director of training or the vice-president of a company or how to get past the secretary with your direct-mail piece.

Ask your staff to display or circulate conference brochures when they make sales visits, hold briefings, or attend education fairs. Most important, ask them if they have access to mailing lists that you can use. You may wish to involve your staff in researching possible sources of funding or for developing in-house mailing lists. For example, assign a staff member who is interested in research to research professional directories in your library for developing in-house mailing lists. Use this person to contact associations to find out whether subgroups in the association would be interested in your specialized topic.

Another valuable source of attendees is the Yellow Pages. Have a staff member create a data base by simply entering names and/or organizations from the Yellow Pages. This is especially helpful when you do not have professional list services in your area or you need local participants for a very specialized program.

Many offices within organizations have display racks or tables for materials and would be happy to include your brochures. Assign a staff member the responsibility of finding these hospitable organizations. Do not forget the front desk at the student union and the general information desk of the university, hospital, museum, chamber of commerce, or adult education center. The local library is also an excellent place in which to display continuing education materials.

Certificate Programs

A good promotional tool for certificate programs is the career night. The career night is similar to the briefing except that it places greater emphasis on career outcomes and job opportunities after completion of the program. It is essential at these sessions that the speakers be interesting and that current students as well as graduates attend and speak about the program. Very often, potential students have real fears about the difficulty of the program, the extent of the homework, and/or the type of evaluation to which they will be subject. Testimonials from students rather than faculty are very reassuring. Emphasis on the practical applications of the program is very important.

Incorporate networking opportunities into career nights by promoting an informal atmosphere and scheduling time for questions and answers and for the participants to share career plans with each other. Often, during the talk over refreshments, potential students sell each other on the merits of the program. Include any staff members who are graduates of your certificate programs on the agenda. Personal recommendations are extremely valuable in convincing hesitant students to register for certificate programs.

Another marketing technique for certificate programs is the program information session. These are program-specific meetings run by the director of the certificate program to answer questions and provide information on a regular basis to the working professional who is a potential student. Usually the sessions are held monthly at noon or at 6 P.M. at a central location. Staff members play an important part; they arrange information tables and displays and also answer questions. Very often, student portfolios or slides of student projects are shown. In addition, tours of classrooms, studios, and/or computer labs should be conducted by the staff for potential students.

Use all your staff to market certificate programs to local civic groups, service clubs, and professional business organizations. Professionals in continuing education should be active in community affairs. We, as leaders, must encourage our staff to join local groups (Fischer, 1984). Mary Lindenstein Walshok discusses the importance of this involvement in detail in Chapter Seventeen. Encourage staff to make presentations on the opportunities and benefits of your programs in the civic organizations to which they belong. Many organizations actively seek individuals who can talk about continuing education in general and about certain career opportunities in particular. If you offer real estate or tax programs, information systems programs, legal assistance programs, or some of the many test review courses, take advantage of the personal contacts your staff may have. Your staff can talk about the merits of continuing education and certificate programs without offending these local service clubs and business groups.

In using staff for this type of marketing, it is important to give them time off to attend meetings, serve on committees, and mingle with attendees at seminars and events. Staff should be encouraged to become visible, active members of groups.

For example, a program director of a landscape design certificate program at a university was offered the opportunity to host a talk show on gardening for a local radio station. This visibility and her personal response to many questions from listeners have led to greater interest in the certificate program and have identified this program director with the certificate program in a very positive way. The result has been an increase in registrations for the landscape design program.

Members of advisory boards for certificate programs should be treated as extended staff. Involve them in the total marketing effort by asking them to write copy for newsletters and brochures. Ask them to serve as a liaison with corporate trainers to recruit potential students and potential qualified faculty in specialty areas. In choosing members for these boards try to achieve the widest representation possible. Then expect these new members to contribute to your program; for example, do not hesitate to ask them for help in finding mailing lists for your programs.

The graduation ceremony is another selling opportunity. Allow students to bring family and/or friends to the graduation program. Have your staff there to greet the attendees. Make the evening worthwhile with inspiring speakers and impressive certificates. At the reception, communicate the advantages of your program to interested friends and family.

Once again, program alumni can be an invaluable aid to the selling effort. Invite alumni to graduation programs. Those who have successfully completed your program are the best salespersons you can find. Ask them to speak at graduation programs, not only at career nights, and feature them in your regularly published continuing education newsletter.

Staff Development

Staff development includes global elements as well as skill-specific elements. Staff development should be concerned with the growth of the whole person, personally and professionally.

A good manager includes staff development in the long-range planning of the organization. Listed here are some examples of how staff development sessions can be used to encourage employees to become salespersons.

1. *Plan general, more global, development sessions for all staff.* Include some social activities and make the time available as part of the regular workday. These sessions should be announced in advance and adequately planned so that support staff as well as professional staff will be able to attend. A good manager tries to minimize the distinctions between professional and support staff. Build a winning team where everyone plays a vital role. In a small staff, it is even more critical that support staff function as professionals. At these general meetings, communicate the importance of the institutional mission and how vital it is for all staff to contribute to the health of the organization. An example of the inclusion of support staff in general staff development is the story of a woman in a continuing education organization whose official position was secretary but who really functioned as the fiscal officer and budget manager. She was shy and had never been included in professional development by previous managers. She was asked to begin attending conferences and meetings. By paying for her to attend professional development conferences, she was encouraged to make many more positive contributions to the organization. These contributions were worth far more than the price of her registration fee and travel expenses.

2. *Plan regular development sessions for the professional managers.* These sessions should be more than marketing meetings. They should address the major concerns of the organization and how everyone can contribute to its success. You can build alliances within the organization by inviting guest speakers from other units, especially when they are directly involved with the continuing education programs. For example, in colleges and universities, some deans feel that continuing education staff members do not really understand or appreciate

faculty members. Rather than ignoring this attitude, take a positive approach and ask these deans to share their interpretations of the importance of the faculty role. The continuing education managers will learn to appreciate the importance of the faculty and will reflect a more positive attitude about the academic point of view to the rest of the continuing education staff. This should, in turn, be followed by a more cooperative attitude on the part of many faculty when you need them to provide their teaching services. In the health care field, physicians can be asked to speak to continuing education staff involved with marketing wellness programs. These physicians can discuss the importance of illness prevention and the costs involved for the patient and the hospital. Those marketing the wellness programs will have a more dynamic point of view and will be more effective as they speak to local groups about the savings, in terms of both dollars and human suffering, derived by subscribing to wellness programs.

3. *Involve your staff in specific training programs designed to enhance specific marketing skills.* Send members to seminars and conferences on personal marketing and ask them to share what they learned in a roundtable discussion. Purchase books and subscribe to periodicals. Circulate among your staff relevant articles that you find as a result of your professional reading.

An effective technique for stimulating creativity in marketing, especially in generating new personal approaches to marketing, is to hold regular small group breakfasts for staff members. Plan these meetings early enough in the morning and at a convenient location, and the result will be active participation in discussion of the most effective approaches to personal sales. Some staff member is bound to be more effective than others in using personal marketing techniques. This person will motivate others to become involved in personal selling.

Managers in most organizations are very generous with their time and resources and will be pleased to host your staff member for a day or two to observe and learn firsthand how the experts perform. If you are willing to offer a return invitation, you may gain immeasurably for only the cost of travel. Although it is not likely that another manager in the same city will give away specific marketing information, even close neighbors can act as mentors to your staff, which will be very helpful to you in marketing and promotion. For example, I recently asked a staff member to extend a personal vacation in another state to visit an institution with an excellent reputation for marketing. The staff member was pleased to do this and returned with more ideas and more enthusiasm for marketing than I could have possibly anticipated. It was worth every cent.

Staff Training in Marketing and Promotion. Do not underestimate the importance of your staff as they interact with your customers when they come through the door or when they call in for more information. Teach them how to answer telephone questions with the ultimate goal of converting inquiries to registrations. Provide them with printed material, highlighting the key concepts, so that they can respond to questions about your programs with ease. Teach staff to probe the callers' interests and to key their responses to those interests. You will need to have regular telephone debriefings to determine the most effective approach for special events such as conferences.

If you are going to use telemarketing, either as a major part of your marketing effort or as a supplement to direct mail, you need to plan very carefully. Develop a script and have the staff members who will be answering the telephone rehearse. Try audiotaping to monitor progress and improve performance. Great care should be taken in training and managing those assigned to dealing with customers—the prospective students. In Chapter Twenty-Five, B. Ray Holland offers excellent advice on planning successful telemarketing efforts. In addition, helpful hints on tracking publicity and advertising are offered in chapters Eighteen and Twenty-Three.

You can provide staff development on a cost-effective basis. Combine efforts with another leader in your organization or in your city. If you collaborate you may be able to afford the speaker neither of you could afford alone. Arrange for a very stimulating staff development training session with an expert on marketing. Cooperate with another administrator in your organization when planning staff development programs. You will build bridges and gain internal visibility by providing opportunities for others.

Pitfalls. The worst error is to overlook your staff as promoters of your program. Ensure that your staff is able to promote all of your programs should the opportunity arise. For example, we had a conference for which we had few registrants. We were working very hard trying to reach potential attendees. We did everything we could think of doing, but we neglected to ask one of our department managers for help. Later, after the event was judged less than a success, the department head volunteered that she could have called at least thirty-five personal contacts in the community and followed up with a personal letter inviting them to attend. We were astounded and very upset that we had overlooked an obvious person who could have helped us.

Provide receptionists with the information they need to speak knowledgeably about a program. Many callers will not make a second phone call if their questions are not answered during the first call. Many of us use student help or part-time help at our reception desk. Be sure that they are provided with brochures highlighting essential data and/or a script. Telephone personnel should be equipped to track the advertising source that led to the call. If your organization spends large amounts of money on direct mail and/or advertising, you will be unhappy to miss even one piece of information. Provide cards and/or other forms to make it easy to document all calls.

Reward Structure. Remember that when you ask your staff to participate in the marketing process, you must also inform them of the reward structure for the success of that program—praise, certificates, attendance at meetings, letters of recognition, attendance at a social activity, and so on. Do not forget those who offered good ideas and worked, possibly on their own time. Simple handwritten thank you notes are greatly appreciated. Positive reinforcement goes far in developing a winning team.

People who work for you want to share in the ultimate results of the organizational effort—increased registrations and quality programs. Often, we exhort people to make an effort to bring in the registrations, but we neglect to inform them of what this effort means to the organization. For example, how often do we take time to share the importance of each registration for our programs with the receptionists or secretaries? Do they know just what each new participant is worth in terms of dollars to the organization? How many more people are needed to reach the break-even point? If you have frequent meetings with key staff and talk about the importance of each registration, you will find they have increased enthusiasm and involvement in your programs, whether they are credit degree programs, conferences, or certificate programs. Assign each person in the reception area of your office one program to learn thoroughly. All receptionists should know enough about all the programs to answer most questions, but each one should have detailed knowledge of one program in particular. They will feel a special pride when you ask them to field questions as the resident expert.

How does involving the staff in the total marketing enterprise lead to organizational development and renewal? Successful organizational renewal and continued growth and development are ongoing tasks in all continuing education organizations. Their accomplishment is sometimes a mystery and a source of great frustration. Some general guidelines can be established as far as the marketing and promotional activities are concerned:

1. Constantly evaluate your publications for effectiveness and rate of return and then compare them with the publications of your competitors. How do your printed pieces look? Are you proud of them? Do they communicate the image of the organization to the outside world? Plan regular review sessions of all your printed materials. Allow enough time in a setting away from the phones for your staff to critique these important examples of your outreach program. On occasion, invite in a publication specialist from an external organization or a faculty member from your graphic arts department. A fresh point of view is necessary and will provide you with many creative ideas.

2. Try to instill a feeling of pride in all staff regarding all printed material—brochures, catalogues, advertisements, flyers, and posters. Give the artist or designer credit for creative efforts. As a group, select the best pieces to submit for review in contests or by in-house experts. If you receive an award, display it and share the credit with all who participated in the creation.

3. Plan a field trip to a printer who will give your staff a guided tour and a minicourse on the printing process. This trip serves two purposes: (1) the printer becomes more familiar with your needs, and (2) the continuing education organization staff learn more about the printing process. They will be more knowledgeable as they talk with clients and will relate more sympathetically with the promotion staff as they work to prepare printed materials.

4. Arrange for the staff to visit an advertising agency. Learn about display

ads, ad placement, costs, production, the creative process, and product management. A visit to a top advertising agency is worth the travel time and money.

5. Plan a staff development session with a professional list manager. Learn about the intricacies of coding, sorting, selling, cleaning, and servicing lists. Learn how to compile your own lists. Appoint one staff member to be the in-house list expert. The entire marketing process from list management to print production and media advertising is an exciting one and the staff will respond to the challenge to get involved. An energized and knowledgeable staff is necessary to compete in the continuing education arena today.

6. Encourage the marketing staff to belong to professional associations and attend meetings to personally promote the programs, set up display tables and racks at a variety of locations, and participate in college fair or career day programs designed to exhibit programs offered by several institutions. Encourage networking in professional organizations and with groups likely to be supportive of continuing education.

Involving the entire staff in the marketing effort, from planning through production, from budgeting to analysis of effectiveness, will be beneficial to the organization. It will engender creative ideas, more individual effort to research target audiences, and more involvement with the total process, resulting in feelings of ownership and pride. By giving staff more responsibility and sharing more of the good results with them, you will promote team spirit and your products and services will improve.

The Marketing Image and the Culture of Your Organization

One of the most important things any continuing education leader must do early is to develop an understanding of the culture of the parent organization. Organizational culture is "a pattern of basic assumptions—invented, discovered, or developed by a given group as it learns to cope with its problems of external adaptation and internal integration—that has worked well enough to be considered valid and, therefore, to be taught to new members as the correct way to perceive, think, and feel in relation to those problems" (Schein, 1985, p. 9). Whether new to the organization or a veteran, you need to probe the internal values and style of operation of your organization as well as the strengths and weaknesses of its programs. You need to have an intimate working knowledge of your organization (Keller, 1983).

You must learn what drives the organization. Is it student enrollments, total tuition revenues, academic excellence of the programs, community outreach and public service, or some combination of these? What are the important rituals of the organization? What is the dominant ethos? How does continuing education contribute to the shared beliefs and patterns of feeling and actions of the parent institution? If you are perceived as an accepted member of the culture as well as a strong partner in the enterprise assisting the institution to reach its goals in a manner compatible with the culture, you will have a much better chance of improving continuing education's reputation and image internally.

The importance of serving the mission of the parent organization must be communicated to all staff members. Chapter Seventeen provides a comprehensive analysis of the many ways to achieve this goal.

Summary

Involvement of all staff in the total marketing enterprise has very positive results for the continuing education organization. The energization, the discovery of creativity, and the generation of enthusiasm justify the effort. In addition, it saves time and money, results in more productive marketing campaigns, ensures quality programs, and contributes positively to the health and vigor of the continuing education organization. The relationship with the parent institution is improved as continuing education is perceived to be an effective force for promoting the goals and values of the entire institution.

25

Successful Telemarketing Techniques for Continuing Education

B. Ray Holland

Telephone marketing is an effective promotional technique that for some time has been used successfully in the business world (Roman, 1976). It is increasingly being used by continuing education organizations as a cost-effective way to increase registrations. This chapter provides practical tips on how to design and implement a successful telemarketing operation in your continuing education organization.

Why Telemarketing?

Telephone marketing can have a significantly positive effect on a potential participant's decision to enroll in a continuing education program, and can often increase your enrollment dramatically. For example, telephoning a pool of past participants in continuing education programs, after a direct-mail piece has been received, can generate up to four times the response elicited by the mail alone.

Past program participants are usually receptive to being telephoned at home in the evening. Past participants have purchased at least once and form a pool of interested people from whom repeat registrations can be obtained. Talking directly to immediate past participants can provide for intermittent personal contact on a systematic basis. This gives your former participants an opportunity to express their opinions about their experience with you. This also can provide you with information about satisfaction levels, so that you can quickly and adequately respond to complaints and suggestions. The incremental by-product of this valuable customer information can be helpful in augmenting market research, particularly as it relates to testing for interest in new offerings. Thus, the bottom line is improved through increased registrations and improved profit margins.

Planning for Telemarketing

Like all other promotional efforts, telephone marketing requires attention to strategic planning to be successful. In telephone marketing it is absolutely necessary that you get started properly. The author has found at the University of Alabama at Birmingham and at Kennesaw State College that modeling on the private sector experience was a foundation for success. At least four publications from the private sector are must reading before you undertake a telephone marketing project: (1) *Telephone Marketing: How to Build Your Business by Telephone* by Murray Roman; (2) *Successful Telephone Selling in the '80s* by Martin D. Shafiroff and Robert L. Shook; (3) *Reach Out and Sell Someone* by Gary S. Goodman; (4) *Telephone Techniques That Work* by Charles Bury. Each is a practical approach to doing it right. In addition, get the appropriate institutional approval and support for any new telemarketing effort. Many institutions engaged in continuing education are by nature conservative. As a result, many administrators may be aware of only the negative stereotypes associated with the telemarketing of commercial products and services. Experience has shown, however, that former program participants generally react positively to a phone call from an education organization when the call follows a direct-mail piece.

Organize Your Effort. Prospects should be lined up in advance. Use your current participants as your prospect pool. They know you and your services. Registration forms, computer printouts, or uniform-sized information cards can be used to record demographic data and enrollment patterns.

The more you know about your prospects the better you can serve them, so the data you will need to know before phoning them should be collected early, should be reliable, and should be studied carefully. These data include name, address, and telephone number. Also ask what past programs or courses they took because many people prefer particular categories of courses and will want to know about similar new ones. Your prospects' enrollment patterns will tell you if there is seasonality to their enrollment behavior and will give you clues about the probability of their enrolling at a given time. You may discover that some prospects have price limitations, and so on.

Set Your Goals. Be sure that you know what you want to accomplish and how you plan to measure success. Several factors have been found to be critical to effective financial and enrollment evaluation:

1. *Sales.* The number of people enrolled as a result of being telephoned.
2. *Income.* The total course fees for which telephoned people register.
3. *Expenses.* Generally, only the cost of purchasing experienced, part-time

telephone marketers. When volunteer help is used, often expenses are reduced but so are caller productivity and registrations.

4. *Percent of expense with respect to income.* You will want to determine this factor and set a corresponding goal after you have some experience and can calculate a reasonable rate.

5. *Reaches.* The number of people with whom you talk. Reaches affect sales volume.

6. *Conversion rate.* This figure becomes more realistic as you gain experience, but setting a goal number of registrations per 100 people called is essential. A good conversion rate for a first-time telemarketing operation is one that is based on a cost recovery basis; however, experience has shown that a conversion rate of 5 to 20 percent is realistic.

7. *Cost per student.* You want to be able to compare this figure and the conversion rate with your direct-mail performance.

Document. Determine the factors you will use to record your telemarketing results and prepare the appropriate documents to plot your data. There are at least nine categories in which data should be gathered and recorded. The call summary sheet in Exhibit 25.1 should reflect these categories.

1. *Interested/sent catalogue.* Some people, although not objecting to being telephoned at home in the evening, prefer to register by other means or are unprepared to register at the time of the call. Their interest is genuine. Record their interest and follow up with another direct-mail piece.

2. *Already registered.* Tally those who have already registered through other means.

3. *Not interested.*

4. *Second calls.* Record a second or third attempt to call a prospect without contact.

5. *Sales you registered.* Tally actual registrations received by phone.

6. *Total calls completed.* Sum of all categories *except* busy/no answer and bad number.

7. *Busy/no answer.*

8. *Bad number.*

9. *Total calls attempted.* Sum of all nine categories.

Accurate data tracking and analysis is the key to good managerial evaluation of your telephone marketing objectives. For instance, a high rate of already registered may indicate you are telephoning too long after the direct-mail piece has been received by your prospects. You will find that the already registered category will decrease over time as your students come to better appreciate the service nature of telemarketing, but do not assume that if you do not call, prospects will automatically find other means of registering; experience has shown that telephone marketing can boost registrations by as much as 35 percent over direct mail alone. Also, a high rate of bad numbers could signal that you

Exhibit 25.1. Call Summary Sheet.

Caller _____

Date _____

| Date | Completed Calls | | | | | Incomplete Calls | | Total Calls Attempted |
	Interested/ Sent Catalogue I/C	Already Registered AR	Not Interested NI	Second Calls SC	Sales You Registered R	Total Completed Calls	Busy/No Answer B/NA	Bad Number BN	

have a problem with recording initial registrations. Or, if you consistently fail to achieve your goal for registrations, you may have set an unrealistic goal or may have an employee performance problem. The ability to objectively evaluate your telemarketing efforts is critical.

Telemarketing Personnel

Recruit top-notch telephone marketing personnel. Use experienced callers, perhaps part-timers, whose performance can be sustained over a three- to four-hour period each night for as many nights as are necessary to call your prospect pool. Then train your callers. Leave nothing to chance. If you do not feel qualified, get a professional telemarketer to conduct training sessions on effective use of voice, opening lines, handling objections, closing of sales, and effective listening.

Timing of Call. Generally, the best time to call is in the evening between 6:00 and 9:00 P.M. You may find, however, that professional development seminars and conferences sell well when you call prospects during the day at the workplace. As you gain experience, the best time to call in your marketplace will become obvious.

Telephone Marketing Script. A very important aspect of any telemarketing program is development of an effective script for your callers to follow. This is important for three reasons. First, it brings a uniformity to the telemarketing program and ensures that people called will receive the same sales approach. Second, it makes it easier for your callers to feel comfortable in telephoning people they do not know. Third, a well-constructed and professionally delivered script increases your conversion rate.

The following sample script has been used successfully by the continuing education program at the University of Alabama at Birmingham. The script was designed to be used after direct-mail announcements of the continuing education program had been sent.

"Hello, may I speak with [name of the prospect]? This is [name of caller] calling from the University of Alabama at Birmingham's Office of Continuing Education. The reason I am calling, Mr./Ms. [name of prospect], is to see if you have registered for a course for the winter term."

If the response is yes, say: "Good! I hope that you enjoy your course. Mr./Ms. [name of prospect], is there another course that you would like me to register you for now over the telephone?" *If "yes," follow the regular registration procedures. If "no," thank the person and go to the next prospect.*

*If the person says no, he or she has not registered for a course,
say:* "Well, Mr./Ms. [name of prospect], we are calling former
students to make it convenient for them to register for noncredit
courses. I see that you took [name of the course] last term and that
you are interested in [subject matter]. Will you be taking another
[subject matter] course or one of our over forty courses being offered
for the first time this term?" *If "no," go to the Overcoming
Objections Script.*

If yes, say: "Good!" Is the catalogue of courses that you
received in the mail close by? *If yes, ask them to get it. If no,
continue with this script.*

*If they are interested in the subject matter, make suggestions
from similar subjects in the catalogue. If they are interested in
another type of course, make suggestions from new courses from the
catalogue. Once the person makes a decision to take a course, say,*
"Good! I am pleased that you are going to take advantage of this
opportunity. I will register you for your course right now." *Refer to
registration card and ask for appropriate information.*

Note: Always ask, "Will you be using your VISA or your
MasterCard to pay for your course fee?" *Be sure to thank the person
you talked with, whether there was a registration or not. If there was
a registration, say:* "Thank you, Mr./Ms. [name of prospect], we
look forward to seeing you [date and time of course]." *If there was
no registration, say:* "Thank you, Mr./Ms. [name of prospect], we
look forward to seeing you next term."

The script will probably continue to evolve as more is learned about
responses and selling techniques. For example, callers should always identify
themselves and give the reason for the call immediately. This puts the person
receiving the call at ease, because the call is from someone they know. Satisfied
past participants identify with you and your program. Capitalize on this.
Repeating the name of the person called is also helpful in establishing rapport. It
is now a truism in effective selling that to a person the most beautiful word in any
language is his or her own name.

You may notice that the "reason for the call" is to make it convenient for
the former participants to register. This is a call designed to serve the participant's interest. Make this genuine.

All customer-centered businesses have high rates of repeat business. This is
one of the most important reasons for referring to past courses at the beginning of
the call. It shows you know and care about your participants and their interests,
and it reinforces their prior choices and decisions.

Guidelines for Using the Script. On the surface you are selling something, but really you are discovering and meeting the needs of the people who have previously participated in your programs. Keep this fact uppermost in your mind as you guide your past participants through a beneficial decision-making process. Unless you can meet a need, your call is unlikely to result in a registration. Follow these helpful guidelines:

1. *Listen.* Failure to listen is probably the most serious mistake made by telephone marketers. Over the telephone, all communication is auditory, so the only way to understand your past participant's message is to **listen to it.** Remember, you cannot talk and listen at the same time. Concentrate by focusing on the other person's words. Ask questions if you do not understand, and practice repeating what you think the person means. A training session on listening skills before the telemarketing program begins is a good idea, even for experienced callers.
2. Welcome the concerns of past participants. Concerns tell you where to go with the conversation. If the caller can answer a person's concern to his or her satisfaction, you are almost certain to get a registration.
3. Repeating something the person says is a compliment and shows that you are listening and paying attention. Repeating also gives you time to think about what you will need to say next.
4. Practice modeling the other person's speaking rate. People enjoy talking with others who talk as they do.
5. Ask for the registration. Give the person credit for making a good choice from several options, all of which are acceptable to you. Continuing education participants enroll for their reasons, not yours.
6. Make sure the person knows that a registration has taken place, the price of the course, the method of billing or charge that is to be used, the due date for payment, the date, time, and location of the course, and any cancelation or no-show policy.

When these guidelines are effectively followed, communication is the result. You have succeeded in helping a prospect select an offering he or she wants and needs, and the prospect has provided you with valuable information that you can use to better serve your participants.

Overcoming Objections. If a person voices a concern or objection, it is most important that you do not become discouraged. In fact, you should welcome concerns because they focus in on areas that need more of your attention. If you listen closely, you will be able to classify concerns quickly into one of four areas: no need, no money, no hurry, no time. When you have successfully classified the respondent's concern, repeat and verify the concern and then handle it. If the concern is *no need,* ask additional questions to get some agreement or to discover another need. When *no money* is a problem, prove the value of continuing education by demonstrating that the benefit is much greater than the price or by pointing out discounts and potential financial aid. If the hesitation to register is *no hurry,* point out the risk of waiting if offerings fill early. No time objections can be effectively handled by having attractive scheduling options and by pointing them out.

Kennesaw State College in the University System of Georgia and the University of Alabama at Birmingham have used the following script successfully, but you will want to develop one designed particularly for your programs and market.

> *When the response is negative, say:* "I see, Mr./Ms. [name of prospect]. So that I can better understand, could you please tell me the reason you do not wish to take a continuing education course at this time?" *If the objection is time related:* "You know, Mr./Ms. [name of prospect], our courses are scheduled at times convenient for busy people like you. I see that you took [name of course] on [date and time] last term. Mr./Ms. [name of prospect], we have several courses scheduled on [date and time] this term that you may be interested in, such as [make suggestions from list]. Which one do you prefer this term?" *If the objection is related to money, say:* "You know, Mr./Ms. [name of prospect], you can charge your fee to either VISA or MasterCard. Also, we have a convenient two-part payment plan that a number of our students use. Which of these do you prefer, Mr./Ms. [name of prospect]?"

> *If the objection is no hurry, say:* "Some courses reach maximum enrollment very quickly. You don't want to miss out on this opportunity." *Or:* "Your early registration could make the difference in whether the course you want makes it. Now is the right time to make your selection."

> *If the objection is no need, say:* "A personal investment in [training, personal enrichment, professional development, whatever you are selling] is an investment in your future, Mr./Ms. [name of prospect]. Keeping up with rapidly changing trends is a must in today's workplace. There are opportunities all through your catalogue for you to enrich your life, to learn something new, or to gain new insights about yourself and others." *Point out several options from the catalogue. Then say:* "Which one do you prefer, Mr./Ms. [name of prospect]?"

> *If objections are not overcome, thank the student and go on to your next prospect.*

The Most Frequently Made Mistakes

Telemarketing is a proven, effective means to increase registrations and to better serve continuing education users. It requires careful planning, specific measurable goals, and trained, well-supervised callers. It is not something to be rushed into. Know who your prospects are before you begin and know 95 percent of what you are going to say before you pick up the phone. By all means, know the benefits of continuing education as well as proven methods of properly handling concerns and objections. Always ask for the registration. From opening the call smoothly, to handling objections, to closing the sale, know what you are doing and avoid the following common mistakes.

Selection of the Wrong Personnel. There will be a temptation to use your staff, volunteers, or students for telemarketing campaigns. The myth of cost savings that this implies is unsubstantiated by experience. A reputable temporary service can provide bright, energetic, and experienced telephone marketers at competitive rates. Their higher productivity and conversion rates will most surely offset any cost savings realized by using inexperienced personnel. Also, special incentives and bonuses are often easier to use and to get past bureaucratic rules when employing temporary or contractual help.

Inappropriate Timing of Calls. Phoning at the wrong time of the day can destroy the effectiveness of your telemarketing program. Schedule evenings, and phone your prospects preferably between 6:00 and 9:00 P.M. Daytime calling reduces reaches, and phoning at work is often considered an interruption, except when selling professional development seminars and conferences. Let your own experience guide you here.

Cold Calling. Don't! Calling people who have never used your service nor participated in your programs is a waste of valuable telemarketing resources. Experience has proven that conversion rates are very low, and the effort is not cost effective. Too much time is spent in reassuring the prospect that you are reputable and in introducing your institution and its programs. Stay with past participants who know and appreciate you.

Boiler Room Method. The boiler room approach, where all callers are crammed into one often noisy room, is associated with questionable phonathons and solicitations. If possible, place the caller alone in an office and periodically monitor his or her performance. This reinforces the person-to-person advantage of telephoning. Your prospect is reassured of the service nature of the call. Importantly, isolation allows for close observation of individual performance and for confidential critique.

Failure to Supervise. Have competent and well-trained supervisors monitor and make suggestions throughout the calling period. Make absolutely sure that your customer service focus is adhered to and that your callers represent your program in the very best light. Evaluate as you proceed, not just afterward. You must be prepared to shut down an unsuccessful effort before it costs you too much, but, more importantly, you need to build on success *as it occurs*.

Summary

The best thing about telemarketing is that it works! Next to a live salesperson, the telephone is the most direct and personal direct-response medium available in today's marketplace. It is even more effective when used in combination with other media, such as direct mail. And, when compared with the high cost of face-to-face sales calls or of large direct-mail campaigns, the cost of telemarketing is very reasonable. At the University of Alabama at Birmingham, where telemarketing in continuing higher education was introduced, conversion rates continue to average over fourteen registrations per one hundred reaches at a cost slightly greater than $4.00 per registration. Kennesaw State College has reached a conversion rate three times higher than that attained through direct mail alone.

A criticism sometimes heard about telephone marketing is that it simply alters patterns of registration. In other words, if they had not been telephoned, they would have used some other method of registration. Experience at both the University of Alabama at Birmingham and Kennesaw State College shows that the intervention of telephone marketing boosted registrations 35 percent over direct mail alone. Experience at these two institutions demonstrates that telemarketing dramatically increases both registrations and profit margins. If these are goals that you share, you should consider a carefully planned telemarketing operation. Determine for yourself its cost effectiveness by following the suggestions in this chapter. Like all other marketing efforts, telemarketing requires planning and organization. You must know exactly what you want to accomplish and why. Define your goals clearly and quantitatively in solid customer service-oriented terms. Select your personnel to obtain your objectives and provide them with the essential tools, including participants' demographics and enrollment history, to support the calling effort. Put into the hands of each caller a thoroughly familiar, close-the-sale script to give direction and to project professionalism. Train. Train. Train. Leave nothing to chance. See that performance is documented and criteria are set against which you will evaluate the effectiveness of your telemarketing effort. If you do it right, you will increase registrations, raise user satisfaction levels, augment your market research, and improve your profit margin.

Telephone marketing works!

26

Exhibiting at Conferences, Conventions, and Trade Shows

Susan Coats

This chapter discusses three ways in which continuing education organizations can use exhibits effectively. First, many continuing education organizations plan conferences where exhibits related to the program content are an integral part of the entire conference experience. Second, continuing education organization may exhibit at conferences, conventions, and trade shows planned by others. In such cases, the purpose of the exhibit is usually to advertise the programs and services of the continuing education organization. Third, continuing educators often use exhibits in such public places as libraries, museums, chambers of commerce, and shopping malls. The exhibit is usually designed to stand alone and contain literature that people may take with them.

Quality, organization, and professionalism are marketing principles that apply to the planning and production of successful exhibits. These principles apply to the smallest information booth as well as to the cast-of-thousands trade show exhibits.

The principles and suggestions discussed in this chapter help ensure that exhibits are successful and that they focus time, money, and energy in the right direction. Guidelines are provided along with two lists of companies that specialize in the exhibition business. One list is a shopping guide to prebuilt exhibit systems; the other highlights the top ten companies in the exhibit business, who design exhibits to meet individual needs.

Setting Goals

The first step to a successful exhibit is goal setting. It is the basis on which the exhibit strategy is planned.

1. Review the mission and philosophy of your organization and parent institution. Chapters Two, Six, and Thirty-One discuss this issue in detail. Plan exhibits to enhance this mission and philosophy.

2. With a clear focus on the mission and philosophy, decide what benefits you expect to receive from the exhibit. For example, are you striving for sales and revenue, name recognition and publicity, increased participation, new market areas, product introduction and information, education for a specialized field of interest, or dissemination of information?

3. Project the goals into benefits to attendees and apply this to the marketing mix of the exhibit strategy. Chapter Nine is an overview of the issues to consider in the marketing mix. For exhibits, this includes such considerations as product, size, location, content of message, and price.

4. Decide on the most effective place to display the exhibit, such as at a conference, convention, trade show, library, museum, or shopping mall, or in-house as a component of a program you sponsor.

5. Evaluate exhibits by comparing the results with the goals. Successful planning of future exhibits can be enhanced by such an evaluation.

With your goals clearly in mind, you can use the following guidelines to plan exhibits.

Guidelines for Planning Exhibits

Space. Unless you own the facilities, you will often find it necessary to purchase or reserve space at least six months in advance to secure a good location. This applies whether you are exhibiting at a large trade show or at your local library. Good exhibit space is scarce. Those fortunate enough to choose a location should consider the flow of traffic and accessibility. Usually, large trade shows do not reserve space more than a year in advance and retain the right to relocate an exhibit according to their needs.

If you exhibit locally at a library, museum, chamber of commerce, shopping mall, or other public place, you may be given free space; however, if you exhibit at a conference or trade show there will probably be a charge. Inquire about charges, deposits, exact location, size, traffic flow, furniture required, setup arrangements, and statistics on previous exhibits and their success. Confirm all arrangements in writing. If the situation calls for occupancy on a first-arrival basis, plan to be there before anyone else.

Size. Size considerations center on three important factors: number of attendees, exhibit storage space, and total number of personnel staffing the exhibit at any one time.

Good planning requires an estimate of expected attendance. To arrive at this estimate, obtain a list of attendees and exhibitors from the organizer of the previous show, if there was one. This will enable you to prepare handouts and arrange for exhibit staffing.

The size of the exhibit is determined by design preference, expected attendance, number of participating exhibits, storage, and staff. Design is influenced by whether information will be disseminated by staff or attendees will pick up information from an unstaffed exhibit.

Budget. Keep in mind that exhibiting is big business. Although they should not have to cost a fortune, exhibits can be expensive depending on your goals and the financial resources available to reach these goals.

The Trade Show Bureau has broken down the exhibit dollar spent at an average trade show:

Exhibit space rental	21%
Exhibit construction	21%
Show services	21%
Transportation	13%
Refurbishing	12%
Special personnel	5%
Specialty advertising	2%
Miscellaneous	5%
Total	100%

This breakdown does not include personnel costs for planning and staffing the exhibit, which average 34 percent of the total exhibit expense, and include salaries, travel, hotels, and miscellaneous expenses. The average cost for an exhibit booth at a trade show or large convention is $10.67 per square foot (range $1.75–$26.78 per square foot). These percentages are only basic information for budget preparation; careful calculations are necessary to meet individual needs.

Staffing. The decision to staff the exhibit depends on the estimated number of attendees, the hours the exhibit area is open, and the size of the exhibit. To test your staff and attendee projections in relation to the actual square footage of the exhibit area, stage the exhibit event ahead of time. Select a large area where the floor space of the booth can be measured to scale and marked off with tape or chalk. Next, place the actual projected number of people into the workable areas and simulate typical exhibit activity. From this model, you can project the number of staff needed.

The staff must project an image designed to enhance the continuing education organization sponsoring the exhibit. The product of an exhibit is quality information and service. Attendees look for product excellence. Make sure that the staff includes people who can communicate well with a variety of personality types and interest groups. The staff must be well trained and knowledgeable about the goals of the organization as well as the goals of the exhibit. In this way they will be able to relate the programs, products, services, and information in the exhibit to the attendees' needs. In addition, they will be able to follow through on all requests for information and commitments. To present the best possible professional image, establish guidelines for dress, breaks, smoking, eating, personal visits, phone calls, and neatness.

Product Demonstration. Always use a professional service approach to establish rapport with attendees during an exhibition. Exhibit marketing can have a powerful impact on the potential customer. Therefore, consistency in all areas of delivery is important. Put yourself in the shoes of the attendees. Instead of using the hard sell, analyze and understand their needs and relate your programs and services to these needs. The underlying objective here is to establish mutual trust and to build a long-term business relationship that benefits all parties.

The Most Frequently Made Mistakes. To avoid the mistakes commonly made in exhibiting, review this list when planning the exhibit.

1. Management of the exhibit should be in the hands of a highly motivated, energetic individual who has been successful in understanding and dealing with a wide variety of people.
2. Allot extra time for design and construction of an exhibit. A timetable that is too tight could make it difficult or impossible to meet the opening deadline.
3. Budget at least 12 to 20 percent more for exhibit costs than anticipated. This allows for miscellaneous cost overruns.
4. Hire good craftspeople, professionals, and skilled workers to execute your exhibit.
5. Do not cut corners by sacrificing design standards and quality in brochures and other visual aids.
6. Seek legal advice in contract and liability matters before signing a contract.
7. Investigate charges for shipping, installation, dismantling, and on-site service contracts.

These guidelines cover the basic elements whatever the size or cost of the exhibit.

Professional Help in Exhibit Preparation

The exhibit industry provides such a vast array of services that it is possible to contract out all services and show up the day before the exhibit at a major convention or trade show for 100,000 people. This is not a recommendation. It serves only to illustrate the possibilities. The following operational and service areas need to be considered to deal effectively with commercial exhibit companies in the industry.

Convention Bureaus. Contact the convention bureau in the city where you are planning an exhibit to get acquainted with the professional exhibit services offered in that city. The range of services offered differs from city to city, but convention bureaus can usually help with all your needs, from logistics and services to union contract specifications and transportation. Convention bureaus can also help in the establishment of credit if notified in advance.

Exposition Managers. These professionals are in charge of the show. They may represent another organization sponsoring the show, a company, or a professional group. Normally they provide an office for general contact and a registration desk for exhibitors.

Exposition Service Contractors. The exposition service contractor is hired by and reports directly to the exposition manager. The contractor physically installs, dismantles, decorates, and provides materials for exhibits; in other words, the contractor is in charge of job site production. The exposition manager handles billing and planning with the exhibitors, and usually an on-site desk supervisor is available to handle problems. A list of these services should be included in a packet of information sent to you ahead of time.

At many large shows exhibitors bring in their own contracted people who operate under a separate agreement, under the contract regulations set forth by the exposition management. Carefully check your overall contract with the exposition service contracting firm. It usually will prohibit direct solicitation by outside contractors who are in direct competition with those companies hired by the exposition management. As an exhibitor, it is important to know that contracting options usually do exist; however, often you must investigate these options on your own.

The following companies specialize in designing modular exhibits as well as large displays for trade shows. The advantage of modular displays is that they are easy to assemble and dismantle, they are lightweight, and they are designed so that they can easily be packed in a car or checked as luggage on a plane. Call or write for complete literature on the wide variety of display systems offered by these companies. All of them are willing to work with you in individualizing their prebuilt display systems to your needs.

Channel-Kor Systems, Inc.
P.O. Box 2297
Bloomington, IN 47402
(800) 242-6567

David Brace Displays, Inc.
4401 Walden Avenue
Lancaster, NY 14086
(716) 685-1500

Dimension Work, Inc.
595 Supreme Drive
Bensenville, IL 60106
(312) 860-9800

Downing Displays, Inc.
115 West McMicken Avenue
Cincinnati, OH 45210
(513) 621-7888

The Exhibit Star
10720 North Stemmons
Dallas, TX 75220
(214) 358-0400

EXPOPLUS System
Division of Chroma Copy International
423 West 55th Street
New York, NY 10019
(212) 399-2420

ExpoSystems
3203 Queen Palm Drive
P.O. Box 5086Y
Tampa, FL 33675
(800) 237-4531
Florida: (800) 238-3976

Faga Systems
31260 Cedarvalley Drive
Westlake Village, CA 91362
(818) 706-3117

Featherlite Exhibits
7312 32nd Avenue North
Minneapolis, MN 55427
(800) 328-4827
Minnesota: (612) 537-5533

GEM Systems
2260 South 3600 West
Salt Lake City, UT 84119
(801) 974-5616

Herrington Display Ltd.
1312 Maple
West Des Moines, IA 50265
(515) 224-4781
(800) 255-2255

Iver Display Systems
110 Pennsylvania Avenue
Bangor, PA 18013
(215) 588-7255

Matrix Exhibits
1610 J. P. Hennessey Drive
LaVergne, TN 37086
(615) 793-3230

Midland Professional Displays
P.O. Box 247
Atlantic, IA 50022
(712) 243-4344

Nimlok Exhibit Systems
6104 Madison Court Morton
Grove, IL 60053
(312) 470-0240

Nomadic Structure, Inc.
7700 Southern Drive
Springfield, VA 22150
(703) 866-9200

Outline
250 Turnpike Street
Canton, MA 02021
(617) 821-2200

PERRYGRAF
Division of Denney–Reyburn Company
19365 Business Center Drive
Northridge, CA 91324-3552
(818) 993-1000
FAX (818) 993-7572

Professional Displays, Inc.
738 Arrowgrand Circle
Covina, CA 91722
(800) 222-6838
California: (800) 843-3533

ShoTEL Displays
301 Chestnut Street
St. Paul, MN
(612) 222-7317

ShowTopper Exhibits
The Godfrey Group, Inc.
P.O. Box 10247
Raleigh, NC 27605-9990
(919) 782-7914

Siegal Display Products
P.O. Box 95
Minneapolis, MN 55440
(612) 340-1493

Skyline Displays, Inc.
P.O. Box 11408
St. Paul, MN 55111-0408
(800) 328-2725
Minnesota: (612) 894-3240

Starrion Display Systems, Inc.
2323 North Milwaukee Avenue
Chicago, IL 60647
(312) 342-5151
(800) 782-1558

TechExhibit
Technical Exhibits Corporation
6155 South Oak Park Avenue
Chicago, IL 60638
(312) 586-3377
FAX (715) 685-9778
Ask for Toni

Xibitron, Inc.
P.O. Box 28019
1701 East Edinger Avenue
Santa Ana, CA 92799
(714) 543-0942

Insist on a quality product whether you decide on a prebuilt or a custom-designed system. Creativity and originality may be explored more with a custom system, but the standard display material and presentation will still allow latitude for creative planning.

Hotels. Some hotels have good exposition space. In these instances, many conferences and conventions invite exhibitors to set up tables and small displays. This provides an opportunity to market programs and services of a continuing education organization on a more intimate level. Coordination of such an exhibit is handled directly with the event chairperson or the convention service manager of the hotel. Such exhibits are usually set up in a conference room or a large hallway. Use the same basic planning guidelines discussed earlier. A small display should be handled just as skillfully and professionally as a large one.

Convention Centers. These centers are built especially for meetings and expositions and vary greatly in facility size, number of buildings, and architectural style. Sometimes, private management firms operate the center for a city or certain geographic area and at times city employees are convention workers. Dealings with the convention center will depend on the management structure and the number of services offered. It is important to make inquiries regarding these details.

Legal Implications

Because of the many different services and contracts, an understanding of the legal issues is necessary before execution of an exhibit. For example, the type of insurance needed for an exhibit depends on the contract and the facility where the exhibit is held. Liability is an issue that deserves serious attention, and a lawyer should review any contract or policy before it is signed. One reason is that few exhibitors know how to look for hidden clauses that restrict liability in favor of the other party. In addition, a signed application for space becomes a binding contract to all the terms listed in the prospectus once it is returned to the sponsors. Further, an exhibitor's liability should be limited to one's own negligence and not that of other exhibitors and the facility management. These are only a few of the legal aspects.

At large expositions, exhibitors are usually required to provide insurance certificates before the opening. In addition, all suppliers and contractors to the exhibit premises should be able to produce proof of insurance to the management before entry to the premises. Union contract clauses differ from one city to another and from one exhibit facility to another.

The exhibit staff should know how to handle emergencies and should be familiar with fire and safety equipment and exits. The exhibit area should be constructed under city building and safety codes. It is especially important to ensure that all materials used in the display are fireproof.

Professional Help in Exhibit Management and Design

Several organizations provide expert information on all aspects of exhibition management. The following list provides the names and addresses of some of these professional groups.

Convention Liaison Council
1575 I Street, NW
Washington, DC 20005
(202) 626-2723

Exhibit Designers and Producers Association
1411 K Street, NW, Suite 801
Washington, DC 20005
(202) 393-2001

International Exhibitors Association
5103-B Backlick Road
Annandale, VA 22003
(703) 941-3725

National Association of Exposition Managers
334 East Garfield Road
P.O. Box 377
Aurora, OH 44202
(216) 562-8255

Trade Show Bureau
P.O. Box 797
8 Beach Road
East Orleans, MA 02643
(617) 240-0177

Health Care Exhibitors Association
5775 Peachtree–Dunwoody Road, Suite 500D
Atlanta, GA 30342
(404) 252-3663

A call or letter to these organizations will bring you complete information on the wide variety of services they offer. For example, the Exhibit Designers and Producers Association is made up primarily of businesses engaged in designing, building, servicing, and transporting exhibits. The International Exhibitors Association has chapters in fourteen regional hub cities and is committed to professionalism in the industry; they offer a variety of educational and informational publications. The National Association of Exposition Managers, in cooperation with Georgia State University in Atlanta, established the first exposition management degree program at the academic level in 1984. NAEM has thirteen chapters and is dedicated to upgrading the exhibit industry. The Trade Show Bureau publishes a variety of statistical reports that are excellent for research studies. These include publications analyzing audience characteristics, sales topics, show categories, exhibitor profiles, and marketing.

The previously mentioned organizations, along with the following top ten exhibition design businesses, can provide useful services. These companies were chosen for their design ability, size, longevity, financial stability, participation in the market, and reputation.

Berm Studios, Inc.
404 Industrial Park Drive
Yeadon, PA 19050
(215) 622-2100

The Derse Company
1234 North 62nd Street
Milwaukee, WI 53213
(414) 257-2000

Design and Production, Inc.
7110 Rainwater Place
Lorton, VA 20079
(703) 550-8640

Design South, Inc.
2235 DeFoor Hills Road, Northwest
Atlanta, GA 30318
(404) 696-9105

Exhibitgroup Chicago
2800 Lively Boulevard
Elk Grove Village, IL 60007
(312) 595-2000

Exhibit Place
12442 Knott Street
Garden Grove, CA 92614
(714) 891-4020

Fritkin–Jones Design Group, Inc.
4020 West Glenlake
Chicago, IL 60646
Telephone (312) 463-1700

General Exhibits and Displays
4925 West Lawrence Avenue
Chicago, IL 60630
(312) 736-6699

Giltspur Expo Industries
4616 Henry Street
Pittsburgh, PA 15213
(412) 621-3700

Structural Displays
12-1233 Ard Avenue
Long Island City, NY 11106
(718) 274-1136

Summary

Exhibit marketing is a powerful management strategy that has been proven successful at conferences, conventions, and trade shows. Success in this area is achieved by using a comprehensive approach to planning and by learning from an already established industry. Use of the guidelines discussed in this chapter, the right marketing mix, and professional standards of quality will ensure your success in planning effective exhibits that meet your educational and marketing goals.

27

Involving Clients in the Development and Marketing of Programs

Richard B. Fischer

According to Peters and Austin (1985), "The surviving organization is the adaptive organization. The adaptive organization is one that is in touch with the outside world via living data" (p. 6). Although this statement was written in the context of for-profit business organizations, it is also applicable to continuing education providers. It is too easy to get caught up in day-to-day logistical activities or to become bogged down in the organizational bureaucracy and out of touch with the outside world—the client. In this discussion the client is the adult learner. Continuing educators, whether they work in museums, hospitals, industry, or educational institutions, must avoid the trap of assuming that they know what the adult learner wants and needs. It is important to involve the adult learner in helping adult educators to understand and measure the needs of the marketplace and, therefore, to market their programs more effectively.

Many companies, from Hewlett–Packard and DuPont to the Big Eight accounting firms and banks, have experienced the strategic advantage of focusing on the client. With almost missionary zeal, they involve clients in the design, development, and marketing of products. It is simply good business strategy. This chapter explores ways to involve the adult learner in the development and marketing of programs. The value of this strategy lies not only in its potential to improve the effectiveness of marketing, but also in its potential to improve the effectiveness of the learning that takes place.

Marketing the Program or Programming the Market

Continuing educators generally have two fundamental development strategies. One involves creation of an entirely new audience or generation of a new need for a particular educational program for which no audience or need existed previously. This strategy is marketing the program. The other strategy is development of programs to meet an identified need or to communicate information about an existing educational program to an already identified interest group. This strategy is programming the market (Frandson, 1974). Too often, the strategy is to market the program without first determining whether a need exists, who needs the program, and how to communicate with the potential learners.

In discussing marketing, one should be careful not to lose sight of the duality of the marketing function. Educational marketing should focus, first, on satisfying the customer's needs and, second, on persuading the customer to buy (Fischer, 1984). In continuing education, marketing is the combination of activities required to direct the flow of educational programs and services from the source to the final user in a form, place, time, and cost that are best able *to satisfy the client's needs*. The last five words are, of course, the most important.

To involve clients in the process, it is necessary to determine who the client is. Who will make the decision to participate? Is it the client who is making the decision to participate, or is a supervisor, spouse, or parent making the decision to send them? Who is the sender and who is the sendee? Obviously, this information is important in identifying which person should represent the client in the development and marketing of programs. There are several simple ways to determine the answers to these questions. In response to telephone or in-person inquiries from clients, find out who initiated the inquiry. Is the potential registrant an individual who has been directed to attend? If the decision to attend has been made by someone else, ask for the decision maker's name. Answers to these questions can often be obtained through a registration form designed to collect the data. Note this example of a section on a registration form:

1. Did you ask to attend this course or were you sent? _____ ask _____ sent
2. If you were sent, who sent you?
   [ ] immediate supervisor   [ ] senior management
   [ ] training director   [ ] other
   Sender's name _____
   Title _____
   Work telephone _____

These data are important because they indicate how advertising copy should be slanted. For example, if it is determined that most attendees ask for permission to attend, the copy should provide the client with a list of benefits that they can use to convince their supervisor it is a good idea to send them. If most clients are sent, the copy should be written in a style that emphasizes the benefits the organization will receive by sending employees. The data also provide the continuing educator with names of organizational decision makers who can be called on at a later date, or who can be sent thank you letters for sending their employees to the program.

The Classical Andragogical Approach. Although an interest in client involvement may appear new to the for-profit business community, the concept of
involving adults in the design process has been a basic tenet of classical adult
education since the coining of the word "andragogy" (Knowles, 1970). Knowles
points out that in traditional educational patterns, adults tend to come into
educational and training programs expecting to be treated like children. He
concludes that when adults are able to participate in the design of learning and
find they can make significant contributions, their motivation to learn increases
dramatically, as does their desire to participate in the learning process. As this
personal desire increases, so does a willingness to encourage others to participate.
Marketing becomes a helping function, not a selling function.

Knowles also highlights the importance of using the experiences of adults
to enhance the richness of the learning design. These principles of adult learning
are built into a seven-step andragogical process (Knowles, 1970, p. 10), which
serves as a foundation for the process of adult education. The process is based on
the resources and interests of individual learners and the needs of the institutions
and organizations of which they are a part. The early steps of the procedure focus
on establishing a climate for learning and a process for mutual planning and
needs identification. Although much has been written since 1970 about Knowles'
process, no writer has disputed the importance of involving the potential learner
in the process of designing and marketing educational programs. Houle (1972)
outlined eleven different educational design situations, only one of which did not
involve a collaborative effort with the client. In that one situation, clients
designed their own learning experiences without any external help.

How Client Involvement Can Enhance Program Development and Marketing

Certain techniques can be used that will both increase clients' involvement
and contribute to program development and marketing efforts.

Use Clients' Expertise to Identify Program Content. For example, although
program planners do not need to be medical doctors to plan continuing
education for physicians, it is important when designing such a program to
involve physicians in the planning discussion to clarify needs and to help the
program planner understand technical terminology and relate on a professional
basis to the client group. Members from the client group can serve in this role.
Clients can identify those areas of intellectual or skill development that they feel
are needed to meet their personal or organizational goals. Learning is a process of
internalization and adults learn most effectively when the content is related to
their own needs, interests, and values. Continuing educators, therefore, do not
have to be content experts. Rather, they should be experts in the process of
helping others identify content needs.

*Build a Marketing Plan Using Clients' Community and Professional Communi-
cation Channels.* Clients can help identify others like themselves who will also

benefit from a structured educational program. They can identify the channels of communications through which these prospective students seek information. For example, who are the opinion leaders in the community whose endorsement might be sought? What clubs, organizations, or meeting locations do prospective students frequent? Who are the supervisors who support further job-related training? Are there professional journals or trade newspapers that are valued? Are there company and organization newsletters that could be used to advertise the program? By involving police chiefs in the planning of law enforcement training programs, one program planner utilized the clients' technological communication channel and thereby gained access to the North American interlinking police teletype network. Announcements of training programs co-sponsored by various police departments were transmitted on the network as "all points bulletins." Thousands of police agencies were reached at no cost to the program as a result of client input.

Develop Client Ownership of the Program. Involvement in the design of the educational program allows clients to feel that the experiences have been developed *by* them, not *for* them. They will feel a stake in its acceptance and success because it is their program. They will usually "talk it up" among their peers, encourage participation, participate themselves, and approach the educational program with an open, positive attitude. Often, programs designed by someone else evoke such comments as "They don't know our problems," "Do we have to go?" "This is going to be a waste of time." These negative preconceptions are significant barriers to a successful learning experience and, by developing client ownership of programs, these negative reactions can be avoided. One very successful university refuses to do any supervisory training until both supervisors and management have worked together to design the training program.

Generate Ideas and Anticipate Points of Conflict. The process of involving clients in program development and marketing often is a significant learning experience in and of itself. In discussing training needs, new ideas can be introduced to broaden the participants' perspective of what skills may be needed to complete a task. Content areas that may be sensitive, taboo, or too advanced for the intended audience can be identified and discussed. Thus, the process can reduce potential conflict before such conflict can become a barrier to the learning or marketing activity. Often, the client's initially stated training need is not the real issue. It is not uncommon for clients to request training at a manufacturing site not to improve employees' skills, but to divert attention from unionization attempts or other labor management conflicts.

Boost Marketing Effort. When clients have participated in a program's development, they are knowledgeable about its details and benefits and can serve as valuable sources of information to others. Once someone has devoted time and energy to developing a program to meet their needs, people are eager to see the program be successful as a way of reaffirming their own judgment of worth. Clients can also be helpful in other ways.. Their names and positions can be used in promotional material to provide legitimacy to a program. Other clients will assume that if Mary Doe or John Jones is on the planning committee, it must be a good program. Clients can also be used as sources of referrals to leaders in other organizations. Involved clients will use their informal communication networks to make others aware of the program. They will identify other individuals and groups with similar needs who can be contacted to participate. They can provide access to in-house publications, associations, and trade mailing lists. Their support can be used as public endorsements or testimonials as well as in publications and news releases. They can be used for telephone solicitations and personal appeals to other members of the peer group. And, finally, they can be counted on to register and participate themselves.

What Information Is Needed?

As one begins to involve clients in the design and marketing of programs, the initial planning task is to spend some time considering what specific information is needed and how best to use the data that are collected. Use the following short list of questions to help define the focus. The answers may suggest which of the many formal and informal information-gathering techniques will be most useful for a particular program's development and marketing.

1. Exactly what does one need to know?
2. Will the information make a difference in designing or marketing the program?
3. How will the information be gathered?
4. How will the information be summarized and used?

It is important to be aware that much of the data gathered from client involvement is qualitative as opposed to quantitative (Stone, 1984). Qualitative measures do not usually generate hard facts or numerical data, but rather help confirm ideas or develop initiative directions. Quantitative measures employ highly structured statistical techniques as a result of responses from large population samples.

Consider also that information from clients will tend to group into three kinds of data: Primary data are firsthand, previously unrecorded information about needs of individuals or organizations. They are the most valuable data and can usually be obtained only through involvement of the adult learner in the process. Secondary data are compiled by an individual other than the original source, for example, the hospital administrator who asks the nursing supervisors for a list of their department's training needs. Tertiary data are usually extracted from published literature, census data, or broadly applied surveys. For example, a national survey of nursing school deans might yield a list of competencies needed by registered nurses. Although all of these sources are of value, they must be considered within the context of a specific learning situation. Usually, development of a continuing education program occurs within a specific surrounding place, time, and sponsor. This context influences how data may be collected and who might be involved in the process.

Assess the information provided by clients from this important context perspective. Consider the following questions. The answers will affect how you approach the program's development and marketing.

1. Is this client representative of the specific population to be served?
2. To what extent is the client knowledgeable about the content needs, background, and capabilities of other clients in the population?
3. How is the representative client viewed by others? Is he/she a respected member of the peer group or a maverick? Do others seek this person's advice?
4. Is the client willing to accept a role of high visibility in endorsing the program?
5. Can the client commit the resources of others in supporting the program? Will the client commit his or her own resources of time and money?
6. Does the client stand to benefit personally from the success of the program? Will this be detrimental to the program?
7. Will the absence of the client in the planning process be detrimental?

Large brokerage or insurance firms frequently volunteer their professionals to help plan and market personal financial planning courses. Before accepting such help, assess the context in which the help is offered using the preceding questions. Maybe the insurance firm is more interested in obtaining potential client lists than in helping to educate the public? Maybe the investment philosophy of the brokerage firm is too narrow and self-serving to provide students with a true representation of investment strategies? An understanding of the client's context will help eliminate these planning biases.

Techniques for Involving the Client

Often the situation dictates the method and timing of gathering data from the client. Where potential clients can be easily identified in advance, a variety of primary data collection techniques can be used. It may not always be possible, however, to identify the client prior to the beginning of the program. In this case, client input can be gathered at the start of the program. Here are some successful techniques for assessing clients' interests and needs. These techniques represent the "program the market" approach and may be particularly valuable in program development.

Written Surveys. This method involves collecting data from clients through use of a written questionnaire or interview. Surveys are particularly useful when quantitative data are needed, the information sought is reasonably specific and familiar to the respondents, there is a high need for administrative convenience, and there is need to gather data from a large client base.

The disadvantage is that the return rate on surveys may be low, the learners may misinterpret questions, and there is no opportunity to probe responses. In general, respondents to mail surveys tend to be college graduates who actively voice their opinion on many issues and come from higher socioeconomic norms. Thus, your responses may not be representative of the general population if that is what you are seeking. It is helpful in using mail surveys to make it very easy for clients to respond. Use prepaid, self-addressed envelopes. Response rates also improve if you use an odd-sized envelope so it stands out, a paper that absorbs ink well, a light, unobtrusive color, and multiple-choice or checklist questions. It is also helpful to collect some basic demographic data for comparison groupings of responses.

By promising to send respondents a free gift, such as a pen with your organization's logo, you are more likely to get a response with names and addresses for future marketing follow-up.

Interviews. Although more costly and time consuming than surveys, interviews have several advantages. In interviewing, questions can be explained or answers probed further. Interviews can very effectively be conducted over the telephone. Most people are very receptive if they think their opinion has been sought on some important matter. For large continuing education organizations, structured telephone interviewing can also create positive public relations. Most prospective adult students are pleasantly surprised to have a large institution call them for their opinion.

Interviews should be structured with a specific set of question guidelines including some open-ended responses. Make it clear from the start of the conversation that nothing is being sold and clearly identify who it is that is calling. A successful opening line might be, "Hello, my name is John Doe from the YMCA. We are considering a new stress management program and are seeking opinions from community leaders about the idea. Do you have a few minutes to talk?" Most people are flattered to be asked their opinion and will gladly talk. If interviewees seem impatient or indicate they are busy, inquire if there is a time when they can be called back because you really want *their* opinion. In any verbal interview situation, avoid making judgments when given responses. (Appendixes I to IV include some sample questions that have been successfully used for both written surveys and structured telephone interviews.)

Of course, the in-person interview is probably the most effective way to involve the client. This type of interview can occur one-on-one in an administrator's office; however, it is more likely to occur in one or more of the following types of group activities.

Planning Groups or Advisory Boards. Most people are willing to volunteer some of their time in the interest of professional development or community service. Use of advisory boards or planning groups can be very effective in involving potential clients. However, there are several important considerations in the care and feeding of planning groups or advisory boards. The convener of such groups must remember to be responsive to both the tasks that need to be accomplished and the membership and maintenance needs of the group. Members of a group will continue to participate only as long as they feel the group is accomplishing something worthwhile and they feel good about belonging to the group.

When inviting people to become members of a planning group, do so in person or by telephone. Do not delegate the task to a junior staff person. Invitees need to feel their involvement is so important that the top person invited them personally. Follow up the oral invitation with a written confirmation clearly outlining group expectations, frequency of meetings, and expected duration of the appointment. (Appendix VI is a sample confirmation letter.)

Respect the members' time commitment by being prepared for each meeting. Provide members a written agenda in advance, clear directions to the meeting location, a starting *and* ending time, and information on how they can be reached during the meeting in case of an emergency.

Help members get to know each other. Provide name tags or place cards and have members introduce themselves at the first meeting. Give every member a list of the names, addresses, and telephone numbers of all other members. Encourage members to know each other on a personal as well as a professional basis. While introducing members, you might ask each person to share something personal about themselves that others do not know. Allow time at each meeting for informal interaction among the members. A brief refreshment or dessert period at the end of the session can serve this purpose.

Devise some method to recognize members for their participation. Public news releases announcing the person's membership in the group or a letter of congratulations from the CEO or president of your organization are appropriate. Recognition dinners, symbolic gifts such as coffee mugs, certificates of appreciation, and inclusion of their name on letterhead stationary or promotional material are all ways to indicate appreciation and encourage continued participation.

Open Houses and Public Hearings. Sometimes it is difficult to determine exactly who the client might be for a new program. In such instances publicly advertised open houses or hearings may encourage those with interest in the subject to identify themselves. Care must be taken in such presentations not to imply the need to rubber stamp a final program, but to encourage input from the client that will impact the final plan. Attendees need to be encouraged to nominate themselves for positions on advisory boards or to submit names of others. At the minimum, they might be asked to jot down ideas that they feel are related or to set up a larger meeting with the program leader to discuss details.

Events. Many events can be staged to encourage the client to become more involved with a program. Invite selected community or professional leaders to RSVP breakfasts or luncheons to discuss mutual issues. Hold briefings or miniprograms focusing on content areas that might be expanded to longer programs. Use evaluation forms or questionnaires at the event to gather information. Honors days or receptions for outstanding current students and clients offer another opportunity for informal needs assessment. Look for opportunities to wander around during registration periods, class breaks, social events, and college nights to talk informally with potential clients. Stage career nights or special adult education exhibits at local shopping malls. The possibilities are endless.

Focus Groups. One of the techniques commonly used by many marketers to involve clients is the focus group (Stone, 1984). Usually, a focus group consists of eight to twelve clients representing the target audience for a particular program. These clients meet together for discussion under the direction of a moderator. The discussion is usually informal but follows a predetermined structure. Participants are often given some token gift for their participation at the conclusion of the session.

Focus groups can be used to generate ideas, for example, "How would you increase minority enrollments in our program?" They could be used to identify problems and issues: "What skills do you think are most important for tomorrow's small business owner?" Focus groups can determine perceptions: "Which of these promotional publications do you like the most and why?" They can also be helpful in developing background for further research: "Why did you choose to enroll in our program?"

Contrary to popular beliefs, focus groups do not have to be conducted by high-priced consultants using one-way mirrored rooms. The objective is to gain firsthand some prospective clients' reactions. With a little preplanning anyone can conduct a focus group. For example, a continuing education organization decided to use several focus groups to get a feel for the effectiveness of their quarterly course catalogue. They wanted to know how the adult learner used the catalogue. Specifically they wanted answers to these questions: Is the catalogue easy to use? Is it well organized and readable? What perceptions do readers have of the parent organization as a result of the publication? About 40 adults were randomly selected from the current registration list and each was called and invited to attend a two-hour evening focus group. A brief explanation was given of the nature of the focus group. About half of those called accepted or were available to attend and two groups of ten were formed. At the session, each group was given a copy of the organization's latest catalogue and catalogues from three other similar programs. After studying the catalogues, each participant was asked the following:

1. Write a one-word reaction to each of the catalogues.
2. Why did you choose that word?
3. Do you use the catalogue to choose courses?
4. How do you go about looking for a course in the catalogue?
5. Do you save the catalogue or discard it after you have made your course selection?

6. How would you change the appearance, organization, or content of the catalogue?

Discussion followed each question.

The sessions were tape-recorded for thorough review at a later time. Participants were given a china coffee mug with the institution's name as a token of appreciation for their time. Results from even this small sample were helpful in redesigning promotional material. Focus groups are an excellent means of *qualitatively* assessing issues or areas of interest. However, one must be careful in drawing *quantitative* conclusions without employing more exacting sampling techniques. The major drawback of focus groups is that results are not strictly projectable to the larger market of clients (Kotler and Murphy, 1987).

Visits to Clients. One-on-one field visits and the development of ongoing personal communication linkages are other important aspects of involving clients in program development or marketing activities. Adult educators must be visible parts of the various constituencies they intend to serve. This means adopting a proactive strategy of becoming involved with the clients' activities, clubs, organizations, and businesses. Priority needs to be given to listening to those one serves, visiting their work sites, and establishing personal communication linkages.

The first step in implementing a strategy of personal contact is to develop an organized method of making visits. Identify the major client groups that will be served. They may be client groups from a church, employees from the adult educator's company, or area businesses and organizations. Make a list of each potential client contact including the name or title, address, and telephone number of the contact person, and any pertinent information about the group. Set a goal on how many visits per week can be accomplished. Then pick up the telephone and schedule some appointments.

Ask clients to give their opinion, share their ideas, or help review a proposal. People will almost always respond to a request for help because it is a low risk for them. They are not making a commitment to buy or support anything. Try such approaches as "I'd be interested in your opinion about our plans to . . ." or "I'd like to ask your help in reviewing a proposal on . . . May I stop by for a few minutes and brief you on the contents?" (Fischer, 1984). By visiting clients at their location and getting them to talk about program ideas, you have involved them. Based on their responses and enthusiasm, it may be a simple step to get their commitment to serve on a planning board or inform others of the program.

Additional Techniques. There are additional ways to involve the client:

- Offer to do free surveys of training needs for businesses, organizations, or departments within an organization.

- Subscribe to organization newsletters and ask for in-house publications. Many of these communications will gratefully publish news releases.
- Invite clients to be guests at one of the programs you sponsor. Provide their transportation and spend the day with them.
- Ask clients to write letters of support for programs or agree to be listed as a co-sponsor.
- Use a peer invitation approach. Ask a leader from the client group to write a letter recommending the program to others (see Appendix VII).
- Develop a list of willing, previous clients who agree to talk on behalf of the program.
- Invite client groups to hold meetings at the sponsoring organization's site, without charge if possible. Make a point of meeting the group, welcoming them as guests, and providing them with take-home information packets.
- Offer to speak at or provide speakers for monthly meetings of client groups.

Helpful Suggestions for Working with Client Groups

Here are several suggestions that may help you avoid some of the common problems in working with client groups.

1. Write an agenda for client meetings and distribute it well in advance. It should focus on the tasks to be addressed, set priorities within given time constraints, and prepare for active participation in the process. Such advance preparation also demonstrates that you and your organization are task oriented, highly organized, and dependable.
2. Let clients know in advance how they will be expected to contribute. Are they expected to supply information, make a report, or lead a discussion? Make a point of involving every client in the discussion. If clients have been quiet during a meeting, call on them to get their participation. Ask them an open-ended question such as "What are your ideas on the suggestions that have been made?" Avoid closed-end questions such as "Do you agree with the plan that was presented?" that allow clients to give a simple "yes" or "no" answer.
3. Respect people's time. Begin and end meetings on time.
4. Keep the size of client groups relatively small and an odd number. Groups of nine to twelve persons seem to be optimal. This allows everyone to get to know each other and encourages participation. An odd-numbered size prevents votes from ending in ties.
5. Arrange the meeting space of planning groups to maximize eye contact among the clients. Eye contact is often a critical factor in facilitating the flow of communications and in developing group cohesiveness. Arranging chairs in a circle or placing tables in a "U" shape are preferable to typical theatre style seating.
6. Make it easy for late arrivals to join the group. Often, client members are delayed for meetings because of work schedules or traffic. Leave an open

chair and place handout materials near the door so latecomers will not disrupt the group or feel embarrassed.

7. Listen, don't talk. As many adult educators and trainers have strong platform speaking skills, keeping silent once you have convened the group can be difficult. Let the client group work through problems even if the adult education leader already knows the proper outcome. The problem-solving process will be valuable and give clients a sense of worth that will help develop group cohesiveness.

8. If the client group is quiet or nonresponsive, break the group down into two- or three-person discussion groups to explore individual issues and report back to the larger group. Another technique is to go to each client and ask for one idea or question. List the comments on a flipchart or blackboard. Keep circulating around the table until there are no more comments. Then synthesize or group the comments together under several broad categories that can serve as guidelines for group discussion.

9. To keep the discussion from getting off track, use such expressions as "Let's take a look at how we are doing" or "What I hear you saying is . . ." to help summarize participants' thoughts.

10. Set high expectations and standards for the group and set yourself as the model for excellence. Poorly written communications, misspelled names, and last-minute invitations to meetings set a poor tone for client input.

11. Do not take client participation for granted. Too often, client groups are initiated with a flurry of activity, but are then slowly ignored until interest withers away. Keep members aware of even the smallest progress in program development or marketing. Make sure they receive a quantity of promotional material. Encourage them to circulate the material to colleagues. Send them copies of class lists, summaries of evaluations, results of marketing efforts, and even copies of texts and course handout materials. Look for articles or newspaper clippings related to the program or the clients' personal interests and send them copies. Most importantly, do not forget to send thank you notes after meetings or when the client has helped in some way.

12. Do not overuse the same client. Client enthusiasm for participation will diminish if the tasks become repetitive or if the appointment on the advisory board becomes a life sentence. The shorter the appointment period, the more likely the opportunity to attract good clients to participate and to make effective use of meeting time.

Summary

As Kotler (1985) has pointed out, three major tasks are involved in analyzing the marketplace. First, one must determine the potential size of the market. Second, one must determine what target groups of clients make up the potential market. And third, one must identify the characteristics of the clients, their needs and interests, and where they seek information. What are their channels of communications? Active involvement of the client in each of these tasks is a relatively low-cost method of gathering additional information and testing assumptions about market strategies. Not only will the results be beneficial, but the interaction and involvement with a wide spectrum of adult learners will be an interesting, stimulating and very enjoyable experience for the adult educator. It will help keep in perspective the human element in the program development and marketing function.

The following appendixes provide sample questionnaires and letters that will be helpful in working with clients. Each appendix explains how best to use the form.

APPENDIX I

This typical general interest survey instrument is usually used when there is a need to survey a large client group to obtain some indication of broad areas of interest.

Sample Interest Questionnaire

We need your help. The Community Center has decided that one of the important new services it will offer its neighbors is a program of continuing education for adults. We want to provide the courses, clubs, and other kinds of activities that *you* want. Will you let us know your desires by checking the column that most nearly reflects the way you feel? Then please place this form in the postage-paid envelope enclosed and mail it right back to our program committee. Thanks.

Short Course (10 weeks)	Good Idea	Inter-ested	Will Enroll
Your Career			
Fashion Design	___	___	___
Drafting	___	___	___
Starting Your Own Business	___	___	___
Writing for Profit	___	___	___
How to Enjoy Retirement	___	___	___
Your Home			
Making Home Repairs	___	___	___
Buying and Selling a Home	___	___	___
Landscaping	___	___	___
Creative Cooking	___	___	___
Antiquing	___	___	___
Know Thyself			
Discovering Your Aptitudes	___	___	___
Logical Thinking	___	___	___
Understanding Your Emotions	___	___	___
Better Human Relations	___	___	___
Creative Problem Solving	___	___	___
Preparation for Marriage	___	___	___
Keep Fit			
Fencing	___	___	___
Golf	___	___	___
Bowling	___	___	___

Short Course	Good Idea	Inter-ested	Will Enroll
Skiing	___	___	___
Yoga	___	___	___
Exercising at Home and Office	___	___	___
Keep Current			
Practical Politics	___	___	___
The Law and You	___	___	___
What It's Like to Be Black	___	___	___
Negro History	___	___	___
The New Math	___	___	___
The Youth Scene	___	___	___
Enjoy Leisure			
Understanding Art	___	___	___
Enjoying Music	___	___	___
Acting and Drama	___	___	___
Playing String Instruments	___	___	___
Improving Your Dancing	___	___	___
Fun with Chess	___	___	___
Arts and Crafts	___	___	___
Painting for Fun	___	___	___
Learn More			
Rapid Reading	___	___	___
Public Speaking	___	___	___
Vocabulary	___	___	___

Sample Interest Questionnaire (Cont'd.)

Clubs (check those you would be most interested in joining)

Hikers	_____	Painting	_____	French	_____
Dance	_____	Bridge	_____	Spanish	_____
Discussion	_____	Riding	_____	Russian	_____
Couples	_____	Camping	_____	German	_____
Speakers	_____	Music	_____	Swedish	_____
Camera	_____	Travel	_____	Italian	_____

General Information

1. What would be the best time of day for course or club meetings for you?

5:00 P.M.	_____	6:30 P.M.	_____	8:00 P.M.	_____
5:30 P.M.	_____	7:00 P.M.	_____	8:30 P.M.	_____
6:00 P.M.	_____	7:30 P.M.	_____	Other	_____

2. What would be the best day of the week for course or club meetings for you?

Sunday	_____	Tuesday	_____	Thursday	_____	Saturday	_____
Monday	_____	Wednesday	_____	Friday	_____		

3. What is your occupation? _____

4. Where do you work?

Downtown	_____	East Side	_____	South Side	_____
West Side	_____	North Side	_____	Other	_____

Please give your name and address if you want further information.

Name _____

Home Address _____

Telephone   Home _____   Business _____

_____

APPENDIX II

Once some specific interest areas have been identified, using the survey in Appendix I, the following survey can help clients focus their interest priorities.

Sample Topic Preference Scale Survey

On a scale of 1 to 5, circle the number that best describes your interest in the following topic areas.

	Low Interest		*Some Interest*		*High Interest*
1. Books of the Bible, textual study	1	2	3	4	5
2. Doctrines of the church, confessional study	1	2	3	4	5
3. Ethical issues	1	2	3	4	5
4. Social issues	1	2	3	4	5
5. Personal/spiritual sharing	1	2	3	4	5
6. Evangelism	1	2	3	4	5
7. Basic religious/philosophical questions	1	2	3	4	5
8. Other _____	1	2	3	4	5

The data obtained from this questionnaire together with the judgments of the committee will be summarized and used in planning and designing programs.

APPENDIX III

This is another example of a survey instrument that can be used to help clients focus their interest priorities.

Sample Client Interest Survey

Dear Doctor:

In order to continue to develop the excellent Continuing Dental Education programs conducted thus far, we would like to request that you check those topics that are of high interest to you. To the right of each topic is a space to write in the name of a particular speaker you would recommend to teach that topic, if you have someone in mind. Thank you for your assistance.

Highly Interested	Topic	Suggested Speaker
_____	Minor tooth movement	_____
_____	Orthodontics for the GP	_____
_____	Medical update for the dentist	_____
_____	Endodontics	_____
_____	Removable prosthodontics	_____
_____	Fixed prosthodontics	_____
_____	Adhesive composites	_____
_____	Dental emergency care	_____
_____	Occlusion	_____
_____	Pharmacology	_____
_____	Electrosurgery	_____
_____	Periodontics	_____
_____	Pain control	_____
_____	Anesthesia and analgesia	_____
_____	Kinesiology	_____
_____	TMJ	_____
_____	Dental materials	_____
_____	Nutrition	_____
_____	Oral pathology	_____
_____	Financial planning	_____
_____	Pedodontics	_____
_____	Prevention dentistry	_____
_____	Radiology	_____

A. Would you attend an in-depth two-day presentation?   ___ Yes   ___ No

B. Topic Areas

Highly Interested	Topic	Suggested Speaker
	Medical update/dental treatment: The patient with	
_____	medical problems	_____
_____	The future of dentistry	_____
_____	Practice management	_____
_____	_____	_____
_____	_____	_____

C. Which days do you prefer?

    ___ Wednesday/Thursday
    ___ Thursday/Friday
    ___ Friday/Saturday
    ___ Saturday/Sunday
    ___ Other _____

D. Comments _____

APPENDIX IV

This instrument is useful in collecting data from advisory groups. It has some use as a follow-up to the first advisory group meeting. Ideas presented at the first meeting are summarized and given more focus with this questionnaire. In addition, the data collected can start to give a better picture of the target population. Use of this questionnaire also ensures that even quiet members of the advisory group have an opportunity for input.

Sample Advisory Committee Questionnaire

I. General Information
    A.   Name _____
    B.   Affiliation _____
    C.1. Number of medical technologists employed in your location/lab ____
    C.2. To the best of your knowledge, please break down and list the number of people at each of the following educational levels.
         ____ No degree or certification (P.J.T.)
         ____ High School + C.L.A. certificate
         ____ High School + H.T. certificate
         ____ Associate degree + M.L.T. certificate
         ____ Bachelor's degree
         ____ Bachelor's degree + specialized certificate
         ____ Bachelor's degree + M.T. certificate
         ____ Bachelor's degree + C.T. certificate
         ____ Master's degree
         ____ HEW examination
         ____ Other _____
    D.   Does your institution have a policy to reimburse expenses and registration fees? ____ If yes, what are its limits? _____
II. Course Information
    At the last meeting, the following were suggested as possible courses. Please indicate major topics that you feel should be covered in such courses. Be as specific as possible.
    A.   Statistics for the Bench Technologist

    1. _____   6. _____

    2. _____   7. _____

    3. _____   8. _____

    4. _____   9. _____

    5. _____   10. _____

    B.   Laboratory Safety and Procedures

    1. _____   6. _____

    2. _____   7. _____

    3. _____   8. _____

    4. _____   9. _____

    5. _____   10. _____

C. Refresher Course

1. _____   6. _____

2. _____   7. _____

3. _____   8. _____

4. _____   9. _____

5. _____   10. _____

D. Toxicology

1. _____   6. _____

2. _____   7. _____

3. _____   8. _____

4. _____   9. _____

5. _____   10. _____

E. Human Relations—Dealing with Patients

1. _____   6. _____

2. _____   7. _____

3. _____   8. _____

4. _____   9. _____

5. _____   10. _____

F. Teaching Techniques in Allied Health

1. _____   6. _____

2. _____   7. _____

3. _____   8. _____

4. _____   9. _____

5. _____   10. _____

G. Instrumentation

1. _____   6. _____

2. _____   7. _____

3. _____   8. _____

4. _____   9. _____

5. _____   10. _____

H. Cost Containment

1. _____   6. _____

2. _____   7. _____

3. _____   8. _____

4. _____   9. _____

5. _____   10. _____

I.   Means of Effective Communication

1. _____   6. _____
2. _____   7. _____
3. _____   8. _____
4. _____   9. _____
5. _____   10. _____

J.   Laboratory Management/Supervision

1. _____   6. _____
2. _____   7. _____
3. _____   8. _____
4. _____   9. _____
5. _____   10. _____

K.   Scientific Sessions/Assemblies

1. _____   6. _____
2. _____   7. _____
3. _____   8. _____
4. _____   9. _____
5. _____   10. _____

L.   Legal Requirements

1. _____   6. _____
2. _____   7. _____
3. _____   8. _____
4. _____   9. _____
5. _____   10. _____

III.   Miscellaneous

A.   Have members of your laboratory participated in any outside professional development activities? _____ If yes, please explain. _____

B.   Does your hospital/lab provide any in-service? _____ If yes, please explain. _____

C.   List speakers and/or topics you or others would recommend.

         Speaker   Topic

_____   _____

_____   _____

                                         Thank you very much.

APPENDIX V

In this sample of a structured telephone interview, the interviewer uses the questions as a guide in talking with clients. The responses are not read or listed with the client, but they represent the most likely client answers. This makes it easy for the interviewer to categorize and check off answers.

Sample Questions for Structured Telephone Interviews

The following questions were developed as part of a structured telephone survey of part-time undergraduate degree students.

1. Which category would best describe your major aim at the time that you first registered as a part-time student (in other words, "Professional Objective" from the computer)?
   A. General Education Development _____
   B. Admission—Undergraduate _____
   C. Admission—Graduate _____
   D. Readmission (dropped, probation, action pending) _____

2. Employment status during the academic year:
   A. Employed full-time (30 hours or more per week) _____
   B. Employed part-time (less than 30 hours) _____
   C. Unemployed but seeking work _____
   D. Not in the work force _____

3. At present you are employed as
   A. Professional (doctor, engineer, accountant, etc.) _____
   B. Manager/administrator _____
   C. Clerical or sales (bookkeeper, secretary, clerk, etc.) _____
   D. Skilled, semiskilled labor services _____
   E. Other _____

4. What is your relationship to other members of your household?
   A. Head of household (main source of family financial support) _____
   B. Co-head of household (share in financial support of family) _____
   C. Spouse of head of household _____
   D. Son or daughter of head of household _____
   E. Other _____

5. Did any of the following represent your major aim at the time that you first registered as a part-time student?
   A. Admission—Undergraduate   Yes _____ No _____
   B. Admission—Graduate   Yes _____ No _____
   C. Readmission   Yes _____ No _____

6. People have different reasons for registering initially as a part-time student instead of as a matriculated full-time student. Please rate the importance of each of the following factors as they influenced your decision to initially register as a part-time rather than a full-time student:

	Not Important 1-3	Somewhat Important 4-6	Very Important 7-9
A. The need to improve your academic record before matriculating	_____	_____	_____

B. Other demands on your time   _____ _____ _____
(such as job, family, etc.)
C. Indecision about your educational _____ _____ _____
or career objective
D. Limited financial resources   _____ _____ _____
E. The need to develop self-   _____ _____ _____
confidence about yourself as a
student
F. A desire to postpone having to   _____ _____ _____
complete paperwork and other
administrative details involved in
matriculating

7. Please rate the usefulness of the following sources of advisement and information.

	Not Used	Not Useful	Somewhat Useful	Very Useful
A. ACCESS Center	____	____	____	____
B. Other University offices and personnel (who?)	____	____	____	____
C. Other students	____	____	____	____
D. University publications	____	____	____	____
E. Other source (specify).	_____
Comments?	_____

8. Have you talked to an academic adviser counselor? Yes ____ No ____

9. How many times have you met with an adviser?
A. 0 ____   C. 2 ____   E. 4 or more ____
B. 1 ____   D. 3 ____

10. How would you rate the registration information and assistance you received?
A. Very helpful ____   C. Not helpful ____
B. Somewhat helpful ____   D. Not applicable ____

11. How long do you estimate it will take to complete your degree?
A. Less than one year ____   C. 3-4 years ____ E. 7 or more years
B. 1-2 years ____   D. 5-6 years ____

APPENDIX VI

This is a model confirmation letter to members of advisory groups clearly stating expectations, setting a professional image for the institution, and at the same time expressing appreciation to board members.

Sample Confirmation Letter to Clients
Invited to Be Members of an Advisory Board

Dear _____ :

Thank you for agreeing to serve for a two-year term on the Advisory Board for the Center's new Advanced Certificate in Gerontology.

You know better than anyone the increasing need to develop competent professionals with the special skill to work in the field of gerontology. We feel the availability of a professional certificate program is an important element in meeting this need. The program will involve a minimum of 250 contact hours of graded instruction; thus, you can be assured that those who graduate will indeed have been challenged and responded accordingly.

As a member of the Advisory Board we seek your input into the design of instructional content, identification of leaders in the field to instruct the program, assistance in establishing supervised field experiences, recognition of the certificate as an employment criterion, and active encouragement and funding of your employees who wish to participate.

The Advisory Board will have two regularly scheduled meetings each year. The meeting site will rotate between counties. Other meetings will be called only as necessary. Advice and assistance will be frequently requested via telephone or one-on-one discussions.

The first, and perhaps most critical, meeting will be [date] and [time] at [address]. In preparation for this meeting, you are asked to critically review the attached proposal and come prepared to dicuss.

Enclosed is a list of those who have accepted invitations to join the Advisory Board.

We are indebted to you for taking time to help the Center implement this new career program. Please don't hesitate to call if you have questions.

John Doe
Program Coordinator
Center for Continuing Professional Education

APPENDIX VII

This model invitation letter demonstrates how members of advisory groups or identified client leaders can be used to market programs. Such peer letters serve as testimonials and can give instant credibility to the program sponsor.

Sample Peer Invitation

Getting clients to write promotional letters to other members of their peer group can be an effective marketing tool. Here is a model letter taken from an actual case at the University of Delaware.

Dear Training Officer:

I am pleased to announce that on September 20 and 29, the Anytown Department of Police in cooperation with the University of Delaware will host a two-day seminar specifically designed for female law enforcement officers. The seminar is entitled "YOU: The Female Law Enforcement Officer." The objectives of the seminar are as follows:

1. To enable the female law enforcement officer to better understand the psychology of women in general and the psychology of law enforcement women in particular.
2. To assist the female officer in dealing with her minority status within the law enforcement environment.
3. To help the female officer discover new ways of reducing the stresses of law enforcement work and the demands of personal life.

Since many of the topics to be discussed will be of a highly personal nature, the seminar will be open only to female officers. The instructor will be Dr. Jane Doe, a clinical psychologist who has worked with female law enforcement personnel for the past twelve years and who has also served as the psychologist for the Anytown Department of Police. A detailed outline of the program is enclosed for your information.

The cost for this seminar is $300.00. If you desire to register any of your personnel, please nominate candidates on your departmental letterhead stationery and forward the listing to our training office. Enclose your check payable to the University of Delaware. The University of Delaware will accept agency vouchers and purchase orders. All nomination letters as well as checks or purchase orders should be returned by September 22, 198X.

> Anytown Department of Police
> 1000 First Street
> Anytown, Delaware 1999X

We sincerely hope that your agency will be able to send female officers of all ranks to this seminar. If you have any questions, please do not hesitate to contact me.

> Sincerely,
> Sandra Smith, Chief of Police

Making Marketing Work in Your Organization

Part Seven deals with practical suggestions for making marketing work in your organization. Dennis P. Prisk begins with Chapter Twenty-Eight, in which he explains how to organize and staff a marketing office. He analyzes general organizational patterns necessary for success, including the advantages and disadvantages of centralized versus decentralized marketing offices. Also discussed are the interoffice relationships between program units and the marketing office by which marketing plans can be developed and implemented successfully.

In Chapter Twenty-Nine, Prisk analyzes the complex issues of budgeting for marketing activities and staff costs associated with marketing. He considers such issues as subsidization of the marketing office, level of service expected from a small marketing office, equipment needed, and recovery of direct marketing costs. Of particular interest is the sample electronic spreadsheet he has developed for monitoring and analyzing the cost effectiveness of marketing activities. This model can easily be adapted by any continuing education organization.

Doe Hentschel concludes Part Seven with Chapter Thirty, in which she demonstrates how to gain organizational support for marketing. She analyzes reasons for lack of support for marketing in some continuing education organizations, how sources of conflict over marketing can be resolved so that support can be achieved, and how change strategies can be used to reduce this conflict. Gaining institutional support for marketing from a parent organization is often difficult, but her chapter provides a thoughtful, practical analysis of how to overcome the obstacles and develop this support.

Thus, Part Seven emphasizes many practical ways to formalize the marketing function in your continuing education organization. Hints are given for budgeting, managing organizational conflict associated with the marketing function, and developing a system that builds total organizational support for marketing.

28

How to Organize and Staff the Marketing Office

Dennis P. Prisk

To date, there has not emerged an ideal model for organizing and staffing a marketing office within a continuing education organization. Just as continuing education is diverse in its organizational pattern, so too are the approaches to marketing. There are, however, two general concepts on which a marketing effort may be developed: a centralized structure and a decentralized structure. A variety of combinations also exist.

A centralized model is one in which one office manages all of the marketing and promotion for the continuing education organization. The Office of Marketing within the University of California, Los Angeles, Extension Division exemplifies this approach. There are major advantages to the centralized approach:

1. One office produces publications, disseminates information, and projects the image. This may serve as a unifying force for the continuing education organization and thus contribute to a unanimity of purpose.
2. Similar to program specialists, specialists in advertising, graphics, research, mailing, and multimedia can be located in one office.
3. In proposing marketing strategies, the marketing office can, as a neutral party, identify potential weaknesses in the educational product and//or recommend improvements in product, presentation, or targeting.
4. Allocation of resources (equipment, staff, and effort) is not duplicated.
5. News media, both print and electronic, may respond more efficiently if the information comes from a single reliable source. A centralized marketing

office also is convenient for the news media because there is only one office, and preferably one contact, to call for information.

6. Costs associated with marketing—materials, supplies, advertisements, personnel—can be more effectively monitored and controlled from a single office.
7. A uniform yet flexible tracking system to assess the cost effectiveness of marketing strategies can be developed.
8. A centralized marketing and communications staff is a resource for the entire spectrum of instructional programs.

The centralized office also has several disadvantages:

1. Market planning is one step removed from those responsible for program development.
2. Work from all divisions must be managed on the basis of a schedule and, therefore, may necessitate longer lead times. Last-minute requests must be minimal to permit control and quality of results.
3. Continuous attention must be given to resource allocation—equipment, staff, and space—if the office is to maintain a high level of customer satisfaction.
4. Directors and/or their staffs do not have direct control over the office of marketing and communications staff, thereby losing some prerogatives.
5. Because another layer of bureaucracy is added to the organization, communication to external agencies may be slowed by the need to gain internal clearance.

A decentralized model is one in which the marketing and promotion of individual programs are handled by each program office. The University of Kansas' Division of Continuing Education illustrates this approach. Note these major advantages to the decentralized structure:

1. Program managers have a higher sense of ownership. They have direct control over how their programs are marketed.
2. Program managers do not compete with other offices in prioritizing marketing projects. They prioritize their own programs.
3. Resources related to marketing and promotion can be distributed throughout the continuing education organization, thereby benefiting the programs directly.
4. There is a greater ability to schedule last-minute projects that require a marketing plan. Program managers do not have to make workload decisions based on the availability of a marketing specialist.
5. A potential negative effect on interorganizational relations is avoided in the event of an ineffective marketing office.
6. There is one less unit for the top management of the continuing education organization to supervise.

7.   Program managers may directly employ special consultants for their activities as the need arises.

There are, however, disadvantages to the decentralized marketing office:

1.   The potential exists for unevenness in promotional material. Perception of what is quality varies among individuals. This cannot be overstressed.
2.   It is unlikely that top management will receive consistent feedback on the effectiveness of programs from a marketing perspective.
3.   Development of a uniform tracking system to assess the cost effectiveness of marketing strategies is less likely to occur.
4.   The potential for quality of expression and presentation may be less because marketing is only one of several skills a programmer must possess.
5.   There is the potential for a duplication of effort in writing news releases, securing and maintaining mailing lists, doing market research, and editing/writing copy, and other tasks.
6.   There is likely to be confusion among internal and external agencies over whom to call for news articles or general information or to clarify inaccuracies.

Between the two ends of the continuum—centralized and decentralized marketing—there exist a myriad of organizational arrangements that combine the elements of both, for example, having an advertising agency or retainer to provide assistance as needed; having a full-time coordinator employed by the continuing education division available to consult with the program managers; and having editors on staff aid in proofing brochure, advertisement, or press release copy. At Illinois State University, for example, the College of Continuing Education employs a coordinator of publicity/promotions, who oversees the planning and coordination of print pieces. But the market strategies for individual programs, as well as budget allocations, are determined by the program managers. Mailing lists are provided by the client; no commercial lists are purchased. Thus, Illinois State University has combined elements of both approaches by maintaining a limited marketing staff and allowing the programmers to exercise discretion in promoting their activities.

Centralized marketing offices are organized in various ways. In some instances, an assistant/associate dean/director serves as the chief administrative officer. In other cases, a director reports directly to the chief executive officer of the continuing education organization or the associate executive officer. Figure 28.1 indicates one pattern of organization for a centralized office.

Typically, the staff responsibilities in a centralized operation comprise implementation of alternative approaches to marketing; maintenance of an organizationwide mailing list system; creation of a tracking system to measure marketing effectiveness; monitoring of demographic and psychographic trends to aid in planning; and analysis of campaign strategies for program offices in terms of budgets. Other responsibilities include supervising the writing and editing of

Figure 28.1. Department of Marketing, UCLA Extension.

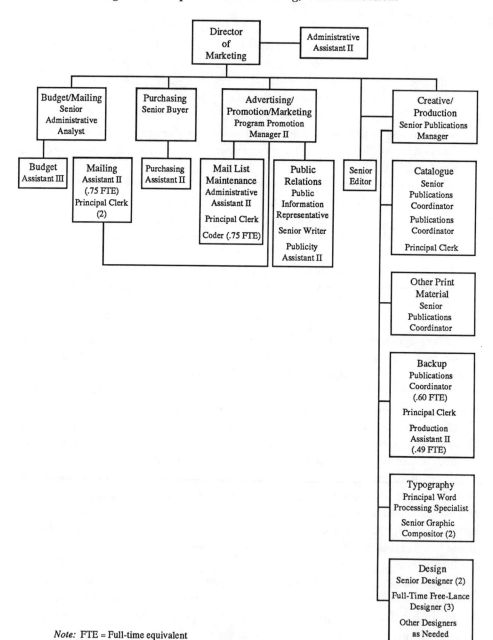

Note: FTE = Full-time equivalent

Reprinted by permission of UCLA Extension.

copy for brochures, press releases, and advertisements; monitoring trends in the use of technology; overseeing market reserach; and being generally accountable for the quality of promotional pieces. Often, the centralized office functions in production of all printed materials; graphic design of publications or displays; creation and/or production of instructional materials; maintenance of media relations, both print and broadcast; development and placement of advertisements; preparation of news releases; acquisition and maintenance of mailing lists; and development and maintenance of a tracking system.

In a decentralized approach to marketing and promotion, the program directors are responsible for their own marketing strategy. They also have the flexibility to bring in consultants when needed. A decentralized structure, such as that used by the University of Kansas, requires the employment of staff with some knowledge of marketing and promotion. Figure 28.2 is the organizational chart of the Division of Continuing Education at the University of Kansas. All of the responsibilities and functions associated with a centralized office are dispensed throughout the program offices.

Creating a Centralized Marketing Office

Establishment of a marketing and communications office within a continuing education organization is, at best, a difficult process. There is no patented formula. Much depends on the institutional environment, the history of the continuing education organization, the nature of previous or existing marketing efforts, as well as the personalities of the staff. What is clear is that a marketing and communications office cannot be established or maintained without the total commitment of the person who heads the continuing education organization. Through both difficult and pleasant times, the head of the organization must be unwavering in support. The existing staff must be persuaded that it is in their best interest to create a central pool of marketing specialists, individuals to whom the programmers can turn when assistance is needed, to promote a program or develop new initiatives. This can be a delicate process, especially when many programmers believe they are equally skilled in the areas of marketing and promotion.

Gaining the support of the central administration in the parent organization for establishing a marketing office may largely depend on whether additional funds are requested to support new positions or the organization intends to reallocate funds internally. The case that is developed and the manner in which it is presented are determining factors in obtaining the necessary approvals.

This author is committed to a centralized marketing office for the following reasons:

1. Such an office can develop standards of quality expected by the institution and demanded by the public.

Figure 28.2. Division of Continuing Education, University of Kansas.

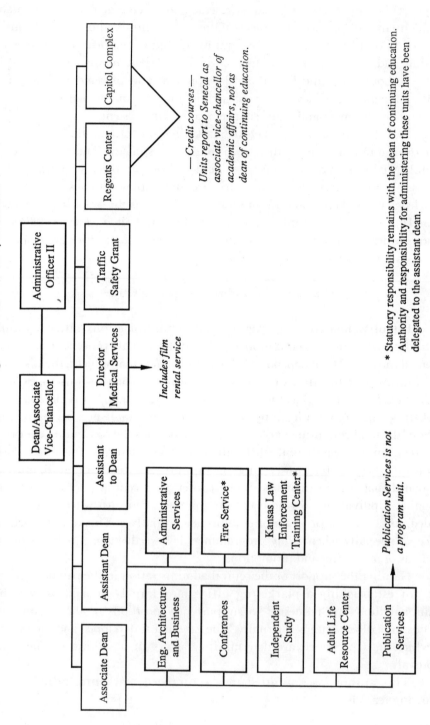

— Credit courses —
Units report to Senecal as associate vice-chancellor of academic affairs, not as dean of continuing education.

Includes film rental service

Publication Services is not a program unit.

* Statutory responsibility remains with the dean of continuing education. Authority and responsibility for administering these units have been delegated to the assistant dean.

Reprinted by permission of the Division of Continuing Education, the University of Kansas.

2.   The office can utilize the continuing education organization's resources more effectively by consolidating previously duplicated staff and functions.
3.   The office's professional staff can assist the entire organization as well as each office by making the most of each promotion dollar.
4.   Market research, tracking systems, and mailing list maintenance, the areas crucial to successful market penetration, can be more effectively and efficiently coordinated through one office.
5.   Sustained, well-planned, and professionally executed publicity and public relations campaigns on behalf of the continuing education division and its individual programs are more likely to yield a higher degree of positive results than would otherwise be the case.
6.   Full-time specialists in marketing and communications are more likely to keep abreast of changes in that field than are program planners.
7.   The chief administrative officer for continuing education has one office to hold accountable for the quality of published material.

Although several models exist for centralizing an office of marketing and communications, the one described herein is based on an account executive model. At the University of Alabama College of Continuing Studies, the Office of Marketing and Communications consists of a director, two account executives, a graphic designer, two secretaries, a mailing list coordinator, a research assistant, and part-time assistants, both students and professionals.

Each program division is assigned an account executive who follows the promotion of programs from initial planning, through the production of materials, to the execution of mailings, publicity, and follow-up. In short, the account executive serves as the liaison between the client (programmer) and vendors. The account executive assists in assessing the client's marketing, communication, and creative needs. Figure 28.3 illustrates the organization of the Office of Marketing and Communications at the College of Continuing Studies.

Common Problems

As is the case with new ventures, not all problems can be seen in the planning stages. This is no less true in establishing a marketing office. Remain aware of the following common problems.

Clearly state the functions of the office. This may appear to be obvious but clarity of purpose is highly important. For example, in the case of a repeat program, where a minimum of changes are required from the previous brochure, who should have the responsibility—the program office or marketing? State institutions often require that publication material be put on bid. Who is responsible for preparing the specifications for the bid? Is the program office or the marketing office responsible for acquiring mailing lists? Who sees to it that the lists are periodically updated and purged? A clear understanding at the outset of the roles of the marketing office and the individual program offices will minimize the confusion.

Figure 28.3. Office of Marketing and Communications, College of Continuing Studies, University of Alabama.

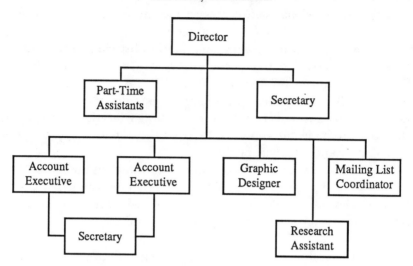

Reprinted by permission of the University of Alabama College of Continuing Studies.

Determining who has final authority for marketing is perhaps one of the most sensitive issues related to a marketing office. As previously stated, many programmers feel they possess the requisite marketing skills. Programmers, rightfully so, have a sense of ownership over something they have developed and are reluctant to turn it over to someone else to promote. At the same time, marketing specialists feel they have the expertise needed to promote a program successfully. Generally speaking, differences over format, graphics, and strategy are resolved through negotiation between the programmer and the marketing staff. In those instances in which there is an impasse, the final decision should rest with the marketing office, unless that decision has a negative impact on the program budget. If that is the case, the program staff must be given the opportunity to make the final decision.

When establishing a service unit such as a marketing office, the chief administrative officer for continuing education should develop a realistic time line for implementation. Employing staff, developing policies and procedures, and establishing a budget all take time. What is important is to gain agreement from the continuing education organization's staff that at some point, whether it is in 12, 18, or 24 months, a marketing office will be fully operational. Functions of the office can be added incrementally until it provides a full range of marketing and promotional services. In the interim, the program staff may retain some marketing responsibilities.

Allocating sufficient resources to support a marketing office is a prerequisite to a successful operation. Once the scope of the office of marketing and communications is determined, a staffing pattern must be identified, and searches begun to fill the positions. A budget for both operations and advertising needs to be developed. Appropriate office space, always a critical issue, must be found. This space must include not just room for staff but also storage space, especially to hold brochures as they await distribution. Technology is an important and growing dimension of an office of marketing and communications. Type of equipment and adequate space are essential to the efficiency of the office.

Identifying the total resources necessary for a marketing office, and making the commitment, should be viewed as an investment in the long-term success of the continuing education organization. At the outset, those involved in deciding to create an office of marketing and communications should also create a plan for growth. As the profit centers (programs) of the continuing education organization grow, the support offices, such as marketing, need to be of adequate size to aid this expansion. Growth should not occur at such a level that it outruns the ability of marketing to support programs. Thus, a plan for growth for the office of marketing and communications is directly related to the organization's strategic planning process.

The marketing office must be knowledgeable about and aware of the goals and objectives of each program office. The marketing office needs to be in a position to know of new or modified goals so that adjustments can be proposed in the marketing and promotion plan. Effective market research and analysis of the data can provide the basis for decisions regarding (1) the degree of satisfaction of the existing customer base, (2) new market penetration, (3) promotion of loss leaders, and (4) selection of appropriate media. This information can be utilized to determine the long-range needs of the office of marketing and communications. This then becomes the basis for a rational plan for growth.

Interoffice Relationships

It is inevitable in any organization that differences will arise among staff over the interpretation and implementation of policies and procedures. Determining a procedure for resolving these differences will necessarily make for a more effective organization. It is important to keep in mind that policies are guidelines. Flexibility is a cornerstone for minimizing problems. Guiding the marketing and program staffs through a responsibility matrix can be an important step in this process. Depending on the issue, some of the staff may only need to be consulted, others simply informed, some staff may be responsible, and others may be the decision makers, for example, the policy issue of who contacts printers for service:

Issue	Responsible	Informed	Consult	Decide
Contacting commercial printers	Marketing staff (account executive)	Program officer	University purchasing	Marketing director

If a program manager contacts a printer directly, contrary to policy, the director of the Office of Marketing and Communications and the director of the Program Division should meet to resolve the issue.

Clearly defining the role of the marketing staff can mitigate the degree of conflict over who is responsible for various aspects of marketing. For example, should programmers contact printers directly to determine the status of their projects, or is this a responsibility of the marketing office? Who has primary responsibility for interfacing with the Purchasing Department? A clipping service is invaluable in determining what articles are being carried by what newspapers. Who is responsible for engaging this service, the program staff or marketing? Marketing research is a prerequisite for the long-term success of the continuing education organization. Is marketing responsible or are the program offices responsible? Or should marketing research permeate the entire organization and therefore become everyone's responsibility?

Again, the issue is one of clarifying the responsibilities of the staff as they relate to the marketing function. The process may take much time and effort initially but it will be worthwhile in the long run.

A communications audit for any organization is one method to determine the clarity with which directions are given and staff assignments determined. Such an audit is especially important for a support unit like marketing. Analysis of policy documents, memoranda, minutes from staff meetings, telephone conversations, and planning meetings can aid in determining the strengths and weaknesses in staff interactions within the continuing education organization. Ineffective communication in this important function can lead to unnecessary confusion among other staff members. More importantly, the marketing office must communicate in such a way that its clients perceive a genuine concern for their programs. A communications audit, undertaken periodically, can yield the type of data that will promote improvements in the effectiveness of the marketing office.

To assess the effectiveness of the marketing office a periodic evaluation by a professional consultant is essential. It is important to address such issues as the appropriateness of the scope and mission of the office, the smooth flow of work, proper management of projects, and the feasibility of lead times. Also to be considered is whether or not program managers know what to expect of marketing and vice versa. And finally, the consultant can offer opinions on whether the office is properly organized, what skills and competencies need to be added, if any, and whether the resources of the office are adequate to meet the scope and mission of the office. From these questions other issues will emerge so that the consultant, staff, and continuing education administrators can develop a comprehensive review of the operation.

Summary

This chapter has analyzed some organizational and staffing patterns for marketing programs offered by a continuing education organization. As we have seen, the key to the success of the marketing effort is an understanding of the goals of the continuing education organization and its relationship to the parent institution. Excellence in communicating the image of continuing education within the parent institution should be a product of the marketing office's daily operation. Marketing should contribute to the planning processes used by the continuing education organization's programmers, especially as it relates to the public's response to programs.

Whether this occurs within a centralized or a decentralized framework, achieving the goals with a reasonable investment of resources is the ultimate measure of success for the marketing function.

29

Budgeting for Marketing Activities and Staff Costs

Dennis P. Prisk

No matter what the organizational structure of the marketing function in a continuing education organization, there are often institutional constraints that govern its activities. For example, must a continuing education organization utilize the parent institution's printing services? Will the organization be required to use specific services of the institution's public relations office, such as photography? Can a continuing education organization enter into a personal services contract with a private consultant to produce a slide/sound presentation or must this be contracted through the parent institution's public relations office?

Restraints (such as those just mentioned), local conditions, and size and scope of the continuing education organization are some of the factors that impinge on budget decisions for marketing and promotion. No one formula will work for everyone. It is important that the circumstances within which the continuing education organization must function be recognized and understood.

The figures and dollar amounts referred to in this chapter are intended only to serve as guidelines. They should serve simply as a starting point in budgeting for marketing activities.

Subsidizing the Marketing Office

To subsidize a marketing office, the continuing education organization will need to consider those costs associated with personnel, operation, equipment, and office space. Often, the primary expenditure taken into account is personnel, that is, the number of staff required for a marketing office and their salary levels. Surprisingly, other areas usually become the highest cost factor over time.

The level of services a marketing office is charged with providing will determine the number and type of staff. At the University of Alabama, the College of Continuing Studies' Office of Marketing and Communications is charged with providing a full range of marketing and promotional services for the College. The office consists of eight full-time staff plus three to four part-time assistants. The combined salary for 1987–1988 was $133,882. The full-time staff comprises a director, two account executives, one graphic artist, two secretaries, a research assistant, and a mailing list coordinator. The part-time staff consists of a graphic artist, editor/writer, and students who perform a variety of tasks. The College consists of a full-time staff in excess of 100. It has an operating budget of approximately $4 million and annually serves more than 22,000 people in credit and noncredit programs.

The operating costs for the office, such as telephone, supplies, postage, and travel, amount to approximately $10,000 annually. Because of a charge-back system, which will be discussed later in this chapter, a significantly larger allocation is not necessary.

The area that requires a considerable expenditure of marketing funds, initially and continuously, is equipment. Some of the major acquisitions of the University of Alabama's College of Continuing Studies' Office of Marketing and Communications have been an Argyle stat camera with safelight, a Xerox telefax machine, IBM XTs, dot matrix printers with regular and wide carriages, one smartlaser printer, IBM PS/2 computers, an IBM ProPrinter II, an Apple MacIntosh II desktop publishing system, an Apple PC 5.25 disk drive to communicate with the IBM PC, an art waxer, drafting boards, and a slide viewing screen. This list of equipment is not exhaustive. Rather, it is simply intended to indicate that some basic equipment must be dedicated to the marketing office. Such items are cost effective and assist the staff in managing their workload more efficiently. For example, stats are photographic reproductions in black and white with little or no distortion of line. Produced commercially, they cost $7 to $17 each, depending on size. Stats produced in-house cost 63 cents each. As a result, we save a minimum of $7,600 per year by maintaining this in-house capability. The computers are used for spreadsheet processing to prepare weekly status reports of all projects, with a separate entry for each item of work in progress. Without the status reports there would be no way of managing the department's workload and no way for the staff to track their progress or prioritize tasks. Lotus 1,2,3 spreadsheet software is used to create tracking reports on the numerical and financial results of conference marketing efforts. Without the computers, the measurement of marketing and project expenses against revenues would be labor intensive and not a good use of staff time.

During the next three to five years, this marketing office will need to add more staff in the areas of writing/editing, graphics, and clerical. Inherent with additional staff is the need for more computers, printers, and other special equipment.

Space is one of the most important, and sensitive, issues confronting any organization. It can be an inhibiting factor in program growth and development, especially for a continuing education organization. Thus, the allocation of space for a marketing office may be the most serious consideration for the chief continuing education administrator. Adequate office space for the staff and part-time assistants is an obvious first step. The graphic artist will require special consideration, for example, adequate natural lighting. Space for production of camera-ready art, transparencies, and the like will need to be allocated. Moreover, extra storage space is needed to accommodate large quantities of brochures. At the University of Alabama, the College's Office of Marketing and Communications occupies approximately 2,500 to 3,000 square feet. If the continuing education organization anticipates having its own offset press, providing bulk mailing services, and adding a photographic development laboratory, an additional 2,000 square feet will be required. As the needs of marketing grow, additional space may be necessary.

Recovery of Direct Marketing Costs

The National University Continuing Education's 1984–1985 Survey of Institutional Members indicated that 33 percent of those who responded subsidize marketing and promotion from continuing education's budget (Prisk, 1986, p. 29). In 21 percent of the participating institutions, marketing and promotion receive a subsidy from the parent institution. Thus, more than 50 percent of the respondents indicated that continuing education's marketing and promotion efforts receive some form of subsidy.

The recovery of marketing costs associated with individual programs is frequently discussed. A review of more than a dozen continuing education marketing and promotion offices suggests that there is no cost recovery pattern. In some instances a charge-back is assessed each program budget for such direct costs as printing, postage, typesetting, mailing list acquisition, and advertising. At one institution the annual average cost per program for these expenses is 17 percent of gross revenues (range 8–31 percent); another averages 12 percent of gross revenues for all programs. Typically, when direct marketing expenses are charged to each program budget, there is no overhead assessed. That is, the continuing education organization allocates funds for the marketing staff and other operating expenses.

Another method is to fund a marketing office's overhead plus expenses for marketing and promoting individual programs. Under this arrangement, each program is carefully evaluated before an allocation is made from a central marketing fund. In this case, each office within continuing education needs to anticipate its total marketing costs for the year, which then becomes the basis for determining the overall amount to be set aside.

A continuing education organization at one institution allocates 10 percent of anticipated income for marketing its programs. At yet another, 6 to 7.5

percent of the annual budget is utilized to fund marketing's overhead plus all marketing costs for individual programs.

Whether the continuing education organization has a fully subsidized marketing office, or one whose overhead only is funded, will depend on the circumstances of continuing education at a particular institution. Whatever is effective and appropriate for the unique needs of a continuing education organization is the most important consideration.

At the University of Alabama's College of Continuing Studies, staff salaries and operating expenses for the Office of Marketing and Communications are funded by the College. Direct program expenses are charged back to the sponsoring College office. In this way, the marketing staff and program manager can determine the particular needs of each activity and budget marketing/ promotion accordingly. Further, all staff members learn the economics of marketing. In those cases where an institution chooses to allocate all marketing costs from a central fund, there is the potential to overlook some marketing expenses. This makes it difficult to affix a true cost to marketing initiatives.

Setting aside a pool of funds for special publications is an important but difficult decision. Whether 10 percent of the organization's expense budget or a stated amount such as $30,000 is allocated to the marketing function is not the issue. The important thing is that discretionary money is needed to support special activities and publications. These may include continuing education's annual report, newsletter, occasional statistical reports, or a slide/tape presentation on the continuing education organization. Moreover, there will be times when it is necessary to augment the marketing budget for special programs. Although it is not possible to arrive at a specific amount that is generally applicable, the College of Continuing Studies attempts to set aside $25,000 to $40,000 annually for special publications.

Reviewing the literature for this chapter did not reveal any continuing education organization that used the services of an advertising agency for all of their marketing and promotion needs. The NUCEA's Survey of Member Institutions, 1984–1985, revealed that only 2.8 percent of the participating continuing education organizations used advertising firms (Prisk, 1986, p. 27). The data were insufficient to indicate the degree to which these organizations used an advertising agency. Typically, an external firm is used for special projects.

Guidelines for Program Budgeting

Each of us will utilize different guidelines or criteria to determine the amount spent per program on marketing. Although assessing the dollars (or percentage of revenues) to invest also depends on local conditions such as labor costs, printing, and institutional support, the following guidelines may be useful.

Closed Markets. A closed market may be defined as one in which the continuing education organization is offering a program exclusively to a client group. For example, a state's Purchasing Agents Association engages the services of a university's continuing education organization to manage its annual conference. As there is a clearly defined market for this program and there is no competition from other providers, the marketing costs are minimal. Usually, in such a case, the association places an advertisement in its newsletter at no cost. The number of direct-mail pieces is well defined, and the mailing list should be reliable. The list is often made available at little or no cost. In these circumstances, no more than 4 to 8 percent of the direct costs of the program should be spent on marketing. Thus, if the association's annual conference incurs $10,000 in direct expenditures, $400 to $800 should be committed to marketing.

New Programs. Whether marketing to new or existing audiences, new programs incur the greatest risk. They also require the greatest investment of time, money, and energy (Willard and Warren, 1986). Such ventures often have a high profile, and, therefore, a more careful analysis of the market potential is required. At the same time, part of the process of market positioning is being at the front end of a new product cycle. For example, in Chapter Nine, Judith K. Riggs discusses in detail the concept of market cycles. What needs to be understood and accepted by the chief continuing education administrator is that taking such risks inevitably results in some misfires. Consequently, it is essential that some risk capital be set aside to underwrite new, untested ventures. The amount is directly related to the number of high-risk initiatives undertaken annually. The amount spent on marketing new programs should be 25 to 40 percent of anticipated expenses. For example, a program expenditure budget of $25,000 would necessitate an outlay of $6,250 to $10,000 for marketing and promotion.

Repeat Business. Less risky than new programs, but not as predictable as closed-market offerings, are repeat programs. These constitute the mainstay of the continuing education organization. An excellent example of a successful repeat program is the Federal Tax Clinic at the University of Alabama, now in its forty-second year. The format is a proven success, the constituent base is clearly defined, the two-day length is sufficient for the content, and the planning process is well established. Moreover, because the program occurs at the same time each year, the professionals who attend actually anticipate the marketing efforts. Clearly, in such an instance, the cost to market this repeat program is not as high as that for a new venture. Similarly, other programs that occur semiannually, such as the CPA Review or a week-long alcohol and drug abuse school, seldom require special or unique marketing. Still, quality promotional pieces are produced to market them. Appropriate costs to market and promote repeat programs should range between 12 and 16 percent of the expenditure budget for that particular activity.

Existing Programs—New Markets. Expanding an existing inventory of successful programs to new markets often involves less risk than creating new programs for existing markets. It may also lead to greater program growth in a shorter period. Development time, as well as location of excellent instructors, has been achieved. One example is an expert witness testimony seminar. For many years forensic specialists have testified in criminal cases, as have psychologists. Thus, the use of experts in the judicial process is not new. However, with the recent proliferation of liability cases, members of other professions are being called to serve as expert witnesses. A program developed for the nursing profession on the techniques of being an expert witness in a judicial proceeding has proved to be successful. The same program, with minor adjustments, can be offered to personal property appraisers, dietitians, and educators, among others. The amount spent to explore new markets for existing programs should range between 18 and 25 percent of the expected expenditure. Generally, these types of programs would cost more to market than repeat programs, but far less than new ventures.

Figure 29.1 displays the relative costs associated with these four types of programs. The charts reflect the shifts in programmatic costs associated with each type of program. These shifts are generally affected by the expenditure for marketing. For example, 6 percent is spent on marketing for closed-market programs and 5 percent on supplies. The chart for expanding existing programs to new markets shows that 19 percent was spent on marketing and 10 percent on supplies. Keep in mind that these are only guidelines. Local market conditions, the institution's market share, the position of continuing education in the marketplace, and local production costs are among the factors that impinge on marketing and promotion costs.

Tracking

Regardless of the amount spent on marketing each of the various types of programs, it is essential to develop an effective tracking system. Only in this way can a cost-benefit analysis be conducted to determine what is or is not working effectively. Further, it is another way that both program and marketing staff can fully understand the costs associated with marketing. Over time, such data aid the staff in the long-range planning process.

Two chapters in this handbook have provided excellent suggestions for tracking. In Chapter Eighteen, Joann Condino demonstrates how to track the results of publicity efforts. And in Chapter Twenty-Three, Maris A. St. Cyr discusses effective ways to track advertising. The following discussion builds on these ideas and illustrates the use of an electronic spreadsheet on a personal computer to track direct-mail efforts.

Whatever system you use, it is important that it take into account the special needs of your continuing education organization for analyzing the results of marketing efforts.

At the University of Alabama's College of Continuing Studies such a system is in place and is continuously refined. Table 29.1 is the tracking report for a Human Resources Management Conference that the College sponsors annually. To understand the categories, a key has been developed by the College's Office of

Figure 29.1. Programmatic Expense Mix.

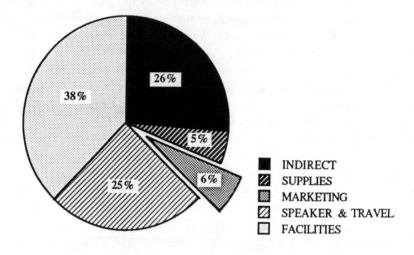

CLOSED MARKET PROGRAMS

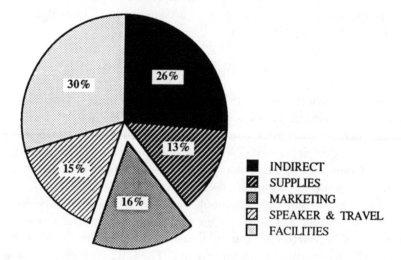

REPEAT PROGRAMS

EXISTING PROGRAMS TO NEW MARKETS

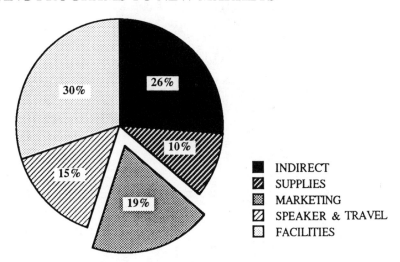

NEW PROGRAMS

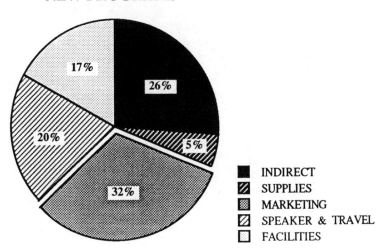

Table 29.1. Tracking Report, Human Resources Management Conference.

List	Code	Number	Printed	Registered	Gross $	Gross %	#/M	$/M	List/Ad Cost	Label Cost	Postage/Insert	Printing/Type	Marketing Cost	Gross Market Costs
ASTD	A	1,541	1,600	5	$795.00	3.2%	3.24	$515.90	$56.57	$14.94	$138.87	$167.19	$377.57	$417.43
ASPA	B	3,662	3,700	13	$1,925.00	7.7%	3.55	$525.67	$138.98	$35.51	$330.00	$386.62	$891.11	$1,033.89
TN, GA, MS FLp. 100+	C	5,000	5,000	3	$436.00	1.8%	0.60	$87.20	$187.38	$48.48	$450.58	$522.45	$1,208.89	($772.89)
MS, 50–99	P	921	1,000	1	$155.00	0.6%	1.09	$168.30	$162.00	$8.93	$83.00	$104.49	$358.42	($203.42)
UEC, 100+ (AL, TN)	R	3,649	3,700	38	$5,800.00	23.3%	10.41	$1,589.48	$0.00	$35.38	$328.83	$386.62	$750.83	$5,049.17
UEC, 50–99 (AL, TN)	S	3,216	3,300	12	$1,725.00	6.9%	3.73	$536.38	$0.00	$31.18	$289.81	$344.82	$665.81	$1,059.19
In-house lists*	T	2,856	2,900	79	$11,515.00	46.3%	27.66	$4,031.86	$0.00	$27.69	$257.37	$303.02	$588.08	$10,926.92
Unknown	—		800	18	$2,510.00	10.1%	0.00	0.00	$44.73	$0.00	$0.00	$0.00	$44.73	$2,465.27
Query	—			0	0.00	0.0%	0.00	0.00	$0.00	$0.00	$0.00	$83.59	$83.59	($83.59)
Total		20,845	22,000	169	$24,861.00	100.0%	8.11	$1,192.66	$589.66	$202.11	$1,878.46	$2,298.80	$4,969.03	$19,891.97

Other Income	$2,475.00
Total Income	$27,336.00
Overhead	$5,312.58
Profit	$6,844.62

Net Income	$12,157.20
Net/Total	44%
Marketing Costs/Total	18%
Profit/Total	25%

*HRM, 2,030; big-business conversion list, 360; health care (personnel director), 346; management development, 120.

Marketing and Communications. In viewing Table 29.1 from left to right, refer to the description of each category in the key following the table.

List	The mailing list through which the audience was reached. The designation "unknown" is used for registrations received for which the source of initial contact with the registrant is not known.
Code	Letter code for each mailing list utilized. The corresponding code is printed on the registration form of the printed piece and noted for tracking purposes when the registration form is returned.
Number	Number of brochures distributed via the named mailing list.
Printed	Number of copies of the brochure that were printed and coded for distribution via the named mailing list.
Registered	For each mailing list, the number of persons registered for a program who did not later cancel. Registrations are identified by the code on each registration form.
Gross $	By code, the number of gross revenue dollars in registration fees collected.
Gross %	Amount of fees collected, by each code, as a percentage of the total registration fees collected.
#/M	For each mailing list, the number of persons who registered per thousand brochures distributed.
$/M	For each mailing list, the number of registration dollars collected per thousand brochures distributed.
List/Ad Cost	For each mailing list, the cost of the mailing list not including the cost of affixing labels, sorting, postage, inserting, typesetting, or printing.
Label Cost	For each mailing list, the cost of attaching mailing labels to printed pieces and preparing those printed pieces for bulk mailing or other methods of distribution.
Postage/Insert	For each mailing list, the cost of postage, bulk shipping or delivery, insertion in other publications, and other similar expenses.
Printing/Type	For each mailing list, the costs of typesetting and printing and/or other costs of preparing a message for distribution in the brochure.
Marketing Cost	For each mailing list, the total costs of preparing and distributing the brochure. It is the sum of List/Ad Cost, Label Cost, Postage/Insert, and

	Printing/Type. In the rare instances when there are other marketing costs, they may be added into this column with footnoted explanations.
Gross Market Costs	For each mailing list, the figure obtained by subtracting Marketing Cost from Gross $. This figure can be either positive or negative. The total for this column represents the money available to cover the costs of staging the program and the organization's overhead costs (35 percent).
Other Income	Income that is derived from sources other than registration fees, such as exhibitor fees.
Total Income	Total revenue obtained from the operation of a program, including registration fees and sponsorships.
Overhead	Amount allocated to cover the costs of organizational facilities, staffing, and operations. (This figure is currently 35 percent of total direct program expenses in the College of Continuing Studies at the University of Alabama.)
Profit	Amount of income remaining for discretionary use after total of Gross Market Costs column and Overhead are subtracted from Total Income.
Net Income	Residual income after total of Gross Market Costs column is subtracted from Total Income, but before Overhead costs are considered.
Net/Total	Percentage of the Total Income from a program that was Net Income after direct expenses and before deduction of the amount earmarked for Overhead.
Marketing Costs/Total	Percentage of the Total Income from a program that was utilized for marketing that program.
Profit/Total	Percentage of the Total Income remaining as profit after all expenses, including Overhead, are deducted.

Thus, in the example given in Table 29.1, the ASTD mailing list was coded A and contained 1,541 names. Sixteen hundred brochures were printed, yielding five registrants. They accounted for $795.00 in gross income or 3.2 percent of the total registration fees; 3.24 people registered per thousand brochures mailed to ASTD members. The $515.90 represents the monies collected per thousand brochures. It costs $56.57 to purchase the list; $14.94 to affix labels; $138.87 for postage, bulk rate; and $167.19 to print the 1,600 brochures. The marketing costs ($56.57, $14.94, $138.87, and $167.19) total $377.57; the gross income minus the marketing cost is $417.43 ($795 minus $377.57). The conclusion is that it is cost effective to use this list. The total program marketing cost of 18 percent of total income is an appropriate expenditure for a repeat program.

Avoiding Common Mistakes

Program managers and members of the marketing staff continuously learn from their successes as well as failures. Since budgeting is a crucial aspect of the program process, it must be carefully analyzed. Therefore, these common mistakes should be reviewed in the hope of avoiding them.

Institute Effective Audience Analysis. Often, programmers do not precisely identify their potential audience. This leads to an unrealistic budget for the purchase of mailing lists. The number of brochures printed, plus the postage, may be unnecessarily high. As there are in excess of 10,000 business mailing lists, in addition to those maintained by professional associations, community agencies, and the continuing education organization itself, highly targeted audience identification becomes critical.

Often, too little time is spent analyzing the same, or similar, previous programs. In hurried times it is easier to simply repeat the format, marketing, and pricing plan. This leads to a level of complacency that, over time, results in customer dissatisfaction and a reduction in the number of registrations or potential loss of the program.

The existing customer base is often taken for granted by even the best continuing education organization. As a result, it is assumed that once an individual has attended a program, he or she will return for the same, or another, activity. When this happens, rather than doing more to cultivate existing customers, a disproportionate amount of energy is spent on identifying new customers. It is important to bring equal levels of sophistication to analysis of the market for both types of clientele. Periodic communication with those who attended an annual conference will cause them to feel they have not been forgotten. For example, several months after an annual program, participants could be sent a summary of the evaluations. Next, they should receive a one-page flyer announcing the theme and key presenters of the next conference. This could be followed by a preliminary program of the next conference. Finally, a copy of the final conference brochure could be sent.

Soliciting comments from former participants, analyzing the previous program, and continuously cultivating the current customer base will create higher-quality programs, as well as greater audience satisfaction.

Concentrate on Costs, Not on Potential Earnings. Program managers and the marketing staff alike are often too conservative in budgeting. They are often reluctant to put enough dollar power behind a marketing strategy. Concern that the program simply breaks even can cause the staff to overlook a potentially larger market. By analyzing primarily the *cost* of printing, rather than recognizing the benefits of the return on a larger investment, a greater market share may be lost. Although continuing educators often claim to be risk takers, this is not necessarily the case when investing more dollars than might otherwise be invested in marketing. Spending more does not imply the most expensive paper, four-color art, or a saddle-stitched brochure. Rather, there should be a closer correlation between the quality of the publication and the program it is promoting.

When it is anticipated that a program will be repeated, the more cost-effective route is to invest more money the first time the program is offered. The design elements are in place, an overall marketing strategy has been developed, and the primary as well as secondary audience has been cultivated. The point is to spend more on marketing those programs that have potential for a high financial gain.

Experiment with Mailings and Advertisements. As in the case with offering loss leaders to test a new product, experimenting with marketing techniques is equally as important in continuing education. To penetrate untested markets, recapture markets lost previously; in general, retaining or gaining a competitive edge requires different approaches to marketing and promotion. For example, ten years ago telemarketing was in its infancy. It is now estimated that by the turn of the century, eight million people will be involved in selling products over the telephone (*FutureScan*, 1986). From 1984 to 1985, approximately $93 billion was spent on business-to-business advertising in marketing. Of that amount, $27 billion was spent on telemarketing ("The 1986 Starmark Report," 1986, p. 6). We are entering an area of increasing use of telemarketing for continuing education. Telemarketing uses may fall into one of the following categories: to assess client satisfaction in recently completed programs; to solicit enrollments for programs; to provide general information on events taking place on campus. In Chapter Twenty-Five, B. Ray Holland shows how to use telemarketing techniques effectively in a continuing education organization and mentions some institutions that do so. Two other institutions using telemarketing effectively are Virginia Commonwealth University and New York University. However, few continuing education divisions employ telemarketing on a consistent, organized basis. Most are still exploring the concept.

Joint sponsorship of advertisements is also cost effective. Figure 29.2 is an example of an advertisement shared by the University of Alabama and the University of Georgia to promote the same program. This joint advertisement made it cost effective to promote the program in the *Wall Street Journal*. With regional editions of the *Journal*, the ad reached those professionals whom we felt would attend from the southeast. Moreover, it was an opportunity for two universities to collaborate on a similar program.

Marketing multiple programs to the same audience is efficient and it saves money for postage, envelopes, and handling charges. For example, brochures for programs entitled "New Directions in Critical Care Nursing," "The Challenge of Oncology Nursing," "The AIDS Phenomenon: Issues Facing Health Care

Figure 29.2. Example of a Joint Advertisement.

You, too, can become a professional consultant
And earn independence, profits, and prestige.

A two-day seminar, led by professional consultant Lynda Falkenberry at the universities listed below, will teach you how to:

- maximize your creative skills and energy
- start up a consulting business
- market your skills, talents, and achievements
- write proposals that sell

Call now to register or to receive a free brochure.

The University of Georgia, September 22-23, 1987
David Payne, (404) 542-2241

The University of Alabama, September 25-26, 1987
Tom Wingenter, (205) 348-6222 or 1-800-452-5971 (in Alabama)

Used by permission.

Professionals,'' and ''Innovative Nursing Care of the Seriously Mentally Disabled'' will be mailed together from the University of Alabama's Office of Marketing and Communication to workers in the health care industry, particularly the nursing professions. Previously, these may have been sent separately. The important issue illustrated by this example is to be as creative in approaching marketing and promotion as in program design. All of us have entered a new marketing environment. Increased competition, continued development of new technologies, and market fragmentation along nontraditional lines have combined to usher in a set of market conditions that is often confusing and complex.

Summary

All institutions are unique, as are the communities in which they are located. These circumstances make it difficult to develop a formula for budgeting marketing costs that is effective for every continuing education organization. Guidelines can assist a continuing education organization in determining reasonable amounts to expend on marketing and promotion. However, no one formula will work for all organizations. Personnel, operating equipment, and allocation of space all need to be considered in determining the cost of establishing a marketing function.

30

Gaining Institutional Support for Marketing

Doe Hentschel

The notion of having to gain organizational support for marketing is contradictory. If the institution supports the activity, support for marketing should automatically follow. But the fact is that this *is* a big issue, one that virtually all continuing educators have faced or will face in the course of their careers.

Reasons for Lack of Support

There are many reasons for the lack of support that is so frequently demonstrated by organizations engaged in continuing education. Most often, the conflict is between the continuing education organization and the parent institution, but occasionally the conflict is an internal one within the organization itself. Before it is possible to plan strategies for reducing that conflict and gaining support for marketing activities, the sources of conflict should be understood.

Conflicts Related to Image. Marketing creates a visible statement about the identity or image of the organization. One of the most common conflicts arises when the image portrayed by the continuing education organization is perceived to be at odds with the image that the parent institution wishes to portray. For example, if a college seeks to convey an elitist image and wants to attract full-time residential students from high socioeconomic groups, support for continuing education advertisements that market the college as a learning center for commuting adult students seeking career changes will be difficult to obtain. The incongruity between images in this example is obvious, but much subtler contradictions can cause just as much resistance to well-designed marketing plans.

Conflicts Related to Goals. Conflicts related to goals result in opposition as well. If a university defines its mission as preparing professionals for their careers, but the continuing education organization sees its goal as providing avocational programs for the community, there may be a perceived contradiction, or even competition, between goals that must be resolved before the institution will support marketing efforts for continuing education.

Sometimes, continuing education goals appear irrelevant to institutional goals and, therefore, not important enough to the overall organizational mission to justify support. If, for example, the institution needs more students to live in the dormitories because of a high and costly vacancy rate, but continuing education seeks support for a major marketing campaign to promote evening courses to commuting, part-time students, it is quite likely that there will be resistance, opposition, or at best neglect when it comes to placing priority on the marketing needs of continuing edudcation.

A related problem occurs when continuing education's goals are viewed as marginal to the main purpose of the institution. Even though printing a catalogue to replace in-house announcements is a priority for the training department in business, if the company is faced with stiff competition for its products from foreign manufacturers, the organization's decision makers may not see the training department's need as central to the task at hand and may be reluctant to divert necessary resources for the catalogue.

Conflicts Related to Values and Norms. Marketing is a relatively new concept in education and service organizations, and some of the lack of support for marketing activity can be understood as a conflict between old and emerging organizational values. If organizational values do not include "selling," any kind of marketing activity may be criticized. In this context, we might not be too surprised to find a hospital administrator questioning the necessity of developing video advertisements promoting the patient education programs for the hospital's closed-circuit TV channel.

When organizational norms lead to slow-paced activity and/or seasonal activity not in step with the continuing education organization's pace and/or calendar, numerous conflicts are likely. A typical frustration in academic organizations occurs when the university print shop closes down between December 20 and January 15 to handle major maintenance on its machines, but continuing education needs brochures for its March programs printed during that period.

When the institutional norms include a high degree of regulation, but continuing education is seen as having more autonomy and/or flexibility than other offices, conflicts may arise that are not directly related to the issue of marketing, but rather are evidence of institutional jealousy or the felt need on the part of top administration to regain control over the continuing education operation. It is common, for instance, for all units at a public university to be required to use the university print shop for all publications. This sometimes results in bureaucratic delays and hurdles as well as increased costs and poorer quality than printing done by commercial printers. In many such institutions, the funding source of continuing education allows more flexibility in regard to some of the state regulations. This flexibility, coupled with their ever-present demand for quick and cost-effective response, makes it possible for continuing education to use commercial printers. The more restricted offices within the parent institution may bring pressure on policy makers to restrict continuing education by playing on the administrators' fears that the continuing education organization is operating outside their authority.

Conflicts Related to Resources. Most continuing educators would probably indicate that lack of support for their marketing efforts is exhibited in battles related to resources. One of the more common symptoms of such conflict is when the continuing education marketing budget is viewed as excessive in terms of the total institutional budget. It is not unusual for the dean of continuing education in a college or university to be asked to explain why continuing education spends more on advertising than the rest of the institution combined. If the dean responds defensively, the lack of support is likely to solidify. In a slightly different case of conflict of resources, the continuing education marketing budget may be viewed as excessive and inappropriate by policy makers in the organization. For example, the board of directors of a nonprofit organization may be concerned that too much money is being spent on advertising rather than direct services to clients.

As marketing gets more sophisticated and costly, self-supporting units may confront internal resistance to spending the money needed to produce high-quality marketing pieces. A program coordinator may assert that mimeographed announcements are perfectly adequate to advertise a workshop and that the cost of a brochure will raise the cost of the program so much that attendance will be discouraged.

Frequently, limitations in human resources cause problems for continuing education administrators. Support units frequently are not adequately staffed to provide the quick response needed, and every continuing educator has at least one war story about a design for a brochure sitting for weeks on the artist's desk because too many other jobs (many of which had no urgent deadlines) were logged in ahead of it. Similarly, limited human resources frequently make it difficult for the continuing education organization to meet lead times required by the publication unit. The result is a backlog on both ends and what appears to be lack of support to get the job accomplished.

Quite probably, there would be fewer problems in gaining support for continuing education marketing if there were unlimited human and fiscal resources at the organization's disposal. However, this is rarely the case. As a result, the allocation of those resources may be viewed as inadequate by the continuing education office which, in turn, interprets this as evidence of lack of support. More than likely, however, the allocation of those resources is a reflection of other factors that call to question the validity of the resource needs of continuing education or that reflect the priorities of decision makers who may have a perspective or value system different from that of the continuing education administrator. Conflicts in image, goals, and norms are rarely consciously recognized by the conflicting parties, often because image, goals, values, and norms are not clearly understood. The first challenge for the continuing educator facing conflicts related to resources is to be sure that the conflict is not really a symptom of a less obvious problem.

Analyzing the Source of Conflict

Failure to analyze the real source of conflict can lead to the use of inappropriate strategies with people who cannot really help anyway. As frustrated as we might feel on many occasions when we desperately need help, special consideration, extra money, or just understanding and trust, we need to retrain ourselves not to react without analysis. The following seven steps provide helpful guidelines for this analysis.

1. *Identify the support you need.* The first step in this analysis should be to examine what kind of support is needed or, conversely, how marketing efforts are being blocked. Are creative ideas being stifled? Are suggestions being ignored or marketing plans being opposed? Are decisions affecting continuing education's marketing being made elsewhere in the organization without adequate input from your office? Are your marketing activities, decisions, staffing patterns, and/or budget being questioned and challenged? Do you need more human and/ or fiscal resources, and are you unable to get them? Are the organization's policies and/or procedures unworkable and are you ineffective in getting adaptations of those you have sought to change? Each of these questions points to a different need, and you should ask yourself these and other questions in your effort to understand your support needs as fully as possible.

2. *Identify the source of conflict.* Once you have identified your needs, the next step is to determine the source of the conflict. If there is resistance to your efforts, does the conflict appear to be related to image, goals, organizational values, norms, or resources? Remember that resistance or lack of support may not emanate from the most obvious causes. Resistance to addition of another graphic artist to your marketing staff may appear to be a resource issue, but on closer examination it may be more related to the reluctance of your superior to allow the continuing education marketing staff to increase when the organization is considering consolidating all marketing functions in a centralized unit. The issue then is a conflict of goals; your goal of increased efficiency conflicts with the organization's goal of increasing centralized control. Your plan to advertise on city buses may be denied for reasons that appear to be related to cost, but such advertising may actually be unacceptable to your organization because it is not interested in attracting commuter students to its traditional campus. This conflict

related to image may never be articulated openly. Indeed, it may not even be consciously understood by the vice-president who asks how much these ads will cost, what results similar campaigns conducted by other institutions have had, and what impact you expect to see in enrollments as a result.

3. *Determine the organization's image and the image of continuing education.* Because an organization's image, goals, norms, and values are so complex and are often not clearly expressed, and because so many conflicts over marketing support are actually conflicts related to these factors, a bit of detective work may be needed in this step of the analysis. Regardless of what your initial thoughts are about the source of conflict, begin your analysis by writing down anything and everything you know about the institution's image. Listen to what your chief executive officer says in speeches. Analyze public statements made by organization spokespersons. Read publications of other offices within the institution and any information disseminated to external constituencies, especially those that affect funding. Academic institutions will seek to convey their desired image to their alumni, their boards of trustees, governing boards, potential donors, and prospective students. Organizations in the private sector will do the same with their stockholders and their clients as well as their employees. In both types of organization, staff orientation manuals can be a gold mine for information about what the employer thinks of itself. All institutions sell themselves through their newsletters, membership brochures, and annual reports.

Consider the organization's historical image as well as its present image. Look for any clues you can find about how that image might change in the future. Image is a fuzzy picture that is extremely susceptible to environmental and personality changes. A women's college that has previously marketed itself as a special environment in which young women can learn to expect the best of themselves and realize their full potential should be highly supportive of a major marketing campaign targeted at returning adult women seeking the same opportunity and climate. But if the president is considering going coeducational to relieve enrollment declines, your campaign to create heightened visibility for the all-women environment may be blocked. Because the president would not want anyone to suspect she is considering admitting men to the school while the issue is still being studied, you may not be given the real reason behind the rejection of your marketing plan. Your clues should have been those enrollment statistics that call for a significant effort to reposition the college in the marketplace and a survey of alumnae that asks, among other things, how strongly they support the concept of single-sex education. Such a question could very well have been an attempt to ascertain the strength of potential opposition to the change to a coeducational college.

Having gathered enough data to form a fairly reliable statement of the parent institution's image, you should conduct a similar exercise to determine what the image of continuing education is and has been. It is not at all unusual for continuing educators to have developed their organizations, along with their images, totally separate from the parent institution. Often this results from the "stand-alone" posture of such organizations. Often it just happens because no one is talking about image with anyone else. Occasionally it happens because continuing education has no clear image, except that of trying to be everything to everybody and respond to whatever program possibilities come along. Regardless of the reason, do not be surprised if you discover that your analysis of image points out major differences, some of which may even be contradictory to the image of your parent institution.

4. *Determine goals.* Similar homework is required to determine the goals of the institution. Even in the post–management-by-objectives era, goal statements may not be the easiest verbage to find or interpret. And even those organizations whose goals seem obvious ("make a profit," "provide quality health care," "teach adults to read") have numerous goals that operate at different levels to make goal attainment possible in the broadest sense. Thus, the manufacturer who wants to make a profit ought also to have goals related to a well-trained work force and cost efficiency. The community hospital will need to recruit and train volunteers. The literacy center needs to create community awareness and generate funding. Sometimes, the institution's decision makers may not recognize some of these goals, but your analysis should be as thorough as you make it. Previously unstated—but authentic—goals may become part of your arsenal to gain support for marketing your programs.

Your analysis of goals may also identify some goals that are contradictory. A college experiencing enrollment problems may seek to rectify that by changing its image from that of a second-rate school to that of a highly selective institution. Appropriate goals would be to raise admission standards and keep class sizes small, thus creating an opportunity for individual attention and a small student/teacher ratio. A concurrent goal, however, is to stabilize the enrollment so that a faculty retrenchment can be avoided. Increased enrollment of part-time adults could stabilize the enrollment, but since those adults will probably want to enroll in high-demand courses, those classes will become even more overcrowded. Many organizations have no idea that these contradictory goals exist. However, if your goals for continuing education are in conflict with any of them, your marketing plans will be affected.

Have you clearly articulated the goals of your continuing education organization? If you have been operating under an informal assumption related to goals, now is the time to sharpen those statements. This will enable you to identify potential goal conflicts that may be creating resistance to your marketing plans. In addition, it will enable you to be more effective in relating your goals to the stated and unstated goals of the organization.

5. *Analyze values and norms.* Having completed this careful analysis of image and goals, doing the same for organizational values and norms naturally follows. Consider factors like management philosophy and style, formal and informal reward systems, communication patterns, the various power structures, the opinion leaders, and the fiscal situation of the organization. It is important to understand how decisions are made, by whom they are made, and in what context they are implemented. Ideally, norms and values are related and support the

image and goals of the organization. But in reality, organizations, like people, are changeable, contradictory, and even occasionally schizophrenic. The more difficulty you have experienced in gaining support for marketing, the less consistency you are likely to find among image, goals, values, and norms. If there were perfect consistency, your organization's image, goals, values, and norms would have developed from those of the parent institution, and your marketing needs would most likely be readily supported.

If you do discover conflict arising from any of these sources, you have some difficult questions to ask yourself. Are you willing to redefine your organization's image so that your marketing efforts will support and enhance the image of the parent institution? Can you relate your image to that of the parent institution to reduce the conflict? Can your marketing efforts assist the institution in clarifying its image instead of confusing it further? Can your goals be changed to support rather than compete with the institutional goals? Are you able to relate your organization's values to the values of the parent institution? As you reexamine every instance in which you feel continuing education is in conflict with the parent institution, can you find any in which some specific changes in the continuing education organization would make it possible to follow the rules everyone else lives with? Have you inadvertently been using the wrong channels within the institutional structure, thereby antagonizing the real power brokers? If so, are you willing and able to build bridges and develop new communications links with those who can be helpful?

If you cannot or will not do these things, then you can probably anticipate continued resistance and accompanying high levels of frustration. There are no strategies for success in these instances, only strategies for survival, because continuing education will continue to be perceived as threatening the identity of the parent institution. You may have to swallow some pride, give up a favorite cause, or generate enthusiasm for an idea that has been unattractive to you to bring continuing education into sync with the parent institution. But the reality is that these basic conflicts create situations in which the institution cannot afford to support your marketing, and that battle will be waged continually and never won by continuing education.

6. *Determine your resource needs.* If you have not identified conflicts related to the preceding factors, then, and only then, should you move on to analyze whether or not the lack of support is really a result of limited resources. Make a list of the resources you need—money, people, talent, time, space, access to equipment; the list should be inclusive. Then ask yourself who controls that resource, and look first within your own office. Is it possible to reallocate money within your own budget to generate enough to support your marketing efforts? Is it possible to increase fees to generate more? Can marketing costs be passed on to co-sponsors? Can an internal reorganization lead to more cost-effective marketing, economy of scale, better use of skills and talents? Unless you are sure that your resource needs cannot be met by restructuring those resources you do control, it is asking for resistance to seek additional resources from the parent institution. It is not uncommon, especially in colleges and universities, for

continuing education to be perceived as being "independently wealthy." Although such is not frequently the case, we must be sure that we have used all the resources under our control before seeking support from outside.

7. *Identify your target.* Once you have identified the source of the resistance, it is then possible to identify your real target for reducing the conflict. If the conflict is related to image, your strategy will be directed to those who perceive that your marketing is in conflict with the institutional image. In the case of the elitist college opposed to a commuter-school image, your targets might be the vice-president for public relations and the admissions director. If the college has an enrollment problem, your plan may be to relate your goal of enrolling commuter students to reducing the decline in enrollments. In this case, the administrator responsible for enrollment management, the fiscal officer, and even the president may be your targets. Although these people may not be the ones directly blocking your marketing plan, if they can see the relationship between your plan to place ads on buses and their goal to stabilize enrollment, they will most likely use their power to clear the way for you.

In many situations, the targets may be people within the continuing education organization itself. Conflicts related to values and norms might best be reduced by adaptations in continuing education. For example, in the problem with the college print shop that closes down for maintenance between semesters, the most useful target may be the program development staff in continuing education. If they could reorient themselves to plan the spring schedules earlier, the publication could be finished before the shop shuts down. If they are too overloaded with activity during the fall to devote sufficient time to spring program development, a thorough examination of staffing, job descriptions, and expectations is probably in order. Thus, the solution may turn out to be more related to resources than norms. The target then might be managers of the units involved, or possibly your superior who has the authority to approve additions to your staff.

Using Change Strategies to Reduce Conflict

Gaining support for marketing efforts requires reducing the conflicts that exist—not escalating them or creating others. Analysis of the type of conflict we are facing, a clear understanding of what we really need, and an accurate identification of who the targets of our efforts should be must precede the planning of strategies for gaining support. If we approach the conflict from the wrong perspective or direct our efforts toward the wrong person or group, we can make matters worse and destroy working relationships within the parent institution. Continually emphasizing the differences between the needs or programs of the continuing education organization and those of the parent institution can backfire by calling attention to those differences and raising questions of relevance, marginality, values, and unity within the organization. Since gaining support means that we will have to bring about change, an analysis of the specific situation from a perspective growing out of change literature is one of the most helpful approaches to employ.

Zaltman, Florio, and Sikorski (1977, pp. 71–76) present a relatively simple typology of change strategies, which lends itself easily to this analysis. The three types of strategies they identify are power strategies, rational strategies, and manipulative strategies. Power strategies involve the use, promise, or withholding of rewards and/or punishments to bring about the desired change. Power strategies require that we employ tactics designed to communicate how those rewards and punishments will be applied. Rational strategies depend on logic and reasoning to inform people of the need for the change and the appropriateness of the specific change being proposed. Thus, informational tactics will be used. Manipulative strategies involve adding to or deleting from the environment those factors that make it easier for people to make the change. Manipulative strategies require persuasive tactics to demonstrate the desirability of the change to the target group or individual. In many instances, a combination of strategies will be the most effective approach to bringing about the change. Success, however, is highly dependent on choosing the right strategy for the situation. The most common mistake made by continuing educators is using change strategies inappropriate in the specific situation.

Power Strategies. Power strategies can be used only when it is possible to gain support or overcome resistance through the use of reward and/or punishment or restriction. In situations where we are attempting to gain support from superiors or other units of the organization, it is not likely that continuing education will control the rewards and sanctions that would have an effect on the target of our change efforts. The continuing education organization's function is most often coordinating, facilitative, and collaborative. It is often dependent on other organizations for the essential resources needed to accomplish its goals. Attempting to force support in these instances is obviously futile, and the recognition of their own powerlessness is the source of much of the frustration felt by continuing educators in such situations. Often overlooked, however, is the potential power of continuing education to affect institutional goal attainment. For example, an institution with enrollment problems can be led to see that successful marketing of continuing education will result in the needed enrollment increases. The highest-level administrators may then choose to use their power to implement needed changes at all levels within the institution to support the marketing plans of continuing education.

Within the continuing education organization itself, the capacity to employ power strategies often exists. It is essential to understand, however, that changes that occur because the target is responding to a desire for a reward (such as a merit award) or the fear of a sanction (such as losing one's job) are far more tenuous than those changes implemented because the target recognizes the value of the change itself. Zaltman, Florio, and Sikorski (1977) suggest that guidelines for using power strategies would include their use only under the following conditions:

1. If the change must be forced because there will be significant resistance to an essential change.
2. If the change must occur rapidly and other strategies will take too long.
3. If resources are limited, thus limiting options.
4. If consensus is unlikely and the process of seeking it would be disruptive or dysfunctional to the institution.

In all of these situations, not only are power strategies appropriate, they may be the only kind that will be effective in the short run. To enhance the long-term acceptance of the change, other strategies that enable the target individual or group to value the change for its inherent qualities should be employed as follow-up.

Rational Strategies. Rational strategies can be used when people are logical and can be convinced by the facts that the change is in their best interests. Although we might like to believe that this would include most situations in our organizations, only in apolitical situations are facts and logic dependable and universally agreed on. Whenever people are even partially motivated by struggles over their own or organizational power, position, and influence, those agendas will interfere with logic and cloud otherwise clear thinking.

Zaltman, Florio, and Sikorski (1977) make it clear that rational strategies are appropriate to use only when all of the following apply:

1. There is a clear discrepancy between what is occurring and what should occur, and the person or unit blocking the desired action does not have sufficient knowledge of ways to reduce that discrepancy.
2. There is no conflict (real or perceived) between the institution's goals and values and the goals and values espoused by continuing education.
3. The communication lines are open and what is needed is communicable.
4. What is needed in the way of support is well understood and feasible given environmental conditions as they are perceived by all parties.

Attempting to use rational strategies when all of these conditions do not exist is a common error made by continuing educators trying to gain support for marketing. It is important to remember that rational strategies focus solely on providing information intended to enlighten the target. The underlying assumption is that if the target had all the facts, support would be forthcoming. The war stories continuing educators share about battles fought repeatedly with unreasonable colleagues who "have their heads buried in sand," "are blocking for the sake of blocking," "are on power trips," "refuse to listen to the facts," and "are a menace to the institution" usually follow unsuccessful attempts to employ rational strategies when the problem was not lack of information.

Manipulative Strategies. The word "manipulative" strikes fear into the hearts of humanistic managers. It smacks of Machiavellian intent to control the minds and behavior of others, a motive that is contradictory to the open sharing and collaborative goal attainment such managers value. The fact is that there is nothing inherently evil about creatively adapting the environment and the situation causing conflict in ways that will reduce the conflict. Learning to recognize when and how we can manipulate resources, events, and other environmental elements can lead to the support we seek for our marketing efforts. If we find our path is blocked by a brick wall, we can attempt to knock it down (power strategy) and get a concussion as our reward. We can explain our need to the owners of the wall and ask that they dismantle it to let us pass through (rational strategy) and will undoubtedly wind up having to redesign our route, vowing never to try to do business with those unreasonable people again. Or, we can gather some stones in the vicinity, make a large enough pile to enable us to climb to the top of the wall and then jump to the ground and be on our way. This rearrangement of the resources in the environment (manipulative strategy) enables us to accomplish our goal with no negative consequences for anyone.

Such manipulative strategies can be used whenever we have the ability to change the environment in ways that will cause decision makers to view continuing education marketing activities as more desirable rather than inappropriate, unnecessary, marginal, or otherwise problematic. They are appropriate to use when there are competing forces that make it possible to restructure the environment. The change planner's success depends on having sufficient knowledge of the organizational values and norms, power structures, communication networks, hidden agendas, and resources that must be used in the restructuring process and on having the creativity and skill to rearrange those elements in ways that lead to acceptance of the change.

Applying Change Strategies

Once you have completed your analysis of the source of conflict that is limiting or blocking support for your marketing efforts and have identified the real target for your change strategies, you are ready to choose strategies to apply to the situation. Each situation will be unique and the tools available to you as the change planner will vary as well. A review of the examples of lack of support given earlier in this chapter should serve to illustrate options that might be available in your particular situation.

Conflicts Related to Image. The example of the elitist college opposing your plans to market to potential commuters is not farfetched. It illustrates what can happen when continuing educators fail to recognize the interrelationships between their image and that of the larger institution. While increasing commuter enrollments may very well be an excellent plan for increasing continuing education enrollment and may also address a significant need in the community, it may not be helpful to the health of the institution *as it is being defined by the decision makers*. This is a good example of a situation in which continuing education should reexamine what it is and make changes in its own identity and image that are consistent with the image of the parent institution.

Since such clear-cut images are more the exception than the rule, however, there may very well be possibilities for relating continuing education's image to the broader one. Even in this example, some manipulation of your message might result in gaining support where it was previously withheld. Suppose, for instance, that your advertising campaign featured testimonials from adults in career transition who were changing from positions of high prestige or life-styles associated with high socioeconomic status. Such testimonials would convey an image of the college quite different from that portrayed by testimonials from a young single parent seeking an education to break a cycle of dead-end jobs or a construction worker pursuing a business degree. You might use a statement from a company president who has returned to college to get teacher certification ("I've gotten a lot from society and now I think it's time to give something back"). Similarly, a career volunteer who lives in a wealthy suburb might comment, "After years of working as a volunteer at the Art Institute, I finally decided it was time to learn more about the art that I've come to love, and commuting to Ivy College from River Hills turned out to be easier than I had anticipated." Placing these testimonials in metropolitan or regional magazines read by upper-middle-class adults will be more appropriate than ads in buses, which had been vetoed by your vice-president for institutional relations. Admittedly, this marketing strategy will attract a different kind of adult student, but that is exactly the point. This institution wants to be attractive to a certain kind of student. You want to attract adults. By biasing the content of your ad, you can gain support. Badgering the vice-president with reasons why the college should want adults and statistics about the declining population of traditional students (rational strategy) will not work if "adult" is perceived as contrary to the institution's image of its student body.

Conflicts Related to Goals. Similar strategies can be useful in reducing conflicts related to goals. Once you are sure that your goal is consistent with one or more of the stated or unstated goals of the institution, you should look for ways to bias your message to highlight that relationship. Lack of support for avocational continuing education programs in professionally oriented universities frequently takes the form of limited availability of facilities and/or requirements that the administration of such programs be totally self-supporting. Such barriers can effectively kill programs like a community music program or physical fitness. This may appear to be a resource conflict, which will lead to long hours of negotiation to develop a schedule to use the pool and the weight room and an agreement to subsidize the music program coordinator's salary for a startup period. If the university really does not want to be bothered with these programs, however, the next layer of snags is likely to appear as barriers to marketing efforts such as bureaucratic hoops, which increase costs and/or delay production. A manipulative strategy to consider is changing your target market to emphasize the university faculty and staff. You are then in a position to convey to the university administration that these programs help to make the university an attractive place to work and will make it possible to recruit and retain a highly qualified work force. By collaborating with the music department and the physical education department to provide paid internships for graduate students to serve as instructors in these programs, you also contribute to the departments' goals of providing professional preparation and much needed financial support for their students. Your strategies will now have won the personnel department, the affirmative action office, and two academic departments as valuable allies in your efforts to gain support for marketing your avocational programs.

The college seeking to fill its dormitories may be uninterested in supporting your marketing campaign for evening courses. However, its administration would probably be enthusiastic if continuing education could assist in solving the problem of empty dorms. Converting one of those dormitories to an adult or family residence hall would mean that you could market the college to a new segment of the adult market. The availability of appropriate, affordable on-campus housing for adults and the concurrent reduction of commuting time will surely add to the attractiveness of your evening programs and it is highly probable that the college will gladly allocate some resources toward meeting this newly defined goal of filling one dorm with adults.

The case of the need for an attractive training catalogue to replace mimeographed in-house announcements of programs is an example of continuing education's goals being viewed as marginal to the parent organization's goals. Once again, the most successful strategy is likely to consist of manipulating the message so that the request for support is perceived to be related to the overriding goal. Suppose that your request for funding is accompanied by a design for the cover of that catalogue that not so incidentally calls attention to programs intended to help supervisors learn how they can increase the company's competitive edge. The request for the budget to print it is not likely to get buried on the desk of the vice-president for human resources. This is a manipulative strategy that adds the visual impact of the catalogue cover, connecting the training programs with the company's goal. In contrast, a rational strategy would have been to write a memo requesting the budget for the catalogue because participation in voluntary training programs had been declining and giving enrollment statistics demonstrating that decline.

Conflicts Related to Values and Norms. The use of manipulative strategies to demonstrate the relationship between continuing education's values and the parent institution's values may be possible in many situations. Occasionally, however, deeply ingrained values may be so entrenched that a different strategy may be more effective. For the purposes of illustration, let us suppose that your analysis of the hospital administrator who is opposing development of ads for patient education programs leads you to believe that a manipulative strategy will be unsuccessful. It is possible that a subtle kind of power strategy could be employed instead. Suppose, for example, that the patient education programs were developed with grant support from a foundation, and your administrator had been extremely proud of receiving that grant. You need to point out that the foundation has expectations about how many participants those programs serve and that if you serve a lower number than expected, future funding would be unlikely, or conversely, that extremely high participation would enhance the hospital's chance of future funding. You are employing a power strategy with your superior. You have identified a reward (funding) that the target (the administrator) values and have communicated your ability to affect that reward by generating participants through advertisements. Your case is weakened, of course, if your ability to control or affect the reward is doubted. When this is the case, you can strengthen your credibility with statistics from similar projects in other hospitals and data on marketing strategies and their results. The danger is that you might present such facts in the belief that this information alone would gain the support you need. However, this rational strategy will not be effective in a value conflict. Linking the facts with clear communication of potential rewards changes the strategy to a power strategy and increases the chance of success. Your follow-up task should be to use manipulative strategies over time to reeducate the administrator about the value of marketing and its relationship to providing quality health care to the community. Once that is achieved, you may be able to use rational strategies the next time you need support for marketing a program as long as other necessary conditions prevail.

Conflicts in norms are poignant reminders that the continuing education enterprise often operates in a manner that is not consistent with the parent organization's norms. Many times, the only way to gain support when such conflicts exist is to reduce the demand by making internal changes in the continuing education organization. This means the target for the change may be a subordinate or a subunit within your institution or your superior whose authority may be needed to make changes in your operation. The example of getting the continuing education calendar to coincide with college shutdowns has no easy solution. You may have to employ both power strategies (overtime work, compensatory time off, special recognition, merit pay) and manipulative strategies (staffing changes, scheduling changes, special authorization to use outside printers) to get the task accomplished. The one thing that is virtually certain is that if the conflict is truly one of long-standing norms, rational strategies are probably going to fail except in those situations where the entire institution is in agreement that the need is essential and a suspension of norms is appropriate. That, of course, requires a power strategy imposed from the highest authority and will work only as long as the need is perceived to be of the highest priority and the rewards are valued or the sanctions are feared. If, for example, there is a severe enrollment crisis and a last-minute effort to increase off-campus enrollments requires a large rerun of brochures for a new mailing, the president can decide that the scheduled maintenance in the print shop will be postponed until the brochures are finished. In this instance, a rational strategy demonstrating the need for the brochures would most likely have been effective in gaining the president's support. When the enrollment crisis has been alleviated, even temporarily, the support for suspension of traditional norms will dissipate.

The common resistance that results from internal jealousy over the flexibility and autonomy afforded continuing education in an otherwise bureaucratic environment can best be overcome by the use of manipulative strategies. You must constantly rearrange the environment so that the flexibility you enjoy provides benefits for others who might otherwise seek to restrain continuing education. As an example, there are several ways in which continuing education's ability to generate flexible dollars can help other academic units in an institution that has to live within spartan budget allocations. Setting up special accounts within the continuing education fund for collaborating departments and sharing the profit from successful programs is one way to help those departments supplement their meager travel budgets. In addition, this helps motivate them to continue working with continuing education. Using flexible continuing education dollars to equip a computer lab for the campus benefits everyone and skirts the restricted bureaucratic channels ordinarily required for the purchase of capital equipment. In the meantime, continuing education's flexibility becomes something to be valued and protected by the entire organization rather than a threat to be controlled and restricted.

Conflicts Related to Resources. As indicated earlier, many, if not most, of the conflicts that appear to be related to resources are manifestations of other, less obvious conflicts. The concern about an excessively high advertising budget may stem from a difference in goals (too much money is being spent on the wrong thing), values (continuing education is not very important), or even norms (public institutions do not traditionally have flashy ads). Limited human resources in the continuing education organization and elsewhere in the institution may also reflect the priorities of the parent institution as opposed to availability of resources. Internal resistance to implementing new standards, which appears to be related to the cost of the new approach, may really be a power struggle or a value conflict. In all of these cases, the analysis of the real problem and the identification of the real target will provide guidance as to which strategies are most appropriate.

In the case of a true conflict of resources, the entire repertoire of strategies should be examined. Manipulative strategies may work to convince others that dollars are needed to enable continuing education to achieve its goals. Reeducation, also a manipulative strategy, may be called for to help policy makers understand the relationship between marketing and continuing education programs. In the case of internal resistance to putting money into quality advertising, power strategies may be required, especially if the conflict is disruptive. Follow-up rational strategies showing the program planner how to use alternative budgeting approaches may be helpful. In addition, manipulative strategies that bring compliments about the attractive brochure to the program planner's attention will support the change and reduce resistance in the future.

When institutional resources are truly lacking, and you have stretched your own resources to their limit in every creative way imaginable, you may be successful in gaining support by explaining the situation to those who control the necessary resources. Before attempting this rational strategy, however, you must be sure that all the conditions for using rational strategies exist. In the example of the need for an additional artist, is there clearly a problem in the amount of time it takes to get art work done because of high demand on the artist's time, and is the vice-president responsible for staffing that organization unaware of the fact that adding a part-time artist during peak times would alleviate the problem? Does the institution support the mission of continuing education, and is continuing education's goal of more rapid turnaround consistent with the goals of the institution? Do you have good rapport with the vice-president, and is it acceptable, in the institutional hierarchy, for you to discuss the problem at the vice-presidential level? Do you have your facts and figures straight so that you can clearly communicate how the part-time artist would benefit the institution and what the total cost would be? Do you have every reason to believe that the necessary money is available? If you can answer all of these questions in the affirmative, the simple approach of presenting all these facts to the vice-president may very well result in the support you need. If not, rethink your game plan and focus on an appropriate manipulative strategy to restructure the environment.

Summary

The goal of this chapter has been to demonstrate that gaining institutional support for marketing is more complicated than most continuing educators believe. Attempts to convince those whose support is needed will be unsuccessful unless appropriate strategies are used. Knowing what kind of strategies to employ requires a thorough understanding of the entire organization as well as the need for marketing support. An analysis of the type of conflict that is blocking support should determine whether there is a conflict of image, goals, values, norms, or resources. This makes it possible to identify the people who will be needed for support. Effective use of power strategies, rational strategies, and manipulative strategies will lead to strong support for marketing. Continuing educators should understand how and when to employ these strategies.

Strategies for Ongoing Success in Marketing

Keeping abreast of market changes is an important activity for all continuing education professionals. Part Eight discusses the wide variety of methods used in accomplishing this task. Edward G. Simpson, Jr., in Chapter Thirty-One, shows how to keep abreast of market changes through environmental scanning. He offers hints on how to plan strategically and how to integrate an environmental scanning system into this strategic planning. His identification and analysis of the ten elements of a good scanning system are invaluable. He also provides a comprehensive listing of scanning resources as well as an analysis of the training and orientation of staff participating in the environmental scanning process. Other issues he addresses are costs associated with scanning, evaluation of the success of environmental scanning, development of a probability impact chart, and processing and use of scanning information as part of the total marketing effort.

Chapter Thirty-Two, by Robert G. Simerly, provides seventy-five practical tips for avoiding the most often made mistakes in marketing. Each tip includes an analysis and illustration of what you can do to avoid each mistake. Issues addressed are those associated with registration; advertising and public relations; direct-mail marketing; providing effective service; copy writing, design, typesetting, and printing; image; evaluation; media relations; mailing lists; and program planning.

In Chapter Thirty-Three, Robert G. Simerly continues this theme of avoiding mistakes and describes a ten-step process to ensure marketing success. Issues addressed are development of a research base related to marketing, necessity of writing advertising and public relations copy so that it emphasizes benefits to consumers, integration of marketing concepts into the everyday routine of the organization, and the importance of designing all marketing activities so they enhance the desired image of the organization.

Concluding the handbook is a section entitled Resources. Included are a list of organizations sponsoring workshops, institutes, and seminars on marketing; an annotated bibliography of the most recent marketing books helpful to continuing education professionals; a list of magazines and journals related to marketing; and a list of clipping bureaus. This section is one of the most comprehensive guides to additional marketing resources ever assembled for continuing educators.

Part Eight completes the *Handbook of Marketing* by emphasizing the need to develop adaptive change strategies, by reporting professional tips on avoiding the mistakes most often made in marketing, and by providing a comprehensive resource for professional development related to marketing for continuing education staff.

31

Keeping Abreast of Market Changes

Edward G. Simpson, Jr.

How often have organizational members said, "If only we had seen it coming in time we could have easily changed our strategy"? What is "it"? We could have changed strategy to do what? The "if" statement could apply to the American automotive industry and the shattering impact of imports on its automobile market in this country. It could just as easily apply to faculty and administrators at a small, traditional liberal arts college surrounded by a growing metropolitan area whose citizens demand educational programming with an increased vocational thrust, offered at nontraditional times and locations for part-time commuter students. Change often represents a distasteful and perhaps unacceptable modification of an institution's historical mission. Failure to change can mean extinction.

These examples represent different cultures, magnitudes of scale, and organizations of a very different character. Yet each illustrates a marketing problem that has a negative consequence or signifies a threat. Yet departures from the status quo can offer continuing education organizations new or tremendously expanded market opportunities. This may entail identifying a market segment that will soon require certification of its professional services. An example is found in a state where the expanding need for certified day-care facility operators has led to development of a certificate program to improve child-care competencies in conjunction with appropriate state agencies (Georgia Center for Continuing Education, 1986). Indicators of this need were the ever-increasing percentage of households in which both spouses worked, the increase in single-parent households, and documented cases of negligent care or abuse—all of which fueled legislative debate on the matter.

How then does a continuing education organization "see it coming"? Whether they are large corporations, small colleges, or continuing education organizations in a parent institution, all organizations must confront a disturbing premise about planning. Ryans and Shanklin (1986, p. xi) have illustrated this premise with an observation from the nineteenth-century British prime minister Benjamin Disraeli: "What we anticipate seldom occurs, what we least expect generally happens." Thus, ideally, an organization wants a marketing scheme that discovers the least expected so that anticipated events have an increased likelihood of occurring. To accomplish this an organization needs to examine or scan its environment for developing trends, possible events, and emerging issues (Morrison, 1987), which can present threats or opportunities to its market. The organization can then use these data to develop systematic strategic planning.

Planning Strategically: An Integral Part of Effective Marketing

Setting aside for a moment the possible need to employ psychics and fortune-tellers, organizations initiate environmental scanning projects to help them "see what's coming." This enables the organization to create several possible scenarios that can be discussed with some informed analysis of expectations as to likelihood of occurrence. The environmental scanning process is not a gimmick or fortune-telling device. Instead, it is an integral dimension of an organization's overall strategic plan. And it is the strategic plan that helps determine the organization's scanning focus.

Many writers have contributed models for strategic planning (Kotler and Murphy, 1987; Keller, 1983; Simerly and Associates, 1987) that discuss each component that should be in the plan. Generally, these components (1) describe capabilities in both staff and resources, (2) assess values and organizational culture, (3) examine both internal and external environments, (4) develop a mission statement that articulates the nature of the organization and the broad goals it seeks to achieve, (5) contain a plan with specific objectives and strategies, and (6) provide systematic feedback for monitoring success and failure in carrying out the plan, as well as the need for possible modification. Of critical importance is the understanding that the process is dynamic and constantly evolving.

Keller's (1983) discussion of strategic planning shows marketing analysis as an essential component of developing what he calls the "academic strategy" for a college or university, all of which is preceded by an assessment of environmental trends. As Jain has written (1983, p. 413), "Strategic planning deals with the relationship of the organization to its environment and thus relates to all areas of a business. Among all these areas, however, marketing is most susceptible to outside influences." Kotler and Murphy describe strategic planning as "the process of developing and maintaining a strategic fit between the organization and its changing marketing opportunities" (1987, p. 121). Thus, marketing concerns become pivotal in strategic planning. Clearly, a successful strategic plan and its marketing component depend on an ongoing and accurate evaluation of the organization's internal and external environments. As a result, scanning is a continual and essential process.

Purpose of Environmental Scanning. It is important to clarify the purpose of environmental scanning (Renfro and Morrison, 1984). Questions do arise, however. Why are we attempting to detect change? For what is the organization scanning? What things are scanned? These questions are answered by framing them within the context of the organization's strategic plan, which, as has been noted, encompasses capabilities, mission, and specific objectives. By fully understanding what the organization is trying to accomplish, its members can begin the process of systematically evaluating its environments for circumstances that may hinder or assist the achievement of organizational objectives. The scanner must look for threats to the organization's market and opportunities for the market to grow, realizing that strategic planning's long-term focus makes ongoing environmental analysis critical. The scanning process cannot be relevant to any organization, however, if the data gathered are not pertinent to its mission.

Scanning and the Organizational Environment. Establishing a scanning system, whether in the continuing education division of a state university or in a private enterprise, must begin with organizational acceptance of the concept. Strategic planning does not come naturally to many environments (Keller, 1983). In fact, two major impediments are having to learn a new process and gaining organizational commitment. The scanning process must evolve, because its insertion within a conservative organization is disruptive and potentially expensive (Morrison, Renfro, and Boucher, 1984). The culture of business and industry often permits a more direct and compatible approach to planning, but the impediments are potentially the same.

Environmental scanning systems are adaptable and can be modified in countless ways to accommodate organizational idiosyncrasies. For a continuing education organization particularly, introduction of the concept might be approached successfully by implementing an "educational strategy." Organizational members can be invited to an environmental scanning workshop, the purpose of which is to introduce the topic within the context of strategic planning. Presenters could be members of the organization, but frequently the skepticism accorded prophets in their own land may limit credibility and attention spans. Consequently, consultants or colleagues outside the profession often find a more receptive audience. By making the workshop experience voluntary and open to all, the resistance that is often automatic in coercive or mandated situations can be dissipated. The rank and file can discuss with administrators and each other the benefits and costs to the organization associated with scanning (Simpson, McGinty, and Morrison, 1987).

The elements of such a workshop include (1) defining strategic planning, (2) reviewing the organization's mission, (3) discussing the kinds of information that are useful in carrying out the mission, (4) discussing the need for systematically looking at the world around the organization with respect to threats and opportunities, (5) participating in small group exercises to identify trends or events that could affect the organization, (6) analyzing the probability of occurrence of the items found in Step 5, and (7) discussing with participants their willingness to commit time and energy to such a process. All these activities, particularly the last step, can help management assess commitment and shape strategies for implementation.

Designing the Scanning System

With any information-gathering process, efficiency is increased with the implementation of a logical system to collect, process, store, and retrieve data. The system must be flexible and adaptable. Elements of a good scanning system should include the following:

1. Participation at all levels of the organization, if possible.
2. An understanding of assignments and project responsibilities involving operation, maintenance, and development of a scanning system.
3. Establishment of a practical taxonomy to collect and classify data.
4. Identification and assignment of materials to be scanned with provisions for "wild cards."
5. Training and orientation of the organization's scanners.
6. Information processing, use, and retrieval strategies.
7. Evaluation and review of all data gathered.
8. Documentation of actions taken.
9. Systematic and prompt feedback to the organization.
10. Evaluation.

Organizational Participation. Management covets the ideal scenario of acceptance, understanding, and participation by all employees. Depending on the culture of the organization, winning the commitment of the potential participants may involve a strategy to educate and build consensus as discussed under Scanning and the Organizational Environment. This approach is essential in an academic setting and is becoming increasingly prevalent in the private sector, where the old-fashioned "do it and like it" attitude is being replaced by employee expectations that management be more solicitous of rank-and-file opinions (Deutsch, 1985).

With implementation of an environmental scanning system, it is only logical that the more sources scanned and the more individuals participating, the greater the probabilities that an issue of importance to the organization will be identified. If the organization's members are committed to the belief that their participation in scanning makes the strategic planning process functional, management must decide whether participation will be mandatory or voluntary.

This is a decision affecting only the rank and file. Management must participate by virtue of its responsibility to lead and structure the planning process.

Organizational size can dictate whether widespread participation of organizational members is feasible. Large corporations have the resources and staff to which the task can be given. Major universities, such as the University of Minnesota, also designate scanning teams (Hearn and Heydinger, 1985). Smaller firms and academic groups usually find voluntary participation desirable for several reasons. First, if they are not totally convinced of the idea, members have an opportunity to observe and reconsider. Second, some will react to mandatory scanning as the "straw that breaks the camel's back" in terms of administrative assignments. The negative repercussions that follow can be damaging. Third, those who do participate bring the enthusiasm and commitment of the true believer. The productivity of meetings and assignments will reflect the positive attitudes.

Members of the continuing education organization must understand that they may drop in or out as they see fit but that the process will continue to move inexorably forward, shaping and refining the mission while producing new objectives and strategies. The universal appeal of the participatory and volunteer model is that it lets group members advance the issues they have identified as important to organizational health. In so doing, individuals have a mechanism to persuade peers and management of the importance of a particular issue. Whether successful or not, individuals have been given a voice in deciding the course to be traveled for the future.

Understanding Assignments and Project Responsibilities. Depending on the volume of data produced by the scanning process, there will need to be one person with at least part-time responsibility for coordinating the project. This individual can be assigned such duties as (1) collecting the scanning reports from staff, (2) scheduling meetings to deal with scanning finds, (3) developing needed report formats and processes, (4) tracking and following up on staff assignments, (5) providing minutes or some record of responses to the data, (6) producing periodic status reports for the organization that give necessary feedback, (7) helping recruit and orient new scanners, and (8) storing and retrieving data.

The organization's chief executive, whether dean, director, president, or department head, has the never-ending task and responsibility of reinforcing management's commitment to strategic planning and environmental scanning. This is demonstrated in part by committing staff and other resources to carry out the project. There should also be communication of the management philosophy that a futures orientation for the organization is healthy and must be ongoing.

Individuals who commit to becoming active scanners have the responsibility of providing information within specified cycles of time. Further, when assignments are made arising from the analysis of scanning information, they must be carried out in a responsible fashion.

Establishing a Practical Taxonomy. When an active scanning process is contemplated, the organization's scanners are faced with the "I can't look at and know everything!" syndrome while trying to answer the question posed at this chapter's beginning—What is the "it" for which we are scanning? There is a need to classify information systematically so that it can be easily retrieved (Simpson, McGinty, and Morrison, 1987).

Information overload is a cliche of the 1980s and it is often the reason advanced to describe scanning as hopeless. One can approach environmental scanning from the point of view that there is so much information for individuals and organizations to absorb, adding to it in carefully premeditated fashion via environmental scanning is, indeed, malice aforethought. Of course, such an attitude is self-defeating. Management in many types of organizations, although not consciously advocating this idea, flounders abut in what might be described as a state of terminal "ad hocism." Organizational leaders grasp at straws in the wind, respond in knee-jerk fashion, and finally drown in a sea of environmental threats and opportunities that they never attempted to manage realistically.

The scanning taxonomy can be viewed as a strategy to deal, at least partially, with the problem of classifying information into broad categories, with subcategories as needed. The approach at the University of Georgia Center for Continuing Education groups data into five general classifications loosely described as political, economic, technological, social, and futures (Simpson, McGinty, and Morrison, 1987). Hearn and Heydinger (1985) at the University of Minnesota used the same categories but arranged their acronym to spell STEP. Keller (1983) adds demographics as a broad scanning focus to the general STEP approach. Sources of data have been compiled by Ahumada and Hefferlin based on Jonsen's (1986) six categories of demographic, economic, political, organizational, technological, and sociocultural issues. The final format is perhaps better determined by carefully evaluating various environmental trends and selecting those that the organization feels will most influence its planning (Schmidt, 1987).

Scanning Sources. You can identify the media, conference presentations, and other events to be scanned in many ways. First, review publications that are specific to the profession or business represented by the organization. Look for those that may contain trend analyses or that offer probable future scenarios that may impact the mission and objectives of the organization. The Trend Analysis Program (TAP) in Washington, D.C., reviews numerous sources (Keller, 1983). In higher education, for example, the *Chronicle of Higher Education* offers an assortment of data, analysis, and opinion on just about anything influencing postsecondary education. Such a publication may require a team of scanners who read and report on different scanning categories, to ensure that all areas are examined.

Newspapers are another excellent source of scanning data. The *Wall Street Journal, Christian Science Monitor,* and *USA Today* are fertile sources of trend possibilities (Renfro and Morrison, 1984). In fact, the Naisbitt group's (1982) effort that produced *Megatrends* relied for its trend identification on the analysis of thousands of newspapers. *John Naisbitt's Trend Letter* is another good, general scanning source from which organization-specific information can be gleaned. In addition, readings from *The Futurist* and the *World Future Society Bulletin* should be included as should nonestablishment publications such as the *Village Voice* (Renfro and Morrison, 1984). Publications, TV, radio, and speeches present an unending flow of trend information.

With assignment of scanners to selected sources, the organization's ad hoc nature in dealing with the flow is diminished. Scanners should be asked to volunteer to report on specific media. The project coordinator can then monitor input from people and sources to see if assignments are responsibly completed. From time to time, scanners will undoubtedly be somewhat less than prolific in their reports and a bit of encouragement along with responsible peer pressure can usually get things moving again.

In making decisions on what should be systematically scanned, there is a premeditated choice to exclude and shut off a multitude of sources from the formal process. Consequently, Morrison, Renfro, and Boucher (1984) suggest looking at sources in each of four main taxonomic classifications: social, technological, economic, and legislative/regulatory. Further, they recommend attention be given to publications from special-interest groups that represent the genesis of new issues and trends, such as the Union of Concerned Scientists, the Sierra Club, and Congress Watch.

As noted earlier, the designated scan list, by choice, excludes volumes of possible source materials. There will always be discussion, debate, and fear among scanning team members that something vital is being missed or that another source should be added. The system must, therefore, permit submission of "wild card" ideas—input from sources other than those assigned. Flexibility of this sort may lead to a serendipitous discovery from the general reading, viewing, and listening habits of the team members. The following section on training scanners also makes allowance for the wild card process.

Training and Orientation of Scanners. Members of the organization who have committed to the scanning concept require specific training on (1) what to look for and (2) how to deliver this information to the system. The more scanners an organization has, the more information is scanned. This results in more consensus development, team building, and staff development. Scanners are asked to look for trends, events, and emerging issues as described by Morrison, Renfro, and Boucher (1984) and Simpson, McGinty, and Morrison (1987). A *trend* consists of data that usually represent gradual and extended change in such areas as social issues, technology, politics, and economics. It can be local, regional, national, or international in character and may offer scenarios for the future by identifying possible events and issues. For example, a continuing trade imbalance that increases the deficit of the United States could lead, in conjunction with other variables, to a sudden precipitous decline in the stock market.

An *event* is any confirmable happening that, by its occurrence, definitely alters the future in relation to the past. Such a happening would be the abolition of tenure in a university system.

An *emerging issue* emanates from a trend or event and often requires a response. An example is the matter of universities and colleges being charged by representatives of small businesses with producing large sums of unrelated business income through sales of computers, clothing, and gifts in various institutional auxiliary services. This brings the possibility of class action suits from private business, which could represent a threat to a university revenue source, not to mention public relations difficulties.

Armed with these definitions, scanners can confidently look for trends, events, and emerging issues that may pose a threat to the organization or that contain new programming opportunities for a continuing education division's changing market. Some scanners will be a bit uncertain as to exactly what is meant by an environmental threat. Kotler and Murphy (1987) define an *environmental threat* as "a challenge posed by an unfavorable trend or specific disturbance in the environment that would lead, in the absence of purposeful action, to the stagnation, decline, or demise of an organization or one of its programs" (p. 123). Many threats can be clouds with silver linings that, if identified and compensated for in time, can represent the opportunity for a new market. Scanners can be sensitized to this positive dimension as they learn the format by which they summarize and report their findings.

Scanners have now been given a philosophical base, a taxonomy, scanning sources, and definitions for what it is they are searching. The next step in the methodology is to put the information source into a format that can be processed and used by the organization. One approach that has been used successfully in a continuing education organization of over 250 people, the Georgia Center for Continuing Education, involves the following procedure (Simpson, McGinty, and Morrison, 1987):

1. Scanners write abstracts of the articles they read. These abstracts are typed on a single page, as in Exhibit 31.1. Conciseness is encouraged by asking scanners what they would tell colleagues if only a few minutes were available to share the information in the article. What major points would be made and what examples of trends or events would be cited to show change?
2. Answers to these queries are followed by one or two paragraphs of explanation, which should contain any substantiating statistics.
3. The last portion of the abstract responds to the question, "How will the information in this article affect the organization?"
4. So that others may pursue the issue in detail, a copy of the complete article is attached to the abstract for permanent filing and reference. When abstracts are circulated for review and discussion among scanners, only the one-page summary is reproduced, but the complete article is available for a more thorough review if the scanner wishes.
5. Retrieval of a scanning abstract is facilitated as the one-page summary is headed by an alphanumeric code, a bibliographic entry, the taxonomy entry (which can be supplied by the project manager), and the scanner's name. Formatting can be adapted for computer entry as well.

**Exhibit 31.1. Abstract of Continuing Resource, Georgia Center
Environmental Scanning Project—Director's Office.**

_____/Taxonomy Code (Primary) Cross Ref. Codes _____

Scanner's Name _____

Nature of Resource ____ Publication ____ Conference/Meeting ____ Media ____

Title (Article, Session, Show) _____

Author/Speaker/Reporter _____

Publication/Conference/Network _____

Date _____ Pages _____ Vol. ____ No. ____

Summary _____
(Concise, single-spaced, typed statement that is understandable without reference to the original material)

Implications _____

How might the Georgia Center's programs or management be affected?

Processing and Using the Information. The manager of the scanning project should establish a periodic scanning cycle. In educational organizations, this can follow the academic quarter or semester. Businesses, volunteer groups, nonprofit organizations, and others can establish a cycle convenient to their modes of operation. With scanning abstracts arriving at the project manager's established control point in irregular fashion, failure to have at least three systematic reviews a year can result in elapse of too much time between scanning and response and in too much material to analyze, which can overload the review process.

Scanners should continuously submit abstracts but the project manager will need to (1) stop at some predetermined point, (2) collect those abstracts submitted, and (3) catalogue and compile abstracts in broad groupings suggested from the taxonomy and topics submitted.

Depending on the size of the organization and its scanning philosophy, either a designated team or just one person may process the material. The resulting analysis may go straight to management for interpretation, or it may be processed through a cross section of the organization's members. In the proper organizational circumstances, management can gain a great amount of insight regarding priorities and issues if nonmanagement personnel as well as management personnel have the opportunity to suggest their impressions of threats and opportunities from the scanning material. Management can then separately analyze the abstracts and a comparison can be made of the conclusions reached by the two groups in their evaluations of the same scanning data. This benefit to the overall organization cannot be overemphasized. Although the rank and file have their say, management may have to confront in thoughtful and analytical ways a pronounced divergence of thinking on what is perceived as threatening to the organization. Regardless, scanning will generate so many issues that even the largest of institutions will be unable to address all of them (Morrison, Renfro, and Boucher, 1984).

There must be strategies to produce consensus on the major areas of organizational concern and to limit the number to a manageable total, say six or less. In this way, the organization can realistically develop an action plan for an effective marketing response. Skeptics may comment that reducing an environment filled with threats and opportunities to only a half dozen or fewer cannot possibly be a realistic planning method. However, the salient point is that scanning is a focused and systematic analysis and is better than an ad hoc approach that may have an organization reviewing print media in an unfocused fashion that fails to stimulate action (Kotler and Fox, 1985).

Evaluating and Reviewing Data. The issues about which scanners must forge a consensus can be surfaced through a number of strategies. Several writers have given useful formats for speculating about the probability of occurrence of trends, events, and emerging issues and their impact on the organization, either positive or negative (Kotler and Murphy, 1987; Keller, 1983; Morrison, Renfro, and Boucher, 1984; Simerly and Associates, 1987; Simpson, McGinty, and Morrison, 1987). One useful approach for scanners is to limit the number of possible topics through a modified, nominal group technique. Using this technique, participants are given summaries of scanning abstracts or the actual abstracts and are asked to select their top six. Individual votes are tallied and the six receiving the highest number become the subjects of immediate organizational attention. As the nominal group approach allows a scanner to vote privately without discussion, it can eliminate peer pressure to agree with the most vocal members of the group.

Discussion and evaluation of these topics can employ a probability-impact chart (Morrison, Renfro, and Boucher, 1984).

Morrison, Renfro, and Boucher (1984) also provide useful summaries of techniques for charting impacts and consequences. These include impact networks, the Delphi technique, forecasting, extrapolation of mathematical trends, QUEST, cross-impact analysis, policy-impact analysis, and scenario development. The sophistication of certain approaches may make them impractical for some, but the concepts are valuable to any group of scanners.

Once the organization has identified, by whatever method, those scanning topics with which it will grapple during a particular scanning cycle, a critical element of the process becomes operational. Discussion, debate, and analysis of abstracts and their emerging themes will necessitate action by management through individual and committee assignments to secure additional data, act on any conclusions, implement short-range objectives, and adjust strategy as needed. The responsibility for tasks and the time frame for their completion must be carefully and conscientiously monitored and reinforced by the project manager. The scanning cycles become meaningless unless the subsequent action is implemented in a timely way.

Documentation of Actions and Feedback. In whatever forum the organization designates, there should be discussion and review of actions taken or assigned in previous scanning cycles. This systematically provides for a verbal review, evaluation, and status report on projects. Furthermore, it gives emphasis to an ongoing planning cycle that is reflective and measurable even though it is future directed. Such an approach reaffirms for the organization's members that planning is a permanent fixture in the group's process and it strengthens the philosophical foundation discussed earlier.

A written summary of the scanning topics surfaced, along with actions taken, should be distributed to all levels of the organization after each cycle. This accomplishes several things. It (1) improves communication through feedback, (2) helps to explain any new adjustments in policy, (3) keeps the organization's business and markets before its members, (4) informs members that a systematic planning approach exists, (5) serves as a passive recruiting device for scanners by letting colleagues see what others are accomplishing, (6) reinforces to scanners that their efforts have amounted to something and are important to the organization, (7) documents who has assignments and when they are due, and (8) produces a plan for operating purposes.

Evaluation. Establishing an effective evaluation of environmental scanning is essential. In establishing such evaluation, it is important to deal with a critical issue. Any evaluation of scanning must deal with the reasoning behind the concept separately from the mechanics of the process itself. The evaluation of environmental scanning must then focus on (1) the effectiveness of the system in alerting the organization to threats or opportunities so plans can be adjusted, and (2) the efficiency of the system's procedures.

Addressing system effectiveness can at times be likened to the little Georgia farm boy and the city slicker. Said the latter to the boy, "Why are you putting that scarecrow in a cotton field?" Replied the boy, "Keeps elephants from trampling the cotton." "But, my lad," intoned the city dweller, "there are no elephants in Georgia!" "Works, don't it?" responded the young man.

Scanning may periodically seem a process apart from other issues in the organization. If no disasters befall the organization, if no markets are lost, then perhaps that would have been the situation regardless. If a market segment collapses when the collapse could have been prevented, has scanning failed and should it be abandoned? The answer is "no" to both questions. As with any system, scanning cannot function perfectly, and as the computer experts note, "garbage in, garbage out." Scanning may not catch everything but it should certainly help improve the odds for success. There is always the positive reinforcement that occurs when actions taken are clearly linked to scanning and the results are an outstanding success.

On the matter of organizational acceptance and usefulness as perceived by the scanners, a periodic evaluation can be most helpful. It can be internal (Hearn and Heydinger, 1985; Simpson, McGinty, and Morrison, 1987) or external (Murphy, 1987). Even when universal participation is absent and wide-ranging differences of opinion exist among scanners and nonscanners, positive benefits can accrue to the organization and its strategic planning. As Murphy (1987) found at the University of Georgia's Center for Continuing Education: "Based on field observations, interviews, and survey responses, it is the researcher's conclusion that the environmental scanning process, as conducted at the Georgia Center for Continuing Education, is an important and viable component of the organization's strategic planning process. Furthermore, according to the evidence. . . environmental scanning has increased the Georgia Center's ability to react to and implement change in response to external factors that impact on its mission" (p. 148).

Costs of Operating the System. Establishing and maintaining an environmental scanning process can mean significant costs for the organization (Simpson, McGinty, and Morrison, 1987). These can include costs for (1) the staff required to maintain and operate the system, (2) scanning sources and printed materials, (3) storage space, (4) computer support, and (5) copying and printing costs.

Although these cost factors are significant, the ultimate cost to the organization can be greater if environmental scanning is not employed. The highest cost to the organization will be the time of scanners. This is particularly true if many staff are involved in the process. Depending on the availability of scanning source materials, purchase of new periodicals can also be expensive.

The volumes of data and the need for prompt and efficient retrieval of abstracts and related data make computer support ultimately essential, even if not initially required. Whatever the status of computer support, reproduction demands and printing expand with the size of the organization and the number of scanners. These will likely always be significant cost areas.

Unanticipated Benefits of Scanning. Environmental scanning is designed to benefit the organization's strategic plan; however, there are ancillary benefits for scanners and the organization as a whole (Simpson, McGinty, and Morrison, 1987). The actual process of scanning and abstracting can enhance the critical thinking skills of staff. A scanner must have heightened sensitivities to the organization's needs while reading, must be able to perceive appropriate topics for abstracting, and then must present the salient points in an incisive and convincing manner for colleagues to ponder. This heightened and focused awareness can improve renewal for both the individual and the organization. Further, the demands of the scanning system impose a personal and organizational discipline for dealing with the future and, thus, the fate of the organization. All the while, an important management objective is pursued in that scanning permits across-the-board participation and input by all who wish to make the required effort. Those who make the effort will contribute in a continuing and significant manner to the clarification and empowerment of the organizational mission.

As with any new or experimental system, there will be false starts and adjustments will be required. However, some problem areas and misguided assumptions that can be eliminated are provided in the following brief list.

1. *Assuming that everyone will understand and be supportive of environmental scanning.* Consider the difficulty at times of reaching agreement with one other person on certain issues. Compound that with dozens or hundreds of persons and the problem is obvious. Furthermore, some individuals never choose to be part of the team and some do not have the discipline or interest to try to understand what scanning is about.

To avoid this mistake, be persistent. Continue to offer orientation and training opportunities for new scanning recruits, as described in this chapter. Have management provide continual reinforcement, verbally and in writing. A few naysayers should not be allowed to ruin an otherwise fine effort.

2. *Believing that environmental scanning will tell the organization all it needs to know about the future.* Scanning collects data that are analyzed to present *possible* scenarios or futures if the organization reacts in a particular way. The system does not tell fortunes, nor is it infallible.

During training and orientation sessions, reiterate that scanning does not tell fortunes. Scanners must understand that disorganized, ad hoc environmental analysis is being replaced by a system that seeks only to improve the odds for correct decision making.

3. *Pretending that environmental scanning is easy.* Environmental scanning is *not* easy. To some, reading a few articles, writing a couple of abstracts, and getting together with colleagues for discussion may appear to cause no unusual inconvenience. Proper implementation of the system requires self-discipline and that most precious of resources—time. The care and feeding of scanners and the maintenance of the philosophical premise underlying scanning are neverending and demanding

The truth can be frightening to scanners. Remind them that participation is voluntary, so if things become overwhelming there is an escape hatch—they can quit. Of course, this is not an option for large numbers of people if a system is to be successful. Consequently, if people begin to feel overcommitted, suggest a brief respite or drop-out period with the idea of soon rejoining the project. Subtle reminders from busy colleagues who are actively participating provide a bit of peer pressure that often is very effective. Do not respond to nonparticipants negatively. Give encouragement, show understanding, and, above all, keep selling.

4. *Assuming that environmental scanning is inexpensive.* The costs associated with a scanning project were noted earlier. A project of any consequence demands staff time and that is expensive. If scanning is done properly, other resources will be challenged, such as budgets for purchasing print media, computer time, software, and copying.

Deal with the issue of cost in the early stages of planning the scanning effort. Take the cost areas outlined in this chapter, try to think of others, and talk through them realistically. Do not omit the potential cost to markets and the organization if threats are not identified in a timely fashion. By dealing with the cost issue early in the process and gaining commitment to move ahead, participants can be reminded later that the budget has been legitimized.

5. *Believing that if the project is started in some fashion, you can make up the process as you go along.* Keller (1983) has written that academics "prefer to do very little until near-certainty and rigorous methodologies have been worked out. But life does not allow such delays" (p. 158). This observation should not be interpreted to mean that a process or plan for implementation of each phase of the scanning project should not have been thought through and initially decided on. When scanning orientations take place, the entire process must be explained step by step. Therefore, the process must be designed in advance. The process can and, no doubt, will be changed to accommodate organizational needs and idiosyncrasies but there must be an initial frame of reference. When this is done, scanning should proceed and allow for adjustments to fit the individual needs of the organization.

Summary

Environmental scanning is an essential element of the strategic planning process. As such, members of a continuing education organization must understand the rationale behind scanning. Organizations scan to identify trends, events, and emerging issues that threaten their missions or strategic plans. They also scan to initiate compensating strategies and objectives in a wide variety of areas including marketing.

Scanning should not be attempted without proper training and orientation of scanners, adequate staffing, adequate support and operating systems, and the understanding that the process is time consuming and requires both personal and organizational discipline. The benefits, however, are worth the effort. Scanning helps to develop a futures orientation for the organization. It enhances personal and organizational renewal. It introduces systematic planning and review. It is one of the best techniques available to help an organization adjust its marketing techniques to fit the rapidly changing expectations of the marketplace.

32

Seventy-Five Tips for Avoiding Common Marketing Mistakes

Robert G. Simerly

Each chapter in this handbook presents an in-depth discussion and analysis of important marketing issues. The authors provide practical advice on the implementation of marketing in a wide variety of continuing education organizations. This chapter summarizes that advice in seventy-five concrete tips on registration; advertising and public relations; direct-mail marketing; effective service; copy writing, design, and typesetting; printing; image; evaluation; media; mailing lists; and program planning.

Registration Issues

1. *Generally avoid discounts for early registrations.* This major mistake is made by many program planners. Such discounts make sense and provide benefits only to the program planners. Planners who institute this policy believe that it will encourage people to register earlier and thus it will be possible to plan the work flow in the registration office more effectively. From the standpoint of the participant, however, this policy is punitive. Participants registering after the cutoff date tend to become angry at the sponsoring organization because the registration fee has increased. Therefore, they find it easier not to attend.

The solution is to eliminate the late registration penalty so that everyone pays the same registration fee.

2. *Avoid expensive cancelation penalties.* Again, these penalties meet the need of the sponsoring organization and do nothing to encourage early registration. If people who cancel are penalized, why should they register early?

An expensive cancelation fee encourages participants to wait until the last minute to register. It is not a good marketing strategy.

3. *Make it easy for people to register by boldly displaying your phone number throughout all advertising.* Many continuing education organizations find that at least half of their students register by phone. To make this process as easy as possible, boldly display your phone number throughout brochures; do not include it only with the registration information. You want to convey, throughout your advertising, that registration is easy.

4. *Design the registration form of a direct-mail brochure so that the mailing label is returned with the registration even if a copy of the form is remitted rather than the original.* Mailing labels should always be coded so that on completion of a program, you can determine which list drew the greatest number of registrants. The only way to do this is to place the registration form on the back cover so that the mailing label of the brochure is returned even if a copy of the form rather than the original is remitted. For telephone registrations, the registration clerk should ask the caller to identify the code on the mailing label. Knowledge of the numbers of registrants drawn from the different lists will make it possible to eliminate the less productive lists and increase advertising cost-effectiveness.

5. *Consider the pitfalls in offering team discounts to organizations.* This marketing device is used often, but it is important to plan the program budget to accommodate this team registration, which results in a lower per-person registration. The only failsafe way to do this is to calculate your break-even point on the assumption that all registrants will be members of teams. Let us say that the regular registration fee is $100 per person and the registration for groups of four or more is $75 per person. To calculate the break-even point accurately you must assume that all registrants will take advantage of the team registration of $75 per person. This is the only way to plan a conservative budget. Incidentally, many continuing education professionals find that team discounts do not increase attendance.

6. *Increase the number of registrations by giving participants a place on the program.* Many organizations, particularly academic organizations, cannot afford to pay travel and registration fees for employees to attend conferences and professional meetings. However, they often will make money available for attendance if their people play a key role in the program, for example, present a paper. Therefore, when planning a professional conference, consider a call for papers in the first mailing. Almost everyone whose paper is accepted can be counted on for a confirmed registration. In addition, consider including poster sessions in which attendees can display their latest research findings or tell about their organization. Key registrants can be asked to lead informal swap-shop sessions. In this way, potential registrants can go to their organization to request travel funds that will assist them with the dissemination of their research findings. This works especially well in academic circles, where travel and registration fee money is particularly tight.

7. *Always ask for a registration or a response in advertising.* If you are

going to the expense of sending out advertising, ask for a response. The response may be a call requesting more information, or it may be a registration. Sometimes program planners send out sketchy information in a program announcement, indicating that the official brochure will follow as soon as it is printed. This creates a negative image. Basically, it shows that you are behind in your advertising plans, that you are sending incomplete information until the complete information is available. When this happens, people rarely pay serious attention to the official information. The one exception concerns annual meetings of conventions for associations. Often, in such cases, a flyer is mailed that says, for example, "Mark your calendar for the next annual meeting of the association on May 2." This is appropriate because a loyal group of attendees has evolved for the annual meeting. For a one-time program, however, an announcement to mark your calendar, without information about the program, is almost always ineffective in garnering registrations. In fact, it usually creates a very negative image of disorganization.

8. *Make your registration form easy to complete.* Design the registration form in a brochure or catalogue so that it is easy to use. Do not ask for extra information even though it might be interesting for your organization to have. It is important to make it as easy as possible for the interested person to register. For example, one university continuing education organization uses a long, complicated registration form that asks for age, race, occupational group, and alumnus status at that institution. Even though the form indicates that this information is optional, it creates major psychological blocks in the registration process. Although the sponsoring organization may find this information of interest, the registrant receives no benefit for giving it. Incidentally, the previously mentioned organization's original purpose in requesting the optional information was to build a better data base about program attendees. However, they have found that few registrants take the time to fill out their cumbersome registration form. Therefore, the forms are incomplete and virtually useless for marketing purposes. If you must have this extra information, collect it at the end of the program, when participants are feeling good about you and are willing to assist you with market research.

Advertising/Public Relations

9. *Emphasize program benefits in all written and verbal communication with potential participants.* People attend programs because of their perception of the benefits they will receive. Therefore, in all written and verbal communication with potential participants, emphasize these benefits. State these benefits from the participant's point of view rather than from the point of view of the program planner. Often, important differences exist between these two viewpoints. Chapter Twelve provides a detailed explanation of how to do this.

10. *Print messages on all organizational materials.* Project the image of your organization on all materials. For example, print the organization's name on pens, pencils, and pads included in program registration packets and on

matchbook covers, buttons, and stickers. Print your name and an advertising message on paper napkins, cups, and plates used at coffee breaks. Consider selling T-shirts with the printed name of your organization or a particular program. Print your name at the top of all handouts and other materials. The backs of tent name cards should carry an advertising message. Develop a comprehensive systems approach by examining all materials you distribute to determine where it is appropriate to advertise your organization's name, slogan, or description of services and benefits.

11. *Insert announcements of your programs in calendars of upcoming events in magazines, journals, newsletters, and newspapers.* Usually, there is no charge for inclusion in calendars of upcoming events. Many people read these columns regularly. Remember that most magazines or journals require a three- to six-month lead time to ensure inclusion of an announcement in an issue. This is particularly true of quarterly publications.

12. *Arrange to have your program announcements listed on the cable TV community calendar.* Most cable TV companies offer a community calendar on one of their channels. Dispensing information about community events and educational programs is a requirement for a cable TV license, so you will find such companies to be very receptive to your requests. Many people will see these announcements as they flip through the cable stations searching for an interesting program. Include the name and phone number of the person to call for more information.

13. *Use planning committees to help market programs.* Choose people for program planning committees who are leaders in their fields. They have important contacts. Use planning committee members creatively to enhance your marketing. For example, they may have access to hard-to-secure mailing lists for professional associations, and may even be able to obtain such mailing lists free. They may volunteer to mention your program during upcoming speeches to community and civic groups or to distribute brochures at an annual meeting. They may be available for radio and TV interviews in which they can talk about the program. Planning committee members are valuable resources to your marketing efforts. If they have had a hand in planning an excellent program, they will want to ensure its success. Therefore, they usually are very willing to assist with the program's marketing plan.

14. *Consider using shopping weeklies and giveaway newspapers to market your programs or obtain publicity about your organization.* These weeklies and giveaways can often be an important marketing resource. Naturally, it is important that the tone of the publication be appropriate to the image you want to convey. The readership for these publications is often large and diverse. Do not overlook these publications as an important marketing channel.

15. *Enlist the support of your local chamber of commerce and convention and visitors bureau.* Chambers of commerce and convention and visitors bureaus are dedicated to increasing business in the communities they represent. They are important sources of information, publicity, and assistance. For example, let us say that you are conducting a three-day workshop in another city. The

convention and visitors bureau will probably provide volunteers to handle your registration table, if the registration process is not too large or complicated. In addition, they may staff an information table about local attractions, restaurants, and special events and provide free maps of the city, state, and region. You can frequently obtain specialized mailing lists from local chambers of commerce. Learn how these organizations can assist you with marketing both in your local community and in other cities.

16. *Consider advertising in airline magazines.* Fliers are a captive audience and they tend to read the official airline magazine in the seat pocket. Consider inserting a list of your upcoming programs in such magazines, particularly in those of airlines that fly into your city. Always include a coupon for requesting additional information. In addition, boldly display the name and phone number of the person to call for more information. Many airline magazines include a response card on which readers can circle the number of the ad for which they would like more information. The card then is returned postpaid to the airline, which, in turn, sends you a list of names and addresses of respondents to whom you can send your literature directly. Code your responses so that you can track the effectiveness of your ad. You want to track all responses, particularly those that convert to program registrations.

17. *Advertise upcoming programs in the brochure for a current program.* People you have determined to be in the correct target group to receive a brochure about a specific program are excellent candidates for notification about other upcoming programs. Consider including in the brochure a section entitled "Preview of Upcoming Programs." Offer the reader the opportunity to obtain more information about these programs by checking the appropriate box on the registration/response form or by calling the phone number boldly displayed. In this way, you can build an effective mailing list of people who are predisposed to read information about your organization and its programs.

18. *Exhibit at conferences, conventions, annual meetings, and trade shows.* These events are excellent opportunities to make personal contact and assemble lists of people who have heard about your organization and its programs. If you offer continuing education programs for school administrators, consider exhibiting at the annual meeting of the American Association of School Administrators. If you hold programs for psychologists, consider exhibiting at the annual meeting of the American Psychological Association. A word of warning, however. Check the types of exhibits used by others before attending. Pay particular attention to your competitor's exhibits. Make yours look better and different. Establish an easy technique to capture the names and addresses of people to whom you talk during the meeting; ask them for their business cards or have them fill out a card for a free drawing. Offer buttons for them to wear, and give them information about your organization to take home. Follow up shortly with a mailing that contains a personal letter.

19. *Include brochures of upcoming programs in registration packets.* When people are waiting for a program to begin, they often browse through their registration packets. Include brochures of upcoming programs in these packets.

Code these brochures for tracking purposes. Even if they do not produce many registrants, you may want to continue this procedure as a public relations effort. It keeps the name of your organization and its programs before the public.

20. *At all programs, arrange to advertise your organization and its upcoming events at a display table or booth.* People who attend your programs are the most likely registrants for other programs. Therefore, set up a table or booth at the program to dispense information. Include brochures and calendars of upcoming events. This is an excellent way to increase name recognition for your organization.

21. *In advertising sent to business addresses, always emphasize the benefits that attendance at the program will have on the job.* Such an emphasis encourages superiors to send their subordinates. Copy should underline the payoff for the investment in training and development. State these benefits in terms of how the organization will benefit by the employee's attendance. Put yourself in the shoes of the potential registrant's superior when writing copy to gain an understanding of the possible motivations he or she would have to send people. Chapter Twelve offers many practical tips in this area. Do not assume that people will reach these conclusions by themselves.

22. *Keep extensive files of examples of good and bad marketing ideas.* These files are useful as you work with graphic designers in explaining what you are trying to accomplish with your total marketing plan. In addition, they provide useful tickler files that can be reviewed as you develop plans for marketing new programs or revising existing ones.

23. *Keep track of your marketing costs in relation to gross revenue.* These data are very important to any continuing education organization. Chapter Twenty-Nine illustrates how to set up an electronic spreadsheet on a personal computer to gather such data. To plan for effective marketing, benchmarks must be established with respect to overall spending for marketing. For example, if you find that you are spending only 2 percent of gross revenue on marketing, you may want to plan an increase in next year's budget in the hope that it will generate additional revenue. Some of the most effective continuing education organizations in the country find that they spend between 20 and 30 percent of their gross revenue on marketing. If you are spending less than this, you probably should ask yourself if you are satisfied with your present results. If not, consider planning future budgets to fund more extensive marketing efforts.

24. *Give programs away to create new programs.* Allow people to attend programs free to see how you operate, especially if you are trying to get them to work with you to create new programs. For example, a continuing education organization at a large university invites every new faculty member to lunch at its residential continuing education center. Staff members make personal phone calls to arrange these meetings, pick up each new faculty member, host a lunch, give them a tour of the facilities, talk about the services provided, and drive them back to their offices. This personal attention leads to new friends, creates goodwill, and results in many new programs.

Direct-Mail Marketing

25. *Mail brochures well in advance of the event.* It is almost impossible to mail brochures too early for most continuing education programs. Remember that it usually takes a minimum of two to four weeks for a brochure mailed at bulk rate to travel across country, and this time must be calculated into the total marketing plan. As a general rule, brochures need to be in the hands of potential registrants ten to sixteen weeks before the event. For some events, such as annual meetings or large special programs, an even longer lead time is necessary. This is particularly true for professional development programs, where the registrant must arrange time off from work or where the registrant's employer will be paying his or her way. Securing time off is often a long process, taking up to four to six weeks in many large organizations. As a general rule, brochures should be received ten to sixteen weeks in advance of the program. If brochures are mailed out later than this, the reason should be clear and defensible. Failure to prepare the copy in time is not an adequate reason. If the copy is late, it is almost always better to change the dates of the program than to shorten the ten- to sixteen-week lead time. Chapter Fourteen discusses in detail how to set up a planning and production schedule.

26. *Consider mailing two copies of the same brochure to the same address, spacing the mailings two to three weeks apart.* Mailing two copies of the same brochure to the same person with a two- to three-week interval can increase program registrations as much as 25 percent. Therefore, when developing a total marketing plan for any program, establish a budget to accommodate these mailings. You can always test the idea by doing a split mailing. To one half of a large list, mail only one copy of the brochure. To the other half of the list, mail two copies of the brochure. Code the registration forms and mailing labels. Alert your registration staff to request the tracking code in phone registrations. Compare the results to see how much better the double mailing did. Try this for several programs until you develop a reliable data base, on which to decide whether double mailings represent a good return on the investment. Many program planners find that double mailings produce one of their best returns on investment.

27. *Stagger mailing dates when mailing to multiple lists that may contain duplicate names.* If you are doing a large bulk mailing to several different lists, it is possible that a number of names appear on more than one list. Therefore, rather than doing one mass mailing on the same day to all the lists to get the project out of the way, consider staggering the mailing dates for each list, about five to eight days apart. Those people who receive duplicate brochures or catalogues will receive them on different days. Receipt of such advertisements on different days serves as a positive reinforcement of your program, whereas receipt of four copies of the same brochure on the same day creates a negative image.

28. *Design brochures, catalogues, and other advertising pieces to look different from those of your competitor.* If your competitor happens to have adopted a particular style, do not imitate it. Instead, go for a very different look

that is in line with the tone and image of your organization. This establishes your individual identity in the market. The last thing you want to do is look like the competition. You want instantaneous organizational or program recognition. Experiment until you find the difference that is right for your organization. Never assume that you can maintain that right look forever. When you become successful, the competition will copy you. Then you must change again to remain on the cutting edge.

29. *Mail enough brochures to attract the number of registrants required to break even financially.* Deciding on the number of brochures to mail to break even is always tricky. Although there exist no formulas that guarantee success in this area, professionals in direct-mail marketing have developed some useful guidelines. As a general rule, count on an average of one registrant per thousand brochures mailed to a general mailing list. If you have a targeted mailing list, for example, a list of all registered nurses in a city for a program on improving patient care, you can generally count on two to five registrants per thousand brochures mailed. Greater responses would represent above-average success. These guidelines are general. It is important to develop a data base in your own organization by monitoring the number of registrants relative to the number of brochures mailed. You will then be able to develop more reliable break-even estimates for your programs. Chapter Ten contains an extensive analysis of this issue.

30. *Schedule large mailings to avoid the December holidays.* Post offices across the country are very busy from December 1 until January 5. Avoid this period for any large mailings of advertising. You cannot ensure that advertising pieces, especially bulk mail, mailed during this period will reach the destination on time. In addition, so many people are busy with holiday plans and end-of-year reports that they often disregard the advertising received at this time.

31. *If people attend annual programs out of habit, you often do not need to develop extensive and expensive advertising programs unless your aim is to increase the number of registrants dramatically.* Annual programs tend to develop a loyal following of participants who attend whether a modest announcement in a newsletter or an expensive brochure is used to advertise the program. Get to know the history of the organization and the attendees of repeater programs. This will enable the program planner to determine the extent of advertising needed for such programs. Two questions are important: (1) Are we satisfied with the number of attendees and (2) do we want to increase the attendance? If the answer to both is "no," spend money for things other than extensive advertising.

32. *Include envelope stuffers in all outgoing communications.* Registration acknowledgments, bills, invoices, thank you letters, and invitations to speakers are all important components of the total marketing effort. Consider including envelope stuffers in all of these. One envelope stuffer could describe the organization and how to gain access to its services. Another stuffer could contain information about upcoming programs. Yet another stuffer could be testimonials

from satisfied clients with the name and phone number of the person in the organization to call to discuss a program idea.

Providing Effective Service

33. *Allow people to register without payment.* Insisting on payment with registration discourages registrations. This tactic meets only the needs of the program planner. The registrant should register quickly and easily while he or she is still in the mood. Almost no one defaults on payments for continuing education programs. Allow registrants to pay their fees by check, credit card, or purchase order, or bill them later. Occasionally, it may be appropriate to offer installment payments, depending on the cost and the individual needs of your program.

34. *Try to convert inquiries into actual registrations.* Those who take the initiative to inquire about your program, either by letter, in person, or over the phone, are predisposed to registering. They are your best prospects. Their agenda during inquiries is to gain more information and obtain satisfactory answers to their questions. The agenda of the program planner and all office staff should be to convert such inquiries into registrations. After answering all their questions, offer them an easy way to register, for example, by saying, "We're glad that you called and we hope that you will be attending our program. In fact, to ensure you a place in the program I'm going to sign you up. Naturally, there is no obligation on your part. If you find for any reason that you cannot attend all you have to do is call and let us know that you'd like to cancel your registration. In the meantime, however, you are assured a place in the program." If the caller finds this acceptable, then acknowledge the registration within twenty-four hours with a personal note. In most cases, up to 90 percent of such registrants remain active and actually attend the program. Why? You have answered their questions and made it easy for them to register and attend. You have also given them personal attention.

35. *Acknowledge registrations promptly.* When someone registers for your program, acknowledge the registration promptly, within twenty-four hours. This communicates that yours is a responsive organization. You can also use this acknowledgment to communicate that you are pleased that they will be attending the program. Follow-up information, such as information about hours, special events, and parking, can be sent to confirmed registrants. Remember, this communication with the registrant is an excellent opportunity to convey a positive image, as well as to confirm the registration. Establish a positive image of real people who are pleased to be working with the registrant. In addition, enclose additional information about your organization and its comprehensive continuing education programming in the confirmation. One continuing education organization that serves 75,000 people annually prints information about the organization on the reverse side of all invoices. Information about other upcoming programs is also enclosed with each acknowledgment. Assume that there is no such thing as a blank side to any piece of paper you send out in the

acknowledgment. It is strategic advertising space that can be used to communicate positive images about your organization.

36. *Train all staff to answer the phone and respond to inquiries.* The person answering the phone is a key salesperson in your organization. What do you do to improve their sales techniques? Are they trained effectively to convert inquiries into registrations? Can they handle complaints without becoming defensive? What image do they project as they interact with clients? For example, during the past month, I had the following experiences in telephone calls with continuing education organizations. One secretary put me on hold because the person I wanted to talk to was on the other line. I waited five minutes and hung up. If the person answering the phone had been trained to be service oriented, she would have gotten back to me to inquire whether I wanted to wait or wanted the person to return my call. While I was talking to the secretary at another office, I heard a phone ring in the background. She said, "I'm going to put you on hold for a moment while I answer the other phone." What she communicated was that other messages took priority over mine. In a call to another continuing education office, I could hear rock music playing loudly in the background. In yet another office, I could not get through to the person I wanted to talk to until I had given my name and organizational affiliation twice and had explained to the secretary why I wanted to talk to the person. Such barriers do not communicate a customer service orientation. How people are handled on the phone, regardless of their reason for calling, should be an important part of an organization's overall marketing plan.

37. *Give refunds immediately.* When refunds are in order for cancelations or for dissatisfaction with a program, process these refunds immediately. Nothing creates ill will faster than having to wait a long time for a refund. If you work in a large organization, such as a university, where refunds are processed by central accounting, you may have to live with the fact that it will take three or four weeks from the time you process the paperwork until the computer generates a check and the accounting office mails it out. If this is the case, notify the customer that the refund paperwork has been processed and of the approximate date to expect their check.

38. *Don't ever say no.* Developing an effective service orientation requires reacting to a wide variety of client needs. To be most effective, develop a staff philosophy illustrated by such statements as "I don't know the answer to that but I'll find out." "Let me see if I can make that work for you." "How can I be most helpful to you?"

39. *Follow the twenty-four-hour rule.* If a person calls to request your help in setting up a continuing education program, be on site within twenty-four hours to discuss the details. Within another twenty-four hours send them additional literature and information. Prospective clients who are thinking of planning programs do not want to wait until you find it convenient to visit. They want instant interest in their project. This applies whether the client is external or internal to your institution.

40. *Develop a total systems approach to marketing the services of your*

organization and the benefits that can be obtained from using these services. Every piece of literature that leaves your office should market your services and serve to reinforce the organization's image of excellence. Therefore, approach marketing from a systems point of view.

Copy Writing, Design, Typesetting, and Printing

41. *Describe accurately and completely the program content in each brochure or catalogue.* Each brochure or catalogue should contain a comprehensive, accurate, and substantive description of program content. A simple list of presentations is usually not adequate. Chapter Twelve explains in detail how to write effective copy. Descriptions of program content should clearly spell out what participants will learn by attending the program. Then, work with the presenters to ensure that they successfully deliver what has been promised.

42. *Have at least one other person review brochure copy before it is sent to the typesetter and after its return.* Before it is typeset, copy should be reviewed by someone not closely involved with the program. After it is typeset, the copy should be read to correct typographical errors.

43. *Establish the principle that after copy has been typeset, no changes will be made except to correct typographical errors.* It is tempting to make substantive changes in copy after it is returned from the typesetters. Excessive changes at this point may delay the printing process one or two weeks and double the typesetting bill. The time to make changes is before the copy has been typeset, not after.

44. *Consider electronic typesetting.* Now that personal computers and word-processing packages are in wide use in continuing education organizations, errors can be considerably reduced by (1) running a computer spelling check on all copy and (2) sending the typesetter copy either on disk or by modem and telephone transmission. This procedure greatly reduces typesetting errors because the copy is not rekeyed. Most typesetters are now equipped to handle this direct transfer of copy from computer disk to their typesetting machines. You can cut your typesetting bill at least in half by adopting this method. The longer the typesetting project, the greater your savings. Also, with this method, you can usually get twenty-four-hour turnaround at the typesetters. It is particularly important that copy not be changed once it is typeset, however, because the changes would have to be done by hand, greatly increasing cost and turnaround time.

45. *Include testimonials in brochure and catalogue copy.* Testimonials by satisfied past participants are effective in communicating the quality of your program. Chapter Twelve provides relevant guidelines. Testimonials—the actual words of past participants—are almost always more effective than the copy you could write. Obtain permission to use the complete name, organizational affiliation, title, city, and state of these past participants. The reader is thus assured of the veracity of the testimonials.

46. *Use a routing box next to the mailing label on all brochures and*

catalogues. This tactic enables the person receiving the publicity to route it throughout the organization to others who may be interested in the program. An easy way to do this is to insert a small box on the side of the mailing label. The copy should read, "Route to . . ." Include sufficient space for the reader to write in the names of several people.

47. *Advertise on the back cover of all brochures and catalogues.* Often, program planners fail to realize that the back cover is important advertising space. The back cover should be just as effective as the front cover in convincing the reader to open the advertising piece and read it. Remember that a person has a fifty–fifty chance of picking up the advertising piece with the back cover facing up. Use the same care in copy writing and design for the back cover as you use for the remainder of the brochure.

Image

48. *Actively plan to convey the image you want in your advertising.* Establish very clearly exactly what image you want your advertising to convey about your program and organization. Then, ensure that all printed material is designed to achieve this image. For example, do you want a conservative image? Or do you prefer an avant-garde image? Do you want a slick look? Do you want boldness? The overall image chosen should be consistent with the overall image of your organization and the particular program being advertised. Therefore, consider the following items: color, paper stock, size and style of print, language, overall graphic design, use of photographs and pictures, headlines, price of the program, and location.

49. *Select special-program locations appropriate to the image of your organization and the content of the program.* This concept is very important. For example, a prestigious national educational organization recently mailed a brochure advertising an upcoming professional development workshop. The content of the workshop was excellent; however, it was held in Miami in January. Although this location is not inappropriate, the cover of the brochure had a large graphic design containing palm trees, beaches, ocean, and sun. The image was appropriate for a family vacation brochure but not for a professional association brochure. It is difficult for employees to obtain permission from their superiors to attend a substantive and serious program when the cover of the brochure so strongly conveys the image of a luxurious winter vacation in the sun. It is important that the description of the location and the graphic images used be consistent with the goals, objectives, and tone of the program. The organization could easily have conveyed a different image in their brochure. Incidentally, the program was not successful.

50. *Avoid sexist and culturally biased approaches in advertising and promotion.* Successful marketers are sensitive to the fact that leaders in the United States are men and women from a wide variety of cultural and ethnic backgrounds. Incorporate this sensitivity into advertising copy and graphics. Continuing education programs are for sales*people,* not salesmen. Use "he and

she," not just "he." Recently, a large, prestigious firm specializing in management development programs sent out a brochure announcing a new program entitled "Effective Supervisory Skills." The cover showed a man walking through the door of an executive suite. The implication drawn from this image is that only men are supervisors. It would have been just as easy to picture a man and a woman walking through the door. In another example, the brochure for a program entitled "Transactional Analysis for Parents" carried photographs of only white parents and children. The brochure would have appealed to a wider audience had it acknowledged our cultural and ethnic diversity and included representative photographs.

51. *Always have a professional photographer take photographs used in advertising.* Nothing is worse than a bold, effective brochure brimming with substantive descriptions of program content but containing photographs that do not match the professional level of the copy and design. Use of a professional photographer will ensure that the photographs are of uniform quality. Snapshots are always inappropriate for use in quality advertising and promotional literature. Remember, the photograph should convey the quality and excellence of your organization. Tell the photographer how you plan to use the photographs. Specify high-contrast glossy prints to ensure top-quality reproduction.

52. *Price programs appropriately.* Many items contribute to the price of a program. Programs must be priced to recover direct and, sometimes, indirect costs. In addition, the price must meet the expectations of the attendees. Consumers often make inferences about the quality of a program from its price. For example, a two-day program on managing the problem employee aimed at midlevel managers probably will not do well if it is priced at $89. Such managers are used to paying a minimum of $150 per program day. Therefore, a price of $300 to $600 is probably more appropriate. A lower price may communicate to prospective registrants that the program is of lower quality than higher-priced programs. The lesson here is to know your group of potential attendees and price according to their expectations.

Evaluation

53. *Use end-of-program evaluation forms to collect useful marketing information.* Evaluation forms provide an excellent opportunity to collect useful marketing information. Collect testimonials that can be used in future brochure copy. Ask people to list the names of friends they think would like to receive information about future programs. Request employers' names and addresses, which you can add to your mailing list. Invite attendees to contact you about arranging in-house programs. Ask them what they found especially helpful about program content and what they would like to see in future programs. Then convert this information into powerful advertising copy and new programs. Ask what months and days of the week are most convenient for them to attend future programs. Find out whether they or their employers paid the registration fee. This information is useful in pricing future programs.

54. *Consider subscribing to a clipping bureau to monitor the effectiveness of your advertising/public relations.* Clipping bureaus read all magazines and newspapers published in the United States. Service for foreign publications is also available. For a monthly fee, they will mail you a copy of any article, ad, or announcement that mentions the name of your organization. Although it is easy for you to monitor paid advertising and obtain copies of newspaper ads, it is more difficult to catch newspaper articles about your program, particularly if you have mailed news releases throughout a state or region. Clipping bureaus help you monitor these articles so that you can determine the effectiveness of your efforts. And here is a special hint. If your continuing education unit is part of a larger organization, for example, a large university, the chances are very good that your organization's main public information office already subscribes to a clipping bureau. Often, it is easy to arrange to have them send you copies of clippings related to your unit. Major clipping bureaus are listed under Resources, at the end of this book.

55. *Continuously evaluate your advertising effectiveness and test-market new ideas.* Strategic thinking is the key to advertising. Constantly develop new strategies. Test new ideas. Experiment through a split mailing to determine what color of ink on brochures draws the most registrants. Does a two-color brochure outdraw a one-color or four-color brochure? Experiment with paper stock. Which results in the most registrants? Do a split mailing in which half of the brochures arrive with a cover letter in an envelope and the other half arrive flat without an envelope. Which mailing draws more registrants? Develop a research data base about your own marketing effectiveness.

56. *Make evaluation forms short and simple.* Program evaluation is important and it can provide very useful information for future marketing. However, at the end of a program, participants are usually so intent on their departure that they are not interested in completing long evaluations. To increase the response rate, make evaluations short and to the point. If the form takes longer than five minutes to complete, it is probably too long. If the number of participants is very large, use optical scan sheets and provide pencils so that the evaluation can be machine scored. Data that cannot be easily tabulated are usually not used for future marketing decisions.

Media Relations

57. *Get to know key media people in your community and stay in touch with them.* Local media people are important contacts. They can help you promote your continuing education programs. Get to know them. Find out what information they would like to have about programs and in what format they want it.

58. *Develop effective public service announcements for radio and television.* Most radio and television stations run a limited number of free public service announcements (PSAs). Develop personal contacts with the people who schedule these PSAs. If yours is a not-for-profit organization, they will be

receptive to airing your announcements. PSAs are an important source of free publicity. All radio and television stations in your area should regularly receive copy for PSAs related to your programs. As your primary reason for placing PSAs is to generate inquiries, include a name and phone number to call for more information.

59. *Invite local media people to attend programs at no charge.* Many continuing education organizations who adopt this policy find that the number of feature and news stories in the local media begins to increase. Even if you do not have a blanket no-charge policy for the media, extend special no-charge invitations to cover specific programs for which you would like news or feature coverage.

Mailing Lists

60. *Maintain computerized lists of past attendees for future mailings.* Past attendees constitute your best source of potential registrants for future programs. Establish methods to ensure that past attendees receive copies of brochures and catalogues for future programs similar to those they have attended. Enclose a cover letter with the brochure or catalogue. Distinguish past attendees by area of interest so that you can zero in on likely prospects for specific programs. Lists of past attendees often outdraw other lists by at least two to one. With personal computers and the wide variety of data-based management software, it is now easy to maintain, code, update, and retrieve such lists. Many software packages manage both the registration process and list maintenance.

61. *Use the local yellow pages as a valuable source of people who should receive advertising.* The Yellow Pages are often overlooked in the construction of mailing lists. For example, if you are offering a two-day program entitled "How the Tax Law Affects Your Business," all business owners in your community are potential registrants. Rent a Yellow Pages mailing list of all businesses in your area.

62. *Update your own mailing lists periodically.* Because of the mobility of our population, mailing lists become outdated quickly, within a maximum of three years. Therefore, update your own lists frequently. More than 30 percent of the people on a list have moved or changed jobs after one year. An easy way to update a list is to mail stamped, self-addressed postcards asking people to return the cards if they would like to remain on the mailing list. At this time, people can also indicate changes of title or address. Allow them space to add the names of friends to the mailing list.

63. *Get on your competitors' mailing list.* You probably are already on the mailing lists of some of your major competitors as a result of your membership in different organizations. However, if you are not on the competitor's mailing list, arrange to be included. In this way, you can easily monitor the direction of their marketing, their course content, their use of presenters, and how far in advance they mail. All good marketing plans should include a systematic analysis of the competition's advertising.

64. *Ask program presenters for their mailing lists or a list of their professional acquaintances.* Program leaders are often excellent sources of names for mailing lists. They can give you rosters of attendees at other programs where they have made presentations. They can list professional colleagues who would like to receive information about upcoming programs, as well as the professional associations to which they belong. If they write books, they may be able to obtain book-buyer lists from their publishers.

65. *Retain the names and addresses of registrants who cancel.* People who cancel their registrations are good prospects for future programs. Obviously, they wanted to attend or they would not have registered. Do not delete these names from your prime list. The cover letter enclosed with the brochure might begin, "We're sorry that a change in plans prevented you from attending our recent program. However, we know that you will want to know about a similar program we have scheduled on September 17." Follow up with a phone call. They will appreciate this individual attention.

66. *Retain the names and addresses of all respondents.* People who write or call for additional information are predisposed to act favorably toward your organization and its programs. Do not discard these names. Incorporate them into your computer list and code them appropriately. Send them information about upcoming programs. Above all, ensure that staff members record, on the appropriate computer list, the names and addresses of all callers to whom they mail a brochure or catalogue. Track the registration rate attained with these lists.

Program Planning

67. *Find your marketing niche and position yourself correctly in the market.* Success in continuing education demands that you position yourself correctly in the market. Create a special marketing niche by making the content of your program different from that of your competition. Provide programs and services not provided by others. If the competition has devoted itself to general programs on the use of electronic spreadsheets on personal computers, perhaps you should develop custom application workshops, for example, a workshop entitled "Using Lotus 1, 2, 3 to Improve Profitability for Your Sales Force." If the competition is offering a series of general updates on the new tax laws, it may be time for you to institute a program entitled "How to Save Money and Make the New Tax Law Work for Your Restaurant." Remember that your market niche and position must be consistent with the organizational image.

68. *Conduct telephone interviews with potential attendees to help structure program content and write effective advertising copy.* One of the best ways to determine program content and write effective copy is to choose ten people at random from potential attendees at a program. Call them, discuss your ideas, and secure their feedback, positive and negative. Ask them what they would expect to learn from such a program. Who would they like to see as presenters? What benefits do they see in attending? These people will write most of your brochure copy. Use the same language they use. If the copy is written from their

point of view, it will ring true with the reader. Ask the interviewees what times they would find most convenient to attend and how much they would be willing to pay for such a program. Ten to fifteen such structured phone interviews should provide a perspective wide enough to be considered reliable and generalizable to a larger population. After the interview, send the participants final typewritten copy, before it is sent to the typesetter, with a note thanking them for their cooperation. Tell them that you are giving them an advance preview of the program. Follow up by sending several printed brochures, asking them to pass the brochures along to interested friends. As many as 90 percent of these people will register for the program. In offering you their opinions, they have committed themselves psychologically to the success of the program. Also see chapters Twelve and Twenty-One.

69. *The fastest growing segment of the population comprises retired people over age 60.* This market is important to continuing education programs. Tapping it will increase revenue for your organization and provide a valuable service for the participants. According to projections, this market segment is projected to continue to grow rapidly through at least the end of the century.

70. *Develop a comprehensive internal marketing plan.* If your continuing education organization is part of a larger, parent institution, develop a comprehensive internal marketing plan. Design this plan (1) to project your image to the many departments within the parent institution, (2) to explain the services you offer and the benefits to people in the parent institution, and (3) to ask people to respond to your messages by requesting more information and/or arranging appointments to discuss new program ideas. This internal marketing plan is as important as any external plan and should be accounted for in the budget.

Miscellaneous

71. *Develop a mission statement to guide all your actions.* Profit is not the goal of marketing. The goal is to *provide a service that will result in profit* or at least in breaking even if you are in the nonprofit sector. There are important and subtle distinctions here. Establishing this priority is more easily accomplished through development of an overarching mission statement to guide the organization. Such a statement facilitates long-range planning. In addition, it provides bases on which daily decisions can be made. Ask the following question constantly: "Are our programs and marketing efforts helping us to achieve our mission?" The best marketers never lose sight of the integral relationship between marketing and organizational mission.

72. *Market video- or audiotapes of program presentations.* Conference and workshop attendees often like to purchase audio- or videotapes of the presentations so that they can review the major ideas presented. They can take the tapes to work and share the ideas with colleagues. Many people listen to audiotapes of conference presentations as they drive to work. In addition, you may be able to

market the tapes to people who could not attend the program. Thus, video- and audiotapes represent a new source of revenue for your organization.

73. *Issue certificates of attendance or achievement.* Such certificates can be an effective component of the overall program marketing plan. Certificates should be professionally designed by a graphic designer and printed on good-quality paper. They should contain appropriate signatures and perhaps even a seal and ribbon used by the organization. To ensure that certificates will be displayed, award either framed certificates or wood-mounted certificates etched in metal that are ready to hang. Do not award certificates indiscriminately. Be sure that your audience is at the appropriate educational level and values such certificates. For example, at a conference where the majority of registrants hold a doctorate, certificates may be inappropriate. However, for a program in which the majority of people are not college graduates and value such certificates, their use is appropriate. Know your audience. An important side benefit, from a marketing point of view, is that displayed certificates keep your organization's name and programs in the public eye.

74. *Plan your time with clients and programs effectively.* According to an old marketing adage, 80 percent of your business derives from 20 percent of your clients. Leverage time and money to maximize this payoff. All clients do not require the same amount of time and attention. It is more cost effective to spend the most time with the people and programs that will produce the greatest payoff—however you measure that payoff.

75. *Ask all staff to make one sales call a month.* Think of everyone on the staff as a salesperson. Professional development and training can be geared to achieving this attitude. By asking each staff member to make one sales call a month, marketing comes to be seen as everyone's responsibility. Staff members can report on their sales calls at regularly scheduled meetings. The impact of this tactic can be quickly calculated. For example, suppose that you have a staff of fifteen and each person makes one sales call a month; this is 180 extra sales calls a year that would not ordinarily be made.

Summary

This chapter has presented seventy-five tips on marketing. These suggestions are *guidelines* that can be adapted to any continuing education organization. It is important to conduct action-oriented research continuously so that these suggestions can be modified to fit your individual needs. You can thus develop the best possible marketing plans for your organization and avoid the common mistakes.

33

A Ten-Step Process to Ensure Success in Marketing

Robert G. Simerly

This handbook provides a comprehensive overview of marketing concepts and techniques that are used successfully by a wide variety of continuing education organizations. The emphasis is on useful ideas that can easily be adapted to meet the individual needs of continuing education organizations. This chapter condenses these major marketing concepts and techniques into a ten-step process. By undergoing this process, a continuing education organization can ensure its survival, growth, and constant renewal in the ever-changing demands of the marketplace. These ten principles are marked by a unifying theme. *Successful marketing is not an event or a specific activity. Rather, it is a process ensuring that an organization reaches its goals and objectives by exchanging its products, services, and knowledge for program registrations.*

Thus, continuing education leaders should strive to adapt the following ten-step process to their organizations.

1. *Establish a marketing-related research base.* The increase in literature on marketing research has resulted in the development of marketing into an academic discipline with specialized language, concepts, techniques, and guidelines for effective practice. To become an effective marketer, one must become a behavioral scientist, who constantly discovers new, effective methods to study human behavior in relation to the products, knowledge, and services offered by the continuing education organization. As a behavioral scientist, the successful marketer tends to avoid prescriptive solutions to problems. Instead, he or she concentrates on developing a research base useful in designing marketing techniques appropriate for the special needs of the organization.

Also important is an organizational data base of reliable information related to the following questions:

- What is our organization's average response rate for direct mail per thousand brochures and/or catalogues mailed?
- What variables tend to increase or decrease this response rate?
- What reliable and systematic processes have we developed to collect data on the public's perception of the quality of our programs and services?
- What is the appropriate marketing mix among direct mail, advertising, public relations, and personal sales?
- How do we institute processes that will enable us constantly to develop program ideas directly related to the various needs of our client groups?
- How do we establish reliable feedback channels to check whether copy and graphic design convey the image and tone we have determined to be appropriate for the organization?
- How do we determine our effectiveness in marketing? Have we agreed on specific measures of effectiveness, or do we tend to assume that no matter how effective our marketing is, we could have done better? How do we get feedback on our effectiveness in handling telephone requests for information and registrations?
- Do we have reliable tracking systems? Can we easily compose mailing lists of past participants to use for new programs?
- What portion of our budget is allocated for marketing? Does the marketing budget need to be increased or decreased?
- How do we compare in marketing effectiveness with other, similar organizations? Do we spend more or less on marketing? Are we more effective or less effective in our marketing efforts? Is the return on marketing investment greater or less than that of the competition?
- What kind of training and development program have we established to keep staff on the cutting edge of excellent practice in marketing? How do we reward staff for excellence in marketing effectiveness?

One of the requirements for successful leadership in continuing education is the use of action-oriented research methods to solve organizational marketing problems. Developing these behavioral science research techniques, learning how to interpret research data and make reliable inferences from them, and building a research base appropriate to the special needs of the organization are skills important to continuing education leaders.

2. *Write advertising copy that emphasizes the benefits participants will receive by enrolling.* It is important to establish positive images with the many publics being served so that they will react positively and register for programs. People pay money to register for a program in exchange for the benefits they believe they will receive by attending. This exchange principle should be firmly established in an organization before programs are designed. Program planners

should constantly ask themselves, "What benefits will participants receive by attending this particular program?"

Once the principle has been established, content and presentations can be designed to ensure that participants receive these benefits, and advertising copy can be written to emphasize these benefits. Thus, potential participants will not have to try to infer what the benefits are.

The most successful marketing efforts are those that guide potential registrants through the advertisement and encourage them to register for the program. There are clearly identifiable reasons to attend and these reasons are grounded in perceptions of the positive benefits to be received.

Often, the exchange principle operates at more than one level. For example, the exchange principle is important to those who decide to attend because of the personal benefits they feel they will receive. They, in turn, may need to convince others of the benefits, typically employers who may be investing in training and development to enhance their organizations.

3. *Integrate marketing concepts into the daily routine.* Successful marketing in continuing education should not be an event. It should be a normal process, part of everyday organizational life. When this attitude is encouraged, staff think strategically about marketing in relation to all programs and services. They assume responsibility for gathering the data that will enable them to market programs and services more effectively.

Incorporating excellence into program design, establishing excellence as a standard of service, and delivering on all established benefits come to be seen as the baseline for program development in the organization. New projects are planned under the guidance of comprehensive marketing plans. The reality of achieving financial goals as well as program goals is firmly established.

Each program unit begins to see itself as responsible for improving marketing efforts. The real difficulties of garnering predictable audience response are discussed openly. The impreciseness of measurement techniques in the behavioral sciences is acknowledged and compensated for. Results become more predictable with the development of a comprehensive data base related to the organization's marketing efforts.

Marketing is demystified as these issues are addressed. People feel better about themselves and their contributions to the organization as their skills increase. Marketing is the thread unifying all organizational units.

4. *Promote a comprehensive service orientation.* With the publication of Peters and Waterman's *In Search of Excellence* (1982), a chord was struck in the consciousness of organizational leaders throughout the country. The nation's businesses responded to the idea that excellence is based on a concern for people that emphasizes service to clients. Such an orientation should form the baseline for all marketing activities in continuing education. It makes it much easier to market both specific programs and the overall image and tone of the organization. And it is essential to development of a responsive and adaptive organization.

In promoting a service orientation in marketing activities, address these questions:

- How can we effectively measure our clients' satisfaction with our programs and services?
- How do we establish an ongoing process that assesses the strengths and weaknesses of our service orientation?
- How do we remain innovative in our approaches to client service?
- How do we develop special market niches for client service that are different from those of our competitors?
- How can we select and train personnel to incorporate client service into their daily routines?

5. *Design all marketing activities so that they enhance the image of the organization.* The public demands excellence in continuing education programs. Often, these images of excellence, often abstract, vary with the individual. Therefore, it is important to develop a clear, consistent, and positive set of images related to the continuing education organization and its programs, staff, and services. When people receive excellent service or increase their job skills by participating in programs, they view the continuing education organization in a positive light.

Therefore, all marketing should be designed to convey a positive message and thus enhance the overall image of the organization. These questions may help:

- Have we established an organizational mission and a set of goals and objectives? Is all marketing directly related to fulfilling this mission and achieving the established goals and objectives?
- Is the image conveyed by marketing activities consistent with the overall tone of the organization?
- Do others interpret the image in the way intended, or do significant inconsistencies exist between the intended response and the actual response? How does the organization reliably test this?
- Are all staff aware of the image the organization wants to convey so that they can direct their actions to projecting this image?
- Is success celebrated so that all staff are made aware of their colleagues' contributions to overall marketing efforts?

Image development should have a clear and consistent relationship to these organizational goals and objectives. If overall organizational goals and objectives are not in place and clearly understood by staff, image development will probably fall below average. However, if the goals and objectives are in place, and if staff have played a major role in establishing them, image enhancement will flow naturally and successfully.

6. *Price programs and services competitively.* The price of a program or service depends on (1) the number of registrants needed to break even according to financial goals, (2) realistic projections of the number of people expected to attend (based on research techniques and data that have proved reliable), (3)

registrants' perceptions of the benefits they will receive relative to what they perceive as a fair price for these benefits, and (4) perceptions of the value of the program or service relative to that of the competition. Pricing is a complex issue.

Too low a price conveys an image of inferiority in relation to the competition. Too high a price can drive off potential registrants, who either cannot afford the program even if they value the benefits or feel that the price is too high in relation to the value they place on the benefits.

It then becomes important to determine the amount people will pay for the programs and services offered by the organization. The answer is tied to the nature of the organization and the expectations of the client groups. For example, Harvard University has established a niche for itself in the continuing education market that emphasizes high-ticket programs based on selective screening of participants for admission. This approach works well for Harvard and is consistent with the overall image the institution wants to convey. Hence, its continuing education efforts have been very successful.

On the other hand, one for-profit continuing education organization has been very successful in developing one-day intensive seminars for secretaries throughout the United States. Their advertising prominently displays a price of $89, and clients are guaranteed their money back, no questions asked, if they are not satisfied with the quality of the program. The organization has been successful with this approach, because it found a special market niche consistent with its image and serviced it well.

Physicians often do not respond positively to modestly priced (for example, $75) continuing education programs, because they are accustomed to paying much higher fees for the quality they expect. On the other hand, nurses see a $75 registration fee as high because they belong to organizations that offer free training and development programs. In addition, nurses must often pay all or part of their registration fee from a salary much lower than that of physicians.

The principle is competitive pricing of programs and services. This involves (1) determining the fee expected by potential registrants, (2) finding out what the competition charges, (3) analyzing the fee needed to break even according to financial goals, and (4) developing and packaging the program so that it fills a marketing niche not currently filled effectively by the competition.

7. *Develop an effective marketing mix of direct mail, public relations, advertising, and personal sales.* Successful marketing depends on analyzing the goals of programs and services, developing market niches designed to fulfill unmet needs, and convincing people that they can fulfill these needs by registering for the continuing education activity. To accomplish this task, a balance must be struck among direct mail, public relations, advertising, and personal sales.

In most organizations, this marketing mix operates at two levels: for individual programs and for the organization as a whole. Effective operation on both levels simultaneously is the essence of a comprehensive marketing mix.

8. *Obtain professional assistance with graphic design.* Most people look at an advertising piece two to three seconds before deciding either to read it or

discard it. Therefore, design advertising so that it immediately attracts the reader's attention and invites him or her to read the entire piece. The reader's attention is attracted by (1) the content of the message and (2) the appearance of the piece. Professional help with graphic design will increase the chance that an advertising piece will intrigue the reader.

Hire one full-time designer or several free-lance graphic designers with whom you can build a long-term relationship. You must often work through several advertising projects before designers understand your organization and the image and tone you want to convey. Do not leave the interpretation of the image and tone up to the designers. Instead, discuss with them your organization and the overall image you want to convey to potential registrants. Explain that you want to emphasize benefits to registrants visually, and note the portions of the copy that emphasize benefits. Discuss illustration of cultural and ethnic diversity and avoidance of sex-role stereotyping in all art work. Stress the need to attain institutional recognition through the advertising. Discuss the research on direct-mail response with designers.

Even the best graphic designers can fail to identify the elements that generate positive reaction to direct-mail advertising. This form of advertising is specialized. Emphasize the need for bold design in line with the institutional image. Use past advertisements as examples of what works and what does not work. Ask designers to prepare rough sketches of major advertising pieces before proceeding to the finished product. In this way, you can make modifications and save money in the long run.

The time spent in developing this collegial, professional relationship with your graphic designer has its payoffs. If the two of you are on the same wavelength you can agree on the goals of each advertising piece. You will develop a common set of concepts and the language to describe these concepts. And above all, the designers will develop a psychological bond with you and the organization. They will commit themselves to the success of advertising projects. They can then recommend new approaches based on their understanding of the overall goals.

9. *Track results.* Tracking of all advertising and public relations efforts is necessary to establishment of a marketing-related research base. The most elaborate marketing plans and expensive advertising pieces are not effective if they do not produce the number of registrants required to break even with respect to the program's financial goals. Therefore, develop methods to track the results of every marketing project. Track all mailing lists to determine which list drew the most responses. The lists resulting in telephone and in-person registrations must also be identified. Design registration forms so that the mailing label, with the appropriate code, is returned with the registration, even if the respondent mails a copy of the registration form. Registration staff must be trained to make the appropriate inquiries during telephone registrations. For example, is the caller responding to a direct-mail brochure or to a newspaper ad? These data must be recorded in a uniform fashion so that they can be easily analyzed.

Tracking also means that the environment must be scanned to determine those program topics that are particularly marketable at the moment and those that have run their course. The public's perceptions of your organization and its programs must be accurately recorded. Is the feedback on the quality of your programs and service negative? If so, how are you dealing with it? Is the feedback positive? How is it dealt with? Both positive feedback and negative feedback are considered in a comprehensive environmental scanning system.

After the tracking data are collected, they must be analyzed and used to make recommendations on future marketing projects. These recommendations must then be transmitted to the staff. Team approaches to the aforementioned tasks are often effective.

10. *Continuously analyze the common marketing mistakes so you can avoid them.* Establish a system that detects problems in their early stages. In this way, the necessary corrective action can be taken before the organization and/or program suffers negative consequences. In monitoring these common mistakes, ask the following questions:

- What variables in the marketing mix are most likely to lead to problems?
- Do you discuss the common marketing mistakes with staff to increase their sensitivity to potential problems, or do you limit such discussions to key program planners?
- Do you reward those staff members who detect the early warning signs of trouble?
- When problems reoccur, do you make the necessary changes, even if it involves addressing complex issues?
- At meetings, do you clearly communicate to staff that their involvement in all marketing activities is a high priority?

Summary

These ten steps are practical suggestions that can be adapted to the individual needs of continuing education organizations. They acknowledge that successful marketing is not a particular event or series of campaigns. Marketing is most successful when it is woven into the daily fabric of organizational life. Excellence in service to clients becomes an overarching organizational goal. All marketing then flows naturally and systematically from this major goal.

Resources

A. Seminars, Workshops,
   and Independent Study Courses
   on Marketing

B. University Executive Development Programs
   in Marketing

C. Annotated Bibliography of Useful Books

D. Magazines and Journals on Marketing

E. Marketing-Related Organizations
   and Associations

F. Specialized Reference Works

G. Clipping Bureaus

Resources

This section lists a wide variety of marketing resources of interest to continuing education professionals.

- Seminars, workshops, and independent study courses on marketing
- University executive development programs in marketing
- Annotated bibliography of useful books
- Magazines and journals on marketing
- Marketing-related organizations and associations
- Specialized reference works
- Clipping bureaus

Continuing education professionals will find this section invaluable in helping them remain current. By browsing through the seminars, workshops, and independent study courses, readers can develop a plan to attend selected programs over a three- or four-year period. After reviewing the lists of useful books and magazines and journals, professionals can compile their own reading lists to enhance their professional development in marketing, ordering books, magazines, and journals for their personal libraries as well as for libraries in their organizations. From the list of professional associations and organizations, they can choose those they would like to join. Thus, this section can assist continuing educators in enhancing their self-directed learning.

A. Seminars, Workshops, and Independent Study Courses on Marketing

A number of organizations regularly offer marketing seminars and workshops. The following list contains some that have proved to be popular with continuing education professionals.

American Demographics' Annual Conference on Trends and Lifestyles
American Demographics, Inc.
P.O. Box 68
Ithaca, NY 14851
(800) 828-1133

This annual conference offers more than fifteen sessions on such important issues as segmenting the market by life-style, attracting the 55-plus market, capturing the spending power of the youth market, using demographics in data base marketing, and responding to the changing needs of the work force. There is an extensive exhibit area at the conference.

American Management Association
135 West 50th Street
New York, NY 10020
(212) 586-8100

The American Management Association sponsors workshops as well as independent study courses on a wide variety of marketing topics. For example, a review of their most recent catalogue reveals such topics as "Strategic Marketing Planning Using Lotus 1,2,3," "How to Analyze the Competition," "Pricing Strategies and Practices," and "Fundamentals of Direct-Mail Marketing." Request their catalogue of workshops as well as their independent study catalogue.

American Society of Association Executives
The ASAE Building
1575 I Street, NW
Washington, DC 20005
(202) 626-2723

The American Society of Association Executives is the association designed to serve professionals who are leaders in many associations throughout the country. ASAE publishes a magazine as well as many other helpful booklets. In addition, ASAE offers many marketing-related conferences and workshops and a national marketing certification program for association executives that involves completion of a specified number of continuing education programs.

American Society for Training and Development
1630 Duke Street
Box 1443
Alexandria, VA 22313
(703) 683-8100

The American Society for Training and Development is designed to meet the needs of professionals in human resource training and development. ASTD publishes a magazine and various directories, such as their training video directory, and also sponsors conferences and workshops throughout the year. Many of their programs address the marketing needs of continuing education professionals.

The College Board
45 Columbus Avenue
New York, NY 10023-6917
(212) 713-8000

The College Board regularly conducts two-day marketing seminars for professionals working with adult learners. Among their past presenters are such professionals as Harold Hodgkinson, Dorothy Durkin, Richard Fischer, Gayle Hendrickson, Mary Hendry, Laurence Smith, Dennis Tarr, and Billy Wireman.

The Continuing Education Forum
14618 Tyler Foote Road, Suite 888
Nevada City, CA 95959
(916) 292-3000

Headed by Francis E. (Skip) Andrew, The Continuing Education Forum is an organization devoted to assisting all types of continuing education program providers do a better job. The organization consults with seminar providers, markets seminars for their own company, prepares brochures for numerous meeting providers, and maintains a national network of experts who can assist continuing education professionals in solving a wide variety of problems.

Gralla Conferences
1515 Broadway
New York, NY 10036
(212) 868-1300

Two Gralla workshops that continuing education professionals will find particularly helpful are "How to Negotiate Hotel Contracts" and "How to Negotiate with the Airlines." Bruce Lucker, president of Lucker & Company, a consulting firm to the hotel, convention, and meeting industries, is one of their presenters. The workshops contain practical information helpful to continuing education professionals who do extensive negotiations with hotels and airlines. Gralla Conferences also offers a wide variety of other programs.

Lakewood Publications and Conferences
50 South Ninth Street
Minneapolis, MN 55402
(612) 333-0471

This organization publishes *Training* magazine, which is related to human resource training and development, and holds conferences and workshops throughout the United States. These programs often have significant sessions devoted to continuing education marketing issues. For example, a recent national conference on training issues had workshop sessions entitled "Marketing, Promoting, and Gaining Support for Training," "The Dollars and $Sense of Training: Can You Justify Them?" and "Powerful Presentations That Get Results."

LERN (Learning Resources Network)
1554 Hayes Drive
Manhattan, KS 66502
(913) 539-5376

LERN conducts a wide variety of marketing programs for professionals. A phone call will put you on a mailing list for upcoming programs. LERN also publishes a number of workbooks, books, and monographs related to marketing for continuing education. Members receive free consulting services, including written critiques of program materials. Three recent LERN workshops offered at major cities throughout the United States were "Designing Brochures for Results," "Advertising and Promotion," and "Marketing Techniques for Office Staff."

The Marketing Federation
7141 Gulf Boulevard
St. Petersburg Beach, FL 33706
(813) 367-5629

Anver Suleiman's name has become synonymous with the marketing of meetings. Teacher, writer, speaker, consultant, and day-to-day practitioner, Suleiman sponsors an annual two-day marketing seminar each year as well as other marketing programs at convenient locations throughout the country. At these programs, a wide variety of marketing experts update issues important to continuing education. The Federation will also custom design a program for your organization.

National Association of Exposition Managers
334 East Garfield Road
P.O. Box 377
Aurora, OH 44202
(216) 562-8255

This group of professionals strives to make the trade show marketing medium the best it can be. The current membership is 2,400 in five different categories. Education has been and continues to be the number one concern. NAEM publishes many helpful works on how to plan and manage the exhibit function. In addition, NAEM holds seminars and conferences throughout the year and publishes a newsletter six times a year and an annual directory entitled "Who's Who in Exposition Management."

National University Continuing Education Association
One Dupont Circle, NW, Suite 420
Washington, DC 20036
(202) 659-3130

The National University Continuing Education Association is an institutional-based membership organization devoted to assisting continuing education professionals in colleges and universities. Members include those who receive the newsletter as well as the various reports and directories published throughout the year. In addition, each fall, NUCEA holds regional conferences for continuing education professionals, and each spring, an annual meeting. NUCEA sponsors seminars, conferences, and workshops on a wide variety of issues related to marketing. In fact, one division of the organization is devoted to people with interests in marketing continuing education programs and services.

Office of Professional Development
Clemson University
P.O. Box 912
Clemson, SC 29633
(803) 656-3983

Ralph Elliott, Director of Professional Development at Clemson, conducts marketing seminars throughout the United States. One of his two-day seminars is entitled "Increasing Registrations and Revenue Through Effective Seminar/ Conference Marketing." He will custom design a marketing program for your continuing education organization.

Performance Seminar Group
11 Commerce Street
Norwalk, CT 06850
(203) 852-0429

The Performance Seminar Group is especially known for its one-day workshops held in major cities. Examples of recent seminars include one-day sessions on "Designing and Preparing Camera-Ready Artwork," "Fundamentals of Direct Mail," and "Techniques for Telephone Marketing." Among their list of presenters are Chip Chapin, David Morris, Horace Klafter, Steven Isaac, and Deanna Maneker.

B. University Executive Development
Programs in Marketing

A number of universities regularly schedule residential marketing programs. Although these programs are not designed to deal specifically with marketing for continuing education, the principles they teach can be adapted to continuing education organizations. These programs range in length from several days to several weeks. A phone call to the following institutions will place you on their mailing lists for upcoming programs.

Harvard Business School
Executive Education Programs
Glass Hall–Soldiers Field Road
Boston, MA 02163
(617) 495-6226

Northwestern University
Executive Programs
Kellogg Graduate School of Management
James L. Allen Center
2169 Sheridan Road
Evanston, IL 60201
(312) 864-9270

Purdue University
Krannert School of Management
State and Grant Streets
West Lafayette, IN 47907
(317) 494-9700

Stanford University
Office of Executive Programs
Graduate School of Business
Stanford, CA 94305-5015
(415) 723-3341

University of California, Berkeley
Executive Education Programs
School of Business
350 Barrows Hall
Berkeley, CA 94720
(415) 642-4735

University of California, Los Angeles
Executive Education
Graduate School of Management
Room 2381
Los Angeles, CA 90024
(213) 825-2001

University of Chicago
Programs for Executives and Professionals
Office of Continuing Education
5835 South Kimbark Avenue
Chicago, IL 60637
(312) 702-1724

University of Illinois, Urbana-Champaign
Executive Development Center
College of Business Administration
205 David Kinley Hall
1407 West Gregory Drive
Urbana, IL 61801
(217) 333-4552

University of Michigan
Executive Education Center
School of Business Administration
Ann Arbor, MI 48106
(313) 763-4229

University of Pennsylvania
The Wharton School
Executive Education
200 Vance Hall
Philadelphia, PA 19104
(215) 898-1776

University of Texas, Austin
Management Development Programs
Graduate School of Business
P.O. Box 7337
Austin, TX 78713
(512) 471-5893

University of Virginia
The Darden School
P.O. Box 6550
Charlottesville, VA 22906
(804) 924-3900

University of Wisconsin, Madison
Executive Development Programs
Communications Program
221 Lowell Hall
610 Langdon Street
Madison, WI 53703
(608) 262-3447

C. Annotated Bibliography of Useful Books

Albrecht, K., and Zemke, R. *Service America! Doing Business in the New Economy*. Homewood, Ill.: Dow Jones-Irwin, 1985.

This book provides an excellent analysis of how an emphasis on the service orientation of an organization can be the best possible marketing strategy. Service management is based on the active management of thousands of "moments of truth." These are the points of interaction between the organization and its clients. Numerous examples illustrate how management of this interaction must be at the heart of all marketing efforts. This book should be required reading for managers in all organizations.

Beder, Hal (ed.). *Marketing Continuing Education*. New Directions for Continuing Education, no. 31. San Francisco: Jossey-Bass, 1986.

This excellent edited source book covers definition and analysis of the market, development of program offerings, promotion of continuing education programs, pricing and fee management, and ethical issues in marketing and continuing education. Readers will find many useful ideas.

Bloch, T. M., Upah, G. D., and Zeithaml, V. *Services Marketing in a Changing Environment*. Chicago: American Marketing Association, 1985.

This edited work emphasizes how services can be marketed, particularly within a larger institutional environment. The importance of tracking service expectations and performance over time is emphasized. The wide variety of articles are designed to help professionals think strategically about the marketing of services.

Block, P. *The Empowered Manager: Positive Political Skills at Work*. San Francisco: Jossey-Bass, 1987.

The central idea of this book is that organizational politics, as we usually see it, tends to work against people accepting additional responsibility in our organizations. Block examines ways in which people can become political in very positive ways. There are many good, practical hints on how to become powerful advocates for our offices in a manner that does not alienate those around us. This book is an important extension of Rosabeth Kanter's ideas presented in *Men and Women of the Corporation*. Her definition of power is the ability to get your fair share of resources in the organization to do the job you were hired to do. This definition of power is very positive. Block suggests many ways to become political without becoming manipulative. Organizational politics also requires that we instill a sense of entrepreneurial spirit in our organizations. According to Block, "Within each of us is the ability to create an organization of our own choosing." This very insightful book gets top marks for its readability and practical tips for success within organizations.

Bobrow, E. E., and Bobrow, M. D. *Marketing Handbook*. Vols. I and II. Homewood, Ill.: Dow Jones–Irwin, 1985.

This excellent handbook covers marketing from A to Z. Volume I is devoted to marketing practices, and Volume II, to marketing management.

Among the topics covered are marketing to the public sector, services marketing, purchase behavior, market surveys, development of marketing goals and strategies, and the impact of the law on marketing.

Book, A. C., and Schick, D. C. *Fundamentals of Copy and Layout*. Lincolnwood, Ill.: NTC Business Books, 1986.

This workbook might be called a first workbook for copy writing. The many useful ideas presented can be adapted from the business world to continuing education programs. Topics include ad research, ad writing, elements of layout, and print and broadcast media. Throughout the workbook are worksheets for practicing the principles presented. A glossary of terms useful to the beginning copywriter concludes the book.

Breen, G. E. *Do-It-Yourself-Marketing Research*. New York: McGraw-Hill, 1977.

The strong point of this excellent, short book is the practical approach it takes to market research. In fact, it even includes sample questionnaires for written responses and structured interview questions for oral responses. It covers evaluation of problems, market research study planning, use of secondary sources, mail questionnaire studies, individual and group interviews, and telephone research. Breen has written an excellent primer on market research applicable to a wide variety of organizations.

Brochure Distribution. Manhattan, Kans.: Learning Resources Network, 1987.

This short work covers the many ways to distribute brochures, including direct mail. There is helpful advice on using racks to display brochures and enlisting children to distribute brochures. Guidelines to increase effectiveness of brochure distribution are also given.

Burnett, E. *The Complete Direct Mail List Handbook*. Englewood Cliffs, N.J.: Prentice-Hall, 1988.

This 736-page handbook is a comprehensive, definitive work on direct-mail marketing. It contains everything you need to know about lists and how to use them for greater profit in your organization. During a career that spans thirty years in direct-mail marketing, Ed Burnett has helped mailers select over two billion names. The thesis of the book is that list selection is one of the most critical factors in guaranteeing success in direct-mail marketing. In addition to providing hundreds of practical hints, Burnett includes a special section on mastering the mathematics of testing mailing lists. This book should be a part of the professional library of every continuing education professional.

Buzzell, R. D. (ed.) *Marketing in an Electronic Age*. Boston: Harvard Business School Press, 1985.

Robert D. Buzzell of the Harvard Business School has edited one of the best collections on preparing for the future of marketing in an electronic age. Among the issues addressed are the changed U.S. media environment, adaptation of advertisers to new electronic media, development of new marketing strategies in the information industry, and the coming revolution in marketing theory. The articles in this book, contributed by various experts in the field, are very thought provoking.

Chapman, E. A., Jr. *Exhibit Marketing: A Survival Guide for Managers.* New York: McGraw-Hill, 1987.

This first full-length book on the use of exhibits as an integral part of effective marketing was written by the person who created the exhibit management system for the AT&T division that markets high-technology equipment. Chapman's exhibiting ideas and concepts have been widely covered in the press. This book contains a wide variety of checklists, forms for budget planning, and suggestions for additional resources. It covers preparation of exhibits, evaluation of exhibits on the basis of cost, measurement of the return on investment, promotional activity before and during the show, and hospitality management. This very practical book is full of many helpful hints on how to produce effective exhibits as an important part of overall marketing.

Crompton, J. L., and Lamb, C. W., Jr. *Marketing Government and Social Services.* New York: Wiley, 1986.

These authors have performed an important service in writing a book aimed at marketing government and social services. They discuss how to decide what business you're in, how to develop a market plan, how to evaluate marketing efforts, how to identify potential markets, and how to price. The sections on advertising, public service announcements, and personal selling are especially helpful.

Desatnick, R. L. *Managing to Keep the Customer: How to Achieve and Maintain Superior Customer Service Throughout the Organization.* San Francisco: Jossey-Bass, 1987.

Desatnick has researched businesses that have become known for their excellent customer service and has extracted the principles that worked. He provides step-by-step details that others can adapt to their organizations. He addresses interview techniques that identify staff with good service potential. In addition, he considers how management training programs can be implemented to encourage a service orientation on the part of all staff. One of his key points is that customer relations mirrors staff relations. You can never hope to produce good customer relations without actively planning for the best possible working environment for staff. This involves helping people to participate in the goal-setting process for the organization, helping people to develop a psychological bond with the organization, and measuring on a regular basis the effectiveness in achieving these aims. The appendix of the book is particularly helpful because it contains a sample job description for a training director, a sample employee opinion survey, a sample exit interview questionnaire, and examples of customer opinion surveys. Also included are a sample internal client survey, management climate and leadership effectiveness survey results, and some general management skill suggestions.

Direct Marketing Creative Guild. *Direct Marketing Design: The Graphics of Direct Mail Response Marketing*. New York: PBC International, Inc., 1985.

Continuing education leaders will find that this book helps them to think strategically about the graphic design process in direct-mail response. There are hundreds of illustrations of bold, effective direct-mail campaigns. Even though the examples are not from the continuing education setting, the principles can be easily adapted to direct-mail marketing for continuing education programs.

Dobmeyer, E. *Registration Techniques to Increase Enrollments*. Manhattan, Kans.: Learning Resources Network, 1986.

This thirty-five-page book contains many very practical tips on what can be done during the registration process to help increase enrollments. It covers the proper location for your registration form on a brochure, use of a second registration form to increase enrollments, and the reasons credit card registrants often sign up for more courses. In addition, it offers hints on registration copy for your brochure, registration methods, incorporation of marketing research into registration, and evaluation of registration policies.

Donnelly, J. H., and George, W. R. *Marketing of Services*. Chicago: American Marketing Association, 1981.

This book comprises the proceedings of the American Marketing Association's 1981 Special Educators' Conference. This was the first AMA conference to deal solely with services marketing; thus, the volume contains articles on services marketing by a wide variety of national experts. Among the issues addressed are the need for marketing management to be different for services, the role of personal selling, the effects of marketing advertising on the quality of professional services, and strategies for marketing professional services. In addition, each article contains an excellent bibliography.

Ehrenkranz, L. B., and Kahn, G. R. *Public Relations/Publicity: A Key Link in Communications*. New York: Fairchild, 1983.

This book is designed to be a basic primer for public relations. It covers such basic topics as press release writing, use of photographs, presentation strategy, contact with the media, press conferences and press parties, and broadcast techniques. It is a useful, how-to-do-it book for those just getting started in public relations.

Elliott, R. D. *House Lists: How to Create a More Responsive In-House Mailing List*. Manhattan, Kans.: Learning Resources Network, 1987.

This book provides an excellent, short analysis of the assembly, mainte-nance, and use of house mailing lists. Of particular help is the step-by-step guide that helps readers to decide whether it is more cost effective to maintain in-house lists or purchase outside lists. This is one of the best short, practical guides to the many variables involved in decisions on house list maintenance.

Elliott, R. D. *Marketing In-House Seminars.* Manhattan, Kans.: Learning Resources Network, 1986.

Elliott has produced a very useful manual for the marketing of in-house seminars. Among the topics covered are techniques, different in-house positioning strategies, effective marketing tips, and generation of inquiries and leads. The manual also contains many practical forms, tips, guidelines, and suggestions on avoiding the mistakes most often made in marketing in-house seminars. This very authoritative and practical work addresses the special needs of a very important aspect of continuing education marketing.

Farlow, H. *Publicizing and Promoting Programs.* New York: McGraw-Hill, 1979.

Very much a how-to-do-it book with many useful ideas on effective publicization and promotion of programs, this book covers such practical topics as publicizing and promoting programs on radio and television, preparing a press release, and developing special-interest mailing lists. The book highlights useful hints on almost every page and discusses how these hints can be implemented within a continuing education setting.

Fenno, B. *Helping Your Business Grow: 101 Dynamic Ideas in Marketing.* New York: American Management Association, 1982.

This highly readable book lives up to its title, by providing many marketing guidelines that continuing educators can adapt to their individual requirements. The thesis is that effective marketers promote their products in relation to the needs of the buyer. All 101 ideas are worth contemplating.

Fischer, R. B. *Personal Contact in Marketing.* Manhattan, Kans.: Learning Resources Network, 1984.

A sixty-two-page guide to the use of personal contact to increase marketing effectiveness, this book explains how to move from the office into the field, how to build ongoing personal linkages, how to rethink office practices such as telephone response, and how to spend more time listening to those you serve. There are many very helpful practical tips throughout this work.

Freedman, L. *Quality in Continuing Education.* San Francisco: Jossey-Bass, 1987.

Although not devoted exclusively to marketing, this book does cover an essential part of program marketing—monitoring the quality of continuing education. Freedman describes how one defines quality, plans for it, and evaluates it in continuing education programs. His analysis provides both theoretical and practical guidelines for improvement of program design, selection of faculty and staff, and internal quality control mechanisms. In addition, he devotes a special chapter to marketing. Continuing education professionals will find many useful suggestions in this book. Quality programs are much easier to market.

Goldman, J. *Public Relations in the Marketing Mix: Introducing Vulnerability Relations.* Chicago: Crain Books, 1984.

In this very good primer on developing effective public relations, the author's thesis is that traditional marketing audits do not reveal an organization's vulnerabilities but, instead, highlight its strengths. Nevertheless, an understanding of one's vulnerabilities is important to development of an effective public relations campaign. This interesting approach has not yet gained wide attention in marketing/public relations circles.

Greenley, G. *The Strategic and Operational Planning of Marketing.* London: McGraw-Hill, 1986.

Greenley's book is unique in that it relates marketing directly to the strategic planning process in organizations. Thus, marketing is presented not as an isolated, specialized act but rather as one of the skills all managers must incorporate into their daily behavior. Among the issues covered are development of a planning framework, setting of organizational objectives and conduct of a strategic audit, development of marketing strategies, and implementation of plans.

Harper, R. *Mailing List Strategies: A Guide to Direct Mail Success.* New York: McGraw-Hill, 1986.

Simply put, this is one of the best, most comprehensive books available on mailing list strategies. Harper is president of Klied Company, Inc., list consultants in New York. She has put together a highly readable, practical book that all continuing education professionals should have in their reference library. Harper addresses why measuring the rate of return on direct mail is both a science and an art, completely analyzes the renting of mailing lists, describes what service companies can do for you, explains how you can do a reliable cost analysis for your organization in relation to rate of return for direct mail, and describes list testing. She is a seasoned pro and includes many practical examples, guidelines, and hints for everyone involved with direct-mail marketing.

Hayes, R. S., and Elmore, G. B. *Marketing for Your Growing Business.* New York: Wiley, 1985.

This very practical primer is intended to assist a small business with its marketing plans. Hayes and Elmore make many helpful suggestions on developing a calendar for marketing, developing a marketing plan, conducting low-cost market research, and planning for an effective overall image. Continuing education providers in smaller organizations will find this book to be particularly helpful.

Heskett, J. L. *Managing in the Service Economy*. Boston: Harvard Business School Press, 1986.

Although not written especially for continuing education professionals interested in marketing, this book provides many practical suggestions on managing effectively in the service economy. Continuing education professionals can adapt these ideas to their own organizations. He presents four major concepts: (1) targeting a market segment, (2) conceptualizing consumers' perceptions of the service, (3) developing an operational strategy, and (4) implementing an effective delivery system for services—a system that transforms vision into action. There is also an excellent chapter on the future of the services industry. Continuing education professionals will find the discussion and analysis quite thought provoking.

Higgins, D. (ed.). *The Art of Writing Advertising*. Lincolnwood, Ill.: NTC Business Books, 1987.

Higgins interviews five professionals in the advertising field: William Bernbach, Leo Burnett, George Griggin, David Ogilvy, and Rosser Reevers. The result is a concise series of good advertising principles and practical advice for today's copywriters. This book offers readers an opportunity to learn the views of top professionals in the field on advertising today and the direction in which it is moving. All of the contributors emphasize the need to look for the unique qualities of the product of service and to communicate these through strong and accurate copy.

Hodgson, R. S. *The Dartnell Direct Mail and Mail Order Handbook*. (3rd ed.) Chicago: Dartnell Corp., 1980.

This third edition of the popular handbook comprises 1,538 pages of straightforward discussion and analysis of effective strategies for direct-mail marketing. It is probably the most comprehensive book ever written on this subject. Public reaction to direct mail, guidelines for direct mail, planning of direct-mail campaigns, and selection and maintenance of mailing lists are thoroughly discussed. Hodgson also analyzes reply cards, letters and envelopes that draw the best responses, and cost savings in the production process.

Holtz, H. *The Direct Marketer's Workbook*. New York: Wiley, 1986.

In this absolutely first-rate book containing practical tips for direct-mail marketing, Holtz covers everything from the needs and motivations of your audience to copy-preparation aids. Particularly helpful is the section on computerizing your marketing operation. Scattered throughout the workbook are helpful forms that can be customized to your individual marketing operation.

Keim, W. A., and Keim, M. C. (eds.) *Marketing the Program*. New Directions for Community Colleges, no. 36. San Francisco: Jossey-Bass, 1980.

This collection of marketing articles is aimed specifically at the community college. Topics include rethinking marketing in the community college,

college strategies for implementing a marketing plan, marketing and the printed media, and market segmentation. The evaluation of marketing practices in community colleges is also considered. This book represents the first collection of articles to address marketing for community colleges. The articles are brief and practical, and a good bibliography is provided.

Kotler, P. *Marketing Management: Analysis, Planning, and Control.* (5th ed.) Englewood Cliffs, N.J.: Prentice-Hall, 1984.

This comprehensive overview of the marketing process addresses strategic planning and the marketing management process; the marketing information system and marketing research; market measurement and forecasting; market segmentation, targeting, and positioning; and marketing strategies during periods of shortages, inflation, and recession. This book is in its fifth edition, attesting to its popularity with marketing students and professionals.

Kotler, P. *Marketing for Nonprofit Organizations.* Englewood Cliffs, N.J.: Prentice-Hall, 1982.

Kotler continues his definition of marketing as the "effective management by an organization of its exchange relations with its various markets and publics." He uses examples from museums, colleges and universities, symphonies, blood banks, churches, and police departments to illustrate how marketing concepts originally developed for the profit sector can successfully be adapted to the nonprofit sector.

Kotler, P., and Andreasen, A. R. *Strategic Marketing for Nonprofit Organizations.* New York: Prentice-Hall, 1987.

This fully revised edition of an excellent work offers practical advice on how to improve your services, communicate effectively, define objectives, and sell your organization's image to the public. Tips are offered on efficient promotion procedures to cut costs, save time, and increase the satisfaction of your target market. In addition, the authors discuss how to design an effective marketing mix and develop a customer orientation appropriate to your organization.

Kotler, P., and Fox, K. *Strategic Marketing for Educational Institutions.* Englewood Cliffs, N.J.: Prentice-Hall, 1985.

Continuing education professionals who work in educational institutions will find this very fine marketing book aimed at a specific segment of the market to be particularly helpful. It provides a comprehensive analysis of the planning tools needed to make institutional marketing more effective without relying on quick fixes or gimmicks. Case studies illustrate effective ways to market educational institutions.

Lacznick, G. R., and Murphy, P. *Marketing Ethics: Guidelines for Managers.* Lexington, Mass.: Lexington Books, 1985.

Although generally geared to the marketing of industrial and business products, this work gives excellent insight into major ethical problems in marketing. Of particular interest to continuing education practitioners are the chapters entitled "Incorporating Marketing Ethics into the Organization" and "Code of Ethics." A sample code of ethics is provided.

Laric, M. V., and Stiff, R. *VISICALC for Marketing and Sales.* Englewood Cliffs, N.J.: Prentice-Hall, 1984.

This excellent work on the use of personal computer electronic spreadsheets for marketing addresses the concept and power of spreadsheet models, problem solving with spreadsheets, cost analysis and pricing, and allocation of promotional resources. The reader is assumed to have a knowledge of VISICALC. Many suggestions and models of a wide variety of marketing applications are offered.

Leffel, L. G. *Designing Brochures for Results.* Manhattan, Kans.: Learning Resources Network, 1983.

This fifty-two-page book gives practical tips on designing brochures and increasing enrollment in continuing education programs. The author, an experienced continuing education marketer, analyzes why some brochures work and others do not and offers guidelines for writing effective copy. This book constitutes a useful nuts-and-bolts approach to brochure design.

Lenz, E. *Creating and Marketing Programs in Continuing Education.* New York: McGraw-Hill, 1980.

This book is particularly helpful because it is written by a continuing education professional for other professionals. Among the topics covered are development and marketing of programs for general and special audiences, and inclusion of grants and contracts in the overall marketing plan. Evaluation of and accountability for continuing education programs are also considered.

Levinson, J. C. *Guerrilla Marketing: Secrets for Making Big Profits from Your Small Business.* Boston: Houghton Mifflin, 1984.

Guerrilla Marketing is for the small business. It approaches marketing from every angle. It emphasizes consistency in message, quality, and cost effectiveness. Levinson provides many practical tips that can be adopted by continuing education organizations. Among the topics covered are the secret to obtaining free research, development of a creative marketing program, use of personal letters and of circulars and brochures, advertising in the classified sector, and newspaper advertising. This very practical book is full of hundreds of ideas adaptable to continuing education organizations.

Ley, D. F. *The Best Seller.* Newport Beach, Calif.: Sales Success Press, 1986.

An important aspect of marketing continuing education programs is the personal selling that occurs between the continuing education organization and its clients. Although this book is not written specifically for a continuing education audience, its principles are easily generalizable. This book provides one of the best analyses of the selling process and offers many practical suggestions for increasing sales effectiveness. According to the American Management Association, "It is the finest book ever written on selling."

Lovelock, C. H. *Services Marketing.* Englewood Cliffs, N.J.: Prentice-Hall, 1984.

Noting that the service sector of our economy is twice as large as the manufacturing sector, Lovelock provides a comprehensive overview of services marketing. He emphasizes the increasingly competitive nature of services marketing and analyzes methods to position your organization in the appropriate market niche in relation to this competition. His thesis is that the special nature of service organizations requires a distinctive approach to marketing strategy.

Lovelock, C. H., and Weinberg, C. B. *Marketing for Public and Nonprofit Managers.* New York: Wiley, 1984.

Managers in public and nonprofit organizations have a set of marketing issues different from those of the for-profit sector. This book does a very fine job of analyzing these differences, discussing specific case histories and examples, and of providing guidelines and strategies for managers of public and nonprofit organizations. In addition, Lovelock and Weinberg highlight the marketing similarities with the for-profit sector and show how many marketing concepts apply equally to both sectors.

Luther, W. M. *The Marketing Plan: How to Prepare and Implement It.* New York: American Management Association, 1982.

In this book, Luther attempts to walk the reader through the development of a marketing plan. There is an emphasis on developing measurable objectives and relating these to overall organizational planning. The author sees development of a marketing plan as an integral part of overall strategic planning. He also considers public relations as a topic separate from advertising and illustrates the importance of integrating this into an overall marketing plan.

McCaffrey, M., with Derloshon, J. *Personal Marketing Strategies: How to Sell Yourself, Your Ideas, and Your Services.* New York: Prentice-Hall, 1983.

Filled with many practical tips on marketing your organization and its services, this book discusses creation of an effective public image, development of relationships, retention of clients, and the setting of marketing and selling goals. The unique feature of this book is its emphasis on the personal aspects of marketing versus organizational aspects. There are many helpful hints on generating commitment and cooperation and on increasing effectiveness daily in your organizational role of marketing ideas and services.

McCann, J. M. *The Marketing Workbench: Using Computers for Better Performance.* Homewood, Ill.: Dow Jones-Irwin, 1986.

This book is geared to product marketing for business. However, it provides a very good overview of the many uses of computers in effective marketing. Differing philosophies and approaches to marketing, marketing trends, and the impact of computers on marketing and management are analyzed. A special section is devoted to identifying future issues related to computers and marketing. The thesis is that all organizations must prepare for the increasing knowledge explosion.

McDonald, M. H. *Marketing Plans: How to Prepare Them—How to Use Them.* New York: Franklin Watts, Inc., 1985.

This excellent work provides a comprehensive conceptual base for developing a marketing plan that includes a detailed analysis of how to do a market audit. Throughout is an emphasis on the integration of marketing into the total planning process. As a result, there is extensive discussion on relating marketing to the establishment of specific organizational goals and objectives. Unique features are an analysis of forecasting and organizing for market planning and specific guidelines for designing and implementing a marketing planning system.

Meyers, G. C., with Holusha, J. *When It Hits the Fan: Managing the Nine Crises of Business.* Boston: Houghton Mifflin, 1986.

Much has been written about organizational change; however, little has been written on crisis management in organizations. Any comprehensive marketing plan should address this important issue. Although not written from a continuing education perspective, this insightful book provides many important lessons for continuing educators. It is written from a practical point of view by a former chairperson of American Motors, who provides a provocative analysis of how to manage crises. The guidelines and analysis can easily be translated to continuing education organizations.

Mitchell, A. *The Nine American Lifestyles: Who We Are and Where We Are Going.* New York: Warner Books, 1983.

In this now classic work in the psychographic literature of marketing, Mitchell has made a major impact on marketing through his VALS (values, attitudes, and life-styles) typology. The VALS typology comprises four comprehensive groups that are divided into nine life-styles. Each life-style is intended to describe a unique way of life directed by values, drives, beliefs, needs, dreams, and special points of view. Such psychographic data have gained wide acceptance among professional marketers during the last five years, and this book is the authoritative volume. The many good ideas in this book have important implications for the way continuing educators market their programs.

Nash, E. L. *The Direct Marketing Handbook.* New York: McGraw-Hill, 1984.

This comprehensive, nine-hundred-page handbook covers every aspect of direct marketing from development of a marketing strategy, to initiation of a planning process, to use of media, to such specific applications as catalogue sales, fund-raising, and international direct marketing. Each of the sixty chapters is written by an expert who has concentrated on synthesizing research into a series of practical guidelines for implementing suggested direct marketing strategies.

Osborne, S. G. *Electronic Direct Marketing*. Englewood Cliffs, N.J.: Prentice-Hall, 1984.

As a result of the explosion of marketing through electronic delivery, continuing educators, especially those in the for-profit sector, increasingly are integrating electronic direct marketing (EDM) into their overall marketing plans. In fact, EDM is the fastest growing of all marketing techniques because of its cost effectiveness in reaching large audiences. EDM includes television and radio advertising, cable TV ads, electronic mail, and telemarketing. This book is a good practical guide to the intricacies of electronic direct marketing.

O'Shaughnessy, J. *Competitive Marketing: A Strategic Approach*. Boston: George Allen & Unwin, 1984.

Another very good introductory marketing text, *Competitive Marketing* addresses why consumers buy, how they choose, and by what are they influenced. Particularly helpful is Part II, which deals with customers, markets, and competition. This analysis of psychographic data and consumer behavior is very thought provoking.

Pentland, L. *Salesbook Spreadsheets*. New York: McGraw-Hill, 1985.

In another excellent book devoted to the use of electronic spreadsheets to predict annual results, forecast sales, monitor cash flow, and figure break-even points and profitability, the reader is assumed to have a knowledge of spreadsheets on personal computers.

Promoting Issues and Ideas: A Guide to Public Relations for Nonprofit Organizations. New York: The Foundation Center, 1987.

This book is one of the best concise public relations guides available for nonprofit organizations. There are helpful hints on everything from speaking before the public to effective lobbying. Utilization of new communications technologies and development of a comprehensive public relations plan are also considered.

Rados, D. L. *Marketing for Nonprofit Organizations*. Boston: Auburn House, 1981.

In an excellent work on marketing for the nonprofit sector, Rados effectively uses case studies to illustrate marketing concepts. He explains how to conduct a market audit, organize a sales force, and effectively introduce marketing concepts into the nonprofit organization. Especially helpful is his discussion of pricing, which includes an analysis of cost-based pricing and demand pricing.

Rapp, S., and Collins, T. *Maximarketing: The New Direction in Promotion, Advertising, and Marketing Strategy.* New York: McGraw-Hill, 1987.

This landmark book is the *Megatrends* and *Future Shock* of marketing. The authors' thesis is that effective marketing is increasingly based on a segmented, decentralized market for which special marketing methods must be devised. They assert that marketing is in a stage of transformation, from mass marketing, to segmented marketing, to niche marketing. This is what Toffler calls the "demassification" of the market. The authors provide a thoughtful, in-depth analysis of the changing American household, the decline of brand loyalty, new ways to shop and pay, the development of data base marketing, the rise of the service economy, and the flowering of the information society. In addition, there is extensive consideration of not only reaching the prospect and making the sale but also of developing a continuing relationship with clients. This very important work should be read by all continuing educators even though it does not deal directly with continuing education programs.

Ries, A., and Trout, J. *Marketing Warfare.* New York: McGraw-Hill, 1986.

The thesis of this book—that there is a direct relationship between tactics in warfare and tactics in marketing—is illustrated by the chapter titles: "The Principle of Force," "The Superiority of the Defense," "The Nature of the Battleground," "Principles of Offensive Warfare." All the examples are drawn from the for-profit sector business world. The point is made that nothing succeeds in marketing like a sound strategy based on creative ways to position yourself in the market and to offer people the benefits they value.

Ries, A., and Trout, J. *Positioning: The Battle for Your Mind.* New York: McGraw-Hill, 1986.

Positioning is a marketing term commonly used to denote that communication can occur only in the right circumstances and at the right time. Ries and Trout have produced an excellent work containing many examples of how organizations have positioned themselves and their products correctly and incorrectly. The principles discussed in this book should be thoroughly studied by continuing educators. Correct positioning of the continuing education organization and its programs is essential. The book offers many practical tips and guidelines on how to accomplish this task most effectively.

Robertson, T. S., Zielinski, J., and Ward, S. *Consumer Behavior.* Glenview, Ill.: Scott, Foresman, 1984.

This book was written primarily for MBAs and advanced undergraduates. As such, it is a good introductory text on consumer behavior. There is an extensive analysis of the logic of consumer-needs satisfaction and the role of consumer behavior in social policy. In addition, there are excellent sections on the methodology of research on consumer behavior, the ways by which consumers process information, the role of cognitive development in consumer behavior, and the use of demographic and psychographic data in marketing.

Strauss, L. *Electronic Marketing: Emerging TV and Computer Channels for Interactive Home Shopping.* White Plains, N.Y.: Knowledge Industry Publications, 1983.

Home shopping has not yet gained wide acceptance for use by continuing education programs. However, electronic marketing/home shopping is growing at an exponential rate in other fields. It is the future. This book provides a good overview of the subject and assists continuing educators in beginning to think strategically about this important new concept. This marketing technique has important implications for continuing education professionals even though these ideas are not currently being implemented in such organizations.

Tapor, R. S. *Institutional Image: How to Define, Improve, Market It.* Washington, D.C.: Council for Advancement and Support of Education, 1986.

This guide is particularly helpful for people in higher education. In fact, it is one of the few works available that deals substantially with the concept of institutional image. Among the important issues addressed are who builds an image, how is a successful image built, how does an institution position itself, and how is a marketing plan implemented. Tapor develops the three R's for image building: research, recognition, and repetition. This book offers many practical suggestions for members of higher education organizations.

Weiers, R. M. *Marketing Research.* Englewood Cliffs, N.J.: Prentice-Hall, 1984.

Weiers thoroughly reviews the many effective ways to conduct market research. Among the topics covered are the design, implementation, and control of the marketing research project and the basics of sampling and measurement. Information collection (for example, survey research), telephone interviews, mail questionnaires, and strategies for reducing nonresponse error are also included.

D. Magazines and Journals on Marketing

The following magazines and journals offer up-to-date material on a wide range of marketing issues.

Advertising Age
740 Rush Street
Chicago, IL 60611

American Demographics: The Magazine of Consumer Markets
108 North Cayuga Street
Ithaca, NY 14850

Communications World
International Association of Business Communications
870 Market Street, Suite 940
San Francisco, CA 94102

Continuing Health Education Memo
S. R. Knapp Associates
North Arlington Atrium
3436 North Kennicott Avenue
Arlington Heights, IL 60004

Direct Marketing Magazine
224 7th Street
Garden City, NY 11530

Direct Marketing News
19 West 21st Street
New York, NY 10010

Direct Marketing Newsletter
Hoke Communications, Inc.
224 Seventh Street
Garden City, NY 11530

The Journal of Business and Industrial Marketing
108 Loma Media Road
Santa Barbara, CA 93103

Journal of Marketing
American Marketing Association
230 North Michigan Avenue
Chicago, IL 60601

The Journal of Service Marketing
108 Loma Media Road
Santa Barbara, CA 93103

Public Relations Journal
Public Relations Society of America
845 Third Avenue
New York, NY 10022

Public Relations News
127 East 80th Street
New York, NY 10021

Target Marketing
North American Publishing Company
401 North Broad Street
Philadelphia, PA 19108

E. Marketing-Related Organizations and Associations

The following organizations and associations serve professionals interested in enhancing their marketing skills. A call to them will bring you literature about membership as well as a list of benefits and upcoming programs.

American Association for Adult and Continuing Education
1112 Sixteenth Street, NW
Suite 400
Washington, DC 20036
(202) 463-6333

American Hotel and Motel Association
888 Seventh Avenue
New York, NY 10106
(212) 265-4506

American Management Association
135 West 50th Street
New York, NY 10020
(212) 586-8100

American Marketing Association
250 South Wacker Drive, Suite 200
Chicago, IL 60606
(312) 648-0536

American Society of Association Executives
The ASAE Building
1575 I Street, NY
Washington, DC 20005
(202) 626-2723

American Society of Engineering Educators
11 Dupont Circle, Suite 200
Washington, DC 20036
(202) 293-7080

American Society for Training and Development
1630 Duke Street
Box 1443
Alexandria, VA 22313
(703) 683-8100

American Telemarketing Association
5000 Van Nuys, Suite 400
Sherman Oaks, CA 91403
(800) 441-3335

Annual Conference for Directors of Management Development Programs
c/o Timothy Sullivan, Director
Center for Management Development
Bryant College
450 Douglas Pike
Smithfield, RI 02917-1283
(401) 232-6205

Association for Continuing Higher Education
c/o College of Graduate and Continuing Studies
University of Evansville
1800 Lincoln Avenue
Evansville, IN 47722
(812) 479-2472

Association of College and University Housing Offices
Central Support Services
101 Curl Drive, Suite 140
Columbus, OH 43210-1195
(614) 292-0099

Business/Professional Advertising Association
Metroplex Corporate Center
100 Metroplex Drive
Edison, NJ 08817
(201) 935-4441

Continuing Health Exchange Network
c/o Diane Pitkin
P.O. Box 35492
Dallas, TX 75235
(214) 879-3789

Direct Marketing Association
6 East 43rd Street
New York, NY 10017
(212) 689-4977

Exposition Service Contractors Association
1516 South Pontius Avenue
Los Angeles, CA 90025
(213) 478-0215

Foundation for Public Relations, Research & Education
310 Madison Avenue, Suite 1710
New York, NY 10017
(212) 370-9353

Hotel Sales & Marketing Association International
1300 L Street, NW, Suite 800
Washington, DC 20005
(202) 789-0089

Institute for Meeting and Conference Management
P.O. Box 14097
Washington, DC 20044
(202) 281-0932

International Association of Business Communications
National Headquarters
870 Market Street, Suite 940
San Francisco, CA 94102
(415) 433-3400

International Exhibitors Association
5103-B Backlick Road
Annandale, VA 22003
(703) 941-3725

Meeting Planners International
Infomart
1950 Stemmons Freeway
Dallas, TX 75207-5018
(214) 746-5222

National Association of Exposition Managers
334 East Garfield Road
P.O. Box 377
Aurora, OH 44202
(216) 562-8255

National University Continuing Education Association
One Dupont Circle, NW, Suite 420
Washington, DC 20036
(202) 659-3130

Product Development and Management Association
Indiana University
801 West Michigan Street
Indianapolis, IN 46223
(317) 274-4984

Public Relations Society of America
33 Irving Place
New York, NY 10003
(212) 228-7228

Sales & Marketing Executives International
Statler Office Tower, Suite 458
Cleveland, OH 44115
(216) 771-6650

Society for Nonprofit Organizations
6314 Odana Road, Suite 1
Madison, WI 53719
(608) 274-9777

F. Specialized Reference Works

All TV Publicity Outlets Nationwide
P.O. Box 1197
New Milford, CT 06776

This directory is a show-by-show listing, including types of public relations materials selected by the producers. In addition, the size of the audience reached by each show and the name and address of the public relations person for each show are listed.

Direct Mail List Rates and Data
Standard Rate and Data Service, Inc.
3004 Glenview Road
Wilmette, IL 60091

This classic reference work for direct-mail marketing is a 1,600-page reference that provides names, addresses, and information on the following:

- Mailing list brokers arranged alphabetically by company name. A professional mailing list broker will work with you to find the best lists to reach the people you want to reach with your message. A professional list broker will define and select your lists and is usually a wise investment for someone inexperienced with direct-mail list selection.
- Mailing list compilers arranged alphabetically by company name and, if applicable, by specialty.
- Mailing list managers arranged alphabetically by company name. The entry for each company includes all lists represented by that list manager.
- Master index section. Lists are indexed according to name of the list, subject matter, and market classification. If you are choosing your own list, this is the section that you probably will use most often.
- Consumer coop mailings and package insert programs. These companies specialize in combining your ad with others in joint mailings, for example, packets containing several different types of coupons. These companies specialize in placing your advertising message as an insert in other mailings.

Direct-mail marketing is an art and a science. One large direct-mail corporation maintains a consumer file of 78,000,000 households; it also maintains nearly four hundred individual and neighborhood characteristics such as age, income, and education that can be used singly or in combination. You can choose among the following twelve variables from the list of four hundred to construct a custom list of potential recipients of information about your continuing education programs:

- Ages of individual family members
- Length of residence
- Sex of head of household
- Dwelling unit type
- Ethnic/religious designation

- Life-cycle identifier such as marital status or mail-order response
- Income level
- Home value
- Owner versus renter
- Educational/occupational data
- Growth and mobility trends
- Index of social position

Many large mailing houses also provide lettershop services and will label, sort, and mail your advertising. Therefore, familiarity with Standard Rate and Data Service's *Direct Mail List Rates and Data* is a must for anyone engaging in extensive marketing of continuing education programs. Lists typically cost from $40 to $75 per thousand names for a one-time use. Lists are available in a wide variety of formats, for example, avery, cheshire, and heat transfer. In addition, multiple lists can often be run through a merge/purge computer program to eliminate duplicate names. This book is the one-stop shopping service for information about direct-mail services and lists.

The Direct Marketing Market Place: The Directory of the Direct Marketing Industry
1033 Channel Drive
Hewlett Harbor, NY 11557
This annual directory, containing seven hundred and twenty pages of information on over 19,000 organizations and key executives, is designed to be an easy-to-use source covering the entire spectrum of direct marketing. You will find listings for companies that sell by mail; advertising agencies; consultants; local, national, and international direct marketing clubs and associations; courses and seminars; printers; computer services; and list brokers.

Editor and Publisher International Yearbook
Editor and Publisher
11 West 19th Street
New York, NY 10011
This yearbook lists the names, addresses, and phone numbers of editors and reporters. It is an excellent source of names for mailing lists for publicity releases. It also is helpful in identifying whom to contact to discuss the possibility of feature or news stories related to continuing education programs.

Encyclopedia of Associations
Gale Research Company
Book Tower
Detroit, MI 48226
This classic three-volume work is invaluable to those compiling mailing lists designed to reach members of associations. It contains the names and addresses of over 15,000 associations, along with information about number of

members, divisions within the association, and annual conferences. Volume One is the basic index of associations. Voluem Two is the geographic and executive index. Volume Three contains new associations and projects and is the periodical supplement service that increases the usefulness of Volume One. This encyclopedia will enable marketers to create effective mailing lists of members of professional associations, who can then be contacted to purchase their lists.

Gale Directory of Publications
(formerly Ayer Directory of Publications)
Gale Research Company
Book Tower
Detroit, MI 48226

This annual publication lists the names and addresses of most public publications in the United States and Canada. Newspapers, magazines, journals, and other publications are listed by state and city. There is also an alphabetical index.

IMS Directory of Publications
IMS Press
Division of IMS Communications, Inc.
426 Pennsylvania Avenue
Ft. Washington, PA 19034

Almost all newspapers and periodicals published in the United States are listed. The directory is arranged by state and by city. It is an excellent source for developing mailing lists for publicity releases, and is also useful for identifying whom to contact to discuss the possibility of feature or news stories related to continuing education programs.

The Professional's Guide to Public Relations Services
Richard Weiners, Inc. Publishers
888 Seventh Avenue
New York, NY 10019

A reference compendium of techniques, names, addresses, and descriptions of public relations organizations. Included are chapters on broadcast monitoring, celebrities and speakers, clipping bureaus, communications and image consultants, editorials, mailing services, media directories, photography, radio, television, and skywriting.

Southern California Media Directory and PCLA Membership Roster
Publicity Club of Los Angeles, Inc.
5000 Van Nuys Boulevard, Suite 400
Sherman Oaks, CA 91403

This annual directory lists addresses and phone numbers of public relations and community organizations, business publications, news services and bureaus, regional and national magazines, newspapers, ethnic and religious publications, college newspapers, television and radio stations, and a local membership roster. Check to see if one is available from your area's publicity club.

Ulrich's International Periodicals Directory (two volumes)
Bowker & Company
245 West 17th Street
New York, NY 10011

This publication lists periodicals by subject and title, vendors, periodicals available on-line, and publications of international organizations, and includes a user's guide. It gives the features of each periodical, including circulation and year first published.

G. Clipping Bureaus

Clipping bureaus read all magazines, newspapers, journals, and newsletters published. By contracting with them, you will be provided with clippings of all articles mentioning your organization. This kind of a tracking system constitutes an excellent way to assess whether your publicity and news releases actually get published. The following is a list of the leading clipping bureaus.

Allen's Press Clipping Bureau
657 Mission Street, Room 602
San Francisco, CA 94105
(415) 392-2353

519 Southwest Third, Room 509
Portland, OR 97204

1331 Third Avenue, Room 511
Seattle, WA 98101

215 West 6th Street, Room 1100
Los Angeles, CA 90013

American Press Clipping Service Inc.
119 Nassau Street
New York, NY 10038
(212) 962-3797

ATP Clipping Bureau, Inc.
(American Trade Press)
5 Beekman Street
New York, NY 10038
(212) 349-1177

Bacon's Clipping Bureau
332 South Michigan Avenue
Chicago, IL 60604
(312) 922-2400

Berliner Research Center, Inc.
Mill Plain Road
Danbury, CT 06810
(203) 744-2333

Bowdens Information Service
624 King Street West
Toronto, Ontario M5V2X9
(416) 860-0794

Bureau International de Presse
Centre de Documentation Internationale
68 East 7th Street
New York, NY 10002
(212) 533-7420

Burrelle's Press Clipping Bureau
75 East Northfield Avenue
Livingston, NJ 07039
(800) 631-1160
New York: (212) 227-5570
New Jersey: (201) 992-6600

Canadian Press Clipping Services
4601 Yonge Street
North York, Ontario M2N 5L9
(416) 221-1660

Congressional Record Clippings
1868 Columbia Road, NW
Washington, DC 20009
(202) 332-2000

Empire State Press Clipping Service
455 Central Avenue
Scarsdale, NY 10583
(914) 723-2792

Home Economics Reading Service Inc.
733 15th Street, NW
Washington, DC 20005
(202) 347-4763

Illinois Press Clip
929 South Second Street
Springfield, IL 62704
(217) 523-5095

International Press Clipping Bureau, Inc.
5 Beekman Street
New York, NY 10038
(212) 267-5450

1868 Columbia Road, NW
Washington, DC 20009
(202) 332-2000

International Press Cutting Bureau
Lancaster House 70
Newington Causeway, London SE1
01-403-0608

Luce Press Clipping Inc.
420 Lexington Avenue, Room 360
New York, NY 10170
(212) 889-6711

Mutual Press Clipping Service, Inc.
1930 Chestnut Street
Philadelphia, PA 19103
(215) 569-4257

New England Newsclip Agency, Inc.
5 Auburn Street
Framingham, MA 01701
(617) 879-4460

New Jersey Clipping Service
75 Northfield Road
Livingston, NJ 07039
(201) 994-3333

New York State Clipping Service
(Division of Burrelle's)
330 West 42nd Street
New York, NY 10036
(212) 967-8210

Newsvertising/Congressional Press Monitoring Retrieval Services
1868 Columbia Road, NW, Suite 402
Washington, DC 20009
(202) 332-2000

Oklahoma Press Association
3601 North Lincoln
Oklahoma City, OK 73105
(405) 524-4421

Packaged Facts
274 Madison Avenue
New York, NY 10016
(212) 532-5533

Pennsylvania Clipping Service
2150 Herr Street
Harrisburg, PA 17103
(717) 238-3843

Press Intelligence, Inc.
1334 G Street, NW
Washington, DC 20005
(202) 783-5810

Pressclips, Inc.
1 Hillside Boulevard
New Hyde Park, NY 11040
(516) 437-1047

Review on File
Walton, NY 13856
(607) 865-4226

Romeike & Curtice Ltd.
Hale House 290–296
Greenlanes, London N13 5T
01-882-0155

Universal Press Clipping Bureau
1613 Farnam Street, Suite 414
Omaha, NE 68102
(402) 342-3178

Vaz Dias International
110 West 40th Street, Room 1405
New York, NY 10018
(212) 838-3897

Virginia Press Services, Inc.
P.O. Box C-32015
Richmond, VA 23261-2015
(804) 798-2715

West Virginia Press Services, Inc.
101 Dee Drive, Suite 220
Charleston, WV 25311
(304) 342-6908

References

Aaker, D. A., and Myers, J. G. *Advertising Management*. Englewood Cliffs, N.J.: Prentice-Hall, 1982.

Aarons, W. F., and Bovee, C. L. *Contemporary Advertising*. (2nd ed.) Homewood, Ill.: Irwin, 1986, pp. 219-231.

Ackoff, R. L. F., Elsa, V., and Gharajedaghi, J. *Creating the Corporate Future: Plan or Be Planned For*. New York: Wiley, 1981.

Ahumada, M. M., and Hefferlin, J. B. L. "Sources of Assistance." In P. M. Callan (ed.), *Environmental Scanning for Strategic Leadership*. New Directions for Institutional Research, no. 52. San Francisco: Jossey-Bass, 1986.

Albrecht, K., and Zemke, R. *Service America! Doing Business in the New Economy*. Homewood, Ill.: Dow Jones-Irwin, 1985.

Alderson, J. "Is Service as Bad as *Time* Says?" *Meetings & Conventions,* July 1987, pp. 50, 57.

Allen, L. A. *Making Managerial Planning More Effective*. New York: McGraw-Hill, 1982.

Alsop, R., and Abrams, B. "Selling God." *The Wall Street Journal on Marketing,* 1986, pp. 223-226.

Andrew, F. E. *A Bibliography on Data Base Marketing*. Nevada City, Calif.: The Continuing Education Forum, 1987.

Andrew, F. E. *Mailing List Magic: How to Choose and Win with the Best Mailing Lists for Your Meeting Marketing*. Nevada City, Calif.: The Continuing Education Forum, 1988.

Arbitron Ratings Company, Inc. *Television Ratings Book, 1987-88, Radio Ratings Book, 1987-88*. New York: Arbitron Ratings Co., Inc.

Atlas, J. "Beyond Demographics." *The Atlantic Monthly,* Oct. 1984, pp. 49, 58.

Atlas of Utah. Provo, Utah: Brigham Young University Press, Weber State College, 1981.

491

Bagge, I. G. "Marketing Continuing Education Programs: The UCLA Approach." *1981 Proceedings*, n.d., pp. 76–84.

Bagge, I. G. "Promotion: Extending the Marketing Mix." *Continuum*, July 1983, pp. 30–41.

Baier, M. *Elements of Direct Marketing*. New York: McGraw-Hill, 1983.

"Balancing Your Media Mix." *Business Marketing*, Aug. 1987, p. 90.

Barban, A. M., Cristol, S. M., and Kopec, F. J. *Essentials of Media Planning: A Marketing Viewpoint*. Chicago: Crain Books, 1976.

Barban, A. M., Cristol, S. M., and Kopec, F. J. *Essentials of Media Planning*. (2nd ed.) Lincolnwood, Ill.: NTC Business Books, 1987.

Beck, A. C., and Hillmar, E. D. *Positive Management Practices*. San Francisco: Jossey-Bass, 1986.

Beder, H. (ed.) *Marketing Continuing Education*. New Directions for Continuing Education, no. 31. San Francisco: Jossey-Bass, 1986.

Bellman, G. M. *The Quest for Staff Leadership*. Glenview, Ill.: Scott, Foresman, 1986.

Belth, I. "The SIC Code Needs Therapy." *Business Marketing*, Aug. 1984, pp. 50, 52.

Benn, A. *The 27 Most Common Mistakes in Advertising*. New York: AMACOM, 1978.

Benn, O. "A Segmentation Approach to the Market." *Marketing and Media Decisions*, May 1984, pp. 134–136.

Bennis, W., and Nanus, B. *Leaders: The Strategies for Taking Charge*. New York: Harper & Row, 1985.

Berkman, H. W., and Gilson, C. *Advertising Concepts and Strategies*. (2nd ed.) New York: Random House, pp. 152–169, 187, 239–240.

Bloch, T. M., Upah, G. D., and Zeithaml, V. *Services Marketing in a Changing Environment*. Chicago: American Marketing Association, 1985.

Block, P. *The Empowered Manager: Positive Political Skills at Work*. San Francisco: Jossey-Bass, 1987.

Bly, R. W. *The Copywriter's Handbook: A Step-by-Step Guide to Writing Copy That Sells*. New York: Dodd, Mead, 1985.

Bobrow, E. E., and Bobrow, M. D. *Marketing Handbook*. Vol. I and II. Homewood, Ill.: Dow Jones-Irwin, 1985.

Bolman, L. G., and Deal, T. E. *Modern Approaches to Understanding and Managing Organizations*. San Francisco: Jossey-Bass, 1984.

Book, A. C., and Schick, D. C. *Fundamentals of Copy and Layout*. Lincolnwood, Ill.: NTC Business Books, 1986.

Boyatzis, R. E. *The Competent Manager: A Model for Effective Performance*. New York: Wiley, 1982.

Bradford, D. L., and Cohen, A. R. *Managing for Excellence: The Guide to Developing High Performance in Contemporary Organizations*. New York: Wiley, 1984.

Brannen, W. H. *Advertising and Sales Promotion: Cost-Effective Techniques for Your Small Business*. Englewood Cliffs, N.J.: Prentice-Hall, 1983.

Breen, G. E. *Do-It-Yourself-Marketing Research.* New York: McGraw-Hill, 1977.

Brochure Distribution. Manhattan, Kans.: Learning Resources Network, 1987.

Brown, W. P., Martin, D., and Schultz, D. E. *Strategic Advertising Campaigns.* (2nd ed.) Chicago: Crain Books, 1984.

Buell, V. P., and Huyel, C. *Handbook of Modern Marketing.* New York: McGraw-Hill, pp. 7-3-7-46.

"Building an Integrated Marketing Strategy." *Business Marketing.* Aug. 1987, p. 46.

Burnett, E. "Rules for Testing Lists." Reprinted from B. Love (ed.) *Folio,* July 1983.

Bury, C. *Telephone Techniques That Sell.* New York: Warner Books, 1980.

Buzzell, R. D. (ed.) *Marketing in an Electronic Age.* Boston: Harvard Business School Press, 1985.

Cabell, D. W. *Cabell's Direction of Publishing Opportunities in Education.* Beaumont, Tex.: Cabell, 1984.

Caples, J. *Tested Advertising Methods.* Englewood Cliffs, N.J.: Prentice-Hall, 1974.

Capon, N. *The Product Life Cycle.* Cambridge, Mass.: HBS Case Services, Harvard Business School, 1978.

Chapman, E. A., Jr. *Exhibit Marketing: A Survival Guide for Managers.* New York: McGraw-Hill, 1987.

Cohen, D. *Advertising, 1988.* Glenview, Ill.: Scott, Foresman, 1988, pp. 75-77.

Cohen, W. A., and Cohen, N. *Top Executive Performance: 11 Keys to Success and Power.* New York: Wiley, 1984.

Cole, R. S. *The Practical Handbook of Public Relations.* Englewood Cliffs, N.J.: Prentice-Hall, 1981.

Colley, R. H. *Determining Advertising Goals for Measured Advertising Results.* New York: New York Association for National Advertising, 1961.

Converse, J. M., and Presser, S. *Survey Questions: Handcrafting the Standardized Questionnaire.* Sage University Paper Series on Quantitative Applications in the Social Sciences, series no. 07-063. Beverly Hills, Calif./London: Sage, 1986.

Cook, T. D., and Campbell, D. T. *Quasi-experimentation: Design & Analysis Issues for Field Settings.* Boston: Houghton Mifflin, 1979.

Cooper, K. J., Stern, H., and Mitchell, A. *Consumer Values and Demand.* Lincoln, Nebr.: Business Intelligence Program, SRI International, 1960.

Corey, R. E. *Marketing Strategy—An Overview.* Cambridge, Mass.: HBS Case Services, Harvard Business School, 1978.

Corey, R. E. *A Note on Pricing Strategy.* Cambridge, Mass.: HBS Case Services, Harvard Business School, 1982.

Corrado, F. M. *Media for Managers.* Englewood Cliffs, N.J.: Prentice-Hall, 1984.

Crompton, J. L., and Lamb, C. W., Jr. *Marketing Government and Social Services.* New York: Wiley, 1986.

Cross, K. P. *Adults as Learners. Increasing Participation and Facilitating Learning.* San Francisco: Jossey-Bass, 1981, pp. 89-90, 120-122, 164-168, 235-241.

Culligan, M. J., and Green, D. *Getting Back to the Basics of Public Relations and Publicity.* New York: Crown, 1982.

Cutler, P. *Marketing for Nonprofit Organizations.* (2nd ed.) Englewood Cliffs, N.J.: Prentice-Hall, 1982, pp. 177–182.

Cutslip, S. M., Center, A. H., and Broom, G. M. *Effective Public Relations.* (6th ed.) Englewood Cliffs, N.J.: Prentice-Hall, 1985.

Daniells, L. M. *Business Information Sources.* (rev. ed.) Berkeley: University of California Press, 1985.

Deal, T. E. "Building an Effective Organizational Culture: How to Be Community-Oriented in a Traditional Institution." In R. G. Simerly and Associates (eds.), *Strategic Planning and Leadership in Continuing Education.* San Francisco: Jossey-Bass, 1987.

Deal, T. E., and Kennedy, A. A. *Corporate Cultures: The Rites and Rituals of Corporate Life.* New York: Addison-Wesley, 1982.

DeBruicker, F., and Summe, G. "Make Sure Your Customers Keep Coming Back." *Harvard Business Review,* Jan.-Feb. 1985, pp. 92, 98.

Demby, E. "Psychographics and from Whence It Came." In W. D.. Wells (ed.), *Lifestyle and Psychographics.* Chicago: American Marketing Association, 1974.

"Demographic Forecasts: Marriage and Money." *American Demographics,* May 1987, p. 70.

"Demographics: Is the Sun Setting on the West?" *Sales and Marketing Management,* Oct. 1987, pp. 78–84.

Derr, C. B. *Managing the New Careerists. The Diverse Career Success Orientations of Today's Workers.* San Francisco: Jossey-Bass, 1986.

Desatnick, R. "Building the Customer-Oriented Work Force." *Training and Development Journal,* Jan. 1987a, pp. 52, 53.

Desatnick, R. L. *Managing to Keep the Customer: How to Achieve and Maintain Customer Service Throughout the Organization.* San Francisco: Jossey-Bass, 1987b.

Deshpande, R. "The Organizational Context of Market Research Use." *Journal of Marketing,* Fall 1982, pp. 91–100.

Deutsch, R. E. "Tomorrow's Workforce: New Values in the Workplace." *The Futurist,* Dec. 1985, pp. 8–11.

Digest of Education Statistics 1985–1986. Washington, D.C.: Office of Educational Research and Improvement, U.S. Department of Education, Center for Statistics, 1986.

Direct Marketing Creative Guild. *Direct Marketing Design: The Graphics of Direct Mail Response Marketing.* New York: PBC International, Inc., 1985.

"Direct Marketing, Postage Hike Expected." *Marketing and Media Decisions,* Aug. 1987, p. 105.

Dobmeyer, E. *Registration Techniques to Increase Enrollments.* Manhattan, Kans.: Learning Resources Network, 1986.

Domeneche, M. (ed.) *Oxbridge Directory of Newsletters.* New York: Oxbridge Communications, Inc., biennial.

Donnelly, J. H., and George, W. R. *Marketing of Services.* Chicago: American Marketing Association, 1981.

Doyle, P., and Saunders, J. "Market Segmentation and Positioning in Specialized Industrial Markets." *Journal of Marketing,* Spring 1985, pp. 24–32.

Duchaine, R. J. (ed.) *Thomas Register of American Manufacturers and Thomas Register Catalog File.* New York: Thomas, annual.

Dunn, S. W., and Barban, A. M. *Advertising: Its Role in Modern Marketing.* New York: Dryden Press, 1986.

Dun's Business Identification Service. Parsippany, N.J.: Dun's Marketing, 280 microfiche cards revised semiannually.

"Economic Forecast." *Marketing and Media Decisions,* Aug. 1987, p. 25.

Edmondson, B. "Colleges Conquer the Baby Bust." *American Demographics,* Nov. 1987a, p. 26.

Edmondson, B. "Inside the Empty Nest." *American Demographics,* Nov. 1987b, p. 24.

Ehrenkranz, L. B., and Kahn, G. R. *Public Relations/Publicity: A Key Link in Communications.* New York: Fairchild, 1983.

Eitel, D. F. "Mission Statements in Continuing Higher Education." *The Journal of Continuing Higher Education,* Summer 1987, pp. 2–4.

Elliott, R. D. *Marketing In-House Seminars.* Manhattan, Kans.: Learning Resources Network, 1986.

Elliott, R. D. *House Lists: How to Create a More Responsive In-House Mailing List.* Manhattan, Kans.: Learning Resources Network, 1987.

Ethridge, J. M. (ed.) *Directory of Directories.* Detroit, Mich.: Gale Research Co., biennial.

Evans, F. J. *Managing the Media: Proactive Strategy for Better Business–Press Relations.* New York: Quorum Bodes, 1987.

Exter, T. "How Many Hispanics?" *American Demographics,* May 1987, pp. 36–39, 67.

Exter, T., and Barber, F. "What Men and Women Think." *American Demographics,* Aug. 1987, p. 34.

Farlow, H. *Publicizing and Promoting Programs.* New York: McGraw-Hill, 1979.

Farris, P. W. *Note on Media Selection.* Cambridge, Mass.: HBS Case Services, Harvard Business School, 1978.

Fenno, B. *Helping Your Business Grow: 101 Dynamic Ideas in Marketing.* New York: American Management Association, 1982.

Ferrell, O. C., and Pride, W. M. *Fundamentals of Marketing.* Boston: Houghton Mifflin, 1982.

Fischer, R. *Personal Contact in Marketing.* Manhattan, Kans.: Learning Resources Network, 1984.

Fischer, R. B. "Successful Marketing Strategies and Techniques." In Q. Gessner (ed.), *Handbook on Continuing Higher Education.* New York: Macmillan, 1987.

Foster, D. W. *Planning for Products and Markets.* London: Longman, 1972.

Foster, K. S. "Continuing Education In-Class Enumeration." Unpublished, Sept. 1981.

Foster, K. S. "Analysis of Education Programming." Unpublished, Apr. 1983.

Foster, K. S. "Correspondence Market Evaluation." Unpublished, Apr. 1984a.

Foster, K. S. "Child Care Survey." Unpublished, Sept. 1984b.

Foster, K. S. "Study on Short Course Potential." Unpublished, Dec. 1985.

Foster, K. S. "DCE Advertising Recall." Unpublished, Sept. 1986.

Foster, K. S. "Correspondence Study Catalog Evaluation." Unpublished, July 1987a.

Foster, K. S. "Analysis of International Studies Potential." Unpublished, Sept. 1987b.

Foster, K. S., and Albiston, D. "Bountiful/University of Utah Student Survey." Unpublished, July 1987.

Foster, K. S., and Safman, T. "Student Attitudes Towards a Semester System." Unpublished, n.d.

Francese, P. K. "How to Manage Consumer Information." *American Demographics,* Aug. 1985, pp. 23-25.

Frandson, P. E.. "Madison Avenue." *The NUCEA Spectator,* June 1974, pp. 8-13.

Freedman, L. *Quality in Continuing Education.* San Francisco: Jossey-Bass, 1987.

FutureScan. Security Pacific Bank, no. 491, July 21, 1986.

Gale Directory of Publications. Detroit, Mich.: Gale Research Co.

Gardner, J. "The Tasks of Leadership." *New Management,* Spring 1987, *4,* 9, 14.

Garlin, R. H. "The New Concept of Marketing." *The Marketing Manual.* Manhattan, Kans.: The Learning Resources Network, 1983.

Garreau, J. *The Nine Nations of North America.* Boston: Houghton Mifflin, 1981.

Garver, J. "New Marketing Approaches to Continuing Education in the 1980's." *Continuum,* Jan. 1983, pp. 1-6.

Geographical Mobility. Washington, D.C.: U.S. Department of Commerce, Bureau of the Census, 1984.

Georgia Center for Continuing Education. "Environmental Scanning Records." Atlanta: University of Georgia, 1986.

Gianni, T. "Marketing Strategy, Marketers Discover What Quality Really Means." *Business Marketing,* Apr. 1987, p. 58.

Goldman, J. *Public Relations in the Marketing Mix: Introducing Vulnerability Relations.* Chicago: Crain Books, 1984.

Goodman, G. S. *Reach Out and Sell Someone.* Englewood Cliffs, N.J.: Prentice-Hall, 1983.

Gordon, O. J. "DCE Course Migration." Unpublished, 1973.

Gordon, O. J. "Adult Learner Assessment." Unpublished, July 1985.

Gordon, O. J. "Analysis of Courses by Section." Unpublished, Sept. 1986.

Gordon, O. J. "Analysis of Courses by Section." Unpublished, Sept. 1987.

Gould, J. S. *How to Publicize Yourself, Your Family, & Your Organization.* Englewood Cliffs, N.J.: Prentice-Hall, 1983.

Govoni, N. M., Eng, R., and Galper, M. *Promotional Management.* Englewood Cliffs, N.J.: Prentice-Hall, 1986.

Greenley, G. *The Strategic and Operational Planning of Marketing.* London: McGraw-Hill, 1986.

Grove, A. S. *High Output Management.* New York: Random House, 1983.

Gruenwald, G. *New Product Development.* Chicago: Crain Books, 1985, pp. 24, 217–219, 297–302, 346–347.

Haley, R. I. "Benefit Segmentation: A Decision-Oriented Research Tool." *Journal of Marketing,* July 1968, pp. 30–35.

Haley, R. I. "Benefit Segments: Backwards and Forwards." *Journal of Advertising Research,* Feb./Mar. 1984, pp. 19–25.

Hall, D. T., and Associates. *Career Development in Organizations.* San Francisco: Jossey-Bass, 1986.

Harper, R. *Mailing List Strategies: A Guide to Direct Mail Success.* New York: McGraw-Hill, 1986.

Harris, P. R. *Management in Transition: Transforming Managerial Practices and Organizational Strategies for a New Work Culture.* San Francisco: Jossey-Bass, 1985.

Hayes, R. S., and Elmore, G. B. *Marketing for Your Growing Business.* New York: Wiley, 1985.

Hearn, J. C., and Heydinger, R. B. "Scanning the University's External Environment: Objectives, Constraints, and Possibilities." *Journal of Higher Education,* 1985, pp. 56, 419–445.

Heskett, J. L. *Managing in the Service Economy.* Boston: Harvard Business School Press, 1986.

Hickson, D. J., and others. *Top Decisions: Strategic Decision Making in Organizations.* San Francisco: Jossey-Bass, 1986.

Higgins, D. (ed.) *The Art of Writing Advertising.* Lincolnwood, Ill.: NTC Business Books, 1987.

Hodgson, R. S. *The Dartnell Direct Mail and Mail Order Handbook.* Chicago: Dartnell Corp., 1980a.

Hodgson, R. S. *Direct Mail and Mail Order Handbook.* (3rd ed.) Chicago: Dartnell Corp., 1980b.

Holland, B. R. *Telephone Marketing as an Effective Means to Enroll Noncredit Continuing Education Students.* Ann Arbor, Mich.: University Microfilms Inc., 1985.

Holtz, H. *How to Succeed as an Independent Consultant.* New York: Wiley, 1983.

Holtz, H. *The Direct Marketer's Workbook.* New York: Wiley, 1986.

Hough, J. (ed.). "A Hotelier Attacks Planners." *Meeting Planners Alert.* Newtown, Mass.: Practice Management Associates, Aug. 1987.

Houle, C. O. *The Design of Education.* San Francisco: Jossey-Bass, 1972.

Household and Family Characteristics. Washington, D.C.: U.S. Department of Commerce, Bureau of the Census, 1985.

Iacocca, L. *Iacocca: An Autobiography.* New York: Bantam Books, 1984.

Ingalls, J. *Trainer's Guide to Andragogy.* Washington, D.C.: U.S. Government Printing Office, 1973.

"International Marketing." *Business Marketing,* Jan. 1987, pp. 48–70.

Jain, S. C. "The Evolution of Strategic Marketing." *Journal of Business Research,* 1983, pp. 11, 409–425.

Johnston, J. S., Jr., and Associates. *Educating Managers.* San Francisco: Jossey-Bass, 1986.

Jones, D., and Associates. "University of Utah Student Survey." Unpublished, May 1985.

Jonsen, R. W. "The Environmental Context for Postsecondary Education." In P. M. Callan (ed.), *Environmental Scanning for Strategic Leadership.* New Directions for Institutional Research, no. 52. San Francisco: Jossey-Bass, 1986.

Kaatz, R. B. *Cable: An Advertisers Guide to the New Electronic Media.* Chicago: Crain Books, 1982.

Kahn, J., and Pearlstein, S. "The Lost Art of Selling: The Founder of Neiman-Marcus on the Decline of Retailing." *Inc.,* June 1987, pp. 44, 48.

Kanter, R. M. *Men and Women of the Corporation.* New York: Basic Books, 1977.

Kanter, R. M. *The Change Masters: Innovation and Entrepreneurship in the American Corporation.* New York: Simon & Schuster, 1983.

Keim, W. A., and Keim, M. C. (eds.). *Marketing the Program.* New Directions for Community Colleges, no. 36. San Francisco: Jossey-Bass, 1981.

Keller, G. *Academic Strategy: The Management Revolution in American Higher Education.* Baltimore, Md.: Johns Hopkins University Press, 1983.

Kelly, T. "Report on the State of Utah Economy, First Security Bank Corporation." February 1988.

Kern, R. "Where Consumers Spend Their Money." *Sales and Marketing Management,* Jan. 1988, pp. 38–43.

Kilmann, R. H. *Beyond the Quick Fix: Managing Five Tracks to Organizational Success.* San Francisco: Jossey-Bass, 1984.

Kilmann, R. H., Saxton, M. J., Serpa, R., and Associates. *Gaining Control of the Corporate Culture.* San Francisco: Jossey-Bass, 1985.

Kinal, D. "Dip Into Several Segmentation Schemes to Paint Accurate Picture of Marketplace." *Marketing News,* Sept. 14, 1984, p. 32.

Kinnear, T. C., and Taylor, J. R. *Marketing Research: An Applied Approach.* St. Louis, Mo.: McGraw-Hill, 1983.

Kirchhoefer, O. (ed.). *Direct Mail List Rates and Data.* Wilmette, Ill.: Standard Rate and Data Service, bimonthly.

Kirkpatrick, D. L. *How to Manage Change Effectively.* San Francisco: Jossey-Bass, 1985.

Knesel, D. C. *Free Publicity, a Step by Step Guide.* New York: Sterling, 1982.

Knowles, M. S. *Modern Practice of Adult Education.* New York: Association Press, 1970.

Knox, A. B. *Adult Development and Learning: A Handbook on Individual Growth and Competence in the Adult Years.* San Francisco: Jossey-Bass, 1977.

Koepp, S. "Pul-eeze! Will Somebody Help Me?" *Time,* Feb. 2, 1987, pp. 48, 55.

Kotler, P. *Marketing for Nonprofit Organizations.* Englewood Cliffs, N.J.: Prentice-Hall, 1982.

Kotler, P. *Marketing for Profit Organizations.* Englewood Cliffs, N.J.: Prentice-Hall, 1984.

Kotler, P. *Marketing Management: Analysis, Planning and Control.* (5th ed.) Englewood Cliffs, N.J.: Prentice-Hall, 1985.

Kotler, P. *Principles of Marketing.* Englewood Cliffs, N.J.: Prentice-Hall, 1986.

Kotler, P., and Andreasen, A. R. *Strategic Marketing for Nonprofit Organizations.* New York: Prentice-Hall, 1987.

Kotler, P., and Bloom, P. N., *Marketing Professional Services.* Englewood Cliffs, N.J.: Prentice-Hall, 1984.

Kotler, P., Ferrell, O. C., and Lamb, C. *Strategic Marketing for Nonprofit Organizations.* Englewood Cliffs, N.J.: Prentice-Hall, 1987.

Kotler, P., and Fox, K. *Strategic Marketing for Educational Institutions.* Englewood Cliffs, N.J.: Prentice-Hall, 1985.

Kotler, P., and Levy, S. "Broadening the Concept of Marketing." *Journal of Marketing,* Jan. 1978, pp. 10–15.

Kotler, P., and Murphy, P. E. "Strategic Planning for Higher Education." In P. Kotler, O. C. Ferrell, and C. Lamb (eds.), *Strategic Marketing for Nonprofit Organizations.* Englewood Cliffs, N.J.: Prentice-Hall, 1987.

Kotter, J. P. *Power and Influence: Beyond Formal Authority.* New York: Free Press, 1985.

Kurtz, D. L., and Boone, L. E. *Marketing.* (2nd ed.) Hinsdale, Ill.: Dryden Press, 1984, p. 190.

Lacznick, G. R., and Murphy, P. *Marketing Ethics: Guidelines for Managers.* Lexington, Mass.: Lexington Books, 1985.

Laric, M. V., and Stiff, R. *VISICALC for Marketing and Sales.* Englewood Cliffs, N.J.: Prentice-Hall, 1984.

Laser, W., and Shaw, E. "How Older Americans Spend Their Money." *American Demographics,* Sept. 1987, p. 36.

Lawler, E. E., III. *High Involvement Management. Participative Strategies for Improving Organizational Performance.* San Francisco: Jossey-Bass, 1986.

Leffel, L. G. *Designing Brochures for Results.* Manhattan, Kans.: Learning Resources Network, 1983.

Lenz, E. *Creating and Marketing Programs in Continuing Education.* New York: McGraw-Hill, 1980.

Lesley, P., and others (eds.) *Lesley's Public Relations Handbook.* (3rd ed.) Englewood Cliffs, N.J.: Prentice-Hall, 1983.

Lesser, J. A., and Hughes, M. A. "The Generalizability Across Geographic Locations." *Journal of Marketing,* Jan. 1986, pp. 18–27.

Levinson, J. C. *Guerrilla Marketing: Secrets for Making Big Profits from Your Small Business.* Boston: Houghton Mifflin, 1984.

Levitt, T. *The Marketing Imagination.* New York: Free Press, 1983.

Lewis, R. "Targeting Through Direct Marketing." *Marketing Communications,* Oct. 1984, pp. 19–26.

Ley, D. F. *The Best Seller*. Newport Beach, Calif.: Sales Success Press, 1986.

Lippitt, G. L. *Organizational Renewal: A Holistic Approach to Organization Development*. Englewood Cliffs, N.J.: Prentice-Hall, 1982.

London, M. *Developing Managers: A Guide to Motivating and Preparing People for Successful Managerial Careers*. San Francisco: Jossey-Bass, 1985.

Long, H. B. *Adult Learning Research and Practice*. New York: Cambridge University Press, 1983, pp. 24, 42, 67, 91, 95, 96–109, 111–124, 228–233.

Lord, W. J., and others. *Functional Business Communications*. Englewood Cliffs, N.J.: Prentice-Hall, 1983.

Lovelock, C. H. *Services Marketing*. Englewood Cliffs, N.J.: Prentice-Hall, 1984.

Lovelock, C. H., and Weinberg, C. B. *Marketing for Public and Nonprofit Managers*. New York: American Management Association, 1982.

Lovelock, D. H., and Rothschild, M. L. "Uses, Abuses, and Misuses of Marketing in Higher Education." Distributed at Harvard University, Summer 1981.

Luther, W. M. *The Marketing Plan: How to Prepare and Implement It*. New York: American Management Association, 1982.

McBurney, D. H. *Experimental Psychology*. Belmont, Calif.: Wadsworth, 1983.

McCaffrey, M., and Derloshon, J. *Personal Marketing Strategies: How to Sell Yourself, Your Ideas, and Your Services*. New York: Prentice-Hall, 1983.

McCann, J. M. *The Marketing Workbench: Using Computers for Better Performance*. Homewood, Ill.: Dow Jones-Irwin, 1986.

McCarthy, E. J. *Basic Marketing: A Managerial Approach*. (3rd ed.) Homewood, Ill.: Richard D. Irwin, 1968.

McCarthy, E. J., and Perreault, W. D., Jr. *Essentials of Marketing*. Homewood, Ill.: Richard D. Irwin, 1985.

McDonald, M. H. *Marketing Plans: How to Prepare Them—How to Use Them*. New York: Franklin Watts, Inc., 1985.

McNutt, D. "Marketing by Objectives." *CASE Currents*, Nov./Dec. 1983.

Maehr, M. L., and Braskamp, L. A. *The Motivation Factor: A Theory of Personal Investment*. Lexington, Mass.: Lexington Books, 1986.

Magnesen, V. "A Short Course in Customer Service." *Training and Development Journal*, Jan. 1987, pp. 52, 53.

Magrath, A. J. "Are You Overdoing Lean and Mean." *Sales and Marketing Management*, Jan. 1988, pp. 46–54.

Makens, J. C. *The Marketing Plan Workbook*. Englewood Cliffs, N.J.: Prentice-Hall, 1985.

Marketing Classes for Adults. Vol. 3, no. 5. Manhattan, Kans.: Learning Resources Network, May 1984.

Marketing Management for Extended Education: Procedures Manual. Long Beach: California State University, 1984.

Marshall, M. V. "Short Note No. 10, Strategic Pricing Concepts." Short Notes on Marketing, Harvard Advanced Management Program, 1980.

Meyers, G. C., with Holusha, J. *When It Hits the Fan: Managing the Nine Crises of Business*. Boston: Houghton Mifflin, 1986.

Miaoulis, G., and Kalfus, M. D. "10 MBA Benefit Segments." *Marketing News,* Aug. 5, 1983, Sect. 1, p. 14.

Mintzberg, H. "The Manager's Job: Folklore and Fact." *Harvard Business Review,* July-Aug. 1975, pp. 49, 61.

Mitchell, A. *The Nine American Lifestyles: Who We Are and Where We Are Going.* New York: Warner Books, 1983.

Mitroff, I. I. *Stakeholders of the Organizational Mind: Toward a New View of Organizational Policy Making.* San Francisco: Jossey-Bass, 1983.

Moore, T. "Different Folks, Different Strokes." *Fortune,* Sept. 16, 1985, p. 65.

Morrison, J. L. "Establishing an Environmental Scanning System to Augment College and University Planning." *Planning in Higher Education,* 1987, *15,* 7–22.

Morrison, J. L., Renfro, W. L., and Boucher, W. I. *Futures Research and the Strategic Planning Process: Implications for Higher Education.* ASHE–ERIC Higher Education Report no. 9. Washington, D.C.: Association for Study of Higher Education, 1984.

"Multimedia Audiences." New York: Simmons Market Research Bureau, n.d.

Murphy, M. F. "Environmental Scanning: A Case Study in Higher Education." Unpublished doctoral dissertation, University of Georgia, Athens, 1987.

Naisbitt, J. *Megatrends: The New Directions Transforming Our Lives.* New York: Warner Books, 1982.

Nash, E. L. *Direct Marketing Strategy, Planning, Execution.* New York: McGraw-Hill, 1982.

Nash, E. L. *The Direct Marketing Handbook.* New York: McGraw-Hill, 1984.

Nelton, S. "Adapting to a New Era in Marketing Strategy." *Nation's Business,* Aug. 1984, pp. 18–23.

Nesbit, M., and Weinstein, A. "How to Size Up Your Customers." *American Demographics,* July 1986, pp. 34, 36, 37.

Newom, D., and Scott, A. *This is PR: The Realities of Public Relations.* (3rd ed.) Rosemont, Calif.: Wadsworth, 1985.

Noel, J. "Managing the Continuing Education Organization in a Mature Market." *The Journal of Continuing Higher Education,* Summer 1985, pp. 17–19.

Norris, J. S. *Public Relations.* Englewood Cliffs, N.J.: Prentice-Hall, Inc., 1984.

Nylen, D. W. *Advertising: Planning, Implementation, and Control.* Cincinnati, Ohio: Southwestern, 1986.

Ogilvy, D. *Ogilvy on Advertising.* New York: Crown, 1983.

"One Nation Divisible." *Marketing and Media Decisions,* July 1987, p. 118.

Osborne, S. G. *Electronic Direct Marketing.* Englewood Cliffs, N.J.: Prentice-Hall, 1984.

O'Shaughnessy, J. *Competitive Marketing: A Strategic Approach.* Boston: George Allen & Unwin, 1984.

Parkhurst, W. *How to Get Publicity, and Make the Most of It Once You've Got It.* New York: Times Books, 1985.

Patti, C. H., and Murphy, J. H. *Advertising Management: Cases and Concepts.* Columbus, Ohio: Grid, Inc., 1978.

Pentland, L. *Salesbook Spreadsheets.* New York: McGraw-Hill, 1985.

Peters, T., and Austin, N. *A Passion for Excellence: The Leadership Difference.* New York: Random House, 1985.

Peters, T. J., and Waterman, R. H., Jr. *In Search of Excellence: Lessons from America's Best-Run Companies.* New York: Warner Books, 1982.

Pfeffer, J. *Power in Organizations.* Boston: Pitman, 1981.

Pfeiffer, W. J., Goodstein, L. D., and Nolan, T. M. *Understanding Applied Strategic Planning: A Manager's Guide.* San Diego, Calif.: University Associates, 1985.

Phillips, J. J. *Improving Supervisors' Effectiveness: How Organizations Can Raise the Performance of Their First-Level Managers.* San Francisco: Jossey-Bass, 1985.

Pinchot, G., III. *Intrapreneuring.* New York: Harper & Row, 1985.

"Planning." *Marketing and Media Decisions,* Jan. 1988, p. 51.

Plummer, J. T. "How Personality Makes a Difference." *Journal of Advertising Research,* Dec. 1984/Jan. 1985, *24* (6), 27–31.

President and Fellows of Harvard College. "Product Policy." Cambridge, Mass.: HBS Case Services, Harvard Business School, 1975.

Prisk, D. P. *A Survey of Institutional Members, 1984–1985.* Washington, D.C.: National University Continuing Education Association, 1986.

The Professional's Guide to Public Relations Services. New York: Richard Weiner, Inc.

Promoting Issues and Ideas: A Guide to Public Relations for Nonprofit Organizations. New York: The Foundation Center, 1987.

"Public Perception of the Division of Continuing Education." Wasatch Opinion Research Corp., unpublished, Nov. 1977.

Quelch, J. A.. "Communications Policy." Cambridge, Mass.: HBS Case Services, Harvard Business School, 1975.

Rados, D. L. *Marketing for Nonprofit Organizations.* Boston: Auburn House, 1981.

Rand McNally Commercial Atlas and Marketing Guide. (119th ed.) New York: Rand McNally, 1988.

Rapp, S., and Collins, T. *Maximarketing: The New Direction in Promotion, Advertising, and Marketing Strategy.* New York: McGraw-Hill, 1987.

Ray, M. L. *Advertising and Communication Management.* Englewood Cliffs, N.J.: Prentice-Hall, 1982.

Raymondo, J. C. "Who's on First." *American Demographics,* Nov. 1987, p. 38.

Renfro, W. L., and Morrison, J. L. "Detecting Signals of Change: The Environmental Scanning Process." *The Futurist,* Aug. 1984, pp. 49–53.

Ridgeway, J. *Successful Media Relations—A Practitioner's Guide.* Brookfield, Vt.: Gower, 1984.

Ries, A., and Trout, J. *Positioning: The Battle for Your Mind.* New York: McGraw-Hill, 1981.

Ries, A., and Trout, J. *Marketing Warfare.* New York: McGraw-Hill, 1986.

Robertson, T. S., Zielinski, J., and Ward, S. *Consumer Behavior.* Glenview, Ill.: Scott, Foresman, 1984.

Roel, R. (ed.) *Direct Marketing.* Garden City, N.Y.: Hoke Communications Inc., monthly.

Roman, K., and Maas, J. *How to Advertise.* New York: St. Martin's Press, 1976.

Roman, M. *Telephone Marketing: How to Build Your Business by Telephone.* New York: McGraw-Hill, 1976.

Rosenfeld, J. "Segmentation Theory in Practice." *Marketing Communications,* Oct. 1985, pp. 84–86.

Rossell, C. (ed.) *Zip Target Marketing.* Philadelphia: North American, monthly.

Russell, C. "A High Yield Investment." *American Demographics,* Mar. 1985, p. 7.

Russell, J. J. (ed.) *National Trade and Professional Associations of the United States.* Washington, D.C.: Columbia Books, annual.

Ryans, C. C., and Shanklin, W. L. *Strategic Planning, Marketing and Public Relations, and Fund-raising in Higher Education.* Metuchen, N.J.: Scarecrow Press, 1986.

Sammon, K. *Planning for Out-of-Home Media.* New York: Traffic Audit Bureau Inc., 1987.

Schein, E. H. *Organizational Culture and Leadership: A Dynamic View.* San Francisco: Jossey-Bass, 1985.

Schmidt, J. W. "The Leader's Role in Strategic Planning." In R. G. Simerly and Associates, *Strategic Planning and Leadership in Continuing Education. Enhancing Organizational Vitality, Responsiveness, and Identity.* San Francisco: Jossey-Bass, 1987.

School Enrollment—Social and Economic Characteristics of Students: 1982. Washington, D.C.: U.S. Department of Commerce, Bureau of the Census, 1982.

Schwartz, D. J. *Marketing Today: A Basic Approach.* New York: Harcourt Brace Jovanovich, 1983.

Schwartz, J. "Hispanic Opportunities." *American Demographics,* May 1987, pp. 56, 58, 59.

Shafiroff, M. D., and Shook, R. L. *Successful Telephone Selling in the '80s.* New York: Barnes & Noble Books, 1982.

Shapiro, B. P. "Concept of the Marketing Mix." Cambridge, Mass.: HBS Case Services, Harvard Business School, 1981.

Shapiro, B. P., and Bonoma, T. V. "How to Segment Industrial Markets." *Harvard Business Review,* May-June 1984, pp. 104–110.

Sherrid, P. "Plain Vanilla Just Won't Do." *Forbes,* Oct. 21, 1985, pp. 146, 147.

Sheth, J. "Marketing Megatrends." *Journal of Consumer Marketing,* Summer 1983, *1* (1), 5, 13.

Sheth, J. N. *Models of Buyer Behavior, Conceptual, Quantitative, and Empirical.* New York: Harper & Row, 1974.

Sheth, J. N. *Winning Back Your Market: The Inside Stories of the Companies That Did It.* New York: Wiley, 1985.

Shostack, G. "Designing Services That Deliver." *Harvard Business Review,* Jan.-Feb. 1984, pp. 130, 136.

Simerly, R. G. *Successful Budgeting for Conferences and Institutes.* Manhattan, Kans.: LERN Publishing, 1984.

Simerly, R. G., and Associates. *Strategic Planning and Leadership in Continuing Education. Enhancing Organizational Vitality, Responsiveness, and Identity.* San Francisco: Jossey-Bass, 1987.

Simpson, E. G., Jr., McGinty, D., and Morrison, J. L. "Environmental Scanning at the Georgia Center for Continuing Education: A Progress Report." *Continuing Higher Education Review,* 1987, *3,* 51.

Sims, H. P., Jr., Gioia, D., and Associates. *The Thinking Organization: Dynamics of Organizational Social Cognition.* San Francisco: Jossey-Bass, 1986.

Sissors, J. A., and Surmanek, J. *Advertising Media Planning.* Chicago: Crain Books, 1980.

Smith, W. L. "Defining and Analyzing the Market." In H. Beder (ed.), *Marketing Continuing Education.* New Directions for Continuing Education, no. 31. San Francisco: Jossey-Bass, 1986.

Smith, W. R. "Product Differentiation and Market Segmentation as Alternative Marketing Strategies." *Journal of Marketing,* July 1956, pp. 3-8.

Southern California Media Directory and PCLA Membership Roster. Sherman Oaks, Calif.: Publicity Club of Los Angeles, Inc.

Srivastva, S., and Associates. *Executive Power.* San Francisco: Jossey-Bass, 1986.

Standard Periodical Directory. New York: Oxbridge Communications, Inc. annual.

Stanton, W. J. *Fundamentals of Marketing.* (7th ed.) New York: McGraw-Hill, 1984.

"The 1986 Starmark Report." *Business Marketing,* Supplement, 1986, pp. 1-19.

State and Metropolitan Area Data Book 1986. Washington, D.C.: U.S. Department of Commerce, Bureau of the Census, 1986.

Statistical Abstract of the United States 1987. Washington, D.C.: U.S. Department of Commerce, Bureau of the Census, 1987, pp. 22-26, 137-150.

Steiner, G. A. *Strategic Planning: What Every Manager Must Know.* New York: Free Press, 1979.

Steiner, G. A., and Miner, J. B. *Management Policy and Strategy.* New York: Macmillan, 1982.

Stevens, A. *The Persuasion Explosions: Your Guide to the Power and Influence of Contemporary Public Relations.* Washington, D.C.: Acropolis Books, 1985.

Stone, B. *Successful Direct Marketing Methods.* Lincolnwood, Ill.: Crain Books, 1984.

"Strategies: A Smorgasbord Approach to Customer Service, the New Wave from Europe." *Sales and Marketing Management,* Nov. 1987, p. 44.

Strauss, L. *Electronic Marketing: Emerging TV and Computer Channels for Interactive Home Shopping.* White Plains, N.Y.: Knowledge Industry Publications, 1983.

"1986 Study of Media and Markets, Sports and Leisure." New York: Simmons Market Research Bureau, n.d.

Suleiman, A. *Developing and Marketing Successful Seminars and Conferences.* New York: Marketing Federation, 1982.

Suleiman, A. S. "Marketing the Facility." St. Petersburg Beach, Fla.: Marketing Federation, 1987.

Surmanek, J. *Media Planning, a Quick and Easy Guide.* Chicago: Crain Books, 1980.

"1988 Survey of Selling Cost." *Sales and Marketing Management,* Feb. 1988.

Tannenbaum, R., Margulies, N., Massarik, F., and Associates. *Human Systems Development: New Perspectives on People and Organizations.* San Francisco: Jossey-Bass, 1985.

Tapor, R. S. *Institutional Image: How To Define, Improve, Market It.* Washington, D.C.: Council for Advancement and Support of Education, 1986.

Tarpey, L. X., Donnelly, J. H., Jr., and Peter, J. P. *A Preface to Marketing Management.* Dallas: Business Publications, Inc., 1979.

Taylor, J. "Development of Psychological Screening Test for University of Utah Division of Continuing Education, Prelim Project." Unpublished, May 1982.

"The Brand Plan." *Marketing and Media Decisions,* Jan. 1987, p. 22.

Townsend, B. "Psychographic Glitter and Gold." *American Demographics,* Nov. 1985, pp. 22-29.

"Trade Show Bureau Research Report Number 2030." East Orleans, Mass.: Trade Show Bureau, Nov. 1986.

Udell, J. G., and Laczniak, G. R. *Marketing for an Age of Change: An Introduction.* New York: Wiley, 1981.

Ulrich's International Periodicals Directory. 2 vols. New York: Bowker, annual.

U.S. Office of Management and Budget. *Standard Industrial Classification Manual.* Washington, D.C.: U.S. Government Printing Office, 1987.

Vorous, G., and Alvares, P. (eds.). *What Happens in Public Relations.* New York: AMACOM, 1981.

Votruba, J. C. "From Marginality to Mainstream: Strategies for Increasing Internal Support for Continuing Education." In R. G. Simerly (ed.), *Strategic Planning and Leadership in Continuing Education.* San Francisco: Jossey-Bass, 1987.

Walshok, M. L. "Developing a Strategic Marketing Plan." In R. G. Simerly (ed.), *Strategic Planning and Leadership in Continuing Education. Enhancing Organizational Vitality, Responsiveness, and Identity.* San Francisco: Jossey-Bass, 1987.

Wasson, J. L. "Psychographics: An Aid to Demographics." *Adweek's Marketing Week,* Sept. 1987, p. 48.

Webster, F. E., Jr. *Industrial Marketing Strategy.* New York: Wiley, 1984.

Weiers, R. M. *Marketing Research.* Englewood Cliffs, N.J.: Prentice-Hall, 1984.

Weilbacher, W. M. *Marketing Management Cases.* London: Macmillan, 1970, pp. 127-149.

Weinstein, A. "Ten Point Program Customizes Segmentation Analysis." *Marketing News*, May 23, 1986, p. 22.

Weinstein, A. *Market Segmentation*. Chicago: Probus, 1987.

Willard, J. C., and Warren, L. A. "Developing Program Offerings." In H. Beder (ed.), *Marketing Continuing Education*. New Directions for Continuing Education, no. 31. San Francisco: Jossey-Bass, 1986, pp. 29–48.

Wilson, A. *The Marketing of Professional Services*. New York: McGraw-Hill, 1972, pp. 89–92.

Wind, Y. "Issues and Advances in Segmentation Research." *Journal of Marketing Research*, Aug. 1978, pp. 317–337.

Winston, M. B. *Getting Publicity*. New York: Wiley, 1982.

Winter, F. W. "Market Segmentation: A Tactical Approach." *Business Horizons*, Jan.–Feb. 1984, pp. 57–63.

Yankelovich, D. "New Criteria for Market Segmentation." *Harvard Business Review*, Mar./Apr. 1964, pp. 83–90.

Yankelovich, D. *New Rules: Searching for Self-fulfillment in a World Turned Upside Down*. New York: Random House, 1981.

Yip, G. S. "Marketing Selection and Direction: Role of Product Portfolio Planning." Cambridge, Mass.: HBS Case Services, Harvard Business School, 1981.

Young, K. E. "Good-bye Security Blanket." *CASE Currents*, Nov./Dec. 1983, pp. 48–52.

Zaltman, G., Florio, D. H., and Sikorski, L. A. *Dynamic Eduational Change*. New York: Free Press, 1977.

Zeithaml, C. P., and Zeithaml, V. A. "Environmental Managements: Revising the Marketing Perspective." *Journal of Marketing*, Spring 1984, pp. 46–53.

Zeithaml, V. A. "The New Demographics and Market Fragmentation." *Journal of Marketing*, Summer 1985, pp. 64–75.

Zotti, E. "Thinking Psychographically." *Public Relations Journal*, May 1985, pp. 26–30.

Index